PORTRAITS

OF THE

GREAT REVIVAL

OF

THE EIGHTEENTH CENTURY

THE FOUNDRY, MOORFIELDS.

PORTRAITS

OF THE

GREAT REVIVAL

OF

THE EIGHTEENTH CENTURY

PAXTON HOOD

AMBASSADOR

BELFAST ♦ GREENVILLE
NORTHERN IRELAND SOUTH CAROLINA

ISBN 1 84030 009 4

AMBASSADOR PRODUCTIONS LTD,
Providence House
16 Hillview Avenue,
Belfast, BT5 6JR
Northern Ireland

Emerald House,
1 Chick Springs Road, Suite 206
Greenville,
South Carolina 29609
United States of America

PREFACE TO THIS EDITION

THE author of the following pages begs that they may be read kindly—and, he will venture to say, *not* critically. Originally published as a series of papers in the *Sunday at Home*, the Committee of the Religious Tract Society suggested that their reprint in this form might be useful; they are only *Vignettes*—etchings. The History of the great Religious Movement of the Eighteenth Century yet remains unwritten; not often has the world known such a marvellous awakening of religious thought; and, as we are further removed in time, so, perhaps, we are better able to judge of the momentous circumstances, could we but seize the point of view.

CONTENTS.

VIGNETTES OF THE GREAT REVIVAL.

CHAPTER I.

THE DARKNESS BEFORE THE DAWN.

IT cannot be too often remembered or repeated that
when the Bible has been brought face to face with
the conscience of corrupt society, in every age it
has shown itself to be that which it professes, and which
its believers declare it to be—"the great power of God."
It is not in this place for us to do more than notice that
it proved itself thus amidst the hoary and decaying cor-
ruptions of the ancient civilisation, when its truths were
first published to the Roman Empire; it proclaimed its
power to the impure but polished society of Florence,
when Savonarola preached his wonderful sermons in St.
Mark's; and effected the same results throughout the
whole German Empire, when Bible truth sounded forth
from Luther's trumpet-tones. The same principle is

illustrated where the great evangelical truths of the New Testament entered nations, as in Spain or France, only to be rejected. From that rejection and the martyrdoms of the first believers, those nations have never recovered themselves even to this hour; and of the two nations, that in which the rejection was the most haughty and cruel, has suffered most from its renunciation.

England has passed through three great evangelical revivals. The first, the period of the Reformation, whose force was latent here, even before the waves of the great German revolution reached our shores, and called forth the pen of a monarch, and that monarch a haughty Tudor, to enter the lists of disputation with the lowly-born son of a miner of the Black Forest. What that Reformation effected in our country we all very well know; the changes it wrought in opinion, the martyrs who passed away in their chariots of fire in vindication of its doctrines, the great writers and preachers to whose works and names we frequently and lovingly refer.

Then came the second great evangelical revival, the period of Puritanism, whose central interests gather round the great civil wars. This was the time, and these were the opinions which produced some of the most massive and magnificent writers of our language; the whole mind of the country was stirred to its deepest heart by faith in those truths, which to believe ennobles human nature, and enables it to "endure as seeing Him who is invisible." There can be no doubt that it produced some of the grandest and noblest minds, whether for service by sword or pen, in the pulpit or the cabinet, that the world has known. Lord Macaulay's magnificently glowing description of the English Puritan, and how he attained, by his evangelical opinions, his stature of strength, will be familiar to all readers who know his essay on Milton.

But the present aim is to gather up some of the facts and impressions, and briefly to recite some of the influences of the third great evangelical revival in our country. We are guilty of no exaggeration in saying that these have been equally deserving historic fame with either of the preceding. The story has less, perhaps, to excite some of our most passionate human interests ; it had not to make its way through stakes and scaffolds, although it could recite many tales of persecution ; it unsheathed no sword, " the weapons of its warfare were not carnal ; " and on the whole, it may be said its doctrine " distilled as the dew ; " yet it is not too much to say that from the revival of the last century came forth that wonderfully manifold reticulation and holy machinery of piety and benevolence, we find in such active operation around us to-day.

All impartial historians of the period place this most remarkable religious impulse in the rank of the very foremost phenomena of the times. The calm and able historian, Earl Stanhope, speaking of it, as " despised at its commencement," continues, " with less immediate importance than wars or political changes, it endures long after not only the result but the memory of these has passed away, and thousands " (his lordship ought to have said millions) " who never heard of Fontenoy or Walpole, continue to follow the precepts, and venerate the name of John Wesley." While the latest, a still more able and equally impartial and quiet historian, Mr. Lecky, says, " Our splendid victories by land and sea must yield in real importance to this religious revolution ; it exercised

a profound and lasting influence upon the spirit of the
Established Church, upon the amount and distribution of
the moral forces of the nation, and even upon the course
of its political history."

Shall we, then, first attempt to obtain some adequate
idea of what this Revival effected, by a slight effort to
realise what sort of world and state of society it was
into which the Revival came? One writer truly remarks,
" Never has century risen on Christian England so void of
soul and faith as that which opened with Queen Anne,
and which reached its misty noon beneath the second
George, a dewless night succeeded by a dewless dawn.
There was no freshness in the past and no promise in the
future ; the Puritans were buried, the Methodists were not
born." It is unquestionably true that black, bad and
corrupt as society was, for the most part, all round, in the
eighteenth century, intellectual and spiritual forces broke
forth, simultaneously we had almost said, and believing,
as we do, in the Providence which governed the rise of
both, we may say, consentaneously, which have left far
behind all social regenerations which the pen of history
has recited before. Of almost all the fruits we enjoy, it
may be said the seeds were planted then ; even those
which, like the printing-press or the gospel, had been
planted ages before, were so transplanted as to flourish
with a new vigour.

Our eye has been taught to rest on an interesting
incident. It was in 1757 the great and good John Wesley,
travelling and preaching, then about fifty years of age, but
still with nearly forty years of work before him, arrived
in Glasgow. He saw in the University its library and its
pictures ; but, had he possessed the vision of a Hebrew

seer, he might have glanced up from the quadrangle of the college to the humble rooms, up a spiral staircase, of a young workman, over whose lodging was the sign and information that they were tenanted by a "mathematical instrument maker to the University." This young man, living there upon a poor fare, and eking out a poor subsistence, with many thoughts burdening his mind, was destined to be the founder of the greatest commercial and material revolution the world has known: through him seems to have been fulfilled the wonderfully significant prophecy of Nahum: "The chariots shall rage in the streets, they shall jostle one against another in the broad ways: they shall seem like torches, they shall run like the lightnings." This young man was James Watt, who gave to the world the steam engine. A few years after he gave his mighty invention to Manchester; and the world has never been the same world since. "By that invention," says Emerson, "one man can do the work of two hundred and fifty men;" and in Manchester alone and in its vicinity there are probably sixty thousand boilers, and the aggregate power of a million horses.

Let not the allusion seem out of place. That age was the seed-time of the present harvest fields; in that time those great religious ideas which have wrought such an astonishing revolution, acquired body and form; and we ought to notice how always, when God sets free some new idea, He also calls into existence the new vehicle for its diffusion. He did not trust the early Christian faith to the old Latin races, to the selfish and æsthetic Greek, or to the merely conservative Hebrew; He "hissed," in the graphic language of the old Bible, for a new race, and gave the New Testament to the Teutonic people, who have ever been its chief guardians and expositors; and thus, in all reviews of the development and unfolding of the religious life in the times of which we speak, we have to notice how the material and the spiritual changes have re-acted on each other, while both have brought a change which has indeed " made all things new."

Contrasting the state of society after the rise of the Great Revival with what it was before, the present with the past, it is quite obvious that something has brought about a general decency and decorum of manners, a tenderness and benevolence of sentiment, a religious interest in, and observance of pious usages, not to speak of a depth of religious life and conviction, and a general purity and nobility of literary taste, which did not exist before. All these must be credited to this great movement; it is not in the nature of steam engines, whether stationary or locomotive, printing presses, or Staffordshire potteries, undirected by spiritual forces, to raise the morals or to improve the manners of mankind.

If sometimes in the presence of the spectacles of ignorance, crime, irreligion, and corruption in our own day, we are filled with a sense of despair for the prospects of society, it may be well to take a retrospect of what society was in England at the commencement of the last century. When George III. ascended the throne the population of England was not much over five millions; at the commencement of the present century it was nearly eleven millions; but with our intensely crowded population of the present day, the cancerous elements of society, the dangerous, pauperised, and criminal classes are in far less proportion, not merely relatively, but really. It was a small country, and possessed few inhabitants; and there are few circumstances which can give us much pleasure in the review; national distress was constantly making itself bitterly felt; it was the age of mobs and riots. The state of the criminal law was cruel in the extreme; Blackstone calculates that for no fewer than one hundred and sixty offences, some of them of the most frivolous description, the judge was bound to pronounce sentence of death. Crime, of course, flourished; during the year 1738 no fewer than fifty-two criminals were hanged at Tyburn; during that and the preceding years, twelve thousand persons had been convicted, within the Bills of Mortality, for smuggling gin and selling it without licence. The amusements of all classes of people were exactly of that order calculated to create a cruel disposition, and thus to encourage crime; bear-baiting, bull-baiting, prize-fighting, cock-fighting: on a Shrove Tuesday it was dangerous to pass down any public streets. This was the day selected for the barbarity of tying a harmless cock to a stake, there to be battered to death by throwing a stick at it from a certain distance. The grim humour of the people took this form of expressing the national hatred to the French, from the Latin name for the cock, *Gallus;* it was in truth a barbarous pun.

With abundant wealth and means of happiness, the people fell far short of what we should consider comfort now; life and liberty were cheap, and a prevalent Deism or Atheism was united to a wild licentiousness of manners, brutalising all classes of society. For the most part, the Church of England had so shamefully forgotten or neglected her duty—this is admitted now by all her most ardent ministers—while the Nonconformists had sunk generally into so cold an indifferentism in devotion, and so hard and sceptical a frame in theology, that every interest in the land was surrendered to profligacy and recklessness, and, in thoughtful minds, to despair. Society in general was spiritually dead. The literature of England, with two or three famous exceptions, suffered a temporary eclipse; such as it was, it was perverted from all high purposes, and was utterly alien to all purity and moral dignity. A good idea of the moral tone of the times might be obtained by running the eye over a few volumes of the old plays of this period, many of them even written by ladies; it is amazing to us now to think not only that they could be tolerated, but even applauded. The gaols were filled with culprits; but this did not prevent the heaths, moors, and forests from swarming with highwaymen, and the cities with burglars. In the remote regions of England, such as Cornwall in the west, Yorkshire and Northumberland in the north, and especially in the midland Staffordshire, the manners were wild and savage, passing all conception and description. We have to conceive of a state of society divested of all the educational, philanthropic, and benevolent activities of modern times. There were no Sunday-schools, and few day-schools; here and there, some fortunate neighbourhood possessed a grammar-school from some old foundation. Or perhaps some solitary chapel, retreating into a bye-lane in the metropolitan city, or the country town, or, more probably, far away from any town, stood at some confluence of roads, a monument of old intolerance; but, as we said, religion was in fact dead, or lying in a trance.

As to the religious teachers of those times, we know of no period in our history concerning which it might so appropriately be said, in the words of the prophet, "The pastors have become brutish, and have not sought the Lord." In the life of a singular man, but not a good one, Thomas Lord Lyttleton, in a letter dated 1775, we have a most graphic portrait of a country clergyman, a friend of Lyttleton, who went by the designation of "Parson Adams." We suppose him to be no bad representative of the average parson of that day—coarse, profane, jocular, irreligious. On a Saturday evening he told Lyttleton, his host, that he should send his flocks to grass on the approaching Sabbath. "The next morning," says Lyttleton, "we hinted to him that the company did not wish to restrain him from attending the Divine service of the parish ; but he declared that it would be adding contempt to neglect if, when he had absented himself from his own churches he should go to any other. This curious etiquette he strictly observed ; and we passed a Sabbath contrary, I fear, both to law and to gospel."

If we desired to obtain some knowledge of what the Church of England was, as represented by her clergy when George III. was king, we should go to her own records ; and for the later years of his reign, notably to the life of that High Church bishop, a learned, active, and amiable man, Dr. Blomfield, Bishop of London, whose memory was a wonderful repository of anecdotes, not tending to elevate the clergy of those times in popular estimation. Intoxication was a vice very characteristic of the cloth : on one occasion the bishop reproved one of his Chester clergy for drunkenness : he replied, " But, my lord, I never was drunk on duty." " On duty !" exclaimed the bishop ; " and pray, sir, when is a clergyman not on duty?" "True," said the other; "my lord, I never thought of that." The bishop went into a poor man's cottage in one of the valleys in the Lake district, and asked whether his clergyman ever visited him. The poor man replied that he did very frequently. The bishop was delighted, and expressed his gratification at this pastoral oversight; and this led to the discovery that there were a good many foxes on the hills behind the house, which gave the occasion for the frequency of calls which could scarcely be considered pastoral. The chaplain and son-in-law of Bishop North examined candidates for orders in a tent on a cricket-field, he being engaged as one of the players; the chaplain of Bishop Douglas examined whilst shaving; Bishop Watson never resided in his diocese during an episcopate of thirty-four years.

And those who preached seem to have rarely been of a very edifying order of preachers; Bishop Blomfield used to relate how, in his boyhood, when at Bury St. Edmund's, the Marquis of Bristol had given a number of scarlet cloaks to some poor old women; they all appeared at church on the following Sunday, resplendent in their new and bright array, and the clergyman made the donation of the marquis the subject of his discourse, announcing his text with a graceful wave of his hand towards the poor old bodies who were sitting there all together: "Even Solomon, in all his glory, was not arrayed like one of these!" This worthy seems to have been very capable of such things: on another occasion a dole of potatoes was distributed by the local authorities in Bury, and this also was improved in a sermon. "He had himself," the bishop says, "a very corpulent frame, and pompous manner, and a habit of rolling from side to side while he delivered him-self of his breathing thoughts and burning words ; on the occasion of the potato dole, he chose for his singularly appropriate text (Exodus xvi. 15) : "And when the children of Israel saw it, they said one to another, It is manna ; " and thence he proceeded to discourse to the recipients of the potatoes on the warning. furnished by the Israelites against the sin of gluttony, and the wickedness of taking more than their share.

When that admirable man, Mr. Shirley, began his evangel-istic ministry as the friend and coadjutor of his cousin, the Countess of Huntingdon, a curate went to the archbishop to complain of his unclerical proceedings : " Oh, your grace, I have something of great importance to communicate ; it will astonish you ! " " Indeed, what can it be ? " said the archbishop. "Why, my lord," replied he, throwing into his countenance an expression of horror, and expecting the archbishop to be petrified with astonishment, " he actually wears white stockings ! " "Very unclerical indeed," said the archbishop, apparently much surprised ; he drew his chair near to the curate, and with peculiar earnestness, and in a sort of confidential whisper, said, " Now tell me— I ask this with peculiar feelings of interest—does Mr. Shirley wear them over his boots ? " " Why, no, your grace, I cannot say he does." " Well, sir, the first time you ever hear of Mr. Shirley wearing them over his boots, be so good as to warn me, and I shall know how to deal with him ! "

We would not, on the other hand, be unjust. We may well believe that there were hamlets and villages where admirable country clergymen realised their duties and fulfilled them, and not only deserved all the merit of

Goldsmith's charming picture, but were faithful ministers
of the New Testament too.   But our words and illustrations refer to the average character presented to us by
the Church; and this, again, is illustrated by the vehement
hostility presented on all hands to the first indications of the
Great Revival. For instance, the Rev. Dr. Thomas Church,
Vicar of Battersea, in a well-known sermon on charity
schools, deplored and denounced the enormous wickedness
of the times; after saying, "Our streets are grievously
infested; every day we see the most dreadful confusions,
daring villanies, dangers, and mischiefs, arising from the
want of sentiments of piety," he continues: "For our own
sakes and our posterity's everything should be encouraged
which will contribute to suppressing these evils, and keep
the poor from stealing, lying, drunkenness, cruelty, or
taking God's name in vain.   While we feel our disease, 'tis
madness to set aside any remedy which has power to
check its fury."   Having said this, with a perfectly
startling inconsistency he turns round, and addressing
himself to Wesley and the Methodists, he says, "We
cannot but regard you as our most dangerous enemies."

When the Great Revival arose, the Church of England
set herself, everywhere, in full array against it; she
possessed but few great minds.   The massive intellects
of Butler and Berkeley belonged to the immediately preceding age.   The most active intellect on the bench of
bishops was, no doubt, that of Warburton; and it is sad to
think that he descended to a tone of scurrility and injustice
in his attack on Wesley, which, if worthy of his really
quarrelsome temper, was altogether unworthy of his
position and his powers.

Thus, whether we derive our impressions from the

so-called Church of that time, or from society at large
we obtain the evidences of a deplorable recklessness of
all ordinary principles of religion, honour, or decorum. Bishop Butler had written, in the "Advertisement"
to his *Analogy*, and he appears to have been referring
to the clerical and educated opinion of his time : " It is
come, I know not how, to be taken for granted by many
persons that Christianity is not so much as a subject
of inquiry, but that it is now at length discovered to be
fictitious ; " and he wrote his great work for the purpose of
arguing the reasonableness of the Christian religion, even on
the principles of the Deism prevalent everywhere around
him in the Church and society. Addison had declared
that there was " less appearance of religion in England
than in any neighbouring state or kingdom, whether
Protestant or Catholic ; " and Montesquieu came to our
country, and having made his notes here, published,
probably with some French exaggeration, that there was
" no religion in England, and that the subject, if mentioned
in society, excited nothing but laughter."

Such was the state of our land, when, as we must think,
by the special providence of God, the voices were heard
crying in the wilderness. From the earlier years of the
last century they continued sounding with such clearness
and strength, from the centre to the remotest corners of
the kingdom ; from the coasts, where the Cornish wrecker
pursued his strange craft of crime, along all the highways
and hedges, where rudeness and violence of every description made their occasions for theft, outrage, and
cruelty, until, as we shall see, the whole nation became,
as if instinctively, alive with a new-born soul, and not in
vision but in reality something was beheld like that seen

by the prophet in the valley of vision—dry bones clothed
with flesh, and "standing up an exceeding great army,"
no longer on the side of corruption and death, but ready
with song and speech, and consistent living, to take their
place on the side of the Lord.

CHAPTER II.

FIRST STREAKS OF DAWN.

IN the history of the circumstances which brought about the Great Revival, we must not fail to notice those which were in action even before the great apostles of the Revival appeared. We have already given what may almost be called a silhouette of society, an outline, for the most part, all dark; and yet in the same period there were relieving tints, just as sometimes, upon a silhouette-portrait, you have seen an attempt to throw in some resemblance to the features by a touch of gold.

Chief among these is one we do not remember ever to have seen noticed in this connection—the curious invasion of our country by the French at the close of the seventeenth century. That cruel exodus which poured itself upon our shores in the great and even horrible persecution of the Protestants of France, when the blind bigotry of Louis XIV. revoked the Edict of Nantes, was to us, as a nation, a really incalculable blessing. It is quite singular, in reading Dr. Smiles's *Huguenots*, to notice the large variety of names of illustrious exiles, eminent for learning, science, character, and rank, who

found a refuge here. The folly of the King of France
expelled the chief captains of industry ; they came hither
and established their manufactures in different departments, creating and carrying on new modes of industry.
Also great numbers of Protestant clergymen settled here,
and formed respectable French churches ; some of the
most eminent ministers of our various denominations at
this moment are descendants of those men. Their
descendants are in our peerage ; they are on our bench
of bishops ; they are at the Bar ; they stand high in the
ranks of commerce. At the commencement of the
eighteenth century, their ancestors were here, just settled
on our shores ; in all instances men who had fled from
comfort and domestic peace, in many instances from
affluence and fame, rather than be false to their conscience or to their Saviour. The cruelties of .that dreadful persecution which banished from France almost every
human element it was desirable to retain in it, while
they were, no doubt, there the great ultimate cause of
the French Revolution, brought amongst us what must
have been even as the very seasoning of society, the salt
of our earth in the subsequent age of corruption. Most
of the children of these men were brought up in the
discipline of religious households, such as that which
Sir Samuel Romilly—himself one of those descendants
to whom we have referred—describes. Dr. Watts's mother
was a child of a French exile. Clusters of them grew
up in many neighbourhoods in the country, notably in
Southampton, Norwich, Canterbury, in many parts of
London, where Spitalfields especially was a French colony.
When the Revival commenced, these were ready to aid
its various movements by their character and influence.

Some fell into the Wesleyan ranks, though, probably, most, like the eminent scholar and preacher, William Romaine, one of the sons of the exile, maintained the more Calvinistic faith, reflecting most nearly the old creed of the Huguenot.

This surmise of the influence of that noble invasion upon our national well-being is surely justified by natural inference from the facts. It is very interesting to attempt to realise the religious life of eminent activity and usefulness sustained in different parts of the country before the Revival dawned, and which must have had an influence in fostering it when it arose. And, indeed, while we would desire to give all grateful honour to the extraordinary men (especially to such a man as John Wesley, who achieved so much through a life in which the length and the usefulness were equal to each other, since only when he died did he cease to animate by his personal influence the immense organisation he had formed), yet it seems really impossible to regard any one mind as the seed and source of the great movement. It was as if some cyclone of spiritual power swept all round the nation—or, as if a subtle, unseen train had been laid by many men, simultaneously, in many counties, and the spark was struck, and the whole was suddenly wrapped in a Divine flame.

Dr. Abel Stevens, in his admirable and most interesting, indeed, charming history of Methodism, from his point of view, gives to his own beloved leader and Church the credit of the entire movement; so also does Mr. Tyerman, in his elaborate life of Wesley. But this is quite contrary to all dispassionate dealing with facts; there were many men and many means in quiet operation, some of

these even before Wesley was born, of which his pre-
hensile mind availed itself to draw them into his gigantic
work; and there were many which had operated, and
continued to operate, which would not fit themselves into
his exact, and somewhat exacting, groove of Church life.

We have said it was as if a cyclone of spiritual power
were steadily sweeping round the minds of men and
nations, for there were undoubted gusts of remarkable
spiritual life in both hemispheres, at least fifty years
before Methodism had distinctly asserted itself as a fact.
Most remarkable was the " Great Awakening " in America,
in Massachusetts—especially at Northampton (that is a
remarkable story, which will always be associated with
the name of Jonathan Edwards).   We have referred to
the exodus of the persecuted from France ; equally remarkable was another exodus of persecuted Protestants
from Salzburg, in Austria.   The madness of the
Church of Rome again cast forth an immense host
of the holiest and most industrious citizens.   At the call
of conscience they marched forth in a body, taking joy-
fully the spoiling of their goods rather than disavow
their faith : such men with their families are a treasure
to any nation amongst whom they may settle.   Thomas
Carlyle has given a glowing historical eulogy to the
memory of these men, and the exodus has furnished
Goethe with the subject of one of his most charming
poems.

Philip Doddridge's work was almost done before the
Methodist movement was known.   It seems to us that
no adequate honour has ever yet been paid to that most
beautiful and remarkably inclusive life.   It was public, it
was known and noticed, but it was passed almost in

retreat in Northampton. That he was a preacher and
pastor of a Church was but a slight portion of the life
which succumbed, yet in the prime of his days, to consumption. His academy for the education of young
ministers seems to us, even now, something like a model
of what such an academy should be ; his lectures to his
students are remarkably full and scholarly and complete.
From thence went forth men, like the saintly Risdon
Darracott, the scholarly and suggestive Hugh Farmer,
Benjamin Fawcett, and Andrew Kippis. The hymns of
Doddridge were among the earliest, as they are still
among the sweetest of that kind of offering to our modern
Church ; their clear, elevated, thrush-like sweetness, like
the more uplifted seraphic trumpet tones of Watts, broke
in upon a time when there was no sacred song worthy of
the name in the Church, and anticipated the hour when
the melodious acclamations of the people should be one of
the most cherished elements of Christian service.

And Isaac Watts was, by far, the senior of Doddridge ;
he lived very much the life of a hermit. Although the
pastor of a city church, he was sequestered and withdrawn
from public life in Theobalds, or Stoke Newington, where,
however, he prosecuted a course of sacred labour of a
marvellously manifold description, intermeddling with
every kind of learning, and consecrating it all to the
great end of the Christian ministry, and the producing
of books, which, whether as catechisms for children,
treatises for the formation of mental character, philo-
sophic essays grappling with the difficulties of scholarly
minds, or "comfortable words" to "rock the cradle of
declining age," were all to become of value when the
nation should awake to a real spiritual power. They are

mostly laid aside now; but they have served more than one generation well; and he, beyond question, was the first who taught the Protestant Christian Church in England to sing. His hymns and psalms were sounding on

ISAAC WATTS.

when John Wesley was yet a child, and numbers of them were appropriated in the first Methodist hymn-book. But Watts and Doddridge, by the conditions of their physical and mental being, were unfitted for popular leaders. Perhaps, also, it must be admitted that they had not that which has been called the "instinct for souls;" they were concerned rather to illustrate and expound the truth of God, and to "adorn the doctrine of Christ our Saviour," by their

PHILIP DODDRIDGE.

lives, than to flash new convictions into the hearts of men. It is characteristic that, good and great as they were, they were both at first inimical to the Great Revival; it seemed to them a suspicious movement. The aged Watts cautioned his younger friend Doddridge against encouraging it, especially the preaching of Whitefield ; yet they both lived to give their whole hearts to it ; and some of Watts's last words were in blessing, when, near death, he received a visit from the great evangelist.

Thus we need to notice a little carefully the age immediately preceding the rise of what we call Methodism, in order to understand what Methodism really effected ; we have seen that the dreadful condition of society was not inconsistent with the existence over the country of eminently ·holy men, and of even hallowed Christian families and circles. If space allowed, it would be very pleasant to step into, and sketch the life of many an interior ; and it would scarcely be a work of fancy, but of authentic knowledge. There were yet many which almost retained the character of Puritan households, and among them several baronial halls. Nor ought we to forget that those consistent and high-minded Christian folk, the Quakers, were a much larger body then than now, although, like the Shunammite lady, they especially dwelt among their own people. The Moravians also were here ; but all these existed like little scattered hamlet-patches of spiritual life ; they were respectably con-servative of their own usages. Methodism brought to religion enthusiasm, and the instinct for souls, united to a power of organisation hitherto unknown to the religious life.

At what hour shall we fix the earliest dawn of the Great Revival ? Among the earliest tints of the " morning spread upon the mountains," which was to descend into the valley, and illuminate all the plains, was the con-version of that extraordinary woman, Selina Shirley, the

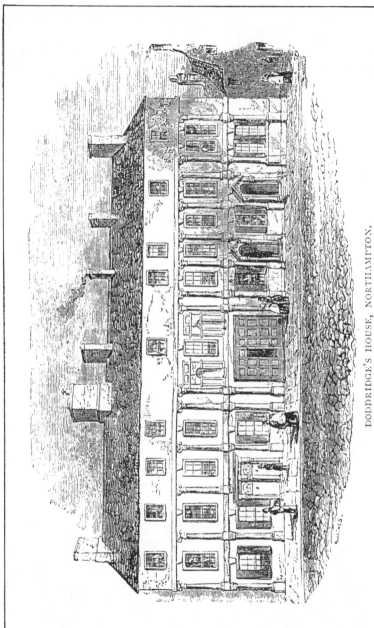

DODDRIDGE'S HOUSE, NORTHAMPTON.

Countess of Huntingdon ; it is scarcely too much to call her the Mother of the Revival ; it is not too much to apply to her the language of the great Hebrew song—"The inhabitants of the villages ceased, they ceased until that I arose : I arose a mother in Israel." She illustrates the difference of which we spoke just now, for there can be no doubt that she had a passionate instinct for souls, to do good to souls, to save souls. Her injunctions for the destruction of all her private papers have been so far complied with as to leave the earlier history of her mind, and the circumstances which brought about her conversion, for the most part unknown. It is certain that she was on terms of intimate friendship with both Watts and Doddridge, but especially with Doddridge. Another intimate friend of the Countess was Watts's very close friend, the Duchess of Somerset ; and thus the links of the story seem to run, like that old and well-known instance of communicated influence, when Andrew found his own brother, Simon, and these in turn found Philip, and Nathanael. It was very natural that, beholding the state of society about her, she should be interested, first, as it seems, for those of her own order ; it was at a later time, when she became acquainted with Whitefield, that he justified her drawing-room assemblies, by reminding her—not, perhaps, with exact critical propriety—of the text in Galatians, where Paul mentioned how he preached "privately to those of reputation." For some time this appears to have been the aim of the good Countess, much in accordance with that pretty saying of hers, that "there was a text in which she blessed God for the insertion of the letter M : 'not *many* noble.'" The beautiful Countess was a heroine in her own line from the earliest days of her conversion : belonging to one of the noblest families of England, she had an entrance to the highest circles, and her heart felt very pitiful for, especially, the women of fashion around her, broken-hearted with disappointment, or sick with *ennui.*

Among these was Sarah, the great Duchess of Marlborough, apparently one of the intimate friends of the Countess; her letters are most characteristic. She mentions that the Duchess of Ancaster, Lady Townshend, and others, had just heard Mr. Whitefield preach, and " What they said of the sermon has made me lament ever since that I did not hear it ; it might have been the means of doing me some good, for good, alas! I do want; but where among the corrupt sons and daughters of Adam am I to find it?" She goes on : " Dear, good Lady Huntingdon, I have no comfort in my own family ; I hope you will shortly come and see me ; I always feel more happy and more contented after an hour's conversation with you ; when alone, my reflections and recollection almost kill me. Now there is Lady Frances Saunderson's great rout to-morrow night ; all the world will be there, and I must go. I hate that woman as much as I hate a physician, but I must go, if for no other purpose than to mortify and spite her. This is very wicked, I know, but I confess all my little peccadilloes to you, for I know your goodness will lead you to be mild and forgiving ; and perhaps my wicked heart may gain some good from you in the end." And then she closes her note with some remarks on " that crooked, perverse little wretch at Twickenham," by which pleasant designation she means the poet, Pope.

Another, and another order of character, was the Duchess of Buckingham ; she came to hear Whitefield preach in the drawing-room, and was quite scandalised. In a letter to the Countess, she says, " The doctrines are most repulsive, and strongly tinctured with impertinence : it is monstrous to be told that you have a heart as sinful as the common wretches that crawl the earth ; this is highly offensive and insulting, and I cannot but wonder that your ladyship should relish any sentiments so much at variance with high rank and good breeding." Such were some of the materials the Countess attempted to gather in her drawing-rooms, if possible to cure the aching of empty hearts. If the two duchesses met together, it is very likely they would be antipathetic to each other ; a prouder old lady than Sarah, the English empire did not contain, but she was proud that she was the wife and widow of the great Marlborough. The Duchess of Buckingham was equally proud that she was the natural daughter of James II. When her son, the Duke of Buckingham, died, she sent to the old Duchess of Marlborough to borrow the magnificent car which had borne John Churchill's body to the Abbey, and the fiery old Duchess sent her back word, " It had carried Lord Marlborough, and should never be profaned by any other corpse." The message was not likely to act as an *entente cordiale* in such an assembly as we have described.

The mention of these names will show the reader that we are speaking of a time when the Revival had not wrought itself into a great movement. The Countess continued to make enthusiastic efforts for those of her own order—we are afraid, with a few distinguished exceptions, without any great amount of success ; but certainly, were it possible for us to look into the drawing-room in South Audley Street, in those closing years of the reign

of George II., we might well be astonished at the brilliancy
of the concourse, and the finding ourselves in the company
of some of the most distinguished names of the highest
rank and fashion of the period.   It was the age of that
cold, sardonic sneerer, Horace Walpole; he writes to
Florence, to his friend Sir Horace Mann, in his scoffing
fashion : " If you ever think of returning to England, you
must prepare yourself with Methodism ; this sect increases
as fast as almost any religious nonsense ever did ; Lady
Fanny Shirley has chosen this way of bestowing the dregs
of her beauty, and Lyttleton is very near making the same
sacrifice of the dregs of all those various characters that he
has worn.   The Methodists love your big sinners as proper
subjects to work upon, and indeed they have a plentiful
harvest."   Then he satirises Lady Ferrars, whom he styles
" General, my Lady Dowager Ferrars."   But, indeed, it is
impossible to enumerate the names of all, or any proportion
of the number who attended this brilliant circle.   Sometimes unhappy events took place; Mr. Whitefield was
sometimes too dreadfully, although unconsciously, faithful.
Lady Rockingham, who really seems to have been inclined
to do good, begged the Countess to permit her to bring
the Countess of Suffolk, well known as the powerful
mistress of George II.   Whitefield " knew nothing of the
matter;" but some arrow "drawn at a venture," and which
probably might have as well fitted many another lady
about the court or in that very room, exactly hit the
Countess.   However much she fidgeted with irritation, she
sat out the service in silence; but, so soon as it was over, the
beautiful fury burst forth in all the stormful speech of a
termagant or virago.   She abused Lady Huntingdon ; she
declared that the whole service had been a premeditated

attack upon herself. Her relatives, Lady Bertie, the celebrated Lady Betty Germain, the Duchess of Ancaster, one of the most beautiful women in England, and who, afterwards, with the Duchess of Hamilton, conducted the future queen of George III. to our shores, expostulated with her, commanded her to be silent, and attempted to explain her mistake ; they insisted that she should apologise to Lady Huntingdon for her behaviour, and, in an ungracious manner, she did so ; but we learn that she never honoured the assembly again with her presence.

What a singular assembly from time to time ! the square dark face of that old gentleman, painfully hobbling in on his crutched stick—face once so handsome as that of St. John, now the disappointed, moody features of the massive, but sceptical intelligence of Bolingbroke ; poor worn-out old Chesterfield, cold and courtly, yet seeming so genial and humane, coming again and again, and yet again ; those reckless wits, and leaders of the *ton* and all high society, Bubb Doddington, afterwards Lord Melcombe, and George Selwyn ; the Duchess of Montague, with her young daughter ; Lady Cardigan, often there, if her mother, Sarah of Marlborough, were but seldom a visitor. Charles Townshend, the great minister, often came ; and his friend, Lord Lyttleton, who really must have been in sympathy with some of the objects of the assembly, if we may judge from his *Essay on the Conversion of St. Paul*, a piece of writing which will never lose its value. There you might have seen even the great commoner, William Pitt, afterwards Earl of Chatham ; but we can understand why he would be there to listen to the manifold notes of an eloquence singularly resembling, in many particulars, his own. And, in fact, where such persons were

present, we might be sure that the entire nobility of the
country was represented.   It might be tempting to loiter
amidst these scenes a little longer.   It was an experiment
made by the Countess; she probably found it almost a failure,
and, in the course of a few years, turned her attention to the
larger ideas connected with the evangelisation of England,
and the training of young men for the work of the
ministry.   She long outlived all those brilliant hosts she
had gathered round her in the prime of life.   But we cannot doubt that some good was effected by this preaching to
"people of reputation."   Courtiers like Walpole sneered,
but it saved the movement to a great degree, when it
became popular, from being suspected as the result of
political faction ;   and probably, as all these nobles and
gentry passed away to their various country seats, when
they heard of the preachers in their neighbourhoods, and
received the complaints of the bishops and their clergy,
with some contempt for the messengers, they were able
to feel, and to say, that there was nothing much more
dreadful than the love of God and His goodwill to men
in their message.

It seems a very sudden leap from the saloons of the
West End to a Lincolnshire kitchen ; but in the kitchen
of that most romantic old vicarage of Epworth, it has
been truly said, the most vigorous form of Methodism
had its origin.   There, at the close of the seventeenth
century, and the commencement of the eighteenth, lived
and laboured old Samuel Wesley, the father of John and
Charles.   Samuel was in every sense a wonderful man,
more wonderful than most people know, though Mr.
Tyerman has done his best to set him forth in a
very clear and pleasant light, in his very entertaining

biography. Scholar, preacher, pastor, and poet was
Samuel; he led a life full of romantic incident, and
full of troubles, of which the two most notable are debts
and ghosts: debts, we must say, in passing, which had
more to do with unavoidable calamity than with any
personal imprudence. The good man would have been
shocked, and have counted it one of his sorest troubles,
could he, in some real horoscope, have forecast what
"Jackey," his son John, was to be. But it was his
wife, Susannah Wesley, the mother of our John, patient
housewife, much-enduring, much-suffering woman, Mary
and Martha in one, saint as sacredly sweet as any who
have seemed worthy of a place in any calendar of
saints, Catholic or Protestant, mother of children, all
of whom were remarkable—two of them wonderful,
and a third highly eminent—it was Susannah Wesley,
whose instinct for souls led her to look abroad over all
the parish in which she lived, with a tender, spiritual
affection; in her husband's absence, turning the large
kitchen into a church, inviting her poor neighbours into
it, and, somewhat at first to the distress of her husband,
preaching to and praying with them there. This brief
reference can only memorialise her name; read John Kirk's
little volume, and learn to love and revere "the mother
of the Wesleys!" The freedom and elevation of her
religious life, and her practical sagacity, it is not difficult
to see, must have given hints and ideas which took shape
and body in the large movement of which her mighty
son came to be regarded, and is still regarded, as the
patriarch. Thus Isaac Taylor says, "The Wesleys' mother
was the mother of Methodism in a religious and moral
sense, for her courage, her submissiveness to authority,

the high tone of her mind, its independence, and its self-control, the warmth of her devotional feelings, and the practical direction given to them, came up, and were visibly repeated in the character and conduct of her sons." Later on in life she became one of the wisest advisers of her son, in his employment of the auxiliaries to his own usefulness. Perhaps, if we could see spirits as they are, we might see in this woman a higher and loftier type of life than in either of those who first received life from her bosom ; some of her quiet words have all the passion and sweetness of Charles's hymns. Our space is too short for many quotations, but take the following words, and the sweet meditation in prose of the much-enduring, and often patiently suffering lady in the old world country vicarage, reads like many of her son's notes in verse : "If to esteem and have the highest reverence for Thee ; if constantly and sincerely to acknowledge Thee the supreme, and only desirable good, be to love Thee, I DO LOVE THEE ! If to rejoice in Thy essential majesty and glory ; if to feel a vital joy overspread and cheer the heart at each perception of Thy blessedness, at every thought that Thou art God, and that all things are in Thy power ; that there is none superior or equal to Thee, be to love Thee, I DO LOVE THEE ! If comparatively to despise and undervalue all the world contains, which is esteemed great, fair, or good ; if earnestly and constantly to desire Thee, Thy favour, Thy acceptance, Thyself, rather than any, or all things Thou hast created, be to love Thee, I DO LOVE THEE !" At length she died as she had lived, her last words to her sons breathing the spirit of her singular life : " Children, as soon as I am released, sing a psalm of praise to God !"

Thus, from the polite circles of London, from the obscure old farm-like vicarage, the rude and rough old English home, events were preparing themselves. John Wesley was born in 1703; the Countess of Huntingdon in 1707: near in their birth time, how far apart the scenery and the circumstances in which their eyes first opened to the light. Whitefield was born later, amidst the still less auspicious scenery of the old Bell Inn, at Gloucester, in 1714. These were undoubtedly among the foremost names in the great palpitation of thought, feeling, and holy action the country was to experience. Future chapters will show a number of other names, which were simultaneously coming forth and educating for the great conflict. So it has always been, and singularly so, as illustrating the order of Providence, and the way in which it gives a new personality to the men whom it designs to aid its purposes. We shall see how, in every part of the country, all unknown to each other, in families separated by position and taste, by birth and circumstances, a band of workers was preparing to produce an entire moral change in the features of the country.

CHAPTER III.

OXFORD: NEW LIGHTS AND OLD LANTERNS.

IT is remarkable that one of the very earliest movements of the new evangelical succession should manifest itself in Oxford—many minded Oxford —whose distant spires and antique towers have looked down through so many ages upon the varying opinions which have surged up around and within her walls. Lord Bacon has somewhere said that the opinions, feelings, and thoughts of the young men of any present generation forecast the whole popular mind of the future age. No remark can be more true, as exhibited generally in fact. Thus it is not too much to say that Oxford has usually been a barometer of coming opinions : either by her adhesion or antagonism to them, she has indicated the pathway of the nearing weather, either for calm or storm. It was so in the dark ages, with the old scholastic philosophy ; it was so in the times immediately succeeding them : in our own day, the great Tractarian movement, with all its influences Romeward, arose in Oxford ; later still, the strong tendencies of high intellectual infidelity, and denial of the sacred prerogatives and rights of the Holy Scriptures, sent forth some of their earliest notes from Oxford. Oxford has been likened to the magnificent conservatory at Chatsworth, where art combines with nature, and achieves all that wealth and taste could command; but the air is heavy and close, and rich as the forms and colours are around the spectator, there is depression and repression, even a sense of oppression, upon the spirits, and we are glad to escape into the breezy chase and among the old trees again. This is hardly true of Oxford; no doubt the air is hushed, and the influences combine to weigh down the mere visitor by a sense of the hoariness of the past, and the black antiquity and frost of ages; but somehow there is a mind in Oxford which is always alive—not merely a scholarly knowledge, but a subtle apprehension of the coming winds—even as certain creatures forebode and know the coming storm before the rain falls or the thunder rolls.

We may presume that most of our readers are acquainted with the designation, "the Oxford Methodists;" but, perhaps, some are not aware that the term was applied to a cluster of young students, who, in a time when the university was delivered over to the usual dissoluteness and godless indifference of the age, met together in each other's rooms for the purpose of sustaining each other in the determination to live a holy life, and to bring their mutual help to the reading and opening of the Word of God. From different parts of the country they met together there; when they went forth, their works, their spheres were different; but the power and the beauty of the old college days seem to have accompanied them through life; they realised the Divine life as a real power from that commencement to the close of their career,

although it is equally interesting to notice how the frame-
work of their opinions changed.   Some of their names
are comparatively unknown now, but John and Charles
Wesley, George Whitefield, and James Hervey, are well-
known; nor is John Gambold unknown, nor Benjamin
Ingham, who married into the family of the Countess
of Huntingdon, of whom we will speak a little more
particularly when we visit the wild Yorkshire of those
days; nor Morgan of Christ Church, whose influence is
described as the most beautiful of the whole, a young
man of delicate constitution and intense enthusiasm, who
visited and talked with the prisoners in the neighbourhood,
visited the cottages around to read and pray, left his
memory as a blessing upon his companions, and was very
early called away to his reward.   This obscure life seems
to have been one most honoured in that which came to
be called by the wits of Oxford, " The Holy Club."

It was just about this time that Voltaire was predicting
that, in the next generation, Christianity would be over-
thrown and unknown throughout the whole civilised world.
Christianity has lived through, and long outlived many
such predictions.   Voltaire had said, " It took twelve men
to set up Christianity ; it would only take one" (humbly
referring to himself) " to overthrow it ; " but the work
of those whom he called the "twelve men" is still of
some account in the world—their words are still of some
authority, and there are very few people on the face of
the earth at this moment who know much of, and fewer
still who care much for the wit of the vain old infidel.
But that Voltaire's prediction was not fulfilled, under the
providential influence of that Divine Spirit who never
leaves us in our low estate, was very greatly owing to this

obscure and despised "Holy Club" of Oxford. These young men were feeling their way, groping, as they afterwards admitted, and somewhat in the dark, after those experiences, which, as they were to be assurances to themselves, should be also their most certain means of usefulness to others.

They were also called Methodists. It is singular, but neither the precise etymology nor the first appropriation of the term Methodist has, we believe, ever been distinctly or satisfactorily settled. Some have derived it from an allusion in Juvenal to a quack physician, some to a passage from the writings of St. Chrysostom, who says, "to be a Methodist is to be beguiled," and which was employed in a pamphlet against Mr. Whitefield. Like some other phrases, it is not easy to settle its first import or importation into our language. Certainly it is much older than the times to which these papers especially refer. It seems to be even contemporary with the term Puritan, since we find Spencer, the librarian of Sion College under Cromwell, writing, "Where are now our Anabaptists and plain pack-staff Methodists, who esteem all flowers of rhetoric in sermons no better than stinking weeds?" A writer in the *British Quarterly* tells a curious story how once in a parish church in Huntingdonshire, he was listening to a clergyman, notorious alike by his private character and vehement intolerance, who was entertaining his audience, on a week evening, by a discourse from the text, Ephesians iv. 14, "Whereby they lie in wait to deceive." He said to his people, " Now, you do not know Greek ; I know Greek, and I am going to tell you what this text really says ; it says, ' they lie in wait to make you Methodists.' The word used here is *Methodeian*, that is really the word that is used, and that is really what

Paul said, 'They lie in wait to make you Methodists '—a Methodist means a deceiver, and one who deludes, cheats, and beguiles." The Grecian scholar was a little at fault in his next allusion, for he proceeded to quote that other text, "We are not ignorant of his devices," and seemed to be under the impression that "device" was the same word as that on which he had expended his criticism. "Now," said he, "you may be ignorant, because you do not know Greek, but we are not ignorant of his devices, that is, of his methods, his deceivers, that is, his Methodists." In such empty wit and ignorant punning it is very likely that the term had its origin.

John Wesley passed through a long, singular, and what we may call a parti-coloured experience, before his mind came out into the light. In those days his mind was a singular combination of High Churchism, amounting to what we should call Ritualism now, and mysticism, both of which influences he brought from Epworth : the first from his father, the second from the strong fascination of the writings of William Law. He found, however, in the "Holy Club" that which helped him. He tells us how, when at Epworth, he travelled many miles to see a "serious man," and to take counsel from him. "Sir," said this person, as if the right word were given to him at the right moment, exactly meeting the necessities of the man standing before him, " Sir, you wish to serve God and to go to heaven : remember you cannot serve Him alone ; you must therefore find companions, or make them. The Bible knows nothing of solitary religion." It must be admitted that the enthusiasm of the mystics has always been rather personal than social ; but the society at Oxford was almost monastic, nor is it wonderful that, with the spectacle of the dissolute life around them, these earnest men adopted rules of the severest self-denial and asceticism. John Wesley arrived in Oxford first in 1720; he left for some time. Returning home to assist his father, he became, as we know, to his father's immense exultation, Fellow of Lincoln College.

In 1733 George Whitefield arrived at Oxford, then in his nineteenth year. Like most of this band, Whitefield was, if not really, comparatively poor, and dependent upon help to enable him to pursue his studies; not so poor, perhaps, as an illustrious predecessor in the same college (Pembroke), who had left only the year before, one Samuel Johnson, the state of whose shoes excited so much commiseration in some benevolent heart, that a pair of new ones was placed outside his rooms, only, however, creating surprise in the morning, when he was seen indignantly kicking them up and down the passage. Whitefield was not troubled by such over-sensitive and delicate feelings ; men are made differently. Johnson's rugged independence did its work; and the easy facility and amiable disposition, which could receive favours without a sense of degradation, were very essential to what Whitefield was to be. He, however, when he came to Oxford, was caught in the same glamour of mysticism as John Wesley. But in this case it was Thomas à-Kempis who had besieged the soul of the young enthusiast ; he was miserable, his life, his heart and mind were crushed beneath this altogether inhuman and unattainable standard for salvation. He was a Quietist—what a paradox !—Whitefield a Quietist ! He was seeking salvation by works of righteousness which he could do. He was practising the severest austerities and renouncing the claims of an external world ; he was living

an internal life which God did not intend should bring to
him either rest or calm ; for, in that case, how could he
ever have stirred the deep foundations of universal
sympathy ?

But that heart, whose very mould was tenderness, was
easily called aside by the sight of suffering ; and there is
an interesting story, how, at this time, in one of his walks
by the banks of the river, in such a frame of mind as we
have described, he met a poor woman whose appearance was discomposed. Naturally enough, he talked with
her, and found that her husband was in the gaol in Oxford,
that she had run away from home, unable to endure any
longer the crying of her children from hunger, and that
she even then meditated drowning herself. He gave her
immediate relief, but arranged with her to meet him, and
see her husband together in the evening at the prison. He
appears to have done them both good, ministering to their
temporal necessities ; he prayed with them, brought them
to the knowledge of the grace which saves, and late on in
life he says, "They are both now living, and I trust will
be my joy and crown of rejoicing in the day of the Lord
Jesus." Happy is the man to whose life such an incident as this is given ; it calls life away from its dreary
introspections, and sets it upon a trail of outwardness,
which is spiritual health ; no one can attain to much
religious happiness until he knows that he has been the
means of good to some suffering soul. Faith grows in us by
the revelation that we have been used to do good to others.

It was about this time that Charles Wesley met Whitefield moodily walking through the college corridors. The
misery of his appearance struck him, and he invited him
to his rooms to breakfast. The memory of the meeting

never passed away; Charles Wesley refers to it in his elegy on Whitefield. In a short time he leaped forth into spiritual freedom, and almost immediately became youth as he was, preacher, and we may almost say, apostle. The change in his mind seems to have been as instantaneous and as luminous as Luther's at Erfurt. Whitefield was at work, commencing upon his own great scale, long before the Wesleys. John had to go to America, and to be entangled there by his High Church notions; and then there were his Moravian proclivities, so that, altogether, years passed by before he found his way out into a light so clear as to be able to reflect it on the minds of others.

To some of the members of this "Holy Club" we shall not be able to refer again; we must, therefore, mention them now. Especially is some reference due to James Hervey; his name is now rather a legend and tradition than an active influence in our religious literature; but how popular once, do not the oldest memories amongst us well know? On some important points of doctrine he parted company from his friends and fellow-students, the Wesleys. John Wesley used to declare that he himself was not converted till his thirty-seventh year, so that we must modify any impressions we may have from similar declarations made by the amiable Vicar of Weston Favel: the term conversion, used in such a sense, in all probability means simply a change in the point of view, an alteration of opinion, giving a more clear apprehension of truth. Hervey was always infirm in health, tall, spectral; and, while possessing a mind teeming with pleasing and poetic fancies, and a power of perceiving happy analogies, we should regard him as singularly

wanting in that fine solvent of all true genius, geniality.
Hence, all his letters read like sermons ; but his poor, infirm
frame was the tabernacle of an intensely fervent soul.
Shortly after his settlement in his village in Northamptonshire, he was recommended by his physician to follow
the plough, that he might receive the scent of the fresh
earth ; a curious recommendation, but it led to a conversation with the ploughman, which completely over-
turned the young scholar's scheme of theology.   The
ploughman was a member of the Church of Dr. Doddridge,
afterwards one of Hervey's most intimate friends.   As
they walked together, the young minister asked the old
ploughman what he thought was the hardest thing in
religion ?   The ploughman very respectfully returned the
question.   Hervey replied, " I think the hardest thing in
religion is to deny sinful self," and he proceeded, at some
length, of course, to dilate upon and expound the
difficulty, from which our readers will see that, at this
time, his mind must have been under the same influences
as those we meet in *The Imitation* of Thomas
à-Kempis.   " No, sir," said the old ploughman, " the
hardest thing in religion is to deny righteous self," and
he proceeded to unfold the principles of his faith.   At
the time, Hervey thought the ploughman a fool, but the
conversation was not forgotten, and he declares that it
was this view of things which created for him a new creed.
Our readers, perhaps, know his *Theron and Aspasia:* we
owe that book to the conversation with the ploughman ;
all its pages, alive with descriptions of natural scenery,
historical and classical allusion, and glittering with
chromatic fancy through the three thick volumes, are
written for the purpose of unfolding and enforcing — to

put it in old theological phraseology—the imputed and imparted righteousness of Christ, the great point of divergence in teaching between Hervey and John Wesley.

Thus the term Methodism cannot, any more than Christianity, be contented with, or contained in one particular line of opinion. Thus, for instance, among the members of the "Holy Club" we find the two Wesleys and others distinctly Arminian—the apostles of that form of thought which especially teaches us that we must attain to the grace of God; while Whitefield first, and Hervey afterwards, became the teachers of that doctrine which announces the irresistible grace of God as that which is outside of us, and comes down upon us. No doubt the doctrines were too sharply separated by their respective leaders. In the ultimate issue, both believed alike that all was of grace, and all of God; but experience makes every man's point of view; as he feels, so he sees. The grand thought about all these men in this Great Revival was that they believed in, and untiringly and with immense confidence announced, that which smote upon the minds of their hearers almost like a new revelation; in an age of indifference and Deism they declared that "the grace of God hath appeared unto all men."

There is a very interesting anecdote showing how, about this time, even the massive and sardonic intellect of Lord Bolingbroke almost gave way. He was called upon once by a High Church dignitary, his intimate friend, Dr. Church, Vicar of Battersea, and Prebendary of St. Paul's, to whom we have already referred as from the first opposed to the Revival, and, to the doctor's amazement, he found Bolingbroke reading Calvin's *Institutes*. The peer asked the preacher, the infidel the professed Christian, what he thought of it. "Oh," said the doctor, "we think nothing of such antiquated stuff; we think it enough to preach the importance of morality and virtue, and have long given up all that talk about Divine grace." Bolingbroke's face and eyes were a study at all times, but we could wish to have seen him turn in his chair, and fix his eyes on the vicar as he said: "Look you, doctor. You know I don't believe the Bible to be a Divine revelation, but those who do can never defend it but upon the principle of the doctrine of Divine grace. To say the truth, there have been times when I have been almost persuaded to believe it upon this view of things; and there is one argument I have felt which has gone very far with me on behalf of its authenticity, which is, that the belief in it exists upon earth even when committed to the care of such as you, who pretend to believe in it, and yet deny the only principle upon which it is defensible." The worn-out statesman and hard-headed old peer hit the question of his own day, and forecast all the sceptical strife of ours; for all such questions are summed in one, Is there supernatural grace, and has that grace appeared unto men? This was the one faith of all these revivalists. The world was eager to hear it, for the aching heart of the world longs to believe that it is true. The conversation we have recited shows that even Bolingbroke wished that it might be true.

To return for a moment to Hervey. His new creed changed the whole character of his preaching. The little church of Weston Favel, a short distance from the town of Northampton, became quite a shrine for pilgrimages; he was often compelled to preach in the churchyard. He was assuredly an intense lover of natural scenery, a student of natural theology of the old school. His writing is now said to be meretricious and gaudy. One critic says that children will always prefer a red to a white sugar-plum,

WESTON FAVEL CHURCH.

and that the tea is nicer to them when they drink it from a cup painted with coloured flowers ; and this, perhaps not unfairly, describes the style of Hervey ; we have prettiness rather than power, elegant disquisition rather than nervous expression, which is all the more wonderful, as he must have been an accomplished Latin scholar. But he had a mind of gorgeous fulness, and his splendid conceptions bore him into a train of what now seem almost glittering extravagances. Hervey was in the manner of his life a sickly recluse, and we easily call up the figure of the old bachelor—for he never married—alternately watching his saucepan of gruel on the fire, and his favourite microscope on the study table of the vicarage. He was greatly beloved by the Countess of Huntingdon, perhaps yet more by Lady Fanny Shirley—the subject of Walpole's sneer. He was, no doubt, the writer of the movement, and its thoughts in his books must have seemed like "butter in a lordly dish." But his course was comparatively brief ; his work was accomplished at the age of forty-five. He died in his chair, his last words, " Lord, now lettest Thou Thy servant depart in peace, for mine eyes have seen Thy most comfortable salvation ;" shortly after, " The great conflict is over ; all is done ;" the last words of all, " Precious salvation." And so passed away one of the most amiable and accomplished of all the revivalists.

We do not dwell at length on the name of John Gambold, because, although ever an excellent and admirable man, he lived the life rather of a secluded mystic, than that of an active reformer. He became a minister of the Church of England, but afterwards left that communion, not from any dissension either from the doctrine or the discipline of the Church, but simply because he found his spiritual relationships more in harmony with

those of the Moravians, of whose Church he died a bishop.
We presume few of our readers are acquainted with his
poetical works ; nor are there many words among them
of remarkable strength. *The Mystery of Life* is certainly
pleasingly impressive ; and his epitaph on himself deserves
quotation :

> " Ask not, ' Who ended here his span?'
> His name, reproach, and praise, was Man.
> ' Did no great deeds adorn his course?'
> No deed of his but showed him worse :
> One thing was great, which God supplied,
> He suffered human life—and died.
> ' What points of knowledge did he gain?'
> That life was sacred all—and vain :
> ' Sacred, how high? and vain, how low?'
> He knew not here, but died to know."

Such were some of the men who went forth from
Oxford ; we shall meet them again, and others of their
company, on whose names we have not dwelt. Meantime,
as the flame of revival was spreading, Oxford again starts
into singular notice ; how the " Holy Club " escaped
official censure and condemnation seems strange to us,
but in 1768 the members of a similar club were, for
meeting together for prayer and reading the Scriptures,
all summarily expelled from the university. Their number
was seven. Several of the heads of houses spoke in their
favour, the principal of their own hall, Dr. Dixon, moved
an amendment against their expulsion, on the ground of
their admirable conduct and exemplary piety. Not a
word was alleged against them, only that some of them
were the sons of tradesmen, and that all of them " held
Methodistical tenets, taking upon them to pray, read,
and expound the Scriptures, and sing hymns at private

houses." These practices were considered as hostile to the Articles and interests of the Church of England, and sentence was pronounced against them.

Of course this expulsion created a great agitation at the time ; and as the moral character of the young men was so perfectly unimpeachable, it no doubt greatly aided the cause of the Revival. Dr. Horne, Bishop of Norwich, author of the Commentary *On the Psalms*—no Methodist, although an admirable and evangelical man—denounced the measure in a pamphlet in the strongest terms. The well-known wit and Baptist minister of Devonshire Square in London, Macgowan, lashed the transaction in his piece called *The Shaver.* All the young men seem to have turned out well. Some, like Thomas Jones, who afterwards became curate of Clifton, and married the sister of Lady Austen, Cowper's friend—found admission into the Church of England ; the others instantly found help from the Countess of Huntingdon, who sent them to finish their studies at her college in Trevecca, and afterwards secured them places in connection with her work of evangelisation. The transaction gives a singular idea of what Oxford was in 1768, and prepares us for the vehement persecutions by which the representatives of Oxford all over the country armed themselves to resist the Revival, whilst it justifies our designation of this chapter, " New Lights and Old Lanterns."

CHAPTER IV.

CAST OUT FROM THE CHURCH—TAKING TO THE FIELDS.

THERE can be little doubt that whatever of latent powers there might be as indicated in the several instances we have set before our readers, it was field-preaching, preaching in the open air, which first gave national distinctiveness to the Revival, and constituted it a movement; and assuredly any occasions of excitement; we have known give no idea whatever of the immense agitations which speedily rolled over the country, from one end to the other, when these great revivalists began their work in the fields. And the excitement continued, rolling on through London, as we said, and through the counties of England, from the west to the north, not for days, weeks, or months merely, but through long years, until the religious life of the land was entirely rekindled, and its morals and manners remoulded; and all this, especially in its origination, without money, no large sums being subscribed or guaranteed to sustain the work. The work was done, not only without might or power, but assuredly in the very teeth of the malevolence of might and of power; nor is

it too much to say that it probably would not have
been done, could not have been done, had the churches,
chapels, and great cathedrals been thrown open to the
preachers.

It seems a singular thing to say, but we should speak
of Whitefield as the Luther of this Great Revival, and of
Wesley as its Calvin. Both in the quality of their work
and in their relation in point of time, this analogy is not
so unnatural as it perhaps seems at first. The impetuosity
and passion, the vehemence and sleepless vigilance of
Whitefield first broke open the way; the calm, cautious,
frequently even nervously timid intelligence of Wesley
organised the work. If Calvinism in itself be, as it has
been truly described, the conservative element of all theology, Wesleyanism was, in a special manner, the conservative element of the Revival. This we shall see, however,
more distinctly, by-and-by; it was Whitefield who began
the work of field-preaching.

We cannot but wonder how a writer, in a recent
number of the *Edinburgh Review*, could say, " It is a great
mistake to complain, as so many do, that the Church
cast out the Wesleys. We have seen at the beginning
how kindly, and even cordially, they were treated by the
leading members of the episcopate." Surely any history
of Methodism gives an emphatic contradiction to this
statement. Bishop Benson, indeed, ordained Whitefield,
but he bitterly lamented to the Countess of Huntingdon
that he had done so, attributing to him what seemed to
the Bishop the mischief of the evangelical movement.
" My lord," said the Countess, " mark my words: when
you are on your dying bed, that will be one of the few
ordinations you will reflect upon with complaisance."

The words were, in a remarkable degree, prophetic; when the Bishop was on his death-bed he sent ten guineas to Mr. Whitefield as a token of his " regard, veneration, and affection," and begged the great field-preacher to remember him in prayer. If the bishops were kind and cordial to the first Methodists, they certainly took a singular way of dissembling their love; for instance, Bishop Lavington, of Exeter, whose well-known two volumes on Methodism are really a curiosity of episcopal scurrility, was in a passion with everything that looked like Whitefieldism in his diocese. Mr. Thomson, the Vicar of St. Gennys, was a dissipated clergyman, a character of known immorality; he was a rich man, and not dependent upon his vicarage. In the midst of his sinful life conscience was arrested; he became converted; he countenanced, and threw open his pulpit to Mr. Whitefield; he became remarkable himself, as he had been before for his ungodliness, now for his devout life and fervent gospel preaching. What made it all the worse was that he was a man of real genius. Now all his brethren in the ministry disowned him, and closed their pulpits against him; and presently Bishop Lavington summoned him to appear before him to answer the charges made against him by his brethren for his Methodistical practices. " Sir," said the Bishop, in the course of conversation, " if you pursue these practices, and countenance Whitefield, I will strip your gown from off you." Mr. Thomson had on his gown at the time—more frequently worn by ministers of the Church then than now. To the amazement of the Bishop, Mr. Thomson exclaimed, " I will save your lordship the trouble!" He took off his gown, dropped it at the Bishop's feet, saying, " My lord, I can preach without a gown!" and before the Bishop could recover from his astonishment he was gone. This was an instance, however, in which the Bishop was so decidedly in the wrong that he sent for the vicar again, apologised to him ; and the circumstance, indeed, led to the entertainment by the Bishop of views which were somewhat milder with reference to Methodism than those which still give notoriety to his name.

Southey, in his certainly not impartial volumes, admits that, for the most part, the condition of the clergy was dreadful ; it is not wonderful that they closed their churches against the innovators. There was, for instance, the Vicar of Colne, the Rev. George White ; when the preachers came into his neighbourhood, it was his usual practice to call his parishioners together by the beat of a drum, to issue a proclamation at the market-cross, and enlist a mob for the defence of the Church against the Methodists. Here is a copy of the proclamation, a curiosity in its way : "Notice is hereby given, that if any man be mindful to enlist in His Majesty's service, under the command of the Rev. Mr. George White, Commander-in-Chief, and John Bannister, Lieutenant-General, of His Majesty's forces for the defence of the Church of England, and the support of the manufactory in and about Colne, both which are now in danger, let him repair to the drum-head at the Cross, where each man shall receive a pint of ale in advance, and all other proper encouragements." Such are some of the instances, which might be multiplied to any extent, showing the reception given to the revivalists by the clergy of the time. But let no reader suppose that, in reciting these things, we are willingly dwelling upon facts not creditable to the Church, or that we forget how many of her most admirable members have made an abundant *amende honorable* by their eulogies since; nor are we forgetting that Nonconformist chapels, whose cold respectability of service and theology were sadly outraged by the new teachers, were not more readily opened than the churches were to men with whom the Word of the Lord was as a fire, or as a hammer to break the rocks in pieces.

Whitefield soon felt his power. Immediately after his ordination, he in some way became for a time an occasional supply at the chapel in the Tower; he found a straggling congregation of twenty or thirty hearers; after a service or two the place was overflowing, and remained so. During his short residence in that neighbourhood the youth continued throughout the whole week preaching to the soldiers, preaching to prisoners, holding services on Sunday mornings for young men before the ordinary service. He was still ostensibly at Oxford; a profitable living was offered to him in London, and instantly declined. He went to Gloucester, to Bristol, to Kingswood. Of course it is impossible to follow Whitefield step by step through his career; we can only rapidly bring out a crayon sketch of the chief features of his work. We shall not therefore attempt to follow him in his voyages to Georgia; voyaging was no pastime in those days, and he spent a great amount of time in transit to and fro on the seas; but our business with him is as the first field-preacher; and Kingswood, near Bristol, appears to have been the first place where this great work was to be tried. It was then, what it is still, a region of rough collieries, the Black Country of the West; the people themselves were of the roughest order. Whitefield spoke at Bristol, to some friends, of his probable speedy embarkation to preach the Gospel among the Indians of America; and they said to him, "What need of going abroad to do this? Have we not Indians enough at home? If you have a mind to convert Indians, there are colliers enough in Kingswood!" A savage race! As to taking to the fields in this instance, it was simply a

GEORGE WHITEFIELD.

necessity; there were no churches from whence the preacher could be ejected. Try to realise it: the heathen society, indoctrinated only in brutal sports; the rough, black labour only typical of the rough, black minds, the rough black souls. Surely he must have been a very brave man; nor was he one at all of that order of apostles

whose native roughness is well fitted, it seems, to challenge
roughness to civility.

Whitefield was a perfect gentleman, of manners most
affectionate and amiable ; altogether the most unlikely
creature, it seems, to rise triumphant over the execrations
of a mighty mob. Again and again we have to remark
that the oratory of Whitefield seems to us almost the
greatest mystery in the history of eloquence : his voice
must have been wonderful ; its strength was overwhelming,
but it was not a roar ; its modulations and inflections
were equal to its strength, so that it had the all-command-
ing tones of a bell in its clearness, and all the modulations
of an organ in its variety and sweetness. Kingswood only
stands as a representative of crowds of other such places,
where savages fell before the enchantment of his sweet
music. Read any accounts of him, and it will be seen
that we do not exaggerate in speaking of him as the very
Orpheus of the pulpit. Assuredly, as it has been said
Orpheus, by the power of his music, drew trees, stones,
the frozen mountain-tops, and the floods to bow to his
melody, so men, " stockish, hard, and full of rage," felt a
change pass over their nature, as they came under the
spell of Whitefield. Yet, perhaps, he would not have
gone to Kingswood had he not been inhibited from
preaching in the Bristol churches. He had preached in
St. Mary Redcliff, and the following day had preached
opening sermons in the parish church of SS. Philip and
Jacob, and then he was called before the Chancellor of the
diocese, who asked him for his licence by which he was
permitted to preach in that diocese. Whitefield said he
was an ordained minister of the Church of England, and
as to the special licence, it was obsolete. " Why did you

not ask," he said, "for the licence of the clergyman who preached for you last Thursday?" The Chancellor replied, "That is no business of yours." Whitefield said, "There

WHITEFIELD AT KINGSWOOD.

is a canon forbidding clergymen to frequent taverns and play at cards, why is that not enforced?" The Chancellor evaded this, but charged Whitefield with preaching false doctrine; Whitefield replied that he preached what he knew to be the truth, and he would continue to preach. "Then," said the Chancellor, "I will excommunicate you!" The end of it was that all the city churches were shut against him. "But," he says, "if they were all open, they would not contain half the people who come to hear. So at three in the afternoon I went to Kingswood among the colliers." Whitefield laid his case in a very respectful letter, before the Bishop, but on he went. As to Kingswood, tears poured down the black faces of the colliers; the great audiences are described as being drenched in tears. Whitefield himself was in a passion of tears. "How can I help weeping," he said to them, "when you have not wept for yourselves?" And they began to weep. Thus in 1739 began the mighty work at Kingswood, which has been a great Methodist colony from that day to this. That was a good morning's work for the cause of Christ when the Chancellor shut the doors of the churches of Bristol against the brave and beautiful preacher, and threatened to excommunicate him. Was it not said of old, "Thou makest the wrath of man to praise Thee?"

Now, then, see him girt and road-ready; we might be sure that the example of the Chancellor of Bristol would be pretty generally followed. The old ecclesiastical corporations set themselves in array against him; but how futile the endeavour! Their canons and rubrics were like the building of hedges to confine an eagle, and they only left him without a choice—without any choice but to fulfil his instinct for souls, and to soar. Other "little brief authorities," mayors, aldermen, and such like, issued their fulminations. Coming to Basingstoke, the mayor, one John Abbott, inhibited him. John

Abbott seems to have been a burly butcher. The intercourse and correspondence between the two is very humorously characteristic; but, although it gives an insight as to the antagonism which frequently awaited Whitefield, it is too long to quote in this brief sketch. The butcher-mayor was coarse and insolent; Whitefield never lost his sweet graciousness; writing to abusive butchers or abusive bishops, as in his reply to Lavington, it was all the same, he never lost his temper, never indulged in satire, never exhibits any great marks of genius, writes straight to the point, simply vindicates himself and his course, never retracts, never apologises, goes straight on.

We have no other instance of a preacher who was so equally at home and equally impressive and commanding in the most various and dissimilar circles and scenes; it is significant of the notice he excited that his name occurs so frequently in the correspondence of that cold and heartless man and flippant sneerer, Horace Walpole, whose allusions to him are usually disgraceful; but so it was, he was equally commanding in the polished and select circles of the drawing-room, surrounded by dukes and duchesses, great statesmen and philosophers, or in the large old tabernacle or parish church, surrounded by more orderly and saintly worshippers, or in nature's vast and grand cathedrals, with twenty or thirty thousand people around him.

From the day when he went to Kingswood, we may run a rapid eye along the perspective of his career—in fields, on heaths, and on commons, it was the same everywhere; from his intense life we might find many scenes for description: take one or two. On the breast of the mountain, the trees and hedges full of people, hushed to profound silence, the open firmament above him, the prospect of adjacent fields—the sight of thousands on thousands of people ; some in coaches, some on horseback, and all affected, or drenched in tears. Sometimes evening approaches, and then he says, " Beneath the twilight it was too much for me, and quite overcame me." There was one night never to be forgotten. While he was preaching it lightened exceedingly ; his spirit rose on the tempest ; his voice tolled out the doom and decay hanging over all nature ; he preached the warnings and the consolations of the coming of the Son of Man. The thunder broke over his head, the lightning shone along the preacher's path, it ran along the ground in wild glares from one part of heaven to the other ; the whole audience shook like the leaves of a forest in the wind, whilst high amidst the thunders and the lightnings, the preacher's voice rose, exclaiming, "Oh, my friends, the wrath of God ! the wrath of God !" Then his spirit seemed to pass serenely right through the tempest, and he talked of Christ, who swept the wrath away ; and then he told how he longed for the time when Christ should be revealed amidst the flaming fire, consuming all natural things. "Oh," exclaimed he, "that my soul may be in a like flame when He shall come to call me !" Can we realise what his soul must have been who could burn with such seraphic ardours in the midst of such scenes ?

So he opened the way everywhere, by his field-preaching, for John Wesley. Truly it has been said, " Whitefield, and not Wesley, is the prominent figure in the opening of the Methodist movement ;" and the time we must assign to this first popular agitation is the winter of 1738-39. The two men were immensely different. To

Whitefield the preaching was no light work; it was not talking. After one of his sermons, drenched through, he would lie down, spent, sobbing, exhausted, death-like: John Wesley, after one of his most effective sermons, in which he also had shaken men's souls, would just quietly mount

WHITEFIELD PREACHING IN LONDON.

his little pony, and ride off to the next village or town, reading his book as he went, or stopping by the way to pluck curious flowers or simples from the hedges; the poise of their spirits was so different. All great movements need two men, Moses and Aaron; the prophet Elijah must go before, "to restore all things." White-

field lived in the immediate neighbourhood and breathed
the air of essential truth ; Wesley looked at men, and saw
how all remained undone until the work took coherency
and shape. As he says, " I was convinced that preaching
like an apostle, without joining together those that are
awakened, and training them up in the ways of God, is only
begetting children for the murderer." Whitefield preached
like an apostle ; the scenes we have described look charming rural scenes, in which men's hearts were bowed and
hushed before him ; but there were widely different scenes
when he defied the devil, and sought to win his victims
away, even in fairs and wakes—the most wild and dissolute
periodical pests and nuisances of the age. We have seen
how rough human nature went down before him, as in the
instance of the man who came with heavy stones to pelt
him, and suddenly found his hands as it were tied, and
himself in tears, and, at the close, went up to the preacher,
and said, " I came here only to break your head, and you
have broken my heart !"

But the roughs of London seem to have been worse than
the roughs of Kingswood ; and we cannot wonder that
men like Walpole, and even polite and refined religious
men, thought that a man who could go right into St.
Bartholomew's Fair, in Moorfields, and Finsbury, take
his station among drummers, trumpeters, merry-andrews,
harlequins, and all kind of wild beasts, must be " mad ; " it
must have seemed the height of fanaticism, like preaching
to a real Gadarene swinery. All the historians of the
movement—Sir James Stephen, Dr. Abel Stevens, Dr.
Southey, Isaac Taylor, and others, recite with admiration
the story of the way in which he wrestled successfully
with the merry-andrews. He began to preach at six

o'clock in the morning; stones, dirt, rotten eggs were
hurled at him. "My soul was among lions," he says;
but the marvellous voice overcame, and he went on speaking, and we know how tenderly he would speak to them, of
their own miseries, and the dangers of their own sins;
the great multitude—it was between twenty and thirty
thousand—"became like lambs;" he finished, went away,
and, in the wilder time—in the afternoon—he came again.
In the meantime there had been organisations to put him
down: here was a man with a long heavy whip to strike
the preacher; there was a recruiting sergeant who had
been engaged with drum and fife to interrupt him. As he
appeared on the outskirts of the crowd, Whitefield, who
well knew how to catch the humour of the people too,
exclaimed, "Make way for the king's officer!" and the
mob divided, while, to his surprise, the recruiting officer,
with his drum, found himself immediately beneath Whitefield; it was easy to manage him now. The crowd
around roared like wild beasts; it must have been a
tremendous scene. Will it be believed—it seems incredible—that he continued there, preaching, praying, singing,
until the night fell? He won a decided victory, and the
next day received no fewer than a thousand notes from
persons, "brands plucked from the burning," who spoke
of the convictions through which they had passed, and
implored the preacher to remember them in his prayers.

This was in Moorfields, in which neighbourhood since,
the followers both of Wesley and of Whitefield have found
their tabernacles and most eminent fields of usefulness.
Many have attempted fair-preaching since Whitefield's day,
but not, we believe, with much success; it needs a remarkable combination of powers to make such efforts successful.

Whitefield was able to attempt to outbid the showmen, merry-andrews, and harlequins, and he succeeded. No wonder they called him a fanatic ; he might have said, " If we be beside ourselves, it is for God, that by all means we may save some ! "

But what we have been especially desirous that our readers should note is, that these more vehement manifestations of Methodism were not the result of any methodised plan, but were a simple yielding to, and taking possession of circumstances ; it was as if "the Spirit of the Lord" came down upon the leaders, and "carried them whither they knew not."

CHAPTER V.

THE REVIVAL BECOMES CONSERVATIVE.

LORD MACAULAY'S verdict upon John Wesley, that he possessed a "genius for government not inferior to that of Richelieu," received immediate demonstration when he came actively into the movement, and has been abundantly confirmed since his death, in the history of the society which he founded. It has been said that all institutions are the prolonged shadow of one mind, and that by the inclusiveness, or power of perpetuity in the institution, we may know the mind of the founder. Much of our last chapter was devoted to some attempt to realise the place and power of Whitefield; what he was in relation to the Revival may be defined by the remark, often made, and by capable critics, that while there have been multitudes of better sermon-makers, it is uncertain whether the Church ever had so great a pulpit orator. In Wesley's mind everything became structural and organic; he was a mighty master of administration; but he also followed Whitefield's example, and took to the fields; and we shall see that very great, indeed, amazing results, followed his ministry.

Many of the incidents which are impressive and amusing show the difference between the men. Whitefield, as we have seen, overwhelmed the people : Wesley met insolence and antagonism by some sharp, concise, and cuttingly appropriate retort, which was remarkable, considering his stature. But both his presence and his words must have been usually commanding : " Be silent, or begone," he turned round sharply and said once to some violent disturbers, and they were obedient to the command.

We have always thought Wesley's rencontre with Beau Nash at Bath a fair illustration of his quiet and almost obscurely sarcastic method of quite sufficiently confounding a troublesome person. Preaching in the open air at Bath, the King of Bath, the Master of the Ceremonies, Nash, was so unwise as to attempt to put down the apostolic man. Nash's character was bad ; it was that of an idle, heartless, licentious dangler on the skirts of high society. He appeared in the crowd, and authoritatively asked Wesley by what right he dared to stand there. The congregation was not wholly of the poor ; there were a number of fashionable and noble persons present, and among them many with whom this attack had been pre-arranged, and who expected to see the discomfiture of the Methodist by the courtly and fashionable old dandy. Wesley replied to the question simply and quietly that he stood there by the authority of Jesus Christ, conveyed to him " by the present Archbishop of Canterbury, when he laid hands on me and said, ' Take thou authority to preach the Gospel!' " Nash began to bustle and to be turbulent, and he exclaimed, " This is contrary to Act of Parliament ; this is a conventicle." " Sir," said

Wesley, "the Act you refer to applies to seditious meetings : here is no sedition, no shadow of sedition ; the meeting is not, therefore, contrary to the Act." Nash stormed, "I say it is ; besides your preaching frightens people out of their wits." "Sir," said Wesley, "give me leave to ask, Did you ever hear me preach ?" "No !" "How, then, can you judge of what you have never heard ?" "Sir, by common report." "Common report is not enough," said Wesley ; "again give me leave to ask is your name not Nash ?" "My name is Nash." And then the reader must imagine Wesley's thin, clear, piercing voice, cutting through the crowd : "Sir, I dare not judge of *you* by common report." There does not seem much in it, but the effect was overwhelming. Nash tried to bully it out a little ; but, to make his discomfiture complete, the people took up the case, and especially one old woman, whose daughter had come to grief through the fop, in her way so set forth his sins, that he was glad to retreat in dismay. On another occasion, when attempts were made to assault Wesley, but there was some uncertainty about his person, and the assailants were saying, "Which is he ? which is he ?" he stood still as he was walking down the crowded street, turned upon them, and said, "I am he ;" and they instantly fell back, awed into involuntary silence and respect.

It is characteristic that while Whitefield simply took to the work of field-preaching, and preaching in the open air, and troubled himself very little about finding or giving reasons for the irregularity of the proceeding, Wesley defended the practice with formidable arguments. It is remarkable that the practice should have been deemed so irregular, or should need vindication, considering that our Lord had given to it the sanction of His example, and that it had been adopted by the apostles and fathers, the greatest of the Catholic preachers, and the reformers of every age. A history of field and street-preaching would form a large and interesting chapter of Church history. Southey quotes a very happy series of arguments from one of Wesley's appeals : "What need is there," he says, speaking for his antagonists, "of this preaching in the fields and streets ? Are there not churches enough to preach in ? " " No, my friend, there are not, not for us to preach in. You forget we are not suffered to preach there else we should prefer them to any place whatever." " Well, there are ministers enough without you." " Ministers enough, and churches enough ! For what ? To reclaim all the sinners within the four seas ? and one plain reason why these sinners are never reclaimed is this : they never come into a church. Will you say, as some tender-hearted Christians I have heard, 'Then it is their own fault ; let them die and be damned !' I grant it may be their own fault, but the Saviour of souls came after us, and so we ought to seek to save that which is lost." He went on to confess the irregularity, but he retorted that those persons who compelled him to be irregular had no right to censure him for irregularity. "Will they throw a man into the dirt," said he, "and beat him because he is dirty ? Of all men living those clergymen ought not to complain who believe I preach the Gospel ; if they will not ask me to preach in their churches, they are accountable for my preaching in the fields." This is a fair illustration of neat shrewdness, the compact, incisive common sense of Wesley's mind. Thus he argued himself into that sphere of labour which justified him in after years in saying, without any extravagance, " The world is my parish."

We have said the Revival became conservative. It is true the Countess of Huntingdon did much to make it so ; but it assumed a shape of vitality, and a force of coherent strength, chiefly from the touch of Wesley's administrative

JOHN WESLEY.

mind. The present City Road Chapel, which was opened in 1776, opposite Bunhill Fields Burial Ground, is probably the first illustration of this fact ; it stands where stood the Foundry—time-honoured spot in the history of Methodism. It stood in Moorfields ; the City Road was a mere lane then. The building had been used by government for

casting cannon ; it was a rude ruin. Wesley purchased it
and the site at the very commencement of his work, in
1739; he turned it into a temple. As the years passed
on it became the metropolitan seat of every holy agency
of Christian usefulness ; it was the cradle of London
Methodism, accommodating fifteen hundred people.
Until within twenty years of Wesley's purchase this had
been a kind of Woolwich Arsenal to the government;
it became a temple of peace, and here came "band
rooms," schoolrooms, book-rooms—the first saplings of
Methodist usefulness.

How truly it has been said by a writer in the *British
Quarterly*, that the most romantic lives of the saints of
the Roman Catholic calendar do not present a more startling succession of incidents than those which meet us in
the life and labours of Wesley. Blessed Raymond, of
Pegnafort, spread his cloak upon the sea to transport him
across the water, sailing one hundred and sixty miles in six
hours, and entering his convent through closed doors ! The
devout and zealous Francis Xavier spent three whole days
in two different places at the same time, preaching all the
while ! Rome shines out in transactions like these :
Wesley does not ; but he seems to have been almost
ubiquitous, and he moves with a rapidity reminding us of
that flying angel who had the everlasting Gospel to preach,
and he shines alike in his conflicts with nature and the still
wilder tempests caused by the passions of men. We read
of his travelling, through the long wintry hours, two hundred and eighty miles on horseback, in six days ; it was a
wonderful feat in those times. When Wesley first began
his itinerancy there were no turnpikes in the country; but
before he closed his career, he had probably paid more,

says Dr. Southey, for turnpikes than any other man in England, for no other man in England travelled so much. His were no pleasant journeys, as of summer days ; he travelled through the fens of Lincolnshire when the waters were out ; and over the fells of Northumberland when they were covered with snow. Speaking of one tremendous journey, through dreadful weather, he says, " Many a rough journey have I had before ; but one like this I never had, between wind and hail, and rain, and ice, and snow, and driving sleet, and piercing cold ; but it is past. Those days will return no more, and are therefore as though they had never been.

> " ' And pain, like pleasure, is a dream ! ' "

How singular was his visit to Epworth, where he found the church of his childhood, his father's church, the church of his own first ministrations, closed against him. The minister of the church was a drunkard ; he had been under great obligations, both to Wesley himself and to the Wesley family, but he assailed him with the most offensive brutality ; and when Wesley, denied the pulpit, signified his intention of simply partaking of the Lord's Supper with the parishioners on the following Sunday, the coarse man sent word, " Tell Mr. Wesley I shall not give him the Sacrament, for he is not *fit*." It seems to have cut Mr. Wesley very deeply. " It was fit," he says, " that he who repelled me from the table where I had myself so often distributed the bread of life, should be one who owed his all in this world to the tender love my father had shown to his, as well as personally to himself." He stayed there, however, eight days, and preached every evening in the churchyard, standing on his father's

tomb; truly a singular sight, the living son, the prophet
of his age, surely little short of inspired, preaching from
his dead father's grave with such pathos and power as
we may well conceive. "I am well assured," he says, "I
did far more good to my old Lincolnshire parishioners
by preaching three days on my father's tomb than I did
by preaching three years in his pulpit!"

WESLEY PREACHING IN EPWORTH CHURCHYARD.

As he travelled to and fro, odd mistakes sometimes
happened. Arrived at York, he went into the church in
St. Saviour's Gate; the rector, one Mr. Cordeau, had
often warned his congregation against going to hear "that

vagabond Wesley" preach. It was usual in that day for
ministers of the Establishment to wear the cassock or
gown, just as everywhere in France we see the French
abbés. Wesley had on his gown, like a university man in
a university town. Mr. Cordeau, not knowing who he was,
offered him his pulpit; Wesley was quite willing, and
always ready. Sermons leaped impromptu from his lips,

EPWORTH CHURCH.

and this sermon was an impressive one; at its close the
clerk asked the rector if he knew who the preacher was.
"No." "Why, sir, it was that vagabond Wesley!" "Ah,
indeed!" said the astonished clergyman; "well, never
mind, we have had a good sermon." The anecdotes of

the incidents which waited upon the preacher in his travels are of every order of humorous, affecting, and romantic interest; they are spread over a large variety of volumes, and even still need to be gathered, framed, and hung in the light of some effective chronicle.

We may suppose our readers to be acquainted with the brilliant passage to which we have already referred, in which Lord Macaulay portrays, as with the pencil of a Vandyke, the features of the great English Puritans. Perhaps, even had the great essayist attempted the task, he had scarcely the requisite sympathies to give an effective portrait or portraits of the early Methodists; indeed, their characters are different, as different as a portrait from the pencil of Denner to one from that of Vandyke, or of Velasquez; but as Denner is wonderful too, although so homely, so the Methodist is a study. The early Methodist was, perhaps, usually a very simple, what we should call an ignorant, man, but he had "the light which lighteth every man that cometh into the world." He was not such an one as the early Puritan or the ancient Huguenot, those children of the camp and of the sword, Nonconformist Templars and Crusaders, whose theology had trained them for the battle-field, teaching them to frown defiance on kings, and to treat with contempt the proudest nobles, if they were merely unsanctified men. The Methodist was not such an one as the stern Ironside of Cromwell; as he lived in a more cheerful age, so he was the subject of a more cheerful piety; he was as loyal as he was lowly. He had been forgotten or neglected by all the priests and Levites of the land; but a voice had reached him, and raised him to the rank of a living, conscious, immortal soul. He also was one for whom Christ

died.   A new life had created new interests in him ; and
Christianity, really believed, does ennoble a man—how can
it do otherwise ?   It gives self-respect to a man, it shows
to him a new purpose and business in life ; moreover, it
creates a spirit of holy cheerfulness and joy ; and thus
came about that state of mind which Wesley made sub-
servient to organisation—the necessity for meetings and
reciprocations.   It has been said that every church must
have some sign or countersign, some symbol to make it
popularly successful.   St. Dominic gave to his order the
Rosary ; John Wesley gave to his Society the Ticket.   There
were no chapels, or but few, and none to open their doors to
these strange new pilgrims to the celestial city.   We have
seen that the churches were closed against them.   We
believe Lord Macaulay to be right when he says, had
John Wesley risen in the Church of Rome, she would
have thrown her arms round him, only regarding him
as the founder of a new order, with certain pecu-
liarities calculated to increase and to extend her empire,
and in due time have given to him the honours of canonisation.

The clergy as a body gathered up their garments and
shrunk from all contact with the Methodists as from a
pestilence.   What could be done ?   Something must be
done to prevent them from falling back into the world.
Piety needs habit, and must become habitual to be safe,
even as the fine-twined linen of the veil, and the ark of
the covenant, and the cherubim shadowing the mercy-seat,
were shut in and all their glory defended by the rude
coverings of badger-skins.   John Wesley knew that the
safety of the converted would be in frequent meetings
for singing and prayer and conversation.   Reciprocation

is the soul of Methodism; so they assembled in each others' houses, in rude and lonely but convenient rooms, by farm-house ingles, in lone hamlets. Thus was created a homely piety, often rugged enough, no doubt, but full of beautiful and pathetic instincts. So grew what came to be called band-meetings, class-meetings, love-feasts, and all the innumerable means by which the Methodist Society worked, until it became like a wheel within a wheel; simple enough, however, in the days to which we are referring. "Look to the Lord, and faithfully attend all the means of grace appointed in the Society." Such was, practically, the whole of Methodism. So that famous old lady, whose bright example has so often been held up on Methodist platforms, when called upon to state the items of her creed, did so very sufficiently when she summed it up in the four particulars of "repentance towards God; faith in the Lord Jesus Christ; a penny a week; and a shilling a quarter." Wesley seems to have summed the Methodist creed more simply still: "Belief in the Lord Jesus Christ, and an earnest desire to flee from the wrath to come." This was his condition of Church fellowship. When the faith became more consciously objective, it too was seized by the passionate instinct, the desire to save souls. This drove the early Methodists out on great occasions to call vast multitudes together on heaths, on moors. Perhaps—but this was at a later time—some country gentleman threw open his old hall to the preachers; but the more aristocratic phase of the Methodist movement fell into the Calvinistic rather than into the Wesleyan ranks, and, as we shall see, subsided into the organisation of the Countess of Huntingdon, which was, in fact, a kind of Free Church of England. The followers of Wesley sought the sequestration of nature, or in cities and towns they took to the streets or the broad ways and outlying fields. In some neighbourhoods a little room was built, containing the germ of what in a few years became a large Wesleyan Society. The burden of all these meetings, and all their intercourse, whether in speech or song, was the sweetness and fulness of Jesus. They had intense faith in the love of God shed abroad in the heart ; and their great interest was in souls on the brink of perdition. They knew little of spiritual difficulties or speculative despair ; their conflict was with the world, the flesh, and the devil ; and in this person, whose features have lately become somewhat dim, and who has wrapped himself in a new cloak of darkness, they did really believe. Wesley dealt with sin as sin, and with souls as souls ; he and his band of preachers had little regard to proprieties, and it was not a polished time ; so, ungraceful and undignified, the face weary, and the hand heavy with toil, they seemed out of breath pursuing souls. The strength of all these men was that they had a definite creed, and they sought to guard it by a definite Church life. The early Methodist had also cultivated the mighty instinct of prayer, about which he had no philosophy, but believing that God heard him, he quite simply indulged in it as a passion, and in it to him there was at once a meaning and a joy. We are not under the necessity of vindicating every phase of the great movement, we are simply writing down some particulars of its history, and how it was that it grew and prevailed. God's ministry goes on by various means, ordinary and extraordinary ; that is the difference between rivers and rains, between dews and lightnings.

A very interesting chapter, perhaps a volume, might be

compiled from the old records of the mere anecdotes—the
very humours—of the persecution attending on the Revival.
Thus, in Cornwall, Edward Greenfield, a tanner, with a
wife and seven children, was arrested under a warrant
granted by Dr. Borlase, the eminent antiquary, who was,
however, a bitter foe to Methodism. It was inquired
what was the objection to Greenfield, a peaceable, inoffen-
sive man; and the answer was, "The man is well enough,
but the gentlemen round about can't bear his impudence;
why, he says he knows his sins are forgiven!" The story
is well known how, in one place, a whole waggon-load of
Methodists were taken before the magistrates; but when
the question was asked in court what they had done, a
profound silence fell over the assembly, for no one was
prepared with a charge against them, till somebody
exclaimed, "They pretended to be better than other
people, and prayed from morning till night!" And
another voice shouted out, "And they've *convarted* my
wife; till she went among they, she had a tongue of
her own, and now she's as quiet as a lamb!" "Take
them all back, take them all back," said the sensible
magistrate, "and let them convert all the scolds in the
town!"

There is a spot in Cornwall which may be said to be
consecrated and set apart to the memory of Wesley; it is
in the immediate neighbourhood of Redruth, a wild, bare,
rugged-looking region now, very suggestive of its savage
aspect upwards of a hundred years since. The spot to
which we refer is the Gwennap Pit; it is a wild
amphitheatre, cut out among the hills, capable of holding
about thirty thousand persons. Its natural walls slant
upwards, and the place has altogether wonderful properties

for the carrying the human voice. Wesley began to preach in this spot in 1762. When he first visited Cornwall, the savage mobs of what used to be called "West Barbary," howled and roared upon him like lions or wild beasts ; in his later years of visitation, no emperor or sovereign prince could have been received with more reverence and affection. The streets were lined and the windows of the houses thronged with gazing crowds, to see him as he walked along ; and no wonder, for Cornwall was one of the chief territories of that singular ecclesiastical kingdom of which he was the founder. When he first went into Cornwall, it was really a region of savage irreligion and heathenism. The reader of his life often finds, usually about once a year, the visit to Gwennap Pit recorded : he preached his first sermon there, as we have said, in 1762 ; at the age of eighty-six he preached his last in 1789. There, from time to time, they poured in from all the country round to see and to listen to the words of this truly reverend father.

The traditions of Methodism have few more imposing scenes. Gwennap Pit was, perhaps, Wesley's most famous cathedral ; a magnificent church, if we may apply that term to a building of nature, among the wild moors ; it was thronged by hushed and devout worshippers. Until Wesley went among these people, the whole immense population might have said, "No man cared for our souls ; " now they poured in to see him there : wild miners from the immediate neighbourhood, fishermen from the coast, men who until their conversion had pursued the wrecker's remorseless and criminal career, smugglers, more quiet men and their families less savage, but not less ignorant, from their shieling, or lowly farm-stead on the distant heath. A strange throng, if we think

WESLEY PREACHING IN GWENNAP PIT.

of it, men who had never used God's name except in an oath, and who had never breathed a prayer except for the special providence of a shipwreck, and who with wicked barbarity had kindled their delusive lights along the coasts, to fascinate unfortunate ships to the cruel cliffs! But a Divine power had passed over them, and they were changed, with their families ; and hither they came to gladden the heart of the old patriarch in the wild glen —a strange spot, and not unbeautiful, roofed over by the blue heavens. Amidst the broom, the twittering birds, the heath flower, and the scantling of trees, amidst the venerable rocks, it must have been wonderful to hear the thirty thousand voices welling up, and singing Wesley's words :

> " Suffice that for the season past,
> Hell's horrid language filled our tongues ;
> We all Thy words behind us cast,
> And loudly sang the drunkard's songs.
> But, oh, the power of grace Divine !
> In hymns we now our voices raise,
> Loudly in strange hosannahs join,
> While blasphemies are turned to praise !"

Such was one of the triumphs of the Great Revival.

CHAPTER VI.

THE SINGERS OF THE REVIVAL.

CHIEF of all the auxiliary circumstances which aided the Great Revival, we believe, beyond a question, was this : that it taught the people of England, for the first time, the real power of sacred song. That man in the north of England who, when taken by a companion who had been converted to a great Methodist preaching, and being asked at the close of the service how he had enjoyed it, replied, " Weel, I didna care sae mich aboot the preaching, but, eh, man ! yon ballants were grand," was no doubt a representative character. And the great and subduing power of large bodies of people, moved as with one heart and one voice, must have greatly aided to produce those effects which we are attempting to realise. All great national movements have acknowledged and used the power of song. For man is a born singer, and if he cannot sing himself he likes to feel the power of those who can. It has been so in political movements : there were the songs of the Roundheads and the Cavaliers. And the greatest religious movements through all the Christian ages have acknowledged the power of sacred

song, even from the days of the apostles, and from the
time of St. Ambrose in Milan. Luther soon found that
he must teach the people to sing. That is a pleasant little
story, how once, as he was sitting at his window, he
heard a blind beggar sing. It was something about the
grace of God, and Luther says the strain brought tears
into his eyes. Then, he says, the thought suddenly flashed
into his mind, " If I could only make gospel songs which
people could sing, and which would spread themselves up
and down the cities!" He directly set to work upon this
inspiration, and let fly song after song, each like a lark
mounting towards heaven's gate, full of New Testament
music. "He took care," says one writer, in mentioning
the incident, "that each song should have some re-
memberable word or refrain; such as ' Jesus,' ' Believe and
be saved,' ' Come unto Me,' ' Gospel,' ' Grace,' ' Worthy is
the Lamb,' and so on."

Until Watts and Doddridge appeared, England had no
popular sacred melodies. Amongst the works of the
poets, such as Sir Philip Sidney, Milton, Sandys, George
Herbert, and others, a few were scattered up and down;
but they mostly lacked the subtle element which constitutes
a hymn. For, just as a man may be a great poet, and
utterly fail in the power to write a good song, so a man
may be a great sacred poet, and yet miss the faculty which
makes the hymn-writer. It is singular, it is almost in-
definable. The subtle something which catches the
essential elements of a great human experience, and gives
it lyrical expression, takes that which other men put into
creeds, sermons, theological essays, and sets it flying, as
we just now said, like "the lark to heaven's gate." It
ought never to be forgotten that Watts was, in fact, the

creator of the English hymn.   He wrote many lines which good taste can in no case approve ; but here again the old proverb holds true, " The house that is building does not look like the house that is built."   And the great number of following writers, while they have felt the inspiration he gave to the Church, have moulded their lines by a more fastidious taste, which, if it has sometimes improved the metre or the sentiment, has possibly diminished in the strength.   We will venture to say that even now there is a greater average of majesty of thought and expression in Watts's hymns than in any other of our great hymn-writers ; although, in some cases, we find here and there a piece which may equal, and some one or two which are said to surpass, the flights of the sweet singer of Stoke Newington.   But the hymns of Watts, as a whole, were not so well fitted to a great and popular revival, to the expression of a tumultuous and passionate experience, as some we shall notice. They were, as a whole, especially wanting in the social element, and the finest of them sound like notes from the harp of some solitary angel.   One cannot give to them the designation which the Wesleys gave to large sections of their hymns, " suitable for experience meetings."   Praise rather than experience is the characteristic of Watts, although there are noble exceptions.   Our readers will perhaps remember a well-known and pleasing instance in a letter from Doddridge to his aged friend.   Doddridge had been preaching on a summer evening in some plain old village chapel in North- amptonshire, when at the close of the service was " given out," as we say, that hymn commencing :

"Give me the wings of faith to rise."

We can suppose the melody to which it was sung to have

been very rude ; but it was, perhaps, new to the people, and the preacher was affected as he saw how, over the congregation, the people were singing earnestly, and melted to tears while they sang ; and at the close of the service many old people gathered round Doddridge, their hearts all alive with the hymn, and they wished it were possible, only for once, to look upon the face of the dear old Dr. Watts.   Doddridge was so pleased that he thought his old friend would be pleased also, and so he wrote the account of the little incident in a letter to him.   In many other parts of the country, no doubt, the people were waiting and wishful for popular sacred harmonies. And when the Great Revival came, and congregations met by thousands, and multitudes who had been accustomed to song, thoughtless, foolish, very often sinful and licentious, still needed to sing (for song and human nature are inseparable, apparently, so far as we know anything about it, in the next world as well as in this), it was necessary that, as they had been "brought up out of the horrible pit and miry clay," "a new song of praise" should be put in the mouth.   John Wesley had heard much of Moravian singing. He took Count Zinzendorf's hymns, translated them, and immensely improved them ; he was the first who introduced into our psalmody the noble words of Paul Gerhardt. Some of the finest of all the hymns in the Wesleyan collection are these translations. Watts was unsparingly used. Wesley's first effort to meet this necessity of the Revival was the publication of his collection in 1739. And thus, most likely without knowing the anecdote of Luther we have quoted above, Wesley and his coadjutors did exactly what the Reformer had done. They gave effect to the Revival by the ordinance of song, and preached the Gospel in sweet words, and often recurring Gospel refrains.

The remark is true that there was no art, no splendid form of worship or ritual; early Methodism and the entire evangelic movement were as free from all this as Clairvaux in the Valley of Wormwood, when Bernard ministered there with all his monks around him, or as Cluny when Bernard de Morlaix chanted his " Jerusalem the Golden." Like all great religious movements which have shaken men's souls, this was purely spiritual, or if it had a secular expression it was not artificial. Loud amens resounded as the preacher spoke or prayed, and then the hearty gushes of, perhaps, not melodious song united all hearts in some litany or Te Deum in new-born verse from some of the singers of the last revival. Amongst infuriated mobs, we read how Wesley found a retreat in song, and over-powered the multitude with what we, perhaps, should not regard melody. Thus, when at Bengeworth in 1740, where Wesley was set upon by a crowd, and it was proposed by one that they should take him away and duck him, he broke out into singing with his redoubted friend, Thomas Maxfield. He allowed them to carry him whither they would ; at the bridge end of the street the mob retreated and left him; but he took his stand on the bridge, and striking up—

> " Angel of God, whate'er betide,
>   Thy summons I obey,"

preached a useful and effective sermon to hundreds who remained to listen, from the text, " If God be for us, who can be against us ? "

But the contributions of Watts and Wesley are so well known that it is more important, in an essay so brief as the present, to notice that as the Revival moved on, very soon other remarkable lyrists appeared to contribute, if few, yet really effective words. Of these none is more remarkable than the mighty cobbler, Thomas Olivers, a "sturdy Welshman," as Southey calls him. He is not to be confounded with John Oliver, also one of the notabilities of the Revival. Thomas was really an astonishing trophy of the movement; before his conversion he was a thoroughly bad fellow, a kind of wandering reprobate, an idle, dissipated man. He fell beneath the power of Whitefield, whom he heard preach from the text, "Is not this a brand plucked out of the fire?" He had made comic songs about Whitefield, and sung them with applause in tap-rooms. As Whitefield came in his way, he went with the purpose of obtaining fresh fuel for his ridicule. The heart of the man was completely broken, and he felt so much compunction for what he had done against the man for whom he now felt so deep a reverence and awe, that he used to follow him in the streets, and though he did not speak to him, he says he could scarcely refrain from kissing the prints of his footsteps. And now, he says at the beginning of his new life, what we can well believe of an imagination so intense and strong, "I saw God in everything : the heavens, the earth and all therein showed me something of Him ; yea, even from a drop of water, a blade of grass, or a grain of sand, I received instruction." He was about seriously to enter into a settled and respectable way of business when John Wesley heard of him ; and although he was converted under Whitefield, Wesley persuaded him to yield himself to his direction for the work of preaching as one of his itinerant band, and sent him into Cornwall—just the man we should think for Cornwall, fiery

and imaginative : off he went, in 1753. He was born in
1725. He testifies that he was "unable to buy a horse, so,
with my boots on my legs, my great-coat on my back,
and my bag with my books and linen across my shoulders,
I set out for Cornwall on foot." Henceforth there were
forty-six years on earth before him, during which he
witnessed a magnificent confession before many witnesses.
He became one of the foremost controversialists when dis-
sensions arose among the men of the Revival. He acquired
a knowledge of the languages, especially of Hebrew, and
was a great reader. Wesley appointed him as his editor
and general proof reader ; but he could never be taught to
punctuate properly, and the punctilious Wesley could not
tolerate his inaccuracies as they slipped through the proof,
so he did not retain this post long. But Wesley loved him,
and in 1799 he descended into Wesley's own tomb, and his
remains lie there, in the cemetery of the City Road Chapel.
He wrote more prose than poetry ; but, like St. Ambrose,
he is made immortal by a single hymn. He is the author
of one of the most majestic hymns in all hymnology. Byron
and Scott wrote Hebrew melodies, but they will not bear
comparison with this one. While in London upon one
occasion, he went into the Jewish synagogue, and he
heard sung there by a rabbi, Dr. Leoni, an old air, a
melody which so enchanted him and fixed itself in his
memory, that he went home, and instantly produced what
he called "a hymn to the God of Abraham," arranged to
the air he had heard. And thus we possess that which we
so frequently sing,

"The God of Abraham praise ! "

It is principally known by its first four verses ; there are twelve. "There is not," says James Montgomery, "in our language a lyric of more majestic style, more elevated thought, or more glorious imagery; it is like a stately pile of architecture, severe and simple in design; it strikes less on the first view than after deliberate examination, but the mind itself grows greater in contemplating it;" and he continues, "On account of the peculiarity of the measure, none but a person of equal musical and poetical taste could have produced the harmony perceptible in the verse." There will, perhaps, always be a doubt whether Olivers was the author of the hymn,

"Lo! He comes with clouds descending."

If Charles Wesley were the author, he undoubtedly derived the inspiration of the piece from Olivers' hymn, "The Last Judgment:" it is in the same metre, and probably Wesley took the thought and the metre, and adapted it to popular service. What is undoubted is that Olivers, who is the author of the metre, is also the author of the fine old tune "Helmsley," to which the hymn was usually sung until quite recent times; the tune was originally called "Olivers."

It is but a natural step from Thomas Olivers to his great antagonist, Augustus Toplady; he also is made immortal by a hymn. He wrote many fine ones, full of melody, pathos, and affecting imagery. Toplady, as all our readers know, was a clergyman, the Vicar of Broad Hembury, in Devonshire. He took the strong Calvinistic side in the controversies which arose in the course of the Great Revival; Olivers took the strong Arminian side. They were not very civil to each other; and the scholarly clergyman no doubt felt his dignity somewhat hurt by the rugged contact with the cobbler; but the quarrels are forgotten now, and there is scarcely a hymn-book in which the hymn of Olivers is not found within a few pages of

"Rock of Ages, cleft for me!"

To this hymn has been given almost universally the palm as the finest hymn in our language. Where there are so many, at once deeply expressive in experience, and subdued and elevated in feeling, we perhaps may be forgiven if we hesitate before praise so eminently high. Mr. Gladstone's translation into the Latin, in the estimation of eminent scholars, even carries a more thrilling and penetrative awe. But Toplady wrote many other hymns quite equal in pathos and poetic merit. The characteristic of "Rock of Ages" is its depth of penitential devotion. A volume might be written on the history of this expressive hymn. Innumerable are the multitudes whom these words have sustained when dying; they were among the last which lingered on the lips of Prince Albert as he was passing; and to how many, through every variety of social distinction, have they been at once the creed and consolation! It is by his hymns that Toplady will be chiefly remembered. For years he was hovering along on the borders of the grave, slowly dying of consumption; and he died in 1778, in the thirty-eighth year of his age. It was his especial wish that he should be buried with more than quiet, that no announcement should be made of the funeral, and that there should be no especial service at his grave: it testifies, however, to the high regard in which he was held that thousands followed him to his burial in Tottenham Court Road Chapel; and when we know that his dear friend Rowland Hill conducted the service, we can scarcely be surprised, or offended, that he broke through the injunctions of his friend, and addressed the multitude in affectionate commemoration of the sweet singer.

Toplady we should regard as the chief singer of the

AUGUSTUS TOPLADY.

Revival, after Charles Wesley, although entirely of another order; not so social as meditative, and reminding us, in many of his pieces, of the characteristics we have attributed to Watts. His midnight hymn is a piece of uncommon sublimity; portions of it seem almost unfit for congregational singing; but for inward plaintive meditation, for reading in the evening family prayer, when the hushed stillness of night is over the household, and the pilgrim of life is about to commit himself to the unconsciousness of sleep, the verses seem tenderly suggestive:

> " Thy ministering spirits descend,
>   And watch while Thy saints are asleep;
>   By day and by night they attend,
>   The heirs of salvation to keep.
>   Bright seraphs despatched from the throne,
>   Fly swift to their stations assigned;
>   And angels elect are sent down
>   To guard the elect of mankind.
>
>   Their worship no interval knows:
>   Their fervour is still on the wing;
>   And, while they protect my repose,
>   They chant to the praise of my King.
>   I, too, at the season ordained,
>   Their chorus for ever shall join;
>   And love and adore without end
>   Their gracious Creator and mine."

We have noticed in a previous chapter, that when Whitefield separated himself from Wesley, the Revival took two distinctly different routes. We only refer to this again for the purpose of remarking that as Toplady was intensely Calvinistic in his ideas of the method of Divine grace, so his hymns, also, reflect in all its fulness that creed; yet they are full of tenderness, and well calculated frequently to arouse dormant devotion. " Your harps, ye trembling saints;" " Emptied of earth I fain would be;" " When languor and disease invade;" " Jesus, immutably the same;" " A debtor to mercy alone," and many another, leave nothing to be desired either on the score of devotion, poetry, or melody.

In a far humbler sphere, but representing the same faith and fervour as Toplady, and also carried away young, was Cennick. In an article in the *Christian Remembrancer*, on English hymnology, written very much for the purpose of throwing contempt on all the hymn-writers of the Revival, Cennick is spoken of as " a low and violent person ; his hymns peculiarly offensive, both as to matter and manner." Some exceptions are made by the reviewer for " Children of the Heavenly King." We may presume, therefore, that to this writer, " Thou dear Redeemer, dying Lamb," is one of the " peculiarly offensive." This is not wonderful, when in the next page we read that " the hymns of Newton are the very essence of doggerel." This sounds rather strange, as a verdict, to those who have felt the particular charm of that much-loved hymn, " How sweet the name of Jesus sounds ! "

It is not without a purpose that we refer to this paper in the *Christian Remembrancer*—evidently by a very scholarly hand—because its whole tone shows how the sacred song of the Revival would be likely to be regarded by those who had no sympathy with its evangelical teaching. The writer, for instance, speaking of Wesley's hymns, doubts whether any of them could possibly be included by any chance in English hymnology ! " Jesus, lover of my soul," is said, " in some *small* degree to approximate to the model of a Church hymn ! " Of the Countess of Huntingdon's hymn-book, the writer says, " We shall certainly not notice the raving profanity ! " It is not necessary further either to sadden or to irritate the reader by similar expressions ; but the entire paper, and the criticisms we have

cited, will show what was likely to be the effect of the
hymns of the Revival on many similar minds of that time.
In fact, the joy of the Revival work arose from this, that
no person, no priest, nor Church usage, was needed to inter-
pose between the soul and the Saviour. Faith in Christ, and
His immediate, personal presence with the soul seeking
Him by faith, as it was the burden of the best of the
sermons, so it was, also, of all the great hymns.

The origin and the authors of several eminent hymns are
certainly obscure. To Edward Perronet must be assigned
the authorship of the fine coronation anthem of the Lamb
that was slain : " All hail the power of Jesu's name ! "

Another, which has become a universal favourite, is
" Beyond the glittering starry globe." This is a noble and
inspiring hymn ; only a few verses are usually quoted in
our hymn-books. Lord Selborne divides its authorship
between Fanch and Turner. We have seen it attributed to
Olivers ; this is certainly a mistake. The *Quarterly Review*,
in a very able paper on hymnology, reproducing an old
legend concerning it, traces it to two brothers in a humble
situation in life, one an itinerant preacher, the other a
porter. The preacher desired the porter to carry a letter
for him. " I can't go," said the porter, " I am writing a
hymn." " You write a hymn, indeed ! Nonsense ! you go
with the letter, and I will finish the hymn." He went, and
returned, but the hymn was unfinished. The preacher had
taken it up at the third verse, and his muse had forsaken
him at the eighth. " Give me the pen," said the porter,
and he wrote off,

> " They brought His chariot from above,
>   To bear Him to His throne ;
> Clapped their triumphant wings, and cried,
>   ' The glorious work is done ! ' "

Unfortunately the author of the paper in the *Quarterly Review* appears never to have seen the hymn in its entirety. The verse he cites is not the eighth, but the twenty-second, and it has been mutilated almost wherever quoted ; the verse itself is part of an apostrophe to the angels, recalling their ministrations round our Lord :

> " Tended His chariot up the sky,
>   And bore Him to His throne ;
> Then swept your golden harps and cried,
>   ' The glorious work is done ! ' "

Whoever wrote the hymn had the imagination of a poet, the fine pathos of a believer, and a strong lyrical power of expression.

Anecdotes of the origin of many of our great hymns of this period are as interesting as they are almost innumerable : those of which we are speaking are hymns of the Revival— to speak concisely—perhaps commenced with the Wesleys, and closed with Cowper and Newton. It must not be supposed that there were no singers save those whose verses found their way into the Wesleyan or other great collections of hymns ; there were James Grant, Joseph Griggs, especially notable, Miss Steele, the author of a great number of hymns of universal acceptance in all our churches, and which are more like those of Doddridge than any other since his day. Then there was John Stocker,—but we would particularly notice Job Hupton, the author of a hymn which has never been included in any hymn-book except *Our Hymn Book*, edited by the author of this volume, but which is scarcely inferior to " Beyond the glittering starry sky."

" Come, ye saints, and raise an anthem,
  Cleave the skies with shouts of praise.
Sing to Him who found a ransom,
  Ancient of eternal days.
Bring your harps, and bring your odours,
  Sweep the string and pour the lay :
View His works ! behold His wonders !
  Let hosannas crown the day ! "

The hymn is far too long for quotation. Job Hupton was
a Baptist minister in the neighbourhood of Beccles, where
he died in 1849, in the eighty-eighth year of his age, and
the sixty-fifth of his ministry.

Thus there was set free throughout the country a spirit
of sacred song which was new to the experience of the
nation : it was boldly evangelical ; it was devoted, not to
the eulogy of Church forms and days ; there was not a
syllable of Mariolatry ; but praise to Christ, earnest meditation upon the state of man without His work, and the
blessedness of the soul which had risen to the saving
apprehension of it. This forms the whole substance of the
Divine melody. It has seemed to some that the most
perfect hymn in the English language is, " Jesus ! lover of
my soul." Sentiments may differ, arising from modifications of experience, but that hymn undoubtedly is the very
essence of all the hymns which were sung in the days of
the Great Revival. For the first time there was given to
Christian experience that which met it at every turn.
Watts found such a choir, and such an audience for his
devotions, as he had never known in his life ; and " Charles
Wesley," says Isaac Taylor, " has been drawing thousands
in his wake and onward, from earth to heaven." The
hymns met and united all companies and all societies.
The bridal party returned from church, singing,

> " We kindly help each other,
> Till all shall wear the starry crown."

If they gathered round the grave, they sang;—and what a variety of glorious funereal hymns they had! But that was a great favourite :

> " There all the ship's company meet,
> Who sailed with their Saviour beneath ;
> With shoutings each other they greet,
> And triumph o'er sorrow and death."

Few separations took place without that song,

> " Blest be the dear uniting love,
> That will not let us part."

While others became such favourites that even almost every service had to be hallowed by them ; such as,

> " Jesus ! the name high over all,
> In hell, or earth, or sky ; "

while an equal favourite almost, was,

> " Oh, for a thousand tongues to sing
> My great Redeemer's praise ! "

They must soon have become very well known, for so early as 1748, when a sad cluster of convicts, horse-stealers, highway robbers, burglars, smugglers, and thieves, were led forth to execution, the turnkey of the prison said he had never seen such people before. The Methodists had been among them ; they had all yielded themselves to the power of " the truth as it is in Jesus," and on their way to Tyburn they all sang together,

> " Lamb of God ! whose bleeding love
> We now recall to mind,
> Send the answer from above,
> And let us mercy find ;
> Think on us, who think of Thee,
> And every struggling soul release ;
> Oh ! remember Calvary,
> And let us go in peace ! "

The hymns found their way to sick beds. The old Earl of Derby, the grandfather of the present peer, was dying at Knowsley. He had for his housekeeper there a Mrs. Brass, a good and faithful Methodist ; the old Earl was fond of talking with her upon religious matters, and one day she read to him the well-known hymn, "All ye that pass by, to Jesus draw nigh." When she came to the lines,

> " The Lord in the day of His anger did lay
> Our sins on the Lamb, and He bore them away,"

the Earl looked up and said, "Stop ! don't you think, Mrs. Brass, that ought to be, ' The Lord in the day of His *mercy* did lay ? ' "

The old lady did not admit the validity of his lordship's theology ; but it very abundantly showed that his experience had passed through the verse, and reached to the true meaning of the hymn. An old blind woman was hearing Peter McOwan preach. He quoted these lines :

> " The Lord pours eyesight on the blind ;
> The Lord supports the fainting mind."

The poor old woman was not happy until she met the preacher, and she said, "But are there really such sweet verses ? Are you sure the book contains such a hymn ?" and he read the whole to her. It is one by Watts :

> " I'll praise my Maker while I've breath."

Innumerable are the anecdotes of these hymns; they inaugurated really the rise of English hymnology; and it is not too much to say that, as compared with them, many more recent hymns are as tinsel compared with gold. A writer truly says: " They sob, they swell, they meet the spirit in its most hushed and plaintive mood. They roll and bear it aloft, in its most inspired and prophetic moods, as on the surge of more than a mighty organ swell ; among the mines and quarries, and wild moors of Cornwall, among the factories of Lancashire and Yorkshire, in chambers of death, in the most joyous assemblages of the household, they have relieved the hard lot, and sweetened the pleasant one; and even in other lands soldiers and sailors, slaves and prisoners, have recited with what joy these words have entered into their life."

Thus the great hymns of this period grew and became a religious power in the land, strangely contradicting a verdict which Cardinal Wiseman pronounced some years since, that "all Protestant devotion is dead." While we give all honour to the fine hymns of Denmark and Germany, many of the best of which were translated with the movement, it may, with no exaggeration, be said that the hymnology of England in the eighteenth century is the finest and most complete which the history of the Church has known.

CHAPTER VII.

THE HERESY OF LAY PREACHING, AND SOME OF THE LAY PREACHERS.

THERE came with the work of the Revival a practice, without which it is more than questionable if it would have obtained such a rapid and abiding hold upon the various populations and districts of the country; this was lay preaching. But the designation must have a more inclusive interpretation than we generally apply to it; we must understand by it rather the work of those men who, in contradistinction to the great leaders of the Revival—men of scholarship, of universities, and of education—possessed none of these qualifications, or but in a more slight and undisciplined degree. They were converted men, modified by various temperaments; they one and all possessed an ardent zeal; but, in many instances, we shall find that they were as much devoted to the work of the ministry as those who had received a regular ordination. It is singular that prejudices so strong should exist against lay preaching and preachers, for the practice has surely received the sanction of the most ancient usages of the Church, as even Dr. Southey admits, in his notes to the *Life of Wesley*. Thus, in the history of the Church, this pheno-menon could scarcely be regarded as new. Orders of preaching friars; "hedge-preachers," "black, white, and grey," with all their company; disciples of Francis, Dominic, or Ignatius, had spread over Europe during the dark and mediæval ages. Although this rousing element of Church life had not found much expression in the churches of the Reformation, yet with the impulse of the new Revival, up started these men by multitudes. The reason of this was very simple. There is a well-known little anecdote of some town missionary standing up in a broad highway preaching to a multitude. He was arrested by a Roman Catholic priest, who asked him from the edge of the crowd by what authority he dared to stand there? and who had given him the right to preach? The man had his New Testament in his hand; he rapidly turned to the last chapter of it, and said, "I find it written here, 'Let him that heareth say, Come!' I have heard, and I would say Come!" The anecdote represents suffi-ciently the rise and progress of lay preaching in the Revival. There first appeared, naturally, a simple set of men, who, in their different spheres, would, perhaps, lead and direct a prayer-meeting, and round it with some pious and gentle exhortation. We have already pointed out the necessity soon felt for frequent and reciprocative services; these were not the lay preachers to whom we refer; but in this fraternal form of Church fellowship, the lay preacher had his origin.

Wesley imposed restrictions upon his helpers which he soon found himself compelled to renounce. John Wesley

was a strong adherent to the idea of Church order. The
first lay preacher in his communion who leapt over the
traces was Thomas Maxfield. It was at the Foundry in
Moor Fields. Wesley was in Bristol, and the intelligence
was conveyed to him. He appears to have regarded it as
a serious and dangerous innovation. The great and good
Susannah Wesley, his mother—now past threescore years
and ten—infirm and feeble, was yet living in the Chapel
House of the Foundry. To her John hurried on his arrival
in London; and after his affectionate salutations and
inquiries, he expressed such a manifest dissatisfaction and
anxiety that she inquired the cause. With some indigna-
tion and unusual abruptness, he said, " Thomas Maxfield
has turned preacher, I find ; " and then the wise and saintly
woman gave him her advice. She reminded him that,
from her prejudices against lay preaching he could not
suspect her of favouring anything of the kind ; " but take
care," she said, " what you do respecting that young man,
for he is as surely called of God to preach as you are."
She advised her son to hear Maxfield for himself. He did
so, and at once buried all his prejudices. He exclaimed
after the sermon, " It is the Lord, let Him do what seemeth
Him good!" and Thomas Maxfield became the first of a
host who spread all over the country.

It may be supposed that the Countess of Huntingdon
very naturally shared all Wesley's prejudices against lay
preaching ; but she heard Maxfield preach, and she wrote
of him, " God has raised one from the stones to sit among
the princes of the people. He is my astonishment ; how
is God's power shown in weakness!" and she soon set herself to the work of supplying an order of men, of whom
Maxfield was the first to lead the way. By-and-by came

another innovation : the lay evangelists at first never went into the pulpit, but spoke from among the people, or from the desk. The first who broke through this usage was Thomas Walsh ; we will say more of him presently. He was a man of deep humility, and his life reveals entire and extraordinary consecration ; but he believed himself to be an ambassador for Christ ; and he walked directly up into the pulpit, never questioning, but quite disregarding the usual custom. The majesty of his manner, his solemn, impressive, and commanding eloquence, forbade all remark ; and henceforth all the lay preachers followed his example. There arose a band of extraordinary men. Let the reader refer to the chronicles of their lives, and the effects of their labours, and he will not suppose that he has seen anything in our day at all approaching to what they were.

Local preachers have now long been part of the great organisation of Methodism. But in the period to which we refer, it must be remembered that the pen had not commenced the exercise of its more popular influence. We have seen that there were few authors, few journalists, very few really popular books ; these men, then, with their various gifts of elevated holiness, broad and rugged humour, or glowing imagination, went to and fro among the people, rousing and instructing the dormant mind of the country. Then it was Wesley's great aim to sustain interest by variety. Wesley himself said that he believed he should preach himself and his congregation asleep if he were to confine his ministrations to one pulpit for twelve months. We would take the liberty to say in reference to this, that it would depend upon whether he kept his own mind fresh and wakeful during the time. He writes, however : " We have found by long and constant experience, that a frequent change of teachers is best ; this preacher has one talent, that another. No one whom I ever knew has all the talents which are needful for beginning, continuing, and perfecting the work in a whole congregation ; neither," he adds, " can he find matter for preaching morning and evening, nor will the people come to hear him ; hence he grows cold, and so do the people ; whereas if he never stays more than a fortnight together in one place, he may find matter enough, and the people will gladly hear him."

This certainly gives an idea but of a plain order of services ; and, no doubt, some of Wesley's preachers were of the plainest. There was Michael Fenwick, of whom Wesley says, "he was just made to travel with me—an excellent groom, *valet de chambre*, nurse, and, upon occasion, a tolerable preacher." This good man was one day vain enough to complain to Wesley, that although he was constantly travelling with him, his name was never inserted in Wesley's published *Journals*. In the next number he found himself immortalised with his master there. "I left Epworth," writes Wesley, "with great satisfaction, and about one preached at Clayworth. I think none were unmoved but Michael Fenwick, who fell fast asleep under an adjoining hayrick."

A higher type of man, but still of the very plain order of preachers, was Joseph Bradford. He also was Wesley's frequent travelling companion, and he judged no service too servile by which he could show his reverence for his master. But on one occasion Wesley directed him to carry a packet of letters to the post. The occasion was very extraordinary, and Bradford wished to hear Wesley's sermon first. Wesley was urgent, and insisted that the letters must go. Bradford refused ; he would hear the sermon. "Then," said Wesley, "you and I must part!" "Very good, sir," said Bradford. The service was over. They slept in the same room. On rising in the morning, Wesley accosted his old friend and companion, and asked if he had considered what had been said, that they must part. "Yes, sir," replied Bradford. "And must we part?" inquired Wesley. "Please yourself, sir," was the reply. "Will you ask my pardon?" rejoined Wesley. "No, sir." "You won't?" "No, sir." "Then I will ask yours," replied the great man. It is said that Bradford melted under the words, and wept like a child. But we must not convey the idea that the early preachers were generally of this order. "In a great house there are vessels to honour and vessels to dishonour." "Vessels of dishonour" assuredly were none of these men : but there were some who attained to a greatness almost as remarkable as the greatness of the three, Whitefield and the Wesleys.

What a man was John Nelson! His was a life full of singular incidents. It was truly apostolic, whether we consider its holy magnanimity, the violence and vehemence of the cruel persecutions he encountered, or his singular power over excited mobs ; reminding us sometimes of Paul fighting as with wild beasts at Ephesus, or standing with cunning tact, and disarming at once captain and crowd on the steps of the Castle at Jerusalem. Then, although he was but a poor working stonemason, he had a high gentlemanly bearing, before which those who considered themselves gentlemen, magistrates and others, fell back abashed and ashamed. He was one of the prophets of Yorkshire ; and many of the large Societies at this day in Leeds, Halifax, and Bradford owe their foundation to him. It seems wonderful to us now, that merely preaching the word of truth, and especially as John Nelson preached it, with such a cheerful, radiant, and even heavenly manner, should bring out mighty mobs to assault him. The stories of his itinerancy are innumerable, and his life is really one of the most romantic in these preaching annals. At Nottingham, while he was preaching, the crowds threw squibs at him and round him ; but, as he was still pursuing his path of speech, a sergeant in the army pressed up to him, with tears, saying, " In the presence of God and all this company, I beg your pardon. I came here on purpose to mob you, but I have been compelled to hear you ; and I here declare I believe you to be a servant of the living God !" He threw his arms round Nelson's neck, kissed him, and went away weeping ; and we see him no more. Perhaps more remarkable still was his reception at Grimsby. There the clergyman of the parish hired a drummer to gather a great mob, as he said, "to defend the rights of the Church." The storm which raged round Nelson was wild and ferocious ; but it illustrates the power of this extraordinary man over his rudest hearers, that after beating his drum for a long time, the poor drummer threw it away, and stood listening, the tears running down his cheeks.

Nelson was a man of immense physical strength ; his own trade had fostered this, and before his conversion he had, no doubt, been feared as a man who could hit out, and hit hard. As the most effectual means of silencing him, he was pressed for a soldier ; but John was not only a Methodist, he had adopted the Quaker notion that a Christian dare not fight ; and he seems to have been a real torment to the officers and men of the

JOHN NELSON AT NOTTINGHAM.

regiment, who indeed marched him about different parts of the country, but could not get him either to accept the king's money or to submit to drill. An officer put him in prison for rebuking his profanity, and threatened to chastise him. Nelson says, " It caused a sore temptation to arise in me ; to think that a wicked, ignorant man should thus torment me, and I able to tie his head and heels together. I found an old man's bone in me ; but the Lord lifted up the standard within, else should I have wrung his neck and set my foot upon him."

At length, after three months, the Countess of Hunting-don procured his discharge. The regiment was in New-castle. He preached there on the evening of the day on which he was liberated, and it is testified that a number of the soldiers from his regiment came to hear him, and parted from him with tears. He was arrested as a vagrant, without any visible means of living. A gentleman instantly stepped forward and offered five hundred pounds bail ; but the bail was refused. He was able to prove that he was a high-charactered, industrious workman ; but it availed nothing. Crowds wept and prayed for him as he was borne through the streets. " Fear not ! " he cried, " oh, friends ; God hath His way in the whirlwind, and in the storm. Only pray that my faith fail not ! " It was at Bradford. They thrust him into a most filthy dungeon. The authorities would give him no food. The people thrust in food, water, and candles. He shared these with some wretched prisoners in the same cage, and he sang hymns, and talked to them all night. He was marched off to York ; but there the excitement was so great when it was known that John Nelson was coming a prisoner that armed troops were ordered out to guard him. He says,

"Hell from beneath was moved to meet me at my coming!" All the windows were crowded with people—some in sympathy, but most cheering and huzzaing as if some great political traitor had been arrested; but he says, "The Lord made my brow like brass, so that I could look upon all the people as grasshoppers, and pass through the city as if there had been none in it but God and me."

Such was John Nelson. These anecdotes are sufficient to show the manner of man he was. He has been truly called "the proto-martyr of Methodism." But it is not in a hint or two that all can be said which ought to be said of this noble and extraordinary man. His conversion, perhaps, sank down to deeper roots than in many instances. The thoughts of Methodism found him perplexed with those agonising questions which have tormented men in all ages, until they have realised the truth as it is in Jesus. His life was guilty of no immoralities; he had a happy, humble home, was industrious, and receiving good wages; but as he walked to and fro among the fields he was distressed, "for," he said, "surely God never made man to be such a riddle to himself, and to leave him so." He heard Wesley preach. "Then," he says, "my heart beat like the pendulum of a clock, and I thought his whole discourse was aimed at me;" and so, in short, he became a Methodist, and a Methodist preacher; and among the noble names in the history of the Church of Christ, in his own line and order, it may be doubted whether a nobler name can be mentioned than that of John Nelson.

Quite another order of man, less human, but equally divine, was Thomas Walsh. His parents were Romanists, and he was intended by them for the Romish priesthood; and he appears to have been an intense Romanist ascetic until about eighteen years of age. He had a thoughtful and exceedingly intense nature, and his faith was no rest to him. In his dilemma he heard a Methodist preacher speak one day from the text, "Come unto Me, all ye that labour and are heavy laden, and I will give you rest." It appears to have been the turning-point of a remarkable life.

"The life of Thomas Walsh," says Dr. Southey, "might almost convince a Catholic that saints were to be found in other communions as well as in the Church of Rome." Walsh became a great biblical scholar; he was an Irishman, he mastered the native Irish, that he might preach in it; but Latin, Greek, and Hebrew became familiar to him; and of the Hebrew, especially, it is said that he studied so deeply, that his memory was an entire concordance of the whole Bible. His soul was as a flame of fire, but it burnt out the body quickly. John Wesley says of him, "I do not remember ever to have known a man who, in so few years as he remained upon earth, was the instrument of converting so many sinners." He became mighty in his influence over the Roman Catholics. The priests said that "Walsh had died some years ago, and that he who went about preaching, on mountains and highways, in meadows, private houses, prisons, and ships, was a devil who had assumed his shape." This was the only way in which they could account for the extraordinary influence he possessed. His labours were greatly divided between Ireland and London, but everywhere he bore down all before him by a kind of absorbed ecstasy of ardent faith; but he died at the age of twenty-seven. While lying on his death-bed he was oppressed with a sense of despair, even of his salvation. The sufferings of his mind on this account were protracted and intense; at last he broke out in an exclamation, " He is come! He is come! My Beloved is mine, and I am His for ever!" and so he fell back and died. Thomas Walsh is a great name still in the records of the lay preachers of early Methodism.

All orders of men rose: different from any we have mentioned was George Story, whose quiet, but earnest and reasonable nature, seems to have commanded the especial love of Southey. He appears never to have become what some call an enthusiast; but he interestingly illustrates, that it was not merely over the rugged and uninformed minds that the power of the Revival exercised its influence. Very curiously, he appears to have been converted by thinking about Eugene Aram, the well-known scholar, whose name has become so celebrated in fiction and in poetry, and who had a short time before been executed for murder at York. Story was impressed by the importance of the acquisition of knowledge, and Aram's extraordinary attainments kindled in his mind a sense of admiration and emulation; but, as he thought upon his life, he reasoned, "What did this man's learning profit him? It did not save him from becoming a thief and a murderer, or even from attempting his own life." It was an immense suggestion to him; it led him upon another track of thinking. The Methodists came through his village; he yielded himself to the influence, and Dr. Southey thinks "there is not in the whole biography of Methodism a more interesting or remarkable case than his." He became a great preacher, but disarmed and convinced men rather by his calm, dispassionate elevation of manner, than by such weapons as the cheerful *bonhomie* of Nelson, or the fervid fire of Walsh.

But we are, perhaps, conveying the idea that it was only

beneath the administration of John Wesley that these great lay preachers were to be found. It was not so ; but no doubt beneath that administration their itinerancy became more systematic and organised. Whitefield does not appear to have at all shared Wesley's prejudices on this means of usefulness ; but those men who fell beneath the influence of Whitefield, or the Countess, seem soon to meet us as settled ministers, in many, if not in all instances. Among them there are few greater names in the whole Revival than those of Captain Jonathan Scott and the renowned Captain Toriel Joss. Captain Scott was a captain of dragoons, and one of the heroes of Minden ; he was converted by the instrumentality of William Romaine, who, in spite of his prejudices against lay preaching, encouraged him in his excursions, in which he spoke to immense crowds with great effect. Fletcher, of Madeley, said, "his coat shames many a black one." He was a gentleman of an ancient and opulent family, and the Countess, who, naturally, was delighted to see people or her own order by her side, felt herself greatly strengthened by him. It was said, when he preached at Leeds the whole town turned out to hear him ; and he was one of the great preachers of the Tabernacle in Moorfields, during more than twenty years. But yet a far more famous man was Toriel Joss. He was a captain of the seas, and had led a life which somewhat reminds us of Newton's. He was a good and even great sailor, but he became a greater preacher. Whitefield said of these two men, that " God, who sitteth upon the flood, can bring a shark from the ocean, and a lion from the forest, to show forth His praise." Joss was a man of property, with a fair prospect of considerable wealth, when he renounced the seas and became one of the great lay preachers. Whitefield insisted that he should abandon the chart, the compass, and the deck, and take to the pulpit. He did so. In London his fame was second only to that of Whitefield himself. He became Whitefield's coadjutor at the Tabernacle, where, first as associate pastor, and afterwards as pastor, he

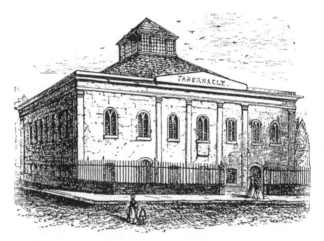

TABERNACLE, MOORFIELDS.

continued for thirty years. The chapel at Tottenham Court Road was his chief field, and John Berridge called him "Whitefield's Archdeacon of Tottenham."

We cannot particularise others: there were Sampson Staniforth, the soldier, Alexander Mather, Christopher Hopper, John Haime, John Parson—and these are only representative names. There were crowds of them; they travelled to and fro, with hard fare, throughout the land. Their excursions were not recreations or amusements. Attempt to think what England was at that time. It is a fact that they often had to swim through streams and wade through snows to keep their appointments; often to sleep in summer in the open air, beneath the trees of a forest. Sometimes a preacher was seen with a spade strapped to his back, to cut a way for man and horse through the heavy snow-drifts. Highwaymen were abroad, and there are many odd stories about their encounters with these men; but, then, usually, they had nothing to lose. Rogers, in his *Lives of the Early Preachers*, tells a characteristic story. One of these lay preachers, as usual on horseback, was waylaid by three robbers; one of them seized the bridle of his horse, the second put a pistol to his head, the third began to pull him from the saddle—all, of course, declaring that they would have his money or his life. The preacher looked solemnly at them, and asked them "if they had prayed that morning." This confounded them a little, still they continued their work of plunder. One pulled out a knife to rip the saddle-bag open; the preacher said, "There are only some books and tracts there; as to money, I have only twopence halfpenny in my pocket;" he took it out and gave it them. "All that I have of value about me," he said, "is my coat. I am a servant of God; I am going on His errand to preach; but let me kneel down and pray with you; that will do you more good than anything I can give you." One of them said, "I will have nothing to do with anything we can get from this man!" They had taken his watch; they restored this, and took up the bags and fastened them again on the horse. The preacher thanked them for their great civility to him; "But now," said he, "I will pray!" and he fell upon his knees, and prayed with great power. Two of the rascals, utterly frightened at this treatment, started off as fast as their legs could carry them; the third—he who had first refused to have anything to do with the job—continued on his knees with the preacher; and when they parted company, he promised that he would try to lead a new life, and hoped to become a new man.

Should the reader search the old magazines and documents in which are enshrined the records of the early days of the Revival, he will find many incidents showing what a romantic story is this of the self-denials, the difficulties, and enthusiasm of these men, whose best record is on high —most of them faithful men, like Alexander Coates, who, after a life of singular length and usefulness in the work, went to his rest. His talents were said to be extraordinary, both in preaching and in conversation. Just as he was dying, one of his brethren called upon him and said, "You don't think you have followed a cunningly-devised fable now?" "No, no, no!" said the dying man. "And what do you see?" "Land ahead!" said the old man. They were his last words. Such were the men of this Great Revival; so they lived their lives of faithful usefulness, and so they passed away.

CHAPTER VIII.

A GALLERY OF REVIVALIST PORTRAITS.

IF we were writing a sustained history of the Revival, we might devote some pages, at this period, to notice the varied forms of satire and ribaldry by which it was greeted. While the noble bands of preachers were pursuing their way, instructing and awakening the popular mind of the country, not only heartless and affected dilettanti, like Horace Walpole, regarded it with the condescension of their supercilious sneers, but for the more popular taste there was *The Spiritual Quixote*, a book which even now has its readers, and in which Whitefield and his followers were held up to ridicule; and Lackington, the great bookseller, in his disgraceful, but entertaining autobiography, attempted to cover the Societies of Wesley with his scurrility. It was about the year 1750 that *The Minor* was brought out on the stage of the Haymarket Theatre; the author was that great comedian, but most despicable and dissolute character, Foote. The play lies before us as we write; we have taken it down to notice the really shameless buffoonery and falsehood in which it indulges. Whitefield is especially libelled and burlesqued.

The Countess of Huntingdon waited personally on the Lord Chamberlain, and besought him to suppress it ; it was not much to the credit of his lordship's knowledge, that he declared, had he known the evil influence of the thing before it was licensed, it should not have been produced, but being licensed, it was beyond his control. Then the good Countess waited on David Garrick ; Garrick knew and admired Whitefield ; he received her with distinguished kindness and respect, and it is to his honour that, through his influence, it was temporarily suppressed. It seems a singular compensation that the author of this piece, who permitted himself to indulge in the most disgraceful insinuations against one of the holiest and purest of men, a few years after was charged with a great crime, of which he was, no doubt, quite innocent, and died a broken-hearted and beggared man.

Another of these disgraceful stage libels, *The Hypocrite*, appeared at Drury Lane in 1768 ; in it are the well-known characters of Dr. Cantwell, and Mawworm, and old Lady Lambert. There is more of a kind of genius in it than in *The Minor*, but it was all stolen property, and little more than an appropriation from Molière's *Tartuffe* and Cibber's *Nonjuror*. All these things are forgotten now ; but they are worthy of notice as entering into the history of the Revival, and showing the malice which was stirred in multitudes of minds against men and designs, on the whole, so innocent and holy. Was it not written from of old, "The carnal mind is enmity against God ? "

But as to the movement itself, companions-in-arms, and of a very high order alike for valour and character, crowded to the field ; we have referred to several distinguished laymen; it is at least equally important to notice that while the leaders of the Church were, as a body, set in array against it—while archbishops and bishops of that day frowned, or scoffed and scorned, there were a number of clergymen whose piety, whose wit and eloquence, whose affluent humour, whose learning, whose intrepidity and sleepless variety of labour, surround their names, even now as then, with a charm of interest, making every life as it comes before us a readable and delightful recreation. Some of them were assuredly oddities; it is not long since we made a pilgrimage to Everton, in Bedfordshire, to read the singular epitaph, on the tomb in the churchyard, of one of the oddest and most extraordinary of all these men. Even if our readers have read that epitaph, it will do them no harm to read it again:

Here lie
The earthly remains of
JOHN BERRIDGE,
Late Vicar of Everton,
And an itinerant servant of Jesus Christ,
Who loved his Master, and His work,
And after running on His errands many years,
Was called up to wait on Him above.
Reader,
Art thou born again?
No salvation without a New Birth!
I was born in sin, February, 1716,
Remained ignorant of my fallen state till 1730,
Lived proudly on Faith and Works for Salvation
Till 1751.
Was admitted to Everton Vicarage, 1755.
Fled to Jesus alone for refuge, 1756.
Fell asleep in Christ Jesus, January 22, 1793.

With the exception of the date of his death, it was written by the hand that moulders beneath the stone it is characteristic that its writer caused himself to be buried in that part of the churchyard where up to that time only those had been interred who had destroyed themselves, or come to an ignominious end. Before his death he had often said that he would take this effectual means of consecrating that unhallowed spot.

This epitaph sufficiently shows that John Berridge was an original. Southey says of him that he was a buffoon and a fanatic. Southey's judgments about the men of the Revival were frequently as shallow as they were unjust; he must have felt a sharp sting when, as doubtless was the case, he heard the well-known anecdote of George IV., who, on reading Richard Watson's calm reply to Southey's attacks on the Methodist leaders, exclaimed, as he laid down the book, "Oh, my poor Poet Laureate!" He deserved all that and a good deal more, if only for the verdict we have quoted on Berridge. So far as scholarship may test a man, John Berridge was most likely a far deeper scholar than Dr. Southey; he was a distinguished member of Clare Hall, Cambridge, and for many years read and studied fourteen hours a day; but he was an uncontrollable droll and humourist; pithy proverbs fell spontaneously along all his speech. As one critic says of his style, "it was like granulated salt." As a preacher, he was equal to any multitudes; he lived among farmers and graziers, and the twinkling of his eye, all alive with shrewd cheerfulness, compelled attention even before he opened his lips. The late Dr. Guthrie, not long before his death, thought it worth his while to republish *The Christian World Unmasked; pray Come and Peep;* and it is characteristic of Berridge throughout.

After his conversion, his Bishop called him up and

threatened to send him to gaol for preaching out of his parish. Our readers may imagine with such a man what sort of conference it was, and which of the two would be likely to get the worst of it : "I tell you," said the Bishop, "if you continue preaching where you have no right, you are very likely to be sent to Huntingdon Gaol." "I have no more regard for a gaol than other folks," said he ; "but I would rather go there with a good conscience than be at liberty without one." The conference is too long for quotation, but Berridge held on his way ; he became one of the most beloved and intimate friends of the Countess of Huntingdon ; and if he shocked his bishop by preaching out of his own parish, he must have roused his wrath by preaching in her ladyship's chapel in London, and throughout the country. His letters to the Countess are as characteristic as his speech, or any other of his writings. Thus he writes to her about young Rowland Hill, "I find you have got honest Rowland down to Bath ; he is a pretty young spaniel, fit for land or water, and he has a wonderful yelp ; he forsakes father and mother and brethren, and gives up all for Jesus, and I believe he will prove a useful labourer if he keep clear of petticoat snares." No doubt, Berridge sometimes seemed not only racy, but rude ; but his words were wonderfully calculated to meet the average and level of an immense congregation. While he lived on terms of fellowship with all the great leaders of the movement, he was faithful as the vicar of his own parish, and was the apostle of the whole region of Bedfordshire.

With all his shrewd worldly wisdom, Berridge had a most benevolent hand ; he was rich, and devoted far more than the income of his vicarage to helping his poor neighbours, supporting itinerant ministers, renting houses and barns for preaching the Gospel, and, however far he travelled to preach, always disbursing his expenses from his own pocket. How he would have loved John Bunyan, and how John Bunyan would have loved him! It is curious that within a few miles of the place where the illustrious dreamer was so long imprisoned, one should arise out of the very Church which persecuted John, to do for a long succession of years, on the same ground, the work for which he was persecuted.

From the low Bedford level, what a flight to the wildest spot in wild Yorkshire, Haworth, and its venerable old parish church, celebrated now as a classic region, haunted by the memory of the author of *Jane Eyre*, and all the Brontë family ; but in the times of which we are writing, the vicar, William Grimshaw, was quite as queer and quaint a creature as Berridge. A wild spot now—a stern, grand place; desolate moors still seeming to stretch all round it ; though more easily reached in this day, it must indeed have been a rough solitude when William Grimshaw became its vicar, in 1742. He was born in 1708 ; he died in 1763. He was a man something of the nature of the wild moors around him. When he became the pastor of the parish, the people all round him were plunged in the most sottish heathenism. The pastor was a kind of son of the desert, and he became such an one as the Baptist, crying in the wilderness. The people were rough, they perhaps needed a rough shepherd ; they had one. The character of Grimshaw is that of a rough, faithful, and not less beautiful shepherd's dog. On the Sabbath morning he would commence his service, giving out the psalm, and having taken note of the absentees from the congrega-

HAWORTH CHURCH.

tion, would start off, while the psalm was being sung, to drive in the loiterers, visiting the ale-houses, routing out the drinkers, and, literally compelling them to come into the parish church. One Sabbath morning, a stranger riding through Haworth, seeing some men scrambling over a garden wall, and some others leaping through a low window,

GRIMSHAW'S HOUSE.

imagined the house was on fire. He inquired what was the matter. One of them cried out, "The parson's a coming!" and that explained the riddle. Upon another occasion, as a man was passing through the village, on the Sabbath day, on his way to call a doctor, his horse lost a shoe. He found his way to the village smithy to have his loss repaired. The blacksmith told him that it was the Lord's day, and the work could not be done unless the minister gave his permission. So they went to the parson, who, of course, as the case was urgent and necessary, gave his consent. But the story illustrates the mastery the vicar attained over the rough minds around him. He was a man of a hardy mould. He was intensely earnest. He not only effected a mighty moral change in his own parish, but Haworth was visited every Sabbath by pilgrims from miles round to listen to this singular, strong, mountain voice ; so that the church became unequal to the great congregations, and he often had to preach in the church-yard, a desolate-looking spot now, but alive with mighty concourses then. It is said that his strong pithy words haunted men long after they were spoken, as in the well-known instance of the infidel nobleman, who, in an affected manner, told him he was unable to perceive the truth of Christianity. "The fault," said the rough vicar, "is not so much in your lordship's head as in your heart."

Grimshaw was the first who kindled in the wild heights of Yorkshire the flames of the Revival. His mind was stirred simultaneously with others, but he does not appear to have received from either Whitefield or Wesley the impulses which created his extraordinary character, though he, of course, entered heartily into all their work. They visited Haworth, and preached to immense concourses there. As to Grimshaw himself, in the most irregular manner, he preached in the Methodist conventicles and dissenting chapels in all the country round. He effected an entire change in his own neighbourhood. He put down the races ; he reformed the village feasts, wakes, and fairs. He was often expecting suspension, and at last he was cited

WILLIAM GRIMSHAW.

before the Archbishop, who inquired of him as to the number of his communicants. " How many," said his grace, " had you when you first went to Haworth ?" " Twelve." " And how many now ?" " In the summer, about twelve hundred." The astonished Archbishop turned to his assistants in the examination, and said, " I really cannot find fault with Mr. Grimshaw when he brings so many people to the Lord's Table." Southey is also complimentary, in his own way, to this singular clergyman, and says, " He was certainly mad !"

It was what Festus said to Paul ; but the madness of the pastor of Haworth was a blessing to the farms and cottages of those wild moorlands. He was a child of nature in her most beautiful moods, glorified by Divine grace. The freshness and buoyancy of the heath his foot so lightly pressed, and the torrents which sung around him, were but typical of his hardy naturalness and beauty of character. Truly it has been said, it was not more natural that the gentle lover of nature should lie at the foot of Helvellyn, than that this watchman of the mountains should sleep at the foot of the hills amongst which he had so faithfully laboured. We have seen that he died comparatively young. His last words were very characteristic. Robert Shaw, an old Methodist preacher, called upon him ; he said, " I will pray for you as long as I live, and if there is praying in heaven, I will pray for you there ; I am as happy as I can be on earth, and as sure of glory as if I were in it." His last words were, " Here goes an unprofitable servant ! "

The wild Yorkshire of that day took up the Revival with a will ; and Henry Venn, of Huddersfield, we suppose, has even transcended by his usefulness the fame of either

Berridge or Grimshaw; he was born in 1724, and died in
1797. His life was genial and fruitful, and to his church
in Huddersfield the people poured in droves to listen to
him. It has been said his life was like a field of wheat, or
a fine summer day. And how are these to be painted or
put upon the canvas? He could scarcely be called eccentric, excepting in the sense in which earnestness, holiness,
and usefulness are always eccentric. His influence may be
said, in some directions, to continue still. He was one
of the indefatigable coadjutors of the Countess in all her
work, and towards the close of his life he came to London
to throw his influence round young Rowland Hill, by
preaching for some time in Surrey Chapel.

In another district of Yorkshire, a mighty movement
was going on, commencing about 1734. Benjamin Ingham,
whom we met some time since at Oxford, as a member of
the Holy Club, was living at Ossett, near Dewsbury. He
had married Lady Margaret Hastings, a younger sister of
the Countess of Huntingdon. He had received ordination
in the Church of England, but his irregularities had forced
him out. Like the Wesleys, in the earlier part of his
history, he became enchanted with the devotional life of
the Moravians, and at this period he introduced with
marvellous results a modified Moravianism into the West
Riding of Yorkshire. He founded as many as eighty
Societies; but he appears to have attempted to carry out an
impossible scheme, the union of the Moravian discipline
and doctrine with his idea of Congregationalism. His
influence over the West Riding for a long time was
immense; but, most naturally, divisions arose, and the
purely Moravian element separated itself into its own
order of Church life, while the Methodist element was

absorbed in the great and growing Wesleyan Societies. He was a friend of Count Zinzendorf, who was his guest for a long time at Ledstone House. The shock which his Society sustained, and the death of Lady Margaret, his admirable and beloved wife, were blows from which the good man never recovered ; but the effects of his usefulness continued, although he passed ; and if the reader ever visits the little Moravian Colony and Institution of Fulneck, near Leeds, in Yorkshire, he may be pleased to remember that this is also one of the offshoots of the Great Revival.

It is a sudden leap from the West Riding of Yorkshire to Truro, the charming little capital of Western Cornwall. We are here met by an imperishable and beautiful name, that of Samuel Walker, the minister ; he was born in 1714, and died in 1761. His influence over his town was great and abiding, and Walker of Truro is a name which to this day retains its fragrance, as associated with the restoration of his town from wild depravity to purity and exemplary piety.

How impossible it is to do more than merely mention the names of men, every action of whose lives was consecrated, and every breath an ardent flame, all helping on and urging forward the great work of rousing a careless world and a careless Church. What an influence had William Romaine, who for a long time, it has been said, was one of the sights of London ; it was rather drolly put when it was said, " People came from the country to see Garrick act and to hear Romaine preach." Nor let our readers suppose that he was a mere sensational orator ; he was a great scholar. We hear of him first as the Gresham Professor of Astronomy, and the editor of the four volumes of Calasio's *Hebrew Concordance;* then he caught the

evangelic fire ; he became one of the chaplains of the
Countess of Huntingdon, and, so far as the Church of the
Establishment was concerned, he was the most considerable light of London for a period of nearly fifty years ;
and very singular was his history in this relation, especially
in some of the churches whose pulpits he filled. It seems
singular to us now how even his great talents could obtain
for him the place of morning lecturer at St. George's,
Hanover Square ; but the charge was soon urged against
him that he vulgarised that most fashionable of congregations, and most uncomfortably crowded the church. He
was appointed evening lecturer at St. Dunstan's in Fleet
Street; but the rector barred his entrance into the pulpit,
seating himself there during the time of prayers, so that
the preacher might be unable to enter. Lord Mansfield
decided that, after seven in the evening, the church was
not the rector's, but that Mr. Romaine was entitled to the
use of it ; then, at seven in the evening, the churchwardens
closed the church doors, and kept the congregation outside, wearying them in the rain or in the cold. At length,
the patience of the churchwardens gave way before the
persistency of the people and the preacher ; but it was an
age of candles, and they refused to light the church, and
Mr. Romaine often preached in a crowded church by the
light of one candle. They paid him the merest minimum
which he could demand, or which they were compelled to
pay ; sometimes only eighteen pounds a year. But he
was a hardy man, and he lived on the plainest fare, and
dressed in homespun cloth. He was dragged repeatedly
before courts of law, but he was as difficult to manage
here as in the church ; he brought his judges to the
statutes, none of which he had broken. Every effort was

made to expel him from the Church, but he would not be cast out; and at last he appears to have settled himself, as such men generally do, into an irresistible fact. He became the Rector of St. Ann's, Blackfriars. There he preached those sermons which were shaped afterwards into the favourite book of our forefathers, *The Life, Walk,*

ST. ANN'S, BLACKFRIARS.

and Triumph of Faith. Born in 1714, he died in 1795. His last years were clothed with a pleasant serenity, although, perhaps, some have detected in his character marks of a severity, probably the result of those conflicts which, through so many years, he had with such remarkable consistency sustained.

And surely we ought to mention, in this right noble band, John Newton; but he brings us near to the time when the passion of the Revival was settling itself into organisation and calm; when the fury of persecution was ceasing; Methodism was becoming even a respectable and acknowledged fact. John Newton was born in 1725, and died in 1807. All his sympathies were with the theology and the activities of the revivalists; but before he most singularly found himself the Rector of St. Mary Woolnoth and St. Mary Woolchurch, he had led a life which for its marvellous variety of incident reads like one of Defoe's fictions. But his parlour, in No. 8, Coleman Street Buildings, on a Friday evening, was thronged by all the dignitaries of the evangelical movement of his day. As he said, " I was a wild beast on the coast of Africa, but the Lord caught me and tamed me; and now you come to see me, as people go to look at the lions in the Tower." A grand old man was John Newton, the young sailor transformed into the saintly old rector; there he sat with few traces of the parson about him, in his blue pea-jacket, and his black neckerchief, liking still to retain something of the freedom of his old blue seas; full of quaint wisdom which never, like that of his friend Berridge, became rude or droll; quietly sitting there and meditating; his enthusiastic life apparently having subsided into stillness; while the Hannah Mores, Wilberforces, Claudius Buchanans, and John Campbells, went to him to find their enthusiasm confirmed. The friend of Cowper, who surely deserves to be called the Poet Laureate of the Revival—himself the author of some of the sweetest hymns we still sing; the biographer of his own wonderful career, and of the life of his friend and brother-in-arms, William Grimshaw; one of

ST. MARY WOOLNOTH.

the finest of our religious letter-writers ; with capacities within him for almost everything he might have thought it wise to undertake, he now seems to us appropriately to close this small gallery we have attempted to present. When the spirit of the Revival was either settling into firmness and

REV. JOHN NEWTON.

consolidation, or striking out into those new and marvellous fields of labour—its natural outgrowth—which another chapter may present succinctly to the eye, John Newton, by his great experience of men, his profound faith, his steady hand and clear eye, became the wise adviser and fosterer of schemes whose gigantic enterprise would certainly have astonished even his capacious intelligence.

In closing this chapter it is quite worth while to notice that, various as were the characters of these men, and of their innumerable comrades, to whom we do homage, although we have no space even to mention their names, their strength arose from the certainty and the confidence with which they spoke ; there was nothing tentative about their teaching. That great scholar, Sir William Hamilton, says that "assurance is the *punctum saliens*, that is the strong point, of Luther's system ;" so it was with all these men, "We speak that we do know, and testify that we have seen ;" it was the full assurance of knowledge ; and it gave them authority over the men with whom they wrestled, whether in public or private. Whitefield and Wesley alike, and all their followers, had strong faith in God. They were believers in the personal regard of God for the souls of men ; and every idea of prayer supposes some such personal regard, whether offered by the highest of high Calvinists, or the simplest Primitive Methodist ; the whole spirit of the Revival turned on this ; these men, as they strongly believed, were able, by the strong attractive force of their own nature, to compel other minds to their convictions. Their history strongly illustrates that that teaching which oscillates to and fro in a pendulous uncertainty is powerless to reform character or influence mind.

CHAPTER IX.

BLOSSOMS IN THE WILDERNESS.

THUS, our preceding chapters have, assuredly, shown that the Great Revival was creating over the wild moral wastes of our country a pure and spiritual atmosphere, and its movements and organisations were taking root in every direction. Voltaire, and that pedantic cluster of conceited infidels, the Bolingbrokes, Middletons, and Mandevilles, Chubbs, Woolstons, and Collinses, who prophesied that Christian faith was fast vanishing from the earth, were slightly premature. It is, indeed, interesting to notice the contrast in this period between our own and the then most unhappy sister-kingdom of France : there, indeed, Christian faith did seem to be trodden underfoot of men. While a great silent, hallowed revolution was going on here, all things were preparing for a tremendous revolution there. It was just about the time that our Revival was leavening English society that Lord Chesterfield summed up what he had noticed in France, in the following words : " In short, all the symptoms which I have ever met with in history previous to great changes and revolutions in government, now exist and daily increase in France." The words were spoken several years before that terrible Revolution came, which conducted the King, the Queen, and almost all the aristocracy, respectability, and lingering piety of the nation to the scaffold. It was a wonderful compensation. A few years before, a sovereign had cast away from his nation, and from around his throne, all the social elements which could guard and give dignity to it ; how natural, then, that the whole *canaille* of the kingdom should rush upon the throne of his successor, and cast it and its occupant into the bonfire of the Reign of Terror !

But with us, from some cause, all was different. This period of the Revival has been truly called the starting-point of our modern religious history ; and, somehow, all things were singularly combining to give to our nation a new-born happiness, to create new facilities for mental growth and culture, and to enlarge and to fill our cup of national joy. It will be noticed that these things did not descend to the nation generally from the highest places of the land. With the exception of the sovereign, we cannot see many instances of a lively interest in the moral well-being of the people. Other exceptions there were, but they were very few. From the people themselves, and from the causes we have described, originated and spread those means which, amidst the wild agitations of revolution, as they came foaming over the Channel, and which were rather aided than repressed by the unwisdom of many of our governments and magistrates, calmed and enlightened the public mind, and secured the order of society, and the stability of the throne.

The historians of Wesleyanism—we will say it respectfully, but still very firmly—have been too uniformly disposed to see in their own society the centre and the spring of all those amazing means of social regeneration to which the period of the revival gave birth. Dr. Abel Stevens specially seems to regard Methodism and Wesleyanism as conterminous. It would seem from him that the work of the printing-office, the book or the tract society, schools and missions, and the various means of social amelioration or redemption, all have their origin in Wesleyanism. We may give the largest honour to the venerable name of Wesley, and accept this history by Dr. Stevens as the best, yet as an American he did not fully know what had been done by others not in the Connexion. There was an immense field of Methodism which did not fall beneath the dominion of Wesley, and had no relation to the Wesleyan Conference. The same spirit touched simultaneously many minds, quite separated by ecclesiastical and social relations, but all wrought up to the same end. It is true these papers have been greatly devoted to reminiscences of the great preachers, and illustrations of the preaching power of the Revival, but our readers know that the Revival did not end in preaching. These voices stirred the slumbering mind of the nation like a thunder-peal, but, as we shall see, they roused to work and practical effort. The great characteristic of all that came out of the movement may be summed up in the often-quoted expression, "A single eye to the glory of God." As one of the clergymen of Yorkshire, earnest and active in those times, was wont to say, "I do love those one-eyed Christians."

We shall have occasion to mention at length the name of Robert Raikes, and that name reminds us not only of Gloucester, but of Gloucestershire ; many circumstances gave to that most charming county a conspicuous place. Lying in the immediate neighbourhood of Bath, it attracted the attention of the Countess. "As sure as God is in Gloucestershire," was an old proverb, first used in monastic days, then applied to the Reformation time, when Tyndale, the first translator of the English New Testament, had his home in the lovely village of North Nibley; but it became yet more true when Whitefield preached to the immense concourses on Stinchcombe Hill; when Rodborough and Ebley, and the valley of the Stroud Water were lit up with Revival beacons, and when Rowland Hill established his vicarage at Wotton-under-Edge; then, in its immediate neighbourhood, arose that beautiful Christian worker, the close friend of George Whitefield, Cornelius Winter; and from his labours came forth his most eminent pupil, that great preacher, William Jay.

And the Revival took effect on distinct circles which certainly seemed outside of the Methodist movement, but which yet, assuredly, belonged to it; the Clapham Sect, for instance. "The Clapham Sect" is a designation originating in the facetious and satiric brain of Sydney Smith, than whom the Revival never had a more unjust, ungenerous, or ungracious critic; but the pages of the *Edinburgh Review*, in which the flippant sting of speech first appeared, years afterwards consecrated the term and made it historical in the elegant essay of Sir James Stephen. By his pen the sect, with all its leaders, acts, and consequences, are pleasantly described in the *Essays on Ecclesiastical Biography;* and surely this was as much the result of the Great Revival as the "Evangelical succession" which calls forth the exercise in previous pages of the same interesting pen; it was all a natural evangelical succession, that of which we have spoken before, as enthu-siasm for humanity growing out of enthusiasm for Divine truth. Men who have become fairly impressed by a sense of their own immortality and its redemption in Christ, become interested in the temporal well-being and the eternal welfare of others. It has always been so, and is so still, that men who have not a sense of man's immortal welfare have usually cared but little about his temporal interests. Hospitals and churches, orphanages and mis-sionary societies, usually grow out of the same spiritual root.

With the memory of the paper to which we have referred before us, and the oppressive sense of our diminishing space, we scarcely need ask our readers to accompany us to the pleasant little village of Clapham, and its sweet, sequestered Common, then so far removed from the great metropolis; surrounded by the homes of wealthy men, merchants, statesmen, eminent preachers, all of them infected with the spirit of the Revival, and all of them noteworthy in the story of those means which were to shiver the chains of the slave, to carry light to dark heathen minds, and to hand out the Bible to English villages and far-off nations. But, thus, we have been desirous of con-veying throughout to our readers the impression that those were times of a singular and almost simultaneous spiritual upheaval; it was as if, in different regions of the great lake of humanity, submerged islands suddenly appeared from beneath the waves; and it is not too much to say that all those various means which have so tended to beautify and bless the world, schemes of education, schemes for the im-provement of prison discipline, schemes of missionary enter-prise for the extension of Christian influence in the East

Indies, the destruction of slavery in the West Indies, and the abolition of the slave trade throughout the British Empire ; Bible societies and Tract societies, and, in fact, the whole munificent machinery and organisation of our day, sprang forth from that revival of the last century. It seems now like a magnificent burst of enthusiasm ; yet, ultimately it was based upon only two or three great elements of faith : the spiritual world was an intense reality ; the soul of every man, woman, and child on the face of the earth had an endowment of immortality ; they were precious to the Redeemer, they ought, therefore, to be precious to all the followers of the Redeemer. Charged with these truths, their spirits inflamed to a holy enthusiasm by them, from parlours and drawing-rooms, from the lowly homes and cottages of England, all these new professors appeared to be in search of occasions for doing good ; the schemes worked themselves through all the varieties of human temperament and imperfection ; but, looking back, it must surely be admitted that they achieved glorious results.

If the reader, impressed by veneration, should make a pilgrimage to Clapham Common, and inquire from some one of the oldest inhabitants which was the house in which John Shore, the great Lord Teignmouth, the first President of the Bible Society, lived, his soul within him might be a little vexed to be informed that yonder large building at the extreme corner of the common, the great Roman Catholic Redemptionist College, is the house. There were canvassed and brooded over a number of the schemes to which we have referred. Thither from his own house, close to the well-known " Plough "—its site now covered by suburban shops—went the great Zachary Macaulay, sometimes accompanied by his son, a bright, intelligent lad,

JOHN THORNTON.

afterwards known as Thomas Babington Macaulay. John Shore had been Governor of India, at Calcutta. On the common resided also, for some time, William Wilberforce. These were the great statesmen who were desirous of organising great plans, from which the consummating prayer of David in the 72nd Psalm should be realised. Then there was another house on the common, the mansion of John Thornton, which seemed to share with that of Lord Teignmouth the honours of these Divine committees of ways and means. Before the establishment of the Bible Society, Mr. Thornton had been in the habit of spending two thousand pounds a year in the distribution of Bibles and Testaments—a very Bible Society in himself. It is, perhaps, not too much to say, there was scarcely a thought which had for its object the well-being of the human family but it found its representation and discussion in those palatial abodes on Clapham Common. There were Granville Sharp and Thomas Clarkson ; thither, how often went cheery old John Newton, to whom, first of all, on arriving in London, went every holy wayfarer from the provinces, wayfarers who soon found their entrance beneath his protecting wing, and cheery introduction to these pleasant circles. Beneath the incentives of his animating words, the fervid earnestness of Claudius Buchanan found its pathway of power, and *The Star of the East*—his great sermon on " Missions to India,"— was first seen shining over Clapham Common ; and it was the same genial tongue which encouraged that fine, but almost forgotten, man, John Campbell, in the enterprise of his spirit, to pierce into the deserts of Africa. We may notice how great ideas perpetuate themselves into genera- tions, when we remember that it was John Campbell who first took out Robert Moffat, and settled him down in the field of his wonderful labours.

Sir James Stephen, in his beautiful paper, is far from exhausting all the memories of that Clapham Sect. There was another house, not in Clapham, but not far removed— Hatcham House, as we remember it—a noble mansion, standing in its park, opposite where the old lane turned off from the main road to Peckham. There lived Joseph Hardcastle—certainly one of the Clapham Sect—Wilberforce's close and intimate friend, a munificent merchant prince, in whose offices in the City were held for a long time all the earliest committee meetings of the Bible Society, the Religious Tract Society, and the London Missionary Society, and from whom appear to have emanated the first suggestions for the limitation of the powers of the East India Company in supporting and sanctioning, by the English Government, Hindoo infanticide and idolatry. Among all the glorious names of the Clapham Sect, not one shines out more beautifully than that of this great Christian gentleman.

Perhaps a natural delicacy withheld Sir James Stephen from chronicling the story of his own father, Sir George Stephen ; and there was Thomas Gisborne, most charming of English preachers of the Church of England evangelical school ; and Sir Robert Grant, whose hymns are still among the sweetest in our national psalmody. But we can do no more than thus say that it was from hence that the spirit of the Revival rose in new strength, and taking to itself the wings of the morning, spread to the uttermost parts of the earth.

CHAPTER X.

THE REVIVAL BECOMES EDUCATIONAL.— ROBERT RAIKES.

IN this year of 1880 is celebrated in England and America the centenary of Sunday-schools. The life and labours of Robert Raikes, whose name has long been familiar as "a household word" in connection with such institutions, have, therefore, an especial interest at this season.

Gloucestershire, if not one of the largest, is certainly one of the fairest—as, indeed, its name is said to imply : from *Glaw*, an old British word signifying "fair"—it is one of the fairest, and it ought to be one of the most famous, counties of England. Many are its distinguished worthies : John de Trevisa was Vicar of Berkeley, in Gloucestershire, and a contemporary with John Wycliffe, and, like him, he had a strong aversion to the practices of the Church of Rome, and an earnest desire to make the Scriptures known to his parishioners ; and in Nibley, in Gloucestershire, was born, and lived, William Tyndale, in whose noble heart the great idea sprang up that Christian Englishmen should read the New Testament in their own mother-tongue, and who said to a celebrated priest, "If God spares my life, I will take care that a plough-boy shall know more of the Scriptures than you do." The story of the great translator and martyr is most interesting. Gloucestershire has been famous, too, for its contributions to the noble army of martyrs, notably, not only James Baynham, but, in Gloucester, its bishop, John Hooper, was in 1555 burnt to death. In Berkeley the very distinguished physician, and first promulgator of the doctrine of vaccination, Dr. Edward Jenner, the son of the vicar, was born ; and from the Old Bell, in Gloucester, went forth the wonderful preacher George Whitefield, to arouse the sleeping Church in England and America from its lethargy. The quaint old proverb to which we have already alluded—"As sure as God is in Gloucestershire "—was very complimentary, but not very correct ; it arose from the amazing ecclesiastical wealth of the county, which was so rich that it attracted the notice of the papal court, and four Italian bishops held it in succession for fifty years ; one of these, Giulio de Medici, became Pope Clement VII., succeeding Pope Leo X. in the papacy in 1523. This eminent ecclesiastical fame no doubt originated the proverb ; but it acquired a tone of reality and truth rather from the martyrdom of its bishop than from the elevation of his predecessor to the papal tiara ; rather from Tyndale, William Sarton, and his brother weaver-martyrs, than from its costly and magnificent endowments ; from Whitefield and Jenner rather than from its crowd of priests and friars.

Thus Gloucestershire has certainly considerable eminence among English counties. To other distinguished names must be added that of Robert Raikes, who must ever be regarded as the founder of Sabbath-schools. It is not intended by this that there had never been any attempts made to gather the children on the Sabbath for some kind of religious instruction—although such attempts were very few, and a diligent search has probably brought them all under our knowledge ; but the example and the influence of Raikes gave to the idea the character of a movement ; it stirred the whole country, from the throne itself, the King and Queen, the bishops, and the clergy ; all classes of ministers and laymen became interested in what was evidently an easy and happy method of seizing upon the multitudes of lost children who in that day were " perishing for lack of knowledge."

Mr. Joseph Stratford, in his *Biographical Sketches of the Great and Good Men in Gloucestershire,* and Mr. Alfred Gregory, in his *Life of Robert Raikes*—to which works we must confess our obligation for much of the information contained in this chapter—have both done honour to the several humbler and more obscure labourers whose hearts were moved to attempt the work to which Raikes gave a national importance, and which from his hands, and from his time, became henceforth a perpetual institution in the Church work of every denomination of Christian believers and labourers. The Rev. Joseph Alleine, the author of *The Alarm to the Unconverted,* an eminent Nonconformist minister of Taunton, adopted the plan of gathering the young people together for instruction on the Lord's day. Even in Gloucestershire, before Raikes was born, in the village of Flaxley, on the borders of the Forest of Dean—Flaxley, of which the poet Bloomfield sings :

"'Mid depths of shade gay sunbeams broke
  Through noble Flaxley's bowers of oak ;
  Where many a cottage, trim and gay,
  Whispered delight through all the way : "

in the old Cistercian Abbey, Mrs. Catharine Boevey, the
lady of the abbey, had one of the earliest and pleasantest
Sabbath-schools. Her monument in Flaxley Church,
erected after her death in 1726, records her "clothing
and feeding her indigent neighbours, and teaching their
children, some of whom she entertained at her house, and
examined them herself." Six of the poor children, it is
elsewhere stated, "by turns dined at her residence on
Sundays, and were afterwards heard say the Catechism."

We read of a humbler labourer, realising, perhaps, more
the idea of a Sabbath-school teacher, in Bolton, in Lancashire, James Hey, or "Old Jemmy o' th' Hey." Old
Jemmy, Mr. Gregory tells us, employed the working days
of the week in winding bobbins for weavers, and on
Sundays he taught the boys and girls of the neighbourhood to read. His school assembled twice each Sunday,
in the cottage of a neighbour, and the time of commencing
was announced, not by the ringing of a bell, but by an
excellent substitute, an old brass pestle and mortar. After
a while, Mr. Adam Compton, a paper manufacturer in the
neighbourhood, began to supply Jemmy with books, and
subscriptions in money were given him ; he was thus
enabled to form three branch establishments, the teachers
of which were paid one shilling each Sunday for their
services. Besides these there are several other instances :
in 1763 the Rev. Theophilus Lindsey established something
like a Sunday-school at Catterick, in Yorkshire ; at High
Wycombe, in 1769, Miss Hannah Ball, a young Methodist

lady, formed a Sunday-school in her town; and at
Macclesfield that admirable and excellent man, the Rev.
David Simpson, originated a similar plan of usefulness;
and, contemporary with Mr. Raikes, in the old Whitefield
Tabernacle, at Dursley, in Gloucestershire, we find Mr.
William King, a woollen card-maker, attempting the
work of teaching on a Sunday, and coming into Gloucester
to take counsel with Mr. Raikes as to the best way of
carrying it forward. Such, scattered over the face of the
country, at great distances, and in no way representing
a general plan of useful labour, were the hints and efforts
before the idea took what may be called an apostolic
shape in the person of Robert Raikes.

For, notwithstanding the instances we have given, Mr.
Raikes must really be regarded as the founder of Sunday-
schools as an extended organisation. With him they
became more than a notion, or a mere piece of local
effort; and his position and profession, and the high
respect in which he was held in the city in which he lived,
all alike enabled him to give publicity to the plan : and
before he commenced this movement, he was known as a
philanthropist; indeed, John Howard himself bears something like the same relation to prison philanthropy which
Raikes bears to Sunday-schools. No one doubts that
Howard was the great apostle of prisons; but it seems
that before he commenced his great prison crusade, Raikes
had laboured diligently to reform the Gloucester gaol. The
condition of the prisoners was most pitiable, and Raikes,
nearly twenty years before he commenced the Sunday-
school system, had been working among them, attempting their material, moral, and spiritual improvement,
by which he had earned for himself the designation of

the " Teacher of the Poor" Howard visited Raikes in Gloucester, and bears his testimony to the blessedness and benevolence of his labours in the prison there; and the gaol appears not unnaturally to have suggested the idea of the Sunday-school to the benevolent-hearted man. It was a dreadful state of society. Some idea may be formed of it from a paragraph in the *Gloucester Journal* for June, 1783, the paper of which Raikes was the editor and proprietor: it is mentioned that no less than sixty-six persons were committed to the Castle in one week, and Mr. Raikes adds, " The prison is already so full that all the gaoler's stock of fetters is occupied, and the smiths are hard at work casting new ones." He goes on to say : " The people sent in are neither disappointed soldiers nor sailors, but chiefly frequenters of ale-houses and skittle-alleys." Then, in another paragraph, he goes on to remark, " The ships about to sail for Botany Bay will carry about one thousand miserable creatures, who might have lived perfectly happy in this country had they been early taught good principles, and to avoid the danger of associating with those who make sobriety and industry the objects of their ridicule."

From sentences like these it is easy to see the direction in which the mind of the good man was moving, before he commenced the work which has given such a happy and abiding perpetuity to his name. He gathered the children ; the streets were full of noise and disturbances every Sunday. In a little while, says the Rev. Dr. Glass, Mr. Raikes found himself surrounded by such a set of little ragamuffins as would have disgusted other men less zealous to do good, and less earnest to disseminate comfort, exhortation, and benefit to all around him, than the founder of Sunday-schools. He prevented their running about in wild disorder through the streets. By and by, he arranged that a number of them should meet him at seven o'clock on the Sunday morning in the cathedral close, when he and they all went into the cathedral together to an early service. The increase of the numbers was rapid; Mr. Raikes was looked up to as the commander-in-chief of this ragged regiment. It is testified that a change took place and passed over the streets of the old Gloucester city on the Sunday. A glance at the features of Mr. Raikes will assure the reader that he was an amiable and gentle man, but that by no means implies always a weak one. He appears to have had plenty of strength, self-possession, and knowledge of the world. He also belonged to, and moved in, good society; and this is not without its influence. As he told the King, in the course of a long interview, when the King and Queen sent for him to Windsor, to talk over his system with him, in order that they might, in some sense, be his disciples, and adopt and recommend his plan: it was "botanising in human nature." "All that I require," said Raikes, to the parents of the children, "are clean hands, clean faces, and their hair combed." To many who were barefooted, after they had shown some regularity of attendance, he gave shoes, and others he clothed. Yes, it was "botanising in human nature;" and very many anecdotes show what flowers sprang up out of the black soil in the path of the good man.

All the stories told of Raikes show that the law of kindness was usually on his lips. A sulky, stubborn girl had resisted all reproofs and correction, and had refused to ask forgiveness of her mother. In the presence of the mother, Raikes said to the girl, "Well, if you have no regard for yourself, I have much for you. You will be ruined and lost, if you do not become a good girl ; and if you will not humble yourself, I must humble myself on your behalf, and make a beginning for you ;" and then, with great solemnity, he entreated the mother to forgive the girl, using such words that he overcame the girl's pride. The stubborn creature actually fell on her knees, and begged her mother's forgiveness, and never gave Mr. Raikes or her mother trouble afterwards. It is a very simple anecdote ; but it shows the Divine spirit in the method of the man ; and the more closely we come into a personal knowledge of his character, the more admirable and lovable it seems. Thus literally true and beautiful are the words of the hymn :

> " Like a lone husbandman, forlorn,
>   The man of Gloucester went,
> Bearing his seeds of precious corn ;
>   And God the blessing sent.
>
> Now, watered long by faith and prayer,
>   From year to year it grows,
> Till heath, and hill, and desert bare,
>   Do blossom as the rose."

Mr. Raikes was a Churchman ; he was so happy as to have, near to his own parish of St. Mary-le-Crypt, in Gloucester, an intimate friend, the Rector of St. Aldate's—a neighbouring parish in the same city—the Rev. Thomas Stock, whose monument in the church truly testifies that " to him, in conjunction with Robert Raikes, Esquire, is justly attributed the honour of having planned and instituted the first Sunday-school in the kingdom." Mr. Stock was but a young man in 1780, for he died

ROBERT RAIKES AND THE SULLEN SCHOLAR.

in 1803, then only fifty-four years of age; he must have been, at the time of the first institution of Sunday-schools, a young man of fine and tender instincts. He appears, simultaneously with Mr. Raikes's movement, to have formed a Sunday-school in his own parish, taking upon himself the superintendence of it, and the responsibility of such expenses as it involved. But Mr. Stock says, in a letter written in 1788, "The progress of the institution through the kingdom is justly attributed to the constant representations which Mr. Raikes made in his own paper of the benefits which he saw would probably arise from it." At the time Mr. Raikes began the work, he was about forty-four years of age; it was a great thing in that day to possess a respectable journal, a newspaper of acknowledged character and influence; to this, very likely, we owe it, in some considerable measure, that the work in Gloucester became extensively known and spread, and expanded into a great movement. But he does not appear to have used the columns of his newspaper for the purpose of calling attention to the usefulness and desirability of the work until after it had been in operation about three years; in 1783 and 1784, very modestly he commends the system to general adoption.

It is remarkable that in the course of two or three years, several bishops—the Bishop of Gloucester, in the cathedral, the Bishops of Chester and Salisbury, in their charges to the clergy of their dioceses—strongly commended the plan. All orders of mind poured around the movement their commendation; even Adam Smith, whom no one will think likely to have fallen into exaggerated expressions where Christian activity is concerned, said, "No plan has promised to effect a change of manners with equal ease and simplicity, since the days of the apostles." The poet Cowper declared that he knew of no nobler means by which a reformation of the lower classes could be effected. Some attempts have been made to claim for John Wesley the honour of inaugurating the Sunday-school system ; considering the intensely practical character of that venerated man, and how much he was in advance of his times in most of his activities, it is a wonder that he did not ; but his venerable memory has honours, certainly, in all sufficiency. He wrote his first commendation of Sunday-schools in the *Arminian Magazine* of 1784. He says, " I find these schools spring up wherever I go ; perhaps God may have a deeper end therein than men are aware of ; who knows but that some of these schools may become nurseries for Christians ?" Prophetic as these words are, this is fainter and tardier praise than we should have expected from him ; but in 1787 he writes more warmly, expresses his belief that these schools will be one great means of reviving religion throughout the kingdom, and expresses " wonder that Satan has not sent out some able champion against them." In 1788 he says : " I verily think that these schools are one of the noblest specimens of charity which have been set on foot in England since the days of William the Conqueror."

Some estimate may be formed of the rapidity with which the movement spread, when we find that in this year, 1787, the number of children taught in Sunday-schools in Manchester alone, on the testimony of the very eminent John Nichols, the great printer and anecdotist, was no fewer than five thousand. It was in this year also, 1787, that Mr. Raikes was visiting some relatives in the neighbourhood of Windsor. He must have attained to the dignity of a celebrity; nor is this wonderful, when we remember the universal acceptance with which his great idea of Sunday-schools had been honoured. The Queen invited him to visit her, and inquired of him, he says, "by what accident a thought which promised so much benefit to the lower order of people as the institution of Sunday-schools, was suggested to his mind?" The visit was a long one; he spent two hours with the Queen— the King also, we believe, being present most of the time —not so much in expounding the system, for that was simple enough, but they were curious as to what he had observed in the change and improvement of the characters among whom he worked; and we believe that it was then he told the King, in the words we have already quoted, that he regarded his work as a kind of "botanising in human nature;" this was a favourite phrase of his in describing the work. The result of this visit was, that the Queen established a Sunday-school in Windsor, and also a school of industry at Brentford, which the King and Queen occasionally visited. We think it may be taken as an illustration of the native modesty of Mr. Raikes's own character that he never referred in his paper to this distinguished notice of royalty.

Do our readers know anything of Mrs. Sarah Trimmer? A hundred years ago, there was, probably, not a better-known woman in England; and although her works have long ceased to exercise any influence, we suppose none, in her time, were more eminently useful. Pious, devoted, earnestly evangelical, if we speak of her as a kind of lesser Hannah More, the remark must apply to her intellectual character rather than to her reputation or her usefulness. Almost as soon as the Sunday-school idea was announced, she stepped forward as its most able and intrepid advocate ; her *Economy of Charity* exercised a large influence, and she published a number of books, which, at that time, were admirably suited to the level of the capacity which the Sunday-school teacher desired to reach ; she was also a great favourite with the King and Queen, and appears to have visited them on the easy terms of friendship. The intense interest she felt in Sunday-schools is manifest in innumerable pages of the two volumes which record her life ; certainly, she was often at the ear of the royal pair, to whisper any good and pleasant thing connected with the progress of her favourite thought. She repeatedly expresses her obligation to Mr. Raikes ; but her biographer only expresses the simple truth when he says : " To Mr. Raikes, of Gloucester, the nation is, in the first place, indebted for the happy idea of collecting the children of the poor together on the Sabbath, and giving them instruction suited to the sacredness of the day ; but, perhaps, no publication on this subject was of more utility than the *Economy of Charity*. The influence of the work was very visible when it first made its appearance, and proved a source of unspeakable gratification to the author."

It will not consist with the contracted space of our pages to enter at greater length into the life of Robert Raikes ; but we trust that we have said sufficient to show that the term which has been applied to him of "founder of Sunday-schools," is not misapplied. He was a simple and good man, on whose heart, as into a fruitful soil, an idea fell, and it became a realised conviction. Look at his portrait, and instantly there comes to your mind Cowper's well-known description of one of his friends,

" An honest man, close-buttoned to the chin,
Broadcloth without, and a warm heart within."

No words can better describe him—not a tint of fanaticism
seems to shade his character; he had a warm enthusiasm
for ends and aims which commended themselves to his
judgment. It is pleasant to know that, as he lived when
the agitation for the abolition of the slave trade was commencing, he gave to the movement his hearty blessings
and best wishes. At sixty-seven years of age he retired
from business; no doubt a very well-to-do man, for he was
the owner of two freehold estates near Gloucester, and he
received an annuity of three hundred pounds from the
Gloucester Journal. He died at his house in Bell Lane, in
the city of Gloucester, where he had taken up his residence
when he retired from active life; he died suddenly, in his
seventy-sixth year, in 1811. Then the family vault in
St. Mary-le-Crypt, which sixty years before had received
his father's ashes, received the body of the gentle philanthropist. He had kept up his Sunday-school work and
interest to the close; and he left instructions that his
Sunday-school children should be invited to follow him
to the grave, and that each of them should receive a
shilling and a plum cake. On the tablet over the place
where he sleeps an appropriate verse of Scripture well
describes him : " When the ear heard me, then it blessed
me; and when the eye saw me, it gave witness to me :
because I delivered the poor that cried, and the fatherless,
and him that had none to help him. The blessing of him
that was ready to perish came upon me : and I caused the
widow's heart to sing for joy."

It seems very questionable whether the slightest shade
can cross the memory of this plain, simply useful, and

unostentatious man.   And it ought to be said that Anne
Raikes, who rests in the same grave, appears to have been
every way the worthy companion of her husband.   She
was the daughter of Thomas Trigg, Esq., of Newnham, in
Gloucestershire; the sister of Sir Thomas Trigg and Admiral
John Trigg.   They were married in 1767.   She shared
in all her husband's large and charitable intentions, and
when he died he left the whole of his property to her.

RAIKES'S HOUSE, GLOUCESTER.

She survived him seventeen years, and died in 1828, at the
age of eighty-five.

The visitor to Gloucester will be surely struck by a
quaint old house in Southgate Street—still standing
almost unaltered, save that the basement is now divided
into two shops.   A few years since the old oak timbers
were braced, stained, and varnished.   It is a fine specimen
of the better class of English residences of a hundred
and fifty years since, and is still remarkable in the old

city, owing very much to the good taste which governed their renovation. This was the printing-office of Robert Raikes, a notice in the *Gloucester Journal*, dated August 19, 1758, announcing his removal from Blackfriars Square to this house in Southgate Street. The house now is in the occupation of Mrs. Watson. The house where Raikes lived and died is nearly opposite. It will not be difficult for the spectator to realise the pleasant image of the old gentleman, dressed, after the fashion of the day, in his blue coat with gold buttons, buff waistcoat, drab kersey-mere breeches, white stockings, and low shoes, passing beneath those ancient gables, and engaged in those various public and private duties which we have attempted to record. A century has passed away since then, and the simple lessons the philanthropist attempted to impart to the young waifs and strays he gathered about him have expanded into more comprehensive departments of know-ledge. The originator of Sunday-schools would be astonished were he to step into almost any of those which have branched out from his leading idea. It is still ex-panding ; it is one of the most real and intense activities of the Universal Church ; but among the immense crowds of those who, in England and America, are conducting our Sunday-school classes, it is, perhaps, not too much to say, that in not one is there a more simple and earnest desire to do good than that which illuminated the life, and lends a sweet and charming interest to the memory, of Robert Raikes.

CHAPTER XI.

THE ROMANTIC STORY OF SILAS TOLD.

DR. ABEL STEVENS, in his *History of Methodism*, says, " I congratulate myself on the opportunity of reviving the memory of Silas Told ; " and speaks of the little biography in which Silas himself records his adventures as " a record told with frank and affecting simplicity, in a style of terse and flowing English Defoe might have envied."

Such a testimony is well calculated to excite the curiosity of an interested reader, especially as the two or three incidents mentioned only serve to whet the appetite for more of the like description. The little volume to which he refers has been for some years in the possession of the author of these *Vignettes*. It is indeed an astonishing book ; its alleged likeness to Defoe's charmingly various style of recital of adventures by sea and by land is no exaggeration, whilst as a piece of real biography it may claim, and quite sustain, a place side by side with the romantic and adventurous career of John Newton ; but the wild wonderfulness of the story of Silas seems to leave Newton's in the shade. Like Newton, Told was also a seer of visions and a dreamer of dreams, and a believer in special providences; and well might he believe in such who was led certainly along as singular a path as any mortal could tread. The only other memorial besides his own which has, we believe, been penned of him—a slight, brief recapitulation—well describes him as honest, simple, and tender. Silas Told accompanied, in that awful day, numbers of persons to the gallows, and attempted to console sufferers and victims in circumstances of most harrowing and tragic solemnity: he certainly furnished comfortable help and light when no others were willing or able to sympathise or to help. John Wesley loved him, and when Silas died he buried him, and says of him in his *Journal:* "On the 20th of December, 1778, I buried what was mortal of honest Silas Told. For many years he attended the malefactors in Newgate without fee or reward; and I suppose no man, for this hundred years, has been so successful in that melancholy office. God had given him peculiar talents for it, and he had amazing success therein; the greatest part of those whom he attended died in peace, and many of them in the triumph of faith." Such was Silas Told.

But before we come to those characteristic circumstances to which Wesley refers, we must follow him through some of the wild scenes of his sailor life. He was born in Bristol in 1711; his parents were respectable and creditable people, but of somewhat faded families. His grandfather had been an eminent physician in Bunhill Row, London; his mother was from Exeter; she bore the somewhat unmusical and unpleasant name of Suckabitch—a name, we may presume, she was not indisposed to change. Silas says the tradition connected with the origin of the name was that in the time of the kings of the West Angles, one of the kings, being out on a certain day hunting with one of his nobles, discovered a male infant in a wood, with no one near it but a large bitch, its keeper having left the child and gone into the woods.   The King took the child home, gave him his name, brought him up, and settled upon him, when he reached maturity, a large estate round the spot where he was found; and the name and estate seem to have gone together until within a generation or two of the birth of Silas.

Silas was educated in the noble foundation school of Edward Colston in Bristol.   The life of this excellent philanthropist was so remarkable, and in many particulars so like his own, that we cannot wonder that he stops for some pages in his early story to recite some of the remarkable phenomena in Colston's life.   Silas's childhood was singular, and the stories he tells are especially noticeable, because in after-life the turn of his character seems to have been especially real and practical.   Thus he tells how, when a child, wandering with his sister in the King's Wood, near Bristol, they lost their way, and were filled with the utmost consternation, when suddenly, although no house was in view, nor, as as they thought, near, a dog came up behind them, and drove them clear out of the wood into a path with which they were acquainted; especially it was remarkable that the dog never barked at them, but when they looked round about for the dog he was nowhere to be seen.   Careless children, out for their own pleasure, they sauntered on their way again, and again lost their way in the wood—were again bewildered, and in greater perplexity than before, when, on a sudden looking up, they saw the same dog making towards them; they ran from him in

fright, but he followed them, drove them out of the laby-
rinths, and did not leave them until they could not possibly lose their way again.   Simple Silas says, " I then
turned about to look for the dog, but saw no more of
him, although we were now upon an open common.   This
was the Lord's doing, and marvellous in our eyes."

When he was twelve years of age, he appears to have
been quite singularly influenced by the reading of the
Pilgrim's Progress ; and late in life, when writing his
biography, he briefly, but significantly, attempts to re-
produce the intense enjoyment he received — the book
evidently caught and coloured his whole imagination.
At this time, too, he was very nearly drowned, and
while drowning, so far from having any sense of terror,
he had no sense nor idea of the things of this world,
but that it appeared to him he rushingly emerged out
of thick darkness into what appeared to him a glorious
city, lustrous and brilliant, the light of which seemed to
illuminate the darkness through which he had urged his
way.   It was as if the city had a floor like glass, and yet
he was sure that neither city nor floor had any substance ; also he saw people there ; the inhabitants
arrayed in robes of what seemed the finest substance,
but flowing from their necks to their feet ; and yet he
was sensible too that they had no material substance ;
they moved, but did not labour as in walking, but glided
as if carried along by the wind ; and he testifies how he
felt a wonderful joy and peace, and he never forgot the
impression through life, although soon recalled to the world
in which he was to sorrow and suffer so much.   It is quite
easy to see John Bunyan in all this ; but while he was thus
pleasantly happy in his visionary or intro-visionary state,

a benevolent and tender-hearted Dutchman, who had been among some haymakers in a field on the banks of the river, was striking out after him among the willow-bushes and sedges of the stream, from whence he was brought, body and soul, back to the world again.   Such are the glimpses of the childhood of Silas.

Then shortly comes a dismal transition from strange providences in the wood, and enchanting visions beneath the waves, to the singularly severe sufferings of a seafaring life.   Our ships in that day have left a grim and ugly reputation surviving still.   The term "sea-devil" has often been used as descriptive of the masters of ships in that time. Silas seems to have sailed under some of the worst specimens of this order.   About the age of fourteen he was bound apprentice to Captain Moses Lilly, and started for his first voyage from Bristol to Jamaica.   "Here," he says, "I may date my first sufferings."   He says the first of his afflictions "was sea-sickness, which held me till my arrival in Jamaica ; " and considering that it was a voyage of fourteen weeks, it was a fair spell of entertainment from that pleasant companion.   They were short of water, they were put on short allowance of food, and when having obtained their freight, while lying in Kingston harbour, their vessel, and seventy-six sail of ships, many of them very large, but all riding with three anchors ahead, were all scattered by an astonishing hurricane, and all the vessels in Port Royal shared the same fate.   He tells how the corpses of the drowned sailors strewed the shores, and how, immediately after the subsidence of the hurricane, a pestilential sickness swept away thousands of the natives. "Every morning," he says, "I have observed between thirty and forty corpses carried past my window ; being very near death myself, I expected every day to approach with the messenger of my dissolution."

During this time he appears to have been lying in a warehouse, with no person to take care of him except a negro, who brought him every day Jesuit's bark to where he was laid in his hammock.

"At length," he says, "my master gave me up, and I wandered up and down the town, almost parched with the insufferable blaze of the sun, till I resolved to lay me down and die, as I had neither money nor friend ; accordingly, I fixed upon a dunghill in the east end of the town of Kingston, and being in such a weak condition, I pondered much upon Job's case, and considered mine similar to that of his ; however, I was fully resigned to death, nor had I the slightest expectation of relief from any quarter ; yet the kind providence of God was over me, and raised me up a friend in an entire stranger. A London captain coming by was struck with the sordid object, came up to me, and, in a very compassionate manner, asked me if I was sensible of any friend upon the island from whom I could obtain relief ; he likewise asked me to whom I. belonged. I answered, to Captain Moses Lilly, and had been cast away in the late hurricane. This captain appeared to have some knowledge of my master, and, cursing him for a barbarous villain, told me he would compel him to take proper care of me. About a quarter of an hour after this, my master arrived, whom I had not seen before for six weeks, and took me to a public-house kept by a Mrs. Hutchinson, and there ordered me to be taken proper care of. However, he soon quitted the island, and directed his course for England, leaving me behind at his sick quarters ; and, if it should please God to permit my recovery, I was commanded to take my passage to England in the *Montserrat*, Captain David Jones, a very fatherly, tender-hearted man : this was the first alleviation of my misery. Now the captain sent his son on shore, in order to receive me on board. When I came alongside, Captain Jones, standing on the ship's gunwale, addressed me after a very humane and compassionate manner, with expressions to the following effect : ' Come, poor child, into the cabin, and you shall want nothing that the ship affords ; go, and my son shall prepare for you, in the first place, a basin of good egg-flip, and anything else that may be conducive to your relief.' But I, being very bad with my fever and ague, could neither eat nor drink."

A very pleasant captain, this seems, to have sailed with ; but poor Silas had very little of his company. However, the good captain and his boatswain put their experiences together, and the poor boy was restored to health, and after some singular adventures he reached Bristol. Arriving there, however, Captain Lilly transferred him to a Captain Timothy Tucker, of whom Silas bears the pleasing testimony, " A greater villain, I firmly believe, never existed, although at home he assumed the character and temper of a saint." The wretch actually stole a white woman from her own country to sell her to the black prince of Bonny, on the African coast. They had not been long at sea before this delightful person gave Silas a taste of his temper. Thinking the boy had taken too much bread from the cask, he went to the cabin and brought back with him his large horsewhip, " and exercised it," says Silas, " about my body in so unmerciful a manner, that not only the clothes on my back were cut to pieces, but every sailor declared they could see my bones; and then he threw me all along the deck, and jumped many times upon the pit of my stomach, in order to endanger my life; and had not the people laid hold of my two legs, and thrown me under the windlass, after the manner they throw dead cats or dogs, he would have ended his despotic cruelty in murder." This free and easy mode of recreation was much indulged in by seafaring officers in that time, but this Tucker appears to have been really what Silas calls him, "a bloodthirsty devil;" and stories of murder, and the incredible cruelties of the slave-trade lend their horrible fascination to the narrative of Silas Told. How would it be possible to work the commerce of the slave-trade without such characters as this Tucker, who presents much more the appearance of a lawless pirate than of the noble character we call a sailor?

Those readers who would like to follow poor Silas through the entire details of his miseries on ship-board, his hairbreadth escapes from peril and shipwreck, must read them in Silas's own book, if they can find it; but we may attempt to give some little account of his wreck, upon the American coast, in New England. Few stories can be more charming than the picture he gives of his wanderings with his companions after their escape from the wreck, not because he and they were destitute, and all but naked, but because of the pleasant glimpses we have of the simple, hospitable, home-life in those beautiful old New England days—hospitality of the most romantic and free-handed description.

We will select two pictures, as illustrating something of the character of New England settlements in those very early days of their history. Silas and his companions

were cast on shore, and had found refuge in a tavern
seven miles from the beach ; he had no clothing ; but the
landlord of the tavern gave him a pair of red breeches,
the last he had after supplying the rest. Silas goes on :
"Ebenezer Allen, governor of the island, and who dwelt
about six miles from the tavern, hearing of our distress,
made all possible haste to relieve us ; and when he arrived
at the tavern, accompanied by his two eldest sons, he took
Captain Seaborn, his black servant, Joseph and myself
through partiality, and escorted us home to his own
house.   Between eleven and twelve at night we reached
the Governor's mansion, all of us ashamed to be seen ;
we would fain have hid ourselves in any dark hole or
corner, as it was a truly magnificent building, with wings
on each side thereof, but, to our astonishment, we were
received into the great parlour, where were sitting by the
fireside two fine, portly ladies, attending the spit, which
was burdened with a very heavy quarter of house-lamb.
Observing a large mahogany table to be spread with a fine
damask cloth, and every knife, fork, and plate to be laid in
a genteel mode, I was apprehensive that it was intended
for the entertainment of some persons of note or distinction,
or, at least, for a family supper.   In a short time the joint
was taken up, and laid on the table, yet nobody sat down
to eat ; and as we were almost hid in one corner of the
room, the ladies turned round and said, ' Poor men, why
don't you come to supper ? '   I replied, ' Madam, we had
no idea it was prepared for us.'   The ladies then entreated
us to eat without any fear of them, assuring us that it was
prepared for none others ; and none of us having eaten
anything for near six and thirty hours before, we picked
the bones of the whole quarter, to which we had plenty of

rich old cyder to drink : after supper we went to bed, and enjoyed so profound a sleep that the next morning it was difficult for the old gentleman to awake us. The following day I became the partaker of several second-hand garments, and, as I was happily possessed of a little learning, it caused me to be more abundantly caressed by the whole family, and therefore I fared sumptuously every day.

" This unexpected change of circumstances and diet I undoubtedly experienced in a very uncommon manner ; but as I was strictly trained up a Churchman, I could not support the idea of a Dissenter, although, God knows, I had well-nigh by this time dissented from all that is truly good. This proved a bar to my promotion, and my strong propensity to sail for England to see my mother prevented my acceptance of the greatest offer I ever received in my life before ; for when the day came that we were to quit the island, and to cross the sound over to a town called Sandwich, on the main continent, the young esquire took me apart from my associates, and earnestly entreated me to tarry with them, saying that if I would accede to their proposals nothing should be lacking to render my situation equivalent to the rest of the family. As there were very few white men on the island, I was fixed upon, if willing, to espouse one of the Governor's daughters. I had been informed that the Governor was immensely rich, having on the island two thousand head of cattle and twenty thousand sheep, and every acre of land thereon belonging to himself. However, I could not be prevailed upon to accept the offer ; therefore the Governor furnished us with forty shillings each, and gave us a pass over to the town of Sandwich."

Such passages as this show the severe experiences

through which Silas passed ; they illustrate the education
he was receiving for that life of singular earnestness and
tenderness which was to close and crown his career ; but
we have made the extract here for the purpose of giving
some idea of that cheerful, hospitable, home life of New
England in those then almost wild regions which are now
covered with the population of towns.

Here is another instance, which occurred at Hanover, in
the United States, through which district Silas and his
companions appear to have been wending their way,
seeking a return to England.   "One Sunday, as my
companions and self were crossing the churchyard at the
time of Divine service, a well-dressed gentleman came out
of the church and said, 'Gentlemen, we do not suffer any
person in this country to travel on the Lord's day.'   We
gave him to understand that it was necessity which constrained us to walk that way, as we had all been shipwrecked on St. Martin's Vineyard, and were journeying
to Boston. The gentleman was still dissatisfied, but quitted
our company and went into church.   When we had gone
a little farther, a large white house proved the object of
our attention.   The door being wide open, we reasonably
imagined it was not in an unguarded state, without
servants or others ; but as we all went into the kitchen,
nobody appeared to be within, nor was there an individual
either above or below.   However, I advised my companions to tarry in the house until some person or other
should arrive.   They did so, and in a short time afterwards
two ladies, richly dressed, with a footman following them,
came in through the kitchen ; and, notwithstanding they
turned round and saw us, who in so dirty and disagreeable
a garb and appearance might have terrified them exceed-

ingly, yet neither of them was observed to take any notice of us, nor did either of them ask us any questions touching the cause of so great an intrusion.

"About a quarter of an hour afterwards, a footman entered the kitchen with a cloth and a large two-quart silver tankard full of rich cyder, also a loaf and cheese ; but we, not knowing it was prepared for us, did not attempt to partake thereof. At length the ladies coming into the kitchen, and viewing us in our former position, desired to know the reason of our malady, seeing we were not refreshing ourselves ; whereupon I urged the others to join with me in the acceptance of so hospitable a proposal. After this the ladies commenced a similar inquiry into our situation. I gave them as particular an account of every recent vicissitude that befell us as I was capable of, with a genuine relation of our being shipwrecked, and the sole reasons of our travelling into that country ; likewise begged that they would excuse our impertinence, as they were already informed of the cause ; we were then emboldened to ask the ladies if they could furnish us with a lodging that evening. They replied it was uncertain whether our wishes could be accomplished there, but that if we proceeded somewhat farther we should doubtless be entertained and genteelly accommodated by their brother —a Quaker—whose house was not more than a distance of seven miles. We thanked the ladies, and set forward, and at about eight o'clock arrived at their brother's house. Fatigued with our journey, we hastened into the parlour and delivered our message ; whereupon a gentleman gave us to understand, by his free and liberal conduct, that he was the Quaker referred to by the aforesaid ladies, who, total strangers as we were, used us with a degree of hospitality impossible to be exceeded; indeed, I could venture to say that the accommodations we met with at the Quaker's house, seeing they were imparted to us with such affectionate sympathy, greatly outweighed those we formerly experienced.

"After our banquet, the gentleman took us up into a fine spacious bed-chamber, with desirable bedding and very costly chintz curtains. We enjoyed a sound night's rest, and arose between seven and eight the next morning, and were entertained with a good breakfast; returned many thanks for the unrestrained friendship and liberality, and departed therefrom, fully purposed to direct our course for Boston, which was not more than seven miles farther. Here all the land was strewed with plenty, the orchards were replete with apple-trees and pears; they had cyder-presses in the centre of their orchards, and great quantities of fine cyder, and any person might become a partaker thereof for the mere trouble of asking. We soon entered Boston, a commodious, beautiful city, with seventeen spired meetings, the dissenting religion being then established in that part of the world. I resided here for the space of four months, and lodged with Captain Seaborn at Deacon Townshend's; deacon of the North Meeting, and by trade a blacksmith." He gives a glowing and beautiful description of the high moral and religious character of Boston; here also he met with a stroke of good fortune in receiving some arrears of salvage for a vessel he had assisted in saving before his last wreck. Such are specimens of the interest and entertainment afforded in the earlier parts of this pleasant piece of autobiography. But we must hasten past his adventures, both in the island of Antigua and among the islands of the Mediterranean.

It is not wonderful that the great sufferings and toils of Silas should, even at a very early period of life, prostrate his health, and subject him to repeated vehement attacks of illness. He was but twenty-three when he married ; still, however, a sailor, and destined yet for some wild experiences on the seas. Not long, however. A married life disposed him for a home life, and he accepted, while still a very young man, the position of a schoolmaster, beneath the patronage of a Lady Luther, in the county of Essex. He was not in this position very long. Silas, although an unconverted man, must have had strong religious feelings ; and the clergyman of the parish, fond of smoking and drinking with him—and it may well be conceived what an entertaining companion Silas must have been in those days, with his budget of adventures—ridiculed him for his faith in the Scriptures and his belief in Bible theology. This so shocked Silas, that, making no special profession of religion, he yet separated himself from the clergyman's company, and shortly after he left that neighbourhood, and again sought his fortune, but without any very cheerful prospects, in London.

It was in 1740 that a young blacksmith introduced him to the people whom he had hitherto hated and despised—the Methodists. He heard John Wesley preach at the Foundry in the Moor Fields—the cradle of Methodism in London—from the text, "I write unto you, little children, for your sins are forgiven you." This set his soul on fire ; he himself became a Methodist, notwithstanding the very vehement opposition of his wife, to whom he appears to have been very tenderly attached, and who herself was a very motherly and virtuous woman, but altogether indisposed to the new notions, as many people considered them. He improved in circumstances, and became a responsible managing clerk on a wharf at Wapping. While there Mr. Wesley repeatedly and earnestly pressed him to take charge of the charity school he had established at the Foundry. After long hesitation he did so ; and it was here that while attending a service at five o'clock in the morning, he heard Mr. Wesley preach from the text, " I was sick, and in prison, and ye visited me not." By a most remarkable application of this charge to himself, Silas testifies that his mind was stirred with a strange compunction, as he thought that he had never cared for, or attempted to ameliorate the condition, or to minister to the souls of the crowds of those unhappy malefactors who then almost weekly expiated their offences, very often of the most trivial description, on the gallows. It seems that the hearing that sermon proved to be a most remarkable turning-point in the life of Silas. Through it he became most eminently useful during a very remarkable and painful career ; and his after-life is surrounded by such a succession of romantic incidents that they at once equal, if they do not transcend, and strangely contrast with his wild adventures on the seas.

And here we may pause a moment to reflect how every man's work derives its character from what he was before. What thousands of sailors, in that day, passed through all the trials which Silas passed, leaving them still only rough sailor men ! In him all the roughness seemed only to strike down to depths of wonderful compassion and tenderness. Singular was the university in which he graduated to become so great and painful a preacher ! How he preached we do not know, but his words must have been warm and touching, faithful and loving, judging from their results; and as to his pulpit, we do not hear that it was in chapels or churches—his audience was very much confined to the condemned cell, and to the cart from whence the poor victims were "turned off," as it was called in those days. In this work he found his singular niche. How long it often takes for a man to find his place in the work that is given him to do; and when the place is found, sometimes, how long it takes to fit nicely and admirably into the work itself! what sharp angles have to be rubbed away, what difficulties to be overcome! It is wonderful, with all the horrible experiences through which this man had passed, and spectacles of cruelty so revolting that they seem almost to shake our faith, not merely in man, but even in a just and overruling God, that every sentiment of religion and tenderness had not been eradicated from his nature; but it would appear that the old gracious influences of childhood—the days of the *Pilgrim's Progress*, and the wonderful vision when drowning beneath the waters, had never been effaced through all his strange and chequered career, although certainly not untainted by the sins of the ordinary sailor's life. The work in which he was now to be engaged needed a very tender and affectionate nature; but ordinary tenderness starts back and is repelled by cruel and repulsive scenes. Told's education on the seas, like that of a surgeon in a hospital, enabled him to look on harrowing sights of suffering without wincing, or losing in his tender interest his own self-possession.

It ought not to be forgotten that John Howard, the great prison philanthropist, belongs to the epoch of the

Great Revival. Of him Edmund Burke said, "He had visited all Europe in a circumnavigation of charity, not to survey the sumptuousness of palaces, or the stateliness of temples ; not to collect medals or to collate manuscripts, but to dive into the depths of dungeons and to plunge into the infections of hospitals." About the year 1760, when he began his consecrated work, Silas Told, as a prison philanthropist upon a smaller, but equally earnest scale, attempted to console the prisoners of Newgate.

Shortly after hearing that sermon to which we have alluded, a messenger came to him at the school to tell him that there were ten malefactors lying under sentence of death in Newgate, some of them in a state of considerable terror and alarm, and imploring him to find some one to visit them. Here was the call to the work. The coincidences were remarkable : John Wesley's sermon, his own aroused and tender state of mind produced by the sermon, and the occasion for the active and practical exercise of his feeling. So opportunities would meet us of turning suggestions into usefulness, if we watched for them.

The English laws were barbarous in those days ; truly it has been said that a fearfully heavy weight of blood rests upon the conscience of England for the state of the law in those times. Few of those who have given such honour to the noble labours of John Howard and the loving ministrations of Elizabeth Fry ever heard of Silas Told. In a smaller sphere than the first of these, and in a much more intensely painful manner than the second, he anticipated the labours of both. He instantly responded to this first call to Newgate. Two of the ten malefactors were reprieved ; he attended the remaining eight to the gallows. He had so influenced the hearts of all of them in their cell that their obduracy was broken down and softened—so great had been his power over them, that locked up together in one cell the night before their execution, they had spent it in prayer and solemn conversation. "At length they were ordered into the cart, and I was prevailed upon to go with them. When we were in the cart I addressed myself to each of them separately. The first was Mr. Atkins, the son of a glazier in the City, a youth nineteen years of age. I said to him, 'My dear, are you afraid to die?' He said, 'No, sir; really I am not.' I asked him wherefore he was not afraid to die? and he said, 'I have laid my soul at the feet of Jesus, therefore I am not afraid to die.' I then spake to Mr. Gardner, a journeyman carpenter; he made a very comfortable report of the true peace of God which he found reigning in his heart. The last person to whom I spoke was one Thompson, a very illiterate young man; but he assured me he was perfectly happy in his Saviour, and continued so until his last moments. This was the first time of my visiting the malefactors in Newgate, and then it was not without much shame and fear, because I clearly perceived the greater part of the populace considered me as one of the sufferers."

The most remarkable of this cluster was one John Lancaster—for what offence he was sentenced to death does not appear; but the entire account Silas gives of him, both in the prison and at the place of execution, exhibits a fine, tender, and really holy character. The attendant sheriff himself burst into tears before the beautiful demeanour of this young man. However, so it was, that he was without any friend in London to procure for his body a proper interment; and the story of Silas admits us into a pretty spectacle of the times. After the poor bodies were cut down, Lancaster's was seized by a surgeons' mob, who intended to carry it over to Paddington. It was Silas's first experience, as we have seen ; and he describes the whole scene as rather like a great fair than an awful execution. In this confusion the body of Lancaster had been seized, the crowd dispersed—all save some old woman, who sold gin, and Silas himself, very likely smitten into extraordinary meditation by a spectacle so new to him— when a company of eight sailors appeared on the scene, with truncheons in their hands, who said they had come to see the execution, and gazed with very menacing faces on the vacated gallows from whence the bodies had been cut down. " Gentlemen," said the old woman, " I suppose you want the man that the surgeons have got ?" " Ay," said the sailors, "where is he ?" The old woman gave them to understand that the body had been carried away to Paddington, and she pointed them to the direct road. Away the sailors hastened—it may be presumed that Lancaster was a sailor, and some old comrade of these men. They demanded his body from the surgeons' mob, and obtained it. What they intended to do with it scarcely transpires; it is most likely that they had intended a rescue at the foot of the gallows, and arrived too late. However, hoisting it on their shoulders, away they marched with it off to Islington, and thence round to Shoreditch ; thence to a place called Coventry's Fields. By this time they were getting fairly wearied out with their burden, and by unanimous consent they agreed to lay it on the step of the first door they came to : this done, they started off. It created some stir in the street, which brought down an old woman who lived in the house to the step of the door, and who exclaimed, as she saw the body, in a loud, agitated voice, " Lord! this is my son John Lancaster!" It is probable that the old woman was a Methodist, for to Silas Told and the Methodists she was indebted for a decent and respectable burial for her son in a good strong coffin, and decent shroud. Silas and his wife went to see him whilst he was lying so, previous to his burial. There was no alteration of his visage, no marks of violence, and says Told, "A pleasant smile appeared on his countenance, and he lay as in a sweet sleep." A singularly romantic story, for it seems the sailors did not know at all to whom he belonged ; and what an insight into the social condition of London at that time!

Told did not give up his connection with his school at the Foundry, but he devoted himself, sanctioned by John Wesley and his Church fellowship, to the preaching and ministering to all the poor felons and malefactors in London, including also, in this exercise of love, the work-houses for twelve miles round London ; he believed he had a message of tender sympathy for those who were of this order, "sick and in prison." It seems to us, who know how much he had suffered himself, strange that the old sailor possessed such a loving, tender, and affectionate heart ; and yet he tells how, in the earlier part of these very years, he was haunted by irritating doubts and alarms : then came to him old mystical revelations, such as those he had known when drowning, reminding us of similar instances in the lives of John Howe and John Flavel ; and the noble man was strengthened.

He went on for twenty years in the way we have described ; and the interest of his autobiography compels the wish that it were much longer ; for, of course, the largest amount of his precious life of labour was not set down, and cannot be recalled; and readers who are fond of romance will find his name in connection with some of the most remarkable executions of his time.

A singular circumstance was this : Four gentlemen—Mr. Brett, the son of an eminent divine in Dublin ; Whalley, a gentleman of considerable fortune, possessed of three country-seats of his own ; Dupree, "in every particular," says Silas, "a complete gentleman ;" and Morgan, an officer on board one of His Majesty's ships of war—after dinner, upon the occasion of their being at an election for the members for Chelmsford, proposed to start forth, and, by way of recreation, rob somebody on the highway. Away they went, and chanced upon a farmer, whom they eased of a considerable sum of money. The farmer followed them into Chelmsford ; they were all secured, and next day removed to London ; they took their trials, and were sentenced, and left for execution. Told visited them all in prison. Morgan was engaged to be married to Lady Elizabeth Hamilton, the sister of the Duke of Hamilton. She repeatedly visited her affianced husband in his cell, and Told was with them at most of their interviews. It was supposed that, from the rank of the prisoners, and the character of their offence, there would be no difficulty in obtaining a reprieve ; but the King was quite inexorable : he said, "his subjects were not to be in bodily fear in order that men might gratify their drunken whims." Lady Elizabeth Hamilton, however, thrust herself several times before the King ; wept, threw herself on her knees, and behaved altogether in such a manner that the King said, "Lady Betsy, there is no standing your importunity any further ; I will spare his life, but on one condition—that he is not acquainted therewith until he arrives at the place of execution ;" and it was so. The other three unfortunates were executed, and Lady Elizabeth, in her coach, received her lover into it as he stepped from the cart. It is a sad story, but it must have been a sweet satisfaction to the lady.

Far more dreadful were some cases which engaged the tender heart of Silas. A young man, named Coleman, was tried for an aggravated assault on a young woman. The young woman herself declared that Coleman was not the man ; but he had enemies who pressed apparent circumstances against him, and urged them on the young woman, to induce her to change her opinion. She never wavered ; yet, singular to say, he was convicted and executed. A short time after the real criminal was discovered, by his own confession ; he was also tried, condemned, and executed, and the perjured witnesses against poor Coleman sentenced to stand in the pillory.

But one of the most pitiful and dreadful cases in Silas Told's experience was that of Mary Edmondson, a sweet young girl, tried upon mere circumstantial evidence, and executed on Kennington Common, for the supposed murder of her aunt at Rotherhithe. She appears to have been most brutally treated ; the mob believed her to be guilty, and received her with shocking execrations. Whether Silas had a prejudice against her or not, we cannot say ; it is not likely that he had a prejudice against any suffering soul ; but it so happened, he says, as he had not visited her in her imprisonment, so he entertained no idea of seeing her suffer. But as he was passing through the Borough, a pious cheesemonger, named Skinner, called him into his shop, tenderly expressed deep interest in her present and future state, and besought him to see her ; so his first interview with her was only just as she was going forth to her sad end.

Silas shall tell the story himself: " When she was brought into the room, she stood with her back against the wainscot, but appeared perfectly resigned to the will of God. I then addressed myself to her, saying, ' My dear, for God's sake, for Christ's sake, for the sake of your own precious soul, do not die with a lie in your mouth ; you are, in a few moments, to appear in the presence of the holy God, who is of purer eyes than to behold iniquity. Oh, consider what an eternity of misery must be the position of all who die in their sins !' She heard me with much meekness and simplicity, but answered that she had already advanced the truth, and must persevere in the same spirit to her last moments." Efforts were made to prevent Told from accompanying her any farther, and the rioters were so exasperated against her that Told seems only to have been safe by keeping near to the sheriff along the whole way. The sheriff also told him that he would be giving a great satisfaction to the whole nation, could he only bring her to a confession. " Now, as we were proceeding on the road, the sheriff's horse being close to the cart, I looked up at her from under the horse's bridle, and I said, ' My dear, look to Jesus.' This quickened her spirit, insomuch that although she had not looked about her before, she turned herself round to me, and said, ' Sir, I bless God I can look to Jesus—to my comfort.'"

Arrived at the place of execution, he spoke to her again solemnly, " Did you not commit the fact ? Had you no concern therein ? Were you not interested in the murder?" She said, " I am as clear of the whole affair as I was the day my mother brought me into the world." She was very young, she had all the aspects of innocence about her. The sheriff burst into tears, and turned his head away, exclaiming, "Good God! it is a second Coleman's case!"

At this moment her cousin stepped up into the cart, and sought to kiss her. She turned her face away, and pushed him off. She had before charged him with being the murderer—and he was. When subsequently taken up for another crime, he confessed the committal of this. Her aunt had left to Mary, in the event of her death, more money than to this wretch. The executioner drew the cart away, and Mary's body—leaning the poor head, in her last moments, on Silas's shoulder—dear old Silas, her only comfort in that terrible hour—fell into the arms of death. But he tells how she was cold and still before the cart was drawn away.

But perhaps a still more pitiful case was that of poor Anderson, who was hanged for stealing sixpence : he was a labouring man, and had been of irreproachable character. He and his wife—far gone with child—were destitute of money, clothes, and food. He said to his wife, " My dear, I will go out, down to the quays ; it may be that the Lord will provide me with a loaf of bread." All his efforts were fruitless, but passing through Hoxton Fields, he met two washerwomen. He did not bid them stop, but he said to one, " Mistress, I want money." She gave him twopence. He said to the other, "You have money, I know you have." She said, " I have fourpence." He took that. Insensible of what might follow, as of what he had done, he walked down into Old Street : there, the two women having followed him gave him in charge of a constable. He was tried, sentenced to death, and for this he died.

"Never," says Told, "through the years I have attended the prisoners, have I seen such meek, loving, patient spirits as this man and his wife." Told attended him to execution, and sought to comfort the poor fellow by promising him to look after his wife; and most tenderly did Told and his wife redeem the promise, for they took her for a short time into their own home. Told obtained a housekeeper's situation for her, and she became a creditable and respected woman. He bound her daughter apprentice to a weaver, and she, probably, turned out well, although he says, "I have never seen her but twice since, which is many years ago."

Our readers will, perhaps, think that it is time we drew these harrowing stories to a close; but there are many more of them in this brief, but most interesting, although forgotten autobiography. They are recited with much pathos. We have the story of Harris, the flying highwayman; of Bolland, a sheriff's officer, who was executed for forging a note, although he had refunded the money, and twice afterwards paid the sum of the bill to secure himself. A young gentleman, named Slocomb, defrauded his father of three hundred pounds; his father would not in any way stir, or remit his claim, to save him. Told attended him and thought highly of him, not only because he expressed himself with so much resignation, but because he never indulged a complaint against him whom Told calls "that lump of adamant, his father." With him was executed another young gentleman, named Powell, for forgery. Silas Told also attended that cruel woman, Elizabeth Brownrigg, who was executed for the atrocious murder of her apprentices. And of all the malefactors whom he attended she seems to us the most unsatisfactory.

We trust our readers will not be displeased to receive these items from the biography of a very remarkable, a singularly romantic and chequered, as well as singularly useful career. References to Silas Told will be found in most of the biographies of Wesley. Southey passes him by with a very slight allusion. Tyerman dwells on his memory with a little more tenderness; but, with the exception of Stevens, none has touched with real interest upon this extraordinary though obscure man, and his romantic life and labours in a very strange path of Christian benevolence and usefulness. He was known, far and near, as the "prisoners' chaplain," although an unpaid one. He closed his life in 1778, in the sixty-eighth year of his age. As we have seen, John Wesley appropriately officiated at his funeral, and pronounced an affectionate encomium over the remains of his honoured old friend and fellow-labourer.

CHAPTER XII.

FRUIT.

ILLUSTRATING what we have said before, it remains to be noticed, that nearly all the great societies sprang into existence almost simultaneously. The foremost among these,* founded in 1792, was the Baptist Missionary Society. It appears to have arisen from a suggestion of William Carey, the celebrated Northamptonshire shoemaker, who proposed as an inquiry to an association of Northamptonshire ministers, "whether it were not practicable and obligatory to attempt the conversion of the heathen." It is certainly still a moot question whether Le Verrier or Adams first laid the hand of science on the planet Neptune; but it seems quite certain that, when one of God's great thoughts is throbbing in the heart of one of His apostles, the same impulse and passion is stirring another, perhaps others, in remote and far-away scenes. Altogether unknown to William Carey, that same year the

---

* It is not implied that these were the first modern missionary agencies. The Moravians had already sent the Gospel into many regions. There were Swedish and Danish Missionary Societies also at work. The Society for the Propagation of the Gospel had, as long before as the time of the Hon. Robert Boyle, been at work in America.

WILLIAM CAREY.

great Claudius Buchanan was dreaming his divine dreams about the conquest of India for Christ, in St. Mary's College, Cambridge. Undoubtedly the honour of the first consolidation of the thought into a missionary enterprise must be given to William Carey and his little band of obscure believers.

At the close of Carey's address, to which we have referred, a collection was made for the purpose of attempting a missionary crusade upon Hindostan, amounting to £13 2s. 6d. The wits made fine work of this: the reader may still turn to Sydney Smith's paper in the *Edinburgh Review*, in which the idea and the effort are satirised as that of "an army of maniacs setting forth to the conquest of India." But this humble effort resulted in magnificent achievements; Carey and his illustrious coadjutors, Ward and Marshman, set forth, and became stupendous Oriental scholars, translating the Word of Life into many Indian dialects. Then came tempests of abuse and scurrility at home from eminent pens. We experience a shame in reading them; but it shows the catholicity of spirit pervading the minds of Christ's real followers, that Lord Teignmouth, and William Wilberforce, and Dr. Buchanan, were amongst the ablest and most earnest defenders of the noble Baptist missionaries. We are able to see now that this mission may be said to have saved India to the British Empire. It not only created the scholars to whom we have referred, and the bands of holy labourers, but also the sagacity of Lord Lawrence, and the consecrated courage of Sir Henry Havelock. We are prepared, therefore, to maintain that we are indebted more to William Carey and his £13 2s. 6d. than to the cunning of Clive and the rapacity of Warren Hastings.

Another child of the Revival was born in 1795—the London Missionary Society. But it would be idle to attempt to enumerate the names either of its founders, its missionaries, or their fields of labour; let the reader turn to the names of the founders, and he will find they were nearly all enthusiasts who had been baptised into the spirit of the Revival—Rowland Hill, Matthew Wilks, Alexander Waugh, William Kingsbury, and, notably, Thomas Haweis, the Rector of Aldwinckle and chaplain to the Countess of Huntingdon. Nor must we omit the name of David Bogue, that strong and eloquent intelligence, whose admirable and suggestive work on *The Divine Authority of the New Testament*, sent to Napoleon in his exile at St. Helena by the Viscountess Duncan, was, after the Emperor's death, returned to the author full of annotations, thus seeming to give some clue to those religious conversations, in which the illustrious exile certainly astonishes us, not long before his departure.

It is the London Missionary Society which has covered the largest surface of the earth with its missions, and it is not invidious to say that its records register a larger range of conquests over heathenism and idolatry than could be chronicled in any age since the first apostles went upon their way. We have only to remember the Sandwich Islands, and the crowds of islands in the Southern Seas, with their chief civiliser, the martyr of Erromanga; Africa, from the Cape along through the deep interior, with Moffatt and Livingstone, whose celebrated motto was, "The end of the geographical feat is the beginning of the missionary enterprise;" China and Robert Morison; Madagascar and William Ellis, and many other regions and names to justify our verdict.

In 1800 the Church Missionary Society came into existence. "What!" said the passionate and earnest Rev. Melville Horne, in attempting to arouse the clergy to missionary enthusiasm; "have Carey and the Baptists had more forgiven than we, that they should love more? Have the fervent Methodists and patient Moravians been extortionate publicans, that they should expend their all in a cause which we decline? Have our Independent brethren persecuted the Church more, that they should now be more zealous in propagating the faith which it once destroyed?" And so the Church Missionary Society arose; and in 1804, the Bible Society; in 1805, the British and Foreign School Society; in 1799, the Religious Tract Society, which, since its foundation, has probably circulated not less than five hundred millions of publications. The Wesleyan Missionary Society—which claims in date to take precedence of all in its foundation in the year 1784 —was not formally constituted till 1817. Every one of these, and many other such associations, alike show the vivid and vigorous spirit which was abroad seeking to secure the empire of the world to the cause of Divine truth and love.

And, meantime, what works were going on at home? Education and intelligence were widely spreading; simple academies were forming, like that founded by the Countess of Huntingdon at Trevecca, where the minds of young men were being moulded and informed to become the intelligent vehicles of the Gospel message—eminently that of the great and good Cornelius Winter, in Gloucestershire; and that of David Bogue at Gosport; while, in the north of England, arose the small but very effective colleges of Bradford and Rotherham; and the now handsome Lanca-

shire Independent College had its origin in the vestry of
Mosley Street Chapel, where the sainted William Roby,
as tutor, gathered around him a number of young men,
and armed them with intellectual appliances for the work
of the ministry.

Some of the earliest efforts of Methodism, and some of
the most successful, had been in the gaols, and among the
malefactors of the country—notably in the wonderful
labours of Silas Told, whose extraordinary story has been
recited in these pages. Silas passed away, but an angel
of light moved through the cells of Newgate in the person
of Elizabeth Fry, as beautiful and commanding in her
presence as she was holy in her sweet and fervid zeal.
Now began thoughts too about the waifs and strays of the
population—the helpless and forgotten ; and the great and
good John Townshend, an Independent minister, laid the
foundation of the first Deaf and Dumb Asylum, the noble
institution of London.

In the world of politics, also, the men of the Revival
were exercising their influence, and procuring charters of
freedom for the mind of the nation. Has it not been ever
true that civil and religious liberty have flourished side by
side ? A blight cannot pass over one without withering
the other. The honour of the repeal of the Test and
Corporation Acts is due to the Great Revival : the Tolera-
tion Act of those days was really more oppressive on
pious members of the Church of England than on Dissenters ; they could not obtain, as Dissenters could, a
licence for holding religious services in their houses,
because they were members of the Church of England.

William Wilberforce owed his first religious impressions
to the preaching of Whitefield ; with all his fine liberality

of heart, he became an ardent member of the communion of the Church of England. It seems incredible to us now that he lived constantly in the expectation—we will not say fear—of indictments against him, for holding prayer-meetings and religious services at his house in Kensington Gore. Lord Barham, the father of the late amiable and excellent Baptist Noel, was fined forty pounds, on two informations of his neighbour, the Earl of Romney, for a breach of the statute in like services. That such a state of things as this was changed to the free and happy ordinances we behold around us in our day, was owing to the spirit which was abroad, giving not only freedom to the soul of the man, but dignity and independence to the social life of the citizen. Everywhere, and in every department of life, the spirit of the Revival moved over the face of the waters, dividing the light from the darkness, and thus God said, " Let there be light, and there was light."

CHAPTER XIII.

AFTERMATH.

THE effects of that great awakening which we have thus attempted concisely, but fairly, to delineate, are with us still ; the strength is diffused, the tone and colour are modified. One chief purpose has guided the pen of the writer throughout : it has been to show that the immense regeneration effected in English manners and society during the later years of the last century and the first of the present, was the result of a secret, silent, most subtle spiritual force, awakening the minds and hearts of men in most opposite parts of the nation, and in widely different social circumstances. We would give all honour where honour is due, remembering that " Every good gift and every perfect gift is from above." There are writers whose special admiration is given to some favourite sect, some effective movement, or some especially beloved name ; but a dispassionate view, an entrance—if we may be permitted so to speak of it—into the camera, the chamber of the times, presents to the eye a long suc-cession of actors, and brings out into the clear light a wonderful variety of influences all simultaneously at work to redeem society from its darkness, and to give it a higher degree of spiritual purity and mental and moral dignity.

The first great workers were passing away, most of them, as is usually the case, dying on Pisgah, seeing most distinctly the future results of their work, but scarcely permitted to enter upon the full realisation of it. In 1791, in the eighty-fourth year of her age, died the revered Countess of Huntingdon; her last words, "My work is done; I have nothing to do but to go to my Father!" No chronicle of convent or canonisation, nor any story of biography, can record a more simple, saintly, and utterly unselfish life. To the last unwearied, she was daily occupied in writing long letters, arranging for her many ministers, disposing of her chapel trusts; sometimes feeling that her rank, and certain suppositions as to the extent of her wealth, made her an object on which men were not indisposed to exercise their rapacity. Still, as compared with the state of society when she commenced her work, in this her closing year, she must have looked over a hopeful and promising future, as sweet and enchanting as the ineffably lovely scenery upon which her eyes opened at Castle Doddington, and the neighbouring beauties of her first wedded home.

In 1791, John Wesley, in his eighty-eighth year, entered into his rest, faithfully murmuring, as well as weakness and stammering lips could articulate, "The best of all is, God is with us!" Abel Stevens says, "His life stands out, in the history of the world, unquestionably pre-eminent in religious labours above that of any other man since the apostolic age." It is not necessary, in order to do Wesley sufficient honour, to indulge in such invidious comparisons. It is significant, however, that the last straggling syllables which ever fell from the pen in his beloved hand, were in a letter to William Wilberforce, cheering him on in his efforts for the abolition of slavery and the slave trade. Charles Wesley had preceded his brother to his rest in 1788, in the eightieth year of his age.

Thus the earlier labourers were passing away, and the

JOHN WESLEY'S TOMB, CITY ROAD.

work of the Revival was passing into other forms, illustrating how not only "one generation passeth away, and another cometh," but also how, as the workers pass, the work abides. It would be very pleasant to spend some time in noticing the interior of many old halls, which were

JOHN WESLEY, M.A.
BORN JUNE 17, 1703; DIED MARCH 2, 1791.

CHARLES WESLEY, M.A.
BORN DECEMBER 18, 1708; DIED MARCH 29, 1788.

"THE BEST OF ALL IS, GOD IS WITH US."

"I LOOK UPON ALL THE WORLD AS MY PARISH."

THE WESLEY MONUMENT, WESTMINSTER ABBEY.

now opening, at once for the entertainment of evangelists, and for Divine service ; prejudices were dying out, and so far from the new religious life proving inimical to the repose of the country, it was found to be probably its surest security and friend ; and while the efforts were growing for carrying to far-distant regions the truth which enlightens and saves, anecdotes are not wanting to show that it was this very spirit which created a tender interest in maintaining and devising means to make more secure the minister's happiness at home.

From many points of view William Wilberforce may be regarded as the central man of the Revival in its new and crowning aspect ; as he bore the standard of England at that great funeral which did honour to all that was mortal of his friend William Pitt, on its way to the vaults of the old Abbey, so, as his predecessors departed, it devolved on him to bear the standard of those truths and principles which had effected the great change, and which were to effect, if possible, yet greater changes. By his sweet, winning, and if silvery, yet enchaining and overwhelming eloquence, by his conversation, which cannot have been, from the traditions which are preserved of it, less than wonderful, and by his lucid and practical pen, he continued to give eminent effect to the Revival, and to procure for its doctrines acceptance in the highest circles of society. It is perhaps difficult now to understand the cause of the wonderful influence produced by his *Practical View of Christianity;* that book itself illustrates how the seeds of things are transmitted through many generations. It is a long way to look back to the poor pedlar who called at the farm door of Richard Baxter's father in Eaton-Constantine, and sold there Richard Sibbs's *Bruised Reed* but that was the birth-hour of that great and transcendently glorious book, *The Saint's Everlasting Rest.* *The Saint's Everlasting Rest* was the inspiration of Philip Doddridge, and to it we owe his *Rise and Progress of Religion in the Soul.* Wilberforce read that book, and it moved him to the desire to speak out its earnestness, pathos, and solemnity in tones suitable to the spirit of the Great Revival which had been going on around him. A young clergyman read the result of Wilberforce's wish in his *Practical View of Christianity,* and he testifies, "To that book I owe a debt of gratitude; to my unsought and unexpected introduction to it, I owe the first sacred impressions which I ever received as to the spiritual nature of the Gospel system, the vital character of personal religion, the corruption of the human heart, and the way of salvation by Jesus Christ." And all this was very shortly given to the world in those beautiful pieces, which it surely must be ever a pleasure to read, whether for their tender delineation of the most important truths, or the exquisite language, and the delightful charm of natural scenery and pathetic reflection in which the experiences of *The Young Cottager, The Dairyman's Daughter,* and other "short and simple annals of the poor," are conveyed through the fascinating pen of Legh Richmond.

In this eminently lovely and lovable life we meet with one on whom, assuredly, the mantle of the old clerical fathers of the Revival had fallen. He was a Churchman and a clergyman, he loved and honoured his Church and its services exceedingly; but it seems impossible to detect, in any single act of his life or word of his writings, a tinge of acerbity or bitterness. The quiet and mellowed charm of his tracts—which are certainly among the finest pieces of writing in that way which we possess—appear to have pervaded his whole life. Brading, in the Isle of Wight, has been marvellously transformed since he was the vicar of its simple little church ; the old parsonage, where little Jane talked with her pastor, is now only a memory, and no longer, as we saw it first many years since, a feature in the charming landscape ; and the little epitaphs which the vicar himself wrote for the stones, or wooden memorials over the graves of his parishioners, are all obliterated by time. Several years since we sought in vain for the sweet verse on his own infant daughter, although about thirty-five years since we read it there :

> "This lovely bud, so young and fair,
> Called hence by early doom,
> Just came to show how sweet a flower
> In Paradise should bloom."

But these little papers of this excellent man circulated wherever the English language was spoken or read, and the spirit of their pages penetrated farther than the pages themselves ; while they seem to present in a more pleasant, winning, and portable form the spirit of the Revival, divested of much of the ruggedness which had, naturally, characterised its earlier pens.

Indeed, if some generalisation were needed to express the phase into which the Revival was passing, at this, the earlier part of the present century, it should be called the "literary." Eminent names were appearing, and eminent pens, to gather up the elements of faith which had moved the minds and tongues of men in past years, and to arrest the conscience through the eye. This opens up a field so large that we cannot do justice to it in these brief sketches.

To name here only one other writer ;—Thomas Scott, the commentator on the Bible, and author of *The Force of Truth*, is acknowledged to have exerted an influence the greatness of which has been described in glowing terms by men such as Sir James Stephen and John Henry Newman.

CHARLES SIMEON.

No idea can be formed by those of the present genera-tion of the immense influence Charles Simeon exercised over the mind of the Church of England. He was the leader of the growing evangelical party in the Church ; his doctrines were exactly those which had been the favourite on the lips of Whitefield, Berridge, Grimshaw, and Newton. His family was ancient and respectable, he was the son of a Berkshire squire. He had been educated at Eton, and afterwards at King's College, Cambridge ; he became very wealthy. His accession to the life of the Revival seemed like an immense addition of natural influence : he was faithful and earnest, and, in the habits of his mind and character, exactly what we understand by the thorough English gentleman ; almost may it be said that he made the Revival "gentlemanly" in clergy-men. He opened the course of his fifty-six years' ministry in Cambridge amidst a storm of persecution ; the church-wardens attempted to crush him, the pews of his church were locked up, and he was even locked out of the building. Through all this he passed, and he became, for the greater part of the long period we have mentioned, the most noted preacher of his town and university; and he published, certainly, in his *Horæ Homileticæ* a greater number of attempts at opening texts in the form of sermons, than had ever been given to the world. Simeon devoted his own fortune and means for the purchase of advowsons, in order that the pulpits of churches might be filled by the representatives of his own opinions. No history of the Revival can be complete without noticing this phase, which scattered over England, far more extensively than can be here described, a new order of clergymen, who have maintained in their circles evangelical truth, and have held no inconsiderable sway over the mind of the country.

We only know history through men ; events are only possible through men, of whose mind and activity they are the manifestation. This brief succession of sketches has been very greatly a series of portraits standing out prominently from the scenery to which the character gave effect; but of this singular, almost simultaneous movement, how much has been left unrecorded! It remains unquestionably true that no adequate and perfectly impartial review of the Revival has ever yet been written.

The story of the Revival in Wales, what it found there, and what it effected, is one of its most interesting chapters. How deep was the slumber when, about 1735–37, Howell Harris began to traverse the Principality, exhorting his neighbours concerning the interests of their souls! another illustration that it was not from one single spring that the streams of the Revival poured over the land. It was rather like some great mountain, such as Plinlimmon, from whose high centre, elevated among the clouds, leap forth five rivers, meandering among the rocks in their brook-like way, until at last they pour themselves along the lowlands in broad and even magnificent streams, either uniting as the Severn and the Wye, or finding their separate way to the ocean. Whitefield found his way to Wales, but Howell Harris was already pouring out his consecrated life there; to his assistance came the voice of Rowlands, "the thunderer," as he was called. Scientific sermon-makers would say that Harris was no great preacher; but he has been described as the most successful and wonderful one who ever ascended pulpit or platform in the Principality. By the mingling of his tears and his terrors, in seven years he roused the whole country from one end to the other, north and south; communicating the impulse of his zeal to many like-minded men, by whose impassioned

BOSTON ELM.

words and indefatigable labours the work was continued with signal and lasting results.[*]

If the first throbbings of the coming Revival were felt in Northampton, in America, in 1734, beneath the truly awful words of the great Jonathan Edwards, it was from this country it derived its sustenance, and assumed organisation and shape. The planting of Methodists in New England is a story as long and individual as that which we have just referred to in Wales. The Boston Elm, a venerable tree near the centre of Boston Park, or common, whose decayed limbs are still held together by clamps or rivets of iron, while a railing defends it from rude hands, is an object as sacred to the traditions of Methodism in the United States, as is Gwennap Pit to those of our Methodism in Western England. There Jesse Lee, the first founder of Methodism in New England, commenced the work in 1790, which has issued in an organisation even more extensive and gigantic than that which is associated with the Conference in this country. Stevens, to whose history of Methodism we have so often referred, has also told the story of the Methodist Episcopal Church in the United States of America. As those States have inherited from the mother country their language, their literature, and their principles of law, so also those great agitations of spiritual life to which we have concisely referred, crossed the Atlantic, and spread themselves with power there.

To return to our own land, it is not within our province to attempt to enumerate all the sects, each with its larger or lesser proportion of spiritual power, religious activity, and general acceptance among the people, to which the

[*] See a series of papers on "Welsh Preaching and Preachers" in the *Sunday at Home,* for 1876.

Revival gave birth ;—such as the large body of the Bible
Christians of the West of England ; the Primitive Methodists of the North, those who called themselves the New
Connection Methodists, or the United Free Church Association.   All these, and others, are branches from the great
central stem.   Neither is it in our province to notice how
the same universal agitation of religious feeling, at exactly
the same time, gave birth to other forms, not regarded with
so much complacency ;—such as the rugged and faulty faith
and following of that curious creature, William Huntington,
who, singular to say, found also his best biographer in Robert
Southey ; or the strangely multifarious works and rational-
istic development of Baron Swedenborg, which have, at
least, the merit of giving a more spiritual rendering to the
Christian system than that which was found in the prevalent Arianism of the period of their publication.   Turn
wherever we may, it is the same.   There was a deeper
upheaving of the religious life, and far more widely spread,
than perhaps any age of the world since the time of the
apostles had known before.

A change passed over the whole of English society.
That social state which we find described in the pages of
Fielding and Smollett, and less respectable writers, passed
away, and passed away, we trust, from our shores for ever.
The language of impurity indulged with freedom by the
dramatists of the period when the Revival arose, and read,
and read aloud, by ladies and young girls in drawing-rooms,
or by parlour firesides, became shameful and dishonoured.
In the course of fifty years, society, if not entirely purged
—for when may we hope for that blessedness ?—was
purified.   A sense of religious decorum, and some idea
of religious duty, took possession of homes and minds

which were not at all impressed, either by the doctrines or the discipline of Methodism. All this arose from the new life which had been created.

It was a fruitful soil upon which the revivalists worked. There was a reverence for the Bible as the word of God, a faith often held very ignorantly, but it pervaded the land. The Book was there in every parish church, and in every hamlet; it became a kind of nexus of union for true minds when they felt the power of Divine principles. Thus, when, as the Revival strengthened itself, the great Evangelic party—a term which seems to us less open to exception than "the Methodist party," because far more inclusive—met with the members of the Society of Friends, they found that, with some substantial differences, they had principles in common. The Quakers had been long in the land, but excepting in their own persons—and they were few in number—they had not given much effect to their principles. Methodism roused the country; Quakerism, with its more quiet thought, gave suggestions, plans, largely supplied money. The great works which these two have since unitedly accomplished of educating the nation at home, and shaking off the chain of the slave abroad, neither could have accomplished singly; the conscience of the country was prepared by Evangelic sentiment. In taking up and working out the great ideas of the Revival, we have never been indifferent to the share due to members of the Society of Friends. We have already spoken of Elizabeth Fry, to whom many of the princes of Europe in turn paid honour, to whom with singular simplicity they listened as they heard her preach. There are many names on which we should like a little to dwell; missionaries as arduous and earnest as any we have mentioned, such as Stephen Grellet, Thomas Shillitoe, and Thomas Chalkley. But this would enter into a larger plan than we dare to entertain. Our object now is only to say, how greatly other nations, and the world at large, have benefited by the awakening the conscience, the setting free the mind, the education of the character, by bringing all into immediate contact with the Word of God and the truth which it unveils.

Situated as we are now, amidst the movements and agitations of uncertain seas of thought, wondering as to the future, with strong adjurations on every hand to renounce the Word of Life, and to trust ourselves to the filmy rationalism of modern speculation; while we feel that for the future, and for those seas over which we look there are no tide-tables, we may, at least, safely affirm this, that the Bible carries us beyond the highest water-mark; that, as societies have constructed themselves out of its principles they have built safely, not only for eternal hope, but for human and social happiness also; and we may safely ask human thought—which, unaided and unenlightened by revelation, has had a pretty fair field for the exercise and display of its power in the history of the world—to show to us a single chapter in all the ages of its history, which has effected so much for human, spiritual, intellectual, and social well-being, as that which records the results of the Great Revival of the Last Century.

THE END.

Medical bacteriology

a practical approach

TITLES PUBLISHED IN
THE
PRACTICAL APPROACH
SERIES

Series editors:
Dr D Rickwood
Department of Biology, University of Essex
Wivenhoe Park, Colchester, Essex CO4 3SQ, UK
Dr B D Hames
Department of Biochemistry, University of Leeds
Leeds LS2 9JT, UK

Affinity chromatography

Animal cell culture

Antibodies I & II

Biochemical toxicology

Biological membranes

Carbohydrate analysis

Cell growth and division

Centrifugation (2nd Edition)

Computers in microbiology

DNA cloning I, II & III

Drosophila

Electron microscopy
in molecular biology

Gel electrophoresis of nucleic acids

Gel electrophoresis of proteins

Genome analysis

HPLC of small molecules

HPLC of macromolecules

Human cytogenetics

Human genetic diseases

Immobilised cells and enzymes

Iodinated density gradient media

Light microscopy in biology

Lymphocytes

Lymphokines and interferons

Mammalian development

Medical bacteriology

Medical mycology

Microcomputers in biology

Microcomputers in physiology

Mitochondria

Mutagenicity testing

Neurochemistry

Nucleic acid and
protein sequence analysis

Nucleic acid hybridisation

Oligonucleotide synthesis

Photosynthesis:
energy transduction

Plant cell culture

Plant molecular biology

Plasmids

Prostaglandins
and related substances

Protein function

Protein sequencing

Protein structure

Spectrophotometry
and spectrofluorimetry

Steroid hormones

Teratocarcinomas
and embryonic stem cells

Transcription and translation

Virology

Yeast

Medical bacteriology

a practical approach

Edited by
P M Hawkey
Department of Microbiology,
University of Leeds,
Leeds LS2 9JJ, UK

D A Lewis
Public Health Laboratory,
Royal United Hospital,
Combe Park,
Bath BA1 3NG, UK

IRL PRESS
——at——
OXFORD UNIVERSITY PRESS
Oxford New York Tokyo

IRL Press
Eynsham
Oxford
England

© IRL Press at Oxford University Press 1989

First published 1989

British Library Cataloguing in Publication Data
Medical bacteriology
  1. Medicine, Bacteriology
  I. Hawkey, P.M. (Peter M.)
  II. Lewis, D.A. (Deirdre A.)   III. Series
  616'.014
  ISBN 0-19-963008-9
  ISBN 0-19-963009-7 Pbk

Library of Congress Cataloging-in-Publication Data
Medical bacteriology: a practical approach / edited by P.M. Hawkey, D.A.Lewis.
       p.   cm. — (Practical approach series)
  Includes bibliographies and index.
  1. Diagnostic bacteriology—Laboratory manuals.   I. Hawkey,P.M. (Peter M)
  II., Lewis, D.A. (Deirdre A.)   III. Series.
    [DNLM: 1. Bacteriology—laboratory manuals.   QW 25 M489]
  QR67.2.M43   1989
  DNLM/DLC
  for Library of Congress
  ISBN 0 19 963008 9
  ISBN 0 19 963009 7 (Pbk)

Previously announced as:
ISBN 1 85221 065 6 (hardbound)
ISBN 1 85221 064 8 (softbound)

Typeset and printed by Information Press Ltd, Oxford, England.

Foreword

'. . . confess . . . is it not *life*, is it not *the thing*?—Could any man have written it—who has not lived in the world?'

Lord Byron to his publisher, John Murray

The strongest impression that I take from reading this book is of being in the thick of the daily work of a bacteriology laboratory. The sections, comprehending the main specimen types and necessary investigations, deal with choice of methods, the methods themselves, recipes, suppliers of media, wrinkles, interpretation and reporting to clinicians. Clearly, they are written by people who have had to make these choices, use these methods and conduct this liaison, and the editors are to be congratulated on maintaining the essentially practical flavour implied by their title. Where method choice depends on local conditions this is indicated.

I warmly welcome this book and commend it to established microbiologists as a sounding board for the regular reviews they conduct of their own laboratory's methods. It will also serve as a reference book for less frequently encountered needs, such as the requirement for selective methods for isolation of individual pathogens causing hospital infection. It will be of particular value to newly appointed consultant microbiologists, who may avoid much telephoning of colleagues, reading in the library and frank trial and error by consulting this book.

The main examination for the Membership of the Royal College of Pathologists concentrates on this kind of expertise, and this book may become required reading in preparation for this examination.

David C.E. Speller

Preface

This book is part of a series of practical manuals describing biochemical and molecular biological techniques. The series editors have decided to extend the scope of the series to include medical microbiology and thus this book, together with *Medical Mycology: A Practical Approach*, goes part way to fulfilling this aim.

Our remit has been to describe detailed methods in medical bacteriology and not cover aspects of microbiology, but where possible other texts have been suggested. The methods described in each chapter reflect the personal choice of the author(s) and therefore all available methods may not be included.

In the United Kingdom there are few practical manuals describing methods in medical microbiology. Those that do exist treat specimen processing separately from identification of the likely bacterial pathogens, whereas the arrangement in this book is such that methods are described as they would be required in the processing of a specimen, from its receipt to the issue of the final report. Thus the book forms a good guide for the 'apprenticeship' type of practical training used in medical microbiology.

The book should be of value to medically qualified microbiologists studying for membership of the Royal College of Pathologists, scientists studying for the examinations of the Institute of Medical Laboratory Scientists and students studying for BSc degrees in Medical Microbiology. In the USA it should be of use to candidates taking the examinations of the American Board of Medical Microbiology. We would hope the book will find a place next to the laboratory methods file in all clinical microbiology laboratories.

We are grateful to Professor D.C.E.Speller for his helpful advice in the formative stages of this book. Our thanks go to all the authors for working so hard to produce chapters with current and relevant information. Thanks are also due to the Departments of Photography and Medical Illustration at Leeds General Infirmary for help with illustrations and to Mrs N.W.Hedley for invaluable help in typing manuscript drafts.

Finally we wish to thank medical and scientific staff from within our departments and outside for reading and commenting on chapters.

Peter M.Hawkey
Deirdre A.Lewis

Contributors

L.Booth
Public Health Laboratory, General Hospital, Southampton SO9 4XY, UK

D.Brown
Public Health Laboratory, Addenbrooke's Hospital, Hills Road, Cambridge CB2 2QW, UK

A.C.Bushell
Department of Microbiology, Withybush Hospital, Haverford West, Dyfed, UK

P.M.Cockcroft
Public Health Laboratories, East Wing, St Mary's General Hospital, Milton Road, Portsmouth PO3 6AQ, UK

A.J.Davies
Sandwell District General Hospital, Lyndon, West Bromwich, West Midlands B71 4HJ, UK

R.Freeman
Department of Bacteriology, University of Newcastle upon Tyne Medical School, Framlington Place, Newcastle upon Tyne, NE2 4HH, UK

P.M.Hawkey
Department of Microbiology, University of Leeds, Leeds LS2 9JJ, UK

A.Holt
Department of Microbiology, Southmead Hospital, Bristol BS10 5NB, UK

W.A.Hyde
Lab M Ltd, Topley House, PO Box 19, Bury BL9 6AU, UK

A.E.Jephcott
Gonococcal Reference Laboratory, Bristol Public Health Laboratory, Myrtle Road, Bristol BS2 8EL, UK

D.A.Lewis
Public Health Laboratory, Royal United Hospital, Combe Park, Bath BA1 3NG, UK

J.A.Lowes
Public Health Laboratory, General Hospital, Southampton SO9 4XY, UK

S.R.Palmer
PHLS Department of Epidemiology, Cardiff Royal Infirmary, Cardiff CF2 1S2, UK

S.J.Pedler
Department of Microbiology, Royal Victoria Infirmary, Queen Victoria Road, Newcastle upon Tyne NE1 4LP, UK

D.S.Reeves
Department of Microbiology, Southmead Hospital, Bristol BS10 5NB, UK

Contents

Abbreviations

ABC	antibody-coated bacteria
AFB	acid-fast bacillus
BFP	biological false positive
CAPD	continuous ambulatory peritoneal dialysis
CFT	complement fixation test
CFU	colony-forming unit
CIE	counterimmune electrophoresis
CLED	cysteine lactose electrolyte-deficient (agar)
CNS	coagulase-negative staphylococci
CSF	cerebrospinal fluid
EPEC	enteropathogenic *E.coli*
ETEC	enterotoxigenic *E.coli*
FTA	fluorescent treponemal antigen
IFAT	indirect fluorescent antibody test
IPD	intermittent peritoneal dialysis
MIC	minimum inhibitory concentration
MRSA	methicillin-resistant *Staphylococcus aureus*
MSU	midstream urine
NVS	nutritionally variant streptococcus
OSC	optimal sensitizing concentration
PDE	peritoneal dialysis effluent
RDS	Rapid Diagnostic Sera
THA	treponeme haemagglutination
TPHA	*Treponema pallidum* haemagglutination test
VDRL	Venereal Disease Reference Laboratory
ZN	Ziehl–Neelsen (test)

CHAPTER 1

Bacteriology of urine

DEIRDRE A.LEWIS

1. INTRODUCTION

The urinary tract above the level of the distal urethra is normally sterile but infection at any site within the tract is possible, from the kidney to the urethra, the commonest site of infection being the urinary bladder. In general micro-organisms gain access to the urinary tract from neighbouring sites, most commonly the perianal region, resulting in ascending infection, although spread by the haematogenous route is usually responsible for infections by *Salmonella* spp. and *Mycobacterium tuberculosis*.

The aim of laboratory diagnostic procedures in urinary tract infection should be the detection of the abnormal presence of bacteria at any site within the tract together with evidence of inflammation. In this chapter I present the practical aspects of the laboratory diagnosis of urinary tract infection from the time of specimen collection, which is not normally performed in the laboratory but in a clinical setting, to that of issuing the final laboratory report.

2. SPECIMEN COLLECTION AND TRANSPORT

2.1 Collection

As the bladder is the commonest site of infection in the urinary tract, bladder urine is the specimen most frequently examined and such specimens should reflect as accurately as possible the type and number of bacteria present in the bladder itself. In the collection of urine the problem of contamination of the sample by commensal flora adjacent to the urethra exists and unfortunately these organisms are just the type that cause urinary infections. Thus scrupulous care in the collection of samples is required. Contamination of samples is a particular problem in female patients. There are three main types of urine sample: the midstream urine (MSU) which is appropriate for the majority of patients; catheter specimens of urine, which may be required from people who have poor control of bladder emptying, such as the elderly and patients with neuropathic bladders; and suprapubic aspirates (SPA), which are the best samples from babies and young children. Often specimens of urine collected in a bag applied around the perineum of infants are submitted for culture but these are usually unhelpful unless no bacteria are grown because contamination is very likely and bacteria may even have the opportunity to multiply.

Collection of urine from patients with neuropathic or ileal bladders presents difficulties in interpretation and should be performed only if there is an indication for treatment, such as a pyrexia or constitutional upset. In the case of ileal bladders collection of urine should be by careful catheterization of the stoma. Culture of urine from the kidneys

Table 1. Method for collection of MSU.

Preferably collect the first specimen of the day.

1. (i) *For females*. Clean the external genitalia with soap and water and then holding the labia apart pass urine, discarding the first part of the stream.
    (ii) *For males*. Cleaning the external genitalia is unnecessary but retract the foreskin in uncircumcized males and discard the first part of the stream.
2. Place a sterile container[a] in the line of flow and collect a midstream sample of at least 20 ml.
3. After completing micturition, transfer urine aseptically to a specimen container. When boric acid is used fill the container to the mark indicated.
4. Send the specimen plus the request form to the laboratory as soon as possible.

[a]Urine could be collected directly into the specimen container, but getting the correct volume may be difficult if boric acid is used.

is sometimes required, and specimens for this are obtained following ureteric catheterization through a cystoscope.

At one time is was thought necessary always to collect urine from females by using a catheter but when it was recognized that the process of catheterization introduced a risk of infection this generally stopped. A midstream specimen of urine (for method see *Table 1*) is collected, because the first passage of urine should remove commensals from around the urethra, and urine collected later should be relatively free from contaminants. It has been found that the reliability of a positive result from a clean voided sample in females is 80% after one sample, 90% from two consecutive samples and 100% if three samples give the same results. In males, a single sample only is required because contamination is much less likely. In practice it is often not possible or appropriate to collect more than one sample or urine from a patient with symptoms and thus problems of overtreatment have to be accepted.

The timing of collection of samples is important. The first sample of the day is the best because bacteria will have had an opportunity to grow in the bladder overnight and it is much more likely that significant numbers will be detected in this sample than in one collected later in the day.

For the diagnosis of renal tuberculosis the collection of random clean morning specimens gives a higher yield of positive results than the collection of urine over 24 h (1). The current recommendation is to culture three clean first morning specimens, which increases the likelihood of detecting patients who are only intermittently positive.

2.2 **Transport**

Having collected as good a urine sample as possible, it is then important that there should be minimal delay before culture. For the culture of tubercle bacilli, delay is less important, although urine should be delivered to the laboratory each day or stored refrigerated until the last sample is collected. For other samples, urine should be cultured within 1 h of collection, but if there is a delay the specimen may be refrigerated at 4°C. Because of the delay in transport of specimens to the laboratory some laboratories supply containers with boric acid (2), in order to retain the bacterial count of the sample. Having collected the midstream urine sample in a sterile receptacle, urine is then transferred to the boric acid container which is filled to a given mark so that the final concentration is 1.8% w/v. It is important that this concentration is achieved because boric acid has some antibacterial activity. In fact even at a concentration of 1.8% w/v it may decrease the number of organisms, particularly of some *Pseudomonas* spp. (3). Because of the necessity to collect at least 15 ml of urine, the method may pose problems when urine is being collected from babies and small children.

Probably the best method for eliminating the effects of delay in urine culture is to use the dip-inoculum technique (4). Here the patient should proceed as follows.

(i)   Collect a midstream urine in a sterile receptacle (see *Table 1*).
(ii) Dip the small plastic slide carrying culture media into the urine.
(iii) Allow it to drain and then place it in a closed sterile container for transport to the laboratory. It is best not to collect the specimen by micturating directly on to the spoon because the uneven distribution of bacterial growth which may result makes interpretation difficult.

The plastic slide may carry a variety of culture media, but one of the most popular combinations is MacConkey agar on one side and cysteine lactose electrolyte-deficient (CLED) agar on the other. Immediate culture by this method eliminates the problem of multiplication and perhaps also the survival of some organisms between collection and examination in the laboratory. The disadvantages of this method are, firstly, cost; secondly, if it is used as the sole method of culture, quantitation and identification of organisms are more difficult than when urine is spread on larger agar plates. Also, as no urine sample is received, cell counts cannot be performed.

3. SELECTION FOR PROCESSING AND RAPID SCREENING METHODS

Although visual examination of the urine may not be a reliable method of detecting bacteriuria, inasmuch as cloudy urine is more likely to be due to crystals or leukocytes rather than bacteria, urine that is completely clear can usually be relied upon to indicate that there is not a significant bacteriuria (see Section 6). In a busy microbiology laboratory and when it is necessary to cut costs it may be acceptable practice to discard such midstream urine samples. Cell counts on these specimens will also be forfeited if this is done.

3.1 Enzymatic methods

The most common enzymatic screening tests for the detection of bacteriuria or pyuria include glucose oxidase, nitrate reductase (Greiss test) and leukocyte esterase. These are often used as bedside tests because they are easy to perform, being dipstick tests, rapid and inexpensive, but they have problems and should be interpreted with caution. None of the tests for detecting bacteriuria will be able to differentiate between a true urinary infection and contamination.

(i) *Glucose oxidase*. Bacteria metabolize glucose normally present in urine in low concentrations (2 to 10 mg 100 ml^{-1}) and so a positive glucose oxidase test is indicated by the absence of glucose. The test is highly sensitive but gives false positives, and false negatives occur in diabetic patients, whose urine contains much higher concentrations of glucose than normal. False negatives will also occur in infections caused by bacteria which do not metabolize glucose.

(ii) *Nitrate reductase (Greiss test)*. This has been used as an indicator of urinary tract infections for many years. Nitrate is reduced to nitrite by nitrate reductase, which is

3

present in the Gram negative bacilli which commonly cause urinary tract infections. The test, however, has poor sensitivity when performed on randomly selected urine samples (5) and is best performed on the first sample of the day. The test will not detect bacteria which do not reduce nitrate and urinary nitrite alone is not a reliable indicator of urinary tract infection.

(iii) *Leukocyte esterase.* This is a dipstick method for the detection of pyuria (6). The method is sensitive (88−94%) for detecting white blood cell counts of more than 10 per mm^3, but vitamin C, phenazopyridine and high levels of protein may interfere with the tests.

4. MICROSCOPY

Microscopy of urine may be performed on centrifuged or uncentrifuged urine. There are great advantages in the latter because it is extremely difficult to standardize centrifugation techniques, which are also time-consuming and often messy procedures. However, many laboratories have continued to centrifuge urine in order to detect casts in the deposit. The necessity for this is now in question because of the introduction of new methods. The three methods mentioned here are for unstained and uncentrifuged urine, and the last is suitable for the detection of casts.

4.1 Methods

4.1.1 Unstained urine

(i) *The haematocytometer chamber (Fuchs − Rosenthal or Neubauer) method* (see Chapter 2). This is an accurate method for quantifying the cellular content of urine, but is more accurate than is really required for routine purposes. Its main disadvantages for repeated use are that it is laborious and time-consuming and the chambers have to be cleaned and disinfected between use. Breakage of counting chambers is also relatively expensive.

(ii) *The three-coverslip counting chamber method.* This method (7) provides in effect a disposable counting chamber and is sufficiently accurate for routine purposes. It is quick, cheap, easy to use and requires no special equipment. It is not suitable, however, for the examination of uncentrifuged urine for casts. The method is given in *Table 2* and the preparation shown diagrammatically in *Figure 1*.

(iii) *The microtitre tray and inverted microscope method.* This method, attributable to Rant and Shepherd (Public Health Laboratory, Norwich), is a significant advance in methodology. Firstly, it is an excellent method for detecting casts in uncentrifuged urine and indeed gives better results than when the urine is centrifuged, presumably because some casts disintegrate on centrifugation. Secondly, it is clean, quick and very reproducible. The procedure is given in *Table 3*. Modifications have been made to the method to incorporate culture, by filling some wells with CLED (see 5.1). The urine in transferred from the microscopy well to the culture well by using a multipoint inoculator (8).

4.1.2 Staining of uncentrifuged urine and urinary sediment

Although not in common use as a routine procedure in the UK, staining of uncentrifuged urine is a rapid and inexpensive method for estimating bacteriuria at $\geq 10^5$ colonies

Table 2. The three-coverslip counting chamber method for microscopy of urine.

A. *Requirements*

1.   Counting chamber (*Figure 1*), see below for preparation.
2.   Pipettes.
3.   Light microscope with ×10 and ×40 objectives.

B. *Calibration of microscope* should be done to allow conversion of result from 'cells per field' to 'cells per mm^3'. Proceed as follows.

1.   Dilute a sample of blood 1 in 10 000 and 1 in 100 000 (v/v) with physiological saline and determine the red cell count on both diluted samples with a haematocytometer chamber. The counts should be in the ranges 200–500 and 20–50 per mm^3 respectively.
2.   Set up both samples in a three-coverslip preparation and examine in turn with ×10 and ×40 objectives (see below).
3.   Count the total number of red cells in at least 10 microscope fields and calculate the average number of red cells per field.
4.   Repeat the process several times and determine the mean of the results.
5.   Obtain the necessary conversion factor (*N*) for each objective using the following calculation:

$$N = \frac{\text{Cells per mm}^3}{\text{Average cells per field}}$$

C. *Procedure*

Prepare the counting chamber as follows.
1.   Take a 3 × 1 inch glass slide and with a grease pencil draw two parallel lines about 1 cm apart at right angles to the long axis of the slide[a].
2.   Lay 2 Chance No. 1 coverslips (7/8″ × 7/8″ square) on either side of the compartment, just outside the grease pencil marks, and anchor them to the slide by applying a trace of moisture to the centre of the underside of each. Then proceed as follows.
3.   Take the coverslip preparation and place a loopful of well-mixed uncentrifuged urine into the compartment.
4.   Drop a third coverslip to form a bridge between the first two coverslips. The underside of the third coverslip comes into contact with the urine drop and the preparation is ready for examination[b].
5.   Examine the specimen with the ×10 microscope objective and count the number of white and/or red cells in a field.
6.   Look at 10 separate fields and calculate the average number of both types of cell per field.
7.   Calculate the number of cells per mm^3 by multiplying the average number by the conversion factor *N*.
8.   Examine the specimens under the ×40 objective to confirm the nature of the cells counted and note the numbers and variety of bacteria and other formed elements present.
9.   If the specimen is more cellular or contains a dense deposit, use this objective for counting and apply the different conversion factor appropriate to it.

[a]The compartment may be subdivided with another line, as shown in *Figure 1*, to allow two samples to be set up at the same time, or may be subdivided even further, if desired.
[b]Check each coverslip for distortion by a glance at the image reflected in one face of the coverslip.

ml^{-1}. One or more organisms per oil immersion field has a sensitivity of 85–95% when correlated with a colony count of $>10^5$ ml^{-1}. Staining of urinary sediment is clearly a more tedious and time-consuming procedure because it requires centrifugation of 10 ml of urine for 5 min followed by examination of 1–2 drops of stained sediment. However, the test is sometimes useful as an adjunct to the more routine methods described in 4.1.1. In the event of no growth in the presence of pyuria, or organisms

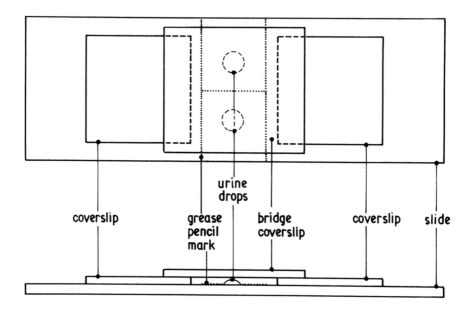

Figure 1. Diagrammatic representation of the three-coverslip counting chamber method for urine microscopy.

Table 3. The microtitre tray and inverted microscope method for urine microscopy.

Requirements

1.   Fixed volume pipette (60 μl).
2.   Disposable plastic tips.
3.   Flat-bottomed plastic microtitre tray.
4.   Inverted microscope with $\times20$ objective lens.

Procedure

1.   Attach a disposable tip to the pipette and draw up 60 μl of urine from a well-mixed sample. Dispense into the appropriate well of the microtitre tray.
2.   Allow about 5 min for the cells to settle and then examine under $\times20$ objective of the inverted microscope. Count the number of white and/or red cells per field and convert to number of cells mm^{-3} by multiplying by conversion factor N (see *Table 2*).
3.   Note the presence of bacteria and any other formed elements. In particular note the presence of casts and identify their character.

being seen in the uncentrifuged urine, this will confirm bacteriuria and, in the case of Gram stain, help to identify the organisms. The reasons for no growth may be that the organisms are unable to grow on the standard media or atmosphere used for culture, or are inhibited by the presence of antibiotic. Another use of the Gram stain is to indicate the type of organisms causing an infection, when this information is required urgently. Staining methods which have been applied in this way are

(i)   Gram stain (for method see Appendix I).

(ii) Acridine orange (9,10). This does not offer any real advantage over the Gram stain.

Unless there is very strong suspicion of renal tuberculosis it is best not to apply the Ziehl—Neelsen stain for acid fast bacilli (Appendix I) to urine because of the relatively common positive findings, which relate to the presence of commensal mycobacteria, such as *M.smegmatis*, rather than pathogens. Such results are very confusing to the clinician, who is left uncertain as to whether or not the patient should be treated. Urine should be cultured for acid-fast bacilli (see 5.2.4), without microscopy.

4.1.3 *Automated microscopy*

Microscopic examination of urine has been automated. The Yellow IRIS (International Remote Imaging Systems Inc.) has a flow microscope in which an uncentrifuged urine specimen is presented to a video camera. Aliquots of the flowing specimens are taken as stop-motion pictures by a video camera. An image processing computer recognizes the individual particle images by size. Analysis of a sample takes 1—4 min. Other cellular elements besides white blood cells and bacteria are also recognized. The method is well standardized, but there are problems with sensitivity and it is very expensive.

4.2 Interpretation of findings on microscopy

Microscopy findings should be interpreted with caution. Leukocytes will be found in all forms of inflammation, and in females leukocytes found in a urine specimen may have come from the vagina. Differences in urine flow will result in different cell counts and white cells will disintegrate in alkaline urine. Thus in infections caused by *Proteus* spp. and particularly when there is a delay in examination of urine there may be no apparent pyuria. Conversely, pyuria will continue after treatment of a urinary tract infection and, whilst organisms should disappear within 24—48 h, pus cells will continue to be seen several days after successful treatment.

However, in spite of these reservations about the interpretation of leukocytes in the urine, the investigation is of use in the diagnosis of urinary tract infection. Little (11) showed that a concentration of 10 leukocytes mm^{-3} corresponded to a white cell excretion rate of 150 000—200 000 per hour, which is considered the upper limit of normal. An explanation should be sought for an increase in white cell excretion and certainly contamination of the specimen from elsewhere should be excluded if culture proves negative. Persistent pyuria in the presence of sterile urine should alert the clinician to the possibility of tuberculosis, tumour or foreign body in the genito-urinary tract.

Haematuria is not a normal finding, although red cells found in the urine may have come from elsewhere such as the vagina. When associated with inflammation as in urinary tract infection, leukocytes are almost invariably present. Haematuria as an isolated finding is more commonly associated with stones or tumour or occasionally with tuberculosis or fungal infections of the urinary tract.

Bacteria may be seen on urine microscopy and the detection of motile bacilli is usually predictive of a positive culture. This finding may be useful therefore in the selection of specimens for performing primary sensitivity tests, thus providing a more rapid result (8.2). If the organisms are seen on routine microscopy but do not grow, it may be an indication for performing a Gram stain on centrifuged deposit, as already mentioned,

7

or selecting alternative culture methods.

The detection of casts and some crystals in urine can be helpful in the diagnosis of conditions other than urinary infection. Such conditions may be associated with few clinical signs and thus microscopy may be a useful tool in diagnosis. Good photomicrographs of the abnormalities which may be seen in unstained urine are provided by Lippman (12).

5. CULTURE

5.1 **Choice of media**

It is important that the media chosen for urine culture are able to support the growth of all urinary pathogens and commensal bacteria, so that contamination may be detected. Also, lactose fermentation should be identifiable by a colour change and *Proteus* spp. should be inhibited from swarming. A combination of blood agar and MacConkey agar has been used. The former permits growth of urinary pathogens and commensals of the genital tract but differentiation cannot be made between lactose fermenters and non-fermenters, and swarming of *Proteus* spp. is not inhibited. On the other hand, MacConkey's medium is an indicator medium for lactose fermentation, with lactose-fermenting organisms forming red colonies whilst non-fermenters do not change the colour of the medium (the indicator in MacConkey's medium is neutral red). Also, it inhibits the swarming of *Proteus* spp. However the disadvantages of this medium are, firstly, it inhibits the growth of many Gram-positive species, and secondly it is characteristically rather variable in its inhibitory properties and may alter from batch to batch. A medium which fulfils all the requirements for a single urine culture medium is CLED (cysteine lactose electrolyte-deficient) agar (13), and it is widely used for this purpose. The indicator in CLED is bromothymol blue, and colonies of lactose fermenters become yellow.

5.2 **Culture methods**

5.2.1. *Streak plate method (standard loop)*

This method necessitates the use of a standard bacteriological loop which delivers a fixed volume of urine to an agar plate. Laboratories may vary in the size of loop they use, but 2 μl is common. A larger volume of urine is required if suprapubic aspirates or ureteric catheter specimens are being examined, because of the importance of low counts. This method is simple and quick and is used most commonly in diagnostic microbiology laboratories in the UK (see *Table 4* and *Figure 2*).

5.2.2 *Screening method: filter paper strip* (14)

This method is suitable for large-scale screening of urines such as occurs in an antenatal clinic. Some laboratories screen all their urine specimens and only proceed to full culture if the screening test reveals a significant growth. In this case the urine is stored under refrigeration until the result is known. Alternatively, a subculture may be made from the growth on the screening plate.

5.2.3 *Culture for 'fastidious' micro-organisms*

The culturing of urine for 'fastidious' organisms is a contentious subject and for a full

Table 4. Urine culture methods.

A. *Streak plate method (standard loop)*

1. Mix the urine well and holding a 2 μl loop (Medical Wire Co. Ltd) vertically charge it with urine.
2. Streak urine on an agar plate to obtain single colonies (*Figure 2*) or, having transferred urine to the centre of the plate, spread it by using a swab and turntable so that the inoculum is spread to the periphery.
3. Incubate the plate overnight at 37°C, in an aerobic atmosphere with or without additional CO_2. One colony on the plate represents 500 living organisms per ml in the original specimen.

B. *Screening method: filter paper strip*

1. Mix the urine well and dip a standard strip of sterile blotting paper (e.g. Bacteruritest strip, Diamed Diagnostics Ltd) into the urine up to the mark 12 mm from the end. The paper is of standard porosity and therefore each strip delivers the same quantity of urine.
2. Remove the excess fluid by touching the side of the jar, and then touch the surface of a well-dried plate[a].
3. Incubate the culture at 37°C aerobically overnight. More than 25 colonies on the plate are equivalent to more than 100 000 bacteria per ml of urine.
4. If the result indicates a significant growth, subculture directly from the growth or culture the refrigerated urine, as described above. Another option would be to obtain a fresh specimen.

[a]In this method large square Petri dishes may be used (100 mm × 100 mm) to culture approximately 30 specimens of urine.

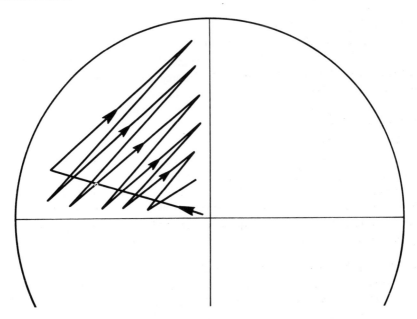

Figure 2. Method of streaking urine to obtain single colonies, using one agar plate for four samples.

account of the arguments for and against the reader is referred to chapters by Maskell (15) and Hamilton-Miller *et al.* (16) respectively. On the one hand, Maskell (15) claims that 50% of urine cultures on CLED from women with urinary symptoms are negative

Table 5. Culture for 'fastidious' micro-organisms.

1. Perform microscopy as in *Table 2* or *3* and culture 2 μl urine on CLED agar, using a standard loop.
2. Incubate the plate overnight at 37°C aerobically, in an atmosphere containing 7% CO_2.
3. Read the plate and if there is no growth but the urine contained pus cells, or the patient had true symptoms of lower tract infection, reincubate for a further 24 h.
4. Read the reincubated plate, counting the colonies (if any) and identifying the organisms (7.1). If there is a pure growth of a 'fastidious' organism and it is present in a count of at least 10^4 ml^{-1}, report its presence.
5. Perform sensitivity tests (8.1) if the patient is symptomatic.
6. If the patient is asymptomatic, or the organisms are present in a low count, or there is an apparently sterile pyuria at 48 h, request a further specimen for culture on additional media. In the case of no growth in the original specimen, enquire about antibiotic treatment at the time of that specimen,
7. Culture repeat specimens on CLED agar and chocolated blood agar[a], for incubation in 7% CO_2 and on blood agar for anaerobic incubation[b].
8. If pyuria is still present and no 'fastidious' organisms are isolated, request three early-morning specimens of urine for culture for *M.tuberculosis*.

[a]It may be necessary to use chocolated blood agar and incubate in CO_2 when culturing urine from children since *H.influenzae* has sometimes been implicated in urinary tract infection.
[b]Anaerobic culture on blood agar may be indicated in patients who have considerable tissue destruction in the bladder, such as carcinoma of the bladder. Necrosis of tissue will lower the oxygen content and thus favour the growth of anaerobes.

after overnight incubation in air and many of these yield growth of 'fastidious' organisms in high counts ($> 10^4$ ml^{-1} of urine), often apparently pure, if reincubated for a further 24 h in 7% carbon dioxide. The majority of cultures yield lactobacilli, but *Streptococcus milleri* and corynebacteria are also isolated. Many of these organisms do not survive well in the bladder and are not isolated from suprapubic aspirates. Maskell claims that they are responsible for the urethral syndrome, that is, inflammation of the urethra and paraurethral tissues. She also feels that 'fastidious' organisms such as corynebacteria and streptococci are responsible for prostatic infections in males. She hypothesizes that, since these organisms are often isolated from people who have had prior antibiotic therapy, there is a selection of commensal flora which are resistant to various antibiotics, resulting in a distortion of the balance of commensal flora.

On the other hand, Hamilton-Miller and colleagues (16) do not feel that the case has really been made for the role of lactobacilli in the urethral syndrome. They feel that what is seen is probably colonization, not infection, by these important vaginal commensals. If culture is performed on an unselected population the recovery of lactobacilli is very low, only $1-5\%$, and this is insufficient justification for the extra laboratory expense in looking for these organisms on a routine basis.

However, Maskell's advocation of the role of 'fastidious' organisms in urinary tract infection has led her to propose a regimen for the culture of such organisms, and this is given in *Table 5*.

5.2.4 *Culture for M.tuberculosis*

This is indicated when there is a clinical suspicion of renal tuberculosis or there is persistent unexplained sterile pyuria, particularly in an elderly patient. The method is given in *Table 6*.

Table 6. Culture for *M.tuberculosis*.

1.	Spin the urine[a] at 1800 *g* for 30 min in sealed universal bottles and buckets. After centrifugation open the buckets in a Class I safety cabinet.
2.	Pour off supernatant and decontaminate the deposit by adding an equal volume of 4% w/v of sulphuric acid and leave for 30 min. Then fill the container to the top with distilled water.
3.	Centrifuge again as in step 1. Decant the supernatant and with a disposable pipette inoculate 0.4 ml of the deposit on to suitable media[b].
4.	Incubate slopes horizontally, at 37°C in air for 1 week and then examine. If negative, reincubate standing vertically and examine weekly for up to 8 weeks.
5.	Confirm mycobacterial colonies by Ziehl−Neelsen staining (Appendix I).

[a]Three early-morning specimens of urine should be submitted to increase the likelihood of detecting *M.tuberculosis*.
[b]Usually Lowenstein-Jensen's medium, (i) with pyruvate, (ii) with glycerol, as slopes in screw-capped bottles.

6. THE CONCEPT OF SIGNIFICANT BACTERIURIA

In 1957, Kass (17) showed that a count of 100 000 colony-forming units (CFU) per ml or higher of a single species in a midstream specimen of urine was almost invariably indicative of bladder bacteriuria, when he compared colony counts of *E.coli* in cultures of bladder urine collected by catheter with those in midstream urines from the same women. It was following this work that the term 'significant bacteriuria' was defined as the presence of at least 100 000 CFU ml^{-1} in two fresh carefully collected midstream urine specimens. However, too strong an emphasis has been placed on these criteria; indeed Kass found that some women with counts of 10^4 CFU ml^{-1} and even less had bladder infections, although when the first early morning specimen was collected counts usually rose to 10^5 ml^{-1} or higher. Actually, bacteriuria is usually characterized by counts well in excess of 10^6 CFU ml^{-1}.

It has been suggested that the presence of pyuria together with a count of $> 10^2$ CFU ml^{-1} should be used as criteria for a diagnosis of urinary infection, particularly in women with the acute urethral syndrome (18). However, unless the laboratory can be sure that specimens have been collected and transported correctly, there is a great danger of overdiagnosis if these lower counts are accepted as being significant. Nevertheless, it is true that too rigid an adherence to Kass's criteria may lead to both over- and under-diagnosis. Factors which may cause the latter are the following.

(i)   A rapid rate of flow of urine due to a high fluid intake and frequent bladder emptying can dilute the bacterial content at least tenfold (19).
(ii) If the site of infection is other than in the bladder, for example renal stones or prostate; in these cases counts may be less than 10^5 CFU ml^{-1}.
(iii) Bacterial pathogens other than *E.coli* may have different growth rates (20).
(iv) The pH of the urine or the presence of antibacterial agents may depress the counts.

On the other hand urinary infection may be overdiagnosed because in stale urine a high count may merely be the result of multiplication of organisms.

The interpretation of cultures of midstream urine is a problem because of potential contamination from periurethral tissues or from the urethra itself, or from the vagina or bowel. Clearly when urine is collected aseptically from the renal pelvis, ureters or bladder, the diagnosis of significant bacteriuria can be made regardless of the number

Table 7. Interpretation and reporting of results.

A. *Midstream urines*

1. Count the number of colonies and multiply by the factor to establish CFU ml^{-1} urine, e.g. if a 2 μl standard loop was used, multiply by 500.
2. Establish whether or not the culture is pure by colonial morphology and if necessary Gram stain (see Appendix I) and identify bacteria (*Tables 8* and *9*).
3. *Examples of reports*:

    With a pure culture (e.g. a lactose-fermenting coliform, such as *E.coli*)
    (i)   If $>10^5$ colonies per ml report:
          $>10^5$ ml^{-1} coliforms (significant growth)[a]
          Perform and give results of antimicrobial sensitivities (for choice, *Table 10*).
    (ii) If 10^4-10^5 colonies per ml report:
          10^4-10^5 ml^{-1} coliforms (equivocal result)[a]
          Comment: suggest a repeat specimen[b].
          Perform sensitivities but withhold from clinician.
    (iii) If $<10^4$ colonies per ml report:
          $<10^4$ ml^{-1} coliforms (of doubtful significance)[a]

    With a mixed culture
    (i) $>10^5$ colonies per ml report:
          $<10^5$ ml^{-1} mixed culture including .....[c]
          Comment: indicates contamination
          Suggest a repeat specimen[d].
    (ii) If $<10^5$ colonies per ml report:
          $<10^5$ ml^{-1} mixed culture, indicates contamination.

B. *Urinary catheters and ileal conduit specimens*

1. Report the number of CFU ml^{-1} in the specimen and the identity (*Tables 8* and *9*) of the organisms in pure or mixed cultures (as above).
2. Perform sensitivities on isolates (for method see Chapter 7) or perform primary sensitivity on the urine, to give an overall picture if there is a mixed growth (Section 8.2).
3. Only report sensitivities if there is a history of pyrexia, otherwise withhold the information from the clinician.
4. If no history of pyrexia is given, comment on the inadvisability of giving antibiotics to apyrexial catheterized patients.

[a]These comments are optional and on occasions may be misleading.
[b]Unless pyuria present, in which case it may be significant and sensitivities should be performed and reported.
[c]Give predominant organism types.
[d]Only repeat if pyuria present.

of organisms found. In the case of bladder urine this applies to specimens collected by catheter or from suprapubic aspirates. Interpretation and reporting of specimens is given in *Table 7*.

6.1 Interpretation and reporting of specimens from patients with indwelling catheters and ileal conduits

Cultures under these circumstances are often mixed and impossible to interpret unless something is known of the reasons for sending the specimen. If the patient has a pyrexia then any of the organisms cultured may be significant and for this reason it is usually wise to perform sensitivities on organisms isolated from catheter specimens, but not to report them unless the patient has a pyrexia or other evidence of extension of infection to the kidneys or bloodstream (21). It has become common clinical practice for samples of urine to be sent for testing when a catheter is removed. This is not a worthwhile procedure unless the patient is symptomatic (22). The concept of significant bacteriuria does not apply to these specimens, and thus although many laboratories report the number of organisms per ml as a matter of convenience, no special significance can be assigned to this. Indeed, it has been found that counts of 10^2 CFU ml^{-1} or more is a more valid index of infection when patients are catheterized and have urinary tract symptoms, although these counts usually increase to at least 10^5 CFU ml^{-1} within a few days (23).

6.2 Interpretation and reporting of suprapubic aspirate and ureteric catheter specimens

There should be no problem with contamination of these specimens and so the concept of significant bacteriuria does not apply and indeed low numbers of organisms may be present, e.g. 10^2 CFU ml^{-1}. In this case purity is more important than a high count of bacteria. A mixed growth, particularly of more than two species, does suggest contamination. Sensitivities should be performed and reported on any pure growth from these specimens.

6.3 Interpretation of cultures for 'fastidious' organisms

Maskell (24) states that while the role of fastidious organisms in the urinary tract is still uncertain it is only possible to suggest diagnostic criteria of significance. At present she reports the presence of these organisms if they are isolated in pure culture in a count of at least 10^4 ml^{-1}. She admits that the quantitative criterion is purely arbitrary.

7. IDENTIFICATION OF BACTERIA

Ideally all significant cultures should be fully identified to species level but this is not usually really necessary or practicable in a busy diagnostic laboratory. Some laboratories may choose to identify all organisms, but most will elect to compromise. In any laboratory the reason for identifying bacteria needs to be defined. Examples of such reasons are as follows.

(i) Different species of organisms such as staphylococci are pathogens in different clinical situations: *Staphylococcus saprophyticus* affects young women in the community, whereas *S.epidermidis* affects mainly instrumented or catheterized hospital patients (25).

(ii) Full identification and even typing may be useful in establishing whether repeated infections are due to relapse or reinfection. However, too much reliance cannot be placed on this as reinfection with the same species may occur, and even serotyping may not be conclusive.

(iii) The prevalence of particular species and their antimicrobial sensitivites may be monitored.

(iv) Biochemical identification and possibly typing will be required to recognize and define an episode of cross-infection in hospital. It is usually possible to provide routinely the information needed by the clinician to diagnose and treat individual patients. Laboratories can identify urinary isolates into broad groups using

Table 8. Identification of Gram-negative bacilli.

1.	Look for colonies characteristic of Gram-negative bacilli; these will usually be larger and more translucent than colonies of Gram-positive cocci. If in doubt perform a Gram stain (Appendix I).
2.	Differentiate between lactose-fermenting and lactose-non-fermenting organisms. On CLED medium lactose fermenters form yellow colonies, whereas on MacConkey agar they form red colonies.
3.	If lactose-fermenting colonies are found they are given the general term 'coliforms'.
4.	If lactose-non-fermenting colonies are found perform a urease test (see Chapter 6, Table 3). If urease positive in 2–4 h call the organism *Proteus* sp. (There is a further clue to the identification of *Proteus* sp. in that they are usually resistant to nitrofurantoin, a resistance that is otherwise uncommon in Enterobacteriaceae.)
5.	If the organism is a lactose-non-fermenter with a characteristic sensitivity pattern, i.e. resistant to oral first-line antibiotics, but sensitive to gentamicin, perform an oxidase test (see Chapter 4, 4.1). If oxidase-positive call it *Pseudomonas* sp.
6.	If the organism is urease- and oxidase-negative, perform slide agglutination tests with polyvalent 'O' and 'H' antisera to see if it is a salmonella. If these are positive, perform full serology and identification[a] (see Chapter 6, Sections 4.5 and 4.6).
7.	If all the above tests are negative call the organism a lactose-non-fermenting coliform.
8.	If the organism has an unusual sensitivity pattern or is multiresistant, including resistance to aminoglycosides[b], identify it to species level, using a computer-assisted system such as API (see Chapter 6, Section 4.6). Similarly, fully identify any organism suspected of being involved in cross-infection.

[a]Either a patient has an acute salmonella infection or is a chronic carrier.
[b]Usually a good marker for plasmid-associated resistance which may be transferable from one bacterium to another.

Table 9. Identification of Gram-positive cocci.

1.	Look for colonies characteristic of Gram-positive cocci. If in doubt perform a Gram stain (Appendix I).
2.	If Gram-positive cocci are identified perform a catalase test to differentiate between staphylococci (positive) and streptococci (negative).
3.	If the organism is catalase-positive, perform a slide coagulase test, or a Staphaurex test (Wellcome Diagnostics) and a DNase test. If coagulase, Staphaurex and DNase positive, call it *Staphylococcus aureus* (see Chapter 5, Section 4.1.4).
4.	If the organism is coagulase, Staphaurex and DNase negative see if it is sensitive to novobiocin by the disc method (see Chapter 7). Perform this test at the same time as the DNase test. If sensitive to novobiocin call it *Stachylococcus epidermis*, if resistant call it *Str.saprophyticus*.
5.	If the organism is catalase-negative it is a streptococcus. If the colony is characteristic of *Streptococcus faecalis*[a] call it *Str.faecalis*. If there is doubt perform a bile aesculin test[b]. If it hydrolyses bile aesculin the medium will turn black. Then call it *Str.faecalis*.
6.	If the organism is bile aesculin-negative note its appearance on blood agar. Perform these two tests at the same time. If the colony is β-haemolytic, determine the Lancefield group (see Chapter 5, Section 4.1.4) and report as *β-haemolytic streptococcus* with its Lancefield group.
7.	If the organism is haemolytic or non-haemolytic (and not *Str.faecalis*) report it as such. It is not usually necessary to identify it further.

[a]*Str.faecalis* is the commonest streptococcus infecting the lower urinary tract.
[b]Prepared by dissolving 1 g aesculin, 0.5 g ferric citrate (filter sterilized) in 1000 ml of bile agar at 55°C. Prepare bile agar by adding 10 g of dehydrated ox bile to 1000 ml nutrient agar and sterilizing at 115°C for 20 min. When cooled to 55°C, add 50 ml of sterile horse serum.

considerably abbreviated identification procedures which are given in *Tables 8* and *9*.

Yeasts can be readily recognized by Gram-staining. They should be identified and sensitivities to agents such as 5-fluorocytosine should be performed if the organism is considered to be of clinical significance, for example if isolated in pure culture from a catheter specimen of urine from a sick, especially immunosuppressed, patient, when it may signify a systemic yeast infection. Counts of 10^3 ml^{-1} may be significant.

7.1 Identification of 'fastidious' or capnophilic organisms

It should be possible to place organisms in broad groups as follows.

(i)   If the organism is an obligate anaerobe (rarely isolated from urine, but may be found in association with bladder tumours) this should be identified where possible, using a computer-assisted system, for example RapID ANA (Innovative Diagnostic Systems Inc).

(ii) If the organism is capnophilic, perform a Gram stain to differentiate lactobacilli, which are large Gram-positive bacilli, from other Gram-positive organisms.

(iii) If it is not possible by Gram stain to differentiate easily between corynebacteria and capnophilic streptococci, such as *Streptococcus milleri* or *S.mitis*, do a catalase test. Streptococci are catalase-negative and corynebacteria catalase-positive.

(iv) If the organism is a pleomorphic Gram-negative bacillus it may be *Haemophilus* sp., in which case perform an X and V test (see Chapter 3, Table 13).

8. SENSITIVITY TESTING

For methods of both qualitative and quantitative sensitivity testing of antimicrobials, see Chapter 7. In this section I shall describe some of the principles of antibiotic sensitivity testing of urinary isolates, such as the choice of agents to be tested and the use of primary sensitivity testing.

8.1 Choice of first-line and second-line agents for sensitivity testing

Antibiotics which are excreted in a microbiologically active form in the urine are required for the treatment of most infections of the urinary tract, especially those of the lower tract. The choice of agents will be governed by whether the patient requires oral or parenteral antibiotics. For example, patients in the community usually require oral agents because of the difficulties of administering drugs by other routes. On the other hand hospitalized patients, particularly those on surgical wards or in intensive care, may require parenteral antibiotics. In general, however, laboratories choose to test mainly oral agents as their first line and follow this with parenteral agents as the second line, if a lot of resistance is seen to the first-line antibiotics, i.e. an organism sensitive to less than two agents. The request form should always be read carefully to see if a particular antibiotic is intended for therapy so that if possible this may be included. When disc diffusion tests are performed, six agents are tested to a plate (see *Table 10*).

The testing of nalidixic acid and nitrofurantoin is a useful adjunct for identification. All Gram-positive bacteria are resistant to nalidixic acid, whereas most coliforms are sensitive, and so it can be used to help differentiate between, for example, *Streptococcus faecalis* and a coliform. Also, all *Proteus* spp. are usually resistant to nitrofurantoin,

Table 10. Selection of antimicrobial agents for testing.

A. *General use, including for Enterobacteriaceae*

1. *First line*: select six from following:

(i) *Commonly used agents*

Ampicillin
Trimethoprim
Nitrofurantoin
Cephalexin/Cephradine
'Augmentin' (clavulanate-
potentiated amoxycillin)

(ii) Less commonly used agents
Sulphonamide[a]
Nalidixic acid
Gentamicin[b]

2. *Second line*: select six from following:

(i) *Cephalosporins*	Cefamandole[c]
	Cefuroxime[c]
	Ceftizoxime[c]
	Cefotaxime[c]
	Ceftazidime[c]
(ii) *Aminoglycosides*	Gentamicin[c]
	Tobramycin[c]
	Netilmicin
	Amikacin
(iii) *Monobactam*	Aztreonam
(iv) *Carbapenem*	Imipenem
(v) *4-Quinolone*	Ciprofloxacin

B. *For Pseudomonas spp.*

Select six from following:

Azlocillin[c]	Gentamicin[c]
Piperacillin[c]	Tobramycin[c]
	Amikacin
Carbenicillin[d]	Aztreonam
Ceftazidime	Imipenem
	Ciprofloxacin

[a]Some laboratories test sulphonamide and trimethoprim separately, others trimethoprim only.
[b]Testing of this agent on specimens from hospitalized patients will identify gentamicin-resistant isolates associated with nosocomial infection.
[c]Only test one agent from the group.
[d]Available as ester, 'carfecillin', for oral use. 4-Quinolones are only other oral agents for pseudomonas infections.

whereas most other coliforms are sensitive. The choice between agents grouped together in *Table 10* will depend upon the antibiotic-prescribing policy of the particular hospital.

If staphylococci are isolated, then the choice of agents will differ from those in *Table 10*. Penicillin should be tested rather than ampicillin because by the use of a low content disc (2IU), resistance is more reliably detected. For the same reason methicillin should be tested at 30°C as a marker for both cloxacillin/flucloxacillin and cephalosporin sensitivity. Among the first-line set of antibiotics for staphylococci, novobiocin may be included so that a separate plate will not have to be used.

Another agent which may be used for Gram-positive organisms, including capnophiles, is tetracycline, although this should not be used in patients with renal impairment, children or pregnant women.

8.2 **Primary sensitivity testing**

Urine may be used as the inoculum for a sensitivity test set up at the same time as the primary culture. For details of the method see Chapter 7, Section 2.6. The major advantage of this is that the results can be reported the following day along with the culture result. Also, the sensitivity results are more representative because they are performed on what has grown from the urine and not from what has been selectively picked for subculture. However, the disadvantages are, firstly, that the inoculum is not controlled and thus may produce too heavy or light a growth; secondly, the culture may be mixed and greater caution must be exercised in reporting on mixed growths. Thus, although there are obvious advantages in performing primary sensitivities they do require the observer to be prepared to discard them if the inoculum is not right or they are mixed, and repeat the test on colonies picked from the primary culture plates. If these rules are adhered to then primary sensitivity testing is a reliable method and is widely used.

It is clearly unnecessarily expensive and time-consuming to perform primary sensitivities on all urines received, and most laboratories will use specific criteria for performing them. These will vary from one laboratory to another but include such things as significant pyuria and the presence of motile bacteria. Some specimens, such as bag urines, will not be used for primary sensitivity testing because contamination is very common. Whatever the criteria adopted there will always be occasions when secondary testing is required.

8.3 **Reporting of sensitivities**

Most laboratories perform a form of selective reporting of sensitivities as part of their antibiotic prescribing policy. For example, if ampicillin is considered the first-line β-lactam antibiotic for the treatment of urinary tract infection, and the organism is sensitive, then other β-lactams included in first-line testing, such as cephalexin or 'Augmentin', may not be reported. Similarly, although gentamicin may be tested in the first-line group, it is unlikely to be reported for patients in the community. To some extent each report will be tailored to the information available.

Selective reporting is very desirable in certain circumstances, such as urinary infection in pregnancy, when certain agents are contraindicated. In this situation, β-lactams are the most appropriate agents. Selective reporting is not entirely aimed at restricting the use of antibiotics, although it may be used for this purpose, but rather to offer guidance to the clinicians to use the most appropriate agents. Various factors determine this, including proven safety of the agents and their cheapness.

9. FURTHER TESTS

9.1 **Detection of antimicrobial substances in urine**

Often there is no mention on the request form that a patient is taking antibiotics, or was taking them 48 h before the urine was collected. Under such circumstances it is difficult to interpret the absence of growth of bacteria in the presence of many white cells. In some laboratories it has become routine practice to screen all urines for the presence of antimicrobial substances. The method is not well standardized, but the basis is as follows.

(i) Mix 0.5 ml of an overnight culture of *E.coli* NCTC 10418 with 100 ml molten agar (e.g. DST, Oxoid), cooled to 50°C. *Bacillus* sp. has been used instead as the indicator organism, but there are advantages in having a mixed inoculum of say *E.coli* and *B.pumilis*, so that a wider range of antibiotics are detected. For the inoculum of *B.pumilis* use a spore suspension as described in Chapter 8.

(ii) Pour the agar into a 25 cm × 25 cm square assay plate which is suitable for screening 100 urines. Allow to set and dry thoroughly.

(iii) Using a 10 × 10 template, place 2 μl loopful of urine onto the appropriate spot and repeat until 100 urines have been inoculated.

(iv) Incubate plate overnight and examine for zones of inhibition around the urine spots, indicating the presence of antimicrobial substances.

A similar method has been used with six test organisms, *E.coli* NCTC 10418, *Klebsiella aerogenes*, *Morganella morganii*, *Streptococcus faecalis*, *Staphylococcus aureus*, *Micrococcus* sp., in order to attempt to identify the antimicrobial agent present by the pattern of inhibition (26).

9.2 Antibody-coated bacteria in urine

Antibodies coating bacteria may be detected in urine, and this forms the basis of the antibody-coated bacteria (ACB) assay, where antibodies attached to bacteria are visualized with the aid of fluorescein-labelled anti-immunoglobulin. The test was first described in 1974 (27,28) when it showed good discrimination between upper and lower urinary tract infections in adults, the presence of ACB being associated with the former. Subsequent studies have given more variable results. A correlation has been found however, between abnormalities of the upper tract and a positive ACB test (29). For a critical review see Mundt and Polk (30). The test is not part of routine practice in the UK.

10. AUTOMATED METHODS

A number of automated or semi-automated rapid screening tests for the detection of bacteriuria have been evaluated recently. Such methods include the following.

(i) *Colorimetric filtration*. A sample of urine is passed through a filter and if cells are present they are trapped on the filter. Safranin O dye is used to stain the trapped cells. This procedure has been adapted for use with a semi-automated instrument, the Bac-T-Screen (Vitek Systems Inc.) and gives a result in 1 min.

(ii) *Bioluminescence*. This is based on the enzymatic bioluminescent reaction of adenosine 5'-triphosphate (ATP) from bacteria with luciferin and luciferinase, which is measured by a luminometer. The Lumac Bacteriuria Screening Kit comprises such a method.

(iii) *Photometry*. In these tests growth is required prior to detection and therefore detection times are somewhat delayed (30 min to 13 h). Urine is diluted in a broth medium and incubated at 35 − 37°C, allowing any bacteria present to grow. The resulting turbidity is detected by changes in light transmission which are measured photometrically. Abbott Laboratories and Organon both produce photometric systems, and all the growth-dependent systems have the additional capacity for organism identification and antimicrobial sensitivity testing.

(iv) *Particle analysis.* Here the impedance changes are measured, caused by particles passing through an orifice, which forms the only electrical contact between a pair of electrodes. These changes are seen as pulses, and the number of pulses equals the number of particles observed and the height of the pulse is proportional to the volume of the particle. Thus by drawing a known volume of diluted urine solution through the orifice, the number of particles present as well as their size distribution can be determined. The Ramus system produced by Orbec is based on this principle.

All the above are rapid screening methods, that is, they detect the presence of bacteria more quickly than culture and incubation and they screen out negatives, eliminating the need for culture. They cannot discriminate between pure and mixed cultures and thus all urines in which bacteria are detected need to be cultured. A large proportion of urines, perhaps 80% received in the laboratory, are negative, and so these systems would save on labour. However, when the expense of the equipment is weighed against the expected benefits, many laboratories are deterred from purchasing them.

11. REFERENCES

1. Kenney,M., Loechel,A.B. and Lovelock,F.J. (1960) *Am. Rev. Respir. Dis.*, **82**, 564.
2. Porter,I.A. and Brodie,J. (1969) *Br. Med. J.*, **2**, 353.
3. Johnston,H.H., Moss,M.V. and Guthrie,G.A. (1978) In *The Bacteriological Examination of Urine: Report of a Workshop on Needs and Methods. Public Health Laboratory Service Monograph Series No. 10.* Meers,P.D. (ed.) H.M. Stationery Office, London, p. 22.
4. Mackey,J.P. and Sandys,G.H. (1965) *Br. Med. J.*, **2**, 1286.
5. James,G.P., Paul,K.L. and Fuller,J.B. (1978) *Am. J. Clin. Path.*, **70**, 671.
6. Perry,J.L., Matthews,J.S. and Weesner,D.E. (1982) *J. Clin. Microbiol.*, **15**, 852.
7. Hilson,G.R.F. (1964) *J. Clin. Path.*, **17**, 571.
8. Tuck,A.C. (1987) *Med. Lab. Sciences*, **44**, 290.
9. Hoff,R.G., Newman,D.E. and Staneck,J.L. (1985) *J. Clin. Microbiol.*, **22**, 513.
10. Lipsky,B.A., Plorde,J.J., Tenover,F.C. and Brancato,F.P. (1985) *J. Clin. Microbiol.*, **21**, 176.
11. Little,P.J.A. (1964) *Br. J. Urol.*, **36**, 360.
12. Lippman,R.W. (1957) In *Urine and the Urinary Sediment, A Practical Manual and Atlas*, 2nd edn, Charles C. Thomas, Springfield, Illinois.
13. Mackey,J.P. and Sandys,G.H. (1966) *Br. Med. J.*, **1**, 1173.
14. Leigh,D.A. and Williams,J.D. (1964) *J. Clin. Path.*, **17**, 498.
15. Maskell,R. (1986) In *Microbial Disease in Nephrology.* Asscher,A.W. and Brumfitt,W. (eds), John Wiley, Chichester.
16. Hamilton-Miller,J.M.T., Brumfitt,W. and Smith,G.W. (1986) In *Microbial Disease in Nephrology.* Asscher,A.W. and Brumfitt,W. (eds), John Wiley and Sons Ltd, Chichester.
17. Kass,E.H. (1957) *Arch. Int. Med.*, **100**, 709.
18. Stamm,W.E., Counts,G.W., Running,K.R., Fihn,S., Turck,M. and Holmes,K.K. (1982) *N. Engl. J. Med.*, **307**, 463.
19. Cattell,W.R., Kelsey Fry,I., Spiro,F.I., Sanderson,J.M., Sutcliffe,M.B. and O'Grady,F. (1970) *Br. J. Urol.*, **42**, 290.
20. Anderson,J.D., Eftekhar,F., Aird,M.Y. and Hammond,J. (1979) *J. Clin. Microbiol.*, **10**, 766.
21. Gillespie,W.A. (1986) *J. Antimicrob. Chemother.*, **18**, 149.
22. Davies,A.J. and Shroff,K.J. (1983) *J. Hosp. Infect.*, **4**, 177.
23. Stark,R.P. and Maki,D.G. (1984) *N. Eng. J. Med.*, **311**, 560.
24. Maskell,R. (1982) In *Urinary Tract Infection, Current Topics in Infection Series 3*, Edward Arnold, London, p.29.
25. Mitchell,R.G. (1968) *J. Clin. Path.*, **21**, 93.
26. Millar,M.R. and Langdale,P. (1985) *J. Clin. Microbiol.*, **21**, 741.
27. Thomas,V., Shelokov,A. and Forland,M. (1974) *N. Eng. J. Med.*, **290**, 588.
28. Jones,S.R., Smith,J.W. and Sanford,J.P. (1974) *N. Eng. J. Med.*, **290**, 591.
29. Rumans,L.W. and Vosti,K.L. (1978) *Arch. Int. Med.*, **138**, 1077.
30. Mundt,K.A. and Polk,B.F. (1979) *Lancet*, **2**, 1172.

CHAPTER 2

Bacteriology of normally sterile body fluids

ROGER FREEMAN

1. INTRODUCTION

The recovery of a bacterium from these specimens should always be considered significant until proven otherwise. Organisms should be identified to species level, not an arduous task as most infections are caused by a single species. Whilst culture of the infecting bacteria will allow identification and antibiotic sensitivity testing to be carried out, these infections are often serious and a rapid diagnosis is required to ensure correct chemotherapy. Various strategies have been adopted to accelerate culture results and detect the presence of bacteria without the need to grow them (often relying on the detection of bacterial antigens or products). This chapter describes methods for the examination of the various categories of normally sterile body fluids and interpretation of these data. For the sake of brevity the examination of urine has been dealt with in Chapter 1.

2. METHODS FOR THE EXAMINATION OF BLOOD

2.1 Principles of blood culture

2.1.1 Number and timing of blood cultures

The timing of blood cultures in the continuous bacteraemia of endocarditis is probably not important, but in most other conditions the bacteraemia is intermittent and related to the fevers and rigors which follow the appearance of organisms in the blood by 30−60 min (1). Unless the fevers and chills follow a regular pattern, blood cultures should be taken as near to the onset of a spike of fever as possible.

In endocarditis, only a small number of samples are needed to isolate an organism, but 3 sets should be taken in order to help distinguish contamination from true infection (*Figure 1*). If the first few cultures are negative in suspected endocarditis, do not persist, since further samples are unlikely to be rewarding (2).

The diagnosis of other conditions may be helped by repeated cultures, although more than 6 sets are unnecessary. Three sets, taken not less than 1 h apart, will give a success rate of 99%, compared with 80% for one set (3). Thereafter the success rate will not improve. Single sets may be adequate in neonates, in whom the density of bacteraemia is higher (4). The sending of large numbers of repeat blood cultures from the same patient, whether positive or negative, should be avoided since they simply waste laboratory time.

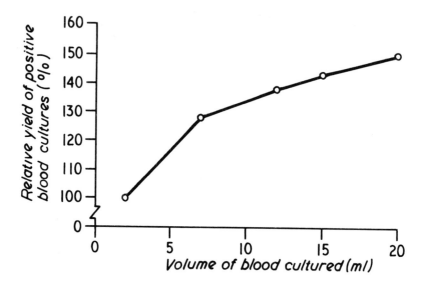

Figure 1. Relative yield of positive blood cultures with increasing volumes of blood cultured between 2 and 20 ml (after A.L.Bisno, *The Diagnosis of Infective Endocarditis*).

Table 1. Taking a blood culture.

1.	Ensure that the blood culture bottles have attained ambient temperature and are not chilled.
2.	Select the venepuncture site and clean it with ethyl alcohol, followed by an iodine-containing agent. Use liberal amounts of both.
3.	Allow ample time for drying and do not touch the cleaned area thereafter except with sterile gloves.
4.	Have an assistant remove the covering material ('Viscap') from the bottle top and wipe the penetrable diaphragm with antiseptic, again allowing adequate time for drying.
5.	Perform the venepuncture and inoculate an adequate amount of blood (see 2.1.3) into each bottle. If it proves impossible to obtain more than a small sample, inoculate fewer bottles rather than distributing very small quantities into several.
6.	Where blood is taken at the same venesection for other tests (e.g. haemoglobin, white blood cell count) insist that the blood culture bottles are inoculated first.
7.	Mix the contents of the bottles gently after inoculation.

2.1.2 *Collection of the sample*

Ward-based staff should be encouraged to take the samples (*Table 1*) since this ensures familiarity with the procedure and increases the amount of clinical interest and information.

2.1.3 *Size of the sample*

The number of bacteria present in the blood of bacteraemic patients is often less than 1 per ml. In endocarditis the levels may be even lower. *Figure 2* shows the relative increase in yield of positive blood cultures per ml of blood cultured in a series of over 1000 cases of sepsis in one centre and suggests that at least 10 ml of blood must be taken in an adult patient. Increasing the volume to 20 ml may produce a further modest

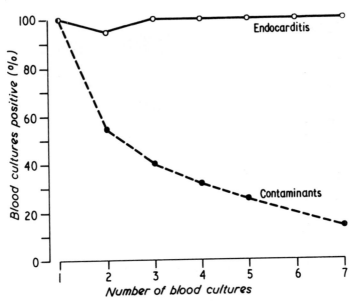

Figure 2. Demonstration of the value of multiple independent blood cultures in distinguishing between contamination and the bacteraemia of infective endocarditis (after A.L.Bisno, *The Diagnosis of Infective Endocarditis*).

yield and should be encouraged in endocarditis. Even when an adequate sample has been obtained it should not be surprising if only some bottles of several inoculated become positive.

Adequate results may be obtained from much smaller volumes in infants, especially neonates (4).

2.1.4 *Recovering organisms from the blood sample*

The various methods which have been devised for the recovery of organisms from blood samples all attempt to satisfy four essential aims:

(i) the creation of the richest possible culture medium to allow the recovery of very small numbers of even very fastidious bacteria;

(ii) the removal, or neutralization, of any substances inimical to bacterial growth, including both natural components of blood and extraneous factors, such as antibiotics;

(iii) the minimizing of both ward-based and laboratory-based contamination;

(iv) the earliest possible detection of the presence of bacteria in the system.

Although many different means of achieving these aims have been devised, the conventional broth-culture technique is still the one most often used and it will now be described in detail. Other methods will then be briefly described.

2.2 Conventional broth blood cultures

2.2.1 *Choice of medium*

The theoretical range of bacteria to be recovered from the blood is unending and no single medium will isolate all bacteria. Certain unusual and extremely fastidious bacteria

23

Figure 3. Some commonly used broth blood culture systems. From left to right: simple bottled media; lab M anaerobic bottle with integral agar paddle; Septicheck (Roche) aerobic paddle system which is attached in the laboratory; Signal system (Oxoid) with the gas capture device in position.

demand specialized media and are not included in a 'routine' system. These are described in section (iii) and should be taken when specific conditions are clinically suspected.

Most systems in common use employ separate media for the isolation of aerobic and anaerobic bacteria, although the Oxoid Signal system (*Figure 3*) uses only one bottle. The Signal system uses a gas capture device which is connected to the culture bottle on receipt in the laboratory. It gives similar results to the radiometric methods but may miss some fastidious organisms (5). It has been found that media ingredients which promote the growth of some bacteria may be inhibitory to other groups of bacteria, so the eventual choice of media will inevitably be a compromise.

(i) *Media for aerobic bacteria.* Use nutrient broth or glucose broth as the basis of the medium. Remember the addition of the sample will convert this medium into 'human blood broth' which is a very rich medium indeed, capable of supporting the growth of many fastidious aerobes and facultative anaerobes. The choice of nutrient broth varies, but good examples are Nutrient Broth No. 2 (Oxoid Ltd) or Columbia Broth.

The glucose concentration should be limited to 0.1% when it promotes the growth of streptococci, coliforms and yeasts, at concentrations greater than 1% the acid generated by growth can kill the bacteria.

The relative volumes of blood sample and medium should be arranged such that a dilution of at least 1 in 5, and preferably 1 in 10, is achieved. A dilution factor of at least 1 in 15−30 is necessary to remove the antibacterial effects of normal human blood, but the addition of sodium polyethanol sulphonate (Liquoid) allows the more modest

Table 2. A recommended broth blood culture set.

		Volume of medium	Liquoid (%)	Volume of blood added (dilution)	Incubation	Organisms
1. Carbon dioxide bottle	Nutrient broth[a]	10 ml	0.05	5 ml (1 in 3)	Air plus 10% carbon dioxide	Strict aerobes and facultative anaerobes[b]
2. Aerobic bottle (diphasic medium)	Glucose (0.1%) broth	50 ml	0.05	5 ml (1 in 11)	Air	Strict aerobes and facultative anaerobes
3. Anaerobic bottle	Fastidious anaerobe broth (Lab M)	75 ml	–	5 ml (1 in 16)	Cap tight	Strict anaerobes and facultative anaerobes

[a]Prepared according to the method given in ACP Broadsheet 81 (9).
[b]Including carboxyphilic organisms such as *Brucella abortus* and *Haemophilus aphrophilus*.

dilution to produce the same effect. Ensure that the concentration of Liquoid does not exceed 0.05% since it may have deleterious effects on certain species at a higher concentration. The addition of 1% gelatin to blood culture media will eliminate the inhibitory effect of Liquoid on susceptible bacteria such as *Neisserria gonorrhoeae* (6).

A variation on the aerobic broth medium is the diphasic medium in which a nutrient agar slope is incorporated into the bottle in addition to the broth. Frequent tipping of the bottle so that the broth phase regularly re-inoculates the agar slope obviates the need for subculture. This technique is often recommended for culture of potentially dangerous organisms (e.g. *Brucella* spp.) since it offers containment and may also reduce laboratory-introduced contamination. By removing the need for regular subculturing, savings in time and material may be made, but must be offset against increased material costs. Several commercial systems are available such as the Septicheck (Roche) and Hy-Pbc-Flask® (Lab M).

If using a 3-bottle set (*Table 2*) incubate one of the aerobic media in CO_2 by loosening the cap and placing the bottle in an atmosphere containing 10% CO_2. This will promote the growth of carboxyphilic organisms such as the more unusual haemophili and some strains of *Streptococcus mutans*.

Tryptic soya broth and brain heart infusion broth are often recommended on the premise that richer media will facilitate the growth of more fastidious bacteria. These more expensive media are unnecessary, since the addition of the sample enriches a nutrient broth base sufficiently for most purposes, and a lethal effect on pneumococci has been ascribed to both tryptic soy and brain heart infusion broths (8). The latter medium has also been shown to inhibit *Brucella* spp. (9). Bile salts need not be added to media to isolate *Salmonella* spp.

(ii) *Media for anaerobic bacteria.* Again, studies have shown that no single medium is ideal for the isolation of all anaerobes, but recent interest in anaerobic bacteria has led to significant improvements in media. If anaerobic media are to be used in volumes of less than 100 ml, it is necessary to add substances capable of producing a reducing atmosphere. The addition of thioglycollate salts will achieve this, but different thioglycollate preparations produce variable results. For instance, USP thioglycollate has been shown to promote the growth of *Bacteroides* spp. and then kill the growing organism (10). Two media with excellent performances in the isolation of strict anaerobes are Thiol broth (Difco) and Fastidious Anaerobic Broth (Lab M); either may be used. Liquoid is not added to anaerobic media, since it has been shown to inhibit anaerobic streptococci (11).

(iii) *Specialist media*. The principal special medium encountered is that for the isolation of brucellae. A diphasic system (called by many 'Castenada's medium') is used in which the broth and slope consist of serum dextrose medium. This is incubated at 37°C in an atmosphere containing 10% CO_2 for up to 6 weeks, inoculating the slope within the bottle regularly. This system has the advantage that containment is provided by the diphasic bottles. All subcultures and subsequent procedures must be performed within a safety cabinet. The previously preferred liver infusion broth and agar for the isolation of brucellae is no longer considered necessary (12).

2.2.2 *Composition of a routine blood culture set*

Table 2 lists a suggested range of media for a routine blood culture set, such sets are a compromise and variations on this theme are widespread and largely acceptable.

2.2.3 *Duration of incubation*

Complete clinical information will have an influence on the length of incubation. If the clinical diagnosis is septicaemia (the old pathological distinctions between 'bacteraemia', 'septicaemia' and 'pyaemia' are irrelevant clinically), the broths should be incubated for 7−10 days. All the common pathogens, such as staphylococci, coliforms and so on, will be isolated within the first 2−3 days.

If endocarditis is suspected, the period should be prolonged to 3 weeks; pyrexia of unknown origin is treated likewise.

2.2.4 *Detection of a positive blood culture*

This relies on three methods which must be combined.

(i) Inspect the undisturbed bottles daily. Note the appearance of turbidity, gas production and look for the development of 'colonies' on the sedimented blood layer, or in the case of biphasic bottles on the agar surface. Do not assume that the culture is negative just because the supernatant broth is clear. Many organisms will first declare their presence on the surface of the blood layer before the broth becomes turbid.

(ii) Gram stain any suspicious looking bottles. This will confirm the presence of organisms and also remains the quickest and most helpful test to allow presumptive identification and guidance of therapy. Inform the ward or, better, go and see the patient at this stage.

(iii) A programme of routine subculturing must be undertaken even if inspection of the bottles fails to show any suggestion of growth. The semi-automatic incorporation of this facility into machine-based blood culture systems (Section 2.3) was originally taken to be one of the major advantages of such systems. Recently modifications to manual systems have been shown to be just as effective and much cheaper (13,14).

Subcultures performed within $12-18$ h of receipt will detect $50-60\%$ of all positives, but subcultures performed within 6 h of receipt are probably not worthwhile, detecting only 30% (13). A study has shown that 4-pm subculturing will achieve a similar yield of positive cultures to a 10-pm subculture without incurring the additional expense and inconvenience (14). The following scheme for routine subculture can be followed.

(i)   Examine each bottle daily as described in (i) above, performing Gram stains and subculture on any with visual indicators of growth.

(ii)   Subculture all bottles on day 0 by ensuring that subculture is performed twice each day, at 9 am and 4 pm. Newly received cultures should thereby be sampled within $7-17$ h of receipt at one of these times. Where diphasic aerobic medium is included in the routine set of blood cultures, flood the agar slope with the broth phase twice at the times indicated. Perform further routine subcultures on days 1, 3 and 7 (this will not be necessary if a diphasic medium is used).

2.2.5 Subculturing

(i)   Avoid the common trap of assuming that growth in only one medium means nothing. As discussed earlier, the small numbers of bacteria present in many blood culture inocula will often lead to this result regardless of the nutritional or other requirements of the organisms.

(ii)   Perform subculturing in a room or area specially set aside for the purpose; a laminar flow cabinet is the ideal. Ensure that adequate space is available so that all technical procedures can be unhurried and easily performed. Exclude other staff whilst subculturing is proceeding and minimize movement. All these procedures will help to minimize laboratory-based contamination. It has been suggested that a safety cabinet should be used. Whilst this is essential for the subculture of specimens thought likely to contain dangerous pathogens (e.g. *Brucella* spp.), the confined space may lead to compromises in technique for routine specimens.

(iii)   Sample the broth cultures using either a needle and syringe (the only method possible with Oxoid Signal type) or a long sterile Pasteur pipette. When using the latter, ensure that sampling includes the sedimented layer and not just the supernatant broth. Place one drop of broth on the various media to be inoculated, allow the liquid to soak into the medium and then spread with a sterile loop. *Table 3* sets out a list of suitable media for the subculturing of the various broths. If Gram stains have been positive, use the information from them to set up appropriate direct sensitivity tests.

2.2.6 Contamination

Contamination arises in three distinct ways. The first two mechanisms are ward-based and, therefore, not directly controlled by the laboratory. However, the regular presence of the microbiologist on the wards will greatly help in minimizing these.

(i) *Cross-contamination.* Blood culture bottles may become cross-contaminated with saprophytic bacteria (common examples are *Pseudomonas maltophilia* and *Flavobacterium* spp.) from non-sterile containers for other tests (15). Blood cultures

Table 3. Summary of broth blood culture subculture plate procedures.

Bottles	Reason for subculture	Pathogens sought	Subcultured on to	Atmosphere of incubation	Details of incubation of plates
Anaerobic bottle	1. ROUTINE	Anaerobes	Blood agar	Hydrogen + 10% CO_2	2 days
	2. Looks positive[a]	Anaerobes +	Blood agar +	Hydrogen + 10% CO_2	Up to 5 days
		aerobes	blood agar	Air + 10% CO_2	Up to 5 days
	3. If Gram-negative bacilli seen and patient has abdominal sepsis	*Bacteroides* + coliforms	+ kanamycin or neomycin Blood agar +	As for (2) Hydrogen + 10% CO_2	Up to 5 days
			MacConkey's agar	Air	2 days
Liquoid CO_2 bottle	1. ROUTINE	Aerobes (especially CO_2-dependent strains)	Blood agar	Air in 10% CO_2	2 days
	2. Looks positive[a]	Aerobes (CO_2-dependent)	Blood agar	Air + 10% CO_2	Up to 5 days in moist state
	3. Organisms seen in Gram but no growth on blood plates after 2 days incubation—resubculture	+ nutritionally variant bacteria (Section 2.2.4)	12% Fresh blood agar + chocolate agar	Air + 10% CO_2 Air + 10% CO_2	
Glucose broth bottle	1. ROUTINE	Aerobes	Blood agar	Air + 10% CO_2	2 days
	2. Looks positive[a]	Aerobes + anaerobes	Blood agar + blood agar	Air + 10% CO_2 Hydrogen + 10% CO_2	Up to 5 days Up to 5 days

[a]When bottle looks positive, appropriate primary antibiotic sensitivity plates are also included.

should either be performed as a separate procedure, or blood culture bottles always inoculated before any other containers (*Table 1*).

(ii) *Skin organisms.* Contamination may arise from the skin organisms of the patient. To minimize this, the necessity for good aseptic and antiseptic practice at the time of venepuncture should be stressed to the ward staff. When more than one set of blood cultures are to be taken separate venepuncture sites should be used. Contamination with skin organisms should be suspected when typical organisms (coagulase-negative staphylococci and/or diphtheroids) are isolated within 1−3 days but only from one set of cultures and not another. It is important to remember that the pathogens *Streptococcus mutans* and *Listeria monocytogenes* may exhibit diphtheroid morphology and that J−K group diphtheroids can cause serious disease in compromised patients. Unfortunately, the isolation from blood cultures of skin-type organisms is not uncommon, and their significance must be assessed as described in *Table 4*.

Table 4. Procedure for the assessment of blood culture isolates thought to be contaminants.

1.	Visit the patient. Patients with septicaemia are ill; those in whom the positive culture results from contamination are often well and lack other markers of serious sepsis (high white cell count, plasma viscosity and C reactive protein).
2.	If in doubt, request further cultures, stressing the need to take them from different sites (*Figure 1*).
3.	Ensure that the ward staff are not taking blood for culture via an indwelling intravenous line or similar device. While it may be helpful to do this in an attempt to prove colonization of such a line, peripheral blood cultures taken from an uncannulated vein must always be taken as well, since the bacteria concerned are often present only within the line.
4.	If a series of well-taken cultures continues to yield a possible contaminant, consider the possibility that the infection is genuine. Obtain additional evidence that this may be the case by trying to prove that the isolates are identical. Various methods exist for typing such isolates; many are given in Chapter 11, Section 4. Widely varying sensitivity profiles will suggest that they are not identical. Small differences may not be significant.
	If the isolate is a coagulase-negative staphylococcus, identify it down to species level using a biochemical profile system, such as API-Staph (API Ltd). Demonstration that the series of isolates comprises various species will strongly suggest that they are all contaminants. The commonest species encountered is *S. epidermidis*, and the API-Staph profiles within this species are very similar, so plasmid profiling may be necessary (Chapter 11, Section 4.7).
5.	Examine the positive bottles very carefully as they become positive. In genuine coagulase-negative staphylococcal bacteraemia and especially endocarditis the bacteria often grow as micro-colonies on the sedimented blood layer rather than causing turbidity in the broth. The supposition is that this is due to agglutination and flocculation by pre-formed antibody. This appearance in a series of such bottles strongly suggests that the isolates are not contaminants.

(iii) *Laboratory-based contamination*. This arises after the first, or subsequent, routine subculture. The range and types of bacteria isolated usually suggest this source and the isolation of the same organism from patients with widely varying clinical conditions should alert the microbiologist.

Occasionally bacteria other than those commonly associated with skin contamination appear in blood cultures; these can cause confusion. Clostridia, especially *Cl. perfringens*, may be isolated from blood cultures. The likely source of these is the patient's skin; it is claimed that these spores are found more commonly on the skin of patients than on the skin of healthy people (16). The patient should be visited to ensure that the cultures are not from a case in which clostridial septicaemia is likely (e.g. portal pyaemia). Take further samples using adequate disinfection with an iodine-based antiseptic.

2.2.7 *Antimicrobial agents in blood cultures*

Dilution of blood containing antibiotics when added to blood culture medium will enable sensitive bacteria to grow. The addition of 50 mg l^{-1} of *p*-aminobenzoic acid will inactivate sulphonamides, and Thiol broth (for anaerobes) will neutralize penicillins, allowing streptococci to grow (17).

However, it is sometimes necessary to attempt to isolate bacteria from the blood of a patient who is already treated with antibiotics. β-Lactam antibiotics may be destroyed with β-lactamase, using the commercially available broad spectrum enzyme (Whatman) which will destroy both penicillins and cephalosporins (18). The enzyme should be dispensed into aliquots to be added to a blood culture bottle and stored frozen at $-20°C$ until required. One 5 ml vial of freeze-dried enzyme reconstituted with 5 ml of sterile water can be dispensed into aliquots of 100 μl using aseptic techniques. When added to up to 100 ml of broth this will provide sufficient β-lactamase activity to neutralize likely concentrations of β-lactam antibiotics. Add the enzyme in an aseptic manner after the receipt of the culture. This is just as effective as adding it to the broth prior to inoculation, and avoids confusion on the wards.

Many methods for the neutralization or removal of other antibiotics have been devised; most are of limited use due to cost and variable efficiency. A commercially produced blood culture bottle containing a range of inactivators including resins, the Antibiotic Removal Device (ARD), is simple to use (19) and could be used by laboratories on an occasional basis.

2.2.8 *Adjuncts to the broth culture system*

Various technical modifications to different stages in the broth culture system have been advanced from time to time. These include the use of acridine orange staining (20) as a method of increasing the sensitivity of Gram stains, centrifugation of aliquots from the bottles prior to Gram staining (21), and lysis of the blood sample plus centrifugation of the resultant fluid prior to inoculation (22). All these modifications have received favourable reports in some hands, but in general have not stood the test of time, or are still being evaluated, and pending this should not be regarded as part of a routine system.

2.2.9 *Trouble-shooting broth blood culture systems*

Occasionally bacteria are seen in the Gram film or a bottle is turbid but the subcultures stubbornly fail to yield an organism. Under these circumstances the procedure should be as follows.

(i)   Consider whether or not the full range of subculture media and atmospheric conditions have been used.

(ii)   If no inadvertent omissions to the standard system have occurred, plan a strategy for the isolation of more fastidious bacteria. At this point the information available from a positive Gram stain will be invaluable.

(iii)   The most common problem is that Gram-positive cocci can be seen in films from the bottles but without growth on subculture. This is strongly suggestive of a nutritional variant streptococcus (NVS). Such strains often require supplementation of subculture media with one or more vitamins, most commonly pyridoxal (23). A simple method of isolating the organism by providing a large range of extra nutrients is to cross-streak. Repeat the subcultures onto the usual media and immediately after inoculation of the media apply a streak of *Staphylococcus aureus* across the plates and then incubate the plates. NVS will grow as satellite growths near the streak. It is possible to supplement chemically defined media with a range of individual vitamins and other growth factors to define the dependence more precisely (24).

(iv)   In the absence of any bacteria being seen in the Gram stain but where the bottle appears to be positive, consider other possibilities. These include *Legionella* spp., *Campylbacter* spp. and mycoplasmata (particularly *Mycoplasma hominis*). Make subcultures onto the specialized media devised for these organisms and incubate.

taking particular care to observe any unusual atmospheric or temperature requirement.

2.2.10 *Characterization of isolates*

All significant blood culture isolates should be identified to species level if possible. Whilst a number of commercial identification kits exist (API 20E, API-Staph, etc.) it is important to carry out basic tests such as the Gram stain, oxidase and catalase tests before proceeding to these specialized identification systems. This is particularly important as most systems offer a computer database to provide a 'best-fit' identification which may be erroneous. It is only by the use of independent tests combined with experience that faulty results in these identification systems will be spotted. Some organisms isolated will not be suited to a commercial identification kit, and reference should be made to a standard work on the identification of clinically important bacteria (25,26).

A check should always be made that Gram-negative bacilli isolated from blood cultures do not slide agglutinate with polyvalent salmonella 'O' antisera prior to formal identification.

The antibiotic sensitivity of isolates should be determined as described in Chapter 7; in order to provide a rapid result a 'direct' sensitivity test should be performed using the blood culture broth as the inoculum. The test can be repeated with a carefully standardized inoculum the following day if necessary.

2.3 **Alternative methods to broth cultures**

Although there have been several attempts to replace blood cultures by the detection of bacterial antigens or chemical markers in blood, these have remained experimental and unhelpful. Examples include the *Limulus* lysate test for endotoxin, gas–liquid chromatography for volatile products of certain bacteria and counter-immunoelectrophoresis for capsular antigens. Apart from technical limitations, which are considerable, none of these methods achieves the recovery of the live bacteria to determine antibiotic sensitivity patterns.

A second category of techniques involves concentration of the blood sample used as the inoculum. Several methods have been devised, but all have drawbacks and it is doubtful whether they are better than existing methods (27).

The final category of methods is the automated or semi-automated systems for the detection of bacterial growth. These have found favour in recent years and at least one system offers a real alternative to broth cultures.

All the currently available methods use a conventional broth system with automated detection of growth. Bioluminescence and microcalorimetry have been employed for detection, but monitoring the production of CO_2 by the growing culture is the only method sufficiently developed to be currently commercially available.

2.3.1 *CO_2 detection systems*

The earliest version of this method involves the detection of radioactive CO_2 produced by the growing culture from ^{14}C-labelled substrates in the broth medium (Bactec®). The instrument samples gas from the headspace in the bottle, and when a predetermined

$^{14}CO_2$ concentration is reached (the 'growth index') the bottle is identified as provisionally positive. Subculture, identification and sensitivity testing are then performed in the usual way. Bottles are incubated independently of the instrument and the system is an automated substitute for the daily visual inspection. Results seem to be equivalent to those achieved by a well-run conventional system but offer no advantage in speed of detection over a conventional system adopting an early inspection routine (13). It is, however, convenient and less labour-intensive than conventional methods. Disadvantages include the disposal of radioactive material, the tying of the laboratory to one supplier and type of medium and the capital and running costs of the equipment— conventional systems are considerably cheaper (13). Sensitivity and specificity of the radiometric system are not significantly different. Laboratory-based contamination should be lower, although there are reports of pseudobacteraemia due to these machines (28).

A recently introduced version of the Bactec® machine uses infrared detection of CO_2, eliminating the problem of radiation exposure.

2.3.2 *Impedance – conductance*

Apart from the CO_2 detection systems, the only other automated method of monitoring growth in blood culture broths which is commercially available uses impedance – conductance (Malthus) (29). Growing bacteria produce alterations in the flow of alternating current as a consequence of their metabolism, and this is detected. The potential advantage of this method is that the electrical changes to be detected can be monitored 'on-line' (i.e. continuously), leading to very early detection of growth, but the currently-available equipment is expensive and cumbersome.

3. METHODS FOR THE EXAMINATION OF CEREBROSPINAL FLUID

3.1 **Introduction**

The correct examination of cerebrospinal fluid (CSF) is a vital task in any bacteriology department. Since bacterial meningitis is an uncommon disease, the bacteriologist must not only examine the specimen but also advise on the interpretation of the results, both bacteriological and biochemical. He should not recoil from offering unbidden advice on the preferred antibiotic treatment of this disease, as it may well be the first case which the junior medical staff on the ward have managed.

3.2 **Bacteriological aspects of specimen collection**

Adequate skin disinfection is important and liberal use of a suitable iodine-containing preparation followed by an adequate interval for drying is advisable. Separate specimens are preferable for biochemical and bacteriological analyses to avoid inadvertent contamination of CSF samples if tests are done in the wrong order. It is important to take the CSF into sterile 'one-use' containers (either disposable, or, if not, a container which has never been used before) since recycled sterilized containers may harbour debris from previous samples which can cause great confusion in stained smears.

Table 5. Procedure for microscopy of CSF, the total cell count.

Perform a total cell count on the uncentrifuged fluid using a Fuchs — Rosenthal counting chamber as follows.

1. Using a sterile glass Pasteur pipette add 1 drop lytic staining fluid (100 mg crystal violet, 1 ml glacial acetic acid, 50 ml water and 40 μl 5% w/v phenol) to 10 drops of CSF, and mix well.
2. Place a drop in the counting chamber and apply the cover slip, pressing firmly either side until an interference pattern appears.
3. Count the number of cells in the entire ruled area and divide this total by 3 to obtain the number of cells per mm^3 of diluted CSF (*Figure 4*). The slight error introduced by this approximation is small compared to dilution errors.
4. Attempt to make a differential count between polymorphs and lymphocytes on the fluid in the counting chamber. Since the staining fluid used should lyse red cells, the distinction between them and lymphocytes should be easy. However, ensure that the staining fluid used on each occasion is fresh or at least recently prepared, so that its lytic power is assured. A check on the validity of the differential count can be made subsequently on centrifuged material (*Table 6*).
5. If the CSF sample appears blood stained, or if the clinician indicates a suspicion of intracerebral haemorrhage, repeat the count on unstained CSF in order to count the number of red cells. In obviously blood stained CSF a useful shortcut is to ask the haematology staff to examine the specimen on a Coulter counter to count rapidly the red cells.
6. Note the apparent presence of any bacteria in the counting chamber, but be very wary of attaching too much significance to any suspicious particles seen. Small particles undergoing Brownian movement can look very similar.
7. Note also any debris in the specimen. The presence of occasional starch granules from gloves may indicate possible contamination.

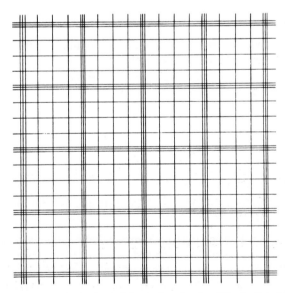

Figure 4. The ruled area of the Fuchs-Rosenthal counting chamber. The depth is 0.2 mm and the entire ruled area is 16 mm^2, the volume therefore being 3.2 mm^3.

3.3 Microscopy

Prior to microscopy the macroscopic appearance of the specimen should be noted, looking particularly for turbidity, blood-staining and xanthochromia, then the procedure described in *Tables 5* and *6* should be followed.

33

Table 6. Procedure for microscopy of CSF, the Gram stain and differential count.

1.	Place a small amount of the CSF into a sterile centrifuge tube or universal container and centrifuge at 1800 g for 10 min. Observe the appearance of the supernatant fluid before discarding, xanthochromia is easily seen.
2.	Use the sediment to make smears on three sterile, new glass slides. Never use cleaned old glass slides for CSF smears, since it is possible that previous material may still adhere and give rise to false-positive Gram stains. Several drops of sediment should be placed on one spot on the slide, each being allowed to dry before the next is added, thus concentrating any bacteria present.
3.	Gram stain the first slide, using 1% carbol-fuchsin as the counterstain (Appendix I); this increases the chances of staining small numbers of Gram-negative bacteria and examine carefully using a $\times 40$ objective and $\times 90$ oil-immersion objective. Note in passing the types of white blood cell seen, and be prepared to spend 5 min searching the whole of the stained area (which should preferably be circumscribed with a 'diamond' mark) before declaring the examination negative.
4.	Stain the second smear with Giemsa's stain and examine the deposit, noting the distribution of the different white blood cell types. Although this slide cannot be used to enumerate these cells, identification of the types is easy and the percentage distribution can be applied to the total count (from the counting chamber). If in doubt about the identity of the white blood cells, save the slide and have it examined by a haematologist or cytologist. Although unusual, leukaemic meningitis may still present with all the clinical appearances of bacterial meningitis. The demonstration of lymphoblasts in the CSF sample may be the initial diagnostic clue. Bacteria present in the film will be stained blue by the methylene blue and their morphology can be noted.
5.	Use the third smear to perform a stain for acid-fast bacilli (Appendix 1). Again, be prepared to spend 5 min searching the slide before declaring the examination negative.

3.4 Culture

(i)   Use the remainder of the centrifuged deposit to inoculate the following media:

    (a)   blood agar, to be incubated aerobically;

    (b)   heated blood (chocolate) agar plate, to be incubated in an atmosphere of 10% CO_2;

    (c)   blood agar, to be incubated anaerobically;

    (d)   place a few drops of the deposit into 2 ml of Brewer's medium or Brain Heat Infusion with 10% added sterile horse serum to provide an enrichment culture.

(ii)   Incubate all media at 37°C, examining the plates after overnight incubation and then daily up to 48 h.

(iii)   Incubate the broth for 48 h performing subcultures onto the range of media described at 24 and 48 h.

The three classical pathogens (*Neisseria meningitidis, Streptococcus pneumoniae, Haemophilus influenzae*) should be expected in most cases. However, no organism isolated from CSF should be disregarded. Although contaminants are possible, most commonly from the skin or plate contaminants, all isolates should be thoroughly investigated and fully identified before making a final report. Two particular traps are the following.

(i)   Coagulase-negative staphylococci (CNS) isolated from CSF should always lead to an appraisal of the patient and the clinical information. In children (and now some adults) with CSF shunt devices used in the management of internal hydrocephalus, CNS are the commonest infecting organisms. Do not be put off by the relative paucity of white cells in such CSF samples which is typical (30).

(ii) Never dismiss a coryneform rod in CSF as a 'diphtheroid' contaminant. *Listeria monocytogenes* can look very similar to a diphtheroid in Gram films and in culture on certain media, and all such bacteria should be checked (31). Simple tests such as the presence of β-haemolysis and ability to grow on Tellurite agar, together with 'tumbling motility' at room temperature should alert laboratory staff to this organism.

In infants, especially neonates, coliform bacilli and Lancefield Group B streptococci will be found, and rarely *Pasteurella* spp. Following neurosurgical operations, a wide range of organisms may be isolated, including *Staphylococcus aureus*, CNS, coliforms and fungi.

3.5 Additional tests

These fall into two categories.

3.5.1 *Tests on bacterial isolates*

Each isolate should be identified and typed as completely as possible. This is particularly important for isolates of *Neisseria meningitidis*, but also applies to the other two common pathogens. *Haemophilus influenzae* and *Streptococcus pneumoniae*. In most cases this will involve enlisting the help of a reference laboratory. The accumulation of such individual results on a national basis becomes very important in identifying trends in epidemiology and sensitivity, patterns which individual centres will never have sufficient data to detect.

3.5.2 *Tests on CSF*

The most popular additional tests applied to culture-negative CSF are those detecting bacterial antigens in the fluid. At least three different methods have been devised: counterimmune electrophoresis (CIE), co-agglutination (Phadebact® CSF Test; Pharmacia Diagnostics AB) and passive agglutination of latex particles sensitized with high-titre antiserum to capsular antigens. The latter two methods are much quicker than CIE and more convenient since they require little equipment, but CIE is more flexible as any source and range of antisera can be used. Little difference in sensitivity exists between the methods, but their usefulness can be questioned. Both false positive and negative results occur periodically so their use should be restricted to culture-negative specimens with some additional evidence of infection, such as pleocytosis.

3.6 Interpretation of the results

As previously mentioned, it frequently falls to the bacteriologist to collate the immediate results on CSF samples and to make an initial judgement on the likelihood of meningitis.

The classical interpretations of the three 'simple' tests, cell count, glucose concentration and protein, are shown in *Table 7*. It is important to bear in mind that these categories are but guidelines and that certain caveats must be applied.

3.6.1 *Cell count*

Whilst numerous polymorphs are usually observed in bacterial meningitis, infection

Table 7. Expected results of basic tests on CSF in the common forms of meningitis.

Type of meningitis	Cell count	CSF glucose	CSF protein
Bacterial	High, almost all polymorphs	Very low	Increased
Viral	Raised, almost all lymphocytes except first 24 h	Normal	Normal or slightly raised
Tuberculous	Raised, almost all lymphocytes	Low	Increased

of shunt devices with CNS does not always follow this pattern (32).

The classical lymphocytosis is not always present in viral meningitis. In the first 24 h of viral meningitis, polymorphs may be present, or the first CSF sample may contain no cells at all. In both cases, subsequent samples later in the illness will show the typical lymphocytosis.

3.6.2 *Glucose concentration*

It should be remembered that the CSF glucose 'normal range' refers to non-diabetic patients. A CSF glucose level well within this 'normal' range may be very abnormal in a patient with hyperglycaemia or hypoglycaemia. The microbiologist should insist on knowing the blood glucose level of the patient at, or near, the time of lumbar puncture before making any assessment of the CSF glucose concentration.

Occasionally, slightly low CSF glucose concentrations occur in severe viral meningitis, due often to Coxsackie virus infections. This, taken with a moderate number of polymorphs (see above), can cause confusion.

3.6.3 *Traumatic taps*

Sometimes the CSF sample is contaminated with a small amount of blood because the operator has damaged a tiny blood vessel during the puncture. There are two ways of resolving this problem. If possible, the operator can take two or three sequential samples. The later samples will contain less and less blood and the cell count can be performed on the second or third sample. Unfortunately, the taking of several samples is not always possible or desirable, for instance in small children. If only one (blood contaminated) sample is available, proceed as follows.

Perform a red cell count on the sample and then, using the lytic staining fluid (Section 3.3), count the white cells. Allow one white cell for an appropriate number of red cells, based on the peripheral blood count at the time. Subtract the 'allowed' number of white cells, approximately 1 per 500 red cells; if a significant excess of white cells remains, report that there is a pleocytosis in the CSF.

Note that in very small children the density of bacteraemia may be very high and the contamination of CSF samples with a small amount of peripheral blood may give rise to a positive CSF culture in the absence of true meningitis.

Table 8. Procedure for the diagnosis of tuberculous meningitis.

1.	On standing, the CSF from cases of TBM may form a very fine clot ('spider web coagulum'); use it after careful removal for the staining procedures.
2.	If the clot is not present, centrifuge the sample at 1800 *g* for 20 min and make ZN or auramine phenol stained films (Appendix I). Examine the film for a least 5 min before reporting it as negative.
3.	Use the remainder of the deposit to inoculate Lowenstein−Jensen's medium, pyruvate egg medium and Kirschner's liquid medium (Chapter 3, Section 3.3.2). A good method for the latter is to add the liquid to the remnants of the deposit in the specimen bottle, since mycobacteria may adhere to glass.
4.	CSF normally does not require any prior treatment before culture for TB. In those rare cases in which TB culture is justified in the presence of other organisms in the CSF, add 20 μl of 5% w/v H_2SO_4 to the deposit before inoculating the TB culture media. Allow 15−20 min for the H_2SO_4 to work.
5.	It is common for patients undergoing antituberculous therapy for TBM to have CSF collected several times during the course of treatment. Do not be alarmed to find that the lymphocytosis does not immediately resolve. It may rise in the first few days or weeks, although over a long period the pleocytosis does resolve with further fluctuations.

3.7 Tuberculous meningitis (TBM)

Clinicians periodically make enquiries to the laboratory about the diagnosis of TBM. They are, quite rightly, very concerned to exclude this life-threatening but treatable condition. However, the limitations in the laboratory diagnosis of this condition must be accepted (*Table 8*). The absence of acid-fast bacilli in a Ziehl−Neelsen smear of the centrifuged CSF deposit (or in a smear stained with auramine phenol and examined under UV light) does not exclude the diagnosis.

4. METHODS FOR THE EXAMINATION OF PERITONEAL DIALYSIS EFFLUENTS

Continuous ambulatory peritoneal dialysis (CAPD) is now an important therapy for end-stage renal failure, over 2000 patients being treated in the UK in 1984. Its major complication, and the one most likely to limit its usefulness, is peritonitis. Failure to control peritonitis is so serious that much effort is devoted to the investigation of this condition. Similar techniques can be applied to specimens received from patients undergoing intermittent peritoneal dialysis (IPD) for acute renal failure.

4.1 Definition of CAPD peritonitis

Peritonitis in CAPD is defined as:

(i) the presence of cloudy effluent with more than 100 white blood cells mm^{-3}, whether clinical symptoms (usually fever and/or abdominal pain) are present or not (33), or

(ii) the presence of organisms in the fluid together with abdominal pain (34).

In CAPD peritonitis the commonest finding is cloudy effluent (99%), then abdominal pain (96%). Systemic abnormalities are less common (fever 35%, leucocytosis 25%). Awareness of these clinical features is important in the laboratory because of the temptation at ward level to send samples of peritoneal dialysis effluent (PDE) from patients with non-specific symptoms but with no marker of CAPD peritonitis.

A firm attitude should be adopted, and only specimens taken from patients with either cloudy effluent or abdominal pain should be examined. Occasionally PDE samples will be cloudy due to fibrin or chyle (35), but in general a visually cloudy effluent is a good indication that excess white blood cells will be found on laboratory examination.

4.2 Sampling PDE

It is important to obtain an adequate sample. Ideally the whole bag should be examined, but this usually proves impracticable. A sample from the bag is obtained on the ward as follows:

(i)   Disinfect a portion of the wall of the bag or the port with alcohol, taking care to allow at least 2 min for the alcohol to dry and exert its effect.

(ii)   Collect at least 30 ml of fluid through the disinfected area using a needle and syringe, placing the sample into sterile containers with a careful aseptic 'no-touch' technique.

(iii)   In the event of any delay before the sample is sent to the laboratory, hold it at 4°C , but try to avoid the need for this.

4.3 Processing the sample

4.3.1 *Cell counts and culture*

Enumeration of the white blood cells will help to confirm a diagnosis of peritonitis. On a stained preparation a differential count is performed so that the presence of large numbers of eosinophils can be detected when present.

Gram stains will be positive in only 25−30% of PDE samples from which organisms are subsequently isolated. Nonetheless the simplicity and rapidity of the Gram stain, together with the value of the information gained when it is positive, make it well worthwhile.

In culturing PDE the laboratory is in a dilemma. Firstly, the number of bacteria may be as low as one colony-forming unit ml^{-1} (36) so that special techniques such as centrifugation, filtration, broth enrichment and pour plates will be required to maximize the detection rate. Secondly, all such methods involve extra manipulations and greatly increase the risks of contamination and false positive cultures.

A routine scheme for the examination of PDE samples is set out in *Table 9*. Using such a system the rate of positive cultures should approach 90%, although this figure will apply only to correctly taken and appropriate samples. Repeat samples taken during therapy of CAPD peritonitis should be discouraged unless there is clearly no clinical response to treatment or the effluent remains cloudy after 48−72 h of therapy.

4.3.2 *Additional techniques*

Several studies have suggested that although the viable count of organisms in PDE fluid is very low, substantial numbers of bacteria may be present within the polymorphs. Logically, lysis of the white blood cells might be expected to release these organisms, increase the viable count, detect additional organisms and, occasionally, lead to bacteria being detected when conventional methods are completely negative. At least two studies suggest that this is so (37,38). Lytic agents employed include Triton X and Saponin, both methods resulting in improved results; however increased contamination may occur.

Table 9. Routine bacteriological examination of PDE sample.

1.	Using an identical method to that in *Table 5* for CSF samples, perform a white blood cell count on the uncentrifuged sample.
2.	From the original sample of 30 ml take 20 ml and centrifuge at 1800 g for 10 min. From the spun deposit prepare 2 fixed smears. Perform a Gram stain on one and a differential white cell stain on the other (Appendix I).
3.	Using the remainder of the centifuged deposit inoculate two blood agar plates. Incubate one plate aerobically at 37°C for 72 h, examining it for growth at intervals. Incubate the second plate under anaerobic conditions, examining at similar intervals.
4.	An alternative method to (3) is to use filtration.
	(i) Filter the 20 ml of PD effluent through a bacteriological filter (0.45 μm, Millipore Corporation).
	(ii) Cut the filter into two halves using sterile scissors.
	(iii) Place one half of the filter on a blood agar plate for aerobic culture and the other half on a blood agar plate for anaerobic culture as in step 3.
5.	Inoculate the remaining 10 ml of PDE into a two blood culture broths (5 ml into each bottle), one of which should contain an anaerobic medium, and incubate both at 37°C.
6.	Observe the broths for signs of growth and subculture if present. In any case perform routine subcultures at 48 h and after 7 days, using identical media and conditions to step 3.

Acridine orange staining of films may detect intracellular bacteria when the conventional Gram film does not (39). Unfortunately, if subsequent culture cannot confirm the presence of the intracellular bacteria, the information may be of only limited value.

4.4 Interpretation of culture results

Gram-positive organisms (*Staphylococcus aureus*, CNS and, occasionally, diphtheroids predominate. Gram-negative bacilli ('coliforms') account for up to 25−30% of infections.

Identify the isolates as described elsewhere (Chapter 5). Most CNS will be *S. epidermidis* on further testing so the need for detailed identification is doubtful, but the API-Staph system or equivalent may be used.

Expect very little return on the anaerobic cultures but be assiduous in testing for these organisms. On the very rare occasions when faecal anaerobes, especially *Bacteroides* spp., are isolated, suspect perforation of the bowel, either by catheter trauma or as a consequence of intra-abdominal disease.

4.5 Sensitivity testing

Almost all CAPD units initially treat CAPD peritonitis with a limited range of intraperitoneal antibiotics. Common choices are cefuroxime, vancomycin and gentamicin (now, in some units, netilmicin), so these should be tested along with any locally preferred antibiotics.

4.6 Culture-negative peritonitis

Certain possibilities should always be considered when a cloudy PDE is culture-negative.

(i) Early morning effluents often have an increased white cell count (due to the longer overnight dwell time) in the absence of infection.

(ii) Intra-abdominal conditions such as cholecystitis, appendicitis, diverticulitis and

genital infections may produce an increased white cell count in the effluent.
(iii) Menstruation and ovulation may occasionally change the appearance of the effluent, usually due to bleeding.
(iv) Eosinophilic peritonitis is thought to be due to a hypersensitivity reaction to some component of the dialysis system. Suspect this when differential stain shows greater than 15% eosinophils. This condition is not an infection.

If despite all this there is genuine peritonitis but cultures remain negative, consider setting up cultures for unusual organisms. Atypical mycobacteria, *Mycobacterium tuberculosis*, fungi and parasites have all rarely been implicated in CAPD peritonitis. It is most likely, however, that culture-negative CAPD peritonitis is a case of infection with a common organism where the viable count is so low that the cultural technique is inadequate (40). Empirical treatment based on this assumption is usually successful.

5. METHODS FOR THE EXAMINATION OF SEROUS FLUIDS

Microbiology departments occasionally receive samples of serous fluid from a range of body sites. Common examples are ascitic, hydrocoele, pleural, pericardial and synovial fluids. Often these samples have been obtained for other purposes and the task of the bacteriology laboratory is to exclude the unlikely possibility of infection rather than confirm suspected sepsis. If serous cavities are obviously infected, the specimen received is almost always frank pus which should be investigated as outlined in Chapter 5. What follows is a simple system for the examination of fluid from serous cavities which is not pus.

5.1 Examination of non-purulent serous fluids

The scheme set out in *Table 10* can be used for all fluids, but individual sites require occasional extra emphasis.

Table 10. Routine bacteriological examination of non-purulent serous fluids.

1.	Using an identical method to that used for CSF (*Table 5*) perform a white blood cell count on the uncentrifuged sample. Since some fluids (particularly synovial fluid) can be very viscous, it may be necessary to make a preliminary 1 in 10 dilution in sterile isotonic saline and then multiply the observed count by 10.
2.	Centrifuge the remainder of the specimen at 2000 *g* for 15 min and discard the supernatant fluid.
3.	Using the spun deposit prepare 2 fixed smears. Perform a Gram stain on one and a differential white cell stain on the other.
4.	Using the deposit inoculate 3 heated blood (chocolate) agar plates. Incubate one aerobically, one anaerobically and the third in an atmosphere containing 10% CO_2, all at 37°C. It is usually helpful to inoculate also a plate of MacConkey's medium and incubate it aerobically at 37°C. Observe the plates for growth at intervals over 48 h.
5.	Using the remainder of the deposit, inoculate a liquid enrichment medium such as Robertson's cooked meat broth, and incubate it at 37°C. Observe for turbidity, subculturing on to the media described in step 4. In any case, perform routine subcultures at 48 h before discarding.
6.	If tuberculosis is suspected, prepare an additional smear to be stained for acid-fast bacilli and use some of the centrifuged deposit to inoculate the range of media described for the diagnosis of tuberculous meningitis (*Table 8*). It is unnecessary to decontaminate clear serous samples prior to examination for acid-fast bacilli.

5.2.1 *Pleural fluid*

Absolute numbers of white blood cells mm^{-3} are not a particularly valuable parameter in clear pleural fluid, but the differential stain may yield useful information. Lymphocytes and, occasionally, eosinophils suggest tuberculous effusions. It is not uncommon for smears from such conditions to be negative in these circumstances since they most commonly occur in primary tuberculosis. Pleural biopsy material may be more useful.

Detection of any unclassifiable or bizarre cell types should always suggest the possibility of malignancy and lead to the specimen being referred to a cytologist.

Very rarely an apparently hazy pleural fluid proves to contain chyle on microscopy (usually suspected in 'wet preparations') and should be referred for biochemical analysis.

5.2.2 *Pericardial fluid*

The same caveat regarding tuberculosis should be observed, and tissue from the pericardium is often necessary to adequately investigate suspected tuberculous pericarditis.

5.2.3 *Synovial fluid*

Although pyogenic infection of a joint almost inevitably produces a fluid of such purulence that formal cell counts are unnecessary, it is important to realize that many non-infective conditions (for instance, rheumatoid arthritis, crystal synovitis) will often produce cell counts in synovial fluid to 50 000 mm^{-3} or more (41). Intra-articular injections may also lead to high white cell counts in synovial fluid in the absence of infection.

6. REFERENCES

1. Bennett,I.L. and Beeson,P.B. (1954) *Yale J. Biol. Med.*, **26**, 241.
2. Werner,A.S., Cobbs,C.G., Kaye,D. and Hook,E.W. (1967) JAMA, **202**, 199.
3. Crowley,N. (1970) *J. Clin. Pathol.*, **23**, 166.
4. Minkus,R. and Moffet,H.L. (1971) *Appl. Microbiol.*, **22**, 805.
5. Rimmer,K. and Cabot,M. (1988) *J. Clin. Pathol.*, **41**, 676.
6. Staneck,J.L. and Vincent,S. (1981) *J. Clin. Microbiol.*, **13**, 463.
7. Roome,A.P.C.H. and Tozer,R.A. (1968) *J. Clin. Pathol.*, **21**, 719.
8. Waterworth,P.M. (1972) *J. Clin. Pathol.*, **25**, 227.
9. Lacey,B.W. (1957) Association of Clinical Pathologists, Broadsheet No. 81. British Medical Association, London.
10. Szawatkowski,M.V. (1976) *Med. Lab. Sci.*, **33**, 5.
11. Graves,M.H., Morello,J.A. and Kocka,F.E. (1974) *Appl. Microbiol.*, **27**, 1131.
12. Stokes,E.J. (1974) Association of Clinical Pathologists Broadsheet No. 82. British Medical Association, London.
13. Ganguli,L.A., Keaney,M.G.L., Hyde,W.A. and Fraser,S.B. (1985) *J. Clin. Pathol.*, **38**, 1146.
14. Youngs,G.R. and Roberts,C. (1985) *J. Clin. Pathol.*, **38**, 593.
15. Gould,J.C., and Duerden,B.I. (1983) *J. Clin. Pathol.*, **36**, 963.
16. Watt,B. (1983) *J. Clin. Pathol.*, **36**, 968.
17. Shanson,D.C. (1978) In *Modern Topics in Infection*, Williams,J.D., (ed.), Heinemann Medical, London, p. 14.
18. Waterworth,P.M. (1973) *J. Clin. Pathol.*, **26**, 596.
19. Munro,R., Collignon,P.J., Sorrell,T.C. and Tomlinson,P. (1984) *J. Clin. Pathol.*, **37**, 348.
20. Finn,A. (1985) *Br. J. Hosp. Med.*, **33**, 272.
21. McCabe,W.R. and Jackson,G.G. (1962) *Arch. Int. Med.*, **110**, 847.
22. Henry,N.K., McLimans,C.A., Wright,A.J. *et al.* (1983) *J. Clin. Microbiol.*, **17**, 864.

23. Roberts,R.B., Krieger,A.G., Schiller,N.L. and Gross,K.C. (1979) *Rev. Inf. Dis.*, **1**, 955.
24. Bouvet,A., Van de Rijn,I. and McCarty,M. (1981) *J. Bact.*, **146**, 1075.
25. Lennette,E.H. (1985) *Manual of Clinical Microbiology.* 4th edn, American Society for Microbiology, Washington.
26. Cowan,S.T. (1974) *Cowan and Steel's Manual for the Identification of Medical Bacteria.* 2nd edn, Cambridge University Press, Cambridge.
27. Spencer,R.C. (1988) *J. Clin. Pathol.*, **41**, 668.
28. Bradley,S.F., Wilson,K.H., Rosloniec,M.A. and Kauffman,C.A. (1987) *Infection Control.*, **8**, 281.
29. Johnston,H.H. (1983) *J. Clin. Pathol.*, **36**, 973.
30. Cohen,S.J. and Callaghan,R.P. (1961) *Br. Med. J.*, **2**, 677.
31. Cruickshank,R. (1975) In *Medical Microbiology.* Cruickshank,R., Duguid,J.P., Marmion,B.P. and Swain,R.H.A. (eds), Vol. II, Churchill Livingstone, Edinburgh, p. 385.
32. Dormer,A.E. (1966) In *The Therapeutic Use of Antibiotics in Hospital Practice.* Ridley,M. and Phillips,I. (eds), E & S Livingstone, Edinburgh and London, p. 147.
33. Gokal,R., Ramos,J.M. and Francis,D.A. (1982) *Lancet*, **ii**, 1388.
34. Pierratos,A. (1984) *Perit. Dialysis. Bull.*, **4**, 2.
35. Prowant,B.F. and Nolph,K.D. (1981) In *Peritoneal Dialysis* (Atkins,R.C., Thomson,N.M. and Farrell,P.C.). Churchill Livingstone, Edinburgh, p. 257.
36. Rubin,J., Rogers,W.A. and Taylor,H.M. (1980) *Ann. Intern. Med.*, **92**, 7.
37. Gould,I.M. and Casewell,M.W. (1986) *J. Hosp. Inf.*, **7**, 155.
38. Law,D., Freeman,R. and Tapson,J. (1987) *J. Clin. Pathol.*, **40**, 1267.
39. Beardsworth,S.F., Goldsmith,H.J. and Whitfield,E. (1983) *Lancet*, **i**, 348.
40. Spencer,R.C. and Fenton,D.A. (1984) *J. Hosp. Inf.*, **5**, 233.
41. Ward,J., Cohen,A.S. and Bauer,W. (1960) *Arthritis and Rheumatism*, **3**, 522.

CHAPTER 3

Bacteriology of the respiratory tract

LINDA BOOTH and J. ANDREW LOWES

1. INTRODUCTION

The bacteriology of the respiratory tract in disease is complicated by the abundant and varied commensal flora of the upper tract, such that unless special techniques are used, all respiratory tract specimens are contaminated with normal flora. Bacteriological examination, therefore, does not entail the listing of all organisms present together with their antibiotic sensitivities, which would be inappropriate and even misleading. Instead, the findings must be interpreted taking into account the method of specimen collection, the expected flora for a given site and the clinical history of the patient.

2. UPPER RESPIRATORY TRACT

2.1 The nose

The commonest bacterial lesion of the anterior nares is a boil and microbiological sampling of this is rarely necessary. Swabs from the anterior nares are most often taken to detect carriage of certain organisms, often for control of infection purposes, such as:

(i) *Staphylococcus aureus* in a patient or family suffering from repeated staphylococcal infections, or when there is a clustering of staphylococcal wound infections;

(ii) methicillin-resistant *S. aureus* (MRSA) when it has been detected in a patient or group of patients;

(iii) β-haemolytic streptococcus, Lancefield group A, when there is an outbreak of infection, for example on a maternity unit throat swabs will be taken as well;

(iv) *Corynebacterium diphtheriae* when it has been isolated from a throat or other swab from a patient. In these circumstances it is necessary to swab an individual patient with disease and individuals who have had close contact with the patient.

Nasal swabs have also been included in the surveillance screens performed in special 'at risk' groups, such as the immunocompromised patient or neonate. They rarely contribute much to patient management.

Table 1 gives the method of screening for carriage of MRSA. For the method of phage typing of staphylococci, see Chapter 11, Section 4.5.

2.2. The nasopharynx

2.2.1 Collection of specimens

Three types of specimen are taken from the nasopharynx.

(i) Post-nasal swabs—a cotton wool swab is placed through the mouth to the posterior wall, behind the uvula, and a specimen obtained by rubbing the swab against

Table 1. Method of screening for nasal carriage of methicillin-resistant *Staphylococcus aureus*.

1.	Moisten a cotton bud swab in sterile peptone water and collect a sample by rubbing the swab against the anterior nares, rotating the swab as this is done.
2.	Plate out the swab on to blood agar and a selective medium, such as mannitol salt agar (MSA).[a] A more selective plate may also be used: MSA containing 4 mg l^{-1} methicillin.
3.	After inoculating the plates, place the swab into an enrichment broth, such as Robertson's cooked meat with 10% added NaCl.
4.	Incubate plates for 18−24 h and 48 h at 37°C. Incubate MSA with methicillin plates at 30°C for 48 h.
5.	Incubate the enrichment broth for 18−24 h at 37°C and subculture onto blood agar plate, incubating this for 18−24 h and 48 h at 37°C.
6.	Examine plates and test presumptive staphylococcal colonies by performing a tube-coagulase[b] and DNase test (see Chapter 5, Section 4.1.4). *S.aureus* colonies on MSA are bright yellow on the pink medium because of the fermentation of mannitol.
7.	Test colonies for methicillin sensitivity by plating on to sensitivity medium with a 10 µg methicillin disc and incubating for 24−48 h at 30°C (see Chapter 7, Section 2.2.1).

[a]10µg tetracycline and gentamicin discs may be placed in the primary inoculum to help identify MRSA resistant to other antibiotics.
[b]Slide coagulase should not be performed directly from MSA.

the posterior wall. This is the most useful specimen for assessing carriage of meningococci for which the swab should be plated on to a selective medium used for *Neisseria gonorrhoeae* (Chapter 4, Section 4.1.). For the identification of meningococci see Chapter 4, Section 4.1.2.

(ii) Pernasal swabs which are used for the diagnosis of whooping cough, see *Figure 1*. Ideally the specimen should be plated out immediately or placed in specific *Bordetella pertussis* charcoal transport medium (1). A dry swab is most unlikely to permit survival of the fastidious pertussis organisms.

(iii) Nasopharyngeal aspirates, which are obtained via the nose using a fine-bore catheter attached to a sputum trap, to which suction is applied. These are usually used for the diagnosis of viral infections such as those caused by the respiratory syncytial viruses, but can also be used for isolation of *Bordetella spp*.

2.2.2 Laboratory diagnosis of B.pertussis and B.parapertussis

The diagnosis of whooping cough is usually made clinically, and negative bacteriology, particularly from a specimen taken late in the illness, does not exclude the diagnosis. The best chance of isolating *B.pertussis* or *B.parapertussis* is during the early catarrhal stage of the illness.

Traditionally, the culture medium used was Bordet−Gengou or a modification of it, but unfortunately the plates have a very limited shelf life of only about 5 days and so the medium is impractical for laboratories handling only small numbers of specimens intermittently. Charcoal cephalexin blood agar on the other hand has a shelf life of up to 8 weeks. The method for culture and identification of *B.pertussis* or *B.parapertussis* is given in *Table 2*.

Erythromycin and co-trimoxazole may be used to decrease the infectivity of clinical cases and for prophylaxis of unimmunized contacts. Disc sensitivity testing is not performed routinely because slow growth of the organisms makes it difficult to perform accurately.

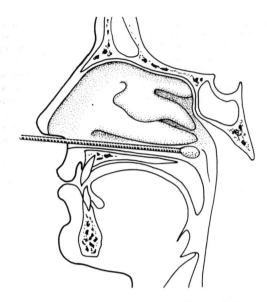

Figure 1. Collection of pernasal swab for isolation of *Bordetella* spp. Guide the swab on a flexible wire horizontally to the back of the nose. If obstruction is encountered, withdraw the swab and reinsert through the other nostril.

Table 2. Method for culture and identification of *Bordetella pertussis* or *B.parapertussis*.

1.	Plate the swab on to Charcoal Cephalexin Blood Agar, streaking out the first two quadrants with a swab and the later quadrants with a loop.[a]
2.	Incubate in a moist atmosphere at 35°C−37°C in air.
3.	Replace the pernasal swab into the transport enrichment medium (if used) and incubate similarly.
4.	Examine the plates for characteristic pearly colonies after 48 h and then daily for 5 days in total.[b]
5.	If the primary plate is negative at 48 h, reculture the swab from the enrichment medium and incubate as before.
6.	Keep the 'post-enrichment' plate for 5 days before discarding as negative.
7.	Gram-stain suspicious pearly colonies (round, smooth, shiny and domed) and examine under the microscope.
8.	Further identify small Gram-negative rods or coccobacilli by agglutination reactions as follows.
	(i) Place a drop of saline on a microscope slide.
	(ii) Pick off a colony from the plate with a wire loop and emulsify it in a drop of saline to produce a cloudy suspension. Then add a drop of appropriate antiserum.[c] Mix well and look for clumping (agglutination).[d]

[a]This is advised given the reduced surface area of the pernasal swab compared with a standard rigid swab.
[b]If fungal contamination is evident, a contaminated area of the agar may be carefully cut out to avoid further obliteration of the plate.
[c]Antisera for *B pertussis* and *B parapertussis* are available from the Division of Microbiological Reagent and Quality Control (DMRQC) of the Public Health Laboratory Service, London, UK.
[d]Occasionally autoagglutination may occur or equivocal reactions may be seen. Subculturing on to antibiotic free media may be helpful and encourage strains to become smooth. It has been suggested that the presence of cephalexin may result in poor development of the type-specific antigen.

2.3 The throat

Infections of the throat may be bacterial or, more commonly, viral in aetiology. The commonest bacterial cause is Lancefield group A β-haemolytic streptococcus

Table 3. Choice of media for culture of throat swabs.

Medium	Organism	Atmosphere	Length of incubation
Blood agar (non-selective)	β-haemolytic streptococci *Corynebacterium haemolyticum*[b] *C.pyogenes*[b]	Aerobic and anaerobic[a]	24–48 h[a]
Crystal violet blood agar (selective)[c]	"	Anaerobic	24–48 h
Tellurite[d] Tinsdale's[e] (selective)	*C.diphtheriae*	Aerobic	24–48 h

[a]The detection of group A β-haemolytic streptococci is enhanced by culturing under anaerobic conditions, using 48 h rather than 24 h incubation and by the use of selective media. However, some laboratories will choose to culture for only 24 h on non-selective media.
[b]For more information about the culture and diagnosis of *C.haemolyticum* and *C.pyogenes*, see another text (2).
[c]An alternative is Colistin, Oxolinic Acid, Blood Agar (see Chapter 11, Table 1).
[d]Colonies which convert tellurite to tellurium (*C.diphtheriae*) acquire a black or grey-black colour.
[e]Tinsdale's medium has been recommended for inexperienced workers. It results in brown haloes and a 'garlicky' smell with colonies of *C.diphtheriae*, *C.ulcerans* and *C.pseudotuberculosis*, but it has a limited shelf life and the brown halo lacks some specificity and sensitivity for *C.diphtheriae*.

(*S.pyogenes*), although groups C and G can also cause pharyngitis. Other bacterial pathogens are corynebacteria, namely *C.diphtheriae*, *C.ulcerans*, *C.haemolyticum*, and *C.pyogenes*. Only the first two produce diptheria exotoxin. *H.influenzae* Pittman type b may be isolated from the throat as the cause of acute epiglottitis but there is usually a concomitant bacteraemia and blood cultures should be taken also. For the diagnosis of *Haemophilus influenzae* infection, see Section 3.2.4.

N.gonorrhoeae may be found in the throat. Usually the patient is asymptomatic but pharyngitis can occur. Screening of throat swabs for gonococci is best confined to specimens from a genito-urinary medicine clinic, unless specifically requested by the clinician. For methodology see Chapter 4, Section 4.1.

2.3.1 Specimen collection and culture of throat swabs

Throat swabs are collected as follows.

(i) Take a cotton wool swab and, depressing the tongue with a spatula, direct the swab to the back of the throat with the other hand and swab the tonsillar area on both sides, rotating the swab as this is done.

(ii) Place the swab in bacterial transport medium if it is not be to plated out immediately.

Choice of media for routine culture of throat swabs is given in *Table 3*. Not all laboratories in the UK culture swabs routinely for *C.diphtheriae*. In those that do not, it is felt that diphtheria is such a rare infection in the UK that the expense is not warranted and they will only culture those swabs where there is some suspicion of diphtheria

Table 4. Culture and identification of β-haemolytic streptococci.

1.	Inoculate a blood agar plate and selective medium, if chosen, with the throat swab, rotating the swab as this is done.
2.	Plate out the swab over the 4 quadrants of the plate and place a Bacitracin ID (identification)[a] disc at the boundary between the inoculum and the second streaked quadrant.
3.	Incubate anaerobically overnight and if there are no suspicious colonies, see below, incubate for a further 24 h.[b]
4.	Look for colonies surrounded by complete clearing of the blood agar (i.e. β-haemolysis). Perform a Gram-stain to confirm that they are Gram-positive cocci. If such colonies appear to be giving a zone of sensitivity to Bacitracin they are 'presumptive' group A β-haemolytic streptococci. This may be reported to the clinician at this stage.
5.	Attempt a direct grouping procedure, such as latex agglutination (see Chapter 5, Section 4.1.4) if there is sufficient growth of the β-haemolytic streptococcus on the primary plate. If this can be done, the result may be reported at this stage.
6.	If there is insufficient growth, pick a β-haemolytic colony with a straight wire and inoculate a blood agar plate. Spread the plate with a loop.
7.	Perform a sensitivity test as described in Chapter 7. Penicillin, erythromycin and tetracycline are the usual antibiotics tested. Incubate this plate and the subculture plate aerobically.
8.	After overnight incubation take the purity plate and perform streptococcal grouping (see Chapter 5, Section 4.1.4). Report group A, C and G streptococci with sensitivities, where appropriate. For groups C and G, comment 'may cause pharyngitis'.
9.	Read and report penicillin and erythromycin sensitivity results. Tetracycline should never be reported for children or pregnant women.

[a]Group A streptococci can be provisionally identified by their sensitivity to bacitracin, but up to 5% of strains are resistant, and up to 15% of group C and G may be sensitive. This level of sensitivity and specificity may be acceptable for specimens from general practice in the absence of an outbreak, although many would prefer to formally group all β-haemolytic streptococci.
[b]Keeping primary culture plates for 48 h results in only a slightly higher yield and since small numbers of colonies may be indicative of carriage rather than infection, 24 h is usually adequate and more convenient.

clinically. The advantage of culturing all swabs is that unsuspected cases will not be missed and the expense can be reduced by using the same plate for several swabs by streaking each swab on a small section of the plate.

The methods for culture of throat swabs for β-haemolytic streptococci and *C.diphtheriae* are given in *Tables 4* and 5 respectively.

Kits are available commercially for detecting group A streptococcal antigen, all offering the advantage over culture of a result within an hour or so. Thus, in general practice a result could be available before the patient leaves the surgery. The C-carbohydrate from the cell wall is extracted from the swab which is then detected with antibody to the group A antigen. Antibody – antigen reaction is demonstrated by a variety of techniques, including latex agglutination and co-agglutination (see Chapter 5, Section 4.1.4). For further details, which vary with each kit, consult the manufacturers' literature.

There are two main methods of testing for the exotoxin of *C.diphtheriae*: guinea pig inoculation and the Elek plate (3). The first is performed only by reference laboratories in the UK. If *C.diphtheriae* is suspected it is therefore most important to involve a reference laboratory at an early stage. Not all strains of *C.diphtheriae* produce toxin, and laboratory efforts should be directed towards detecting toxin-producing organisms in the shortest possible time. The Elek plate method (*Figure 2*) is given in *Table 7*.

Table 5. Culture and identification of *Corynebacterium diphtheriae*.

1.	Plate out the swab[a] onto blood agar (to check quality of specimen collection) and tellurite medium and incubate overnight aerobically.
2.	Examine plates and Gram stain any black or grey-black colonies on the tellurite medium[b] and subculture any Gram positive rods on to Loeffler's slopes. It is advisable to test several colonies even if they appear identical. Reincubate negative plates for a further 24 h.
3.	Incubate slopes for 4−6 h in a 37°C waterbath, then prepare films from the growth and stain for metachromatic ('volutin') granules and bacillary morphology. Suitable stains are Loeffler's methylene blue, Albert's and Neisser's, of which the methylene blue stain is simplest to perform (see Appendix I).
4.	Look for pleomorphic organisms with barred or irregular staining and metachromatic granules, indicating *C.diphtheriae*.[c]
5.	Use some of Loeffler's slope culture for toxin (see *Table 7*) and biochemical testing as follows.

(i) Take some of Loeffler's slope culture with a wire loop and inoculate a range of Hiss's serum water sugars (Southern Group Laboratories) i.e. glucose, maltose, sucrose, trehalose, starch, and a urea slope.

(ii) Take a blood agar plate and place a nitrate-impregnated strip[d] of paper in the middle. Then stab inoculate with a straight wire some of the test culture from the Loeffler's slope and also a positive (e.g. *E.coli*) and negative (e.g. *Acinetobacter anitratus*) control, each approximately 1 cm from the strip.

(iii) Incubate the sugars, starch, urea and blood agar plate overnight in air and read the following day.

(iv) Positive results are shown by red coloration of the medium in the sugar and urea bottles, denoting acidification of the medium in the former and alkalinization in the latter. A positive nitrate reduction test is shown by a large greenish-brown zone of discoloration around the stabbed agar.

(v) For the expected biochemical reactions for the various subspecies of *C.diphtheriae*, see *Table 6*.

6.	Test for antibiotic sensitivity to penicillin and erythromycin as described in Chapter 7.

[a]A throat swab is the normal specimen, but if the diphtheritic membrane is in the larynx or anterior nares then specimens from these sites will be taken. Nose and throat swabs are sent from contacts in an outbreak. Cutaneous diphtheria occurs, especially in the tropics.
[b]The colonies of different subspecies may be characteristic, e.g. *gravis* are typically described as 'daisy heads' and those of *mitis* as 'poached eggs'. However, each laboratory should grow examples of the different strains on their own tellurite medium to become familiar with their characteristic appearances.
[c]Metachromatic granules are usually plentiful in *mitis* strains and scanty in *gravis* and *intermedius* strains. By contrast, non-pathogenic coryneforms tend to have regular morphology and granules are usually absent.
[d]Soak 16 mm wide strips of blotting paper in warm 40% w/v K_2NO_3. Dry in an incubator and autoclave in a glass Petri dish at 10 p.s.i. for 10 min.

2.3.2 *Identification of organisms causing Vincent's angina*

Vincent's angina is an uncommon bacterial infection affecting the mouth as well as the throat. It is a rapidly spreading, indurated cellulitis without abscess formation or lymphatic involvement, which begins in the floor of the mouth, involving the submandibular and sublingual spaces bilaterally. The infection is probably of dental origin in the majority of cases, and is caused by spirochaetes (*Borrelia vincenti*) and anaerobic fusiforms. Identification is made as follows.

(i) Stain a smear from a lesion on a microscope slide with carbol fuchsin or neutral red left for 2 min.

(ii) Examine the slide under the microscope and look for large numbers of fusiforms, red tightly coiled spirochaetes, and many pus cells.

Table 6. Biochemical identification of *Corynebacterium diphtheriae* subspecies, *C.ulcerans* and *C.xerosis*.

	Glucose	Maltose	Sucrose	Starch	Trehalose	Urea	Nitrate
C.diphtheriae (gravis)	A	A	$-^a$	A	–	–	+
C.diphtheriae (mitis)	A	A	$-^a$	–	–	–	$+^c$
C.diphtheriae (intermedius)	A	A	–	–	–	–	+
C.ulcerans	A	A	–	A^b	A^b	+	–
C.xerosis^d	A	A	A	A	–	–	+

A, acid
[a]Rarely, the sucrose may be fermented, producing acid.
[b]Should be read for up to 7 days.
[c]*mitis* strains which are nitrate-negative are referred to as *C.diphtheriae* var. *belfanti*.
[d]Can be distinguished from rare sucrose-positive *C.diphtheriae gravis* strains by the absence of haloes on Tinsdale's medium.

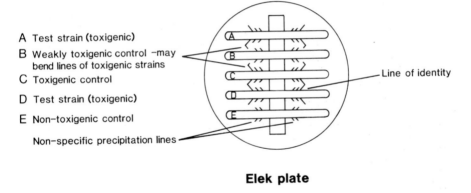

A Test strain (toxigenic)
B Weakly toxigenic control –may bend lines of toxigenic strains
C Toxigenic control
D Test strain (toxigenic)
E Non-toxigenic control

Non-specific precipitation lines

Line of identity

Elek plate

Figure 2. Elek plate method for the detection of toxin production by isolates of *Corynebacterium diphtheriae*.

The organisms may be found in small numbers in swabs from normal throats and mouths.

2.4 The ear

Ear swabs are amongst the least rewarding specimens microbiologically. This is partly because patients are often treated with numerous courses of systemic and topical antibiotics before the swab is taken, making it impossible to interpret the result because of the growth of organisms which would normally be considered secondary colonizers. Ear infections fall into three categories: those of the outer ear (otitis externa), those of the middle ear (otitis media), and those of the mastoid. In practice in the laboratory, all these specimens are handled in much the same way, often because the category is not obvious from the request form. However, it is reasonable not to include anaerobic culture for otitis externa, because anaerobes are uncommon pathogens.

Table 7. Elek method for toxin testing of *Corynebacterium diphtheriae*.

Requirements

1.   Test strain on a Loeffler's slope. More than one colony should be tested.
2.   Control toxigenic strain NCTC 10648 on a Loeffler's slope.
3.   Control weakly toxigenic strain NCTC 3984 on a Loeffler's slope.
4.   Control non-toxigenic strain NCTC 10356 on a Loeffler's slope.

Method (3)

1.   Heat 15 ml pre-prepared Elek's medium in a universal container until molten.
2.   Allow to cool to about 50°C and add 3 ml of sterile horse serum. Mix well and pour into a Petri dish.
3.   Take a strip of filter paper (Whatman's No 1 or No 3) 7 cm $\times$ 1 – 1.5 cm and immerse it in diphtheria antitoxin 500 – 1000 U ml^{-1}. Each new batch of antitoxin should be tested in advance to determine a suitable concentration.
4.   Place the strip across the medium before the agar has fully solidified.
5.   Allow the medium to solidify and then inoculate the test and control strains according to *Figure 2*. An alternative arrangement is Jamieson's modification (3).
6.   After 24 h incubation, examine carefully to detect 'lines of identity' produced when the toxin line (formed by toxin/antitoxin precipitation) of a positive test strain joins the toxin line of a positive control strain to produce an arch[a].

---

[a]If one of the adjacent toxin-producing strains produces toxin more slowly than the other, the arch may be asymmetrical. If a toxigenic strain is adjacent to a weakly toxigenic control, a complete arch may not be seen, but the weakly toxigenic control may cause toxin lines from the toxigenic strain to bend (see *Figure 2*). Non-specific lines may be seen on Elek plates, particularly if incubation is extended beyond 48 h. The toxin lines tend to appear earlier and are sharper.

2.4.1 *Specimens for otitis externa*

The following organisms may be pathogens in acute and chronic otitis externa: β-haemolytic streptococci, *Staphylococcus aureus* and *Pseudomonas aeruginosa*. The last is particulary important in malignant otitis externa, an invasive and necrotizing infection which may be fatal if not treated vigorously by surgery and systemic antibiotics. It usually occurs in the elderly diabetic patient. Milder infections are also seen in divers and users of whirlpool spas. The role of coliforms in chronic otitis externa is not at all clear, as they are usually present as secondary colonizers, particularly after antibiotics have been given. Otomycosis, commonly caused by *Aspergillus niger,* results in the characteristic 'wet newspaper' appearance inside the auditory canal. A method for culture of specimens from otitis externa is given in *Table 8*.

2.4.2 *Specimens from the middle ear and mastoid space following mastoidectomy*

Middle ear contents are only accessible in the event of spontaneous perforation of the eardrum or myringotomy. Rarely, middle ear fluid may be aspirated through the eardrum by tympanocentesis. In the absence of microbiological specimens, as is usually the case in acute otitis media, antibiotics are given on the basis of a knowledge of the common pathogens, which are β-haemolytic streptococci, *Haemophilus* spp., *Staphylococcus aureus* and *Branhamella catarrhalis*. The management of the chronically discharging ear can be a very difficult problem requiring local toilet, antibiotics or surgery. In this condition, an ear swab is the specimen usually received by the bacteriology laboratory. For the method of culture and selection of antibiotics, see *Table 9*.

Table 8. Method for culture of ear swabs from otitis externa.

1.	Inoculate a blood agar and MacConkey plate with the swab and incubate at 37°C aerobically overnight. A Sabouraud plate may be inoculated for yeasts and moulds, although many will appear on a blood agar plate reincubated for 24 h.
2.	Identify staphylococci (see Chapter 5), β-haemolytic streptococci (see *Table 4*) and *Pseudomonas* spp. (see Chapter 5). Note the presence of coliforms. Yeasts and moulds may be identified (4).
3.	Perform sensitivity tests as described in Chapter 7. Topical sensitivities are normally all that are required unless there is a severe infection of the pinna or a severe furuncolosis, in which case systemic antibiotics will be required. The list of topical antibiotics to test is given in *Table 9*.

Report the bacteria growing and their relative proportions. Report sensitivities as follows.

(i) Report topical and systemic sensitivities for *Staphylococcus aureus* and β-haemolytic streptococci. The systemic antibiotics will include penicillin and erythromycin for streptococci and these plus cloxacillin/flucloxacillin for staphylococci.

(ii) Report systemic sensitivities of *Pseudomonas aeruginosa* isolated from malignant otitis externa. These will include an aminoglycoside, antipseudomonal penicillin, ceftazidime and a 4-quinolone, e.g. ciprofloxacin. For uncomplicated pseudomonal otitis externa report topical sensitivities such as polymyxin and gentamicin.

(iii) For isolates other than the above withhold sensitivity results, unless there is a specific indication on the report form to release the information, or there is local agreement with ENT surgeons so to do.

The role of coliforms in chronic middle ear infections can be difficult to assess. It is normally impossible for those in the laboratory to distinguish between colonization of an underlying purulent discharge caused by another microbe (which may be responding to appropriate treatment) and primary infection or superinfection by such organisms. It is our practice to comment that 'the clinical significance of the isolate(s) cannot be assessed on laboratory findings alone' and invite the recipient of the report to discuss the result further with a medical microbiologist if the clinical problem persists.

2.5 The maxillary sinuses

Nose swabs are unsuitable for the investigation of sinus infections. Maxillary antrum wash-out specimens are sometimes received and should be centrifuged, Gram-stained and cultured as for middle ear specimens. Commonly isolated pathogens are pneumococci, *H.influenzae, Staph. aureus, B.catarrhalis* and anaerobes.

3. LOWER RESPIRATORY TRACT

3.1 Specimen collection

3.1.1 *Non-invasive methods*

Collection of expectorated sputum is the only non-invasive method of sampling lower respiratory tract secretions in disease. It is the sample most commonly sent to the laboratory but it is most important that the quality is good. Inevitably the sample will be contaminated with upper respiratory tract flora but, if the specimen has been expectorated, an attempt can be made in its processing to minimize the effects of contamination on the final interpretation. Sputum should be collected under supervision before starting or changing antibiotics, and ideally with the help of a physiotherapist. However, patients with exacerbation of chronic obstructive airways disease can usually produce a sputum sample representative of lower respiratory tract secretions. Patients

Table 9. Method of culture for specimens from otitis media and the mastoid space following mastoidectomy.

1.	Inoculate blood agar, chocolate agar, MacConkey plates and a selective and non-selective anaerobic plate with a swab and prepare a slide for Gram staining, although, if a single swab is received, there may be insufficient material for microscopy.
2.	Perform the Gram stain if sufficient material and comment on the proportions of different organisms and the quantity of pus cells, if present.
3.	Incubate the chocolate agar plate in CO_2 and the blood agar and MacConkey agar in air or CO_2. Examine the plates at 24 h and 48 h. Leave the anaerobic cultures undisturbed and examine at 48 h.
4.	The following colonies should be further identified: those resembling β-haemolytic streptococci, pneumococci, *Haemophilus,* staphylococci, *Branhamella*. (For β-haemolytic streptococci, see *Table 4*; for staphylococci, see Chapter 5; for pneumococci, see *Table 12*; for *Haemophilus* spp., see *Table 13; for Branhamella catarrhalis*, see Section 3.2.4.) It may be unnecessary to identify coliforms, pseudomonads and anaerobes unless the clinical information suggests that these may be important. Perform antibiotic sensitivities as described in Chapter 7. For potential pathogens (see Section 2.4.2) the appropriate systemic antibiotics should be tested.
	Topical sensitivities are often performed on all ear specimens, with antibiotics being chosen which are available as ear drops or ointments, e.g. chloramphenicol, tetracycline (broad-spectrum antibiotics but not appropriate for *Pseudomonas* spp.), framycetin[a], gentamicin[a], polymyxin (suitable for *Pseudomonas* spp.), neomycin[a] (suitable for staphylococci), and bacitracin (suitable for some streptococci and staphylococci). It is sometimes prudent to perform topical sensitivities on coliforms but to withhold this information from the clinician unless it is obviously of relevance.
6.	Report the organisms grown and their relative amounts. Systemic antibiotic and not topical sensitivities are required for acute otitis media. For chronic infections topicals are frequently used (although aural toilet is often all that is required). The exact choice of topicals reported is best agreed locally after discussion with ENT surgeons, particularly as patterns of usage vary considerably. If organisms such as β-haemolytic streptococci, pneumococci, *H.influenzae* are cultured from an ear with evidence of acute inflammation, systemic antibiotics should be used.

[a]Topical eardrops, especially potentially ototoxic aminoglycosides and polymyxin for prolonged periods of time, are controversial in the management of middle-ear disease, although ENT surgeons do use these preparations frequently with apparently no untoward effects. Of undoubted importance, however, is the emergence of resistant organisms when prolonged courses of topical antibiotics are used.

presenting in the early stages of pneumonia may not be able to produce a sputum sample and blood cultures should always be taken.

3.1.2 *Invasive methods*

Transtracheal aspiration is advocated in the USA but rarely performed in the UK. Although often helpful in establishing a microbiological diagnosis, effective clinical management is usually possible without this investigation, which may have serious complications in unskilled hands. The method involves inserting a cannula through the cricothyroid membrane into the trachea, thus bypassing the upper respiratory tract.

Biopsies, brushings and lavage specimens taken during bronchoscopy are usually contaminated by upper respiratory secretions carried into the lower tract by the bronchoscope. Local anaesthetic solutions are used to desensitize the airways and may constitute a large proportion of any aspirates. A bronchial brush enclosed within telescoping inner and outer catheters, the inner of which is plugged, is available for semi-quantitative culture of bronchial secretions and largely overcomes the problems of contamination with upper respiratory secretions if used by a skilled operator [Medi-Tech contamination-free microbiology specimen brush BFW/1.0/70/90, Key-Med (UK) Ltd].

3.2 **Routine microscopy and culture**

Some laboratories will discard specimens which are mucoid without pus on naked eye examination, but this may be unreliable. Most laboratories discard specimens which appear to be only saliva and request a further sample. There is great variation in the method of processing sputum and, because there is no clear consensus, the main methods are detailed below. Specimens should be processed as soon as possible after collection or refrigerated and processed later on the same day. All manipulations on lower respiratory tract specimens, because of the possibility of occult tuberculosis, should be performed in a Class I exhaust protective cabinet in laboratory of containment level 3.

3.2.1 *Specimen preparation*

Two schools of thought exist on the preparation of specimens prior to microscopy and culture: those that homogenize the sample and those that do not. Homogenization to reduce within-specimen sampling error is widely practised but some laboratories feel the extra labour is unjustified and it is better to pick purulent flecks of sputum. Both methods are given below. A method using *N*-acetyl-L-cysteine for homogenization is an alternative to the Sputasol method.

Homogenization

(i)   Add an equal volume of Sputasol (Oxoid Ltd) at working dilution to the specimen and mix.

(ii)   Shake the mixture well and place in a 37°C water bath. Incubate with periodic shaking until liquefaction is complete.

(iii) Plate out sample (*Table 11*) and make a thin smear on a microscope slide.

Direct sampling

(i)   Select a purulent fleck and tease out in sputum pot with a sterile swab.

(ii)   Inoculate plates (*Table 11*) and make a thin smear on a microscope slide.

3.2.2 *Microscopy*

A method for microscopy of sputum is given in *Table 10*.

Comparisons have been made between cultures of transtracheal aspirates and expectorated sputum, and on the basis of these it has been suggested that specimens with many squamous epithelial cells are heavily contaminated by oropharyngeal

Table 10. Method for microscopy of sputum.

1.	Make a thin film on a microscope slide and allow to dry in air, gently heat-fix and stain by Gram's method[a] (see Appendix I).
2.	Examine the film using 100 × magnification (10× eyepiece, 10× objective) and assess the number of squamous epithelial cells and polymorphonuclear leucocytes per low-power field in at least 5 representative fields and then take the average.
3.	Record the quantity of squamous epithelial cells and polymorphs as follows: 0 = 0, 10 = ±, 10−25 = +, 25 = ++ (5).
4.	Examine with high power oil immersion objective and concentrating on purulent areas of the slide, report the abundance and different morphological types of organisms seen (i.e. ±, +, ++, etc.).

[a]Counterstaining with safranin helps in the recognition of intracellular Gram-negative diplococci, particularly relevant because of the role of *Branhamella catarrhalis* in lower-respiratory-tract infection.

secretions. Criteria such as >25 or >10 squamous epithelial cells per low power field of a film prepared from neat sputum have been proposed as a basis for discarding such specimens without culture (5,6). It has been argued that if microscopic criteria are to be used for rejection of specimens, then those with <25 leucocytes per low power field should be discarded because they are unrepresentative of infected parts of the lower respiratory tract (7). However, there should be caution in introducing such a policy because specimens from some patients, such as those with neutropaenia, will not have pus cells and it is not always possible to obtain further specimens in a hurry from a severely ill patient. In order for this kind of policy to be effective, there needs to be good collaboration between clinicians and microbiologists.

3.2.3 *Specimen culture*

After preparation of the sample either by homogenization or direct sampling of purulent material (Section 3.2.1), the specimen is plated out on appropriate media:

(i)   blood agar for pneumococci, branhamella, staphylococci;
(ii)   chocolate agar for *H.influenzae.*

Some laboratories will prefer to use, besides blood agar, a more specific medium for *H.influenzae,* such as chocolate agar with $100-300$ mg l^{-1} bacitracin. Some laboratories use MacConkey agar to facilitate the recognition of *Enterobacteriaceae*, rare but important causes of pneumonia, most commonly hospital-acquired. Methods for sputum culture, which can also be used for endotracheal aspirates, are given in *Table 11*. Transtracheal aspirates can be cultured similarly, but anaerobic culture should be performed as well. Any anaerobes grown will usually be relevant because contamination with upper respiratory tract anaerobes is avoided, unless the catheter is dislodged into the oropharynx, which can happen because coughing is often induced.

Semi-quantitative culture results have been used as one measure of response to treatment of patients with chronic suppurative chest infections (such as cystic fibrosis), along with clinical parameters like temperature, weight gain, and decrease in sputum volume. This is particularly relevant when eradication of infection is not a realistic objective, but a decrease in the microbial load may slow further deterioration of lung function.

3.2.4 *Recognition and identification of isolates*

The main pathogens in lower respiratory tract infections are *Streptococcus pneumoniae, Haemophilus influenzae, Branhamella catarrhalis* and rarely *Staphylococcus aureus.* Members of the Enterobacteriaceae, notably *Klebsiella pneumoniae* and also *Pseudomonas aeruginosa,* can be respiratory pathogens but the recognition and identification of these is dealt with in Chapter 6. The recognition and identification of *S.aureus* is dealt with in Chapter 5 and thus the other three will be described here.

Streptococcus pneumoniae cultured on blood agar in 5% CO_2 overnight produces 0.5 mm round translucent or mucoid colonies with an entire edge, which are initially domed but later partially collapse (due to autolysis) to form the characteristic draughtsman-shaped colony, surrounded by a zone of α-haemolysis (greening of the agar surrounding the colony). Some strains are very mucoid, particularly capsular serotype 3. On microscopy Gram-positive lanceolate diplococci are seen which may

Table 11. Methods for sputum culture.

General method

1. Inoculate appropriate media with a purulent portion of sputum using a swab or with a sterile standard loopful of homogenate (see Section 3.2.1). Using a sterile loop, streak out in 3 further areas, sterilizing the loop after streaking into each area and using the whole plate in a uniform manner to allow relatively standardized reporting.

2. Place an optochin identification disc (which inhibits the growth of pneumococci and aids in their identification) at the junction of the initial inoculum and the first set of streaks on the blood agar plate.[a]

3. Similarly place a bacitracin disc (8 U) on the surface of a chocolated blood agar plate (if a selective medium for haemophilus is not used) to inhibit the growth of Gram-positive organisms.

4. Incubate the plates overnight in CO_2. (The blood agar plate may be incubated in air.) Reincubate if there is no growth. Note the quantity of suspect colonies i.e. pneumococci, *Haemophilus* and *Branhamella*, on the report form.

Semi-quantitative method[b]

1. Plate out 10 μl loopful (standard loop) of an homogenized sputum specimen on one half of a blood agar and chocolated blood agar plate. Mix another 10 μl with 10 ml of phosphate buffer saline. Mix on a vortex mixer and plate out a 10 μl loopful on the other half of each plate.

2. Incubate overnight in CO_2 and read the plate the next day. Reincubate for a further 24 h and re-examine the next day if no growth has occurred, the patient is on antibiotics, or organisms seen on the Gram film have not grown.

3. 500 colonies from the 10 μl loopful of homogenate (i.e. initial dilution) corresponds to 10^5 organisms ml^{-1} in the original specimen. 500 colonies from the 10 μl of diluted homogenate corresponds to 10^8 organisms ml^{-1} in the original specimen.

4. Note quantity of suspect pathogens on the report form.

[a]Some workers recommend the use of a staphylococcal streak on the primary blood agar plate to aid recognition of *Haemophilus* because of its satellitism. However, on highly nutritional agar, such as Columbia agar base, satellitism may not occur, but with other agars organisms other than *Haemophilus* may show satellitism.
[b]This is also appropriate for specimens collected using a microbiological specimen brush at bronchoscopy (3.1.2).

be capsulated. The identity of such colonies is confirmed by an optochin sensitivity or a bile solubility test, as shown in *Table 12*.

Haemophilus spp. on Gram-staining are pleomorphic fine Gram-negative rods. They have requirements for growth, called X and V factors (the former is haemin and the latter NAD). Depending on the species, the requirement is for one or other of these factors or both, as in *H.influenzae*. X factor is contained in blood and V factor is released from red cells when blood is heated in the production of chocolate agar. V factor is also produced by *Staphylococcus aureus*. *Haemophilus* spp. may be provisionally identified by satellitism around a staphylococcal streak on a blood agar plate, and by enhanced growth on a chocolated blood agar. It is, however, a variable phenomenon depending upon the blood agar used; if the V factor content is high, neither phenomenon may be observed. Some corynebacteria and streptococci also satellite, so a Gram stain should be performed to exclude these. *H.influenzae* on chocolated blood agar after 24-h incubation forms $1-2$ mm greyish smooth semi-opaque flat convex round colonies with an entire edge and a characteristic smell. *H.parainfluenzae* forms flat grey semi-opaque colonies with a smooth, rough or wrinkled surface up to 3 mm in diameter. Its role in respiratory tract infection is not yet clearly defined. Confirmation of identity of

Table 12. Methods for the indentification of *Streptococcus pneumoniae*.

A. *Optochin sensitivity test*

1.   If a disc method of sensitivity testing for pneumococci is being used, place an optochin identification disc on the sensitivity plate.
2.   Incubate in CO_2.
3.   A zone of growth inhibition of diameter > 14 mm confirms the identification of a pneumococcus; strains with smaller zones should only be identified as pneumococci if bile-soluble.

B. *Rapid bile-solubility test for presumptive identification*

1.   Touch a loop charged with 2% solution of sodium deoxycholate (pH 7.0) on to a suspect colony on a blood agar plate.
2.   Incubate the plate at 37°C for 30 min.
3.   Observe lysis of the colony if it is a pneumococcus, leaving a zone of α-haemolysis at the site of the colony.

N.B. For these tests use *S.pneumoniae* as a positive control and *S.faecalis* as a negative control.

Table 13. Method for identification of *Haemophilus* spp.

1.   Inoculate evenly 1 or 2 colonies of the strain to be identified with a swab over half the surface of a plate of blood agar base without blood, then turning through 90° inoculate over half the plate again until the whole plate is covered.
2.   Apply discs containing X factor alone, V factor alone and X and V factor together to the surface, about 1 cm in from the edge and equally spaced at 4, 8 and 12 o'clock.
3.   Incubate overnight at 37°C in CO_2, or for up to 48 h if necessary.
4.   Record the growth around the discs. *H.influenzae* is both X- and V-dependent and grows only around the combined XV disc. *Haemophilus* spp. growing around the combined XV disc and the V disc require V factor and include *H.parainfluenzae*.

Haemophilus spp. in the routine laboratory is most usually performed by testing for X and V factor dependence. The method is given in *Table 13*.

Unfortunately blood agar base used for identifying *Haemophilus* spp. varies in its X and V content and also the growth factors can diffuse widely in the agar which can cause erroneous results, for instance *H.influenzae* may be misidentified as *H.parainfluenzae*. The latter problem can be overcome partially by cutting ditches in the agar between the discs, and the former by quality-controlling each batch of medium and sets of discs used with known strains. Tests for the lack of ability to utilize δ-amino-laevulinic-acid for porphobilinogen synthesis (X factor dependence), and an absolute need for V factor tested by detecting growth around a V factor disc on blood agar chocolated by autoclaving to remove all V factor from the medium are recommended for definitive identification (8).

Branhamella catarrhalis is a Gram-negative diplococcus. Unlike *Neisseria* spp., it will grow on unenriched media such as nutrient agar. Colonies are non-haemolytic on blood agar, 0.5−1.0 mm diameter, grey, opaque and smooth. Basic tests for confirmation that should be performed are Gram stain, oxidase, growth on nutrient agar at 35°C and a tributyrin test (butyrate esterase) (9), see Chapter 4, Table 4.

3.2.5 Antimicrobial sensitivity testing

Direct (primary) sensitivity testing with sputum specimens is generally not recommended because it is difficult to control the inoculum. However, direct inoculation of sensitivity plates may be worthwhile if the Gram stain is suggestive of staphylococcal or Gram-negative pneumonia in a patient who is seriously ill, although the tests may need to be repeated.

The following scheme of sensitivity testing is suggested.

(i)   *Streptococcus pneumoniae*: benzylpenicillin, erythromycin and tetracycline.

(ii) *Haemophilus influenzae*: ampicillin, trimethoprim, tetracycline and test for β-lactamase production by nitrocefin test or equivalent (see Chapter 7, Section 2.4.3).

(iii) *Branhamella catarrhalis*: ampicillin, erythromycin, tetracycline and test for β-lactamase production by nitrocefin test or equivalent (see Chapter 7, Section 2.4.3).

If more than one of these organisms are isolated from the same patient with chronic obstructive airways disease, it is sensible to perform and report the same sensitivities of each, testing additional agents if necessary.

Other organisms which may require sensitivity testing, although their isolation is not necessarily significant, are *Staphylococcus aureus*, coliforms and *Pseudomonas aeruginosa*. These may be tested for susceptibility to the following antimicrobials.

(i)   Coliforms: cefuroxime, cefotaxime, gentamicin and ciprofloxacin.

(ii) *Pseudomonas aeruginosa*: gentamicin, azlocillin, ceftazidime and ciprofloxacin.

(iii) *Staphylococcus aureus*: see Chapter 5, Section 4.1.5.

If it is decided to test for amoxycillin/clavulanate and a disc test is used, a low content disc (3 μg) should be selected. This is to detect *H.influenzae*, which will not respond to conventional doses of amoxycillin-clavulanate but will appear falsely sensitive if a high content disc is used. However, such strains will be detected if low content ampicillin discs (2 μg) are used, and they will be found not to produce β-lactamase when tested—therefore it can be assumed that they are amoxycillin/clavulanate-resistant.

3.2.6 *Interpretation and reporting*

If media are inoculated and plated as described in Section 3.2.3, reporting for sputum specimens can be standardized as follows.

(i)   Disregard growth of a potential pathogen in the first and second quadrants.

(ii) Report growths of 5 or more colonies of potential pathogens in the third quadrant as $+++$.

(iii) Report growths of 5 or more colonies of potential pathogens in the fourth quadrant as $++++$. However, a flexible approach is essential, and on occasions low numbers of organisms may be reported. If the specimen was cultured semi-quantitatively, report all potential pathogens present in concentrations of 10^5 ml^{-1} or greater and their approximate numbers per ml. Growths of 10^5-10^6 pneumococci ml^{-1} may be significant, but 10^6 pneumococci ml^{-1} or greater correlates well with blood culture results when they are positive.

(iv) Report no growth if there is no bacterial growth.

The main pathogens are *Streptococcus pneumoniae* and *H.influenzae* and sensitivities of these should be reported if they are present in significant numbers. Growths of

Staphylococcus aureus, β-haemolytic streptococci (with their Lancefield group, see Chapter 5, Section 4.1.4), coliforms and *Pseudomonas aeruginosa* in 'significant' numbers may be reported. Predominant growths of *Branhamella catarrhalis*, if found in conjunction with intracellular Gram-negative diplococci in pus cells on microscopy, should be reported with antibiotic sensitivities. The significance of these isolates will vary and is more likely to be important if they are grown from uncontaminated specimens (see Section 3.2.2). Antibiotic sensitivities should be performed, but it may be best not to report them unless something is known of the clinical circumstances.

Fungi such as *Cryptococcus neoformans*, *Aspergillus* spp. and *Candida* spp., may cause lower-respiratory-tract infections, almost always in immunocompromised patients. For details of culture and identification the reader is referred to another text (4).

The key to improving the quality of sputum reports is to improve the quality of the sample. When samples are collected by interested investigators, results of sputum culture correlate closely with those of transtracheal aspirates. A selective approach to sputum culture based on rejection of samples on criteria based on microscopy has led to some improvement in the quality of specimens sent to the laboratory (10).

3.3 Special microscopy and culture

3.3.1 *Culture of specimens for patients with cystic fibrosis*

This is an example where semi-quantitative culture may be used to good effect (see Section 3.2.3). The main pathogens in cystic fibrosis are *Staphylococcus aureus*, *Haemophilus influenzae*, *Pseudomonas aeruginosa* and in the late stages of disease *P.cepacia*. Sometimes the growth of *P.aeruginosa* swamps other pathogens, necessitating selective culture techniques for the isolation of *S.aureus* and *H.influenzae*. Co-trimoxazole may have been used in therapy, and as a consequence thymine- or thymidine-dependent variants may have been selected (11). This may happen in conditions other than cystic fibrosis. For the isolation of *S.aureus* from a patient with cystic fibrosis, sputum may be inoculated on to a selective plate, such as mannitol salt agar (MSA), and incubated for at least two days in air. MSA should be tested for its ability to support the growth of thymine- or thymidine-dependent strains. These grow on blood agar, but may not be recognized because they grow slowly and display unusual and varied colonial morphology. In addition, they are often 'slide coagulase' negative. Clues to their presence are clusters of Gram-positive cocci seen on Gram stain which fail to be recognized on culture, or *S.aureus* which grows on primary isolation media but not on thymidine-deficient sensitivity testing media.

The isolation of *H.influenzae* may be particularly difficult from the sputum of patients with co-existing colonization with *P.aeruginosa*, and a selective medium containing Oxoid blood agar base no. 2, 1 litre; Haemin (BDH Ltd), 3 mg; and pure bacitracin, 300 mg can be used. A V factor disc is placed in the centre of the second set of streaks and the plates incubated anaerobically (12).

3.3.2 *Microscopy and culture for mycobacterial infections*

Clinical tuberculosis in the UK is caused by *Mycobacterium tuberculosis*, or very rarely *M.bovis*. Other mycobacteria such as *M.kansasii*, *M.xenopi*, *M.avium-intracellulare scrofulaceum* (MAIS complex) and *M.malmoense*, may be associated with pulmonary

Table 14. Preparation of specimens for microscopy for acid-fast bacilli (AFB).

1.	If the specimen is sputum, use a neat or homogenized sample (Section 3.2.1).
2.	If pleural fluid, centrifuge at 2000 *g* for 30 min and examine the deposit.
3.	If tissue, either
	(i) grind in a cotton-wool plugged Griffith's tube with a small volume of sterile saline and disrupt cells by vibrating with glass beads over a vortex mixer[a], or
	(ii) homogenize in a stomacher machine by placing specimen in a plastic bag, sealing it and then placing in another plastic bag.[b]
4.	Prepare smears in the usual fashion, heat-fix on a hot plate, preferably inside the cabinet.

[a]The container must be sealed. Do not allow fluid to swirl up to the top of the container. Wait before opening the specimen in a safety cabinet so that aerosolized particles may settle first.
[b]The specimen must be double-bagged, as splitting may occur.

disease. The MAIS complex is a significant cause of opportunistic infection in patients with the Acquired Immune Deficiency Syndrome. The non-tuberculous infections are referred to as 'mycobacterioses'.

Sputum is the specimen most often sent from the respiratory tract for mycobacterial examination. Early morning specimens are the best because secretions which have pooled overnight in the bronchi are likely to yield the greatest number of bacteria. If the patient is unable to produce sputum, specimens may be collected by bronchoalveolar lavage using a bronchoscope. Pleural fluid and tissue specimens from the respiratory tract may also be obtained. The methods for preparation of specimens of microscopy is given in *Table 14*. Considerable care is required when working with clinical material likely to contain mycobacteria, and specimens should be handled in containment level 3 accommodation. Every laboratory should issue clear instructions for the safe testing of specimens and the following precautions should be taken (13).

(i)   Workers should wear disposable gloves and a gown.

(ii)   All testing must be performed in an approved Category 3 safety cabinet.

(iii)   Disposable loops should be used to avoid spluttering of aerosols created by flaming a loop.

(iv)   Bunsen burners should not be used, unless shielded (Denley) because they disturb the pattern of air circulation through the cabinet.

(v)   Sealed bucket centrifuges should be used and sealed buckets containing the specimens should be opened only inside the safety cabinet.

Slides may then be subjected to staining by the auramine or the Ziehl – Neelsen method (Appendix I). Both utilize the fact that mycobacteria resist decolorization after staining with an arylmethane dye. Auramine staining is recommended for testing large numbers of specimens because a low-power objective is used and permits a larger field of the slide to be examined in the same period of time. Any positives by this method are confirmed by overstaining with Ziehl – Neelsen and examining under oil immersion. The Ziehl – Neelsen method entails heating slides during staining. A variant of this, using Kinyoun's carbol fuchsin (Appendix I) requires no heating and is therefore more convenient. The inclusion of a positive control slide for all methods is indicated for each new batch of stain.

With carbol-fuchsin-based stains, acid-fast bacilli (AFBs) appear red against a blue,

Table 15. Reporting microscopy results when AFBs are seen.

No. of bacilli	Report
0 per 300 fields	Negative for AFB
1−2 per 300 fields[a]	±
1−10 per 100 fields	+
1−10 per 10 fields	++
1−10 per field	+++
10 or more per field	++++

[a]The detection of single bacilli needs very careful consideration. Repeat smears should be prepared and additional specimens obtained if possible.
N.B. Environmental mycobacteria may be present if a specimen container has been washed with tap water.

turquoise or green background, depending on the counter-stain. Only a very experienced worker may be able to detect morphological characteristics which suggest a particular species of mycobacteria, and therefore it is prudent to report only 'acid-fast bacilli seen' together with an index of quantitation. Positive smear results on new patients should be telephoned to the clinician. Microscopy is obviously less sensitive than culture for detecting AFBs and it has been estimated that $5000-10\,000$ bacilli ml^{-1} of sputum are required for positive microscopy. By comparison, $10-100$ AFBs ml^{-1} of sputum may be detected by culture.

When culturing for mycobacteria, it is necessary to minimize overgrowth by contaminants, as mycobacteria are slow-growing. Sputa and post-mortem specimens are treated to remove as many contaminants as possible without prejudicing the survival and growth of mycobacteria. The most common treatment used is sodium hydroxide, and following treatment with this the specimen can either be 'neutralized' by dilution in distilled water or phosphate buffer incorporating a pH indicator such a phenol red, or alternatively the alkalinized specimen can be inoculated onto acidic media. This last procedure, devised by Marks (14), is popular because of its simplicity, and was originally introduced as a method suitable for small laboratories lacking suitable facilities for centrifugation. Other treatments for decontamination are trisodium orthophosphate, which is suitable for lightly contaminated specimens but requires overnight incubation, or sulphuric acid (15), which is suitable for heavily contaminated specimens but is less widely used than sodium hydroxide. Pleural fluids and surgical biopsies are not usually heavily contaminated, and if overnight culture for non-mycobacterial organisms is negative they can be inoculated directly onto neutral media.

The media most often used for mycobacterial work are egg-based, e.g. Löwenstein-Jensen or the Zaher and Marks' modification, acid egg medium (16) in which the phosphate and malachite green concentrations have been changed. Penicillin may be added if the decontamination procedure has not been successful. Some mycobacteria can be inhibited by glycerol, and for *M.bovis* isolation, media should be formulated without glycerol but with added pyruvate. The media are poured as slopes in universal bottles with screw caps to prevent dessication. A liquid medium (Kirshner's) is available which has the additional advantage of being suitable for very small fluid specimens.

The minimum basic method for a laboratory should be the inoculation of alkaline-decontaminated specimens onto acidic media. For specimens which cannot be repeated

Table 16. Method of sputum culture for mycobacteria.

1.	Add an equal volume of 4% NaOH to the specimen and mix at least twice (or continuously on a mechanical agitator) for 20 min.
2.	Inoculate 0.2 ml on to 2 acid egg slopes (4.5 ml of medium per slope) with and without pyruvate and incubate at 37°C.
3.	Examine all cultures weekly. Discard any overgrown with contaminants and set up repeat cultures if possible. Send a report to the clinician requesting further specimens if no clinical material was stored.
4.	If there is a positive culture[a], record whether growth occurs differentially on pyruvate- and non-pyruvate-containing media, the period of incubation and pigmentation, if any.
5.	Perform a Ziehl−Neelsen stain[b], noting if colonies are difficult to emulsify, which is characteristic of *M.tuberculosis*.
6.	If any acid-fast bacilli are demonstrated send out a report but do *not* specify *M.tuberculosis*, even if morphology, etc., is typical.[c]
7.	Extend the incubation period if no growth is apparent at 8 weeks but acid-fast bacilli were seen in the smear for the original specimen. (*M.malmoense* may take up to 12 weeks to grow.)
8.	Subculture any positive isolates on to neutral slopes and send cultures to the local reference laboratory.

[a]Colonies of *M.tuberculosis* are not likely to be visible for 2 weeks and may take up to 8 weeks or so to appear. They are typically buff-coloured, dry and may resemble breadcrumbs.
[b]*M.tuberculosis* typically are evenly stained bacilli, regular in length and may be arranged as serpentine cords.
[c]It is important to notify all new 'culture positive, smear negative' isolates by telephone, as the report is commonly only available after the patient has been discharged and reports may go astray.

Table 17. Method of culture for acid-fast bacilli of tissue, pleural fluid, swabs and pus.

1.	Take tissue and fluid specimens as prepared for microscopy, i.e. homogenized tissue or centrifuged deposit from a fluid. Immerse swabs in 5 ml of 2% NaOH in a universal container for 20 min and treat 'contaminated' pus specimens as for sputum.
2.	Inoculate 0.2 ml of akalinized specimens onto slopes (4.5 ml of medium per slope) as for sputum. Rub treated swabs over acid slopes ensuring a generous inoculum, as a volume of 0.2 ml is optimal to give correct neutralization.
3.	If bacterial contamination is unlikely, as in fresh tissue and pleural fluids, inoculate a pair of neutral LJ slopes (with or without pyruvate) using approximately 0.2 ml.
4.	For specimens which are difficult to repeat e.g. tissue, inoculate Kirschner's medium containing antibiotics (the volume of the inoculum is less critical than for acid egg slopes and may be very small). If the specimen is large, store a small portion at −20°C so that repeat cultures can be set up in the event of contamination of the original cultures.
5.	Incubate all cultures as for sputum and examine in the same way (*see Table 16*).

easily, such as biopsies, they should be inoculated onto acidic or neutral slopes according to the need for a decontaminating procedure, together with Kirschner's medium if there is sufficient specimen. In addition, any remaining specimen may be stored for two weeks to permit repeat cultures to be performed in the event of overgrowth.

The method for sputum culture is given in *Table 16* and for other respiratory specimens in *Table 17*.

Previously a large number of laboratories in the UK, isolating acid-fast bacilli, attempted to perform further identification and sensitivity tests but quality control results were unsatisfactory. Thus the decision was made to centralize the further investigation of mycobacteria to specially designated reference laboratories. The identity of *M.tuberculosis* is confirmed by a lack of pigment production, failure to grow at 25°C and sensitivity of *p*-nitrobenzoic acid. Sensitivity testing for slow-growing organisms requires special methodology which has evolved differently in different countries. The method used in the UK is a modification of the resistance ratio method in which the 'mode' resistance of a number of wild strains is regularly determined. The behaviour of the test strain is then interpreted in relation to this mode. This has been validated by the correlation between *in-vitro* results and *in-vivo* therapeutic response.

Recently a totally new approach to mycobacterial work has been used with success. In 1977, Middlebrook devised a radiometric method whereby the detection of ^{14}C-labelled CO_2 released by metabolism of ^{14}C-labelled palmitic acid indicated viable mycobacteria. The system is commercially available (BACTEC®), see Chapter 2, Section 2.3.1, and its advantage is that it may detect growth earlier than is possible by conventional methods. It has also been adapted for use in identification and sensitivity testing. The system is more expensive than conventional methods and is obviously most appropriate for laboratories using the BACTEC® system for blood cultures. For these reasons its use has been rather limited.

3.3.3 *Special culture for actinomyces and nocardia*

Actinomyces israeli may cause a chronic pulmonary infection which can present like tuberculosis with cavitation, or malignancy. The diagnosis is often unsuspected until sinus formation occurs (see Chapter 5, Section 4.5.3). *Nocardia asteroides* may also cause chronic pulmonary infection or, occasionally in immunocompromised patients, an acute infection with rapid dissemination to other organs. For a culture method, see *Table 18*.

3.3.4 *Special microscopy and culture for Legionella spp.*

Legionella pneumophila causes between 1% and 15% of cases of pneumonia (17). The standard method of diagnosis in most laboratories has been the indirect immuno-fluorescent antibody test on paired sera, but this is by nature a retrospective diagnosis. Direct immunofluorescent examination of respiratory tract specimens is less often performed. Non-cultural methods are discussed in Section 3.4.

Table 18. Method of microscopy and culture for *Nocardia* spp.

Microscopy

Perform a Gram stain on the specimen and look for branching Gram-positive rods.

Culture

1. Culture on to blood agar aerobically and a Sabouraud dextrose plate (without antibiotics), which is particularly suitable for studying the colonial morphology.
2. Examine the plates after 3 days with a plate microscope and then at intervals for 10 days. *Nocardia* colonies range from white to yellow-ochre, orange and pink and their surfaces are usually folded into convoluted patterns (resembling a star, hence *N.asteroides*). Look for aerial mycelia which may give a chalky or downy appearance to the colony macroscopically.
3. Check with a Gram stain of any suspect colonies and perform a modified Ziehl−Neelsen stain for acid-fast bacilli (see Appendix I).
4. Report aerobic Gram-positive acid fast rods as presumptive *Nocardia* sp.[a]

---

[a]Further confirmatory tests for *N.asteroides* include growth at 46°C, positive urease and nitrate reduction and aesculin hydrolysis. Definitive identification is best performed by laboratories with a special interest in *Nocardia* spp.

Legionella culture is performed more commonly now because of improvements in media composition and selectivity and all laboratories should have the ability to culture this genus. Culture offers the advantage of an earlier diagnosis than antibody response and enables speciation and serogrouping to be performed. Culture is more often positive than direct fluorescent antibody (DFA) testing of respiratory specimens (18), but at least 3 days are required for growth to be apparent. Negative DFA does not always exclude *Legionella*, and false positives may occur.

Sputum may be cultured and improvements in media have resulted in increased isolation rates. As only about 50% of patients with legionnaire's disease have a productive cough, other specimens may have to be cultured, including transtracheal aspirates, broncho-alveolar washings, blood, pleural fluid and transbronchial lung biopsies. A detailed account of laboratory methods will be found elsewhere (19).

Infrequently legionellae may be seen on conventional Gram stain, but prolonged counterstaining with carbol fuchsin is recommended (20). It has been suggested that the appearance on Gram stain of pale, small, pleomorphic Gram-negative rods, followed by no bacterial growth after conventional overnight culture should prompt consideration of *Legionella* (21). Culture for legionellae is most appropriate for patients with suspected atypical pneumonia and those with pneumonia who fail to respond to antibiotics or are immunocompromised. Broncho-alveolar lavage may be performed with distilled water rather than saline, as the latter may inhibit recovery of *Legionella* (22). Heat- or acid-treatment of contaminated specimens followed by plating on to selective media helps avoid overgrowth of cultures by contaminants. Various *Legionella* culture media have been devised—the most successful is buffered charcoal yeast extract agar with α-ketoglutarate (BCYEα) (Oxoid Ltd). Selective BCYEα plates containing vancomycin,

Table 19. Method of culture for *Legionella* spp.

1. The various specimen types should be treated as follows.

   (i) *Sputum*: homogenize by shaking with plastic beads.[a] If a Gram stain shows heavy bacterial contamination, the specimen may also be vortex-mixed with an equal quantity of distilled water and then diluted 1 in 100. Heat-treat the homogenized specimen and dilutions if made, by incubating in a water bath at 50°C for 30 min.

   (ii) *Pleural fluid*: centrifuge at 2000 g for 30 min and culture the deposit.

   (iii) *Bronchial washings*: no preparation needed.

   (iv) *Biopsies/tissues*: grind up specimen in a minimum of distilled water.

   (v) *Transtracheal aspirate:* examine a Gram stain and heat-treat specimen, as for sputum, if many organisms are present.

2. Plate the prepared specimen on to selective and non-selective BCYEα.

3. Incubate at 35−37°C in humidified air.

4. Examine plates after 2 days and at intervals until 10 days' incubation is completed. Suspect colonies have a characteristic cut-glass appearance when viewed with a plate microscope. They are 1−2 mm in diameter, flat or convex with complete edges and vary in colour from white to bluish white.

5. Subculture likely colonies on to BCYEα and BCYEα without L-cysteine. Colonies growing only on the complete BCYEα can be identified presumptively as *Legionella* spp., owing to their dependence on L-cysteine.

6. Identify the isolate further by serology, agglutination reactions or direct immunofluorescence, and send to a reference laboratory for confirmation.

[a]It has been found that sodium ions frequently leach from soda glass beads and this inhibits legionellae.

polymyxin and cyclohexamide should be used, together with a non-selective plate, for heavily-contaminated specimens.

Ten days incubation is required for some species of *Legionella* associated with pneumonia (e.g. *L.bozemanii*, *L.dumoffii*, *L.gormanii* and *L.micdadei* (23), although *L.pneumophila* usually grows in 3−5 days.

For the method for *Legionella* culture, see *Table 19*.

3.4 **Non-cultural methods of diagnosis**

3.4.1 *Antigen detection in body tissues and fluids*

Some patients in the early phase of pneumococcal pneumonia, particularly those without pre-existing chronic obstructive airways disease, do not produce sputum, and many

Table 20. Titration of complement and haemolytic serum.

The haemolytic titre of each new batch of complement must be determined by 'chessboard' titration against each new batch of lysin.

1. With a pipette dropper add 2 vols of 25 μl diluent (Ca-Mg buffered diluent, Oxoid Ltd) to each well of a U-bottomed microtitre plate. This represents one vol of serum and one vol of antigen in the CFT. Add a third vol of diluent to the control column in place of complement.

2. Prepare in tubes dilutions of complement with a 20% difference in concentration between each, as follows.

   (i) Set out a row of tubes to cover a series of dilutions from 1 in 30 to 1 in 179.

   (ii) Into the second and each subsequent tube pipette 2 ml diluent. In the first tube make 12 ml of 1 in 30 dilution of complement by adding 0.5 ml preserved complement to 3.5 ml water and then adding 8 ml diluent.

   (iii) From the first tube transfer 8 ml of diluted complement to the second tube; wash the pipette with diluent; mix the contents of the second tube and transfer 8 ml to the third, and so on, to the end of the row, washing out the pipette between each dilution.

3. Add 25 μl of each complement dilution into the appropriate column of the plate.

4. Wrap the plate securely in foil to prevent evaporation and stand at 4°C overnight.

5. Next morning prepare in 1 ml amounts a series of doubling dilutions of haemolytic serum from 1 in 25 to 1 in 800 plus one tube containing 1 ml diluent as a control. Mix each dilution with an equal volume of 4% washed sheep red blood cells, and sensitize for 10 min in a water bath at 37°C or at room temperature for at least 30 min.

6. Remove plates from refrigerator and warm on a 37°C hot-plate for 20 min.

7. Pipette 25 μl volumes of sensitized cells into appropriate row of wells, starting with the control cells without haemolysin and continuing with the highest dilution of haemolysin. Seal with tape and place in incubator room on a hot-plate for 40 min at 37°C, shaking on a microshaker after about 15 min, 30 min and again on removal from incubator.

8. Place plates in refrigerator overnight or for several hours at room temperature until cells have settled and then read.

   0 = no cells remaining i.e. complete lysis
   tr = approximately 10% cells remaining
   1 = approximately 25% cells remaining
   2 = approximately 50% cells remaining
   3 = approximately 75% cells remaining
   4 = approximately 100% cells remaining

   The Optimal Sensitizing Concentration (OSC) of the haemolytic serum is the dilution giving most lysis with the highest dilution of complement.

1 unit of complement (HC_{50}) is the dilution which gives 50% lysis at the optimal sensitizing concentration of the haemolytic serum. In the test proper, 4 units are used ($4HC_{50}$).

patients are treated with antibiotics by their general practitioner before being referred to hospital. Blood cultures should always be taken from patients in hospital with pneumonia, but again only a small proportion are positive. Attempts to detect pneumococcal antigen in sputum, blood and urine may help, and a variety of methods have been used, such as counterimmune electrophoresis (CIE), and agglutination of latex particles or red cells coated with specific antibody (see Chapter 2, Section 3.5.2). Urine specimens can be concentrated before examination using a Minicon B15 concentrator (Amicon Corp.) which concentrates the specimen up to 50-fold (24). Sometimes false positive results are obtained.

In *Legionella* infections, antigen detection in urine using a ELISA has been described and could be a useful rapid test for *L.pneumophila* serogroup 1.

Chlamydia trachomatis (serotypes D−K) are associated with sexually transmitted genital tract infections. Neonates may acquire chlamydial infection following passage through an infected birth canal, resulting in inclusion conjunctivitis and, less commonly, an interstitial pneumonia. Approximately half the neonates with chlamydial pneumonia have a history of conjunctivitis. *C.trachomatis* can be grown from nasopharyngeal secretions and conjunctival smears of concurrent conjunctivitis by the method described in Chapter 4, Section 4.4. Commercial systems based on monoclonal antibodies are available for the detection of elementary bodies by immunofluorescence, or for antigen detection by other methods such as ELISA, facilitating rapid laboratory diagnosis (see Chapter 4, Section 3.1).

3.4.2 *Detection of antibody response in serum*

This has been the mainstay for the diagnosis of atypical pneumonias caused by

Table 21. Titration of antigen and positive control standard antiserum.

It is necessary to obtain the optimal dilution of each antigen and the titre of the corresponding standard antiserum. It is carried out as a 'chessboard' titration in U-bottomed microtitre plates.

1. Using a 1 ml automatic pipette, prepare in tubes serial doubling dilutions of (i) antigen and (ii) antiserum (inactivated at 56°C for 30 min); if antigen and antiserum have not been tested previously, dilutions should range from 1 in 2 for antigen and 1 in 8 for antiserum, otherwise from 4 times previous optimal dilution and titre respectively.
2. Put 1 vol (25 μl) diluent into control wells (antiserum row and antigen column controls).
3. Add 1 vol of each of the antiserum dilutions to each well of the appropriate row, starting at the highest dilution.
4. Add 1 vol of each of the antigen dilutions to each well of the appropriate column.
5. Add 1 vol of complement (4HC$_{50}$) to each well.
6. Put respectively 2, 2, 2, 2 and 3 volumes diluent in five wells for complement controls at 4, 2, 1, 0.5 and 0 (cell control) $\times$ HC$_{50}$. Add indicated dose of complement.
7. Leave plate overnight at 4°C. Next morning warm the plate on 37°C hot-plate for 20 min.
8. Pipette 1 vol of sensitized red cells to each well on the plate. Seal with tape and continue as in *Table 21*.

Reading

The optimal dilution of antigen (OPD) is that which gives most fixation with the highest dilution of serum. This is the dilution to be used in tests with unknown sera. The titre of serum is that dilution which gives a reading[a] of 2 with the optimal dilution of antigen.

[a]A reading of 2 is expected at the titre of the standard serum, but because here the cells are most sensitive to differences in complement concentration, a reading from trace to 3 is acceptable. At twice the titre (i.e. in the preceding well) there should be a reading of 4, and at half the titre (i.e. the well following) there should be a reading of 0−1.

Mycoplasma pneumonia, Chlamydia psittaci and *Coxiella burnetii* (Q fever).

Cultivation of *M.pneumoniae* can be attempted on suitable media but it is rarely performed in the UK. The organism takes approximately 10 days to grow, and

Table 22. Complement fixation test proper.

All sera are stored at $-20°C$ to prevent them from becoming anticomplementary.

1. Heat 1 in 5 serum dilutions (0.2 ml serum, 0.8 ml diluent) at $56°C$ for 30 min to inactivate complement.
2. Titrate the acute and convalescent stage sera in parallel with 1 row for each antigen to be tested.
3. With the reagent dispenser put 1 vol of diluent into wells $2-12$ for each test serum and for each specific reagent control. (It is best to put these controls together on a separate plate when several antigens are being tested.)
4. With the pipette dropper add diluent to 5 complement control wells: 2, 2, 2, 2 and 3 vols respectively for complement at 4, 2, 1, 0.5 and $0 \times HC_{50}$ (cell control).
5. Using the automatic pipette, with a separate tip for each serum, place 0.1 ml of each test serum into the master well (well 1 of each row).
6. Make doubling dilutions with diluters by transferring 25 μl from wells $1-2$ and so on to 8; mix well at each transfer by rotating the diluters 4 times. Blot diluters dry after removal from well 8. Make 3 further transfers of sera from well 1 for (i) non-specific reactivity (with doubling dilutions from wells $9-10$) and (ii) serum controls (1 in 10 dilutions in wells 11 and 12). Blot diluters between (i) and (ii) and clean by flaming, cooling in deionized water and blotting dry.
7. Make doubling dilutions of standard sera from $4 \times$ test titre (4T) to 0.25 test titre (T/4): include serum controls (at 4T in wells 11 and 12).
8. Add 1 vol complement ($4HC_{50}$) to wells $2-11$ in test rows and to wells $2-7$, 9 and 11 in control wells. Add 1 vol complement at $2HC_{50}$ to well 12 of test rows and wells 8, 10 and 12 of control rows; for complement controls add 1 volume 4, 2, 1 and $0.5 \times HC_{50}$ respectively.
9. Add 1 vol of antigen at OPD to test serum dilutions (wells $2-8$) and then to specific reagent row (wells $2-8$).
10. Add appropriate negative antigen control (same dilution as the antigen) to wells $9-10$, and to control negative antigen control (wells $9-10$) of specific reagent control.
11. Add 1 vol of diluent to wells 11 and 12 to make up 3 vols.
12. Wrap plates in foil and stand overnight[a] at $4°C$ and then continue as in *Table 21*, except add 1 vol of 2% sensitized sheep red cells to each well.

Readings

Test: The highest dilution of serum giving a reading of 4 or 3 is taken as the titre.
Controls: Negative antigen control—complete haemolysis.
        Serum control—complete haemolysis.

Layout for plates

(i) Plate with serum dilutions for CF test
     Well 1 = master dilution of test serum
     Well $2-8$ = serum dilutions
     Well $9-10$ = negative antigen control (for non-specific reactions)
     Well $11-12$ = serum control (for anticomplementary activity)
(ii) Plate with reagent controls
     Well 1 = master dilution of specific antiserum
     Well $2-6$ = specific serum dilutions
     Well $7-8$ = antigen control
     Well $9-10$ = negative antigen control
     Well $11-12$ = serum control

[a]The technique of short fixation CFT is the same as the long, except that to allow fixation of complement the tests are incubated for 1.5 h at $37°C$ instead of overnight at $4°C$. The required concentrations of reagents for use may differ and all agents must be standardized under similar conditions to those chosen for performing the diagnostic tests.

overgrowth by contaminants is a problem. For a full account of isolation and identification the reader is referred elsewhere (25). The main test for laboratory diagnosis is the complement fixation test (CFT) to detect a rising antibody titre to *M.pneumoniae*, seen between an acute and convalescent sample. The general principle of the CFT is as follows. The patient's serum is mixed with complement and antigen. If an antigen−antibody reaction takes place, complement is fixed. This is demonstrated by testing for residual complement. Sheep red cells, sensitized with anti-sheep haemolytic serum, are added. If lysis does not occur, complement has been fixed in the first reaction and the test is positive. If there is lysis, free complement is available and the test is negative. A general CFT method which can be applied to all the atypical pneumonias is given in *Tables 21−23*. IgM tests have been described (e.g. using ELISA or immunofluorescence) but are only performed by specialist laboratories. A DNA probe directed against rRNA from *M.pneumoniae* is now available (Gen-Probe Inc.), but it is expensive.

Chlamydia psittaci (a Category 3 pathogen) isolation is hazardous for the laboratory worker and is not performed outside research laboratories. *C.psittaci* infection is usually diagnosed by CFT.

Coxiella burnetii belongs to the *Rickettsiaceae*. Infection is diagnosed by CFT, and phase variation of the CF antigen is unique in *C.burnetii*. The pattern of antibody respose to phase 1 and 2 antigens in conjunction with the clinical findings permits serological recognition of acute or chronic infection and endocarditis. During acute disease, antibody to phase 2 antigens increases, while anti-phase 1 antibodies remain at low levels. In chronic disease, anti-phase 1 antibodies equal or exceed the titre of anti-phase 2 antibodies.

Legionella pneumophila infection is most commonly diagnosed serologically, although culture is becoming more popular. Around 25% of patients may have detectable antibody

Table 23. Method for serological detection of *Legionella pneumophila* infection using an indirect fluorescent antibody test (IFAT) (26).

1.	Apply 5 μl of formolized yolk sac antigen to each 3 mm well of a PTFE-coated microscope slide (Chapter 4, Section 5.1.3). Allow the spots to dry for 20 min in a 37°C incubator. Fix in acetone for 15 min at room temperature.
2.	Make 1 in 16 and 1 in 32 dilutions in PBS of patients' sera. Use a positive control serum diluted 1 in 128 and apply 10 μl of each dilution to an antigen-coated well.
3.	Incubate slides in a moist chamber at 37°C for 30 min.
4.	Wash twice in PBS for 10 min and quickly rinse with distilled water. Dry at 37°C.
5.	Add to each well 5 μl of a 1 in 40 dilution of fluorescein isothiocyanate-labelled conjugate (sheep anti-human whole globulin).
6.	Incubate slides and wash and dry as before.
7.	Examine under a fluorescent microscope and score the intensity of the bacterial fluorescence from − to ±, +, ++, +++.
8.	Titrate further sera showing any fluorescence at a dilution of 1 in 32. The titre of serum is the reciprocal of the highest dilution at which + fluorescence is seen, providing that the positive control gives a result of 1 in 128. If the positive control is reading high or low, adjust the test sera results accordingly.
9.	Interpret as follows: a titre of ≥1 in 16 against serogroup 1 antigen in a patient with pneumonia should alert the clinician to the likelihood of Legionnaire's disease. To confirm the diagnosis a 4-fold rise in paired sera to a titre of at least 1 in 64 or a single titre of ≥1 in 128 with a relevant clinical history is required.

within 2 days of admission to hospital (26), although in some cases up to 6 weeks may be required for seroconversion. The most commonly used method is the indirect fluorescent antibody test (IFAT) (26), using a formolized yolk sac antigen prepared from *L.pneumophila* serogroups 1−6 (DMRQC). The method is given in *Table 23*.

A rapid microagglutination test (RMAT) is also available, and has the advantage of being simpler to perform and giving a result in 30 min (27). This test is suitable for epidemiological purposes when testing large populations and also as a quick diagnostic screening test in individual patients. Positive results should be confirmed by IFAT.

Table 24. Principles of some enzyme immunoassay systems.

All tests require the use of appropriate positive and negative controls.

A. NON-COMPETITIVE ASSAYS

1. *Direct method* (e.g. antigen detection).

(i)   Unlabelled antibody is bound to solid-phase support (plastic microtitre plates, tubes, beads or cuvettes).
(ii)   After adsorption, unbound antibody is removed and untreated binding sites are blocked by certain agents (e.g. bovine serum albumin, gelatin, nonionic detergent).
(iii)   Test serum is added, incubated and unreacted components are removed by washing.
(iv)   Enzyme-conjugated specific antibody is added. Enzyme-labelled antibody binds to antigen captured by the first antibody.
(v)   Unreacted conjugate is removed by washing and enzyme substrate added.
(vi)   Enzymic activity is measured by hydrolysis or oxidation of the substrate to develop a coloured reaction product.
(vii)   Amount of substrate product is judged visually or measured spectrophotometrically or fluorimetrically.
(viii) Reaction product is directly related to concentration of antigen in sample.

2. *Indirect method*

Advantages: Conjugate does not have to be prepared for each antigen being assayed. Greater sensitivity than direct method.

As (i)−(iii) above, then:

(i)   Unlabelled viral antibody, prepared in an animal species different from that used for the production of the viral antibody bound to the solid phase, is added.
(ii)   Unreacted components are removed by washing and enzyme-labelled anti-species gamma globulin against the second antibody is added.
(iii)   Unreacted conjugate is removed and substrate added. Then as (vi) and (vii) above.

3. *Antibody 'capture' method for class-specific antibodies*

Problems in assay of IgM are mainly due to presence and competition of large amounts of IgG in test sera.

(i)   Chain-specific anti-human IgM is adsorbed to the solid phase to 'capture' IgM.
(ii)   Test serum is added and IgM content is bound to the solid-phase.
(iii)   Antigen is added, and antigen bound to specific IgM is detected by enzyme-conjugated specific antibody or in two steps by specific antibody and then enzyme-labelled anti-species gamma globulin.

Positive tests of IgM antibody tests should always be interpreted with caution because of the potential for rheumatoid factor to give false positives.

B. COMPETITIVE ASSAYS (e.g. antibody detection).

(i)   Unlabelled antibody is bound to solid phase and antigen is captured onto this.
(ii)   Test serum is added together with enzyme-conjugated specific antibody. Competition for binding to immobilized antigen occurs between specific antibody in the test serum and conjugated antibody.
(iii)   Unreacted components are removed by washing and enzyme substrate is added.
(iv)   Enzymic activity is measured and is inversely related to the concentration of specific antibody in the test serum.

The RMAT uses an antigen prepared from *L.pneumophila* serogroup 1 which is obtainable from DMRQC.

As a general point, ELISA methods are becoming increasingly popular as a means of non-cultural diagnosis. They are often commercially produced and come with manufacturer's instructions, but they do vary in their basic principles and some examples of these are given in *Table 24.*

4. ACKNOWLEDGEMENTS

We are grateful to several colleagues for helpful discussion and advice especially Dr P.A.Jenkins (PHLS, Mycobacterium Reference Unit, Cardiff) and Dr A.G.Taylor (DMRQC, Central Public Health Laboratory, London).

5. REFERENCES

1. Regan,J. and Lowe,F. (1977) *J. Clin. Microbiol.,* **6**, 303.
2. Coyle,M.B., Hollis,D.G. and Groman,N.B. (1985) In *Manual of Clinical Microbiology.* 4th edn, Lennette,E.H., Balows,A., Hausler,W.J.,Jr and Shadomy,H.J. (eds), American Society for Microbiology, Washington DC, p. 193.
3. Davies,J.R. (1974) In *Laboratory Methods 1. Public Health Laboratory Services Monograph Series No. 5,* Willis,A.T. and Collins,C.H. (eds.), HMSO, London, p.1
4. Evans,E.G.V. and Richardson,M.D. (eds.) (1989) *Medical Mycology: A Practical Approach*, IRL Press, Oxford.
5. Wong,L.K., Barry,A.L. and Horgan,S.M. (1982) *J. Clin. Microbiol.,* **16**, 627.
6. Bartlett,J.G., Ryan,K.J., Smith,T.F. and Wilson,W.R. (1987) *Cumitech 7A, Laboratory Diagnosis of Lower Tract Respiratory Infections,* American Society for Microbiology, Washington DC.
7. Van Scoy,R.E. (1977) *Mayo Clin. Proc.,* **52**, 39.
8. Kilian,M. (1985) In *Manual of Clinical Microbiology.* 4th edn, Lennette,E.H., Balows,A., Hausler,W.J.,Jr and Shadomy,H.J. (eds), American Society for Microbiology, Washington DC, p. 390.
9. Christensen,J.J., Gadeberg,O. and Bruun,B. (1986) *Acta Path. Microbiol. Immunol. Scand. Sect. B.,* **94**, 89.
10. Murray,P.R. and Washington,J.A. (1975) *Mayo Clin. Proc.,* **50**, 339.
11. Sparham,P.D., Lobban,D.I. and Speller,D.C.E. (1978) *J. Clin. Path.,* **31**, 913.
12. Roberts,D.E. and Cole,P. (1980) *Lancet,* **i**, 796.
13. *Code of Practice for the Prevention of Infection in Clinical Laboratories and Post-mortem Rooms* (1978) HMSO, London.
14. Marks,J. (1959) *Monthly Bull. of Min. of Health and PHLS,* **18**, 81.
15. Marks,J. (1972) *Tubercle,* **58**, 31.
16. Zaher,F. and Marks,J. (1977) *Tubercle,* **58**, 143.
17. Macfarlane,J.T., Ward,M.J. Finch,R.G. and Macrae,A.D. (1982) *Lancet,* **ii**, 255.
18. Zuravleff,J.J., Yu,V.L., Shonnard,J.W., Davis,B.K. and Rihs,J.D. (1983) *JAMA,* **250**, 1981.
19. Harrison,T.G. and Taylor,A.G. (1988) *Laboratory Manual for Legionella*, John Wiley, London.
20. Fallon,R.J. (1986) *Med. Lab. Sci.,* **43**, 64.
21. Baptiste-Desruisseaux,D., Duperval,R. and Marcoux,J.A. (1985) *Can. Med. Assoc. J.,* **133**, 117.
22. Edelstein,P.H. and Meyer,R.D. (1984) *Chest,* **85**, 114.
23. Barker,J., Farrell,I.D. and Hutchison,J.G.P. (1986) *J. Med. Microbiol.,* **22**, 97.
24. Ramsey,B.W., Marcuse,E.K., Foy,H.M., Cooney,M.K., Allan,I., Brewer,D., Smith,A.L. (1986) *Pediatrics,* **78**, 1.
25. Razin,S. and Tully,J.G. (eds) (1983) *Methods in Mycoplasmology.* Vols I and II, Academic Press, London and New York.
26. Harrison,T.G. and Taylor,A.G. (1982) *J. Clin. Pathol.,* **35**, 211.
27. Harrison,T.G. and Taylor,A.G. (1982) *J. Clin. Pathol.,* **35**, 1028.

CHAPTER 4

Bacteriology of the genital tract

ALUN J.DAVIES and ANTHONY E.JEPHCOTT

1. INTRODUCTION

Whilst the diagnosis of genital infections by means of bacteriological examination is straightforward in those infections where an organism has a clear pathogenic role, such as is the case in gonorrhoea and syphilis, other infections are encountered where the contribution of diagnostic bacteriology is less clear. Culture of specimens from patients with genital infections may yield organisms such as *Gardnerella* spp., *Listeria* spp. and anaerobic bacteria, which, although capable of causing infections under suitable conditions, do not do so invariably. Unless an organism is generally recognized as a pathogen, its presence in large numbers does not provide evidence of pathogenicity.

Detection of infection in the female genital tract is complicated by the normal microbial vaginal flora and the changes in vaginal flora that occur throughout a woman's life. The laboratory examination of specimens from the genital tract is heavily influenced by the clinical details supplied and the department from which the specimen was sent, so that only organisms relevant to the presenting complaint are sought.

1.1 Normal vaginal flora

(i) *Pre-pubertal.* Immediately post-delivery, circulating maternal oestrogen may result in a microbial flora in babies similar to that in adults. This changes in approximately 2 weeks as the oestrogens are metabolized, so that throughout childhood the vaginal epithelium lacks glycogen, and so carries a scanty background flora of skin organisms and upper respiratory tract commensals.

(ii) *Post-pubertal.* The vaginal epithelium has a high glycogen concentration due to the influence of circulating oestrogens. This is metabolized by lactobacilli to lactic acid, producing a low pH. The vaginal flora may superficially resemble faecal flora due to transient perineal contamination, but many organisms have a very close association with the lower genital tract, e.g. *Bacteroides bivius, Gardnerella vaginalis* and *Mycoplasma hominis* (1). In vaginal secretions, anaerobic bacteria outnumber aerobic by 10^9 to 10^8 ml^{-1}. The commonest anaerobes found are anaerobic or facultatively anaerobic lactobacilli, *Bacteroides* spp. and anaerobic Gram-positive cocci, Diphtheroids and coagulase-negative staphylococci are the commonest aerobic bacteria (2,3). Pregnancy has little effect on this flora, but the number of aerobic bacteria drops in the pre-menstrual week. Cultures from the cervix yield fewer organisms than from the vagina, due to the different epithelia and pH values of the two sites.

One further difficulty in correlating routine laboratory work with the results of carefully controlled studies of the vaginal flora is the problem of sampling. A high vaginal swab (HVS) is the usual specimen received by a routine laboratory, but most studies have used vaginal secretions collected with a calibrated loop or pipette. There is not always a precise correlation between the numbers of bacteria isolated by these more exact techniques with the flora detected by an ordinary swab, so that interpretation of results depends very much on previous experience and knowledge of the likely flora.

(iii) *Post-menstrual women.* The microbial flora alters again at the menopause, with skin and perineal organisms predominating in vaginal culture. Vaginal discharge due to bacterial overgrowth in latter life usually responds to local oestrogen therapy, which alters the pH of the vaginal environment.

1.2 Changes in normal vaginal flora

Vaginal discharge can be physiological or pathological, and there may be fluctuations of a 'normal' discharge associated with ovulation or the use of an intra-uterine device. In assessing the microbiology of vaginal discharge it is simplest to consider:

(i)   organisms normally present in low numbers which can cause symptoms when found as the predominant isolate;

(ii)   organisms not normally isolated, whose presence is usually associated with disease.

The bacteria encountered, together with comments on their significance, are listed in *Table 1*. Note that whilst the yeast *Candida albicans* does not fall within the scope of this book, it is a common cause of vaginal discharge and should be sought; detailed methods for its isolation and identification will be found elsewhere (4).

1.3 Pathogens associated with specific clinical conditions

To ensure efficient use of laboratory time and resources it is important to investigate specimens only for the appropriate pathogen associated with a particular condition. *Table 2* shows the most commonly encountered clinical problems which require examination of an HVS or other specimen from the genital tract and the pathogens likely to cause each of those conditions.

2. COLLECTION AND TRANSPORT OF SPECIMENS

The type of specimen required varies with the presenting complaint. Unfortunately, a specimen commonly received in many laboratories is a low vaginal swab, which yields information about the perineal flora only. A cervical swab, preferably collected with the help of a speculum to avoid perineal contamination, is desirable. Triple swabs are required for *Neisseria gonorrhoeae*, with specimens taken from the cervix, urethra and rectum, and a separate swab for the isolation of *Chlamydia trachomatis*, which should be placed in chlamydia transport medium (Appendix II) immediately and held at 4°C; if not cultured within 24 h the swab should be frozen at −70°C. It is unrealistic to expect to diagnose a microbial cause of pelvic inflammatory disease (PID) from an HVS alone. PID caused by *N.gonorrhoeae* requires an endocervical swab, while chlamydial culture or serology may implicate *C.trachomatis*. A mixture of aerobes or anaerobes from the vagina, possibly after a primary infection with *N.gonorrhoeae*, is responsible for some cases of PID. Fluid from the pouch of Douglas is a more relevant specimen for the investigation of PID than an HVS, but the latter specimen is more likely to

Table 1. Bacteria found in specimens from the vaginal tract.

Organism	Significance and comments
(i) Normally present in low numbers, may cause symptoms when dominant isolate.	
Staphylococcus aureus	Uncommon pathogen, sometimes cause of purulent post-delivery/surgery discharge or the watery discharge of the toxic shock syndrome.
Streptococcus pyogenes (Lancefield gp A *β*.H.S.)	Classical cause of puerperal fever, normally present in large numbers if causing disease. Presence of this bacterium or *Staphylococcus aureus* may indicate nosocomial infection.
Streptococcus agalactiae (Lancefield gp B *β*.H.S.)	Commonly a neonatal pathogen but can cause infection in mother and atrophic vaginitis in older women.
Escherichia coli and other 'coliforms'	Difficult to interpret as colonization with these bacteria can follow antibiotic administration. Large numbers of *E.coli* may accompany anaerobes in post-surgical infections. Heavy introital carriage of *E.coli* has been associated with persistent urinary tract infections.
Listeria monocytogenes	Similar pathogenic role to *Streptococcus agalactiae,* presence in specimens may be significant but must be assessed clinically. Pregnant women more susceptible, outbreaks resulting from contaminated dairy products reported (5).
Clostridium perfringens	Large number isolated following delivery/surgery usually significant (see Chapter 5, Section 3.2/3).
Actinomyces spp.	Associated with IUCD-related infections (see Chapter 5, Section 6.3).
Gardnerella vaginalis	Part of the normal flora, but in association with anaerobic, curved rod-shaped bacteria such as *Mobiluncus curtissii* and *M.mulieris* may cause 'bacterial vaginosis' (previously called non-specific vaginitis) (6,7).
Mycoplasma hominis	A cause of pelvic inflammatory disease and *post-partum* fever when it may be isolated from blood cultures (8). Can be found in asymptomatic individuals, so positive culture results may be difficult to assess. Few laboratories carry out culture or serological tests for this organism.
Ureaplasma urealyticum	Similar constraints to interpretation of positive cultures as *Mycoplasma.* Associated with 'non-gonococcal urethritis' but not routinely cultured.
(ii) Bacteria not normally isolated, substantial pathogenic role.	
Neisseria gonorrhoeae	Presence always indicates disease which may be disseminated. Very occasionally *N.meningitidis* and *N.lactamica* may be isolated from the genital tract of symptomatic patients, careful clinical assessment needed.
Chlamydia trachomatis	Various serotypes: A−C cause trachoma, L1−3 lymphogranuloma venereum and D−K genitourinary infections in adults and pneumonia/conjunctivitis in children.
Treponema pallidum	Causative agent of syphilis, non-culturable. Diagnosis by direct microscopy of lesions (rarely practised) or serology. Many body systems affected, so clinical diagnosis of distinct syndromes important.

Table 2. Pathogens sought in genital specimens grouped by clinical diagnosis.

Group	Clinical diagnosis		Pathogens sought	Suggested media[a]
I	Vaginal discharge	age 15–30	*Neisseria gonorrhoeae*	VCNT
			Trichomonas vaginalis	SAB
			(*Gardnerella vaginalis*)	(BA)
			Chlamydia trachomatis	CHLT
		>50, include	*Streptococcus pyogenes* and *S.agalactiae*	
	Urethral discharge		*N.gonorrhoeae*	
			C.trachomatis	
			S.pyogenes and *Staphylococcus aureus*	
II	Post partum/gynaecological surgery		*S. pyogenes* and *Staphylococcus aureus*	BA
	Septic abortion		*S.agalactiae*	NEO
	Infected Bartholin's gland		*N.gonorrhoeae*	VCAT
			'Coliforms'	MAC
			Clostridium perfringens	
			Mycoplasma hominis	
			Bacteroides spp.	
			anaerobic streptococci	
III	Acute cervicitis (non-puerperal)		All the above plus:	BA
	Vulvovaginitis		*Chlamydia trachomatis*	NEO
	Pelvic inflammatory disease		(*Ureaplasma urealyticum*)	VCAT
	Salpingitis		*M.hominis*	MAC
	Urethritis		*M.genitalium*	CHLT
	Discharge associated with IUCD		*Actinomyces* spp.	

Organism/media in brackets are given a low priority in many laboratories. Vaginal specimens give a poor yield of *N.gonorrhoeae*, culture for this organism optional (G.P. specimens may only be HVS). [a]*Media* SAB - Sabouraud's agar for *C.albicans*. VCNT - Vancomycin, Colistin, Nystatin, Trimethoprim added to chocolate agar incubated in 5% CO_2 for *N.gonorrhoeae*, some laboratories use amphotericin instead of nystatin. As some strains of *N.gonorrhoeae* are sensitive to vancomycin, some laboratories may wish to include a chocolate agar plate *without* antibiotics in addition to VCNT, particularly in culture-negative suspected cases or Gram film positive, culture-negative cases. BA - Blood agar incubated in 5% CO_2. NEO - Neomycin blood agar for anaerobic bacteria. MAC - MacConkey's agar for coliforms. CHLT - Transport media for *Chlam. trachomatis* prior to culture or immunofluorescence.

be sent to the laboratory (9). Urethral swabs from males should be obtained by inserting a cotton wool-tipped wire swab 4 cm into the urethra, rotating and gently withdrawing. The swab should be placed in Stuart's or Amies' transport media (both suitable) and examined in the laboratory that day, although heavily inoculated swabs held in cool conditions may retain culture viability for several days. It is important to ensure that the swabs or transport media used are not toxic to *N.gonorrhoeae*; the addition of activated charcoal can remove toxic substances. A convenient medium and pre-sterilized swab kit (Transwab MW171) is available from Medical Wire and Equipment Ltd.

3. ASSESSMENT OF SPECIMENS IN THE LABORATORY

The clinical details, age of the patient and ward or clinic from which the specimen was sent will determine the way in which it is examined. The scheme in *Table 2* correlates the clinical details with presumed pathogens, and the specimen will then be examined in one of three ways. In group I, *Trichomonas vaginalis, Candida* spp., *N.gonorrhoeae, Chlamydia trachomatis* and, where appropriate, *Gardnerella* spp. are looked for. The second group includes the aerobic and anaerobic bacteria listed, while all the above pathogens are sought in group three as well as, if possible, *M.hominis, Ureaplasma* spp. and *Actinomyces* spp. (rarely). The paucity of clinical details on some forms can cause problems in allocating specimens to one of these groups. One approach is simply to return the form and specimen and ask for relevant clinical details. The problem here is the possible delay in isolating an important pathogen, and microbiology departments should come to an understanding with the departments they serve about the need for full information, including clinical details, recent antibiotic therapy and the age of the patient.

3.1 Microscopy

3.1.1 *Gram films and wet preparations*

Examination of a wet preparation of the swab for *Trichomonas vaginalis* should be performed on all specimens, along with a Gram stain. Examination of a wet preparation is often more useful than a Gram stain. The relative numbers of epithelial cells and pus cells provide helpful information. Infection with trichomonas is usually associated with an increased number of pus cells, the usual finding being approximately one pus cell per epithelial cell. In non-specific vaginitis (NSV) and candidiasis there are usually relatively few pus cells, so that confirmed infection with *Candida albicans* or *Gardnerella vaginalis* and a large number of pus cells should lead to suspicion of a second pathogen.

Endocervical secretions should always be Gram-stained. The cervical discharge usually contains some pus cells, so that large numbers of pus cells are required to diagnose cervicitis. Gram staining for *N.gonorrhoeae* produces many false-negative results, and care must be taken in early infections to distinguish pathogenic intracellular Gram-negative diplococci from extracellular Gram-negative diplococci which may be non-pathogenic *Neisseria* spp. or *Acinetobacter* spp., which can colonize the normal female genital tract. The Gram stain will show the presence of pus cells and may also, in NSV, show the characteristic clue cells, which are epithelial cells studded with 'Gram-variable' diphtheroid-like organisms. The presence of these clue cells and appropriate clinical details should alert the laboratory to culture for *G.vaginalis*. *C.albicans* should be looked for on microscopy, where both spores and mycelia stain Gram-positive.

Examination of Gram-stained smears of exudate can reveal the characteristic Gram-negative diplococci of *N.gonorrhoeae*, often intracellular in early infections, but frequently predominantly extracellular in the later stages. This method is cheap and rapid, and should be carried out in the clinic before the patient leaves. Unfortunately whilst the procedure will detect over 90% of male infections, only 60% of female infections are detected (10). The test can be made more specific and easier to read if an anti-gonococcal fluorescein-conjugated stain is applied. Unfortunately, most commercial reagents lack adequate specificity and fail to penetrate mucus. Autofluorescence of polymorphonuclear cell granules leads to false-positive results, thus rendering this test unsuitable for routine use. Modern monoclonal antibodies have improved specificity but results are still little better than the ordinary Gram film examination.

3.1.2 *Dark-ground illumination microscopy*

As it is not possible to culture *Treponema pallidum* on artificial media, direct microscopy of material from primary lesions and serological tests are the main diagnostic methods used.

Lymph, collected carefully from a suspected primary chancre or a secondary lesion, should be examined by dark-ground microscopy for the presence of spirochaetes. It is difficult to distinguish between *T.pallidum* and the various non-pathogenic commensal spirochaetes commonly found in moist areas of the body. The syphilis spirochaete is non-refractile, white and it has between 6 and 20 waves of 1 μm pitch. It is best recognized by the experienced observer, so every opportunity should be taken to 'learn' the appearance of this organism by first-hand observation. Syphilis spirochaetes may also be demonstrated after fixation of smears using a modified absorbed fluorescent treponemal antigen test (FTA), and in tissues by silver staining.

3.1.3 *Fluorescence microscopy*

Fluorescent labelled antibodies to chlamydia permit the organisms to be directly detected in smears from mucosal surfaces. This technique is particularly appropriate for the examination of small numbers of specimens, and where distance makes transporting a specimen for culture difficult. It also allows for rapid diagnosis, which may be particularly useful in the case of ophthalmic infections, as the procedure takes only 30 min per specimen. Unfortunately, each specimen will require prolonged and careful microscopic examination, which will curtail the number of specimens that can be examined on any day. The test relies upon the specific staining, with fluorescein-labelled monoclonal antibodies, of carefully made smears of genital or ocular mucosal surfaces. Results obtained compare favourably with culture (11, 12, 13). Indeed, because of its good results and its technical simplicity, it is now replacing culture techniques in most laboratories. The specimens must be taken very precisely and must contain cells which are carefully transferred by rolling the swab onto a slide. The antibodies are either directed against the elementary bodies and are predominantly species-specific (Microtrak, Genetic Systems Corporation, Syva UK; Chlamydiaset, Orion Diagnostica, Seward Laboratories) or are genus-specific (Imagen, Boots Celltech) and are directed against the lipopolysaccharide of earlier stages of the life cycle. Clearly, the species-specific

Table 3. Immunofluorescent detection of *Chlamydia trachomatis* antigen.

1.	Reconstitute the FITC-conjugated antibody[a] according to the manufacturer's instructions and date the bottle[b].
2.	Roll the specimen swab firmly across the well of the slide provided in the kit, remove as much material as possible from the swab.
3.	Flood the well with 500µl acetone and allow to evaporate.
4.	Apply 30µl of antibody conjugate to the well to cover the specimen (20µl may be adequate). Do not dilute the reagent.
5.	Incubate for 15 min at room temperature in a moist box (a plastic sandwich box with wet blotting paper is ideal).
6.	Remove the excess antibody conjugate with a Pasteur pipette, gently rinse in distilled water for 10−20 sec.
7.	Drain the slide using blotting paper to remove excess water from *outside* the area of the specimen and allow to air dry.
8.	Add a drop of mounting fluid followed by a coverslip and examine using incident light and 40× objective. Look for the bright green pin-point fluorescent elementary bodies against the dull red fluorescence of the cells. Specimens with no cells cannot be evaluated. Positive specimens should have >5 bodies.

[a]Commercial kits such as Microtrak or Imagen should be used.
[b]Store for a maximum of 3 months at 4°C and use at room temperature.

reagents will tend only to detect genital chlamydia whereas the genus-specific reagent will also react with *C.psittaci* strains. A method for using these kits is given in *Table 3*.

3.2 Detection of antigen in specimens by enzyme immunoassay

Enzyme immunoassay of *C.trachomatis* antigen using ELISA is available as two commercial kits, Chlamydiazyme (Abbott Laboratories) and IDEIA (Boots Celltech Diagnostics Ltd). These tests produce rapid results and are not susceptible to loss of viability of the specimen in transit; initial reports are favourable, however, cross reactions with other bacteria are reported (14). They require a degree of mechanization and are most suited to the larger laboratory which would find the immunofluorescence technique too demanding for the numbers of specimens examined.

Recently a commercial test which detects *N.gonorrhoeae* antigens directly in specimens by an ELISA technique has been marketed. This is the Gonozyme Test (Abbott Laboratories). This has a very high diagnostic success rate in male infections, but in females it is not as good as culture (15). It is thus not acceptable for use as a sole diagnostic test for the individual case, but as it can be automated it could serve well in population screening where large numbers are to be processed.

4. CULTURE

The following sections describe the processing in the laboratory of each type of medium which is described in *Table 2*. Tests for the identification of suspected pathogens are included in each section.

4.1 Selective medium for the isolation of *N.gonorrhoeae*

Whilst VCNT Chocolate Agar is widely used in the UK and some other countries, modified New York City Medium (a nutrient, selective medium containing yeast dialysate and horse-serum) (16) and Thayer-Martin Medium are used in the USA. Swabs should be inoculated as soon as possible after receipt. In the USA, transport/culture systems are quite popular as specimens are often taken in a physician's office rather than a hospital clinic. A number of commercially available systems (such as JEMBEC and Transgrow®) use a directly inoculated purpose-made container of selective culture medium which is provided with its own individual supply of CO_2 (either by a citric acid/bicarbonate mixture or in a pre-gassed bottle) (17,18). This immediately provides the necessary growth conditions, and if the system is incubated before transmission to the laboratory, very rapid results can be achieved. Survival in these systems is as good as other transport media. Culture plates should be incubated at $35-36°C$ in a moist atmosphere of $5\%-10\%$ CO_2. Candle jars require more space than modern CO_2 incubators, but provide entirely adequate growth conditions at minimal cost.

After $24-48$ h incubation, colonies of *N. gonorrhoeae* are small ($0.5-2$ mm), grey, translucent, shiny and convex. They may vary in size, appear sticky when picked off, and will autolyse if left at room temperature for long. Suspect colonies should be screened for the presence of cytochrome oxidase with a spot oxidase test as follows.

(i)   Prepare a $0.3-1\%$ aqueous solution of tetramethyl-*p*-phenylene diamine hydrochloride in sterile water each day (reagent may be pre-weighed in plastic tubes and dissolved freshly each day).

(ii)   Soak a piece of filter paper in the reagent.

(iii)   If a strip of filter paper has been soaked it can be 'blotted' onto the colony. Alternatively, the colony can be rubbed onto the paper with a wooden stick or a platinum loop (Nichrome loops may give a false-positive reaction).

(iv)   A deep purple colour appearing within 10 sec indicates a positive result.

The suspect colony should also be Gram stained, whereupon the Gram-negative cocci, sometimes occurring as diplococci, which have their long axes parallel, will be seen. Isolates fulfilling these criteria, grown on selective media and isolated from a genital site are very likely to be *N. gonorrhoeae*, and a provisional report of 'presumptive *N. gonorrhoeae* isolated' may then be issued. Isolates of *N. gonorrhoeae* will not grow on nutrient agar incubated at $22°C$ for 24 h. It is usual to confirm the identification by carbohydrate utilization and/or serological tests.

4.1.1 *Identification by carbohydrate utilization*

Traditionally the identity has been confirmed by detecting the acidification of glucose-containing media, but not those containing maltose, sucrose or lactose. This is an oxidative and not a fermentative process. It is important that the basal medium is carbohydrate-free (if serum sugars are used, the serum should be checked for maltase activity). Cystine-tryptic digest semi-solid agar can be used, but the serum-free medium of Flynn and Waitkins is excellent (19). The basal medium is usually dispensed into small screw-capped bottles after supplementation with lactose, maltose, glucose or sucrose, although drops of the medium can be dispensed into a sterile petri dish when large numbers of isolates are to be tested and a more rapid result is required.

The inoculated plates or bottles are incubated in $5-10\%$ CO_2 for 24 h with the caps loosened and are then allowed to stand on the bench for 30 min to allow for any acidification due to dissolved CO_2 to dissipate. The disadvantage of this method is that it is slow and requires a heavy, pure growth of gonococci. Further, some meningococci metabolize maltose slowly and may require at least 2 days for acidification of the conventional test system, and some gonococci can be slow to utilize glucose. Increased speed and possibly some increased sensitivity can be obtained by using lightly-buffered solutions of sugars and inoculating these with suspensions of putative gonococci (20). These will reveal pH changes within hours of inoculation but may still cause a delay of at least 1 day for obtaining a pure and sufficient growth of the culture.

Several commercial systems are available for the rapid detection of carbohydrate utilization in lightly buffered media. The MiniTek system (BBL Microbiology Systems) uses filter-paper discs impregnated with carbohydrates which are dispensed into a plastic tray and inoculated with a suspension of the organism. The Quadferm + system (API-System) is a plastic strip with microcapsules containing dehydrated reagents for the carbohydrate utilization, DNase and β-lactamase tests. Each capsule is inoculated with $2-3$ drops of a heavy suspension of the organism in 0.85% w/v saline. The strip is sealed and the results read after 2 h incubation at 37°C. The reactions of commonly encountered neisseriae are listed in *Table 4*.

4.1.2 *Identification by chromogenic detection of pre-formed enzymes*

By employing substrates that produce a coloured product when hydrolysed, enzymes may be detected in *Neisseria* spp. that enable identification to species level. The enzymes detected are γ-glutamyl and prolyl aminopeptidases and β-galactosidase. Reagents are available as commercial kits such as Gonocheck (Du Pont de Nemours Inc.). In this system three substrates are included in a single disposable plastic tube for ease of use.

(i)   Rehydrate substrates with 4 drops of phosphate buffered saline (PBS) (pH 7.2).
(ii)   Inoculate several colonies of the test organism.
(iii) Stopper and incubate at 35°C for 20min.
(iv)   Compare colour produced with the standard on the tube label: blue, *N.lactamica*; yellow, *N.meningitidis*; red, *N.gonorrhoeae*; colourless, *Branhamella catarrhalis*.

The test appears to be as effective as traditional biochemical methods, but is more rapid and may well be increasingly used by laboratories. It should *only* be used on strains isolated from selective media, as certain non-pathogenic neisseriae give similar reactions to those given by *N.gonorrhoeae*.

4.1.3 *Identification by immunological methods*

Identification by immunological means was originally achieved using a slide indirect fluorescence test. This is technically very demanding. The method of choice is now co-agglutination. This provides an excellent check on the results of a biochemical identification or may be used in its place. Commercial kits are available such as the Phadebact® Monoclonal GC Test (Pharmacia Ltd) which uses murine monoclonal antibodies attached to the protein A of a suspension of dead *Staphylococcus aureus*. When the supernatant of a dense boiled suspension of *Neisseria* spp. is added, if the gonococcal specific outer membrane protein (either type 1A or 1B) is present, then the staphylococci will agglutinate (methylene blue is added to make the agglutination easily visible); see *Table 5*. Two pooled monoclonal antibody reagents are provided, one detecting serogroup WI and the other WII/III (these correspond to proteins 1A and 1B), so

Table 4. Characteristics of some human *Neisseria* spp. and *Branhamella catarrhalis*.

Organism	Growth on:		Acid production from:				DNase	Butyrate esterase	γ-Glutamyl aminopeptidase	Propyl aminopeptidase
	Selective media	Nutrient agar at 35°C	Glucose	Maltose	Sucrose	Lactose				
N. gonorrhoeae	+	−	+	−	−	−	−	−	−	+
N. meningitidis	+	−	+	+	−	−	−	−	+	v
N. lactamica	+	+	+	+	−	+[b]	−	−	−	+
N. flavescens[a]	−	+	−	−	−	−	−	−		
N. cinerea	±	+	−	−	−	−	−	−		
B. catarrhalis	±	+	−	−	−	−	+	+	−	−

[a] Produces yellow pigment.
[b] Also gives positive β-galactosidase (ONPG) test.

Table 5. Identification of *N.gonorrhoeae* using Phadebact Monoclonal GC test.

1.	Emulsify sufficient colonies of the suspect isolate in 0.25 ml normal saline to give visible turbidity (a plastic Eppendorf tube is useful).
2.	Heat the suspension in a boiling water bath for 5 min; a collar of expanded polystyrene prevents the tube sinking.
3.	Cool under running water and allow to settle. Mix 1 drop of the supernatant of the suspension with 1 drop of each monoclonal antibody reagent on the card provided in the kit.
4.	Agglutination will occur in one or other of these reagents in 30 sec to 1 min.

providing a degree of strain characterization. Full characterization of the serovar is possible with individual monoclonal antibody reagents, which, when combined with auxotyping, produces a system of strain characterization for research and medicolegal purposes.

4.2 Blood agar and blood agar with neomycin

The aerobic blood agar plate may reveal significant numbers of *Streptococcus pyogenes* and/or *Staphylococcus aureus*. Details of the characteristics and diagnostic tests applied to these organisms are found in Chapter 5, Section 4.1.4.

Listeria monocytogenes will grow on the aerobically incubated blood agar plate producing small, grey colonies with a narrow zone of β-haemolysis. Gram-stained films of the colony reveal pleomorphic Gram-positive rods that on further testing are aesculin-positive and catalase-positive (lactobacilli are usually negative). If a 6-h broth culture incubated at 25°C is examined, the bacilli exhibit characteristic tumbling motility, whereas an identical culture incubated at 37°C shows little or no motility.

Streptococcus agalactiae has surpassed *S.pyogenes* as the major streptococcal cause of neonatal death and *post partum* sepsis. As it is present in the normal vaginal flora, assessment of growth from vaginal swabs is subjective; however, growth from gastric aspirates and deep ear swabs of 'septic' neonates may indicate a significant infection (21). The organism produces larger (compared to Lancefield group A) whitish-grey colonies surrounded by a narrower zone of β-haemolysis. Strains possess the Lancefield group B antigen; see Chapter 5, Section 4.1.4, for details of the method. Most laboratories will rely on the Lancefield grouping; however, if further identification is required, all group B strains will hydrolyse sodium hippurate (Appendix III) and give a positive CAMP test (as described by Christie, Atkins and Munch-Petersen in 1944). The CAMP agent is an extracellular substance that enhances the lysis of red blood cells by staphylococcal β-lysin. Details may be found elsewhere (22).

The anaerobically incubated blood agar plate with neomycin will allow anaerobes such as *Clostridium perfringens*, *Bacteroides* spp. and anaerobic streptococci to be detected. Detailed methods will be found in Chapter 5, Section 3.2. Placing a 5μg metronidazole disc on the second sweep of the plate will provide a zone of inhibition of anaerobic bacteria. Many laboratories may wish to add an anaerobically incubated blood agar plate without neomycin to their set of plates. *Gardnerella vaginalis* might be found growing on such a plate, but as its role in bacterial 'vaginosis' is unclear, not all laboratories will want to pursue it. Full details of its isolation and identification are given elsewhere (6,7). It is a small, non-motile 'Gram variable' bacillus often seen attached in large numbers to squamous epithelial cells. Good haemolysis is seen on human blood bilayer Tween agar which should be incubated in 5% CO_2; strains grow up to a 5 μg metronidazole disc, but not up to a 50 μg disc.

4.3 MacConkey's agar

This medium is selective for members of the *Enterobacteriaceae* and enterococci. The role of such bacteria in vaginal infections is doubtful, but if heavy pure growths are obtained, particularly from patients with retained products of conception, they should be reported as coliforms or enterococci and sensitivity tests performed and reported. Details of the identification of members of the *Enterobacteriaceae* are given in Chapter 6, Section 4.6. However, this should only be undertaken to 'match' a blood culture isolate.

4.4 Chlamydia transport medium

Laboratories handling small numbers of specimens for the identification of chlamydia will probably use direct immunofluorescence (Section 3.1.3). However, those processing larger numbers might use an ELISA method (Section 3.2) or the older, but sensitive, method of culture described in this section. The technique requires the ability to grow McCoy cells in tissue culture and the use of a refrigerated centrifuge. The method is described in detail by Richmond *et al.* (23), but a brief summary is given in *Table 6*.

Table 6. Tissue culture isolation method for *Chlamydia trachomatis*.

1.	Prepare confluent monolayers of McCoy cells on sterile 10 mm diameter glass coverslips (Chance Propper Ltd) in a suitable glass tube which can be centrifuged (e.g. Nunc centrifuge tube 3-62707A).
2.	Inoculate 0.25 ml of the transport medium/culture after agitating the swab.
3.	Centrifuge the tubes for 1 h (34°C, 2000 *g*). This will improve infection. Ensure that the temperature does not rise above 34°C.
4.	Incubate at 35°C for 1 h and then remove the transport medium, replacing it with 1 ml of maintenance medium:

Eagle's minimal essential medium (EMEM)	1.5 ml
Sodium bicarbonate (44% w/v)	5 ml
Fetal bovine serum	1 ml
Glucose (10% w/v in EMEM)	2.5 ml
Vancomycin	100 μg/ml^{-1}
Streptomycin	50 μg ml^{-1}
Cyclohexamide (Sigma)	1 μg ml^{-1}

5.	Incubate cultures for 2−3 days at 35°C.
6.	Aspirate medium, add 1−2 ml methanol to fix and stain with either Giemsa or iodine or use an immunofluorescent technique. For iodine add 1 ml Lugol's iodine for 1−2 min.
7.	Remove coverslip and mount on a slide with iodine−glycerol mounting medium:

Iodine crystals	5 g
Glycerol	50 ml
Distilled water	50 ml

8.	Under bright field microscopy, look for dark red/brown inclusions with a clear halo round the material; starch grains from gloves may give a similar appearance if the iodine stain is used. Immunofluorescent or Giemsa stains obviously do not suffer from this drawback.

5. SEROLOGICAL METHODS

5.1 Serological diagnosis of syphilis

This is the method of choice in later stages of the disease, but tests may not prove positive in early (primary) syphilis, when repeated examinations with appropriate tests should be continued until seroconversion occurs, or until an alternative diagnosis is reached. In the later stages of acquired syphilis a CSF examination should always be carried out to establish the extent of the disease, and in neonatal congenital syphilis a direct search for spirochaetes (in mucosal lesions or *post mortem* specimens such as liver) can be helpful, as interpretation of serological data is difficult because maternal IgG will be present in the baby for 2−3 months. Serological tests use either cardiolipin antigens which detect 'reagin' antibodies or specific *Treponema pallidum* antigens. Selection of which test to perform will be dictated by clinical and laboratory factors. It is important to repeat any positive tests on a new serum sample to avoid clerical errors and to confirm the laboratory findings.

5.1.1 *Venereal Disease Reference Laboratory (VDRL) and allied tests*

Reaginic antibody tests rely for their activity on shared antigenicity of spirochaetes with the lipids in mitochondria. Originally colloidal suspensions of extracts from mitochondria-rich tissues such as heart muscle were used. These have now been superseded by chemically defined mixtures of lecithin and cholesterol (sometimes stabilized with choline), all detecting the same antibodies and known as lipoidal antigens. Early tests included the Wassermann reaction (WR), and Kahn and Price's Precipitation Reaction, but these have been replaced by the Venereal Disease Reference Laboratory (VDRL) test and the Rapid Plasma Reagin (RPR) test.

The VDRL test is a flocculation test carried out on a slide and is read with the aid of a low-power microscope. A carbon-containing VDRL antigen is also available, enabling the test to be read with a light box or automated, when results are read from

Table 7. VDRL test for reaginic antibodies in syphilis.

1.	Use this test in the commercially available kit formats[a] which involve the use of cards or a disposable WHO plate as described below.
2.	Using a programmable automatic pipette[b], take up to 250 μl of the patient's serum and deliver 100 μl into a well, then deliver the remaining 150 μl into a disposable plastic tube and incubate at 58°C for 20 min to provide the serum for the TPHA test which should be performed in parallel to the VDRL test. It is not practicable to do more than 30−40 tests at any one time, as the wells may begin to dry during shaking.
3.	Include in each batch of tests a positive control prepared from a commercial positive control serum standard, diluted according to the manufacturer's recommendation. It is important that the standard is aliquoted and kept frozen until required and then freshly diluted for use each day.
4.	Add 40 μl well-shaken carbon antigen (either from the kit or purchased separately).
5.	Place WHO plate on a rotary shaker and shake for 8 min at 100 r.p.m.
6.	Read the plate over a light box looking for flocculation as in the positive control.
7.	All sera giving positive results to *any* syphilis test should be titrated, particularly if the TPHA test is positive and the VDRL negative, as prozone effects may give false negative results. It is usually sufficient to prepare doubling dilutions of the patient's serum up to 1 in 128.

[a]Obtainable from suppliers such as Oxoid Ltd or Cambridge Biomedical Ltd.
[b]Such as the EDP pipette, Rainin Instrument Co. Inc.

the pattern of flocculated granules of carbon deposited on a ribbon of filter paper. The more recent RPR card test employs a choline-stabilized antigen which contains carbon. This test is performed on white plastic cards. The modifications allow it to be carried out on plasma as well as serum and to be read with the naked eye, so it has tended to replace the VDRL tests.

These tests have many advantages. They become positive early in the course of an infection and remain at substantial titres during the active stages, but fall on successful treatment or in old inactive 'burnt-out' syphilis. Thus they are very well suited to detect clinically active disease, and for this reason, and because they are cheap and simple to perform, are used extensively for screening purposes. They may also be used effectively to monitor the efficacy of therapy in treated cases, because antibody levels reflect antigenic load in the body, and as this falls in the successfully treated case so the antibody titre declines.

Unfortunately, cross-reacting antibodies may also be produced in pregnancy, after immunization or after a variety of acute fevers, especially glandular fever. These are usually of low titre and tend to disappear after a few weeks or months. Sometimes, persistent antibodies appear at a high titre and are often associated with autoimmune disease or clotting defects. These are known as Biological False Positive (BFP) reactions. They can be distinguished from true positive reactions by performing any test which is specific for *Treponema pallidum* infection. Such tests for *T.pallidum* use the actual syphilis spirochaete as antigen. Positive reactions with these occur only after true syphilis infection or after any of the endemic non-venereal treponematoses such as yaws, bejel and pinta. There is no certain way to distinguish between these last infections by serological means.

5.1.2 *Treponema pallidum Haemagglutination Test (TPHA)*

The original specific *T.pallidum* test was the *Treponema pallidum* Immobilization (TPI) test. This relies upon the immobilization of live *T.pallidum* spirochaetes by the patient's serum in the presence of complement. The test is technically difficult and there is a risk of laboratory-acquired infection. It has been superseded by tests using dead whole or fractionated *T.pallidum* which can be stored for long periods, and are free from the risks of infection. They are also much cheaper, as they use far less of the expensive antigen per test. Unfortunately, they are not considered quite as reliable.

The TPHA test detects antibodies which will agglutinate a suspension of red blood cells which have been coated with sonicated *T.pallidum* spirochaetes. It was originally described by Rathlev in 1967 (24), and has now been developed as freeze-dried kits available from various manufacturers such as Mast Diagnostics Ltd. Bovine cells are used and the reaction takes place in a special buffer which contains ox red cell stroma and sonicated non-pathogenic (Reiter's) treponemes in order to avoid non-specific agglutination by antibodies often present in healthy persons, either to ox red cells or to commensal spirochoaetes.

An alternative modification of the TPHA test has been developed in the UK by Sequeira and Eldridge (25). A method for this test based on a commercial kit is described in *Table 8*. This uses avian cells and so avoids the need to add mammalian red cell stroma. The Reiter treponeme sonicate is also omitted, apparently without loss of specificity. This test is known as the THA. Its properties are similar to those of the

Table 8. *Treponema* haemagglutination (THA) test[a].

1.	Take up 190 μl of diluent into the automatic pipette, an air buffer and then 10 μl of heat inactivated serum (*Table 7*) and dispense into the well of a disposable WHO tray.
2.	Transfer 25 μl of 1 in 20 diluted serum to a well of a plastic micro-titre plate with round-bottom wells using a new tip per sample.
3.	Leave the diluted sera at room temperature for 20 min to allow absorption of cross-reacting antigens to occur and then add 75 μl well-mixed THA test cells, previously diluted 1 in 10 with THA diluent, to each well.
4.	Mix by tapping the tray gently, cover and leave undisturbed at room temperature for 60−90 min.
5.	Read tray; negative wells have a tight button of sedimented red cells, the positive wells a well-defined granular ring.
6.	Reconstitute the positive-control serum according to the supplier's instructions, diluted 1 in 10 in saline and treat as in steps 1 to 6. The screening dilution for the sera is therefore 1 in 80 and 1 in 800 for the positive control.
7.	Titrate any positive sera by preparing doubling dilutions of the 1 in 20 diluted serum from step 2 in a micro-titre plate using 25 μl aliquots of THA diluent and 25 μl of diluted serum so that the final dilution of the serum is 1 in 1280. Dilute the positive control serum so that the manufacturer's titre can be reached.
8.	Add 75 μl of THA test cells (diluted 1 in 10 in diluent) to each of the test and positive control dilution wells. Then add 75 μl of THA control cells to 25 μl of 1 in 10 diluted patient's serum to act as an agglutination control. Then test as steps 5 to 7. If agglutination is seen in the agglutination control, report the test as equivocal and perform an FTA-abs.

[a]Reagents for this test are only provided as a standardized kit consisting of absorbing diluent, lyophilized sensitized turkey cells, unsensitized control cells and positive control serum. Do not mix reagents from kit to kit (Don Whitley Scientific Ltd, Shipley, West Yorkshire, UK).

TPHA. Both variants of this test are easy to perform and to read. They tend to become positive rather later in the primary stage, or only in the secondary stage of the disease. Either variant of the test can be used as an ideal complement to the VDRL test for screening and diagnosis and will quickly reveal any BFP reactions.

5.1.3 *Fluorescent Treponemal Antibody test (FTA-abs)*

In early infections the TPHA may be negative, and so a further test is needed in these circumstances; the most appropriate test is the FTA-abs. It is also very useful for confirming an unexpected positive TPHA result. This test employs fixed, whole *T.pallidum* spirochaetes on a slide. These are overlaid with the patient's serum, washed and then treated with a fluorescein-labelled anti-human antibody. It is necessary to use an antiserum which reacts with both IgG and IgM. The slide is subsequently examined by fluorescence microscopy, when positive sera will reveal fluorescent spirochaetes. Originally non-specific anti-treponemal antibody activity (which will otherwise produce spurious positive reactions) was diluted out by performing the test on serum diluted 1:200, but now antibodies are absorbed out by mixing the text serum with a 'sorbent' of heated Reiter treponeme culture filtrate or sonicate. This modification is known as the FTA-abs test. It becomes positive very early during the primary stage of the infection, and as with all the *T.pallidum* tests, once positive it remains so for very many years, if not for the patient's entire life. Details of the test are given in *Table 9*. A simple guide to the interpretation of syphilis serology is given in *Table 10*.

FTA-abs tests are more difficult to perform than the TPHA and are tedious to read in more than small numbers. For these reasons the test is usually reserved for problem

Table 9. Absorbed fluorescent treponemal antigen test (FTA-abs).

A. *Test*

1. Dilute patient's inactivated serum and controls used 1 in 5 in sorbent (Difco Bacto FTA sorbent) i.e. 20 μl serum to 80 μl sorbent.
    The controls will be as follows.
    (i) $++++$ reactive control;
    (ii) $+$ minimally-reactive control [serum (i) diluted in PBS];
    (iii)   non-specific control (to check efficacy of absorption step);
    (iv)   sorbent only;
    (v)   PBS only.
2. Leave at room temperature for 10 min for absorption to occur.
3. Add 20 μl of diluted serum/controls to each spot on the antigen-coated slide[a].
4. Incubate for 20 min at 37°C in a moist chamber.
5. Rinse the slide with PBS using a wash bottle, diverting the jet from the spots and then immerse in PBS in a Coplins stain jar for 10 min, agitating from time to time.
6. Rinse in distilled water and allow to air dry (do not heat).
7. Add 20 μl of fluorescent conjugate [Wellcome Fluorescent Antihuman globulin (sheep)] and incubate for 30 min at 37°C in a moist chamber. Do not refreeze conjugate or store for more than 6 months.
8. Repeat steps 5 and 6.
9. Mount the slide using Difco Bacto FA mounting fluid and a 70 × 20 mm coverslip.
10. Read as soon as possible (if not, store in dark) using non-fluorescent immersion oil and × 100 objective, preferably using incident light, an interference filter (DS500) and a blue barrier filter (LP515).
11. Controls (iii)−(iv) should not have any visible fluoresence, if the patient's serum exhibits fluorescence equal to the $+$ control, report as positive but if the fluorescence is less from the $+$ control, report as negative.

B. *Preparation of FTA-abs slides*

1. Use slides with the antigen already deposited or prepare in the laboratory by soaking at least 20 PTFE-coated slides (C.A.Hendley Ltd) in 70% methanol, followed by polishing with lens tissue.
2. Reconstitute the FTA antigen (Mast Diagnostics Ltd). Draw up into a pipette at least 10 times to break up clumps of treponemes.
3. Dispense 10 μl of the antigen on to each test spot on the slide, air dry for 15 min.
4. Immediately fix in acetone for 10 min (no more than 60 slides 200 ml^{-1}).
5. Allow acetone to evaporate and use slides immediately or pack in aluminium foil at −20°C.

C. *Titration of anti-human conjugates*

1. Dilute 200 μl of reconstituted conjugate twofold serially in PBS from neat to at least 3 dilutions beyond the stated titre.
2. Test each conjugate dilution against a $++++$ positive, $+$ positive and PBS only control using the procedure in A.
3. The working dilution is half the weakest dilution that gives strong fluorescence with the $++++$ positive and weak fluorescence with the $+$ positive. Treponemes in the PBS control area should not be stained by the 1:20 dilution of conjugate.

[a]Most slides have 6 spots, so 1 slide will hold all of the serum/controls for one patient.

sera where the TPHA and VDRL give discordant results. The test can also be made specific for IgG and for IgM classes of anti-treponemal antibody by using immunoglobulin class-specific antisera. Unfortunately, excess IgG will tend to block any IgM in serum, so the tests must be carried out on fractionated sera if reliable results are to be obtained. There are indications that the presence of anti-treponemal IgM is associated with activity of the disease and that only IgG antibodies remain after cure,

Table 10. Serological tests for syphilis and their interpretation.

Test and result			Interpretation[a]
VDRL	TPHA	FTA	
+	−	−	Biological false positive
+	−	+	Early syphilis
+	+	+	Most stages of syphilis
−	+	+	Syphilitic infection at some time[b]. Probably old and inactive or adequately treated.

[a]All positive tests should be repeated before establishing a clinical diagnosis.
[b]No test will differentiate between syphilis and the non-venereal treponematoses.

but this information is not needed in the assessment of adult syphilis. However, serum fractionation is of great importance in the assessment of congenital syphilis in infants.

5.2 Serological diagnosis of chlamydial infections

In most cases of infection, either culture (Section 4.4) or direct immunofluorescence (Section 3.1.3) will be used; however, high levels of genus-specific antibodies are found in systemic chlamydial infections, especially in Lymphogranuloma Venereum (LGV), and psittacosis. These are detected by the complement fixation test. Only very low levels of antibodies are produced in response to mucosal infections by the oculo-genital strains. The test is performed using heated yolk sac (lipopolysaccharide) antigen and is conveniently carried out at the same time as other CFTs are being performed in the laboratory (Chapter 3, Section 3.4.2) by the method of Bradstreet and Taylor (26). It will be positive in patients who are suffering from systemic *Chlamydia trachomatis* infections (such as PID) caused by oculo-genital strains, and will also react in infections with *C.psittaci*, but it will not detect genital mucosal infections.

The micro-immunofluorescence test (27) is usually performed using pools of mixed antigen consisting of elementary bodies from the various serotypes of *C.trachomatis* (28). The egg-grown antigens are spotted on to holes in teflon-coated glass slides, fixed and the exposed to dilutions of patient's sera before staining with fluorescein-conjugated anti-human globulin and examining under a fluorescence microscope. Antibodies detected by this method can result from mucosal infections but will persist for long periods, making it difficult to distinguish between past and current infection (29). However, rising titres, and particularly high levels may be helpful in diagnosing systemic infection, especially if the sites concerned are inaccessible or if prior antibiotic treatment has rendered direct methods inappropriate. Detection of high levels of antibody in an infertile woman will suggest that her infertility may be due to previous chlamydial salpingitis. Specific IgM antibodies can be detected in neonatal chlamydial pneumonitis.

6. ANTIBIOTIC SENSITIVITY TESTING

6.1 Antibiotic sensitivity testing of *N.gonorrhoeae*

It is not necessary at present to test accurately the antibiotic susceptibilities of each gonococcus isolated. Infections are usually treated with a 'one-shot' regime long before results of any test would be available, and treatment failures will reveal themselves at the test of cure. Accurate tests should be carried out from time to time to survey the levels of resistance in the community. These will give a more complete picture of rates of resistance to antibiotics. If they are increasing, this will suggest that currently employed regimes are inadequate and should be modified. It is also necessary to screen all isolates for penicillinase-producing strains, as these will require alternative therapy and will also usually be subjected to more intensive contact tracing than can be given to less resistant infections. This can conveniently be done by incubating a lawn of gonococci on which a 10-unit (6 μg) disc of penicillin has been placed. Any organism with a zone of inhibition of less than 10 mm will prove to be clinically resistant to penicillin and should be investigated further. The bulk of penicillinase-producing gonococci will grow right up to the disc. These can be confirmed by inoculating a spot on to a chocolate plate containing 1 mg l^{-1} ampicillin and which has been previously seeded with a lawn of penicillin-sensitive staphylococci. On incubation of this plate, the staphylococci will only grow in small zones around inoculated penicillinase producing gonococci. One plate can be used for many isolates and should include known controls. Alternatively, chromogenic cephalosporin (Nitrocefin, Oxoid Ltd) or techniques involving pH changes due to hydrolysis of penicillin solutions may be used.

The simplest method is to use a commercial test strip such as Beta-Test (Medical Wire and Equipment Co.) which should be used in the following manner.

(i)   Using an orange-stick, rub 2−3 colonies of the test isolate of *N. gonorrhoeae* over a 2−3 mm^2 area of a test strip, placing the strip on a glass microscope slide, thus providing a convenient backing.

(ii) On either side rub known β-lactamase positive and negative strains.

(iii) Rehydrate the strip with a few drops of saline. (Rubbing the colonies directly on to a wet strip will damage it and may produce a false positive reaction.)

(iv) Within 3 min the positive control, and the test, if it is a β-lactamase producer, will produce a yellow colour around the colonies, whereas the negative control will remain blue.

Certain gonococci which are not penicillinase producers will be detected as resistant by the 10 U disc test. These strains will have high MICs to penicillin (usually in the range of 1−5 mg l^{-1}). These strains are also clinically highly significant, and their detection is an added bonus to the use of the screening procedure.

Where facilities permit, and ideally from time to time in all centres, antibiotic sensitivity tests should be applied to all cultured gonococci. The simplest reliable method employs comparison of inhibition zone sizes obtained with three discs of 0.03, 0.25 and 1 units of penicillin G with those of organisms of known sensitivity (30). Single-disc tests are unreliable for penicillin testing as different rates of growth and many other variables will affect zone diameter. These are controlled to some extent only in the three-disc test.

For greater accuracy plate dilution tests should be employed; the technique of Reyn (31) has proved satisfactory.

Disc diffusion tests are more suitable for antibiotics where a bimodal distribution of sensitivities occurs. This is the case with spectinomycin, streptomycin and kanamycin. When discs are used, the following contents have been recommended (31).

Streptomycin	25 µg
Kanamycin	30 µg
Tetracycline	10 µg
Specinomycin	100 µg or 25 µg

6.2 Antibiotic sensitivity testing of other pathogens

General details of testing of other bacteria will be found in Chapter 7, Section 2.2.1. The testing of staphylococci and streptococci, anaerobic bacteria and coliforms is detailed in Chapter 5, Sections 4.1.5, 3.4 and 5.1.6 respectively. Appropriate antibiotics to test against isolates of *Listeria monocytogenes* are benzylpenicillin, ampicillin, gentamicin, erythromycin and tetracycline.

7. REFERENCES

1. Hill,G.B., Eschenbach,D.A. and Holmes,K.K. (1984) *Scand. J. Urol. Nephrol.*, Suppl. **86**, 23.
2. Goldacre,M.J., Watt,B., Loudon,N., Milne,L.J.R., Loudon,J.D.O. and Vessey,M.P. (1979) *Brit. Med. J.*, **1**, 1450.
3. Masfari,A.N., Duerden,B.I. and Kinghorn,G.R. (1986) *Genitourin. Med.*, **62**, 256.
4. Evans,E.G.V. and Richardson,M.D. (eds) (1989) *Medical Mycology: A Practical Approach*. IRL Press, Oxford.
5. Teberg,A.J., Yonekura,M.L., Salminen,C. and Pavlova,Z. (1987) *Pediatr. Infect. Dis. J.*, **6**, 817.
6. Taylor,E., Blackwell,A.L., Barlow,D. and Phillips,I. (1982) *Lancet*, **1**, 1376.
7. Ison,C.A., Dawson,S.G., Hilton,J., Csonka,G.W. and Easmon,C.S.F. (1982) *J. Clin. Path.*, **35**, 550.
8. Platt,R., Lin,J.S.L., Warren,J.W., Rosner,B., Edelin,K.C. and McCormack,W.M. (1980) *Lancet*, **2**, 1217.
9. Hare,M.J. (1986) *Brit. Med. J.*, **239**, 1225.
10. Barlow,D. and Phillips,I. (1978) *Lancet*, **1**, 761.
11. Tam,M.R., Stamm,W.E., Handsfield,H.H., Stephens,R., Kuo,C.C., Holmes,K.K., Ditzenberger,K., Krieger,M. and Nowinski,R.C. (1984) *New Engl. J. Med.*, **310**, 1146.
12. Thomas,B.J., Evans,R.T., Hawkins,D.A. and Taylor-Robinson,D. (1984) *J. Clin. Path.*, **37**, 812.
13. Alexander,I., Paul,I.D. and Caul,E.O. (1985) *Genitourin. Med.*, **61**, 252.
14. Caul,E.O. and Paul,I.D. (1985) *Lancet*, **i**, 279.
15. Aardoom,H.A., de Hoop,D., Michel,M.F. and Stolz,E. (1982) *Brit. J. Vener. Dis.*, **58**, 359.
16. Young,H. (1978) *J. Clin. Micro.*, **7**, 247.
17. Martin,J.E. and Lester,A. (1971) *HMSHA Health Reports*, **86**, 30.
18. Martin,J.E., Armstrong,J.H. and Smith,P.B. (1974) *Appl. Microbiol.*, **27**, 802.
19. Flynn,J. and Waitkins,S.A. (1972) *J. Clin. Path.*, **25**, 525,
20. Young,H., Paterson,I.C. and McDonald,D.R. (1976) *Brit. J. Vener. Dis.*, **52**, 172.
21. Ferrieri,P., Cleary,P.P. and Seeds,A.E. (1977) *J. Med. Microbiol.*, **10**, 103.
22. McFaddin,J.F. (1980) *Biochemical Tests for Identification of Medical Bacteria*. Williams and Wilkins, Baltimore, p. 18.
23. Richmond,S.J., Bailey,J.M.G. and Mearns,G. (1985) In *Isolation and Identification of Microorganisms of Medical and Veterinary Importance*. Collins,C.H. and Grange,J.M. (eds), SAB Technical Series, Vol. 21, Society for Applied Bacteriology, Academic Press, London, p. 297.
24. Rathlev,T. (1967) *Brit. J. Vener. Dis.*, **43**, 181.
25. Sequeira,P.J.L. and Eldridge,A.E. (1973) *Brit. J. Vener. Dis.*, **49**, 242.
26. Bradstreet,C.M.P. and Taylor,C.E.D. (1962) *Monthly Bulletin of the Ministry of Health and the Public Health Laboratory Service*, **21**, 96.
27. Wang,S.P. and Grayston,J.T. (1971) In *Trachoma and Related Disorders, Caused by Chlamydial Agents*. Nicholson,A. (ed.) Excerpta Medica, Amsterdam, p. 217.
28. Treharne,J.D., Darougar,S. and Jones,B.R. (1977) *J. Clin. Path.*, **30**, 510.
29. Treharne,J.D., Dines,R.J. and Darougar,S. (1977 In *Non-Gonococcal Urethritis and Related Infections*. Hobson,D. and Holmes,K.K. (eds), American Society for Microbiology, Washington DC, p. 249)Public Health Laboratory Service Monograph Series, 1).
30. Wilkinson,A.E., Turner,G.C. and Rycroft,J.A. (1972) In *Laboratory Diagnosis of Venereal Disease*. Wilkinson,E., Taylor,C.E.D., McSwiggan,D.A., Turner,G.C., Rycroft,J.A. and Lowe,G.H. (eds), HMSO, London, p.35.
31. Jephcott,A.E. (1981) *Investigation of Gonococcal Infection*. Association of Clinical Pathologists Broadsheet No. 100, British Medical Association, London.

CHAPTER 5

Bacteriology of superficial and deep tissue infection

ANN C.BUSHELL

1. INTRODUCTION

The range and variety of clinical samples seen and microbes grown from these infections is enormous. The approach will be to outline general methods, concentrating on the major pathogens, and then to examine specific techniques appropriate to different sites of infection with cross-reference to other chapters.

To get the most useful results from these samples it is important to know the *site* (anatomical) and *nature* (primary/secondary, acute/chronic) of the infection. If the sample is of high priority (pus, tissue and some fluids) then the laboratory must liaise with the clinicians to get this information, and must expend maximum effort to get a microbiological diagnosis. If the sample is of lower priority (most 'wound swabs' fall into this category) then the laboratory may legitimately process the sample in a standard, routine manner. The samples which deserve extra effort are not always immediately apparent and it is part of the role of the clinical microbiologist to pick them out.

Finally, intelligent and informed interpretation of culture results and appropriate clinical liaison will make all the difference as far as the clinician (and patient) is concerned between useful and useless laboratory reports.

1.1 Taking good samples

Pus or tissue is always preferable to a swab.

(i) *Pus.* This may be collected in a syringe (with or without a needle). If the pus is very thick it can be 'scooped' up or coaxed into a sterile container using a swab.

(ii) *Swabs.* These must be well loaded, to saturation if possible. Sometimes duplicate swabs are useful, since one can be used for microscopy and the other for culture.

(iii) *Non-discharging lesions* (e.g. cellulitis and early abscesses). These present a problem. Search very carefully for the entry wound and swab this if found. Sometimes a punch biopsy or curettage for culture is indicated. In cellulitis, blood cultures, anti-streptolysin O titre (ASOT) and the clinical picture (characteristic facial lesions in children with *H.influenzae* cellulitis) may be helpful. Fine-needle aspiration biopsy can be useful, as described by Lee *et al.* (1).

(iv) *Open lesions* (such as varicose, ischaemic and diabetic ulcers, burns and pressure sores). Such lesions are nearly always sampled by swabs taken from the surface of the lesion. These swabs yield mixed cultures of bacteria which are often surface colonizers of uncertain pathogenicity.

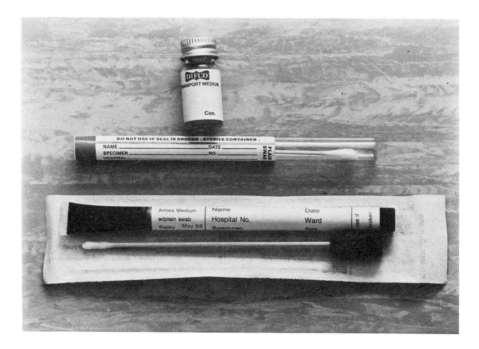

Figure 1. Two examples of swab and transport systems.

1.2 **Transport**

Pus, fluids and tissue should be transported in a suitable sterile container. Swabs may be transported to the laboratory either dry or in transport medium (see *Figure 1*). The latter is preferable unless there is minimal delay in culture. Many types of transport medium are available commercially: they can be obtained in bijoux bottles into which a separate swab may be broken off or pre-packed in a plastic tube accompanied by a swab in a sterile pack. Swabs are available with a range of swab tips (cotton-wool, Dacron), shafts (wood, plastic) and transport media (Amies, Stuarts, and with or without charcoal).

The commercially prepared packs are more convenient and cost about the same as a swab plus separate bijoux.

It is up to the individual laboratory to determine which type of swab is most appropriate. Some of the plastic-shafted swabs can be very flexible and therefore difficult to use. Some transport media show a tendency to 'pull out' of the tube when the swab is withdrawn in the laboratory.

1.2.1 *Transport medium for anaerobic bacteria*

The common pathogenic anaerobes, such as *Clostridium perfringens* and *Bacteroides fragilis* are remarkably tolerant and survive well within pus, fluid and tissue and on a swab in a good-quality transport medium.

More exacting and fastidious anaerobes, such as *Fusobacterium* spp., will also survive well in specimens, and providing they can be cultured within several hours no special attention to transport is usually necessary, although pus and fluids should fill the container in which they are transported.

Fastidious anaerobes will not survive for long on a swab in ordinary transport media, but since they take far longer (5−7 days) to grow than the time for which most laboratories will incubate their routine 'swab' culture plates, it is pointless for general clinical microbiology laboratories to waste time, energy and money on special transport arrangements. For routine swabs, transport is a compromise, as what the laboratory does once it receives the sample has more influence on the culture result.

2. GENERAL METHODS

2.1 Pus

2.1.1 *Macroscopic examination*

The following characteristics should be noted:

(i)   colour—pyocyanin and other pigments, blood staining;
(ii)   consistency—thin and watery or thick;
(iii)   smell—many anaerobes have a foul odour;
(iv)   presence of granules—actinomycosis;
(v)   fluorescence in ultraviolet light—usually only useful on pus from brain or lung abscess (*Bacteroides melaninogenicus* fluoresces red).

2.1.2 *Microscopic examination*

The commonest problem with making films is that the material tends to float or lift off the slide during staining. The following tips may help:

(i)   gently warm the slide first;
(ii)   use a swab rather than a loop to apply the material;
(iii)   keep the smear thin.

Once the material is on the slide, it should be allowed to dry, fixed by passing it several times through a bunsen flame, and then stained using the appropriate stain. A Gram stain (Appendix I) must always be performed on pus; if no organisms are seen then a Ziehl−Neelsen (ZN) stain (Appendix I) should be carried out. Mycobacteria may stain as weakly Gram-positive beaded bacilli. If clostridia are seen, then a spore stain may be useful as spores may be more readily produced in pus than on culture.

The stain results should be telephoned to the clinician if:

(i)   the pus is from an 'important' site (brain, lung, liver);
(ii)   the appearance of the organisms is diagnostic (staphylococci, streptococci, clostridia or fusobacteria);
(iii)   unusual organisms such as mycobacteria, actinomyces or fungi are seen.

2.1.3 *Gas−liquid chromatography (GLC)*

This provides a rapid means of confirming the presence of anaerobes. Many teaching hospital laboratories in the UK have access to GLC equipment which is essential for carrying out research work on anaerobic bacteria. Samples of pus may be examined by GLC as described in Section 3.1; extracts from swabs rarely give satisfactory results.

Table 1. Culture scheme for pus.

Media	Atmosphere	Length of incubation (h)
1. Blood agar	Air or air + 5% CO_2	24
2. MacConkey or CLED agar	Air or air + 5% CO_2	24
3. Blood agar	Anaerobic	24
4. Enriched blood agar (with growth supplements for anaerobes) (see Section 3.2)	Anaerobic	48
5. 'Selective' blood agar, e.g. neomycin blood agar plus metronidazole disc (see Section 3.2)	Anaerobic	48
6. Anaerobic recovery broth, e.g. Robertson's cooked meat, fastidious anaerobe broth (Lab M Ltd)	Air or air + 5% CO_2	24 then subculture to Media 1, 2 and 3

2.1.4 *Direct methods of detecting bacteria*

Methods of antigen detection (see Chapter 2) and nucleic acid detection (gene probes) are not yet available for use on samples from superficial or deep tissue infection. The large range of possible pathogens in such infections makes these methods more difficult to apply than in meningitis, pneumonia or septicaemia. The next few years will no doubt see developments in this field.

2.1.5 *Culture*

A general description of the culture of pus is given below. See Section 3.2 and *Table 3* for the full details of anaerobic culture which are necessary for material from cerebral, liver or lung abscesses. Methods for the culture of mycobacteria can be found in Chapter 3. Clinical information or microscopy of the pus may also indicate whether any other special media are necessary.

(i)   Using a sterile swab or loop to sample the specimen, inoculate the following media: blood agar (aerobic), blood agar (anaerobic, enriched if possible), selective blood agar (e.g. neomycin), MacConkey or CLED, enrichment broth (e.g. Robertson's cooked meat). Then follow the scheme outlined in *Table 1*.

(ii)   If organisms are seen on the Gram film, then 14 days' incubation with terminal subculture of the broth is needed before all the plates are discarded. If no organisms were seen, think again about unusual organisms such as mycobacteria, fungi or actinomyces. Occasionally, bacteria seen on a Gram film fail to grow due to the presence of antimicrobial substances (usually antibiotics). The effect can be detected by applying a filter paper disc soaked in the pus to a lawn of *Staphylococcus aureus* NCTC 6571 and observing whether there is any inhibition of growth.

(iii)   If bacteria have grown on the culture plates, proceed to identify and carry out sensitivity testing, as described in the appropriate section according to the site of the infection. Even when there is a good growth of bacteria on the 24 h plates it is advisable to subculture the broth culture to ensure better recovery of anaerobes.

2.2 Swabs

Wound swabs are by far the commonest type of specimen received from soft tissue infections, and most laboratories receive large numbers every day. Because of this, and also because they are repeatable specimens and they rarely come from life-threatening infections, culture methods are shorter and identification often less detailed than for samples of pus, fluid or tissue.

2.2.1 *Microscopic examination*

Microscopy takes second place to culture unless more than one swab is received from the same site. Only a Gram stain is performed. Swabs are not suitable for examination for mycobacteria except in exceptional circumstances, since all the available material should be used for culture. In many hospital laboratories in the UK routine examination of films from swabs is not carried out.

2.2.2 *Culture*

Swabs should be cultured as outlined in *Table 2*. Any bacterial growth is dealt with as described in Sections 4−9 of this chapter, according to the site of the infection.

2.3 Fluids

The general principles for dealing with a fluid sample are described here. The special processing needed for bile is covered in Section 5.4. Chapter 2 describes methods for cerebrospinal fluid, joint fluid and peritoneal fluid.

Table 2. Culture scheme for routine clinical specimens (e.g. wound swabs).

Media	Atmosphere	Length of incubation (h)
1. Blood agar	Air or air + 5% CO_2	24
2. MacConkey or CLED agar	Air or air + 5% CO_2	24
3. Blood agar	Anaerobic	48
4. 'Selective' blood agar (e.g. neomycin) plus metronidazole disc	Anaerobic	48
Plus (optional)		
5. Recovery broth (e.g. Robertson's cooked meat)	Aerobic	24 then subculture to Media 1, 2 and 3

2.3.1 *Microscopic examination*

(i)   Provided there is sufficient volume, centrifuge the sample for 10 min at 1800 g.
(ii)   Remove all but a drop of the supernatant; re-suspend the deposit in this and make a smear on a slide using a sterile loop or swab.
(iii)   Stain with Gram's stain first; if no organisms are seen, stain with ZN if the clinical details warrant.
(iv)   Telephone a positive Gram film result to the clinician.

2.3.2   *Gas–liquid chromatography*

Fluid samples are suitable for direct gas chromatography, which may be performed if the equipment is available.

2.3.3 *Culture*

The spun deposit is cultured in the same way as pus (*Table 1*). Bile fluid may need to be cultured for enteric pathogens; see Section 5.4.

2.4 **Tissue**

2.4.1 *Microscopic examination*

The tissue should be examined for evidence of pus, and these areas sampled for microscopy, for which three methods are available.

(i)   Press a freshly cut surface of the tissue firmly against a sterile slide. Stain the resulting imprint.
(ii)   Section—a histopathology section can be cut and stained.
(iii)   Ground smear—smear ground or crushed tissue on to a slide, and then stain.

2.4.2 *Culture*

Processing in containment level 3 facilities is recommended to protect the operator from the risk of aerosol infection.

Tissue which is likely to be contaminated, such as samples from superficial lesions or those taken *post mortem* must be washed before being ground up for culture.

(i)   Place a piece of the tissue in a sterile container, add 5 ml peptone water and shake vigorously.
(ii)   With sterile forceps transfer the tissue to a fresh container and repeat the washing process twice.
(iii)   Keep the final peptone water washings for culture. The tissue is now ready for grinding.

Uncontaminated tissue can be ground up without washing.

(i)   With a sterile scalpel blade cut the piece of tissue into 2–3 mm chunks in the lid of a sterile petri dish.
(ii)   Then grind up the tissue with 1 ml peptone water in either a Griffith's tube, a Stomacher or a pestle and mortar.

Tissue (and washings) are cultured in the same way as pus (*Table 1*). Additional anaerobic techniques as described in Section 3.2. may be appropriate (for example for tissue from myonecrosis).

The micro-organisms found in tissue are usually present in smaller numbers than in pus and may be more 'unusual' and difficult to grow. For these reasons, the culture of tissue may need to be prolonged. Relevant information must be obtained from the clinician before culture is undertaken. The additional culture media necessary depends to a great extent on the source and nature of the tissue and this is more fully discussed in Sections 4−9.

3. ANAEROBIC METHODS

3.1 Gas−liquid chromatography

3.1.1 *Use and principle*

GLC is used to detect anaerobic bacteria in clinical material and to identify them when cultured. Fermentation of carbohydrates by anaerobes results in the formation of volatile and non-volatile short-chain fatty acids (VFAs and NVFAs). These can be detected, after extraction, by GLC.

The relative types and amounts of these fatty acids produced varies with both the genus and species (*Figure 2*). The identification of bacteria based on these metabolic pathways is valid because they represent genetically conserved traits.

The extracted volatile components of the sample are carried along with a flow of specially prepared heated gas through a long column packed with material that differentially slows down the flow of the components based on their size and polarity. As the components reach the end of the column they are detected by either a temperature change (thermal conductivity detector) or a change in ionization potential (hydrogen flame ionization detector), which are plotted on a chart recorder as peaks. The peaks are identified by comparison with those obtained from known standards.

3.1.2 *Equipment*

Gas chromatographs are now relatively inexpensive, simple to operate and reliable and are available from various manufacturers (Pye-Unicam, Varian, Perkin-Elmer). The newest gas chromatographs use microprocessor controls to stop and start the analysis, control the baseline and to identify and quantify the peaks. Machines which undertake headspace gas analysis will also reduce the amount of time spent on sample preparation.

GLC analysis of bacterial metabolites is traditionally performed on peptone-yeast-glucose (PYG) broth cultures, and most published identification tables use this for their database. Other liquid media can be used, including thioglycollate broth and chopped meat broth. All these media must be examined, uninoculated, for the presence of VFAs and NVFAs, and caution should be exercised when interpreting patterns from these media when identification tables have been prepared from a PYG base. A method has also been described that uses bacteria grown on blood agar (2). Pus and fluids can be examined directly; a broth extract must be made from swabs.

3.1.3 *Procedure*

The most useful information comes from VFA analysis; this can be supplemented by NVFA analysis, as described in *Table 3*.

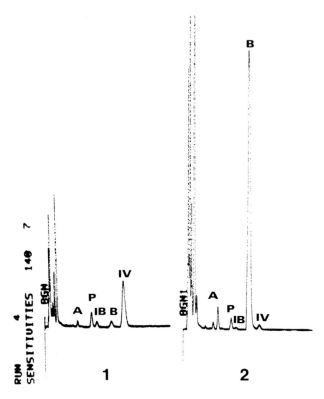

Figure 2. GLC trace using headspace analysis of two species of Gram-negative anaerobic bacteria. The bacteria were grown in FAB and the analysis was performed on a Perkin-Elmer Sigma 36/Sigma 15 machine with an HS6 headspace unit. The column was a ⅛″ × 6′ stainless steel column packed with 10% SP1000/1% H_3PO_4 on Chromosorb WHP 100/120 mesh. Trace 1 is *Bacteroides fragilis* and Trace 2 is *Fusobacterium nucleatum*. Metabolic product abbreviations are as follows: IV, iso-valeric acid; B, butyric acid; IB, iso-butyric acid; P, propionic acid; and A, acetic acid. (Courtesy of Dr P.G.R.Godwin, University of Leeds.)

3.1.4 *Interpretation*

Anaerobes are present in a clinical sample if the trace shows any VFA other than acetic. If only acetic acid is present, this could be due to facultative anaerobes such as *E.coli* *Staphylococcus aureus*. An NVFA trace may then be helpful: if more than lactic or succinic acids are detected then anaerobes are present. *Enterobacteriaceae* produce lactic and succinic acids, so the detection of these two products alone is insufficient.

3.2 **Culture of anaerobes**

Clinical microbiology laboratories should be able to grow and presumptively identify the obligate anaerobes that are commonly associated with human infection. Obligate anaerobes do not use molecular oxygen and their growth is inhibited by it. The amount of oxygen they will tolerate varies from species to species but most human pathogens (as opposed to commensals) are moderate anaerobes (3) which tolerate 2−8% oxygen and exposure to air for a short time. Strict anaerobes, which are inhibited by more than 0.5% oxygen, are found amongst the indigenous flora but are rarely isolated as

Table 3. General procedure for GLC identification of anaerobic bacteria.

1.	Insert the appropriate column in the chromatograph; VFA analysis will require a packing such as Supelco 10% SP1220/1% H_3PO_4 on a Chromosorb WHP 100/120 mesh (Supelco Chromatography Supplies Inc.) packed in a ⅛″ or ¼″ × 6′ stainless steel column. For NVFAs, Supelco SP1000 should be substituted.
2.	Run the appropriate standard solution through the machine for the analysis to be undertaken. The standards can be prepared from the method given in *Table 4*. Treat VFA standard with steps 3−5 and NVFA standard with steps 6−9 before injection.
3.	To extract VFAs from the sample add 200 μl 50% v/v H_2SO_4 to 1 ml of sample (or standard) in a glass tube.
4.	Add 1 ml of ether and mix by shaking.
5.	Centrifuge at 1800 g for 5 minutes and pipette off the top layer into a GLC vial and inject into the chromatograph. Flame ionization detectors will probably only require 12 μl to be injected, thermal conductivity detectors will require about 10−15 μl.
6.	To extract NVFAs add 2 ml of methanol to another sample (or standard) followed by 400 μl of 50% v/v H_2SO_4.
7.	Either incubate at 60°C (for 30 min) or leave at room temperature overnight.
8.	Add 1 ml distilled water and 500 μl chloroform.
9.	Invert gently 20 times and remove the chloroform layer from the bottom of the tube into a GLC vial and inject.

Table 4. Method for the preparation of VFA and NVFA standards for the GLC identification of anaerobic bacteria.

1.	Prepare 100 ml × 100 stock solutions of each acid by making the following volumes/weights up to 100 ml with distilled water:	
	VFAs	
	Acetic	5.7 ml
	Propionic	7.5 ml
	Isobutyric	9.2 ml
	Butyric	9.1 ml
	Iso-valeric	10.9 ml
	Valeric	10.9 ml
	Iso-caproic	12.6 ml
	Caproic	12.6 ml
	NVFAs	
	Pyruvic	6.8 ml
	Lactic (85%)	8.4 ml
	Fumaric	6.0 g
	Benzoic	6.0 g
	Hydrocinnamic	7.5 g
2.	Keep the stock solutions stoppered and refrigerated. When a working standard is required, add 1 ml of each stock solution to a 100 ml volumetric flask and make up to 100 ml with distilled water, keep all standards tightly stoppered.	

pathogens despite correct techniques. Clinical laboratories therefore must direct their time and effort to the reliable culture of the moderate anaerobes such as *Bacteroides fragilis* and *Clostridium perfringens*. The key to successful anaerobic culture is the attainment of an atmosphere with no more than trace amounts of oxygen. The use of reducing agents such as thioglycollate, cysteine and ferrous sulphide in media also enhances growth. Reducing agents have two effects: they lower the redox potential (Eh) and they remove oxygen from the medium.

Table 5. Anaerobic culture scheme for specimens from serious infections, e.g. pus and tissue from brain, liver and lung abscesses, myonecrosis and related infections.

1.	Inoculate on to enriched blood agar—incubate for 48 h and reincubate if there is no growth for a further 5 days.
2.	Inoculate on to selective blood agar + metronidazole disc—incubate for 48 h and reincubate if there is no growth for a further 5 days.
3.	Inoculate into pre-reduced cooked meat broth—incubate *anaerobically* for 48 h, then subculture to: Blood agar—incubate for 48 h aerobically Enriched blood agar—incubate for 48 h anaerobically Selective blood agar—incubate for 48 h anaerobically
4.	Reincubate the broth for a further 5 days and subculture again if no previous growth.
5.	Specimens from myonecrosis, gangrene, etc., put up also a direct Nagler plate (see *Table 10* for details).

3.2.1 *Culture media*

Three types of freshly prepared or pre-reduced media are necessary and should be used routinely for the best results. Solid media should be incubated anaerobically, undisturbed for 48 h. Liquid media can be subcultured after 24 h incubation. A recommended culture scheme is given in *Table 5*.

(i) *Non-selective media.* A good-quality blood agar, such as columbia agar base with $5-10\%$ horse blood, supplemented with 5 mg l^{-1} haemin and 1 mg l^{-1} vitamin K, is recommended. Many other agar bases have been found to be suitable (4), for example anaerobe agar base (Lab M Ltd).

(ii) *Selective media.* This is necessary to avoid missing small numbers of anaerobes in mixed aerobic/anaerobic infections. The selective agent can be incorporated in blood agar or in an enriched blood agar. Selection is achieved by adding antibiotics which inhibit aerobes, especially Gram-negative bacilli. The most popular in the UK is neomycin, but gentamicin and nalidixic acid are acceptable; kanamycin may not be sufficiently selective. Almost all obligate anaerobes are sensitive to metronidazole, and all aerobes are resistant, so this property can be used to facilitate the detection of anaerobes in a mixed culture. Place a 5 μg metronidazole disc on the 'well' of the inoculum on either the selective or the non-selective agar. The selective plate often gives the clearest results.

(iii) *Liquid enrichment media.* Robertson's cooked meat broth and enriched thioglycollate broth are commonly used for enrichment culture. They may be supplemented with vitamin K and haemin and pre-reduced before use either by holding in an anaerobic atmosphere, or by steaming/heating in a boiling water bath for 15 min to drive off oxygen. In practice few laboratories do this; the broths will then reliably grow only bacteria such as *Bacteroides fragilis* or *Clostridium perfringens*. Fastidious anaerobe broth (Lab M Ltd), is also an excellent recovery and enrichment broth (5). Broths should be routinely incubated for 24 h, preferably in an anaerobic atmosphere with a loosened cap, and then subcultured aerobically and anaerobically.

3.2.2 *Anaerobic incubation*

Anaerobic jars are made of plastic or metal with an air-tight clamped lid. The metal

Table 6. Procedure for the use of a gas generator system.

1.	Renew the catalyst in the lid of the jar.
2.	Load the jar with plates.
3.	Open an indicator sachet (a paper strip impregnated with methylene blue); this turns colourless (white) when reduced, which takes 6 h. Place the strip so that it is visible from the outside.
4.	Cut off the corner of the gas generator (a foil envelope) and add 10 ml of tap water with a syringe.
5.	Put the generator in the jar and clamp down the lid, then place the jar in the incubator.
6.	Check after 15−30 min for signs that the generator is working and the jar is air-tight: i.e. condensation on inside of jar and the lid feels slightly warm to touch.
7.	Check the indicator strip at 6 h, or before the jar is opened.

Table 7. Procedure for use of air evacuation system.

1.	Renew the catalyst in the lid of the jar.
2.	Load the jar with the culture plate and an indicator system: either a methylene blue strip or biological indicators—plate cultures of an obligate aerobe and obligate anaerobe.
3.	Clamp down the lid.
4.	Connect one valve to a vacuum pump, the other valve to a mercury manometer, evacuate to about 60 mm of mercury.
5.	Close the valve connecting the jar to the pump, disconnect and reconnect to the anaerobic gas source.
6.	Check that the vacuum is being maintained.
7.	Open the valve to let in the anaerobic gas.
8.	When the manometer has returned to zero, close both valves and disconnect pump and gas.
9.	Leave the jar to stand for 15 min: then check that the catalyst is working by feeling for warmth on the lid and by testing for a secondary vacuum (catalyst action creates reduced pressure) by connecting one valve up to the anaerobic gas and listening for an inrush of gas. If there is no inrush of gas, the catalyst is faulty and must be replaced and the cycle repeated.
10.	Place the jar in an incubator.

jars have two valved vents in their lid. The oxygen in the jar may be removed by two methods.

(i) *Gas generator systems.* These include Gas Pak (Beckton-Dickinson), Gas Kit (Don Whitley Scientific) and Gas Generating Kit (Oxoid Ltd). They are used with a transparent plastic jar and work by producing H_2 and CO_2 following the addition of water to sodium borohydride and sodium citrate. H_2 combines with O_2 in the presence of a catalyst to form water (see *Table 6* for the method of use). CO_2 is necessary for the growth of most anaerobes.

(ii) *Evacuation systems.* This system uses valve-vented metal jars, e.g. BTL, Whitley. The use of this system is described in *Table 7*.

The method relies on the evacuation of air with a vacuum pump from the jar which is then replaced with an anaerobic gas mixture (10% H_2, 5% CO_2, 85% N_2). In the presence of a catalyst, the hydrogen combines with residual oxygen diffusing out from the media to form water.

The gas generator systems are simple, quick, reliable and ideal for out of hours use. The evacuation systems are more tedious to use, and need more equipment, but are cheaper and achieve anaerobiasis more quickly. They are suited to large laboratories with many anaerobic cultures.

An alternative to the anaerobic jar is the anaerobic cabinet. These are air-tight

101

transparent-walled incubator chambers, fitted with glove ports and an air-lock loading port for culture plates. Modern cabinets evacuate and re-fill with anaerobic gas (10% H_2, 5% CO_2, 85% N_2) automatically. They are designed for work to be done inside them, and so provide conditions for research work on the strictest anaerobes. They are not necessary for ordinary routine clinical anaerobic work and are a relatively expensive, luxury addition to the laboratory. Working inside the cabinet using the glove ports requires a certain amount of practice and is unpleasant for long periods. It is all too easy for the cabinet to be used merely as a giant anaerobic jar. It does allow the inspection of anaerobic plates at any time without exposing them to air, and this can be useful when slow-growing anaerobes such as *B.melaninogenicus* are sought in pus specimens (e.g. cerebral abscess).

3.3 Identification of anaerobes

In routine laboratories, even if they have the equipment, time, money and expertise, it is often difficult to know how far to take the identification of anaerobes. In many situations it is sufficient to identify only *B.fragilis* and clostridia to species level and to identify the remaining anaerobes to presumptive genus level, for example *Bacteroides* sp.,' or 'anaerobic cocci'. This is particularly true for specimens which contain a mixed anaerobic flora, such as those from wounds related to gastro-intestinal or gynaecological surgery.

Certain other isolates demand full identification—this includes those from blood culture, brain abscess, myonecrosis and related conditions. In these situations it is wise for those laboratories which are without the equipment (gas chromatography) and expertise to refer isolates to reference centres. It is not within the scope of this book to write a comprehensive guide to the identification of anaerobes, and readers are referred elsewhere (6−8). A brief account follows of some of the more useful methods which are suggested as a minimal approach. The first step in identification is to ensure that the isolate is an obligate anaerobe. All isolates sensitive to a 5 μg metronidazole disc can be assumed to be anaerobes, but the isolate should also be subcultured on to blood agar and incubated in air + 5% CO_2 for 48 h to confirm that it is not capable of aerobic growth.

3.3.1 *Microscopic morphology*

Perform Gram stains of both solid and liquid cultures of the isolate if possible. Note the Gram reaction, cell morphology and presence/absence of spores. Clostridia and peptostreptococci, especially in old cultures, over-decolorize very easily and appear to be Gram negative. In the case of clostridia, cell shape and often the presence of spores makes mis-identification unlikely. Cell morphology can be a helpful aid in identification to genus level. *Bacteroides* spp. are notably very pleomorphic, often irregularly staining, parallel-sided bacilli; fusobacteria have slightly swollen middles and tapering ends, again often very pleomorphic. Branching may be shown by *Actinomyces* spp. and *Bifidobacterium* spp.

Spores show as unstained areas on a Gram stain; occasionally a spore stain (Appendix I) may be helpful: the shape and position of the spores should be noted. *Clostridium perfringens* rarely forms spores in culture and this is a helpful 'negative' finding.

Table 8. Simplified biochemical identification of saccharolytic *Bacteroides* spp. (adapted from ref. 11).

Use a pure culture and check that the Gram stain morphology is correct and carry out the following tests, using *Table 9* to identify the organism.

A. *Sugar fermentation plates.*

1. Pipette 1 ml of one of a 10% sugar solution test (glucose, lactose, sucrose, rhamnose, trehalose, mannitol) over the surface of a carbohydrate-free blood agar plate, and rock the plate to spread the solution over the surface.
2. Tip off the excess and dry the plate in an incubator (30 min).
3. Repeat for each sugar; label the plates.
4. Spot inoculate the organisms on to each sugar plate. Up to 4 organisms can be put on each plate; cut ditches in the agar to separate them. A control organism (e.g. *B.fragilis*) and a control uninoculated agar plate should be included.
5. Incubate for 48 h or until good growth is visible, then using a cork borer remove a plug or agar complete with the colony. To avoid carry-over, flame the cork borer between each plate and each organism.
6. Add 2−3 drops of bromophenol purple to the plug. If the sugar has been fermented, the acid produced changes the indicator from purple to yellow.

B. *Aesculin hydrolysis.*

1. Make up a 0.1% solution of aesculin in cooked meat broth or FAB broth and sterilize.
2. Inoculate, test and control organisms into separate bottles and incubate anaerobically until good growth is obtained.
3. Add 3 drops of 0.1% w/v ferric ammonium citrate to each bottle. A positive reaction is shown by a black colour in the broth.
4. Use a positive control (*B.fragilis*) and a negative control (*B.bivius*).

C. *Gelatin liquefaction.*

1. Add a gelatin disc containing carbon black particles (Oxoid Ltd) to broth culture of the organism and incubate for 48 h.
2. A positive result is indicated by the release of carbon particles into the medium.

D. *Indole production.*

1. Incubate the test and control organisms anaerobically in Indole Nitrate medium (BBL) until good growth is obtained.
2. Add 0.2 ml Kovac's reagent to 3 ml of the culture, shake and allow to stand for 10 min.
3. A positive reaction is shown by a red coloration in the surface layer.
4. Use a positive control; (*B.thetaiotaomicron*) and a negative control (*B.fragilis*).

3.3.2 *Colonial morphology*

Note the size, pigmentation, shape and edge of the colony, any swarming and haemolysis on blood agar.

Some anaerobes can be presumptively identified on the basis of their colonial and microscopic morphology. Examples are:

(i) *Bacteroides melaninogenicus−asaccharolyticus* group—black colonies.

(ii) *Bacteroides ureolyticus*—pitting of agar.

Table 9. Biochemical characteristics of *Bacteroides* spp. encountered in clinical specimens (adapted from refs 10, 11).

Organism	Glucose	Lactose	Sucrose	Rhamnose	Trehalose	Mannitol	Aesculin hydrolysis	Gelatin liquefaction	Indole production
B.fragilis	+	+	+	−	−	−	+	+/−	−
B.vulgatus	+	+	+	+	−	−	+/−	+	−
B.distasonis	+	+	+	+(−)	+	−	+	+(−)	−
B.thetaiotaomicron	+	+	+	+	+	−	+	+/−	+
B.ovatus	+	+	+	+	+	+	+	+	+
B.uniformis	+	+	+	−	+	−	+	+(−)	+
B.melaninogenicus	+	−(+)	+	−(+)	−	−	+/−	+	−
B.intermedius	+	+	+	−	−	−	−	+	+
B.bivius	+	+	−	−	−	−	−	+	−
B.disiens	+	−	−	−	−	−	−	+	−
B.oralis	+	+	+	+/−[f]	−	−	+(−)[e]	+	−
B.asaccharolyticus	−	−	−	−	−	−	−	+	+(−)

Key:
+ >95% strains positive
− >95% strains negative
+(−) 70−95% strains positive
−(+) 70−95% strains negative
+/− 30−70% strains give either result.

(iii) *Clostridium perfringens*—typical double zone haemolysis, no spores.

(iv) *Clostridium tetani*—fine, swarming growth, 'drumstick' bacilli (terminal spores).

3.3.3 *Further conventional tests*

All laboratories must be able to identify *B.fragilis* and pathogenic *Clostridia* spp. The following method will identify most *Bacteroides* spp. (*Table 8* and *9*). An alternative method using antibiotic sensitivity patterns is described elsewhere (9).

Clostridia should be speciated (*Table 10* and *11*) in order to distinguish those which are pathogenic in wound infections, i.e. *Clostridium perfringens, C.tetani, C.novyi A (syn. oedematiens), C.septicum, C.histolyticum, C.bifermentans*, from those which are not. *Clostridium botulinum* is rarely encountered as a wound pathogen and is not discussed further here. *C.tetani* has such characteristic fine swarming growth and drumstick spores that it should be presumptively recognized and the clinicians informed. Toxin testing should be performed either locally or by a reference laboratory.

3.3.4 *New approaches to identification*

Two commercial identification kits containing biochemical tests in pre-packaged form are available: API 20 A (API Lab Products) and Minitek (Becton Dickinson). The test results are scored numerically and the resulting number profile corresponds to a species identification in the analytical index provided. Both kits work best with the saccharolytic

Table 10. Identification scheme for pathogenic clostridia from clinical material.

Use a pure culture and check that the Gram stain morphology is correct and carry out the following tests, using *Table 11* to identify the organism.

1. Egg-yolk agar with antitoxin detects alphatoxin (lecithinase C) by neutralization with specific antitoxin (Nagler reaction) and lipase production. Spread a loopful of antitoxin over one half of an egg-yolk agar plate and allow it to dry for 15 min.
2. Streak the isolate to be tested across the plate from the non-antitoxin side.
3. Streak a positive control on each plate and incubate for 24 h for Nagler reaction, 48 h for lipase detection.
4. *Alpha-toxin-*, or lecithinase C-*producing* organisms produce a diffuse opaque halo in the medium surrounding the colonies, on the untreated half of the plate. On the half treated with antitoxin there is no halo. Note that this opacity diffuses out from the colonies for 2−3 mm.
5. *Lipase-producing* organisms produce a restricted opacity immediately beneath the colonies and a pearly oil-slick layer on top of the colonies. This opacity is not affected by antitoxin (*Figure 3*).
6. Inoculate sugar fermentation plates for the detection of glucose, maltose, sucrose and lactose fermentation (described in *Table 8*). The control organisms should be *Clostridium perfringens*.
7. Add gelatin disc (Oxoid Ltd) to a broth culture of organism to detect gelatin liquefaction and incubate for up to 5 days.
8. Inoculate a Christensen's urea slope to detect urease production.
9. Inoculate a litmus milk.
10. Test for indole production as described in *Table 8*.
11. After 48 h incubation read and record the results of the egg-yolk agar test, sugar fermentation test, urease and litmus milk tests.
12. Check the gelatin liquefaction test and if negative reincubate for further 5 days.

Table 11. Identification of clostridia (adapted from refs 10,12)

Organism	Glucose	Maltose	Lactose	Sucrose	Gelatinase	Urease	Indole	Lecithinase C	Lipase	Litmus milk	Spores
C.perfringens	+	+	+	+	+	-	-	+	-	ACG	rare, N
C.septicum	+	+	+	-	+	-	-	-	-	AC	V
C.novyi (A)	+	+	-	-	+	-	-	+	+	GC	V
C.bifermentans	+	+	-	-	+	-	+	+	-	CD	V
C.sordellii	+	+	-	-	+	+	+	+	-	CD	V
C.sporogenes	+	+	-	-	+	-	-	-	+	D	V
C.histolyticum	-	-	-	-	+	+	-	-	-	D	V
C.tetani	-	-	-	-	+	-	+	-	-	-	T

Key:
+ positive
- negative
A acid (pink)
G gas
C clot

D digestion of clot
T terminal spores
N central spores
ST subterminal spores
V spores variable

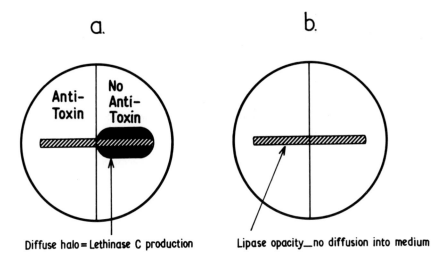

Figure 3. Reactions seen on egg-yolk agar: (**a**) α-toxin producing organism (e.g. *Clostridium perfringens*); (**b**) non-α-toxin-producing organism which does, however, produce lipase (e.g. *Clostridium sporogenes*).

Bacteroides spp. but their overall accuracy is only about 60% even when the recommended supplemental tests are performed (13).

Two new kits using enzyme detection have recently been marketed, the RapID ANA (Innovative Diagnostic Systems Inc.) and the An-Ident (Analytab) or ATB 32A (API Lab Products) in the UK. They give a result after 4 h of aerobic incubation, and provided their cost is competitive they represent a useful new approach. They have been evaluated in the USA and their accuracy to genus level compared to conventional tests is of the order of 95% and species level 80% (14,15). The enzyme kits should be supplemented with egg-yolk agar reactions for the clostridia (*Figure 3*).

3.4 Anaerobic sensitivity testing

For methodology refer to Chapter 7, remember to use appropriate anaerobes as controls. Testing of the following antibiotics is suggested for all species: metronidazole (5 µg); penicillin (1 unit); ampicillin (10 µg); erythromycin (10 µg); Augmentin (20 + 10 µg).

Additional antibiotics to test may include: clindamycin (10 µg); chloramphenicol (10 µg); cefoxitin (30 µg); imipenem (30 µg). Report antibiotics according to the local policy.

4. SKIN AND SOFT TISSUE INFECTIONS

4.1 Pyoderma and cellulitis

These include primary skin infections such as boils, furunculosis, impetigo, cellulitis, erysipelas, infected sebaceous cysts and soft tissue abscesses and erysipeloid.

4.1.1 *Type of samples*

Samples may be pus/pus swabs, the occasional biopsy, curettage, or needle aspirates.

4.1.2 *Expected organisms*

(i)   Common: *Staphylococcus aureus*, typically associated with pustular lesions but also with cellulitis; Group A β-haemolytic streptococci, typically associated with cellulitis.

(ii) Less common: *Haemophilus influenzae* (facial cellulitis in children); other β-haemolytic streptococci, usualy Group G, occasionally Groups F, B, C, but rarely D; anaerobic cocci (infected sebaceous cysts), *Bacteroides* spp., *Clostridium* spp. (anaerobic cellulitis); *Candida albicans* (paronychia, muco-cutaneous candidasis).

(iii) Uncommon: *Erysipelothrix rhusiopathiae* (erysipeploid); *Corynebacterium minutissimum* (erythrasma); *Corynebacterium diphtheriae* (cutaneous diphtheria); *Bacillus anthracis* (anthrax); *Mycobacterium marinum, ulcerans* and *kansasii*; *Pseudomonas mallei* (melioidosis); *P.aeruginosa* (folliculitis); *Sporothrix schenkii* (sporotrichosis); dermatiaceous fungi of mycetoma; *Nocardia* spp.; *Lymphogranuloma venereum* (inguinal lymphadenitis with discharging sinuses).

4.1.3 *Special processing*

Additional processing to that described in Sections 2.1 and 2.2 is necessary only for the uncommon causes. The laboratory needs to be alerted by the clinical details (e.g. foreign travel, occupation).

The following points may be helpful.

Cellulitis in a child	Put up a chocolate agar plate for *Haemophilus influenzae*.
Cellulitis in butcher's or meat/fish handlers	Check all α-haemolytic colonies, they may be *Erysipelothrix rhusiopathiae* which is catalase-negative, H$_2$S-positive.
Chronic infections and infections in immuno-suppressed patients	Do a ZN film if Gram film negative and culture for mycobacteria and nocardia (Chapter 3).
Foreign travel	Consider exotic fungi (e.g. *Sporothrix schenkii*), protozoal infections (e.g. leishmaniasis), and *Corynebacterium diphtheriae*.

Culture and identification methods for the more exotic organisms can be obtained from major texts (6,16,17,18).

4.1.4 *Identification methods*

The identification of the common pathogens *Staphylococcus aureus* and the β haemolytic streptococci is described here. For *Haemophilus* identification see Chapter 3; for anaerobes see Section 3.3.

(i) *Staphylococcus aureus*

(a)   *Pus*: often has little odour and is thick and creamy. The Gram stain shows many polymorphonuclear leucocytes with Gram-positive cocci which are intracellular and/or extracellular, and tend to form clumps or pairs. Dead bacteria stain Gram negative.

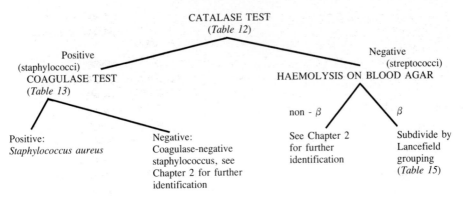

Figure 4. Simplified scheme for the identification of aerobic Gram-positive cocci from clinical specimens.

Table 12. Procedures for performing catalase test.

1.	Place a drop of 3% hydrogen peroxide on a glass slide.
2.	Rub the colony on to a small area of one side of a cover-slip, taking the colonies from blood-free media where possible, as blood is weakly catalase-positive.
3.	Place the coverslip, colony side down, over the drop of hydrogen peroxide.
4.	Positive: bubbles produced, negative: no bubbles.

Alternative method

1.	Using a glass capillary tube 100 mm × 1.5 mm (LIP Ltd) scrape a small amount of the colony into the end of the tube, taking care not to take any of the underlying medium.
2.	Dip the other end of the tube into 3% hydrogen peroxide and allow the tube to half-fill by capillary action.
3.	Invert the tube allowing the hydrogen peroxide to flow down into contact with the bacteria; observe the production of gas.

(b)   *Culture*: at 18−24 h good growth is visible on the blood agar and the CLED or MacConkey plates. The best growth is seen on the aerobic blood plates where the colonies are 1−2 mm in diameter, opaque or creamy white, with a smooth edge. The classical golden colour may take 48 h to become apparent, a narrow zone of β-haemolysis is fairly common. On CLED agar the colonies are often bright yellow; on MacConkey agar, deep opaque pink.

A few strains are CO_2 or nutritionally dependent, and the colonies correspondingly small on ordinary media, especially if not incubated in CO_2.

Identification: the simplified scheme shown in *Figure 4* outlines the steps in the identification of *S.aureus*. Perform Gram stains (refer to Appendix I) and catalase test (described in *Table 12*).

S.aureus is the only member of the family *Micrococcaceae* likely to be encountered in specimens from humans that produces coagulase and this character alone is used in most laboratories to identify the species. The coagulase negative staphylococci and micrococci are important pathogens in certain situations (see Chapter 2).

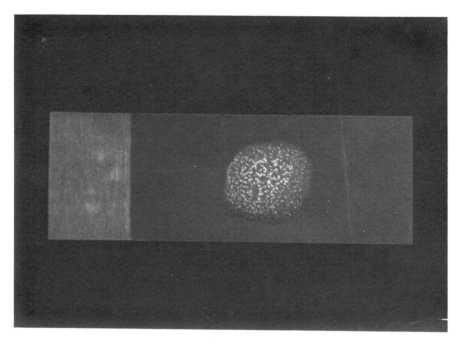

Figure 5. A positive slide coagulase test.

The enzyme coagulase converts fibrinogen to fibrin, so causing the organisms to agglutinate in small quantities of plasma. The slide coagulase test (see *Figure 5*) detects cell-bound coagulase (or clumping factor). Five per cent of strains of *S.aureus* which are slide coagulase negative will produce free coagulase which is detected in the tube coagulase test (see *Figure 6*). In the laboratory, all staphylococci which are slide coagulase negative must have a tube coagulase test carried out. These tests are described in *Table 13*.

Further tests can be carried out where there is doubt about the identification. These are listed below, and whilst not infallible, will aid identification. *S.aureus* is usually positive in these tests; coagulase negative staphylococci are usually negative.

(i)   Production of thermostable deoxyribonuclease (thermonuclease, TNase) (19)—this is a very reliable test but a little time-consuming, so is carried out less often than the simple test for deoxyribonuclease (DNase), see *Table 14*.

(ii) Production of deoxyribonuclease (DNase)—commonly used in the UK, described in *Table 14* (see also *Figure 7*).

Recently several agglutination tests ('Staphaurex'), Wellcome Diagnostics and 'Staph Rapid', Roche) have become available. These tests use either latex particles or sensitized erythrocytes which are coated with purified IgG to detect protein A and with fibrinogen to detect clumping factor. They are slide tests like the slide coagulase. Emulsify a few staphylococcal colonies in a drop of the liquid reagent and look for agglutination—which occurs if the colonies are *S.aureus*. These tests are easy and quick to perform

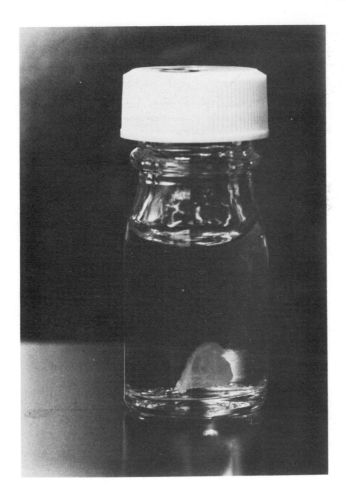

Figure 6. A positive tube coagulase test; the plasma clot can be seen at the bottom of the tube.

(15 sec), sensitive and specific, but are more costly than slide coagulase and tube coagulase.

Laboratories may find them useful but they are too costly as yet to replace the slide coagulase test and not quite as sensitive as the tube test, especially with methicillin-resistant strains (20).

(ii) *β-haemolytic streptococci*. Lancefield groups A (*Streptococcus pyogenes*) and G are the commonest pathogens in soft tissue infections, although groups F, B and C may also be found. These streptococci do not invariably show β-haemolysis, so non-haemolytic or α-haemolytic streptococci which appear to be playing a major part in infection should be grouped and biochemically identified.

(a) *Pus*: usually thin and watery, if present at all, although infections caused by group F streptococci (*S.milleri*) can result in the formation of large amounts of thick pus. The Gram stain shows Gram-positive cocci in short or long chains.

(b) *Culture*: β-haemolysis is seen as a complete clearing of the blood agar medium

111

Table 13. Methods for the detection of staphylococcal coagulase.

A. *Slide coagulase*
This test should not be performed on colonies from high-salt-content media as false positive results may be obtained.

1.   Emulsify several colonies in a drop of water on slide to make a heavy suspension. A second suspension should be prepared alongside to act as a control for auto-agglutination.
2.   Stir in a loopful of undiluted rabbit plasma.
3.   Rock the slide gently for 5 sec; agglutination within 5 sec indicates a positive result (see *Figure 5*).

B. *Tube coagulase*

1.   Add 40 μl of rabbit plasma to 360 μl of normal saline in a small test tube.
2.   Either add 40 μl of an overnight broth culture, or emulsify several colonies straight into the diluted plasma and add a drop of nutrient broth.
3.   Set up controls with each batch of tests:
     Coagulase positive (e.g. NCTC 6571)
     Coagulase negative (e.g. NCTC 7944)
     Uninoculated plasma.
4.   Incubate at 37°C and examine at 1, 3 and 6 h and after overnight incubation. Clotting of the plasma into a gel (see *Figure 6* for appearance) represents a positive result.

Table 14. Presence for the detection of DNase and TNase.

A. *DNase test*

1.   Spot inoculate the organism under test, also a positive control (*Staphylococcus aureus*) and a negative control (*E.coli*) on to DNase agar (Oxoid Ltd, Code CM321).
2.   Incubate overnight.
3.   Flood the plate with 10% v/v HCl; this causes precipitation of nucleic acid which makes the medium cloudy. Where the nucleic acid has been hydrolysed by DNase, there is no precipitation (*Figure 7*).

B. *Rapid TNase test*

1.   Transfer an isolated colony of the organism to be tested to 0.5 ml of brain heart infusion broth and incubate for 2−6 h at 37°C; include negative and positive controls.
2.   Punched wells in TDA medium (Appendix II) (the large end of a sterile Pasteur pipette works well) and fill the wells with the broth culture which has been heated at 100°C for 15 min and cooled.
3.   Incubate the plate at 37°C in an upright position and inspect after 1 h and again after 2 h for the presence of a pink zone around the well. The pink halo is evidence of the breakdown of DNA because toluidine blue dye is blue when complexed with intact DNA but becomes metachromatic (pink) when complexed with nucleotides. A small, clear zone around a well is not indicative of a positive test, since some coagulase-negative staphylococci can destroy the dye without denaturing DNA.

around the colonies, enhanced after anaerobic incubation. α-Haemolyis is seen as a zone of greenish discoloration. Colonies of groups A, B, C and G are whitish-grey and about 1 mm in diameter; group F colonies may be pinpoint in size. Zones of β-haemolysis are largest around group G and C streptococci, Group B streptococci show a narrow zone of haemolysis and the colonies themselves are large and may have a characteristic pink tinge.

(c)   *Identification*: streptococci are identified in the diagnostic laboratory primarily by the simple tests shown in *Figure 4* and their haemolytic action on blood agar,

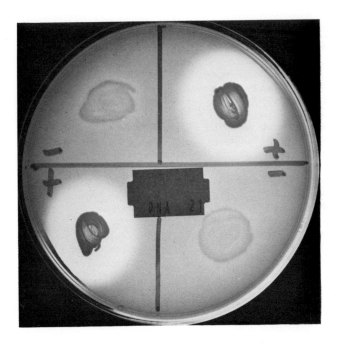

Figure 7. Agar plate DNase test; unaltered DNA has been precipitated with 10% v/v HCl and clear zones where DNA has been denatured are seen around the inocula labelled as positive, which are *Staphylococcus aureus*; the DNase-negative isolates are *S. epidermidis*.

α, β, non-haemolysis or γ and α'. α'-Haemolysis consists of an inner zone of partial haemolysis with an outer zone of complete haemolysis which macroscopically resembles β-haemolysis.

β-Haemolytic streptococci are further identified by the detection of specific cell-wall carbohydrate antigens, first characterized by Rebecca Lancefield. Eighteen distinct antigenic groups are now recognized: groups A−H and K−T. Some groups contain largely one species as defined by their biochemical reactions, for example Group A, *S. pyogenes*; Group B, *S. agalactiae*; but other groups contain a number of species, for example Group C, *S. equisimilis*, *S. dysgalactiae* and *S. equii*. The β-haemolytic streptococci are usually identified only to Lancefield group level and not given species name in most clinical laboratories.

The β-haemolytic streptococci which are pathogenic in man are groups A, B, C, D, F, G and R (acquired from contact with pigs), but rarely any other group. Methods for grouping therefore need detect only these antigens. Some commercial grouping methods exclude groups D (*S. faecalis/faecium*) and F: D because these species can be recognized by their ability to grow on MacConkey's agar and positive aesculin test, and F because these are uncommon outside certain specific clinical conditions. The original Lancefield grouping method is seldom used now outside reference laboratories but is described in *Table 15*. The Lancefield hot acid technique is the reference method for grouping and is the only method available for extracting the type-specific protein antigens used in typing of group A and B streptococci.

113

Table 15. Lancefield grouping method.

A. *Hot-acid extraction*

1.   Culture the organism overnight in 50 ml Todd-Hewitt broth.
2.   Centrifuge and discard the supernatant.
3.   Add 0.4 ml of 0.2MHCl to the packed cells in a centrifuge tube, mix the cells well and place the tube in a boiling water bath for 10 min.
4.   Allow to cool then add one drop of 0.02% w/v phenol red.
5.   Neutralize with 0.2 M NaOH.
6.   Centrifuge and preserve the clear supernatant; this is the antigen extract.

B. *Precipitation*

1.   Allow a 1 cm column of the appropriate anti-serum to run up into a capillary tube (LIP Ltd) by capillary action.
2.   Wipe the outside carefully.
3.   Introduce a similar amount of antigen extract into the tube ensuring that there are no fingerprints on the outside of the tube.
4.   Occlude the top end of the tube once the fluids have run well up the tube.
5.   Occlude the bottom end of the tube with plasticine and stand in a rack.
6.   A positive reaction is indicated by precipitation at the interface within 5 min.

Table 16. Examples of streptococcal grouping kits.

Name	Principle	Groups detected	Manufacturer
Streptex	Latex agglutination	ABCDFG	Wellcome Diagnostics
Phadebact	Co-agglutination	ABCG	Pharmacia Diagnostics
Streptosec	Co-agglutination	ABCG	Organon Teknika Ltd
Oxoid Streptococcal Grouping Kit	Latex agglutination	ABDCFG	Oxoid Ltd

All grouping methods use specific antibodies to detect group antigens and the immunological recognition is visualized by precipitation or agglutination. Most UK laboratories now use commercially produced grouping kits in which grouping is done as slide agglutination. In these kits the group specific antibodies are conjugated to either latex particles or to specially prepared protein A-rich staphylococcal cells. These carrier particles are so large that the agglutination can be seen with the naked eye.

A number of kits are available: they can all be used on small numbers of colonies from solid media, and some have been used with extraction to detect Group A streptococci directly from swabs. The time taken for the tests varies from 1 min to 1 h depending on whether the method includes antigen extraction. Some of the kits available are listed in *Table 16*. The performance and costs are varied and choice is a matter of individual decision.

Cross-reactions can occur with the grouping sera, notably with groups D and G, leading to misidentification. For this reason group D streptococci which have been isolated from a serious infection (e.g. endocarditis) should be further identified using biochemical tests, (API-Strept, API System) or individual tests (6). Pneumococci can on occasions agglutinate with group C antisera. The distinctive colonial morphology of *S.pneumoniae* should prevent confusion but if there is any doubt, identification of the presumed *S.pneumoniae* with optochin and bile-solubility tests should be undertaken.

4.1.5 *Sensitivity testing, interpreting and reporting*

Most patients with pyoderma or cellulitis in the UK are treated empirically with penicillin and/or flucloxacillin or with erythromycin if allergic to penicillin. The intravenous route should be used in serious infections. Topical antibiotics are not recommended.

Direct disc sensitivity testing with appropriate antibiotics is useful if a recognized pathogen is seen on the Gram stain; otherwise the microbiologist should wait for the cultures. Suggested antibiotics to test and report for the common pathogens follow. Any antibiotics that the patient is taking should always be reported (together with comment on appropriateness), also any to which the organism is resistant.

(i) *Staphylococcus aureus*
     First-line antibiotics
     Test: penicillin, erythromycin, tetracycline, fusidic acid, clindamycin, gentamicin, methicillin at 30°C (or other suitable methods for the isoxazolyl penicillins).
     Report: all on local antibiotic policy—but consider not reporting fusidic acid, clindamycin and gentamicin unless the organism is resistant.

Second-line antibiotics: these are tested if the organism is multi-resistant or methicillin resistant, or if there is a clinical reason for doing so.

     Test: vancomycin, rifampicin.
     Consider: teicoplanin, ciprofloxacin, chloramphenicol, cephalosporins. Note that 90% of *S.aureus* isolates are now penicillinase-producing, regardless of origin.
          Telephone the clinician if a methicillin-resistant *S.aureus* is isolated and inform the Infection Control Doctor or Nurse.

(ii) *β-haemolytic streptococci*
     Test: penicillin, erythromycin, tetracycline, clindamycin, cephradine.
     Report: all on local antibiotic policy.

Penicillin is preferred to ampicillin except in enterococcal infections. Streptococci of groups A, B, C and G are usually sensitive to penicillin.

4.2 **Wound infections**

Wound infections follow surgery or trauma that disrupts the skin or mucosal surface (e.g. road traffic accidents and bites). Post-operative wound infections commonly follow gastro-intestinal surgery and some gynaecological surgery, and are discussed further in Sections 5 and 6 respectively.

4.2.1 *Expected organisms*

The type of infecting organism depends on the site and nature of the surgery or trauma.

Wound infections following colo-rectal surgery often contain bacteria from the large bowel (*E.coli, Bacteroides* spp., etc.). Wound infections following bites will contain mouth organisms from the biting animal.

Wound infections are often caused by organisms resident on the skin surface which has been breached. The main culprit here is *S.aureus*, and this is the only constituent of the normal skin flora that is worth looking for *routinely*.

(i) Common: *S.aureus;* β-haemolytic streptococci; *E.coli; Bacteroides fragilis;* *Proteus* spp.; other *Enterobacteriaceae; Cl.perfringens;* anaerobic cocci.

(ii) Less common: micro-aerophilic streptococci; *Pasteurella multocida* (animal bites); other clostridia, other bacteroides; *Fusobacterium* spp.; *Pseudomonas* spp.; *Salmonella* spp.; *Capnocytophaga canimorsus* (formerly DF-2).

(iii) Rare: vibrios (infected marine wounds); *Cl.tetani;* fungi.

4.2.2 *Special processing methods*

None are necessary for the common pathogens. It may be worthwhile to carry out gas chromatography on pus. Inoculation of TCBS (thiosulphate-citrate-bile-sucrose) agar will aid in the recognition of marine vibrios.

4.2.3 *Identification and sensitivity testing*

(i)   Do not carry out sensitivity tests on or identify isolates further than necessary on the normal skin flora (coagulase negative staphylococci, micrococci, diphtheroids, propionibacteria).

(ii)   Identify and carry out sensitivity tests on *S.aureus* and β-haemolytic streptococci: Sections 4.1.4, 4.1.5.

(iii)   Identify to genus level* and carry out sensitivity tests on *Proteus* spp. and *Pseudomonas* spp.: Sections 5.1.3, 5.1.4.

(iv)   Carry out sensitivity tests but do not routinely identify* the lactose fermenting coliforms: Sections 5.1.3, 5.1.4.

(v)   Identify non-lactose fermenting coliforms sufficiently* to exclude salmonella, and carry out sensitivity tests: Sections 5.1.3., 5.1.4.

(vi)   Identify and carry out sensitivity tests on anaerobes: Section 3.3, 3.4.

(vii)   Look for *Pasteurella multocida* in swabs from infected animal bites. Direct microscopy of material from the swab is rarely helpful.
Identification: smooth, greyish colonies on blood agar, poor growth at 18−24 h, colonies reaching 2 mm at 48 h. No growth on MacConkey or CLED agar. Gram stain of colonies reveals Gram-negative cocco-bacilli which are also oxidase-positive and penicillin-sensitive. Complete identification is by API 20E or suitable sugars, urea and indole tests (6).
Sensitivity testing and reporting: test and report penicillin, tetracycline, cephalosporins.

*These organisms should be fully identified to species level and sent for typing (where applicable), if they are found to be multiply antibiotic resistant or they are involved in an episode of cross-infection.

4.2.4 *Interpretation and reporting*

The presence of normal commensal skin flora (apart from *S.aureus*) is common, and although it may be recorded on the report is rarely significant.

The main problem with reporting wound swab cultures is that, apart from the major pathogens such as β-haemolytic streptococci, *S.aureus* and *B.fragilis*, it can be very difficult to judge the pathogenic role of the organisms isolated. This difficulty applies particularly to coliforms, *Proteus* spp. and *Pseudomonas* spp. which are often only colonizing the wound. Many mild post-operative wound infections—those with some reddening or a little serous or even purulent discharge—are not treated by surgeons unless a major pathogen is isolated, as the infection will often resolve. There are occasions when these infections are treated, such as when deep tension sutures or subcutaneous non-absorbable sutures are present, and in clinical conditions where the patient is not fully immuno-competent (e.g. diabetes mellitus). If there is a collection of pus in the wound then surgical drainage is the most important therapeutic step; antibiotics alone will be ineffective. The presence of pathogens in the absence of clinical signs may not require antibiotic treatment (with the possible exception of group A β-haemolytic streptococci). This is particularly relevant for the pathogenic clostridia such as *C.perfringens* which are commonly isolated from wounds as a consequence of faecal contamination.

These problems with interpretation are often left to clinicians to resolve. However, discussion with the clinical microbiologist often ensures appropriate therapy is used. The practical approach in the laboratory is to identify and carry out sensitivity tests on all isolates except the commensal skin flora and those organisms thought to be colonizing the wound as described in Sections 4.2.3 and 5.1.4.

4.3 Gangrene, myositis and fasciitis

Extensive serious infections include gas gangrene (clostridial myonecrosis), necrotizing fasciitis (Fournier's gangrene) and Meleney's synergistic gangrene. *Localized infections* include pyo-myositis (*S.aureus*), infected vascular gangrene (usually a low-grade infection), psoas muscle abscess (*Mycobacterium tuberculosis, S.aureus*).

4.3.1 *Expected organisms*

Anaerobes	Pathogenic clostridia: *Clostridium perfringens, C.septicum, C.novyii, C.histolyticum, C.novyii* A
	Anaerobic cocci
	Bacteroides spp.
Aerobes	Group A β-haemolytic streptococci
	Micro-aerophilic streptococci
	S.aureus
	Rarely, coliforms and other Gram-negative bacilli (diabetic patients usually).

4.3.2 *Special processing*

Process swabs, pus and tissue as described in Sections 2.2, 2.3 and 2.4, respectively. Pay special attention to anaerobic culture (Section 3.2).

4.3.3 *Identification and sensitivity testing*

(i)   Identify and carry out sensitivity testing on all anaerobic isolates: Sections 3.3, 3.4.

Identify and carry out sensitivity testing on *S.aureus* and β-haemolytic streptococci, see Sections 4.1.4 and 4.1.5.

(iii)   Identify and carry out sensitivity testing on other streptococci, see Section 5.1.4.

(iv)   Identify and carry out sensitivity testing on other organisms in diabetic patients or if warranted by the clinical picture.

4.3.4 *Interpretation and reporting*

Since the pathogens involved are well defined and often isolated from normally sterile sites there is rarely any difficulty in interpreting culture results. Coliform organisms are so rarely involved (except in diabetic patients) that unless they are isolated from pus or tissue they are assumed to be secondary invaders or colonizers. Blood cultures are a useful adjunct to diagnosis in the severe infections of this group.

4.4 **Burns, varicose ulcers, ischaemic ulcers, pressure sores**

These lesions are universally colonized with various potentially pathogenic bacteria. This makes interpretation of culture results nearly impossible. The best practical approach is to identify and carry out sensitivity tests as suggested for wound infections. The clinician, sometimes with advice from the clinical microbiologist, decides on clinical grounds when to use systemic antibiotic therapy instead of cleansing and antiseptics. Cellulitis would be a deciding factor, as would accompanying bacteraemia or proposed skin grafting.

4.5 **Sinuses**

Chronic sinuses are associated with the drainage of underlying deep-seated infection. The commonest of these is chronic osteomyelitis, and the processing of such samples is described in Section 7.2. Other conditions in which sinuses are found are all uncommon in the UK and include lymphogranuloma venereum, actinomycosis, *Nocardia* infections, tuberculosis and atypical mycobacterial infection.

Basic laboratory methods for culture and identification of actinomycetes follow, see also Section 6.3. For detailed accounts, see the reference texts (6–8).

4.5.1 *Actinomycosis*

Infected tissue is a hard, granulomatous mass which discharges to the skin surface in multiple sinuses. The usual sites of infection are the jaw (cervico-facial), the ileo-caecal region, the lungs, and in association with intrauterine contraceptive devices (IUDs) (22). Liver and cerebral abscesses have been reported following haematogenous spread.

Pus or tissue biopsy are preferred, but usually all that can be obtained is the dressing from the discharging lesion. Swabs should not be processed unless no other sample can be obtained.

4.5.2 *Microscopic examination*

(i) Place pus, fluid, IUD or dressings in a petri dish and examine for sulphur granules with a plate microscope ($7\times$ to $15\times$ magnification). Sulphur granules are macro-colonies of actinomycete bacteria. They are yellowish white, $0.2-2$ mm in diameter and irregular in shape.

(ii) Crush a granule together with a drop of water between two microscope slides. Remove one slide, heat-fix the preparation and stain with Gram's stain. The typical and diagnostic appearance is a central mass of Gram-positive branching and non-branching filaments surrounded by Gram-negative club-shaped forms.

4.5.3 *Culture*

Culture pus, fluid, tissue on blood agar in air $+\ 5\%\ CO_2$, and anaerobically and in broth medium as described in Section 2.

(ii) To culture a dressing for actinomyces, pick the most contaminated part (complete with granules if seen) and place it in either fastidious anaerobe broth (Lab M), pre-reduced cooked meat broth or thioglycollate broth.

(iii) Incubate, preferably anaerobically with the cap loosened, for 48 h, then centrifuge the broth and culture the deposit as above.

(iv) Incubate culture plates initially for 48 h; if they are sterile reincubate for 5 to 7 days and re-examine. If still sterile then reincubate for a further 2 weeks before discarding.

(v) *Actinomyces israelii* grows on the anaerobic plates only. Smooth strains grow after $2-3$ days and are unremarkable $1-2$ mm white, opaque, smooth colonies. The more typical rough strains usually take $5-7$ days to grow and appear as 1 mm raised, irregular, white, opaque colonies which look like very rough molar teeth.

4.5.4 *Identification*

Typical sulphur granules in clinical material are diagnostic. If absent, definitive identification of actinomyces is more difficult. Gram's stain of colonies shows Gram-positive bacilli, sometimes filamentous and sparsely branching. Formal identification and differentiation from the other anaerobic Gram-positive non-spore-forming bacilli is accomplished by gas−liquid chromatography and biochemical tests (6−8).

4.6 **Fistulae**

Swabs from fistulaes yield the indigenous flora of the underlying viscus as well as skin flora. The interpretation of the bacteriology of such swabs is impossible and has little clinical relevance, since treatment of the bacteria will not 'cure' the fistula. The under-lying cause must be sought.

4.7 **Vesicles and bullae**

Bacterial infections include neonatal scalded skin syndrome and toxic epidermal necrolysis (*S. aureus*); cellulitis with bullae (*β*-haemolytic streptococci); gangrene with bullae (*Pseudomonas aeruginosa, Clostridium* spp.). Viral infections include chickenpox (*Varicella*); shingles (*Herpes zoster*); cold sores and genital herpes (*Herpes simplex*); and orf.

4.7.1 Type of sample

These may be vesicle or bulla fluid, usually in a needle and syringe or a capillary tube (for electron microscopy), and swabs of fluid or base of the blister.

4.7.2 Expected organisms

(i) Common: *Herpes zoster; Herpes simplex.*
(ii) Less common: Group A *β*-haemolytic streptococci; *Clostridium* spp.; *S. aureus*; orf virus.
(iii) Rare: *Pseudomonas aeruginosa.*

4.7.3 Special processing methods

None are needed for the bacterial pathogens. The viral infections may often be diagnosed clinically, but this should be confirmed with electron microscopy of bulla or vesicle fluid and then viral culture. Collect the fluid for electron microscopy with a needle and syringe; for culture take swabs of the base lesions (i.e. containing epithelial cells) into viral transport medium. The reader is referred to textbooks on virology.

4.7.4 Identification and sensitivity testing

Identify and carry out sensitivity tests on group A *β*-haemolytic streptococci and *S. aureus*, see Section 4.1. If the clinical information is suggestive, such as presence of gangrene or immunosuppression, then identify and carry out sensitivity tests on *Clostridium* spp. (Sections 3.3, 3.4) and *Pseudomonas* spp. (Sections 5.1.3, 5.1.4).

4.7.5 Interpretation and reporting

This is usually straightforward, since the clinical picture often suggests the aetiology. Sometimes coliforms, *Pseudomonas* or *Proteus* are isolated from such lesions. This nearly always represents colonization of the wet surface of a broken vesicle or bulla. Rarely *Pseudomonas aeruginosa* is found as a primary pathogen in immunosuppressed patients—a type of ecthyma gangrenosum.

4.8 Suppurative lymphadenitis

Commonly, the infection is an uncomplicated acute pyogenic infection. Rare conditions include tuberculosis, tularaemia, plague, meliodosis, sporotrichosis and glanders. Needle aspirates or lymph node biopsies are the most useful specimens.

4.8.1 Expected organisms

(i) Common: *S. aureus*; group A *β*-haemolytic streptococci.
(ii) Less common: *M. tuberculosis*; *M. bovis.*

(iii) Rare: *Francisella tularensis* (tularaemia); *Yersinia pestis* (plague); *Pseudomonas mallei* (glanders); *Pseudomonas pseudomallei* (meliodosis); *Coccidioides immitis*; *Sporothrix schenkii* (sporotrichosis).

4.8.2 *Special processing*

The aspirate or tissue should be processed as described in Section 2.4. For mycobacteria see Chapter 3, for fungal pathogens see Evans and Richardson (23). Additional culture media will be needed for some of the rare causes listed above, and should be set up if the clinical details suggest this. These are Category 2 pathogens and must be processed under suitable containment. *Yersinia pestis* and *Pseudomonas pseudomallei* will grow on 'ordinary' media. The following are fastidious and need additional media: *Francisella tularensis* requires Dorset's egg medium; *Pseudomonas mallei* requires 4% glycerol blood agar.

4.8.3 *Identification and sensitivity testing*

Identification and sensitivity tests should be performed on *S.aureus* and β-haemolytic streptococci (Sections 4.1.4 and 4.1.5). Provided the tissue or aspirate has not been contaminated by the laboratory, any growth must be regarded as significant and must be fully identified with sensitivity tests. The rare organisms which need special media will not normally be seen on routine culture. Those will grow on routine culture will appear as small, unusual-looking Gram-negative bacilli. Laboratories with no experience of these organisms may wish to refer suspect colonies or even the original specimens to reference centres.

4.9 Chronic ulcers

The following clinical conditions are found: atypical mycobacterial infections, for example swimming-pool granuloma, fish-tank granuloma (*M.marinum*); Buruli ulcer (*M.ulcerans*); sporotrichosis (*Sporothrix schenkii*); glanders (*Pseudomonas mallei*); leishmaniasis and paracoccidioidomycosis (muco-cutaneous ulceration). There are also chronic ulcers associated with the sexually transmitted diseases, syphilis, yaws, chancroid and lymphogranuloma venereum. Samples from these ulcers should be either aspiration or biopsy samples.

Reference should be made to Chapter 3 for mycobacteria; to mycology textbooks for the fungi (23) and to Chapter 4 for the sexually transmitted infections; and to major texts for the remainder. If leishmaniasis is suspected, the aspirate or biopsy should be stained for Leishman−Donovan bodies; see other texts (6,16).

5. INFECTION ASSOCIATED WITH THE GASTRO-INTESTINAL TRACT

5.1 Intra-abdominal abscess

Subphrenic abscess, pelvic abscess, appendix abscess and para-colic abscess will be encountered.

5.1.1 *Expected organisms*

Bacteria from the bowel occur, for example *E.coli; Proteus* sp.; other *Enterobacteriaceae;*

enterococci and other streptococci; *B.fragilis;* anaerobic cocci; and other anaerobes. *S.aureus* is less common and probably follows bacteraemia.

5.1.2 Processing methods

(i)   Process pus and swabs as described in Sections 2.1 and 2.2. Gram stains usually confirm mixed infection but many unexpectedly reveal a pure staphylococcal infection.

(ii)   Gas chromatography is rarely useful since the presence of anaerobes is almost universal.

5.1.3 Identification methods

(i)   Identify enterococci by grouping and by inference from sensitivity tests (enterococci are penicillin- and cephalosporin-resistant but ampicillin-sensitive).

(ii)   Identify *S.aureus* as described in Section 4.1.4.

(iii)   Identify the anaerobes as described in Section 3.3 and the aerobic Gram-negative bacilli as outlined in the scheme shown in *Figure 8*. Full species identification of all the Gram-negative bacilli may be appropriate in certain clinical situations (see 5.6 and 7.1), but it is not routine.

(iv)   Oxidase-negative, fermentative bacilli can be identified using a number of commercial kits, e.g. API 20 (API Laboratory Products).

(v)   Oxidase-positive or non-fermentative bacilli can be more easily identified with kits such as the API 20 NE.

5.1.4 Sensitivity testing and reporting

(i)   Test and report *S.aureus* as described in Section 4.1.5 and anaerobes as described in Section 3.4.

(ii)   Test and report sensitivity of enterococci and other streptococci to penicillin, ampicillin and erythromycin.

(iii)   Test and report sensitivity of aerobic Gram-negative bacilli other than *Pseudomonas* spp. to ampicillin, augmentin, cephradine, cefuroxime, trimethoprim and gentamicin.

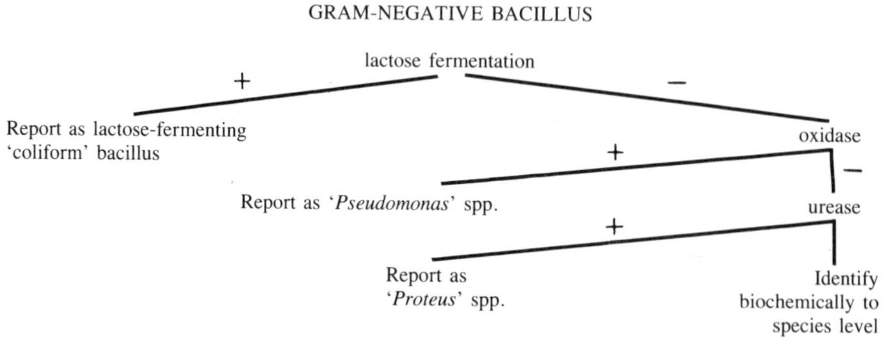

Figure 8. Simple scheme for identification of Gram-negative bacilli in clinical specimens.

(iv) Report all antibiotics on local antibiotic policy. *Second-line antibiotics* (cefotaxime, ceftazidime, netilmicin, piperacillin) are tested if the organism is resistant to more than three of the antibiotics. (Consider amikacin, ciprofloxacin, imipenem, aztreonam.)

(v) *Pseudomonas* spp. should be tested against gentamicin, tobramycin, ceftazidime, azlocillin or piperacillin, and ciproflaxacin. Report all antibiotics on local antibiotic policy. *Second-line antibiotics* are amikacin, imipenem and aztreonam. Antibiotics alone without surgical drainage of the abscess will not be effective.

5.2 Peritonitis

Usually a swab of free peritoneal fluid is received, but occasionally and more helpfully peritoneal fluid itself is sent.

5.2.1 *Expected organisms*

In *primary peritonitis* no apparent focus of infection is evident, the organisms being presumed to gain access from the bloodstream. The commonest isolates are *Streptococcus pneumoniae* and Group A β-haemolytic streptococci. In *secondary peritonitis*, which follows rupture or surgical opening of an abdominal viscus, trauma, or preceding intra-abdominal infection (liver abscess, salpingitis, etc.), the infecting organisms are related to this underlying aetiology. *Escherichia coli*, other *Enterobacteriaceae* and anaerobes (i.e. gastrointestinal tract flora) are the most commonly-encountered isolates. If the underlying problem is connected with the genital tract (as in salpingitis) then *Neisseria gonorrhoeae*, anaerobes or *Chlamydia trachomatis* are more likely to be isolated. Tuberculous peritonitis is extremely rare in the UK and USA.

5.2.2 *Processing methods*

(i) In *primary peritonitis* perform an urgent Gram stain. If negative, or if there is any doubt about the identification of the organisms seen, test the fluid for pneumococcal antigen (using latex/co-agglutination or counter-immunoelectrophoresis). Direct detection of Group A streptococci is possible using latex/co-agglutination techniques.

(ii) Specimens from *secondary peritonitis* are processed as described in Section 2.3 but will need culture on additional media if *N. gonorrhoeae* or *Chlamydia* are suspected; see Chapter 4.

5.2.3 *Identification methods, sensitivity testing and reporting*

For *S. pneumoniae*, *N. gonorrhoeae* and *C. trachomatis* see Chapters 3 and 4; for Group A streptococci, see Sections 4.1.4, 4.1.5; for aerobic Gram-negative bacilli and enterococci, see Sections 5.1.5 and 5.1.4; for anaerobes, see Sections 3.3. and 3.4

5.2.4 *Interpretation*

The precise value of peritoneal swabs in many cases of secondary peritonitis is difficult to assess. They are often taken routinely in acute appendicitis. The bacteriology never influences antibiotic therapy, which is given empirically on clinical indications for short periods, sometimes ending at about the time the full bacteriology results are available.

5.3 **Wound infections**

5.3.1 *Samples and expected organisms*

Almost invariably 'wound swabs' with the occasional sample of pus will be sent to the laboratory. The organisms found in wound infections relate either to the skin or to the site of the surgery (gastro-intestinal tract, genital tract). Of the skin organisms, *S.aureus* is the major pathogen; see Section 4.1. The organisms from the gastro-intestinal tract vary; from oesophagus and stomach they tend to be of mouth and upper respiratory tract type; from the duodenum, mainly streptococcal with a few coliforms and anaerobes; from the ileum, there are more coliforms and anaerobes; from the large bowel, coliforms and anaerobes predominate. Large numbers of coliforms may be found in the stomach and duodenum if the gastric acidity is reduced (usually by H_2 antagonists). Following gynaecological surgery, anaerobes, group B and other streptococci and coliforms are commonly found in wound infections.

5.3.2 *Processing and identification methods and sensitivity testing*

(i)   Process as for pus and swabs in Sections 2.1 and 2.2. No special techniques are necessary.

(ii)   Identify and carry out sensitivity tests on *S.aureus* and β-haemolytic streptococci as described in Sections 4.1.4 and 4.1.5.

(iii)   Identify and carry out sensitivity tests on anaerobes as described in Sections 3.3 and 3.4, and on aerobic Gram-negative bacilli and enterococci as described in Sections 5.1.3 and 5.1.4.

5.3.3 *Reporting and interpretation*

This can be extremely difficult. The decision as to whether to treat a 'wound infection' depends more on the clinical picture than on the organisms isolated, with the exception of β-haemolytic streptococci. Unless the laboratory wishes to have a dialogue with the clinician over every wound swab, it is more practical on culture to identify organisms as far as seems appropriate and perform selected sensitivity tests.

5.4 **Biliary infections**

These include acute cholangitis, acute cholecystitis, empyema of gall bladder, and infection associated with external biliary drainage (T-tubes).

5.4.1 *Type of sample*

Bile collected from a drainage bag is unacceptable; the sample must be from the T-tube catheter itself. Operative specimens of pus, swabs, and bile are often received. Blood cultures may be the only sample that can be sent in acute cholangitis and they are often positive.

5.4.2 *Expected organisms*

Typically gastrointestinal tract organisms, and often a mixed flora, are isolated. The bacteria most commonly encountered are: *E.coli*, *Proteus* spp., other *Enterobacteriaceae*,

B.fragilis, *C.perfringens*, anaerobic cocci, other anaerobes and streptococci, usually enterococci.

In addition, *Pseudomonas aeruginosa* is frequently associated with biliary T-tube drainage, although it is often only colonizing. *Salmonella* spp., including *S.typhi*, may be isolated from biliary carriers.

5.4.3 Processing methods

(i)   Process pus and swabs as described in Sections 2.1 and 2.2
(ii) Bile fluid should be centrifuged at 1800 *g* for 10 min. Make a Gram stain of the deposit and culture as described in Section 2.1.5.
(iii) Set up additional media for enteric pathogens, such as DCLS, DCA or XLD and selenite broth (see Chapter 6), if the clinical details are appropriate.
(iv) Gas chromatography can be carried out directly on bile, and of course pus, and may be worthwhile if the equipment is ready for use.

5.4.4 Identification methods and sensitivity testing

The methods described in Sections 5.1.3 and 5.1.4 are appropriate. Gram-negative bacilli which identify biochemically as *Salmonella* spp. are confirmed as such with serology as described in Chapter 6. Perform the same sensitivity tests for salmonellae as for the other *Enterobacteriaceae* but include chloramphenicol.

5.4.5 Interpretation and reporting

The only samples which pose a problem are those from external biliary drainage—'the T-tube bile' specimens. In common with external urinary drainage, the presence of a foreign body, the catheter, ensures ready colonization with coliforms, *Pseudomonas*, enterococci and occasionally anaerobes. Just as for catheter urine samples, antibiotic therapy is inappropriate unless the patient shows signs of infection; the catheter is to be manipulated (removed or changed) or something is to be injected up the catheter such as X-ray contrast material for a T-tube cholangiogram. There are two approaches the laboratory can take: firstly, to perform sensitivity testing and inform the clinicians that this has been done, but not to report the results unless directly asked to do so; secondly, to perform sensitivity testing, report the results and rely on the clinicians not to use the antibiotics unless they are needed. The best approach depends on local circumstances and each laboratory must decide individually.

5.5 Liver abscess

5.5.1 Type of sample

Pus or other material from a liver aspirate is usually received. Blood cultures are often helpful too.

5.5.2 Expected organisms

Protozoal causes include *Entamoeba histolytica* (amoebic abscess) and *Echinococcus granulosus* (hydatid cyst): these are not discussed further here. Bacterial isolates are frequently multiple, and the commonest are *Streptococcus milleri*, other streptococci, usually enterococci, anaerobes, *E.coli*, and *Enterobacteriaceae*. *Staphylococcus aureus* and Group A streptococci account for less than 20% of cases and are probably secondary to bacteraemia.

5.5.3 *Processing methods*

(i)   Perform an urgent Gram stain and telephone the findings to the clinician.
(ii)   Process basically as for pus (Section 2.1), but pay special attention to anaerobic technique and use prolonged culture (up to 7 days), Section 3.2.
(iii) Direct sensitivity testing may be set up; choose antibiotics with reference to the Gram stain and those listed in Section 5.1.4.

5.5.4 *Identification methods and sensitivity testing*

(i)   All isolates must be identified to species level. Identify and carry out sensitivity testing on streptococci and *S.aureus* as described in Sections 4.1.4 and 4.1.5, anaerobes as described in Sections 3.3 and 3.4. Laboratories without GLC may wish to refer isolates to a Reference Laboratory.
(ii)   Identify and carry out sensitivity testing on *Enterobacteriaceae* and other aerobic Gram-negative bacilli as described in Sections 5.1.3 and 5.1.4, but identify biochemically to species level.

5.5.5 *Interpretation and reporting*

This is straightforward, since any isolate must be considered significant, identified and appropriate sensitivities reported. Antibiotic therapy alone may be successful when micro-abscesses are present, but drainage (either at laparotomy or percutaneously under X-ray guidance), combined with antibiotics, offers the best chance of success.

5.6 **Abscesses**

Perianal abscess, ischiorectal abscess and post-anal abscess are the conditions encountered. Although pus is preferable a swab is usually sent.

5.6.1 *Expected organisms*

These are usually mixed infections involving anaerobes, especially *B.fragilis*, and aerobic Gram-negative bacilli, usually *E.coli*. Commonly *E.coli*, *Proteus* spp., other aerobic Gram-negative bacilli, *B.fragilis*, other anaerobes, and enterococci and other streptococci are encountered. *Staphylococcus aureus* may rarely be encountered, particularly in diabetics.

5.6.2 *Processing and identification methods and sensitivity testing*

(i)   Process as described in Section 2.1. No special techniques are necessary.
(ii)   Identify and carry out sensitivity testing on *E.coli* and aerobic Gram-negative bacilli as described in Sections 5.1.3 and 5.1.4, anaerobes as described in Sections 3.3. and 3.4 and streptococci and *S.aureus* as described in Sections 4.1.4 and 4.1.5.

5.6.3 *Interpretation and reporting*

Surgical drainage of the abscess alone is sufficient in most cases. Antibiotic therapy is needed only in patients with cellulitis or who appear bacteraemic. The most practical approach for the laboratory is to report the results of limited sensitivity testing in the knowledge that they will rarely be of value.

6. GYNAECOLOGICAL AND POST-PARTUM INFECTIONS

6.1 **Post-operative infections**

Wound infections and pelvic abscesses are the most frequent infections encountered. Swabs are nearly always sent, including vaginal swabs, but occasionally pus is received.

6.1.1 *Expected organisms*

These are *E. coli*, other *Enterobacteriaceae*, *Bacteroides fragilis*, other anaerobes, group B streptococci and other streptococci including enterococci and occasionally *Staphylococcus aureus*.

6.1.2 *Processing and identification methods and sensitivity testing*

(i)   Process as described in Sections 2.1 and 2.2. No special techniques are necessary.

(ii) Identify and carry out sensitivity testing on *E. coli* and aerobic Gram-negative bacilli as described in Sections 5.1.3 and 5.1.4, anaerobes as described in Sections 3.3 and 3.4 and streptococci and *S. aureus* as described in Sections 4.1.4 and 4.1.5.

6.1.3 *Interpretation and reporting*

As in all wound infections, the presence of cellulitis or pus is the main guide to treatment. Post-operative vaginal swabs are extremely difficult to interpret unless a heavy growth of a likely pathogen is found.

6.2 **Tubo-ovarian sepsis**

Clinical conditions encountered are salpingitis, tubal abscess, ovarian abscess, pelvic inflammatory disease.

6.2.1 *Type of sample and expected organisms*

A sample of pus taken at operation is the most useful specimen. Free peritoneal fluid or a peritoneal swab are sometimes helpful. Cervical, urethral and rectal swabs are useful adjuncts in the diagnosis of gonococcal infection, as are cervical swabs in chlamydial infection. *Neisseria gonorrhoeae*, group B streptococci, *S. aureus*, *B. fragilis* and other anaerobes and *Chlamydia trachomatis* might be encountered.

6.2.2 *Processing methods*

Culture media must include both selective and non-selective media for *N. gonorrhoeae* (see Chapter 4) as well as media for wound swabs. Special methods are required for detection/culture of *Chlamydia trachomatis* (see Chapter 4).

6.2.3 *Identification methods and sensitivity testing*

Identify and carry out sensitivity tests on *N. gonorrhoeae* as described in Chapter 4 and anaerobes as described in Sections 3.3 and 3.4.

6.2.4 *Interpretation and reporting*

This should pose few problems when samples are taken at operation. Problems arise when the only specimens available in cases of pelvic inflammatory diseases are cervical or vaginal swabs, and these do not yield *N. gonorrhoeae* or *C. trachomatis;* interpretation is then very difficult.

6.3 **Infection associated with intra-uterine contraceptive devices (IUDs)**

Women who have been fitted with an IUD, particularly a tailed device, are at increased risk of pelvic infection (14,15). IUDs act as foreign bodies and their tails provide a route for ascending infection.

6.3.1 *Type of sample and expected organisms*

Cervical swabs are acceptable for actinomycetes culture, but the IUD itself should be cultured wherever possible. *Actinomyces* spp., especially *A. israelii*, will be found, as well as *B. fragilis* and other anaerobes.

6.3.2 *Processing and identification methods and sensitivity testing*

(i)   Culture swabs and IUDs for anaerobes as described in Section 3.2.
(ii)   Culture IUDs and cervical swabs for actinomycetes as described in *Table 17.*
(iii) Identify and carry out sensitivity testing on anaerobes as described in Sections 3.3 and 3.4. Identify *A. israelii* presumptively by microscopic and clonial morphology as described in Section 4.5. Presumptive identification by an immunofluorescent method is described by Traynor *et al.* (22). Full identification can only be accomplished using gas chromatography and biochemical tests.

6.3.3 *Interpretation and reporting*

Anaerobes and actinomycetes should be reported, with sensitivities. Actinomycetes are very often sensitive to penicillin. The prevalence of actinomycetes in the vaginal flora of healthy women without IUDs is very low; prevalence increases with the length of time the IUD has been in place. In many women the actinomycetes seem to be present

---

Table 17. Procedure for the culture of IUDs and cervical swabs for actinomycetes (adapted from ref.22).

1.	Swab the IUD to remove all the pus and debris.
2.	Immerse the swab in 5 ml of a fresh anaerobic broth, agitate it and squeeze all the excess broth out of the swab before removing it.
3.	Make 4 appropriate tenfold dilutions in further 5 ml quantities of broth, i.e. 500 μl added to 5 ml.
4.	Culture 100 μl of each dilution in duplicate as a lawn on blood agar plates containing 5% metronidazole to suppress strict anaerobes.
5.	Incubate at 37°C anaerobically.
6.	Examine at 5 and 10 days.

---

only as superficial colonizers of the endometrium and cause no symptoms. However, the IUD should be removed and examined for actinomycetes if the patient is symptomatic. If *A.israelii* is found the patient should be treated.

If actinomycetes-like organisms are detected in cervical smears the IUD should probably be removed even if the patient is asymptomatic. The need for antibiotic treatment in asymptomatic patients is unknown. The correlation between positive smear microscopy and culture is extremely variable (24).

6.4 Post-partum infections

Endometritis, infected episiotomy wounds and infected caesarian section wounds are the commonest clinical conditions. Post-abortion sepsis and clostridial myometritis occur but are uncommon. Cervical or high vaginal swabs and swabs from the episiotomy or abdominal wound are usually received. Occasionally lochia or endometrial curettings are sent. Blood cultures can be useful in endometritis.

6.4.1 *Expected organisms*

Commonly the same organisms are´ found here as in post-operative gynaecological infections (Section 6.1.). Rarely *Staphylococcus aureus*, group A streptococci and *Clostridium perfringens* are encountered. The latter organism can cause uterine gas gangrene; a very serious infection.

6.4.2 *Processing and identification methods and sensitivity testing*

(i) Process lochia and endometrial curettings as pus (Section 2.1). An urgent Gram stain may be helpful in certain clinical conditions. No special techniques are necessary.

(ii) Identify and carry out sensitivity testing on *E.coli* and aerobic Gram-negative bacilli as described in Sections 5.1.3 and 5.1.4, anaerobes as described in Sections 3.3 and 3.4 and streptococci and *S.aureus* as described in Sections 4.1.4 and 4.1.5.

6.4.3 *Interpretation and reporting*

The interpretation of the significance of *E.coli* and the *Enterobacteriaceae* from post-partum wounds is just as difficult as for any other wound. High vaginal swabs can also pose similar problems in interpretation. Swabs from the cervical os are easier to interpret, there being less chance of contamination with normal vaginal flora at this site. Organisms isolated from the cervix in the presence of pus or a fluid discharge must be considered to be potentially pathogenic. *C.perfringens*, group A streptococci and *S.aureus* must always be reported promptly. *Clostridium perfringens* can be present in the perineum or vagina as a result of faecal contamination or colonization and is not necessarily treated in the absence of clinical signs of infection, but if isolated the clinicians should be informed and its significance discussed.

7. INFECTIONS OF THE SKELETAL SYSTEM

7.1 **Acute osteomyelitis**

7.1.1 *Types of sample*

Pus obtained from direct aspiration at surgery gives the best results. Swabs of pus may be received but should be discouraged. Blood cultures may yield the organism and should always be taken.

7.1.2 *Expected organisms*

S.aureus will be isolated from 90% of cases. Group A β-haemolytic streptococci cause disease in a further 5%, very rarely *Streptococcus pneumoniae* is isolated. *H.influenzae* can cause acute osteomyelitis in children aged 3 months to 5 years, although septic arthritis is a more common presentation than osteomyelitis. Rare causes are *Salmonella* spp. (particularly in children with haemoglobinopathies), *N.meningitidis, E.coli* and *Pseudomonas aeruginosa*. In cases of neonatal osteomyelitis, *S.aureus* is still the most common isolate, although Gram-negative bacilli, pneumococci and Group B streptococci are less frequently encountered.

7.1.3 *Processing methods*

(i)   Process samples as for pus (Section 2.1). Since anaerobes have not been reported in acute osteomyelitis, GLC is not indicated.

(ii)   Perform urgent Gram stains; these are usually positive and should be telephoned to the clinician.

(iii)   Additional culture plates may be set up for neonates (CLED or MacConkey for *Enterobacteriaceae*) and infants and children (chocolate agar for *H.influenzae*).

7.1.4 *Identification methods*

All organisms isolated must be fully identified to species level: specimen contamination by skin commensals is very rare.

(i)   Identify *S.aureus* (Section 4.1.4), β-haemolytic streptococci (Section 4.1.4), *Streptococcus pneumoniae* (Chapter 3) and *H.influenzae* (Chapter 3). Identify all Gram-negative bacilli described in Section 5.1.5, but with full identification to species level.

(ii)   Telephone the culture reports to the clinician particularly if a Gram-negative bacillus is isolated, because in this case the usual empirical antibiotic regimen of flucloxacillin and fusidic acid will not be adequate.

7.1.5 *Sensitivity testing, interpretation and reporting*

Direct disc sensitivity may be set up; the antibiotics tested are chosen on the basis of the Gram stain, and with reference to the lists below. The clinicians will start antibiotic treatment on the basis of the Gram stain or empirically in the knowledge that 90% of cases are due to *Staph.aureus*. Commonly used regimens are flucloxacillin plus erythromycin, or fusidic acid and fusidic acid plus erythromycin. In children under the age of 5 years ampicillin plus flucloxacillin may be used instead, to treat *H.influenzae*, but as up to 25% of type b strains are ampicillin-resistant, cefuroxime or cefotaxime are alternatives (25).

Any antibiotic that the patient is on, and any to which the organism is resistant, should be tested and reported unless they are inappropriate.

(i) *S.aureus*, test and report as described in Section 4.1.5 (i) but note that tetracycline is not recommended for treatment, so there is no need to test or report it.

(ii) *Streptococci and pneumococci*, test and report as described in Section 4.1.5 (ii).

(iii) *Haemophilus influenzae*, test ampicillin, erythromycin, cefuroxime, cefotaxime, chloramphenicol, and report all on the local antibiotic policy (chloramphenicol is not routinely recommended in the UK).

(iv) *Aerobic Gram-negative bacilli* (*Enterobacteriaceae* including *Salmonella* spp.), test and report as described in Section 5.1.4.

(v) *Pseudomonas aeruginosa*, test and report as described in Section 5.1.6.

7.2 Chronic osteomyelitis

7.2.1 *Types of sample*

Wound swabs from the discharging sinus overlying the area of osteomyelitis are commonly received, but are of limited value (26). The best material for culture is granulation tissue or pus from the site of bone infection. Blood cultures are not helpful or of value as most patients will not be septicaemic.

7.2.2 *Expected organisms*

The organisms isolated from tissue specimens of patients with chronic osteomyelitis have changed during the last 30 years. *S.aureus* has become less frequent and the Gram-negative bacilli more frequent and anaerobes are now recognized because culture techniques have improved. This changing pattern reflects nosocomial infection in trauma patients, many of whom have had open operative intervention or internal fixation of fractures.

The following organisms are found: *Staphylococcus aureus*, *Pseudomonas aeruginosa* *E.coli*, *Proteus mirabilis*, and other *Enterobacteriaceae*, *Bacteroides* spp., *Propionobacterium acnes* and anaerobic cocci.

Mixed infections are common, usually *S.aureus* with Gram-negative bacilli. Osteomyelitis caused by *M.tuberculosis* and *Brucella* spp. is uncommon, but should be considered in undiagnosed cases of chronic osteomyelitis.

7.2.3 *Processing and identification methods*

Process pus as in Section 2.1 and tissue as in Section 2.4. Identify *S.aureus* as described in Section 4.1.4, Gram-negative bacilli to species level as described in Section 7.1.4 and anaerobes to species level as described in Section 3.3.

7.2.4 *Sensitivity testing, reporting and interpretation*

S.aureus should be tested and reported as described in Section 4.1.5 (ii), Gram-negative bacilli as described in Section 5.1.4 and anaerobes as described in Section 3.4.

The results of swabs are difficult to interpret due to colonization of the sinus tract with Gram-negative bacilli and skin flora: comparisons of sinus tract and operative specimens show significant disparities (26). Any isolate from tissue or pus should be assumed to be significant. Antibiotics combined with surgical debridement of dead bone can be successful.

8. JOINT INFECTIONS

8.1 **Prosthetic joint infections**

Infections in prosthetic joints are discussed here primarily, acute arthritis is discussed in Chapter 2. Usually a swab is taken from the re-opened joint and sent to the laboratory, preferably with a sample of granulation tissue and fluid from the joint.

8.1.1 *Expected organisms*

These closely resemble those associated with infections of other implanted foreign bodies: prosthetic heart valves, peritoneal dialysis catheters and ventriculo-atrial/ventriculo-peritoneal shunts. The organisms are predominantly normal skin commensals. Coagulase-negative staphylococci are most frequently encountered, but *S.aureus*, coryneforms and skin anaerobes (especially *Propionbacterium acnes*) can be found.

8.1.2 *Processing and identification methods and sensitivity testing*

(i)   Process swabs, tissues and fluid as described in Section 2. Direct microscopy can confirm the presence of organisms but is of limited value in directing therapy since the causative organisms often have unpredictable sensitivities.
(ii) Identify and carry out sensitivity testing of all isolates. The identification and sensitivity testing of coagulase-negative staphylococci, diphtheroids and other such organisms as described in Chapter 2.

8.1.3 *Interpretation and reporting*

This is essentially the same as for the other foreign-body associated infections, and the reader is referred to Chapter 2 for details.

9. CNS INFECTIONS

9.1 **Cerebral abscess**

Meningitis will not be covered here; see Chapter 2 for details. The only acceptable sample from a cerebral abscess is pus collected at operation.

9.1.1 *Expected organisms*

The majority of brain abscesses arise by direct spread from a nearby focus of infection, such as the mastoids, middle ear or the paranasal sinuses. A few arise as a result of haematogenous spread from distant sites of infection (often the lungs or liver) or or following 1° bacteraemia. The organisms found reflect these underlying conditions, and the majority are anaerobic or micro-aerophilic (27).

(i)   Common: *B.fragilis; B.melaninogenicus;* anaerobic cocci; micro-aerophilic streptococci (e.g. *S.milleri*); other *Bacteroides* spp.; aerobic streptococci.

(ii)   Less common: *Enterobacteriaceae; Staphylococcus aureus; Haemophilus influenzae; Fusobacterium* sp.

(iii)   Rare: *Actinomyces* spp.; *Nocardia asteroides*.

9.1.2 *Processing methods*

(i)   Process the pus as described in Section 2.1, with special attention to anaerobic culture as described in Section 3.2. Incubate plates for a minimum of 14 days before accepting a negative result.

(ii)   Make an urgent Gram stain and phone the result to the clinician.

(iii)   Perform urgent gas-liquid chromatography if the equipment is available, but note that pus containing anaerobes is not always foul-smelling.

(iv)   Finally, set up direct sensitivity tests, aerobic and anaerobic, based on the organisms seen on the Gram stain and the antibiotics suggested on Section 9.1.3.

9.1.3 *Identification methods and sensitivity testing*

All isolates should be identified fully, to species level. Help with the identification of anaerobes may be obtained from reference laboratories. Streptococci which are not β-haemolytic can be identified biochemically (e.g. with the API Strep).

Anaerobes, microaerophilic and aerobic streptococci should be tested to penicillin, ampicillin, chloramphenicol and possibly clindamycin. Anaerobes should be tested to metronidazole as well. Other isolates should be tested against the appropriate antibiotics, but in addition chloramphenicol, rifampicin and cephalosporins (cefotaxime and ceftazidime) should be tested, as they penetrate the CNS well.

9.1.4 *Interpretation and reporting*

All isolates with sensitivities should be reported as soon as possible. Sensitivities should be reported without waiting for full identification. Intravenous antibiotics are used, and those with good penetration into brain tissue such as the β-lactams, chloramphenicol and metronidazole are most appropriate. Surgical drainage is complementary to chemotherapy and is performed as soon as the lesion has been localized.

10. EYE INFECTIONS

10.1 **Acute conjunctivitis**

Whilst direct inoculation of plates at the bedside is preferable, swabs from cases of acute conjunctivitis are the most frequently-received ophthalmic specimen. The infection is usually mild, often resolving spontaneously or responding well to antibiotics. However, if some of the rarer causes are not diagnosed, an extensive infection of the whole eye may result rather than local conjunctivitis. Identification of chlamydia will require a swab to be taken in special transport medium (see Chapter 4, Section 4.4), and for trachoma, conjunctival scrapings from the upper lid.

10.1.1 *Expected organisms*

The most commonly isolated bacterial pathogen is *Staphylococcus aureus*, followed by *Streptococcus pneumoniae* (28). *Haemophilus influenzae* may be isolated from mild cases of conjunctivitis when its precise causal role is debatable, unlike *H.aegyptius* which causes acute, contagious conjunctivitis in hot climates. *H.aegyptius* is regarded by some authorities to be a biotype of *H.influenzae*, but because of its distinct pathogenicity others argue for its retention as a separate species (29). More rarely β-haemolytic streptococci, *Enterobacteriaceae*, *Moraxella lacunata* (usually in sandy, hot countries) and *Pseudomonas aeruginosa* (often causing corneal ulcers) are encountered. Ophthalmia neonatorum (purulent discharge from the eye within 3 weeks of birth) is usually due to *Chlamydia trachomatis* rather than *N.gonorrhoeae* as previously. Often no bacterial pathogen is found, as viruses are common causes of acute conjunctivitis, adenovirus (particularly types 3, 7, 8 and 11) causing epidemic keratoconjunctivitis transmitted on hands.

10.1.2 *Processing, identification and sensitivity testing*

(i)   Examine a Gram stain or stain for chlamydiae if appropriate (Chapter 4, Section 3.1.3) of the swab or scrapings.

(ii) Inoculate a blood agar and chocolate blood agar (incubated in 5% CO_2) and incubate for 24 h; if no growth occurs re-incubate for a further 24 h. Direct sensitivities are not normally inoculated. See Chapter 4, Section 4.4 for details of the culture of chlamydiae.

(iii) Identify and carry out sensitivity tests (including chloramphenicol and gentamicin) on *S.aureus* as described in Section 4.1, β-haemolytic streptococci in Section 4.1, *Streptococcus pneumoniae* in Chapter 3, Section 3.2.4, *H.influenzae* in Chapter 3, Section 3.2.4 and *N.gonorrhoeae* in Chapter 4, Section 4.1.

10.1.3 *Interpretation and reporting*

This should pose few problems, as genuinely pathogenic bacteria are usually present in large numbers. In the absence of foreign material, coagulase-negative staphylococci, diphtheroids and viridous streptococci should be regarded as contaminating skin flora. It is usual to report only sensitivities to appropriate topical antibiotics.

10.2 Endophthalmitis

This is a serious infection which may be restricted to certain structures of the globe or involve all of the intraocular contents. Pain in the eye with corneal ulceration, inflammation and pus in the anterior chamber (hypopyon) are typical features. It is most frequently seen following ocular surgery but can also result from penetrating trauma to the eye. Rarely it can arise from haematogenous spread of bacteria to the eye. Superficial swabs are of no value and every attempt should be made to obtain anterior and/or vitreous aspirates.

10.2.1 *Expected organisms*

Staphylococcus aureus and coagulase-negative staphylococci are by far the most commonly encountered pathogens in endophthalmitis following surgery (usually following intraocular lens implantation) (30). Rarely *Pseudomonas aeruginosa* and *Enterobacteriaceae* are encountered, often as a result of peri-operative nosocomial infection. A huge range of bacteria have been described in post-traumatic endophthalmitis, but *Bacillus cereus* is increasingly recognized as a cause of severe disease (31). Metastatic endophthalmitis is caused by bacteria such as *H.influenzae*, *N.meningitidis*, *Nocardia* spp., *B.cereus* and various fungi, particularly *Candida* spp. in intravenous drug users.

10.2.2 *Processing, identification and sensitivity testing*

(i) Process aspirates in the same way as pus (see Section 2.1) and include a chocolate agar plate incubated in 5% CO_2 and a Sabouraud's agar for fungi. Remember to telephone the Gram film result.

(ii) See Section 4.1.4 for details of the identification and sensitivity testing of *S.aureus* and coagulase-negative staphylococci, and other less frequently encountered bacteria in the appropriate section of this book. Aerobic, Gram-positive bacilli, often forming characteristic large rough colonies after 24 h incubation, should be assumed to be *B.cereus*. It is β-haemolytic, produces a lecithinase with a wide zone on egg yolk agar, is resistant to penicillin and produces spores that do not swell the cell. Clindamycin, the aminoglycosides and possibly imipenem are the preferred treatment, so test all of these.

(iii) As only certain antibiotics can be given sub-conjunctivally (e.g. aminoglycosides, methicillin) remember to test these agents, as many antibiotics do not penetrate the eye from systemic or topical administration.

10.2.3 *Interpretation and reporting*

Any growth is likely to be significant (except perhaps some enrichment culture results), and because of the severity of the condition, results should be reported by telephone followed by a written result. Because of the rarity of the condition and the limited number of useful antibiotics, restricted sensitivity reporting is not appropriate.

10.3 **Periocular infections**

These include infections of the eyelids (blepharitis, stye and chalazion), lacrimal duct/sac (canaliculitis/dacryocystitis), and orbital cellulitis. In the first two conditions swabs or scrapings should be obtained; in orbital cellulitis a blood culture must be obtained, as infection is usually haematogenous. Extension of periorbital infection into the cavernous sinus will produce thrombosis with characteristic clinical signs and a high mortality.

10.3.1 *Expected organisms*

Canaliculitis is often caused by *Actinomyces* spp., *Arachnia* spp. or *Fusobacterium* spp., so samples should be processed as pus (Section 2.1). Dacryocystitis may be caused by *Staphylococcus aureus*, β-haemolytic streptococci, *Pseudomonas aeruginosa*, *Streptococcus pneumoniae* and *Chlamydia trachomatis*, and samples should be processed as pus. Infections of the lid are often caused by the same bacteria which cause conjunctivitis (particularly *S.aureus*). Periorbital cellulitis is commonly caused by *H.influenzae* in children (32); *S.aureus*, *Streptococcus pyogenes* and *Streptococcus pneumoniae* being encountered at other ages.

10.3.2 *Processing, identification and sensitivity testing*

(i) Gram stain all specimens. *Actinomyces* spp. and *Arachnia* spp. will be seen as Gram positive branching filaments.

(ii) Process specimens from canaliculitis and dacryocystitis as pus (Section 2.1) and perform identification and sensitivity tests accordingly (Section 2.1).

(iii) Process specimens from lid infections as conjunctival swabs (Section 10.1.2) and further tests as in Section 10.1.3.

Periorbital infections are difficult to diagnose, as the only specimen obtained other than a conjunctival swab (which is usually unhelpful) is a blood culture; process as described in Chapter 2. If operative material is obtained treat it as pus.

10.3.3 *Interpretation and reporting*

Generally moderate or heavy growth of bacteria will be significant. Those with sensitivities to systemic and topical agents should be reported if appropriate. Occasionally, colonizing bacteria such as *Streptococcus viridans* or coagulase-negative staphylococci will be encountered as in conjunctival swabs; these should be ignored.

11. REFERENCES

1. Lee, P.-C., Turnidge,J., McDonald,P.J. (1985) *J. Clin. Microbiol.*, **22**, 80.
2. Wiggins,R.J., Wilks,M. and Tabaqchali,S. (1985) *J. Clin. Pathol*, **38**, 933.
3. Loesche,W.J. (1969) *Appl. Microbiol.*, **18**, 723.
4. Murray,P.R. (1978) *J. Clin. Microbiol.*, **8**, 708.
5. Ganguli,L.A., Turton,L.J. and Tillotson,G.S. (1982) *J. Clin. Pathol.*, **35**, 458.
6. Lennette,E.H., Balows,A., Hausler,W.J. and Shadomy,H.J. (eds) (1985) *Manual of Clinical Microbiology*, 4th edn, Amercian Society for Microbiology, Washington,DC.
7. Willis,A.T. (1977) *Anaerobic Bacteriology Clinical and Laboratory Practice*. 3rd edn, Butterworths, London and Boston.
8.* Holdeman,L.V., Cato,E.P. and Moore,W.E.C. (eds) (1977) *Anaerobe Laboratory Manual*. 4th edn, Virginia Polytechnic Institute and State University, Blacksburg, VA.
9. Leigh,D.A. and Simmons,K. (1977) *J. Clin. Pathol.*, **30**, 991.
10. Willis,A.T. (1977) In *Anaerobic Bacteriology Clinical and Laboratory Practice*, 3rd edn. Butterworths, London and Boston.
11. Duerden,B.I., Collee,J,G., Brown,R., Deacon,A.G. and Holbrook,W.P. (1980) *J. Med. Microbiol.*, **13**, 231.
12. Cowan,S.T. (1974) *Cowan and Steel's Manual for the Identification of Medical Bacteria*. 2nd edn, Cambridge University Press, Cambridge.
13. Rosenblatt,J.E. (1985) *Clinics in Lab. Med.*, **5**, 59.
14. Murray,P.R., Weber,C.J. and Niles,A.C. (1985) *J. Clin. Microbiol.*, **22**, 52.
15. Burlage,R.S. and Ellner,P.D. (1985) *J. Clin. Microbiol.*, **22**, 32.
16. Finegold,S.M. and Baron,E.J. (1986) *Bailey and Scott's Diagnostic Microbiology*. 7th edn., CV Mosby Co., St Louis.
17. Koneman,E.W., Allen,S.D., Dowell,V.R. and Sommers,H.M. (1983) *Color Atlas and Textbook of Diagnostic Microbiology*. 2nd edn, J.B. Lippincott, Philadelphia.
18. *Topley and Wilson's Principles of Bacteriology, Virology and Immunity*, Williams & Wilkins, Baltimore.
19. Barry,A.L., Lachica,R.V.F. and Atchison,F.W. (1973) *Appl. Microbiol.*, **25**, 496.
20. Dickson,J.I.S. and Marples,R.R. (1986) *J. Clin. Pathol.*, **39**, 371.
21. Duguid,H.L.D., Parratt,D., Traynor,R. (1980) *Br. J. Med.*, **281**, 534.
22. Traynor,R.M., Parratt,D., Duguid,H.L.D. and Duncan,I.D. (1981) *J. Clin. Pathol.*, **34**, 914.
23. Evans,E.G.V. and Richardson,M.D. (eds) (1989) *Medical Mycology: A Practical Approach*. IRL Press, Oxford.
24. Jarvis,D. (1985) *J. Infect.*, **10**, 121.
25. Powell,M., Koutsia-Carouzou,C., Voutsinas,D., Seymour,A., Williams,J.D. (1987) *Br. Med. J.*, **295**, 176.

26. Mackowiak,P.A., Jones,S.R. and Smith,J.W. (1978) *JAMA, * **239**, 2772.
27. de Louvois,J. (1980) *J. Clin. Pathol., * **33**, 66.
28. Stenson,S., Newman,R. and Fedukowicz,H. (1982) *Arch. Ophthalmol., * **100**, 1275.
29. Howard,B.J. (1987) In *Clinical and Pathogenic Microbiology*, Howard,B.J., Klaas,J., Weissfeld,A.S., Rubin,S.J. and Tilton,R.C. (eds), CV Mosby Co., St Louis, p. 279.
30. Weber,D.J., Hoffman,K.L., Thoft,R.A. and Baker,A.S. (1986) *Rev. Infect. Dis., * **8**, 12.
31. Davey,R.T. and Tauber,W.B. (1987) *Rev. Infect. Dis., * **9**, 110.
32. Pedler,S.J. and Hawkey,P.M. (1983) *J. Infect., * **6**, 269.
*Available in the UK together with a 1987 supplement from Don Whitley Ltd.

CHAPTER 6

Bacteriology of intestinal disease

STEPHEN J.PEDLER

1. INTRODUCTION

The list of bacteria known or suspected to cause gastro-intestinal infection in human beings is a long and formidable one, and organisms are constantly being added to it. Certain bacteria, such as salmonellae, shigellae and campylobacters, are found sufficiently frequently to be included in the shorter list of bacteria that are looked for routinely in every specimen from a patient with intestinal infection; others, such as enterotoxigenic *Escherichia coli*, may find their way on to this list in the future. The methods used to process faeces specimens in the laboratory may appear complex and confusing, particularly to the trainee in microbiology. The purpose of this chapter therefore is to discuss culture media and technical methods available for faeces bacteriology, and how a specimen of faeces may be processed in the routine laboratory.

Numerous media and methods have been developed for this purpose, and it is not possible to discuss all of them. The exclusion of a particular medium or method does not necessarily imply that it is regarded as unsatisfactory; rather that those methods which are included have been found to be satisfactory in the experience of the author.

It is common practice in many laboratories to examine all faeces specimens for the presence of parasites such as *Giardia lamblia, Entamoeba histolytica* and *Cryptosporidium*. This is a practice which should form part of the standard processing of any faeces specimen from a patient with suspected intestinal infection, but since this book is concerned with bacteriology, technical methods for intestinal parasites are not included here, and the reader should consult another manual (1).

2. BACTERIAL ENTERIC PATHOGENS

Table 1 presents a list of those bacteria known or strongly suspected of causing human intestinal infection. A problem sometimes encountered is deciding when to examine a specimen for one of the less common pathogens, and guidance is given in the table. A discussion of the clinical syndromes and epidemiology of these infections is beyond the scope of this chapter, but will be found elsewhere (2,3).

3. CULTURE MEDIA

A considerable number of selective media are now available for the isolation of pathogenic bacteria from faeces. The aim of this section is to discuss the advantages and disadvantages of the media more frequently used together with the appearance of organisms which grow on them. It should be realized that the stated reactions apply to the majority of strains of a particular species, but that exceptions may occasionally

Table 1. List of bacterial enteric pathogens.

Organism	When to examine
Salmonella spp.	All specimens as part of the standard examination
Shigella spp.	As above
Campylobacter jejuni/coli	As above
Campylobacter laridis	As above
Enteropathogenic *E.coli*	Children under 3 years old
Enterotoxigenic *E.coli*	Traveller's diarrhoea
Enterohaemorrhagic *E.coli*	Bloody diarrhoea and haemolytic uraemic syndrome
Vibrio cholerae, *V.cholerae* non-O1	Travellers from those parts of the world where these infections are endemic or epidemic
V.parahaemolyticus	Travellers returning from abroad; outbreaks of food poisoning associated with shellfish
Yersinia enterocolitica	Clinical details suggestive of *Yersinia* infection
Aeromonas hydrophila, *Plesiomonas shigelloides*	No absolute indication; some laboratories look for these organisms routinely
Clostridium difficile	When requested or clinical details suggestive. Examination should be made routinely in all patients who have diarrhoea and who are taking or have recently taken antimicrobial agents
Clostridium perfringens, *Staphylococcus aureus,* *Bacillus cereus*	Outbreaks of food-borne infection

be seen. In addition to selective plating media, liquid enrichment media and media for identification are also discussed in this section. Further details of media and practical techniques can be found in refs 4−6.

3.1. Media for the isolation of *Enterobacteriaceae*

These media are presented in order of increasing selectivity in *Table 2*. Enrichment media are discussed in Section 3.1.1.

3.1.1 Enrichment media for the isolation of Enterobacteriaceae

(i) *General principles.* Because salmonellae and shigellae may be present in faeces specimens in very small numbers, the routine use of a selective enrichment medium which permits the multiplication of these organisms while inhibiting that of unwanted bacteria is recommended.

(ii) *Choice of medium.* Selenite broth is probably the most widely used enrichment medium, containing sodium selenite as the selective ingredient. It permits the growth of most strains of salmonellae, but some strains of shigellae are inhibited. In an attempt to overcome this problem, Gram-negative broth has been used, which contains a low concentration of sodium desoxycholate as the selective agent. However, this medium is probably insufficiently selective for routine use. Tetrathionate broth is a third possibility, but is much too inhibitory for shigellae. Some strains of salmonellae are also inhibited, particularly if Brilliant Green is included in the formulation. Selenite broth is therefore recommended for general use.

(iii) *Subculture of enrichment media.* Enrichment media should be subcultured to a selective solid medium after incubation. In order to isolate shigellae, a medium of relatively low selectivity should be used; desoxycholate-citrate agar (DCA) or xylose-lysine-desoxycholate agar (XLD) is recommended. If it is desired only to isolate salmonellae (as in a search for *Salmonella typhi*) a more selective medium can be used, such as bismuth sulphite medium.

3.2 **Screening and identification media for the** *Enterobacteriaceae*

Clearly, whichever media are used, the bacteriologist will still be left with a varying number of bacterial strains which might or might not be pathogens. To identify each one of these strains to species level would be time-consuming, expensive and unnecessary. Consequently, a method is needed to screen out organisms not regarded as pathogenic; the small number of organisms which remain may then be identified fully. One approach is to inoculate a short series of biochemical tests with the suspect organism. A suitable range of tests is given in *Table 3*.

If many specimens are being processed the use of individually tubed tests may prove inconvenient. Various composite media have been developed which attempt to carry out several of these tests in one or more tubes. Three of the most widely used of these are described below. A recent innovation has been to look for the presence of certain preformed enzymes. Since this does not depend on bacterial growth in the medium, rapid results are obtained. These tests, which are available in kit form, may eventually replace conventional biochemical tests.

3.2.1 *Kligler's iron agar/triple sugar iron agar*

These two composite media are very similar; Kligler's medium contains two sugars (glucose and lactose) whereas TSI also contains sucrose. The pH indicator is phenol red, and a detection system for H_2S is included. These media are poured as agar slopes, with the total depth of the medium being between 5 and 8 cm. The butt (the deep section of the medium) is inoculated by stabbing with a straight wire, and the surface of the slope is inoculated by streaking.

Organisms which ferment glucose produce acid which initially turns the whole medium yellow. Degradation of protein in the medium leads to the production of alkaline amines, but since this requires the presence of oxygen, it occurs only in the sloped section, which is exposed to the air, and not in the butt. After 24 h, organisms which ferment only glucose produce an acid butt and an alkaline (red) slope. Lactose (and sucrose if present) are present in excess; if either is fermented, sufficient acid is produced to turn the whole medium yellow, regardless of amine production. The production of H_2S will turn the medium black. It is also possible to detect gas production from glucose in these media. This may manifest itself as bubbles of gas in the agar, separation of the agar from the wall of the tube or in some cases complete disruption of the medium. These media cannot readily distinguish salmonellae and shigellae from many strains of the *Proteeae*; for this reason they should be used in conjunction with a test for urease production or the presence of phenylalanine deaminase. Typical reactions in these media are shown in *Table 4*.

Table 2. Selective media for the isolation of the *Enterobacteriaceae*.

Medium	Components	Colonial morphology	Uses
MacConkey's agar	Selective agent: bile salts. Indicator system: lactose plus neutral red pH indicator.	Lactose fermenters red or dark pink; late lactose fermenters pale pink. Non-lactose fermenters colourless or yellow (due to alkaline amine production from protein). Faecal streptococci tiny, magenta colonies.	Low selectivity for salmonellae and shigellae. Can be used for the isolation of *E. coli* and *Yersinia enterocolitica*
Desoxycholate-citrate agar (DCA)	Selective agent: sodium desoxycholate. Indicator systems: lactose plus neutral red; sodium thiosulphate and ferric ammonium citrate as indicator for H_2S production.	Lactose fermenters small, deep pink colonies; late lactose fermenters pale pink or colourless. Non-lactose fermenters colourless, translucent colonies, which may be easily overlooked if small (especially shigellae). H_2S producers may have black-centred colonies.	Relatively low selectivity; useful in isolating shigellae, which may be inhibited by more selective media. Often used when subculturing from liquid enrichment media.
Xylose-lysine-desoxycholate agar (XLD)	Selective agent: sodium desoxycholate. Indicator systems: three fermentable sugars (lactose, xylose, sucrose), plus lysine; pH indicator phenol red (yellow below pH 6.8, red from 6.8 to 8.4, red-purple above 8.4). H_2S detection system as for DCA also included.	Colour changes depend on balance between acid production from sugar fermentation and alkali production from lysine decarboxylation. Organisms which neither decarboxylate lysine or ferment any of the sugars produce colourless, translucent colonies, e.g. the shigellae and some *Proteeae*. Organisms which do not decarboxylate lysine but ferment one or more sugars produce bright yellow colonies, e.g. some *Proteeae*, *Citrobacter* and *Enterobacter* strains. Organisms which decarboxylate lysine but ferment two or three of the sugars produce acid in excess, also giving yellow colonies, e.g. *E. coli* and *Klebsiella*. Salmonellae	Less inhibitory than DCA, general-purpose plating medium. Particularly useful for the isolation of shigellae. May be used when subculturing from selective enrichment media.

Hektoen enteric agar (HEA)	Selective agent: bile salts. Indicator systems: three sugars (lactose, sucrose, salicin); pH indicator is thymol blue (yellow in acid conditions). A dye, acid fuschin, is included. As with DCA and XLD, there is a detection system for H_2S.	decarboxylate lysine, but only ferment xylose, giving colonies which may initially be yellow but which usually turn red after 24 h incubation. Regardless of colour, H_2S producers (*Proteus*, *Citrobacter*, most salmonellae) may yield black-centred colonies. Salmonellae and shigellae do not ferment any of the sugars (apart from rare strains) and give green or blue-green colonies (the colour of the uninoculated medium). Organisms fermenting one or more of the sugars give yellow or orange-yellow colonies (the orange tint is due to the dye). H_2S producers give black-centred colonies.	General plating medium but more selective than XLD. Useful for the isolation of salmonellae.
Bismuth sulphite agar (Wilson and Blair's medium)	Selective agents: bismuth sulphite and Brilliant Green. Indicator system: glucose and ferrous citrate. In the presence of glucose fermentation sulphite is reduced to sulphide, leading to the precipitation of iron sulphide. This gives black colonies and discolouration of the medium under the colony.	Shigellae and most of the *Enterobacteriaceae* other than salmonellae do not grow on this medium. *Salmonella typhi* produces black colonies with a metallic sheen resulting from H_2S production. The medium is often discoloured brown or black under the colony. Most other salmonellae tend to produce grey-black, grey or green colonies, often larger than those of *S. typhi*. The discoloured zone under the colony may be absent. If the strain is an H_2S producer, colonies may have a metallic sheen. Note that the classical appearance of salmonellae on this medium may not be seen if colonies are closely packed together.	Used for the isolation of *Salmonella typhi* and other salmonellae—although occasional strains will not grow on it. Since it does not rely on sugar fermentation for the recognition of possible salmonellae, it is useful for the isolation of biochemically atypical strains such as the Arizona group (late lactose fermenters) and the very rare rapid lactose fermenters. Its main disadvantage is its very short shelf life—no more than 24–36 h after preparation—and many laboratories have for this reason abandoned it for routine use.

Table 3. Screening biochemical tests for salmonellae and shigellae.

Test	Media	Positive result
O-Nitrophenyl galactosidase (ONPG) activity	Tube of *O*-nitrophenyl galactose broth.	Colour change from colourless to yellow.
Urease activity	Urea slope: peptone agar plus urea and phenol red.	Colour change from pale yellow to bright pink.
Motility	Tube of peptone water; after 4−6 h incubation look for motility in a wet preparation.	Motile organisms seen, be careful to distinguish this from Brownian motion, motile organisms move purposefully and in different directions.
Indole production	Tube of peptone water (use the tube set up for motility); after incubation, add Kovac's reagent	Red ring produced on top of the peptone water within the Kovac's reagent.
Hydrogen sulphide production	(1) Tube of peptone water. Insert lead acetate paper between cap and tube.	Blackening of the paper due to the formation of lead sulphide.
	(2) Triple sugar iron agar.	Blackening of the medium due to formation of ferric sulphide.
Carbohydrate fermentation	Sugar media—peptone water plus fermentable carbohydrate plus pH indicator.	Colour change due to acid production (dependent on indicator used).

Note: unless otherwise stated, all tests are incubated for 24 h at 37°C.

Table 4. Reactions in Kligler's iron agar and triple sugar iron agar.

Butt	Slope	H$_2$S	Interpretation
Acid	Acid	No	*E.coli*, *Klebsiella* spp., *Enterobacter* spp., some *Citrobacter* strains
Acid	Acid	Yes	Some *Citrobacter* strains
Acid	Alkaline	No	*Shigella* spp., some *Proteeae*, occasional *Citrobacter* strains
Acid	Alkaline	Yes	*Salmonella* spp., *Proteeae*, some *Citrobacter* strains
Alkaline	Alkaline	No	Non-fermenting bacteria, e.g. *Pseudomonas* spp.

3.2.2 *Kohn's composite media*

This is a two-tube medium.

(i) Tube 1 contains glucose, mannitol and urea, and is poured as a slope similar to TSI/KIA. The pH indicator is phenol red. Organisms which ferment only glucose turn the butt acid (yellow) whilst those which also ferment mannitol (which is present in excess) turn the slope yellow as well. This is the reaction seen with many of the *Enterobacteriaceae*, including *E.coli*, *Citrobacter* spp., *Enterobacter* spp. and *Salmonella* spp. Most strains of *Shigella* spp. also produce this reaction, with the exception of *S.dysenteriae* serotypes 1−10, which do not ferment mannitol. Regardless of sugar fermentation, those organisms which hydrolyse urea (*Proteus* spp., *Morganella morganii* and *Providencia rettgeri*) produce a uniform bright pink colour due to the production of ammonia.

(ii) Tube 2 contains sucrose and salicin, the pH indicator is bromothymol blue, and sodium thiosulphate is included as a sulphur source. The tubed agar is allowed to set vertically, not as a slope. After inoculation, paper test strips for H_2S and indole production are suspended from the top of the tube by wedging them between the wall of the tube and the plug. Fermentation of sucrose and/or salicin (not fermented by the majority of salmonella or shigella strains) turns the blue-green medium yellow. H_2S production turns the appropriate indicator paper black, while the production of indole turns the other paper pink (from pale yellow). It should be noted that neither tube contains lactose, and it is recommended that a test for ONPG activity is set up in conjunction with these tubes.

3.2.3 *Tests for preformed enzymes (API Z)*

These tests detect the presence or absence of enzymes in strains of salmonellae or shigellae. They are available in kit form, and probably the best known is the API Z kit (API System S.A.). The manufacturer's literature should be consulted for full details of how to use this kit. Briefly, the system comprises two plastic cupules (A and B) inoculated from a single colony of a non-lactose fermenter isolated on a selective medium. Cupule A contains substrates for four enzymes not possessed by salmonellae, shigellae or *Yersinia enterocolitica*, plus a test for an esterase specific to the salmonellae. Cupule B is a maintenance cupule should the strain need to be recovered for further identification. An oxidase test can also be performed on the contents of this cupule after recovery of the strain.

Several colour reactions are possible in cupule A; depending on the result obtained, the organism may either be discarded or referred for further identification. The advantage of this approach is that results are available in 2 h, rather than $6-18$ h for the conventional biochemical tests. In addition, it is designed to screen for *Y.enterocolitica* as well as salmonellae and shigellae, unlike other composite media.

3.3 **Media for the isolation of *Yersinia enterocolitica* and pathogens other than *Enterobacteriaceae***

Table 5 presents details of media for the isolation of *Y.enterocolitica* and pathogens other than *Enterobacteriaceae*.

4. SPECIMEN PROCESSING

In this section, methods and techniques are discussed for the processing of a specimen of faeces for salmonellae, shigellae and campylobacters, which are the three groups of organisms looked for routinely in any patient with a gastro-intestinal infection. Methods for other bacteria are found in Section 5.

4.1 **Specimen collection**

4.1.1 *Types of specimen and transport to the laboratory*

Rectal swabs are a poor second best to a specimen of faeces. Whilst there may be difficulties in obtaining specimens from some patients (notably young children and the elderly), there can be no justification for sending rectal swabs from patients with diarrhoea and such specimens should not be accepted.

The most appropriate container for faeces is a wide-mouthed screw-capped plastic

Table 5. Media for the isolation of *Yersinia enterocolitica* and pathogens other than *Enterobacteriaceae*.

Medium	Components	Colonial morphology	Uses
Cefsulodin–irgasan–novobiocin (CIN) agar	Selective agents: sodium desoxycholate, irgasan (a disinfectant) and two antibiotics, cefsulodin and novobiocin. Indicator system: mannitol plus neutral red as pH indicator.	Gram-positive bacteria, *Pseudomonas aeruginosa* and many *Enterobacteriaceae* do not grow on this medium. *Y. enterocolitica* produces medium-sized deep pink colonies (due to mannitol fermentation). Certain *Enterobacteriaceae*—notably *Citrobacter*, *Enterobacter* and *Serratia*—may grow and produce similar colonies. Non-fermenting Gram-negative bacilli (e.g. *Pseudomonas* spp.) may grow, giving colourless or pale yellow colonies.	A selective medium for *Y. enterocolitica*
Campylobacter medium	Blood agar base made selective with three antibiotics, vancomycin, polymyxin B and trimethoprim. Selectivity is increased by incubating at 43°C.	Most other bacteria will not grow on this medium. *Campylobacter jejuni/coli* produces large, flat, glistening grey colonies; often, the long axis of the colony lies along the inoculation streak.	A selective medium for *Campylobacter jejuni/coli*
Thiosulphate–citrate–bile salt–sucrose agar (TCBS)	Selective agents: bile salts, sodium thiosulphate and sodium citrate. Selectivity is increased with a high concentration of sodium chloride and a final pH of 8.6. Indicator systems: sucrose plus thymol blue/bromothymol blue pH indicators. A detection system for H_2S production is included.	Most strains of the *Enterobacteriaceae* are inhibited; some *Proteeae* may grow, giving yellow colonies if sucrose is fermented, with black centres if H_2S is produced. *Vibrio cholerae* (O1 and non-O1 strains) ferment sucrose giving flat, yellow colonies. *V. parahaemolyticus* does not ferment sucrose; colonies are large, blue or blue-green. Note that none of the vibrios produce	This is a selective medium for vibrios.

		H_2S; organisms which do so can be ignored. Faecal streptococci produce small, yellow colonies.	
Alkaline peptone water (APW)	Peptone water base rendered alkaline with a phosphate buffer, giving a pH of 8.6. Many bacteria are inhibited at this pH, but inhibition is incomplete and after 6−8 h incubation initially suppressed bacteria may begin to overgrow any vibrios present.	Not applicable (liquid medium).	A liquid semi-selective enrichment medium for vibrios.
Cycloserine–cefoxitin agar	Blood agar base made selective with two antibiotics, cycloserine and cefoxitin. Older formulations included fructose and egg yolk, neither of which appear to be necessary.	After 48 h incubation, *Clostridium difficile* colonies are large (4−8 mm), greyish-white and flat with a filamentous outline. There is a characteristic smell, similar to paracresol.	A selective medium for *Clostridium difficile*.
Mannitol−salt agar	Selective agent: sodium chloride in high concentration (7.5%). Indicator system: mannitol plus phenol red as pH indicator.	Almost all bacteria except staphylococci and some halophilic vibrios are inhibited. Staphylococci grow well (although colonies are smaller than on blood or MacConkey's agar). *Staphylococcus aureus* ferments mannitol to give yellow zones around the colonies. Most coagulase-negative staphylococci do not give this reaction.	A selective indicator medium for *Staphylococcus aureus*.
Bacillus cereus selective medium	Selective agent: polymyxin B. Indicator systems: egg yolk for lecithinase production; mannitol plus a pH indicator for mannitol fermentation.	*Bacillus cereus* colonies are large and flat with an irregular outline. Colonies are surrounded by an opaque zone of precipitated egg yolk. *Bacillus cereus* does not ferment mannitol and so does not produce an acid reaction in the medium.	A selective indicator medium for *Bacillus cereus*.

pot, containing a small plastic or wooden spoon which fits into the pot when closed. If the faeces are liquid, the pot may be filled to one-third full (no more, in order to avoid spillage when opened); if solid, the spoon is used to collect one spoonful of faeces. Enthusiastic clinicians or nurses who send the entire contents of the bedpan should be discouraged.

Once collected, the specimen may be forwarded to the laboratory by the routine local transport. However, if the delay in reaching the laboratory is likely to be greater than 3−4 h the sample should be refrigerated, since the acid pH which develops will rapidly decrease the viability of any shigellae in the specimen.

4.2 **Microscopy**

Other than a search for parasites (not covered in this chapter) this is not usually done, but occasionally the laboratory may be asked to look for pus cells in the specimen. The following procedure may be used.

(i)   If pus or mucous exudate is present on a solid specimen, mix a small portion with a drop of methylene blue on a slide. A liquid specimen may be examined directly.

(ii)   Cover the drop with a coverslip and examine under the 10× and 40× objectives.

4.3 **Culture**

4.3.1 *Choice of media*

To a great extent this is a matter of personal preference, but it should be noted that no one medium can be regarded as entirely satisfactory for isolating all strains of salmonellae or shigellae. At least two media should be used; suitable combinations would be DCA plus XLD or XLD plus Hektoen's enteric agar. In addition a tube of selenite broth and a selective medium for campylobacters should be inoculated. Laboratories which have a particular interest in *Salmonella typhi* may also wish to include bismuth sulphite agar in the set of media used.

4.3.2 *Culture technique*

(i)   Inoculate a liquid specimen using a bacteriological loop or cotton-tipped swab.

(ii)   If a solid specimen is received, first make a thick emulsion of the specimen in peptone water.

(iii) Either a liquid specimen or the thick emulsion may then be inoculated into the chosen enrichment medium (use about 1 ml of specimen per 20 ml of broth).

(iv)   Incubate all plates (with the exception of the campylobacter plate) in air at 37°C. Incubate the campylobacter medium at 43°C in 5% O_2, 10% CO_2 and 85% N_2. This mixture can be achieved in an anaerobic jar by the use of either a premixed gas supply or a gas-generating kit designed especially for this purpose (for example the CampyPak, BBL Microbiology Systems). It is occasionally recommended that an ordinary anaerobic gas-generating kit be used without putting a catalyst in the jar. This must not be done, as potentially explosive mixtures of oxygen and hydrogen may be generated.

4.4 **Reading the plates**

This section describes how to examine the culture plates after incubation and the setting up and interpreting of screening identification tests. When reading the plates and carrying out further tests, it is essential that all results are recorded on the worksheet accompanying the specimen. This is of course good bacteriological practice with any specimen; but it is perhaps the least interesting part of any investigation and is sometimes overlooked, with dire consequences. In addition, it cannot be emphasized too strongly that when picking colonies for further identification, only isolated single colonies are chosen. Many of the problems which may be encountered stem from a failure to inoculate tests with a pure strain of an organism. If purity cannot be guaranteed, the colony should be subcultured to MacConkey's agar and further investigation carried out the next day. It is not necessary to be an expert bacteriologist to process a faeces specimen correctly, but it is essential to be a careful one.

4.4.1 *The campylobacter plate*

(i) *Examination*

(a)   Examine this plate for colonies suggestive of *Campylobacter* spp. (see *Table 5*). If none are found, reincubate the plate for a further 24 h.

(b)   If suggestive colonies are found, Gram stain them and look for the typical curved or S-shaped Gram-negative bacilli. Perform an oxidase test (see Chapter 4, Section 4.1). Oxidase-positive organisms which grow at 43°C and show typical microscopic morphology can be presumptively identified as *Campylobacter* spp. and a report issued to this effect.

(ii) *Confirmation of identity.* Many general laboratories do not identify these organisms further, but if it is desired to do so, the tests in *Table 6* may be used. Note that hippurate hydrolysis may be used to distinguish between *Campylobacter jejuni* and *C.coli*. Thermophilic and nalidixic-acid-resistant strains from faeces may be reported as *C.laridis*.

(iii) *Sensitivity testing.* When antibiotic treatment is required for campylobacter enteritis, erythromycin is the drug of choice. Gentamicin has been used successfully for the treatment of the occasional systemic infection with *C.jejuni/coli*. Sensitivity testing should be carried out at 37°C on blood agar in the appropriate gaseous environment.

4.4.2 *Media for salmonellae and shigellae*

(i) *Enrichment medium.* The selenite broth (or other enrichment medium) should be subcultured to a DCA or XLD plate and the plate examined after overnight incubation.

Table 6. Identification of *Campylobacter jejuni/coli*.

	Growth at: 25°C	43°C	Catalase	Oxidase	Nalidixic acid	Hippurate hydrolysis
C.jejuni	−	+	+	+	S[a]	+
C.coli	−	+	+	+	S	−
C.laridis	−	+	+	+	R	−

[a]Sensitivity as judged by growth around a 30 μg disc.

(ii) *Examination of solid media.* These plates should be examined for organisms showing colonial morphology and/or colour reactions suggestive of salmonellae or shigellae (see *Table 2*). For each colonial type of suspect colony, one of the following sets of screening tests should be inoculated.

(a)   A short series of biochemical tests (see *Table 3*).
(b)   Kligler's iron agar (or triple sugar iron agar) plus a test for urease production.
(c)   Kohn's tubed composite media plus a test for ONPG activity.
(d)   API Z test kit.

See Section 3.2 for a discussion of these media. KIA or TSI are inoculated by stabbing the butt and streaking the slope; Kohn's medium 1 is inoculated in the same way, medium 2 by stabbing, and the API Z according to the manufacturer's instructions.

If one of the conventional composite media is chosen, the remains of the colony is used to inoculate a purity plate. We have found it useful to use a Petri dish divided in two by a plastic divider (Sterilin Ltd) with one half of the plate containing blood agar and the other MacConkey's agar. Growth on the blood agar may be used for slide agglutination tests if necessary. Setting up a purity plate at this stage will avoid confusion in the interpretation of results later on and also avoids the possibility of discarding a potential salmonella or shigella due to contamination with another organism. Note that since the API Z is read in 2 h, a purity plate will not be available. This means that the utmost care must be taken to ensure that a single colony is used to inoculate the test strip.

(iii) *Reading the screening tests.* The results of the API Z are read 2 h after inoculation. If the reaction is suggestive of *Salmonella* spp., *Shigella* spp. or *Yersinia* spp., the maintenance cupule should be subcultured to MacConkey's agar and blood agar for a purity check and slide agglutinations. Since some pseudomonads may mimic the reactions of potential pathogens in this test, time and media may be saved by performing an oxidase test on cupule B after all subculturing has been done (the oxidase reagent is toxic). Oxidase-positive organisms may be discarded, although it should be remembered that *Aeromonas hydrophila* and *Plesiomonas shigelloides* are regarded by some authorities as causes of diarrhoea. These are identified using the API 20E.

If KIA or TSI and a urease test were used, the purity plate should first be examined. If the culture is not pure, results of biochemical tests are meaningless and should be repeated using a single colony of each non-lactose fermenter on the plate. If the culture is pure, the test should be examined for urea hydrolysis; organisms giving a positive result cannot be a salmonella or shigella and may be discarded. The KIA/TSI slope should then be examined. Interpretation of the possible reactions may be carried out using *Table 4*.

When using Kohn's tubes, the purity of the culture should be checked as above, then medium 1 examined for evidence of urea hydrolysis. If this is absent, the remaining biochemical reactions are read and interpreted using *Table 7*.

It must be understood that the screening tests described here are no more than that—they do not confirm the identity of the organism. For this, further tests are needed as described in Sections 4.5 and 4.6.

Table 7. Biochemical reactions of some enteric Gram-negative bacilli.

	Escherichia coli	Klebsiella	Citrobacter	Enterobacter	Yersinia enterocolitica	Proteus mirabilis	Proteus vulgaris	Morganella morganii	Salmonella typhi	Salmonella spp.	Shigella dysenteriae	Shigella flexneri	Shigella boydii	Shigella sonnei	Vibrio cholerae	Vibrio parahaemolyticus
Motility	+	−	+	+	−	+	+	+	+	+	−	−	−	−	+	+
VP reaction	−	+	−	+	−	v	−	−	−	−	−	−	−	−	v	−
Citrate utilization	−	+	+	+	−	v	v	−	−	+	−	−	−	−	+	+
Urease	−	+	−	−	+	+	+	+	−	−	−	−	−	−	−	−
H₂S	−	−	v	−	−	+	+	−	+	+	−	−	−	−	−	−
Indole	+	−	v	−	v	−	+	+	−	−	v	v	v	−	+	+
LDC	+	v	−	v	−	−	−	−	+	+	−	−	−	−	+	+
ODC	v	−	v	+	+	+	−	+	−	+	−	−	−	+	+	+
PPA	−	−	−	−	−	+	+	+	−	−	−	−	−	−	−	−
ONPG	+	+	+	+	+	−	−	−	−	−	v	−	−	+	+	−
Gas from glucose	+	+	+	+	−	+	+	+	−	+	−	−	−	−	−	−
Acid from:																
mannitol	+	+	+	+	+	−	−	−	+	+	−	+	+	+	+	+
sucrose	v	+	v	+	+	−	+	−	−	−	−	−	−	−	+	−
salicin	v	+	v	+	−	−	−	−	−	−	−	−	−	−	−	−
dulcitol	v	v	v	v	−	−	−	−	−	+	−	−	−	−	−	−

Key: + = most strains positive; − = most strains negative; v = some strains positive, some negative.

4.5 Serotyping of salmonellae and shigellae

4.5.1 *Salmonella serotyping*

The final identification of a salmonella can be regarded as consisting of confirmation of identity by biochemical testing plus determination of serotype. Neither method is adequate when used alone; biochemical tests merely confirm that the organism is a salmonella, but provide no useful information for epidemiological purposes. Serological identification must always be confirmed with biochemical tests due to the presence of similar antigens in other members of the *Enterobacteriaceae*. This section describes practical techniques for salmonella serotyping, but makes no attempt to discuss the theoretical basis of classification by the Kauffman−White scheme. The reader is referred elsewhere for this (7).

(i) *Choice of antisera.* Only a limited number of serotypes are encountered regularly in a general laboratory, and consequently no such laboratory need possess more than a basic set of antisera, as shown in *Table 8*.

(ii) *Initial screening tests.* All suspect organisms should be tested by slide agglutination [for method, see (v) below] against polyvalent-O and polyvalent-H (specific and non-specific phases). If the organism does not agglutinate with polyvalent-O, it should be tested again with Vi antiserum. Vi is a surface antigen and, if present, may mask the underlying O antigens.

Table 8. Antisera for the identification of *Salmonella* serotypes commonly encountered in the UK and USA.

O-antisera	H-antisera
Polyvalent-O, groups A−G	Polyvalent-H, specific and non-specific phases
	Polyvalent-H, non-specific phase
Monovalent O-antisera:	Monovalent-H antisera:
2; 4; 6,7; 8; 9; 3,10;	a; b; c; d; e,h; f,g; g,m;
15; 19,Vi.	i; k; l,v; m,t; r

In the UK an organism which does not agglutinate with the polyvalent-O antiserum groups A−G or with Vi is unlikely to be a salmonella. However, members of rare serogroups not included in the polyvalent-O antisera are occasionally seen. If full biochemical identification still indicates that the organism is a salmonella, it should be sent to a reference laboratory for identification. Conversely, the Vi antigen is also possessed by other members of the *Enterobacteriaceae*, and O antisera occasionally cross-react with organisms other than salmonellae; again, biochemical testing is useful. Negative polyvalent-H agglutination may occur with rare serotypes not included in the polyvalent sera, or the strain may be non-motile (no H antigens present).

(iii) *Determination of serogroup (O antigens)*. If the organism agglutinates in polyvalent-O antiserum, it should be retested with monovalent sera to determine the serogroup. If polyvalent-O agglutination was negative but Vi agglutination was positive, the Vi antigen may be removed and the strain retested, as follows.

(a)   Make a suspension of the organism in 1 ml saline and heat it for 30 min at 100°C.

(b)   Centrifuge in microcentrifuge at 12 000 *g* for 5 min and resuspend the pellet of bacteria in 0.5 ml saline.

(c)   Use this suspension to repeat the O agglutination tests.

Slide agglutination is usually sufficient to determine the O group, but if there is the slightest doubt about the result (e.g. a weak or slow reaction) it should be confirmed with a tube agglutination test [see (vi) below].

(iv) *Determination of serotype (H antigen)*. If the organism agglutinates in polyvalent-H (specific and non-specific) antiserum, test it with polyvalent-H non-specific antiserum. If there is no agglutination (or the reaction is very weak) the organism is in the specific phase and may then be tested with individual antisera or the Rapid Diagnostic Sera (RDS) (see below). Since the serogroup has already been determined, it is not necessary to test every H antiserum straight away—testing should start with those known to occur in that particular serogroup. If there is strong agglutination with polyvalent-H (non-specific) antiserum, the organism is in the non-specific phase and must be changed to the specific phase before the serotype can be determined [see (vii) below]. Because cross-reactions with motile organisms other than salmonellae are common with H antisera, all positive slide agglutination tests for H antigens must be confirmed with a tube agglutination test.

Rapid Diagnostic Sera contain a mixture of antisera to various H antigens, and the pattern of reactions which occur may be used to determine the serotype. This removes the need to test multiple individual antisera. Several different combinations are available from different commercial sources; a popular combination (obtainable from Wellcome

Table 9. Interpretation of reactions using RDS antisera.

Agglutination with RDS:			Indicates H antigen:
1	2	3	
+	+	+	E complex
+	+	−	b
+	−	−	r
−	+	+	k
−	−	+	G complex
−	+	−	L complex
+	−	+	d

Diagnostics and Difco Laboratories) is as follows.

(a)   RDS-1: antisera to b, d, r, and the E complex.

(b)   RDS-2: antisera to b, k, the E complex and the L complex.

(c)   RDS-3: antisera to d, k, the E complex and the G complex.

Note that antiserum to H antigen 'i' is not included and this must therefore be tested separately. This is important because *Salmonella typhimurium*, one of the commonest serotypes seen in the UK and USA, possesses this H antigen. The reaction patterns which occur may be interpreted using *Table 9*.

(v) *Method for slide agglutination test.* When performing these tests, colonies growing on a selective medium should never be used, as erroneous results may be obtained.

(a)   Pick a small amount of growth from a pure culture on a nutrient or blood agar plate and make a smooth, dense suspension in saline on a glass slide. There must be no clumps or particles visible in the suspension.

(b)   To this, add a small loopful of antiserum and mix the two by rocking the slide gently backwards and forwards.

(c)   Look for visible clumping occurring within 60 sec of mixing suspension and antiserum, which indicates agglutination. This is best seen if the slide is held against a dark background such as a black tile.

(d)   Remember that this is a live culture, therefore discard the slide into the bench disinfectant pot.

(vi) *Method for tube agglutination tests.* These are used to confirm the results of slide tests. The aim is to show that the antiserum will agglutinate a suspension of the test organism at a dilution equal to or greater than that stated on the antiserum package. Cross-reactions with other organisms will usually give agglutination only at lower titres than that stated on the bottle. The methods are given in *Table 10*.

(vii) *Method for changing the phase of a Salmonella spp. from non-specific to specific.* Two methods are given in *Table 11* (see also *Figure 1*).

(viii) *Problems encountered in salmonella serotyping.* Difficulties and apparent anomalies are sometimes seen when attempting to determine the serotype of a suspected salmonella. Some of the commoner problems and possible solutions are listed in *Table 12*.

Table 10. Method for tube agglutination tests for salmonellae.

1. Preparation of antigens:
    (i) O-antigens: suspend growth from a nutrient or blood agar plate in 2 ml saline. Heat the suspension for 10 min at 100°C, which removes the flagellae.
    (ii) H-antigens: add a few drops of formalin to an overnight broth culture to kill the organism.
    (iii) Vi-antigen: suspend growth from a plate culture in saline (note—this is a live antigen preparation, and must be handled with care).
2. For each antiserum to be tested, first make a 1/10 dilution of the serum in saline, then set up a rack of seven agglutination tubes.
3. To tubes 2−7, add 200 μl of saline, and to tubes 1 and 2 add 200 μl of the diluted antiserum. Prepare a series of doubling dilutions of antiserum in tubes 2−6, by taking 200 μl from tube 2 and adding it to tube 3. Repeat this process down to tube 6, and discard 200 μl from this tube.
4. Finally, add 200 μl of antigen to all tubes. Tubes 1−6 now contain a series of doubling dilutions of antiserum from 1/20 to 1/640, while tube 7 is a negative control with no antiserum.
5. Incubate the tubes at 50°C in a water bath, and read after 4 h. If the results are negative, incubate at room temperature overnight and read again the next day.
6. Read the tubes in good light against a dark background. Agglutination appears as clumping of the bacteria, which form a deposit on the bottom of the tube, with clearing of the supernatant. It may be necessary to use a hand lens to detect fine traces of agglutination. The result is defined as the highest dilution of antiserum giving visible agglutination.

Table 11. Changing the phase of a salmonella from non-specific to specific.

A. Bridge plate method
   This is the simpler method of the two presented here.
   1. Use a sterile scalpel blade to cut a trough 1 cm wide across a fresh (i.e. moist) blood or nutrient agar plate.
   2. Inoculate one half of the plate with the non-specific phase culture.
   3. Bridge the trough with a strip of moistened sterile filter paper (see *Figure 1a*).
   4. Place a drop of polyvalent-H (non-specific phase) antiserum on the bridge (point *A* on *Figure 1a*) and incubate for 18 h at 37°C.
   5. Motile organisms will migrate across the bridge, but those in the non-specific phase will be immobilized by the antiserum. Subculture from the other half of the plate (point *B* on *Figure 1a*).
   6. The subcultured organisms should now be in the specific phase, but the process may need to be repeated if the organism is still in the non-specific phase.

B. Craigie tube method (see *Figure 1b*)
   1. Prepare 10 ml semi-solid (0.5%) nutrient agar and mix with 3 drops of polyvalent-H (non-specific phase) antiserum.
   2. Pour it into a sterile 30 ml universal bottle, taking care that the upper end of the small inner tube (a length cut from a disposable Pasteur pipette is ideal) is above the surface of the agar. Care must be taken not to disturb the tube, or the motile salmonella in the non-specific phase will 'by-pass' the agar and not be immobilized.
   3. Inoculate the tube at point *A* on *Figure 1b* and incubate for 18 h at 37°C.
   4. Organisms in the non-specific phase will be immobilized by the antiserum, but those in the specific phase will migrate down the inner tube and up onto the surface of the agar, from where they can be subcultured (point *B* on *Figure 1b*).
   5. Repeat the procedure if the organism is still not in the specific phase.

4.5.2 *Shigella serotyping*

(i) *Choice of antisera.* A general laboratory should possess at least polyvalent antisera to the four species of *Shigella*, that is polyvalent *S.dysenteriae* 1−10, polyvalent

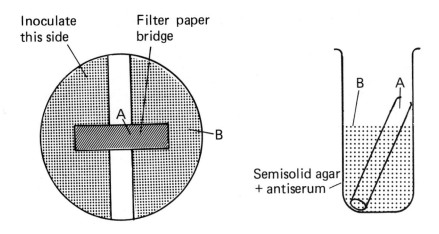

1a Bridge plate method   **1b   Craigie tube method**

Figure 1. Changing the phase of a *Salmonella*.

Table 12. Problems in the serotyping of *Salmonella* strains.

O agglutination	H agglutination	Possible reasons
+	−	(i) The organism is non-motile (e.g. *S.pullorum*).
		(ii) The strain is poorly motile. It is necessary to select the motile sub-population; subculture to a semi-solid (0.5%) agar plate, incubate, and subculture from the spreading edge of the growth obtained.
		(iii) The strain is a rare H type not included in the polyvalent or monovalent sera. Send it to a reference laboratory for identification.
−	+	(i) The organism is not a *Salmonella*; a non-specific antigen−antibody reaction may rarely occur due to the incomplete removal of antibodies from the antiserum other than those directed against the specific H antigen. Recheck the biochemical identification of the organism.
		(ii) The strain belongs to a rarely encountered O group not present in the polyvalent or monovalent sera. Send the strain to a reference laboratory for serotyping.
		(iii) Vi antigen is masking the O antigen. Check agglutination with Vi antiserum.
−	−	(i) This is a rare occurrence and implies that the organism is not a *Salmonella*. Recheck the biochemical identification.
		(ii) A combination of some of the circumstances listed above could also give rise to negative agglutination reactions.
More than one monovalent O antiserum positive	+ or −	(i) The organism may possess O antigens shared between different O groups, or a non-specific antigen−antibody reaction may be occurring. In either case, tube agglutinations should determine the O group to which the organism belongs.
		(ii) The organism is not a *Salmonella*. Recheck the biochemical identification.

S.flexneri, polyvalent *S.boydii* 1−15 and *S.sonnei* phase 1 and 2. It is also useful to keep individual antisera to *S.dysenteriae* ·types 1 and 2, and a panel of antisera to *S.flexneri* serotypes.

(ii) *Determination of serotype.* Suspect organisms should be tested by slide agglutination against the polyvalent antisera, starting with antisera to *S.sonnei*, as this is the commonest species encountered in the UK and USA. If the organism agglutinates with one of the polyvalent antisera, the serotype of the identified species may be determined by slide agglutination with monovalent antisera, if available. The method for slide agglutination is the same as for salmonellae (see Section 4.5.1 above). Tube agglutinations are not usually necessary, but should be performed if there is any doubt about the slide agglutination result, or if biochemical identification is not clearcut (cross-reactions in slide agglutination tests are common, especially with strains of *E.coli*, some of which are biochemically atypical and may resemble shigellae). Antigen for tube agglutination tests is prepared by suspending growth from an agar plate in saline, and adjusting the opacity to the equivalent of about 10^8 organisms ml^{-1} with an opacity standard. The culture is killed with a few drops of formalin, and tube agglutinations carried out as described for salmonellae (*Table 10*).

(iii) *S.flexneri serotyping.* The antigenic structure of *S.flexneri* is complex, and determination of serotype may appear confusing. Consequently serotyping of this species merits a section to itself.

There are six main serotypes of *S.flexneri*, which are determined by the presence of a specific type antigen (labelled I−VI). Subserotypes are determined by the presence of group antigens, which are shared between the six main serotypes. In addition, there are two variants (X and Y) which do not possess a type antigen but do possess different group antigens.

Antisera are available from several commercial sources, but serotyping can be simplified using a panel of eight antisera obtained from Wellcome Diagnostics. In this panel, antisera 1, 2, 4, 5 and 6 are monovalent against the corresponding type antigen (I, II, IV, V and VI). Antiserum 3 contains antisera against type antigen III and also against group antigen 6. This permits differentiation between the subserotypes of serotypes 1 and 4, which vary in their possession of group antigen 6. X antiserum is directed against group antigens 7 and 8, while Y antiserum is directed against group

Table 13. Antigenic structure of *Shigella flexneri* (weak reactions are in parenthesis).

Serotype	Subserotype	Type antigen	Group antigen	Agglutination with Wellcome antiserum
1	1a	I	1,2,4	1 (Y)
1	1b	I	1,2,4,6	1 and 3 (Y)
2	2a	II	1,3,4	2 (Y)
2	2b	II	1,7,8	2 and X
3	3a	III	1,6,7,8	3 and X
3	3b	III	1,3,4	3 and Y
3	3c	III	1,6	3
4	4a	IV	1,3,4	4 (Y)
4	4b	IV	1,3,4,6	4 and 3 (Y)
5	−	V	1,7,8	5 and X (Y)
6	−	VI	1,2,4	6
X variant		−	1,7,8	X
Y variant		−	1,3,4	Y

antigens 3 and 4. The antigenic structure of *S.flexneri* is shown in *Table 13*, which also shows the pattern of reactions which may occur with the Wellcome antisera described above.

4.6 **Biochemical identification**

4.6.1 *Introduction*

The full identification by biochemical testing of a member of the *Enterobacteriaceae* is straightforward if the strain exhibits reactions typical of the species, but can be very difficult with atypical strains. As a result, a full treatment of the subject is beyond the scope of this chapter, and the interested reader is referred to a standard textbook (8,9).

Although the media for biochemical testing may be prepared in the user's own laboratory, many laboratories now find it more convenient to use a commercial kit system for identification of the *Enterobacteriaceae*. Several such kits are available, but in the author's experience the API 20E system (API System S.A.) gives accurate and reproducible results. In this system, a number of tests contained on a plastic strip are inoculated with a suspension of the test organism, and after 24 h incubation the results are combined to produce a 7-digit number (the 'API profile') which may then be looked up in a large database to determine the identity of the organism. It is also possible to obtain a larger database on a floppy disk for use with a microcomputer.

Should the reader wish to attempt identification of a salmonella or shigella from first principles, *Table 7* may be used to determine which tests to set up and the reactions which may be expected. It must be emphasized that the reactions given are those of the majority of strains of a particular species. There will always be some exceptions, and some of the more important of these are discussed below.

4.6.2 *Atypical reactions of the salmonellae and shigellae*

The reactions given in *Table 7* are those seen with the majority of strains of a particular organism. As might be expected, minor differences may be seen, but these do not affect the identification of the organism to genus level. Occasionally more significant variations are seen which might lead to misidentification of an organism, and these will now be described.

(i) *Salmonellae*. Most strains of *Salmonella paratyphi* A do not produce H_2S; this serovar is also LDC-negative and will not grow with citrate as the sole carbon source. *S.pullorum* and *S.gallinarum* are non-motile variants; in addition *S.gallinarum* is ODC-negative and does not produce gas from glucose. The Arizona group (*S.arizonae*; *Salmonella* subgenus III) are ONPG-positive, and may appear as lactose fermenters on media containing this carbohydrate. This clearly causes a problem when using such media, as strains of the Arizona group may be inadvertently discarded. In other respects they behave much as typical salmonellae, and if infection with these organisms is considered possible (for example, during an outbreak), a medium such as bismuth sulphite agar may be used, as it does not rely on failure to ferment lactose as an identifying characteristic. *Salmonella typhi* does not produce gas from glucose.

(ii) *Shigellae*. *Shigella dysenteriae* type 1 is catalase-negative and is thus an exception to the general rule that the *Enterobacteriaceae* are catalase-positive; it also produces a positive ONPG test. The Newcastle and Manchester variants of *S.flexneri* type 6 are atypical in producing gas from glucose, and most strains ferment dulcitol. The Newcastle variant does not ferment mannitol, unlike all shigellae other than *S.dysenteriae*.

4.7 Sensitivity testing of salmonellae and shigellae

4.7.1 *Choice of antimicrobials*

All strains of salmonellae and shigellae should be tested against an appropriate range of antimicrobial agents. For salmonellae, this should include ampicillin, trimethoprim, chloramphenicol and ciprofloxacin. The range for shigellae should include ampicillin, tetracycline, trimethoprim and ciprofloxacin. Technical methods for sensitivity testing are found in Chapter 7, Section 2.

4.8 Reporting to the clinician

4.8.1 *When to report?*

The question of when to report the isolation of a salmonella or shigella is sometimes a difficult one. If the report is made too early and subsequently has to be retracted, not only will the laboratory's credibility suffer, but inconvenience may have been caused to the patient (unnecessary isolation in hospital, or withdrawal from work) and to medical and nursing staff. Alternatively, if the report is issued only after full identification has been made, the patient may not have been isolated or may have continued to work in a sensitive occupation such as food handling, thereby putting others at risk. While rigid rules cannot be laid down, each case being judged individually, a report should never be issued on the basis of screening biochemical tests alone, nor on slide agglutination results without the backup of results from at least some biochemical tests. A provisional report may be issued on the basis of screening tests in composite media plus satisfactory slide agglutinations; to wait for full identification might delay the report for at least one more day. The price which must be paid for early reporting is the recognition that occasional false-positive results will be issued. Such reporting should therefore always be done direct to the clinician by telephone or a visit to the ward, and it should be stressed that the report is provisional and subject to confirmation.

4.8.2 *What to report?*

The isolation of a salmonella from faeces will be provisionally reported as '*Salmonella* sp. isolated—further identification to follow'. A further report will be issued later (possibly several days later) when the full identity of the strain is known. This must be determined and reported in all cases if the fact of isolation is to be of any use for epidemiological purposes, and some common serotypes may also need to be phage- or plasmid-typed. However, all laboratories should be capable of distinguishing *Salmonella typhi* from other serovars and reporting the fact without needing to refer the strain to a reference laboratory before a report is issued.

When reporting the isolation of a shigella, a species name may usually be given on the basis of slide agglutination tests with polyvalent antisera. However, full serotyping of the strain may need the services of a reference laboratory.

Since most cases of enteric infection with salmonellae or shigellae will not benefit from treatment with specific antimicrobial agents, it is common policy not to report sensitivity test results unless the patient has already started specific treatment or unless requested to do so by the clinician. Otherwise, reporting of sensitivity test results may encourage unnecessary and possibly harmful treatment.

5. SPECIMEN PROCESSING FOR ORGANISMS OTHER THAN SALMONELLAE, SHIGELLAE AND CAMPYLOBACTERS

5.1 *Escherichia coli*

5.1.1 *Enteropathogenic E.coli (EPEC)*

EPEC strains may cause diarrhoea in infants and young children, and examination for these organisms has traditionally formed part of the routine processing of faeces from all children aged 3 years or less.

(i) *Culture.* MacConkey's agar (if not already included) and a blood agar plate should be added to the standard set of faeces plates. After incubation, each morphological type of lactose-fermenting colony should be tested by slide agglutination with polyvalent antisera to EPEC (obtainable from Wellcome Diagnostics or Difco Laboratories). Agglutination results may be poor from the MacConkey's plate, and should also be performed using the growth on blood agar. If agglutination occurs with the polyvalent antisera, monovalent sera may be used to identify the serotype.

(ii) *Confirmation of identity.* All suspected EPEC strains should be confirmed by full biochemical testing and by tube agglutination tests. The method for the tube agglutinations is the same as for salmonellae. The antigen for the test is prepared by heating a saline suspension of the organism to 100°C for 1 h, and adjusting the opacity to about 10^8 organisms ml^{-1}.

5.1.2 *Enterotoxigenic E.coli (ETEC)*

(i) *Introduction.* Enterotoxigenic strains of *E.coli* (ETEC) are now regarded as a common cause of traveller's diarrhoea, and in the future the examination of faeces specimens for these strains is likely to be increasingly undertaken by most general microbiology laboratories. ETEC may produce one or both of two different enterotoxins, referred to as heat-stable (ST) and heat-labile (LT) respectively. Diagnosis of infection with ETEC is by demonstrating the ability of strains of *E.coli* isolated from the patient to produce enterotoxin.

At present, detection of ST is not feasible in the general laboratory. Detection of LT may be accomplished by several methods including enzyme-linked immunosorbent assay, reverse passive latex agglutination (VET-RPLA, Oxoid), coagglutination using *Staphylococcus aureus* (Phadebact LT-ETEC, Pharmacia Diagnostics), or by gene probes (Gen-Probe). Unfortunately, these methods are either not yet generally available or are, with the exception of coagglutination, expensive, and until this situation changes the most practical method for a general laboratory processing large numbers of specimens is a tissue culture assay. A method for such an assay, as described by Chapman and Swift (10), is given in *Table 14*. For those laboratories processing small numbers of specimens the coagglutination or RPLA test is recommended.

Table 14. Method for detection of enterotoxigenic *Escherichia coli* LT toxin[a].

1. Materials required: Y1 mouse adrenal cell monolayers; brain-heart infusion broth (BHI) supplemented with lincomycin (concentration: 90 mg l^{-1}); stock solution of polymyxin B (10 g l^{-1}).
2. Inoculate the specimen on to MacConkey's agar; after incubation pick four lactose-fermenting colonies into tubes of 1 ml BHI plus lincomycin and examine each isolate as an individual culture.
3. Incubate the broth at 37°C for 20 h. Then add polymyxin to a final concentration of 100 mg l^{-1}. Incubate broth for a further 4 h.
4. Remove the maintenance medium from the cell monolayer and replace with the crude broth culture. Incubate cells for 30 min. Then remove broth and replace with cell maintenance medium.
5. Reincubate the cell monolayer for 24 h.
6. Examine for typical cytopathic effect of LT, seen as a rounding up of the cells.
7. Confirm the effect as being due to a heat-labile toxin. Retest two portions of the broth culture, one untreated and the other treated by heating to 100°C for 5 min. In the heated culture, the effect should be neutralized.
8. Identify each original isolate, one or more should prove to be *E. coli*. Test each strain of *E. coli* individually for its ability to produce LT.

[a]Method of Chapman and Swift (10).

5.1.3 *E. coli and haemorrhagic colitis*

Recently, *E. coli* (particularly serotype O:157 H:7 which produces a Vero toxin) has been associated with sporadic cases and outbreaks of haemorrhagic colitis and haemolytic uraemic syndrome. One unusual characteristic of this serotype is that, unlike most other strains of *E. coli* and many other *Enterobacteriaceae*, it does not ferment sorbitol. Suspect strains isolated in diagnostic laboratories may therefore be screened for sorbitol fermentation before sending them to a reference laboratory for serotyping and cytotoxin testing. A differential medium, consisting of MacConkey's agar without lactose but with 10 mg l^{-1} of sorbitol has been described for the isolation of non-sorbitol fermenting organisms from faeces (11). Serotypes other than O:157 have been associated with this syndrome, so a screen for free toxin in the faeces should be undertaken if *E. coli* O:157 cannot be identified in an outbreak.

5.2 *Yersinia enterocolitica*

5.2.1 *Isolation*

The isolation of *Y. enterocolitica* from faeces is problematical, partly because the organism grows slowly and may be overgrown by other organisms, and because it grows poorly at 37°C. One approach which has been used to isolate the organism is cold enrichment; a suspension of faeces is made in phosphate-buffered saline, and is kept at 4°C for up to 6 weeks, subcultures to DCA being made at weekly intervals. Since this method may take up to 6 weeks to produce a report, it is not likely to be of use to the individual patient, and is not recommended for routine use. Two alternative methods are described below.

(i) *Use of DCA medium.* A DCA plate is inoculated and incubated at 28−30°C for 48 h. Alternatively, if DCA is included in the standard set of faeces plates used in the laboratory, it may be reincubated at this temperature after it has been examined for salmonellae and shigellae. *Yersinia enterocolitica* appears as a small, translucent non-lactose fermenter which does not produce H_2S; it may easily be overlooked on this medium.

(ii) *CIN agar*. If regular examination for yersiniae is to be made on all faeces specimens, a better approach is to use a specific selective medium; CIN agar is recommended (see *Table 5*). The inoculated plate is incubated at 28−30°C, the optimum growth temperature for *Y.enterocolitica*, for up to 48 h.

5.2.2 Identification

Suspect colonies may be identified by biochemical testing as for other *Enterobacteriaceae*, typical reactions are given in *Table 7*, which gives reactions obtained at 37°C; with *Y.enterocolitica*, results may vary at low incubation temperatures (for example, the organism is motile at 22°C but not at 37°C). It is recommended that all identified strains be sent to a reference laboratory for confirmation of identity and serotyping.

5.3 *Vibrio cholerae* and *V.parahaemolyticus*

5.3.1 Isolation

The following method is that described by Furniss and Donovan (12).

(i)   Inoculate the specimen on to TCBS agar and into 20 ml alkaline peptone water (APW—see *Table 5*).

(ii)   After 6 h incubation inoculate another TCBS plate and APW from the top of the first APW.

(iii)   After overnight incubation examine the TCBS plates and inoculate a third plate from the second APW.

Colonial morphology and colour reactions of *V.cholerae* and *V.parahaemolyticus* are described in *Table 5*.

5.3.2 Identification of V.cholerae

Suspected colonies on the TCBS plate are Gram stained; if they are Gram-negative bacilli, make a heavy subculture to blood agar. This is essential because neither slide agglutination tests nor an oxidase test should be made using growth on TCBS, as erroneous reactions may occur. There should be sufficient growth on the blood agar 6−8 h later for further tests to be made. An oxidase test should be carried out, and the strain tested by slide agglutination with antiserum to *V.cholerae* O1. An oxidase-positive Gram-negative bacillus which grows on TCBS agar with sucrose fermentation and which agglutinates in the above antiserum is presumptively identified as *V.cholerae* O1 (i.e. a potential epidemic strain). The clinician, local public health laboratory and (in the UK) the Medical Officer for Environmental Health must be informed immediately. If the strain does not agglutinate in O1 antiserum but otherwise fulfils the criteria for presumptive identification, it may be a non-O1 strain of *V.cholerae*. These strains may cause sporadic cases of intestinal infection, but are not associated with epidemic cholera.

All strains of *V.cholerae* (O1 and non-O1) should be sent to a reference laboratory for confirmation of identity, serotyping, and (in the case of *V.cholerae* O1) differentiation into classical or El Tor biogroup. Biochemical identification may also be carried out in the general laboratory with the media and tests used for the *Enterobacteriaceae* (results in *Table 7*). Kit systems such as the API 20E may be used, although this system

161

is not specifically intended for use with vibrios. *V.cholerae* non-O1 strains are biochemically identical to *V.cholerae* O1, and ideally should be reported as '*Vibrio cholerae* non-O1 strain'. However, if this is done it will be impossible to convince the clinician that the patient does not have genuine epidemic cholera, and to avoid this, these strains may be reported as 'non-cholera vibrio' even though this is not taxonomically correct.

5.3.3 Identification of V.parahaemolyticus

Subculture suggestive colonies on TCBS to blood agar and CLED medium. *V. parahaemolyticus* is oxidase-positive but will not grow on CLED because it is a halophilic (salt-requiring) vibrio. Organisms meeting these criteria may be fully identified by biochemical testing (*Table 7*). Because this species is halophilic it may not grow in media used for the *Enterobacteriaceae* unless sodium chloride is added to a concentration of 1%. Such modified media are also suitable for the *Enterobacteriaceae*, avoiding the need for duplicate sets of media. When using a kit identification system, the inoculum should be prepared in sterile saline rather than distilled water, as growth of *V. parahaemolyticus* may otherwise be very poor.

5.4 *Clostridium difficile*

5.4.1 Introduction

There are two aspects to the laboratory diagnosis of *Clostridium difficile* infection: isolation of the organism from faeces and demonstration of *C.difficile* cytotoxin in the specimen. Neither can be regarded as entirely satisfactory on its own. *C.difficile* can be isolated from a proportion of the healthy population, which varies with age, being more frequently found in neonates and possibly the elderly. The organism produces two toxins, an enterotoxin and a cytotoxin, but not all strains produce both, and it is possible that the enterotoxin is associated with disease while it is the cytotoxin which is demonstrated in the laboratory. Consequently, both isolation of the organism and detection of the cytotoxin may be undertaken.

5.4.2 Isolation of C.difficile

(i)   Inoculate the specimen on to cycloserine-cefoxitin-containing medium and incubate anaerobically for 48 h.

(ii)   Examine the plate for the characteristic colonies of *C.difficile* (see *Table 5*).

(iii)   Gram stain suggestive colonies and examine the plate under a Wood's light (long-wave UV light). Gram-positive or Gram-variable bacilli which fluoresce yellow-green may be presumptively identified as *C.difficile*. Further identification is not usually necessary, but may be carried out by biochemical testing and gas−liquid chromatography of metabolic products.

5.4.3 Demonstration of cytotoxin in faeces

The materials and method for this investigation are shown in *Table 15*.

Table 15. Method for detection of *Clostridium difficile* cytotoxin in faeces.

1. Materials required: HeLa, human embryonic lung fibroblast or Vero cell monolayers; antiserum to *C.sordellii* toxin, diluted 1/50 in phosphate-buffered saline (PBS)[a]; positive control, e.g. known positive faeces specimen (stored at $-20°C$ until needed) or a broth culture of a toxigenic strain of *C.difficile*.
2. Dilute liquid faeces 1/10. For solid specimens, emulsify a portion of the sample about the size of a small pea in 5 ml PBS. Centrifuge diluted specimen or emulsion at 4000 r.p.m. for 30 min, discard the deposit and use the supernatant for the test.
3. Mix 200 μl of supernatant with 200 μl of *C.sordellii* antitoxin (Wellcome Diagnostics), allow to stand at room temperature for 30 min. If *C.difficile* cytotoxin is present in the specimen, it will be neutralized by the antitoxin.
4. For each specimen, two monolayers are needed. To the first add 100 μl of untreated supernatant plus 100 μl of PBS. To the second add 200 μl of the supernatant/antitoxin mixture.
5. For each batch of tests, set up positive and negative controls (the negative control consists of 200 μl of antitoxin, no supernatant).
6. Incubate all tubes at 37°C overnight.
7. Examine tubes for the typical cytopathic effect (CPE), seen as rounding up and separation of the cells. If human embryonic lung fibroblasts were used, there may also be filamentous projections from the cells. The CPE should be completely neutralized by the *C.sordellii* antitoxin for the result to be indicative of the presence of *C.difficile* cytotoxin.
8. If desired, the titre of toxin in the specimen may be determined by repeating the test with 10-fold dilutions of the supernatant. However, the titre cannot be correlated with the severity of the disease but may decline with successful treatment. It is not recommended as a routine procedure.

[a]Different suppliers' batches of antiserum will vary in their titre.

5.5 'Food poisoning' due to *Clostridium perfringens*, *Staphylococcus aureus* and *Bacillus cereus*

5.5.1 *Introduction*

When investigating an outbreak of food poisoning, it is necessary to obtain both epidemiological (see Chapter 12) and laboratory data in order to identify the source and route of transmission of the agent responsible. There are of course numerous potential causes of 'food poisoning', not all of which are bacterial (or even microbial) in origin. If the nature of the outbreak suggests that the cause may be *Clostridium perfringens*, *Staphlococcus aureus* or *Bacillus cereus*, the laboratory should attempt the isolation of these organisms from faeces. Other specimens may also be collected such as vomit, swabs from utensils, specimens from food handlers and the food itself. Methods for processing these specimens are beyond the scope of this chapter, but procedures are given below for the treatment of faeces specimens.

Since all of these organisms produce disease by the production of an enterotoxin, either in the food or in the intestine, methods for the demonstration of toxin in food or faeces may eventually replace culture methods. At the present time such methods can only be regarded as reference laboratory or experimental procedures.

5.5.2 *Isolation and identification of Clostridium perfringens*

Strains of *C.perfringens* implicated in food poisoning outbreaks were originally described as heat-resistant and non- or weakly haemolytic, but subsequently classical strains have also been associated with the disease. Since almost all of the healthy population carry this organism as part of the normal bowel flora, simple isolation of the organism from

Table 16. Isolation of *Clostridium perfringens* from faeces in suspected food-poisoning outbreaks.

1. Materials required: blood agar containing 100 mg l^{-1} of neomycin (NBA); Robertson's cooked meat medium.
2. Liquid specimens are used directly; make a thick emulsion of a solid specimen in peptone water.
3. Inoculate an NBA plate with the specimen using a calibrated loop (5 μl) in order to obtain a semi-quantitative result.
4. Put 2 ml of the specimen into a tube of cooked meat medium. Heat the tube to 100°C for 1 h.
5. Heat the rest of the suspension to 80°C for 10 min, then subculture to NBA using a calibrated loop.
6. Incubate the tube and plates at 37°C overnight (incubate the NBA plates anaerobically).
7. Next day, subculture the cooked meat medium to NBA, and incubate the plate anaerobically overnight.
8. The procedure in step 4 above will permit detection of heat-resistant strains of *C.perfringens*, but does not give a quantitative result. Step 3 above gives a total viable count of the organism, while step 5 gives a spore count.

faeces is of little help, and a semi-quantitative method must be used. The method is described in *Table 16*. If food is still available, isolation of the organism from food should also be attempted. Confirmation that an outbreak of food poisoning is due to *C.perfringens* is obtained if one (preferably more) of the criteria below is satisfied (13).

(i)   The viable count of *C.perfringens* obtained from faeces is $\geq 10^6$ g^{-1}, see Section 5.5.4.
(ii) Strains of *C.perfringens* from the affected patients are of the same serotype.
(iii) The viable count of *C.perfringens* from the suspected food is $\geq 10^6$ g^{-1}.
(iv) Strains from faeces and food are of the same serotype.

These criteria may not always confirm an episode of food poisoning caused by *C. perfringens*, as well patients in hospitals may have $\geq 10^6$ g^{-1} *C.perfringens* spores in faeces. An outbreak in which spore counts were not useful, but the detection of *C.perfringens* enterotoxin in faeces by both ELISA and RPLA (reverse passive latex agglutination) did enable identification of the affected patients, and the food source has recently been described (14). A recent report has also suggested that enterotoxin-producing strains of *C.perfringens* may cause episodes of infectious diarrhoeal illness in hospital patients in a similar fashion to *C.difficile* (15).

5.5.3 *Isolation of Staphylococcus aureus*

Faeces should be inoculated on to a selective medium such as mannitol-salt agar (see *Table 5*). Suspect colonies may be identified by standard laboratory methods (see Chapter 5, Section 4.1.4).

Staphylococcus aureus may be isolated from the faeces of healthy individuals, so isolation *per se* has little meaning. Strains from the faeces of patients, from food and from food handlers should be phage-typed (Chapter 11, Section 4.5) and tested for enterotoxin production by a reference laboratory. Enterotoxin-producing strains of identical phage types when isolated from the above sources can be assumed to be the cause of the outbreak. Note that *S.aureus* produces enterotoxin in food, not in the intestinal tract, and if the food is subsequently heated the organism may be killed but the toxin left intact. Thus the failure to isolate enterotoxigenic strains of *S.aureus* from faeces does not exclude staphylococcal food poisoning.

5.5.4 *Isolation of Bacillus cereus*

As with *Clostridium perfringens* and *Staphylococcus aureus*, *Bacillus cereus* can be isolated (usually in small numbers) from the stools of a proportion of the healthy population. A semi-quantitative culture method is therefore necessary, together with isolation from the suspected food.

(i)   Liquid specimens may be used directly, otherwise make a heavy suspension of the specimen in peptone water.

(ii)   Prepare 10-fold serial dilutions of the specimen in peptone water by adding 100 μl of suspension to 900 μl sterile saline in a capped sterile tube, mix thoroughly with the pipette and transfer 100 μl to another tube containing 900 μl sterile saline; also plate 100 μl of that dilution onto a selective medium for *B.cereus* (see *Table 5*).

(iii) Change the tip of the pipette for a fresh sterile tip and after mixing the new dilution make a further dilution and plating.

(iv)   Repeat the procedure to provide nine increasing 10-fold dilutions.

(v)   After overnight incubation calculate the viable count of presumptive colonies of *Bacillus cereus* by multiplying the number of colonies on the plate showing $5-30$ colonies by the dilution factor, e.g. 10 colonies on 10^{-5} dilution $= 1 \times 10^6$ CFU ml^{-1}. Remember that if an initial dilution was needed to suspend the faeces then it must be included in the calculation; assume that 1 ml of liquid faeces weighs 1 g. Further confirmation of identity is not usually necessary in the routine laboratory.

Strains of *B.cereus* isolated from faeces and food may be sent to a reference laboratory for serotyping. Confirmation that an outbreak is due to *B.cereus* is obtained if one or more of the criteria below is satisfied (13).

(i)   The viable count of *B.cereus* obtained from food or faeces is $\geq 10^5$ g^{-1}.

(ii)   *B.cereus* is isolated from both food and faeces, and the isolates are of the same serotype.

6. REFERENCES

1. Desowitz,R.S. (1980) *Ova and Parasites: Medical Parasitology for the Laboratory Technologist.* Harper and Row, Hagerstown.
2. Christie,A.B. (1980) *Infectious Diseases: Epidemiology and Clinical Practice.* 3rd edn, Churchill Livingstone, Edinburgh.
3. Mandell,G.L., Douglas,R.G. and Bennett,J.E. (eds) (1985) *Principles and Practice of Infectious Diseases.* 2nd edn, John Wiley, New York.
4. MacFaddin,J.F. (1985) *Media for Isolation – Cultivation – Identification – Maintenance of Medical Bacteria.* Williams and Wilkins, Baltimore.
5. Stokes,E.J. and Ridgway,G.L. (1987) *Clinical Microbiology.* 6th edn, Edward Arnold, London.
6. Cruickshank,R., Duguid,J.P., Marmion,B.P. and Swain,R.H.A. (1975) *Medical Microbiology, Vol. 2: The Practice of Medical Microbiology.* 12th edn, Churchill Livingstone, Edinburgh.
7. Parker,M.T. (1983) In *Topley and Wilson's Principles of Bacteriology, Virology and Immunity, Vol. 2: Systematic Bacteriology.* 7th edn, Wilson,G., Miles,A. and Parker,M.T. (eds), Edward Arnold, London, p. 332.
8. Cowan,S.T. (1974) *Edwards and Ewing's Identification of Medical Bacteria.* 2nd edn. Cambridge University Press, London.
9. Ewing,W.H. (1986) *Cowan and Steele's Manual for the Identification of Enterobacteriaceae.* 4th edn., Elsevier Science Press, New York.

10. Chapman,P.A. and Swift,D.L. (1984) *J. Med. Microbiol.*, **18**, 399.
11. March,S.B. and Ratnam,S. (1986) *J. Clin. Microbiol.*, **23**, 869.
12. Furniss,A.L. and Donovan,T.J. (1974) *J. Clin. Path.*, **27**, 764.
13. Gilbert,R.J., Roberts,D. and Smith,G. (1984) In *Topley and Wilson's Principles of Bacteriology, Virology and Immunity, Vol. 3: Bacterial Diseases.* 7th edn, Wilson,G., Miles,A. and Parker,M.T. (eds), Edward Arnold, London, p. 477.
14. Birkhead,G., Vogt,R.L., Heun,E.M., Snyder,J.T. and McClane,B.A. (1988) *J. Clin. Microbiol.*, **26**, 471.
15. Larson,H.E. and Borriello,S.P. (1988) *J. Infect. Dis.*, **157**, 390.

CHAPTER 7

Antimicrobial susceptibility testing

ALAN HOLT and DEREK BROWN

1. INTRODUCTION

The use of *in vitro* sensitivity testing in clinical laboratories is an attempt to predict the likely *in vivo* response of the infecting organism to a selected range of antimicrobial agents. Such tests are carried out very widely, but their limitations need to be appreciated in that organisms are tested under conditions favouring rapid growth on highly nutritional media and no account is taken of factors outside the organism – antibiotic interaction.

Sensitivity tests are designed to give a result interpreted as sensitive, intermediate or resistant (S, I or R). A patient infected with a sensitive organism should respond to the manufacturer's recommended dosage regimen, whereas one infected with a resistant organism would be unlikely to respond. For an organism categorized as intermediate (or moderately sensitive), there is uncertainty whether or not the patient will respond to standard doses, but he or she will be more likely to respond to higher doses or if concentrations in excess of those in the plasma are obtained at the site of infection. However, it is a term which clinicians generally find unhelpful.

With antimicrobial agents which exhibit a bimodal distribution of sensitivity, for example tetracycline, choosing a cut-off point to differentiate between the sensitive and resistant populations is easily achieved by any of the methods available. Unfortunately, with many agents a bimodal distribution is not seen and the differentiation of the sensitive and resistant populations is unclear. Consequently the choice of breakpoints can be more difficult. Selection of a drug reported as intermediate in preference to an agent noted as sensitive may be determined by potential toxicity and cost as well as pharmacology.

The ideal test of performance of any *in vitro* sensitivity test is the correlation of results with clinical outcome. This is tenuous, however, as with *in vitro* testing it is difficult to take account of variability in pharmacological factors such as absorption, distribution, metabolism, excretion, protein binding, interaction of the chosen agent with other prescribed agents, and patient-related factors such as site and severity of infection, mixed infections, associated illness, immune status and recovery unrelated to treatment.

Data accumulated over fixed time periods are often surveyed locally to produce information on prevalence of resistance for different species. Such information forms the basis for 'best guess' therapy when patients have to be treated before laboratory results are available. The sensitivity pattern may also help in identification of the infecting organism.

2. DISC DIFFUSION METHODS OF ANTIMICROBIAL SENSITIVITY TESTING

The disc diffusion method is the technique most commonly used for routine antimicrobial susceptibility testing. The method is convenient, technically simple, cheap, and, if correctly performed, reasonably reliable. The surface of an agar plate is evenly inoculated with the organism and a filter paper disc containing a defined amount of antimicrobial agent is applied to the inoculated plate. After incubation (usually overnight at $35-37°C$) there is a circular zone of inhibition around the disc as a result of diffusion of the agent into the agar and inhibition of growth of the organism. The size of the zone of inhibition is an indication of the susceptibility of the organism, more resistant organisms giving smaller zone sizes. The size of the zone of inhibition is, however, influenced by technical variables that must be controlled to produce meaningful results. The theoretical aspects of zone formation developed by Cooper and Linton have been interpreted in relation to more recent diffusion procedures by Barry (1,2).

2.1 Factors affecting diffusion tests

These have been extensively reviewed (1−3) and are summarized below.

2.1.1 *Choice of medium*

The culture medium should support the growth of organisms normally tested without being antagonistic to the activity or diffusion of agents. Some of the factors influencing the activity of various antibiotics are shown in *Table 1*.

Supplementation is necessary for some organisms; 5% horse blood is commonly used to supplement media for the growth of streptococci and anaerobes. For *Neisseria* spp. and *Haemophilus* spp., 5% heated (chocolated) horse blood may be added to media. A variety of alternative supplements have been suggested (4−8). Agents which are highly protein-bound, such as fusidic acid and novobiocin, have smaller zones on media containing blood.

The antagonistic effects of thymidine can be avoided by the use of a medium low in thymidine. The effects of thymidine can be eliminated by adding lysed horse blood

Table 1. Factors affecting antimicrobial activity in culture media.

Factor	Agents affected	Effect on activity
Thymidine	Sulphonamides	Reduced
	Trimethoprim	
Raised pH	Aminoglycosides	Increased
	Macrolides	
	Lincosamides	
	Nitrofurantoin	
Lowered pH	Tetracycline	Increased
	Methicillin	
	Fusidic acid	
	Novobiocin	
Monovalent cations	Bacitracin	Increased against staphylococci
(e.g. Na^+)	Fusidic acid	
	Novobiocin	
	Penicillin	Increased against *Proteus* spp.
Divalent cations	Tetracycline	Reduced
(e.g. Mg^{2+} and Ca^{2+})	Polymixins	Reduced against *Pseudomonas* spp.
	Aminoglycosides	

to the medium. Thymidine phosphorylase in the lysed horse blood converts thymidine to thymine, which is around 100 times less antagonistic than thymidine. Excessive thymine can also cause problems, so the medium should preferably be low in both.

Several commercial media are produced specifically for antimicrobial susceptibility testing, and these should be used in routine tests; examples are DST (Oxoid), Iso-Sensitest (Oxoid), SAF (Mast). Mueller−Hinton medium is widely used in the USA, where the medium should conform to published performance standards if used for sensitivity testing (9,10).

2.1.2 *Depth of medium*

Zones of inhibition increase as the depth of agar decreases, and the effect is more marked with very thin plates. Plates should therefore have a consistent level depth of 3−4 mm.

2.1.3 *Inoculum density*

Increasing the inoculum size reduces zone sizes with all antimicrobial agents to some extent. Variation in inoculum size is one of the main sources of error in susceptibility testing.

Most disc diffusion methods recommend an inoculum resulting in semi-confluent growth of colonies. This has the advantage that an incorrect inoculum can be seen and the test repeated. The inoculum is generally acceptable if the density is between almost confluent and colonies separated to the extent that zones cannot be measured.

2.1.4 *Pre-incubation and pre-diffusion*

Pre-incubation of inoculated plates before discs are applied reduces zone sizes, and pre-diffusion of antimicrobial agents prior to incubation has the opposite effect. Although a set pre-diffusion time of 30−60 min may improve reproducibility of tests, attempts to standardize pre-incubation and pre-diffusion times present practical difficulties. The beneficial effects are probably insufficient to warrant the effort required to standardize them, so pre-incubation and pre-diffusion should be avoided.

2.1.5 *Antimicrobial discs*

Commercially produced filter paper discs are almost universally used. Although problems with the discs are occasionally due to manufacturing failures, most faults are related to inadequate handling of discs in the laboratory. High temperature, and particularly high humidity, lead to more rapid deterioration of labile agents, especially β-lactams. Discs should therefore be stored and handled as detailed in *Table 2*.

It is essential to use the disc contents recommended for the method in use. Discs should be in close and even contact with the medium to avoid impaired diffusion of agents into the medium. Multiple discs attached to a circular ring allow several agents to be applied to plates simultaneously, but whether single or multiple discs are used, not more than 6 agents should be tested on a 9 cm plate to avoid unacceptable overlap of zones.

2.1.6 *Incubation*

Plates are incubated at 35−37°C in air unless another atmosphere is essential for growth.

Table 2. Handling and storage of antimicrobial discs.

1. To minimize condensation on discs, warm the containers to room temperature before opening them.
2. If containers are frequently opened, leave them at room temperature during the day and refrigerate them overnight only.
3. Discs, including those in dispensers, should be kept in sealed containers in the dark (some agents, e.g. metronidazole, rifampicin and quinolones, are sensitive to light).
4. Containers should include an indicating desiccant.
5. Store supplies currently in use at $4-8°C$. Store stocks at $-20°C$ if possible, otherwise at $<8°C$.
6. Do not use discs beyond the expiry date given by the maker.

An atmosphere containing additional carbon dioxide should be avoided because this reduces the pH and thus may give false results with some agents. Stacks of plates should be as small as possible, preferably no more than 5 plates high, as plates in the centre of large stacks take considerably longer to warm to incubator temperature than those at the top and bottom.

2.1.7 *Reading of zones*

Reproducibility of reading zones is related to the clarity of zone edges. Hence the reading of tests on sulphonamides and streptococci tends to be most variable. Generally there is an obvious zone edge. Small colonies or a film of growth at zone edges, swarming of *Proteus* spp. into zones, or haemolytic effects on media supplemented with blood should be ignored.

If it is necessary to measure zones, calipers (preferably) or a ruler should be used. For some methods that translate zone size into a category of susceptibility on the basis of fixed zone size breakpoints, a template may be used.

2.2 **Defined methods of disc sensitivity testing**

Defined methods in current use have developed from different directions, and involve different controls and interpretation. Details of several methods are given for comparison in the European Committee for Clinical Laboratory Standards (ECCLS) guidelines for antimicrobial susceptibility testing by diffusion methods (11). It is likely that all these methods will give reasonably reliable results if correctly performed. Few attempts have been made to compare the performance of different defined methods, but no major differences in reliability have been demonstrated.

In the United States a development of the Kirby–Bauer method is widely used and is recommended by the National Committee for Clinical Laboratory Standards (NCCLS) and the World Health Organization (WHO). Variation is controlled by standardization of the technique. The method specifies the medium (Mueller–Hinton), the inoculum (adjusted by comparison with a barium sulphate standard), inoculation method (a swab dipped into the suspension and streaked across the medium or agar overlay), and disc contents. Interpretation is by reference to a table of zone size breakpoints, based largely on regression analysis of data relating zone diameter to the logarithm of the minimum inhibitory concentration (MIC). For discussion of the basis of interpretation of zone sizes and further details of the NCCLS method, the reader is referred to Barry (1,2) and NCCLS (9,10).

Following the recommendations of the WHO-sponsored International Collaborative

Study ('ICS') of Sensitivity Testing (12), 'ICS'-type methods have been developed in several European countries. Although there are variations in the methodology, generally following national guidelines, the control of variation is again based on rigid standardization of all aspects of the technique. As well as specifying medium, inoculum, inoculation method and disc contents, some variations include set periods of pre-diffusion. Interpretation is by reference to a table of zone size breakpoints based largely on regression studies.

In the UK the approach has been fundamentally different. The comparative methods used allow some variation of technique and medium, although within individual laboratories the method is likely to be as closely defined as the standardized methods described above. It is assumed that the effects of variation will be controlled by the method of interpretation, which involves comparison of test zone sizes with the zone sizes of specified control organisms set up at the same time as the test and under identical conditions. Variation affecting the test organism will affect the control in the same way and thus cancel any adverse effect on interpretation. In Stokes' modification of this method, the control is extended by having the control organism on the same plate as the test organism. The criteria for interpretation are not based on any formal evaluation of the relationship of MIC to zone size, but have been developed by relating the results of the tests to clinical effectiveness of the agents, by experience over the years.

2.2.1 *The comparative methods*

The protocol for the preparation of plates is given in *Table 3*.

The inoculum should give semi-confluent growth of colonies on the plates after overnight incubation. Tests with confluent growth or clearly separated colonies should be rejected and repeated. The dry swab method of inoculation is commonly used and is described in *Tables 4 – 6*. Other methods of inoculation are given in *Table 7*.

Plates may be inoculated with the control organism on a separate plate (*Table 5*); with the control organism on the same plate, inoculated using a band plating method (*Table 6; Figure 1*); or with the control on the same plate, inoculated using a rotary plating method (*Table 6; Figure 2*).

In the original descriptions of the comparative method and Stokes' modification the control organism for systemic infections, *Staphylococcus aureus* NCTC 6571, was always used with low content discs. For organisms from the urine, allowance was made for concentration of agents by using a more resistant control, *Escherichia coli* NCTC 10418, and higher content discs for some agents. Strains of *Pseudomonas* spp. were

---

Table 3. Preparation of plates.

---

1. Prepare and sterilize the medium as directed by the makers.
2. If 5% defibrinated horse blood is added for tests on fastidious organisms allow the medium to cool to 50°C before adding the blood. If the medium is not free from thymidine add 5% lysed horse blood for tests on sulphonamides and trimethoprim.
3. Pour the medium into Petri dishes on a flat, horizontal surface to a depth of 3 – 4 mm (17 – 23 ml in an 8.5 – 9 cm circular dish). Use of a medium dispenser will ensure that the depth of agar remains constant.
4. Store poured plates at 4°C and use within 1 week of preparation.
5. Dry plates with the lids ajar so that there are no droplets of moisture on the agar surface. The time taken to achieve this depends on the drying conditions.

Table 4. Preparation of inoculum.

Test strains

1. Prepare a fully grown broth culture (18 h, or 3−5 h if heavily inoculated)
   or
   emulsify several colonies of the test organism in broth to give a suspension of similar density to a broth culture.

Control strains

1. For preparation of pre-impregnated swabs with control organisms, sterilize cotton-wool swabs in screw-capped jars at 160°C for 2 h. [3-inch (7.5 cm) swabs, 'Q-tips', are available from Cheeseborough-Ponds Ltd.]
2. Inoculate the swabs by pipetting a suspension of the organism on the sticks; 20 ml of control suspension is enough for a jar containing about 90 swabs. For *Staphylococcus aureus* NCTC 6571, the control suspension is made by adding approximately 15 drops of an overnight broth culture in 20 ml of nutrient broth. For *Escherichia coli* NCTC 10418 and *Pseudomonas aeruginosa* NCTC 10662, 8 drops of overnight cultures in 20 ml are adequate.
3. Store sealed containers at 4°C.[a]
4. One swab should be used for each plate.

[a]The swabs will keep for a week with no significant changes in the number of organisms (13).

Table 5. Inoculation with control on a separate plate.

1. Make a single streak of a 4 mm loopful of the inoculum across the diameter of a plate.
2. Spread the inoculum with a sterile dry swab over the entire surface of the medium in three directions, 60° apart.
3. Inoculate control organisms[a] on separate plates by the use of pre-impregnated control swabs, again spreading over the entire surface of the medium in three directions.

[a]The controls to use with specific organisms are detailed in Section 3.1.4 and *Table 8*.

tested with a control strain of *P. aeruginosa* (NCTC 10662) because they were of intermediate susceptibility to gentamicin and carbenicillin, and their susceptibility to gentamicin was markedly dependent on the magnesium and calcium content of the medium. In recent years there have been trends towards the use of a single set of disc contents, and the use of control organisms typical of the isolate rather than based on the source of the isolate. These are detailed in *Table 8*.

Additional control strains may be used in particular situations, and details are included in relevant sections. A methicillin-resistant strain of *Staphylococcus aureus* may be used to improve control of methicillin sensitivity tests. *Streptococcus faecalis* ATCC 25922 may be used to check that the thymidine and thymine content of the medium are not too high for trimethoprim and/or sulphonamide tests. A β-lactamase-producing strain of *E. coli* (NCTC 11560) may be used to control discs containing both a β-lactam agent and a β-lactamase inhibitor.

There is concern that with some newer agents the comparative methods tend to report strains falsely resistant because the disc contents used may be inappropriately high and the control organisms too sensitive. No guidelines as to how these problems may be overcome are yet available (The British Society for Antimicrobial Chemotherapy will be producing recommendations for sensitivity testing in the near future).

Table 6. Control on the same plate (Stokes' modification).

Band plating method

1. Apply the control culture[a] in 2 bands on either side of the plate, leaving a central area uninoculated. This is best achieved by the use of pre-impregnated control swabs, but a 4 mm loopful of an inoculum prepared as for test organisms may be transferred to both sides of the plate and spread evenly in the 2 bands with a dry sterile swab.
2. Transfer a 4 mm loopful of the broth culture or suspension of the test organism to the centre of the plate and spread this evenly in a band across the centre of the plate with a dry sterile swab. There should be a gap of 2 mm between the test and control bands.

Rotary-plating method

1. Place the uninoculated plate on a turntable (Denley Ltd) marked with a circle visible through the medium and 15 mm in from the edge of the plate.
2. Use a pre-impregnated control swab to apply the control organism to the centre of the plate. This is achieved by holding the swab on the surface of the medium and moving the swab slowly across the plate as it rotates on the turntable. An uninoculated 1.5 cm band is left around the edge of the plate. The same effect may be achieved by transferring a 4 mm loopful of the control organism to the centre of the plate and spreading evenly with a sterile dry swab as the turntable rotates.
3. Transfer a 4 mm loopful of the test organism to the uninoculated edge of the plate and spread the organism evenly with a sterile dry swab as the plate rotates on the turntable. There should be a 2 mm gap between the test and control organisms.

[a]The controls to use with specific organisms are detailed in Section 3.1.4 and *Table 8*.

Table 7. Alternative methods of inoculation.

Flooding (control on a separate plate only)

1. Prepare a fully grown broth culture (18 h, or 3−5 h if heavily inoculated)
   or
   emulsify several colonies of the test organism in broth to give a suspension of similar density to a broth culture.
2. Dilute the suspension in water:
   1 in 100 for streptococci and *Neisseria* spp.
   1 in 1000 for staphylococci and *Haemophilus* spp.
   1 in 5000 for *Enterobacteriaceae* and *Pseudomonas* spp.
3. Immediately apply 3−5 ml suspension to the medium and tilt the plate to cover the entire surface.
4. Tilt the plate to drain excess inoculum and remove the excess with a Pasteur pipette.
5. Allow the plate to dry.

Wet swab

1. Prepare a fully grown broth culture (18 h, or 3−5 h if heavily inoculated)
   or
   emulsify several colonies of the test organism in broth to give a suspension of similar density to a broth culture.
2. Dilute the suspension 1 in 100 in water.
3. Dip a sterile cotton swab into the suspension and remove excess by turning the swab against the side of the tube.
4. Spread the inoculum over the entire surface of the medium in three directions 60° apart.
5. Allow the medium to dry.

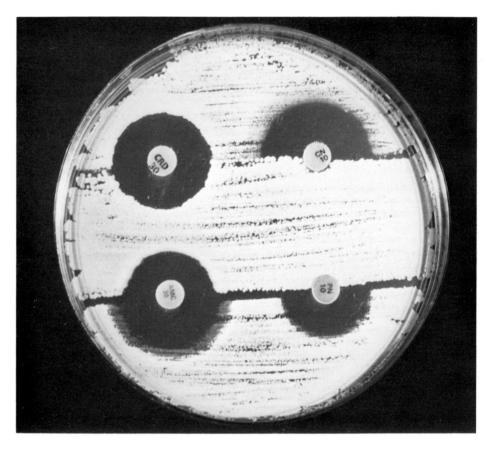

Figure 1. Comparative sensitivity test (Stokes' method) inoculated by the band plating method. The control organism is the 2 outer bands.

Discs should be applied to plates as follows.

(i)   Ensure that the inoculum has dried.

(ii)   Use discs with contents as in *Table 9*.

(iii)   Apply discs to the medium with forceps, a sharp needle, or a dispenser and press gently to ensure even contact.

(iv)   When the control is on the same plate (Stokes' method), apply discs on the line between the test and control organisms. Four discs can be accommodated on a 9 cm diameter plate inoculated by the band method. With the rotary plating method and when the control is on a separate plate, use up to 6 discs.

(v)   Incubate test and control organisms at 35–37°C (30°C may be used for methicillin susceptibility tests (see Section 2.4.2).

If the test zones are obviously larger than the control or give no zone at all, it is not necessary to make any measurement. If there is any doubt, zones should be measured with calipers and a ruler.

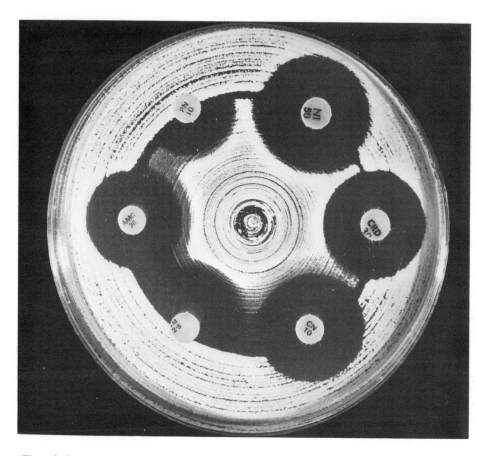

Figure 2. Comparative sensitivity test (Stokes' method) inoculated by the rotary plating method. The control organism is the inner area.

Table 8. Control organisms for the comparative methods.

Control organism	Group of organisms to be controlled
Escherichia coli NCTC 10418	Coliform organisms
Pseudomonas aeruginosa NCTC 10662	*Pseudomonas* spp.
Haemophilus influenzae NCTC 11931	*Haemophilus* spp.
Neisseria gonorrhoeae 'sensitive strain'	*N.gonorrhoeae*
Staphylococcus aureus NCTC 6571	Other organisms that grow aerobically
Clostridium perfringens NCTC 11229	*Clostridium* spp.
Bacteroides fragilis NCTC 9343	Other anaerobic organisms

(i) *Control on a separate plate.* Zone diameters should be measured when possible. If not, measurements should be taken from the edge of the zone to the edge of the disc, in which case adjustment should be made to the criteria for interpretation.

(ii) *Control on the same plate (Stokes' method).* Measure from the edge of the disc

175

Table 9. Suitable disc contents for the comparative methods.

Antimicrobial agent	Disc content
Ampicillin	
Enterobacteriaceae and enterococci	10 μg
Haemophilus and *Branhamella*	2 μg
Augmentin	
Enterobacteriaceae	30 μg
Haemophilus, Branhamella and staphylococci	3 μg
Penicillin	
Staphylococci	2 IU
Streptococci and meningococci	0.25 IU
Piperacillin	30 μg
Mezlocillin	30 μg
Azlocillin	30 μg
Cephalothin	30 μg
Cephalexin	30 μg
Cephadroxil	30 μg
Cephradine	30 μg
Cefuroxime	30 μg
Ceftazidime	10 μg
Cefotaxime	10 μg
Cefsulodin	30 μg
Methicillin	5 μg
Carbenicillin	100 μg
Ticarcillin	75 μg
Gentamicin	10 μg
Amikacin	30 μg
Tobramycin	10 μg
Neomycin	30 μg
Netilmicin	10 μg
Erythromycin	5 μg
Clindamycin	2 μg
Tetracycline	10 μg
Fusidic acid	10 μg
Chloramphenicol	
Enterobacteriaceae	30 μg
Haemophilus, pneumococci and meningococci	10 μg
Colistin	10 μg
Nalidixic acid	30 μg
Nitrofurantoin	50 μg
Sulphafurazole	
Enterobacteriaceae and enterococci	100 μg
Meningococci	25 μg
Trimethoprim	2.5 μg
Cotrimoxazole	25 μg
Spectinomycin	100 μg
Vancomycin	30 μg
Rifampicin	5 μg
Ciprofloxacin	
Pneumococci	5 μg
Other organisms	1 μg
Mupirocin	5 μg

Table 10. Interpretation of disc sensitivity tests.

(i) *Control on a separate plate*
  Sensitive: zone diameter equal to, wider than, or not more than 6 mm[a] smaller than the control.
  Intermediate: zone diameter greater than 10 mm but smaller than the control by more than 6 mm[a].
  Resistant: zone diameter 10 mm or less.

(ii) *Control on the same plate (Stokes' method)*
  Sensitive: zone size (radius) equal to, wider than, or not more than 3 mm[b] smaller than the control.
  Intermediate: zone size greater than 2 mm, but smaller than the control by more than 3 mm[b].
  Resistant: zone size 2 mm or less.

Penicillinase-producing staphylococci showing heaped-up, clearly defined zone edges against β-lactams should be reported resistant irrespective of zone size. Polymyxin diffuses poorly in agar so that zones are small and the above criteria cannot be applied. The intermediate category is not used and in the case of a separate control an isolate is defined as resistant if the zone diameter is >6 mm than the control.

[a]For 'Augmentin' replace 6 mm with 10 mm when the 30 μg disc is used (for *Enterobacteriaceae*) and replace 6 mm with 20 mm when the 3 μg disc is used (for staphylococci, *Branhamella* spp. and *Haemophilus* spp.).
[b]For 'Augmentin' replace 3 mm with 5 mm when the 30 μg disc is used and replace 3 mm with 10 mm when the 3 μg disc is used.

to the edge of the zone. As the control and test organism are adjacent, the difference between the respective zone sizes can easily be seen.

A scheme for interpretation of disc sensitivity tests is given in *Table 10*.

2.3 Selection of agents for routine testing

Agents should be grouped according to the identity of the organism, for example *Enterobacteriaceae, Pseudomonas* spp., staphylococci and streptococci. The choice of agents for testing will differ from one laboratory to another, depending on local preferences. However, similar agents will probably have similar susceptibilities, so only one member of the group need be tested. If one agent in a group is frequently used locally, it would be reasonable to test that in place of the agents listed below, with the exception of anti-staphylococcal β-lactams (ii). When selecting agents for routine testing the following should be remembered:

(i)   Penicillin G is representative of all penicillinase-sensitive penicillins when testing staphylococci.
(ii)   Methicillin or oxacillin are representative of all penicillinase-resistant penicillins and cephalosporins when testing staphylococci.
(iii)   Ampicillin is representative of amoxycillin and ampicillin esters.
(iv)   Combinations of a β-lactam agent and a β-lactamase inhibitor should be tested by the use of discs containing both the inhibitor and the β-lactam agent.
(v)   Cefaclor, cefadroxil, cephalexin and cephradine are similar and only one need be tested.
(vi)   Tetracycline is representative of all tetracyclines (a few tetracycline-resistant strains of *Staphylococcus aureus* and *Enterobacteriaceae* are susceptible to minocycline).
(vii)   Clindamycin is representative of lincomycin. Inducible resistance to these agents

will not be detected in the absence of erythromycin.
(viii) Sulphafurazole is representative of all sulphonamides.
(ix) Colistin is representative of polymyxin B.

2.4 **Specific problems in testing**

2.4.1 *Tests with anaerobic organisms*

The reliability of diffusion susceptibility tests on many anaerobic organisms is questionable, and tests should therefore be limited to rapidly-growing species, i.e. those which will grow on overnight incubation on supplemented medium. Suitable anaerobic control organisms should be included (see *Table 8*).

2.4.2 *Methicillin susceptibility tests with staphylococci*

The expression of resistance is markedly influenced by test conditions, particularly with coagulase-negative staphylococci, and there are considerable differences among strains. The following procedure should be used.

(i) Use 5 μg methicillin discs.
(ii) Incubate tests at 30°C (methicillin/oxacillin only). Tests may be more reliable if incubation is continued for 48 h.

Other important points are:

(iii) Tests may be reliable when incubated at 37°C if the medium contains 5% NaCl. This, however, is medium-dependent, and 5% NaCl may be inhibitory to some strains.
(iv) Resistance may appear as a markedly reduced zone diameter, gradual reduction in colony size up to the disc, a film of growth, or isolated colonies of various sizes within a zone of inhibition.
(v) Some strains which produce large amounts of β-lactamase may give reduced methicillin zone diameters when compared with fully sensitive control strains. Care is necessary to avoid reporting such strains as methicillin-resistant.

2.4.3 *Rapid β-lactamase testing*

Rapid biochemical tests may be used to detect β-lactamase production by *Haemophilus* spp., *Neisseria* spp., *Branhamella* spp. and staphylococci (β-lactamase production may require induction in staphylococci). Several methods have been used (14,15). The most widely used, acidometric and chromogenic substrate methods, are described in *Table 11*.

2.4.4 *Penicillin resistance in Streptococcus pneumoniae*

To detect intrinsic resistance to penicillin in *Streptococcus pneumoniae*, 0.25 U penicillin discs should be used. Methicillin (5 μg) or oxacillin (1 μg) discs are more stable than low content penicillin discs and will reliably indicate intrinsic resistance (16).

2.5 **Quality control**

2.5.1 *External quality control*

Participation in an external quality control scheme provides several benefits:

(i) an independent assessment of performance;

Table 11. Rapid tests for β-lactamase activity in *Neisseria* spp., *Branhamella* spp., *Haemophilus* spp. and staphylococci.

Acidometric test (not suitable for *Branhamella* spp.)

See Chapter 4, Section 6.1.

Chromogenic substrate test

1. Dissolve nitrocefin (Glaxo) in dimethyl sulphoxide to a concentration of 10 g l^{-1} and dilute the solution to 500 mg l^{-1} in 0.05 M phosphate buffer, pH 7.0. (Ready-prepared solution may be purchased from Oxoid Ltd.) Store the solution at 4°C in the dark for up to 1 month.
2. Transfer 50 μl nitrocefin solution to a well in a microtitre tray.
3. Make a dense suspension of several colonies of the test organism in a small volume of saline.
4. Add 50 μl test suspension to the well containing nitrocefin.
5. Set up positive and negative controls by the same method.
6. Incubate at 37°C. A colour change from yellow to red within 30 min indicates production of β-lactamase.

(ii) comparison with other participating laboratories;

(iii) detection of sources of error in testing;

(iv) a stimulus to attain and maintain high standards.

2.5.2 *Internal quality control*

This is used to detect day-to-day variation. Controls strains (*Table 8*) should be used with each test to help detect problems. The strains should be handled as follows.

(i) Store working cultures on agar slopes.

(ii) Subculture them fortnightly.

(iii) Replace them from freeze-dried or frozen cultures (-70°C in glycerol broth) every 2 months, or sooner if contamination is suspected.

The degree of control exercised will depend on the interest and resources of the laboratory. A range of tests of increasing complexity is given below.

(i) Briefly examine control zones to ensure that zone sizes are approximately correct. This approach will indicate major problems.

(ii) Regularly record control zone sizes on a chart, which may be pinned on a noticeboard in the laboratory. Changes in zone sizes indicative of error are clearly seen.

(iii) Establish zone-size limits by recording zone sizes for at least 30 sequential observations. Then, calculate 95% confidence limits (the mean zone size plus or minus 2 standard deviations) and draw the limits on a chart prepared as in (ii) above. Zone sizes should be close to the midpoint of the acceptable range, and no more than 1 in 20 observations would be expected to fall outside the limits.

There are several common errors indicated by control tests.

(i) A gradual decrease in zone sizes may indicate inactivation of labile agents in discs due to improper storage or handling in the laboratory. Test new batches before they are put into routine use.

(ii) A general decrease or increase in zone sizes may indicate too heavy or too light an inoculum.

(iii) Fluctuating zone sizes may indicate errors in measuring or transcribing zone sizes. In particular, different observers may read zone edges differently. Fluctuating zone sizes may also indicate variation in the depth of medium.

(iv) Larger zones with aminoglycoside antibiotics and erythromycin, and smaller zones with tetracycline, methicillin and fusidic acid may indicate that the pH of the medium is too high. The reverse might occur if the pH is too low. Test new batches of medium before they are put into routine use.

(v) Any alteration in zone sizes might indicate contamination or mutational changes in the control strain.

2.6 Primary sensitivity tests

These are tests in which the inoculum is the specimen itself. The use of primary tests is discussed by Waterworth and del Piano (17).

The advantages of primary tests are:

(i) results will be available the next day, 24 h earlier than tests on pure cultures;
(ii) differences in susceptibility may facilitate isolation from mixed cultures;
(iii) small numbers of resistant variants, which might otherwise be missed, may be seen within zones of inhibition.

Care must be exercised to avoid the potential disadvantages of primary testing.

(i) To avoid wasteful tests which show no growth or need to be repeated, carry out primary tests only on specimens from sites that are normally sterile and on urine specimens shown to contain organisms by direct microscopy or by other methods. Direct tests should not be done on specimens that are likely to be heavily contaminated, e.g. from bedsores, ears, varicose ulcers, lesions connected with the large bowel, or on specimens from patients receiving antimicrobial treatment.

(ii) The inoculum cannot be controlled, but many pus swabs and urine specimens contain a density of organisms such that semi-confluent growth of colonies is achieved in most tests if the correct method is used. Repeat tests with incorrect inocula.

(iii) Take care to avoid reporting the susceptibility of commensals.

Primary tests may be done by the comparative methods as described in this chapter, except for the method of inoculation.

(i) Evenly streak pus swabs on the plate in place of the loop and swab method used on pure cultures (*Table 6*).

(ii) With urines a well-mixed specimen replaces the broth culture or suspension of colonies used with pure cultures. Plates may be inoculated with a loop and swab (*Table 6*) or a wet swab (*Table 7*).

(iii) The control organisms used are *Escherichia coli* NCTC 10418 for organisms from urine and *Staphylococcus aureus* NCTC 6571 for other specimens. If, after incubation, the control is seen to be inappropriate (see *Table 8*), the test should be repeated.

(iv) If the inoculum is correct the zones of inhibition of significant pathogenic organisms can be interpreted as for pure cultures (*Table 10*).

3. METHODS FOR DETERMINING MINIMUM INHIBITORY AND BACTERICIDAL CONCENTRATION

The minimum inhibitory concentration (MIC) is determined when a quantitative sensitivity result is required and is the most reliable method for testing slow-growing organisms, such as mycobacteria. The MIC is the lowest concentration of an antimicrobial agent which will inhibit visible growth of the test organism after a suitable period of incubation. Normally serial 2-fold dilutions of antibiotics are tested under defined conditions against a standard inoculum of the test organisms. Tests may be performed by agar or broth dilutions. The latter may be performed using macrodilution, microdilution, or broth plus a low content of agar. All of these techniques, except broth macrodilution, are available commercially in kit form or, with the exception of broth plus a low content of agar, they can be done manually, the dilution series being prepared from solutions made in the laboratory. In order to obtain reliable and reproducible results with any form of MIC test, the factors which may cause variability have to be considered and, as far as is possible, standardized. If a commercial test is used, most of the variable factors will have been standardized, and providing the manufacturer's instructions are carefully followed, reliable results should be obtained. If the tests are to be carried out manually, particular attention must be paid to the following points.

(i) *Preparation of stock antibiotic solutions.* Antibiotic preparations suitable for laboratory use should be obtained from the manufacturers or commercially, as pharmaceutical preparations are often unsuitable. These would normally be supplied in powder form with a quoted potency given in $\mu g\ mg^{-1}$. This must be taken into account during the preparation of stock solutions and is most conveniently done during weighing.

(ii) *Solubility.* Most antibiotics are water-soluble, and sterile distilled water should be used for preparation of stock solutions and further dilution as necessary. Some common agents requiring alternative methods for the preparation of a stock solution are given in *Table 12*.

(iii) *Storage.* Antibiotic powders are normally supplied with instructions for conditions of storage and a date of expiry, and these should always be adhered to. Most powders can be stored in the dark at $4\,^{\circ}C$ over a desiccant, usually silica gel. Stock solutions for most antimicrobials will remain stable at $-70\,^{\circ}C$ for several months, although such solutions should be frozen in aliquots, as thawing and re-freezing is not recommended. Stability of stock solutions of imipenem and clavulanic acid is uncertain, and therefore these should be prepared fresh on each occasion of use.

(iv) *Medium.* It is important that media used for MIC testing should support the growth of the test organisms and be free from constituents which may influence the activity of the agents being tested (Fe^{2+}, Ca^{2+}, Mg^{2+}, thymidine, etc.). It must be established that any supplements added in order to grow more fastidious organisms will not influence the activity of the antimicrobials being tested. There are many 'sensitivity test' media commercially available (see Section 2.1.1). It is advisable to batch test a number of samples from the manufacturer by the 'in use' method, and when a satisfactory batch is selected at least one year's supply should be purchased.

Table 12. Solvents and diluents required for non-water-soluble antibiotics.

Antimicrobial	Solvent	Diluent
Ampicillin/amoxycillin	0.1 M phosphate buffer, pH 8.0	Phosphate buffer, pH 8.0
Aztreonam	Saturated NaHCO$_3$	Water
Ceftazidime	Saturated NaHCO$_3$	Water
Cefotetan	Dimethyl sulphoxide	Water
Chloramphenicol	Absolute ethanol	Water
Erythromycin	Absolute ethanol	Water
Fusidic acid	Absolute ethanol	Water
Moxalactam	0.04 M HCl (2 h)	0.1 M phosphate buffer, pH 6.0
Nalidixic acid	2−3 ml water 5 M NaOH dropwise to dissolve	Water
Nitrofurantoin	Dimethyl sulphoxide	0.1 M phosphate buffer, pH 8.0
Rifampicin	Methanol	Water
Sulphonamide	2−3 ml water then 5 M NaOH to dissolve	Water
Ticarcillin	0.1 M phosphate buffer, pH 6.0	0.1 M phosphate buffer, pH 6.0
Trimethoprim	Concentrated lactic acid to dissolve	Water

(v) *Controls.* In every batch of MIC tests, one or more control organisms should be tested in parallel. The controls may be NCTC/ATCC strains or local isolates, but test results should be accepted only when the control results are within one 2-fold dilution step of expected MICs (see *Table 13*). On repeat testing, MIC values may vary by one dilution from the expected value.

(vi) *Incubation.* MIC tests are usually incubated overnight at 35−37°C. Carbon dioxide enrichment, anaerobic atmosphere or a longer period of incubation are only used when essential for visible growth to occur. When dealing with slow-growing isolates, MIC testing is often the most appropriate form of sensitivity testing, although drug stability during the period of incubation needs to be considered.

As with disc testing, an incubation temperature of 30°C should be used when testing staphylococci against methicillin, and some coagulase-negative strains may require 48 h incubation.

3.1 Preliminary procedures for all manual MIC tests

3.1.1 *Inoculum*

Standardization of the inoculum is necessary in order to obtain reproducible MICs. This can be achieved by dilution of a fully grown broth culture (approximately 1×10^9 CFU ml^{-1}) or by preparation of a suspension of organisms from colonies. The suspension or broth culture is standardized against a turbidity standard by eye, or by use of a spectrophotometer or a nephelometer (a McFarland 0.5 turbidity standard, equivalent to approximately 1×10^8 CFU ml^{-1}, may be made by mixing 0.5 ml 0.048 M BaCl$_2$ with 99.5 ml 0.18 M H$_2$SO$_4$). The suspension can then be further diluted as necessary. For agar dilution MICs, the inoculum is 1×10^4 CFU per spot on the plate. As most multipoint inoculators deliver around 1 μl per spot, the suspension should be diluted to 1×10^7 CFU ml^{-1}. For broth dilution MICs, the final concentration of organisms in the broth is 1×10^5 CFU ml^{-1}. For the agar dilution

Table 13. Expected MIC values for control organisms.

Antibiotics	Staphylococcus aureus NCTC 6571	Escherichia coli NCTC 10418	Pseudomonas aeruginosa NCTC 10662
Amikacin	2	2	4
Ampicillin/amoxicillin	0.06	2	NA
Azlocillin	0.25	8	4
Aztreonam	NA	0.03	4
Carbenicillin	0.5	4	16
Cephalexin	1	4	NA
Cephradine	2	4	NA
Cefotaxime	1	0.015	8
Cefsulodin	NA	NA	2
Ceftazidime	8	0.12	1
Cefuroxime	0.5	1	NA
Chloramphenicol	2	2	NA
Ciprofloxacin	0.12	0.008	0.12
Clindamycin	0.06	NA	NA
Erythromycin	0.12	NA	NA
Fusidic acid	0.06	NA	NA
Gentamicin	0.12	0.5	2
Imipenem	0.03	0.12	2
Methicillin	1[a]	NA	NA
Mezlocillin	0.5	1	8
Nalidixic acid	NA	2	NA
Netilmicin	0.25	0.5	2
Nitrofurantoin	NA	4	NA
Penicillin	0.03	NA	NA
Piperacillin	1	0.5	4
Polymyxin	32	0.25	0.5
Rifampicin	0.008	8	NA
Sulphamethoxazole		16	NA
Tetracycline	0.12	1	NA
Ticarcillin	0.5	1	16
Tobramycin	0.25	0.5	1
Trimethoprim	0.25	0.12	NA
Vancomycin	0.5	NA	NA

Inoculum of 1×10^4 CFU per spot on DST agar.
[a]Inoculum of 1×10^6 CFU per spot, incubation at 30°C.
NA, not applicable.

method, an inoculum density of 1×10^6 CFU per spot should be used when testing β-lactam antibiotics against organisms which produce extracellular β-lactamases. Sharper endpoints are seen with sulphonamide MICs if an inoculum of 1×10^3 CFU per spot is used.

3.1.2 Preparation of stock solution

It is normal practice to produce a dilution series which is based on 1 mg l^{-1} (i.e. 0.5, 1, 2 mg l^{-1} etc.) although closer dilution steps may be used if needed by one of the following:

(i)   using 2/3 rather than doubling dilution steps;

(ii)   using doubling dilutions beginning from more than one starting point;
(iii)   using specific concentrations between the doubling dilution points, for example, 8, 10, 12, 14, 16 mg l^{-1}.

The weight of antibiotic required is calculated thus:

$$\frac{1000}{\text{potency}} \times \frac{\text{volume required}}{\text{(ml)}} \times \frac{\text{concentration required}}{\text{(in 1000 s mg l}^{-1}\text{)}}$$

$$= \text{weight in that volume}$$

Example
If potency $= 852\ \mu\text{g mg}^{-1}\ (85.2\%)$
Final concentration required $= 5000$ mg l^{-1}
Volumes required $= 25$ ml
then

$$\frac{1000}{852} \times 25 \times 5 = 146.7\ \text{mg}$$

i.e. 146.7 mg is dissolved in 25 ml to give 5000 mg l^{-1} stock solution.

3.2 Agar dilution methods

3.2.1 Scheme for making agar dilutions

There are a number of variations in methodology for preparing the working concentrations of antibiotic in agar. Choice of method is largely by personal preference, but will be influenced by

(i)   the number of organisms to be tested (*Figure 3*);
(ii)   the number of agents to be tested;

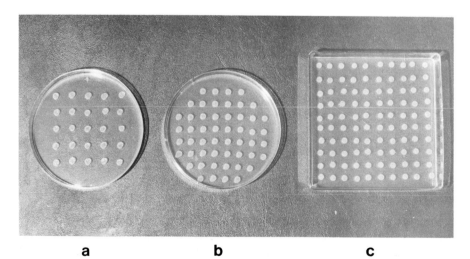

a   **b**   **c**

Figure 3. Various pin configurations for a multi-point inoculator. (**a**) 25 positions; (**b**) 52 positions; (**c**) 100 positions.

Table 14. Method for agar dilution MIC testing of more than 25 strains.

To prepare a range of concentrations 128−0.25 mg l^{-1} in 87 mm Petri dishes using 14 ml glass, disposable, screw-capped blood sample tubes proceed as follows[a].

1. Label 11 tubes and Petri dishes 128, 64, 32,...0.25 and control.
2. From stock solution of 5000 mg l^{-1} take 2.0 ml and add 3.58 ml distilled water. Concentration = 1792 mg l^{-1} (working solution A).
3. Using adjustable volume micropipettes,

   take 1 ml   working solution A into tube labelled 128 mg l^{-1}

   then 0.5   "   "   64

       0.25   "   "   32

       0.125   "   "   16

       0.0625   "   "   8

   Take 0.25 ml of working solution A and add 7.75 ml water.
   Concentration = 56 mg l^{-1} (working solution B).
4. Take 1 ml   working solution B into tube labelled 4 mg ml^{-1}

       0.5   "   "   2

       0.25   "   "   1

       0.125   "   "   0.5

       0.0625   "   "   0.25[b]

   Further dilutions can be prepared by continuing the dilution sequence in the same manner.
5. In turn, top up each tube to the base of the thread with appropriate agar at 50°C. Mix by gentle inversion 3−4 times and pour the entire contents into the corresponding number of Petri dishes, ensuring that the whole base of each plate is covered with agar.
6. Replace lid and allow to set on a level surface undisturbed.
7. If plates are to be used on the day they are poured, use a drying cabinet or incubator to dry them with their lids ajar until the surface of the medium has no visible drops of moisture. Do not overdry the plates, the medium should not appear wrinkled. Seal the plates in plastic bags and store at 4°C for up to 7 days. The amount of drying required will be reduced by storage. Plates should be warmed to room temperature before use.

[a]Different volume containers require different concentrations of working solution A, for example:

Container	*Volume*	*Working solution A*
Universal	28 ml	3584 mg l^{-1}
Urine pot	55 ml	7040 mg l^{-1}

[b]For bottles of different capacity, the same dilution sequence can be employed once the correct concentration of working solution A has been prepared.

(iii)   the size and shape of plates to be used (*Figure 3*);

(iv)   availability of equipment for dispensing media.

If less than 25 organisms are to be tested against a small range of antimicrobials, the antibiotics can be prepared at 20 times the required concentration.

(i)   Add 1 ml of stock solution to a Petri dish.

(ii)   Add 19 ml of molten agar at 50°C by means of an automatic agar dispenser. Manual pipetting of agar lacks accuracy and is tedious.

(iii)   Alternatively, add 1 ml of stock solution to 19 ml molten agar in a universal container and pour into a Petri dish.

If a large number of organisms (>25) and/or a wide range of antimicrobials are to be tested, a more convenient method is to base the preparation of the dilutions on the volume of a suitably sized screw-capped laboratory container when it is filled to the base of the thread. A method for MIC testing on a large scale is given in *Table 14*.

There are methods available, such as 'Adatabs' (Mast Laboratories) which avoid the necessity to weigh out or dilute antibiotics. Set amounts of an antibiotic are bound to an inert carrier substance and are available as tablets. When a tablet is added to 100 ml of molten agar, rapid distribution of antibiotic occurs through the agar to give a known concentration. All labels required for agar bottles and plates come with the tablets, thereby reducing labelling errors. The required number of plates are poured and dried as in *Table 14*.

3.2.2 *Inoculation*

Inocula can be prepared by any of the methods given in Section 3.1.1. Inoculation is normally by means of an automated multipoint inoculator (Denley Instruments Ltd) which delivers a set volume, usually 1 μl, by means of metal pins which transfer inocula from wells in a plastic tray on to the agar surface. The choice of pin configuration and therefore inoculum trays will be determined by the number of organisms to be tested (*Figure 3*). Plates may also be inoculated manually using a wire loop of standard volume.

3.2.3 *Manual reading*

Plates are read for growth by comparison with an antibiotic-free control plate. For most organism−antibiotic combinations, the cut-off between growth and no growth will be sharp and therefore easy to read. Difficulty can be experienced in determining the endpoint if there is a gradual reduction in the degree of growth spread over several dilutions, and care has to be exercised to recognize a mixed culture or contamination from adjacent spots. Single colonies or a barely visible haze of growth should be disregarded, but if a minor amount of growth continues beyond what appears to be the endpoint, contamination is likely and the test should be repeated.

Plates can be read by eye, but if large numbers of tests are being performed this can be time-consuming and tedious, and experience is necessary to achieve consistent results.

3.2.4 *Automated reading*

Automated reading of agar dilution plates is possible, for example with 'Mastascan' (Mast Laboratories), a television camera coupled to a microcomputer. This gives fully automated reading thereby removing the most tedious aspect of this form of test. The degree of growth recognized as the endpoint can be set and will be applied to all plates, thus giving consistency in the reading.

3.2.5 *Spiral plater*

An interesting new development in methodology for quantitative measurement of antimicrobial susceptibility is a spiral plater (Spiral Systems Inc.). After allowing 4−18 h diffusion, this produces a gradient of antibiotic concentrations, decreasing from the centre to the edge of the plate. Test and control organisms (with known MIC values) are streaked in duplicate, radially. The duplicate streaks from each organism are aligned opposite each other. Following overnight incubation, zones of inhibition are measured and MICs can be calculated by reference to the zones obtained with the control strains. A full evaluation of this method is still awaited.

3.3 Broth dilution methods

3.3.1 *Broth macrodilution*

In a clinical laboratory, the MIC test is most commonly performed to test a single isolate against one or a small number of agents, and for this a broth dilution method is particularly suitable. Another advantage of broth over agar dilution is that the former can be converted readily to the bactericidal test. The choice of diluent broth and the dilution scheme to be used are largely a matter of personal preference. Naturally, the test broth must support growth of the test organism, and, including any growth supplement added, should be free of inhibitors to the agents being tested.

The dilution series may be prepared by doubling dilution or more accurately by using master dilutions, particularly if a wide range of concentrations is to be tested. One or a series of control organisms should be tested in parallel with each test strain and the results accepted only if the control results are within one dilution of their expected value. Methods for broth macrodilution are given in *Tables 15–17*. The advantage of the modified Ericsson and Sherris method (*Table 16*) is that there is less opportunity for compounded errors than in the doubling dilution method (*Table 15*).

3.3.2 *Broth microdilution*

There is a wide range of commercial microdilution systems available (*Table 18*). The technique is particularly convenient for testing individual isolates. A fixed volume of the test organism suspended in broth is added to a series of wells, and this reconstitutes the antibiotic to give a full dilution series for MIC determination of a limited set of concentrations for breakpoint tests (see Section 3.4). Some systems include a series of identification tests with the sensitivity tests. The inoculum density and test broth should be prepared in accordance with the manufacturer's recommendations. Reading is usually done by eye, looking for buttons of growth while the plate is placed over a mirror.

Table 15. Broth doubling dilution method: preparation of antibiotic dilutions.

In a sterile universal container:

1. Add 0.16 ml of 1000 mg l^{-1} stock antibiotic solution to 9.84 ml of test broth and mix thoroughly on a vortex mixer, to give 16 mg l^{-1}.
2. Label 9 sterile universal containers as follows: 8, 4, down to 0.03 mg l^{-1}. Add 3 ml of test broth to containers labelled 8, 4, 2, 0.5, etc., down to 0.03 mg l^{-1}. Add 7.75 ml of broth to the container labelled 1 mg l^{-1}.
3. Using a micropipette add 3 ml of 16 mg l^{-1} solution to the bottle labelled 8 mg l^{-1}. Mix by vortexing.
4. Continue the dilution series down to 1 mg l^{-1} using 3 ml transfer volumes and clean pipette tips.
5. Prepare a 0.5 mg l^{-1} solution by adding 0.25 ml of 16 mg l^{-1} solution to 7.75 ml broth and mix by vortexing.
6. Continue the dilution series using 3 ml transfer volumes down to 0.03 mg l^{-1}.
7. Set out two rows of 11 sterile, plugged 7.5 × 1.3 cm tubes in a rack and label for test and control organisms 16, 8, 4, . . . 0.03 mg l^{-1} and growth control. Add 1 extra tube to act as sterility control.
8. Pipette from each antibiotic concentration 1 ml into the 2 corresponding tubes, again using a fresh tip for each concentration.
9. Add 1 ml of broth to each of the 3 control tubes.

Table 16. Broth dilution method, modified Ericsson and Sherris method (12).

---

1. Label 10 sterile universal containers 16, 8, 4, . . . 0.03 mg l^{-1}. Master dilutions are prepared as follows.

   0.16 ml of 1000 mg l^{-1} stock + 9.84 ml broth = 16 mg l^{-1}

   2 ml of 16 mg l^{-1} + 2 ml broth = 8 mg l^{-1}
   1 ml of 16 mg l^{-1} + 3 ml broth = 4 mg l^{-1}
   1 ml of 16 mg l^{-1} + 7 ml broth = 2 mg l^{-1}
   0.5 mg l^{-1} of 16 mg l^{-1} + 7.5 ml broth = 1 mg l^{-1}

   2 ml of 1 mg l^{-1} + 2 ml broth = 0.5 mg l^{-1}
   1 ml of 1 mg l^{-1} + 3 ml broth = 0.25 mg l^{-1}
   1 ml of 1 mg l^{-1} + 7 ml broth = 0.12 mg l^{-1}
   0.5 ml of 1 mg l^{-1} + 7.5 ml broth = 0.06 mg l^{-1}

   2 ml of 0.06 mg l^{-1} + 2 ml broth = 0.03 mg l^{-1}

   Thoroughly vortex mix all dilutions.
2. Set out two rows of 10 sterile plugged 7.5 × 1.3 cm tubes in a rack and label them 16, 8, 4, . . . 0.03 mg l^{-1} plus 3 control tubes.
3. Using a 1 ml micropipette and a sterile tip for each dilution, transfer 1 ml from each master dilution into each of the 2 corresponding tubes.

Table 17. Inoculation of broths for MICs.

Following preparation of broth dilutions as in *Table 15* or *16*, proceed as follows.

1. Prepare inocula of the test and control organisms to produce a final inoculum of 1×10^5 CFU l^{-1}. This can be done by making a 1:200 dilution of an overnight broth culture in sterile saline, or by dilution of a suspension of organisms prepared from growth on a solid medium and the density standardized by the use of a spectrophotometer or a nephelometer or against a McFarland BaSO$_4$ standard.
2. Inoculate the tubes with 1 drop of inoculum and mix by gently shaking the rack. Vortex mix the 2 growth control tubes. Sample 0.1 ml from each control and add to 0.9 ml of sterile saline. Vortex mix and use a standard 2 μl loop to plate on to a suitable medium to check purity and inoculum density (1×10^5 CFU ml^{-1} = 20 colonies).
3. Incubate for 18−24 h at 37°C in air unless an enriched atmosphere is essential for growth of the test strain.
4. Read the tubes for growth while holding them over a mirror. Compare the tests with growth control tubes for turbidity or the presence of buttons of growth.
5. If the bactericidal endpoint is required, subculture 10 μl from those tubes showing no visible growth to a segment of a suitable recovery medium. No growth on the subculture plates signifies a ≥99.9% kill. The incubation time allowed before subculturing is usually 18 h, but may be 4 h, in which case all tubes may have to be subcultured. The control organism serves to check the antibiotic concentration in the dilution series and therefore does not need to be subcultured.
   Results are valid only if:
   (i)   the subcultures taken from control tubes show a pure growth and correct inoculum density;
   (ii) the result obtained for the control organism lies within acceptable limits;
   (iii) the sterility control tubes show no growth.

Many of the commercial systems also offer a fully automated system including the inoculation and reading of plates. Such systems have found little support in the UK largely because of the high cost of equipment and consumables.

Laboratories with a suitable multi-channel dispenser (MIC 2000, Dynatech) can prepare microdilution plates to their own requirements. These can be made in large batches and when sealed should remain stable at −70°C for a minimum of 6 months.

Table 18. Commercial microdilution systems.

Name	Manufacturer	Drug presentation	Breakpoint MIC alone	BP/MIC+ identification	Reading Manual	Automated
Sensititre	Sensititre UK	Dried	+	−	+	+
Sceptor	Becton Dickinson	Dried	+	+	+	
Cobas	Roche	Discs	+	+		+
Autobac	Organon Technica	Discs	+	+		+
Pasco	Difco	Frozen	+	+		
Microscan	American Hospital Supplies	Dried		+	+	+
ATB	API	Dried	+		+	+

3.3.3 Serum bactericidal activity

This is not a method for determining the MIC or MBC of an antibiotic, but the technique has similarities to the broth dilution method.

Doubling dilutions are made of a patient's serum in a suitable nutrient broth. It is most commonly used as a method of monitoring antibiotic therapy in patients with bacterial endocarditis to see at what dilution their serum kills a standard concentration of the organism causing their disease. Bactericidal titres of the serum against the organism should be at least 1 in 4 for pre-dose serum and at least 1 in 8 for a peak (usually 1 h after the dose) post-dose serum (18). However, it has recently been suggested that a peak titre of 1 in 64 is more likely to be associated with cure (19). The method has been applied to other body fluids, such as CSF in meningitis. To perform the test for one sample proceed as follows.

(i) Take 10 sterile tubes and with a micropipette add 1 ml of a suitable broth (such as Iso-Sensitest broth + 5% lysed horse blood or human serum).

(ii) Add 1 ml of patient's serum to the first tube, mix well and then transfer 1 ml to the next tube, changing the pipette tip between each dilution.

(iii) Carry on in this manner to the 8th tube and discard 1 ml of mixture from that, so that there are 1 ml quantities of dilutions of serum from 1:2 to 1:256. If the volume of serum available is small, 0.5 ml quantities may be used or the series may be started at 1:4.

(iv) Prepare the inoculum by taking an overnight broth culture of the organism infecting the patient, and diluting it 1:10 in sterile broth. Add 1 drop of the diluted culture to the first 9 tubes, giving a final inoculum of 1×10^6 CFU ml^{-1}. The 9th tube is the growth control tube and the 10th tube is the sterility control tube.

(v) Mix all tubes on a vortex mixer. Dilute the growth control tube 1:100 in saline and mix again. Inoculate and spread a 2 μl standard loop of this on suitable medium, usually blood agar.

(vi) Incubate tubes and plate overnight at 37°C. The following day, check that the sterility control tube is not turbid and count the colonies on the plate. If the final inoculum was 10^6 CFU ml^{-1}, 20 colonies should be present.

(vii) Look for the cut-off point between a turbid and clear broth in the series of dilutions and the last tube to show turbidity is the serum bacteristatic titre.

(viii) Subculture all the tubes by transferring 10 μl on to a segment of a suitable recovery

Table 19. Breakpoint recommendations of BSAC Working Party.

	Group I: staphylococci, streptococci, B.catarrhalis and H.influenzae		Group II: Enterobacteriaceae and Pseudomonas spp.	
	Low	*High*	*Low*	*High*
Aminoglycosides				
Gentamicin	1	4	1	4
Tobramycin	1	4	1	4
Netilmicin	1	4	1	4
Amikacin	4	16	4	16
Penicillins				
Benzylpenicillin	0.12			
Methicillin	4			
Ampicillin/amoxycillin with or without clavulanate	1		8	
Carbenicillin			32	128
Ticarcillin with or without clavulanate			16	64
Azlocillin			16	64
Piperacillin			16	64
Mezlocillin	2		16	64
Cephalosporins, etc.				
Cephalexin	2	8	2	8
Cephradine	2	8	2	8
Cefuroxime	4		4	16
Cefotaxime	1	8	1	
Ceftazidime	2	8	2	
Ceftizoxime	1	8	1	
Cefsulodin			8	
Aztreonam			8	
Miscellaneous				
Erythromycin	0.5			
Clindamycn	0.5			
Vancomycin	4			
Chloramphenicol	8		8	
Tetracycline	1		1	
Fusidic acid	1			
Rifampicin	1			
Trimethoprim	0.5		0.5	2
Sulphamethoxazole			32	
Ciprofloxacin	1	4	1	4

medium. Spread each with a loop and incubate overnight. The bactericidal titre is the maximum dilution showing 10 colonies or less. This is equivalent to a 99.9% kill.

3.4 Breakpoints in sensitivity testing

In *in vitro* antibiotic sensitivity testing, the laboratory provides information that designates organisms as sensitive, intermediate (moderately sensitive or resistant) or resistant. These categories can be distinguished by the use of *in-vitro* breakpoint antibiotic concentrations. The method used is an abbreviated MIC test where isolates are tested only against 1, 2 or 3 fixed concentrations chosen as 'cut-off' concentrations between the categories of sensitivity. Agar incorporation is the method usually used. The test has gained some popularity in the UK because it is technically simple and suitable for testing large numbers of strains.

In choosing the breakpoints, various considerations, including clinical, pharmacological and microbiological, have to be taken into account, and a working party of the British Society for Antimicrobial Chemotherapy (BSAC) has produced a formula for the calculation of breakpoints (20). A summary of the breakpoint recommendations of the working party is given in *Table 19*.

Control of the breakpoint test is more difficult than conventional MIC tests. As only one to three antibiotic dilutions are tested the choice of control strains is more critical than for diffusion methods. Ideally, control strains should have MICs 4-fold above and below each breakpoint for each agent tested. This is very difficult to achieve without the number of control strains getting unreasonably large. Organisms having MICs very close to a breakpoint concentration should be avoided, as an apparent change in category of sensitivity may be the result of inherent variability of the method rather than incorrect antibiotic content of the test medium.

4. TESTS OF COMBINED ANTIMICROBIAL ACTION

4.1 Chequerboard titration

The interaction of two antimicrobial agents can be studied by performing a chequerboard titration. This is done in broth if a bactericidal endpoint is required, or can be done by agar incorporation, especially if more than one organism is to be tested. The chequerboard test is so named because the test strain is exposed to all concentrations of each agent alone and in all possible combinations of concentrations of the two agents together.

4.1.1 *Chequerboard titration by broth dilution*

A method for performing a chequerboard titration in broth for gentamicin and ampicillin is given in *Table 20*. Each antibiotic is prepared in 10 ml volumes of double the required concentration, so that when mixed with an equal volume of the other agent the required concentration is achieved.

4.1.2 *Chequerboard titration by agar dilution*

This is done in a similar way to the test in broth except that the antibiotic dilutions are prepared in containers according to the number of strains to be tested (see *Table 14*). The antibiotic solutions are prepared at appropriate strengths to allow for the volume of agar to be added.

4.1.3 *Interpretation of chequerboard titrations*

When two antibiotics are combined together the effect may be:

(i)   *synergistic*, when the activity of both drugs together is significantly greater than

Table 20. Chequerboard titration for testing combined antimicrobial action (e.g. gentamicin and ampicillin).

1. Dilute each of the two antibiotic stock 1000 mg l^{-1} stock solutions in broth in sterile universal containers.

    0.64 ml stock solution + 19.36 ml Iso-Sensitest broth = 32 mg l^{-1}

2. In a rack arrange 2 rows of 6 universal containers and add 10 ml of Iso-Sensitest broth to each.
3. With an automatic pipette take 10 ml of the ampicillin 32 mg l^{-1} and add to the first universal container, mix thoroughly and label 'Ampicillin 16 mg l^{-1}'. With a clean pipette tip take 10 ml of the 16 mg l^{-1} solution and add to the next universal container. Mix thoroughly and label 'Ampicillin 8 mg l^{-1}'. Repeat the procedure down to the 6th tube (= 0.5 mg l^{-1}).
4. Starting with the gentamicin 32 mg l^{-1} solution, repeat step 3 using the 2nd row of universal containers to give a range of gentamicin concentrations of 32−0.5 mg l^{-1}.
5. Set out 7.5 × 1.3 cm sterile plugged tubes in an 8 × 8 pattern in racks.
6. Transfer 1 ml of ampicillin 32 mg l^{-1} into each tube in the 1st (top) horizontal row and label each one with its final concentration, e.g. ampicillin 16 mg l^{-1}.
7. Transfer 1 ml of ampicillin 16 mg l^{-1} into each tube in the 2nd horizontal row and label 'Ampicillin 8 mg l^{-1}'. Repeat with the other dilutions.
8. Add 1 ml of sterile broth to the bottom horizontal row and label 'Ampicillin nil'.
9. Transfer 1 ml of gentamicin 32 mg l^{-1} into each tube in the 1st (left hand) vertical row and label 'Gentamicin 16 mg l^{-1}'.
10. Repeat with each gentamicin dilution transferring 1 ml into the corresponding vertical row.
11. Add 1 ml broth to the right hand row and label 'Gentamicin nil'.
12. Dispense a further row of dilutions for each drug alone for testing a suitable control organism, e.g. *E.coli* NCTC 10418.
13. Dilute an overnight broth culture of the test strain 1:200 in broth and add 1 drop to all the tubes (except those for the control organism) to give an inoculum of 1 × 10^5 CFU ml^{-1}.
14. Inoculate the two control series with a similar dilution of the control organism.
15. Shake the racks vigorously to mix the organism with the antibiotic solutions.
16. Use a 2 µl loop to subculture the antibiotic-free control tubes containing the test and control organisms in order to check the inoculum density and the purity of the culture.
17. Incubate all tubes overnight at 37°C in air, unless an enriched atmosphere is essential for growth of the test strain.
18. Read all the tubes for growth and vortex mix. Subculture tubes showing no visible growth by transferring 10 µl on to a segment of a suitable recovery medium and spreading with a loop.
19. Read subcultures for bactericidal endpoints. No growth is equivalent to a ≥99.9% kill.

that of either acting alone in the same concentration;

(ii) *additive*, when the activity of both drugs together shows a minor increase in activity when compared with either acting alone;

(iii) *antagonistic*, when the activity of one drug is reduced by the presence of the other;

(iv) *indifferent*, when the activity of each is unaffected by the presence of the other.

This combined activity can be expressed as the summed fractional inhibitory concentration (εFIC) which is calculated as follows:

$$\epsilon\text{FIC} = \frac{\text{MIC drug A in combination}}{\text{MIC drug A alone}} + \frac{\text{MIC drug B in combination}}{\text{MIC drug B alone}}$$

There is no clear consensus about the interpretation of εFIC values, but synergy is usually taken to be demonstrated by a value of ≤0.7. Hamilton-Miller (21) has suggested a schedule for recommended terminology and numerical criteria for combined antimicrobial activity.

4.2 **Modified chequerboard titration**

In order to determine suitable synergistic combinations of antibiotics it may be sufficient to determine the MIC/MBC of one agent in the presence of one or two fixed concentrations of a second agent. This simple technique is particularly useful when a wide range of antibiotic combinations need to be tested.

To determine the penicillin MIC of an organism in the presence of gentamicin, 1 mg ml^{-1} and 4 mg ml^{-1}, the method is as for a standard MIC test, but the penicillin dilutions are made in broths containing gentamicin at 1 mg l^{-1} and 4 mg l^{-1}. Alternatively the penicillin dilutions can be prepared in 1 ml volumes in triplicate as follows.

(i)   Set 1, the penicillin MIC.
(ii)   Set 2, add 10 μl gentamicin 100 mg l^{-1} to each tube.
(iii)   Set 3, add 10 μl gentamicin 400 mg l^{-1} to each tube.

Sets 2 and 3 give the penicillin MIC in the presence of gentamicin, 1 mg l^{-1} and 4 mg l^{-1} respectively. The addition of gentamicin in this way represents only a 1% increase in volume and any effect on the penicillin concentration can be discounted.

4.3 **Diffusion methods**

The simplest way of demonstrating synergy between two agents is by placing blotting-paper strips, one containing each drug, at right angles to each other on an agar plate uniformly seeded with the test organism. On the single plate the effect of each antibiotic alone can be seen at the ends of the strips and the combined effect over a range of concentrations can be seen in the angle between the strips. The same effect can also be demonstrated using antibiotic discs instead of strips. The distance between the discs is crucial; if it is too great, the effect will not be seen.

Diffusion methods, such as the velvet pad replica plating method and the cellophane transfer method, can be used also to determine combined bactericidal activity of two agents. The methods are rarely used now, and for further details the reader is referred to another text (22).

5. REFERENCES

1.   Barry,A.L. (1976) *The Antimicrobial Susceptibility Test: Principles and Practices.* Lea and Febiger, Philadelphia, p. 163.
2.   Barry,A.L. (1986) In *Antibiotics in Laboratory Medicine.* 2nd edn, Lorian,V. (ed.), Williams and Wilkins, Baltimore, p. 1.
3.   Brown,D.F.J. and Blowers,R. (1978) In *Laboratory Methods in Antimicrobial Chemotherapy.* Reeves,D.S., Phillips,I., Williams,J.D. and Wise,R. (eds), Churchill Livingstone, Edinburgh, p. 8.
4.   Thornsberry,C., Swenson,J.M., Baker,C.N., McDougal,L.K., Stocker,S.A. and Hill,B.C. (1987) *The Antimicrobic Newsletter,* **4**, 47.
5.   Phillips,I. and Warren,C. (1978) In *Laboratory Methods in Antimicrobial Chemotherapy.* Reeves,D.S., Phillips,I., Williams,J.D. and Wise,R. (eds), Churchill Livingstone, Edinburgh, p. 94.
6.   Fallon,R.J. (1978) In *Laboratory Methods in Antimicrobial Chemotherapy.* Reeves,D.S., Phillips,I., Williams,J.D. and Wise,R. (eds), Churchill Livingstone, Edinburgh, p. 99.
7.   Phillips,I. (1978) In *Laboratory Methods in Antimicrobial Chemotherapy.* Reeves,D.S., Phillips,I., Williams,J.D. and Wise,R. (eds), Churchill Livingstone, Edinburgh, p. 103.
8.   Williams,J.D. and Kattan,S. (1978) In *Laboratory Methods in Antimicrobial Chemotherapy.* Reeves,D.S., Phillips,I., Williams,J.D. and Wise,R. (eds), Churchill Livingstone, Edinburgh, p. 106.

9. National Committee for Clinical Laboratory Standards (1984) Performance Standards for Antimicrobial Disc Susceptibility Testing Third Edition. Approved Standard M2-A3. National Committee for Clinical Laboratory Standards, Villanova, PA, USA.
10. National Committee for Clinical Laboratory Standards (1987) Performance Standards for Antimicrobial Susceptibility Testing. Second Informational Supplement M100-S2. National Committee for Clinical Laboratory Standards, Villanova, PA, USA.
11. European Committee for Clinical Laboratory Standards (1988) Guidelines for Antimicrobial Susceptibility Testing by Diffusion Methods. ECCLS Document ISSN, 1011−6265 ECCLS, Lund.
12. Ericsson,H. and Sherris,J.C. (1971) *Acta Pathol. et Microbiol. Scand.,* Section B, Suppl., 217.
13. Felmingham,D. and Stokes,E.J. (1972) *Med. Lab. Tech.,* **29**, 198.
14. Neu,H.C. (1986) In *Antibiotics in Laboratory Medicine,* 2nd edn, Lorian,V. (ed.), Williams and Wilkins, Baltimore, p. 757.
15. Sykes,R.B. (1978) In *Laboratory Methods in Antimicrobial Chemotherapy.* Reeves,D.S., Phillips,I., Williams,J.D. and Wise,R. (eds), Churchill Livingstone, Edinburgh, p. 64.
16. Jacobs,M.R., Gaspar,M.N., Robins-Browne,R.M. and Koornhof,H.J. (1980) *J. Antimicrob. Chemother.,* **6**, 53.
17. Waterworth,P.M. and del Piano,M. (1976) *J. Clin. Pathol.,* **29**, 179.
18. Shanson,D.C. (1982) *Microbiology in Clinical Practice.* John Wright, Bristol and Littleton, MA, p. 349.
19. Reller,L.B. (1986) *Rev. Infect. Dis.,* **8**, 803.
20. Breakpoints in in vitro antibiotic sensitivity testing. Report by a working party of the British Society for Antimicrobial Chemotherapy (1988) *J. Antimicrob. Chemother.,* **21**, 701.
21. Hamilton-Miller,J.M.T. (1985) *J. Antimicrob. Chemother.,* **15**, 655.
22. Waterworth,P.M. (1978) In *Laboratory Methods in Antimicrobial Chemotherapy.* Reeves,D.S., Phillips,I., Williams,J.D. and Wise,R. (eds), Churchill Livingstone, Edinburgh, p. 41.

CHAPTER 8

Antibiotic assays

DAVID S.REEVES

1. INTRODUCTION

For many years after their introduction, antibiotics (for the purposes of this chapter meaning all antimicrobial agents) were only infrequently assayed in samples from patients. Assays have been extensively used in the development and control of antibiotic production, but the methods used are suitable mainly for high concentrations in non-biological matrices (a matrix is the substance, such as plasma, serum or water, in which the antibiotic is prepared or presented), and have an accuracy in excess of that needed for clinical use. The widespread use of gentamicin after its introduction in 1964 proved to be a powerful stimulus for using blood assays since its therapeutic range of concentrations is small. Over the past 20 years there has been an increasing use of antibiotic assays to monitor concentrations in samples from patients, mainly those receiving aminoglycosides (gentamicin and related agents), but also chloramphenicol, vancomycin, antifungal agents and other antibiotics. A variety of techniques have been applied to assays. Initially, most were done by microbiological methods (see Section 5) but non-microbiological techniques are now widely used. Some are based on immunological principles (see Section 6), such as competition for a specific antibody directed against the antibiotic, as in radioimmunoassay. The other widely used technique is high performance liquid chromatography (HPLC) (see Section 7).

2. CLINICAL APPLICATION OF ANTIBIOTIC ASSAYS

2.1 General considerations

Not every patient receiving an antibiotic requires the monitoring of its concentration in blood or other body fluids, and in many types of antibiotic therapy monitoring would needlessly waste resources. Furthermore there must be a relationship, however weak, between concentration and toxicity or efficacy to justify its use.

2.1.1 *Relationship of concentrations to efficacy*

Information on this is scanty. It is known, however, that certain doses of antibiotic (presumably those recommended for normal use) regularly cure infection, and it is also known in general terms the concentrations that such doses produce in the blood. Information is lacking on whether treatment failure is accompanied by low concentrations, but this is not surprising since there are many other factors causing failure and, in any event, concentrations of antibiotics are often well above those needed for therapy because of their low toxicity. Most information relating blood concentrations to efficacy concerns aminoglycosides. This has been reviewed in some detail by Reeves

195

and White (1). For other agents, reliance has to be made on the expected concentrations as known from the published pharmacokinetics of an antibiotic; these have been reviewed by Wise (2) and, for injectable agents, by Reeves and Paton (3). If a patient is unexpectedly failing treatment with an antibiotic to which the infecting pathogen is sensitive, a possible cause may be inadequate concentrations, perhaps due to abnormal pharmacokinetics in a very ill patient, or even the accidental administration of the wrong antibiotic. Similarly, if the patient suffers an ill-effect which may possibly be an adverse reaction of the antibiotic then a measurement of concentrations may show these to be excessively high. Only by readily doing assays can the existence of concentration-dependent effects be established. Certainly when oral therapy is used to treat a serious infection, checks of blood concentration are indicated because of the unreliability of absorption of many agents. Monitoring can also show up failures of compliance and even the prescription or administration of the wrong antibiotics, both causes of otherwise unexplained failure of therapy.

2.1.2 *Relationship of blood concentration to toxicity*

There is rather more substantial evidence of this than with efficacy (1). In particular, there is a reasonable correlation between raised pre-dose ('trough') levels of aminoglycoside and ototoxicity; the correlation with the so-called 'peak' levels is poor, and these are largely done to establish the fact that adequate concentrations are being achieved. There is a reasonable correlation between blood concentration and toxicity for vancomycin, chloramphenicol, erythromycin, benzylpenicillin, and flucytosine (1). There is a very clear connection between high levels of chloramphenicol in the neonate and the frequently fatal 'gray' syndrome, and care should be taken to ensure that levels are in the therapeutic range. In older patients there may be a relationship between levels and bone marrow toxicity, so again plasma concentration monitoring might be justified. Central nervous system irritability leading to fits and coma has been described with benzylpenicillin. Plasma levels were usually over 100 mg l^{-1} and CSF levels over 10 mg l^{-1}.

2.2 **Indications for monitoring**

In view of the frequency of litigation over aminoglycoside toxicity, it is strongly advisable that all patients receiving aminoglycosides have their serum levels monitored. When this is impossible because of unavailability of assays special efforts should be made to monitor concentrations in certain patients or consideration given to using another type of antibiotic.

2.2.1 *Types of patients in whom monitoring of aminoglycoside blood concentration is essential*

These include:

(i)   patients with renal failure, particularly if its degree is changing rapidly or unpredictably;

(ii)   patients with life-threatening infections in whom it is essential to achieve adequate blood concentrations immediately;

(iii)   patients receiving long courses (>7 days) of therapy, since previously stabilized levels may rise after this time;
(iv)   patients with gross obesity, in whom levels tend to be high when dosed according to total body weight;
(v)   patients with pre-existing sensory loss (such as blindness) in whom deafness would provide a disastrous extra burden;
(vi)   patients who have had previous courses of aminoglycosides, since they may already have some vestibular/cochlear damage;
(vii)   patients receiving other drugs which can potentiate ototoxicity (such as frusemide) or renal toxicity (such as some of the older cephalosporins), or inactivate an aminoglycoside (such as carbenicillin).

Assays of non-aminoglycoside antibiotics are sometimes necessary. Chloramphenicol must always be monitored in neonates. Vancomycin, benzylpenicillin and flucytosine monitoring is also recommended in patients with renal failure.

2.2.2 *Situations in which monitoring of concentrations of non-aminoglycoside antibiotics may be advisable*

These include:

(i)   the use of a potentially toxic antibiotic in a patient in whom excretion may be reduced—examples are chloramphenicol in neonates, and benzylpenicillin or flucytosine in renal failure;
(ii)   when a patient with a life-threatening infection fails to respond to therapy with an antibiotic active *in vitro* against the invading pathogen, having excluded other causes for the failure (such as an abscess), assays can provide confirmation that the expected concentrations are indeed present;
(iii)   when giving an antibiotic by a route of uncertain absorption (such as orally) to treat a serious infection (such as bacterial endocarditis);
(iv)   when checking the concentration in a body fluid, such as cerebrospinal fluid, where penetration is poor or uncertain.

3. TAKING SPECIMENS FOR ASSAYS

Using standardized intervals at which blood samples are taken for antibiotic assay after a dose makes it easier to interpret the results and adjust dosage. Although multiple samples taken after a dose would provide more pharmacokinetic information, it is usually impracticable to take more than one post-dose sample and one immediately pre-dose. The former is often termed the 'peak' concentration, although this is clearly a misnomer since the true peak concentration will occur immediately after an intravenous dose of an antibiotic unless it is given as a hydrolysable pro-drug, such as chloramphenicol. The pre-dose sample is taken immediately before a dose and is often called the 'trough' concentration. Following extravascular (intramuscular or oral) administration the blood concentration rises to a maximum and then falls. The interval between the dose and that maximum varies considerably, but is often about 1 h with intramuscular administration. For this reason and others discussed elsewhere (4,5), the sample for the peak concentration is usually taken 1 h post-dose for both intravenous and intramuscular

Table 1. Important points about collecting specimens for assays.

1.	Unless otherwise specifically indicated, always take blood and body fluid samples into plain tubes. Serum is often preferable to plasma for assay.
2.	Collect samples as aseptically as possible, especially for microbiological assays and the determination of inhibitory titres.
3.	Venous blood is preferable, but adequate samples from neonates can be obtained by heel-pricks.
4.	When in doubt, ask the laboratory about the type and minimum volume of sample.
5.	For most antibiotics take the post-dose ('peak') blood sample 1 h after a dose. The pre-dose sample ('trough') is taken just before a dose, often the one immediately preceding the peak sample.
6.	Take the peak sample for antibiotics given intravenously as pro-drugs (chloramphenicol, erythromycin) at 2 h after the dose to allow adequate time for hydrolysis to the active drug.
7.	Do not take the peak sample too early after an intravenous dose. Very high transient concentrations may be found which probably have little relationship to efficacy or toxicity.
8.	The most frequent causes of patently ridiculous results (those which are pharmacokinetically seemingly impossible) are:
	(i) drawing a blood sample back down an intravenous cannula used for giving the antibiotic;
	(ii) failure to give the dose;
	(iii) the dose given at the wrong time;
	(iv) giving an intravenous dose into an infusion tube through which the fluid is running very slowly. The dose will thus take a long time to reach the blood.
9.	When submitting the sample tell the laboratory about all the antibiotics a patient has received in the previous 72 h.
10.	If there is likely to be a delay in the laboratory receiving the sample, seek advice on the stability of the antibiotic in question. Immediate separation of the serum or plasma and its storage at $-20°C$ may be advisable.

administration. This is now recommended in the British National Formulary for aminoglycosides. The important aspects of specimen collection are given in *Table 1*.

4. METHODS OF ASSAY

Assay methods for antibiotics fall into two main types: microbiological and non-microbiological.

(i) *Microbiological methods.* These are based upon response of a population of micro-organisms to differing concentrations of antibiotic. A measurement of response, such as inhibition zone diameter, can be calibrated with known antibiotic concentration in working standards and in that way the concentration of an unknown be determined. The only method now used at all widely for assays in biological matrices is the agar plate diffusion method in which the measured response is zone diameter.

(ii) *Non-microbiological methods.* These employ other principles, such as immunological binding or separation in chromatography (both described below).

4.1 Characteristics of assay methods: microbiological versus non-microbiological methods

In considering whether to use any method, its characteristics must be examined in relation to its intended use. It is particularly important to remember that the needs of an assay for examining samples from normal volunteer studies may differ from those for blood samples from patients with, say, renal failure. The method should therefore always be validated in the circumstances of its use.

4.1.1 *Specificity*

The specificity of an assay may be affected by:

(i)   other antibiotics, perhaps those co-administered with or given previously to the target antibiotic;
(ii) antimicrobially-active metabolites;
(iii) inactive metabolites, which will only affect non-microbiological assays;
(iv) non-antibiotic drugs, which may affect both microbiological assays (such as anti-tumour agents) and non-microbiological assays (such as phenytoin in HPLC).

In samples from patients, problems arise because the requesting clinician fails to inform the laboratory of recent, prior or concomitant antibiotics. Prior antibiotics are a particular problem when they have a long blood half-life or the patient has renal failure. Gross interference by a second, or even a third, antibiotic may be obvious to the laboratory in that it gives rise to a ludicrous result. Lesser interference may, however, pass unnoticed. Clearly microbiological assays are inherently less specific than non-microbiological ones in dealing with mixtures of antibiotics. They do, however, have the advantage of measuring a clinically relevant parameter, the inhibition of a micro-organism, if an appropriate indicator organism is chosen. Thus a *Klebsiella* species is more appropriate for clinical assays of an aminoglycoside than a *Bacillus* species, because the former is less likely to be affected by interfering antibiotics and because it resembles more closely the likely pathogen. A *Bacillus* species is, however, better from samples from pharmacokinetic studies in volunteers because a spore suspension gives more reproducible and a convenient inoculum. Neither microbiological nor non-microbiological assays are entirely specific and this is most likely to become apparent when dealing with complex problems in patients. It is always essential to keep this in mind.

4.1.2 *Precision*

Because microbiological assays depend on a biological response their precision is inherently less good than that of non-microbiological methods. They are, however, capable of giving adequate precision for clinical and pharmacokinetic purposes provided sufficient replication is used, which usually entails putting samples and standards on an assay plate in triplicate. This can give a precision of $10-20\%$ at the 95% confidence limits. Since dilution or protein precipitation of the sample is often a first step in non-microbiological assays they are less susceptible to variation in the sample matrix and thus inherently more precise. This, together with the often sophisticated instrumentation used, makes it easy to obtain a precision of better than 10% at 95% confidence limits.

4.1.3 *Sensitivity*

This is the lowest concentration of antibiotic assayable at the required precision. It may vary with the matrix in which the sample is presented and with the presence of potentially interfering substances. Sensitivity is usually adequate in the microbiological assays of clinical samples since one expects to find sufficient concentrations to inhibit sensitive bacteria. HPLC methods may not easily give sufficient sensitivity, but immunologically based assays usually can.

4.1.4 *Speed*

The minimum time to produce a zone of sufficient readability to give adequate precision is about 5 h with an agar plate diffusion assay when using a *Klebsiella* species as indicator organism. With slower-growing organisms incubation is usually 'overnight' (i.e. about 18 h). For clinical purposes it is highly desirable that an assay result be available before the next dose of antibiotic is due to be given so that it can be appropriately modified. Certainly the result should be available within 2 dose intervals. Non-microbiological assays are often much quicker than microbiological assays, the result for a single sample being available within minutes.

4.1.5 *Range of concentration*

The calibration curve for inhibition zone size versus concentrations for microbiological assays is sigmoid if taken over a wide range of concentrations, and thus it is best only to use the middle part of it. The range of concentrations covered by this part is often about 16-fold. Samples within this range may be assayed directly, but higher concentrations require an initial dilution. This not only introduces a step at which an inaccuracy may occur, but can also lead to an unacceptable delay when an out-of-range sample requires repeating. Non-microbiological assays often have a linear response over a wider range of concentrations, this being particularly true of HPLC, which means that unknown samples from patients can more often be assayed at the first attempt. Furthermore, because of their greater speed, any repeat on a diluted sample will not significantly delay the result.

4.1.6 *Sample size*

For many clinical applications, a sample of up to 1 ml is usually available, but from neonates 100 μl is usual. Since microbiological plate assays need at least a triplicate application of sample to maintain their precision, and each application to the plate (confusingly termed a dose) takes $50-100$ μl, their use for neonatal samples is limited. Sample size is rarely a problem with immunological assays, but may sometimes be so with HPLC to obtain adequate sensitivity.

4.1.7 *Costs*

Agar plate diffusion assays require only inexpensive consumables and equipment when done on the small number of samples sent for clinical purposes, although a small microcomputer is invaluable for recording the zone sizes and calculating the results. Such assays do require skill and experience in the operator to give the best results. Conversely, immunologically based assays usually come in commercial kit form to run on expensive and sophisticated equipment and, since both the consumables and equipment are therefore expensive, a laboratory may have to consider carefully the likely effect on its budget if such an assay is introduced. The degree of skill in the operator of the most sophisticated kit assays is minimal, although some skilled overall supervision is essential. HPLC assays occupy an intermediate position. Consumables are not as expensive as with immunological assays, and in its most basic form the equipment is cheaper. Considerable experience is, however, needed to develop an assay; once it is available then doing individual assays is not difficult.

5. MICROBIOLOGICAL ASSAYS

5.1 Types of microbiological assays

The most widely used is the agar plate diffusion method but others do exist, such as diffusion in agar in a capillary tube, broth dilution, turbidimetry of broth cultures, and rapid methods based on chemiluminescence or urease or ATP production (7,8). The agar plate diffusion method is the most readily accessible for clinical laboratories and also adaptable to a wide variety of antibiotics and will be the only one described in detail (see Section 5.3).

5.2 Preparation and storage of stock standard solutions

All the assay methods described depend for the determination of unknown concentrations on comparison with solutions of known concentration, and the accuracy of the latter is therefore crucial. Stock standards are those prepared directly from a standard antibiotic powder or solution of accurately known potency; they are usually of much higher concentration than the working standards, which are those actually used in the assay

Table 2. Preparation of accurate stock standards.

1.	Never use dosage forms for preparing standards. The drug may be in an inert form (e.g. an ester of chloramphenicol) or contain inert material (e.g. as in tablet). The declared potency may be nominal, and an excess of potency and volume may well be present for solutions.
2.	Obtain antibiotics as 'material for laboratory use' with an accurately declared potency. Manufacturers will usually supply them gratis on request.
3.	Powders may be hygroscopic and therefore acquire moisture from the air, reducing their potency. Antibiotic as a damp powder may also deteriorate more quickly. Always bring a bottle of powder to room temperature before opening it, and weigh out the required powder as quickly as possible. Aminoglycoside powders can be dried at 110°C and should be stored in a desiccator; their potency may be stated 'as is' (i.e. before drying) or 'dry' (i.e. after drying).
4.	If kept dry, most antibiotics remain stable for up to 1 year in airtight containers at 4°C out of the light. If in doubt about stability, consult the manufacturer.
5.	Use a balance which can weigh quickly and accurately to 0.1 mg, and use only scrupulously clean equipment during the weighing.
6.	Weigh out an appropriate amount for making the stock standard a convenient concentration, say 1000 mg l^{-1}. An allowance for stated potency, usually given as μg mg^{-1}, is usually needed. For example, if a solution of 1000 mg l^{-1} is required, 100 mg of antibiotic will be required for 100 ml of solution. If the potency is 900 μg mg^{-1} then the weight of antibiotic needed is 111.11 mg.
7.	Transfer the antibiotic powder completely to a glass volumetric flask by washing with sterile distilled water, and make up to the mark with the same matrix[a].

[a]Some antibiotics do not dissolve easily in water (e.g. chloramphenicol base) and a lipid solvent fully miscible with water will be required (see Chapter 7). Caution is required in subsequent dilutions in aqueous media since precipitation, often apparent as a fine haze, may occur. Since even moderate concentrations of organic solvent may affect a microbiological assay, the only way around the problem may be to decrease the concentration of solute. Providing it does not cause instability, some antibiotics insoluble in water may dissolve better at higher or lower pH values. For example, sulphonamides (weak acids) often dissolve in alkali (e.g. 0.1 M NaOH), and bases like trimethoprim in acid (e.g. lactic acid).

and prepared from the stock standards by dilution into the matrix to be used. The points to be observed for preparing accurate stock standards are given in *Table 2*.

Many antibiotics can be stored in solution without loss of potency for 6 months at $-20°C$. Others keep better at $-70°C$ or over liquid nitrogen. Some antibiotics are not stable in solution and fresh standards must be prepared at regular intervals, even daily. Manufacturers may be able to supply information about stability in solution, or it can be determined experimentally by comparing stored solutions with those freshly prepared. If there is doubt about stability, prepare fresh standards.

5.3 Preparation of working standards

For microbiological assays the matrix must resemble as closely as possible that of the samples of unknown concentration (the tests) including pH, ionic content, and protein concentration and quality. For clinical assays this would ideally be blank (antibiotic-free) material, usually plasma or serum, from the same patient, but this is clearly impracticable. Usually, pooled serum from HBsAg and HIVAb negative healthy donors is used. Each donation should also be tested in a very sensitive antibiotic assay to ensure that it contains no interfering antibiotic. The serum protein binding of antibiotics can vary between animal species, so animal plasma should be avoided if possible for clinical assays. Horse serum of consistent quality may be acceptable but it must be proved to give good results in the assay to be done. Stored sera tends to become alkaline on storage, and this may have a marked effect on the assay of an antibiotic whose activity is strongly affected by pH. For this, standards in fresh serum should be used or the pH of stored serum adjusted back to that of the fresh samples.

Some samples, such as urine or bile, can have very high concentrations of antibiotics and require dilution before assay. They should be diluted in buffer and assayed against working standards prepared in the same buffer. This should be of sufficient molarity to prevent its pH being altered by the addition of the biological material.

Working standards are prepared by diluting the stock standard solution into an appropriate matrix using high-grade volumetric glassware or a highly accurate mechanical diluter. It is often convenient to prepare the working standard of the highest concentration or near to it, and then prepare working standards from it. For example, 1 ml of 500 mg l^{-1} of gentamicin in water (stock standard) is made up to the mark of a 25 ml volumetric flask with working standard matrix, often serum, to give 20 mg l^{-1}. Using 10 ml volumetric flasks the working standards are prepared as follows:

$$0.5 \text{ ml of } 20 \text{ mg } l^{-1} \text{ made up to } 10 \text{ ml } = 1 \text{ mg } l^{-1}$$
$$1.0 \text{ ml of } 20 \text{ mg } l^{-1} \text{ made up to } 10 \text{ ml } = 2 \text{ mg } l^{-1} \text{ etc.}$$

Working standards should never be prepared by doubling dilution from the highest concentration, since any error in dilution may be perpetuated and perhaps magnified.

The range of concentrations of working standards is limited to the relatively small range of linearity or near-linearity of the relationship beween zone diameter and log concentration. The clinical assays described in this chapter are designed to have 5 working standards separated by 2-fold differences, giving a 16-fold range of concentrations overall. The lowest standard concentration is often set by that giving a small but distinct zone under the conditions of the assay.

The storage of standards is discussed in Section 5.2. Working standards may be less stable than stock standards because biological matrices can in themselves cause the breakdown of some antibiotics.

5.4 The agar plate diffusion assay

5.4.1 *Overall principle*

In this method antibiotic diffuses into a sheet of agar from a source (the dose), such as a well or a paper disc, to produce a circular zone of inhibition in the growth of the indicator organism growing in the agar or on its surface, or sometimes both. The diameter of the zone of inhibition is related to the concentration in the dose. Usually the doses are applied just before incubation commences and so, as with susceptibility testing by the disc method, the size of the zone of inhibition depends not only on the concentration and size of the dose but on the inoculum and rate of growth of the indicator organism, and many other factors (8). An outline of the general method is given in *Table 3*.

5.4.2 *Choice and preparation of agar*

The agar must support a good growth of the indicator organism and must resist splitting when poured in large sheets, especially when wells are cut in it. For an antibiotic whose activity is affected markedly by pH, the pH of the agar must match that of the samples. Agar should be prepared in batches and bottled in sufficient amounts for single plates, usually 100 ml, so as to give consistent results.

5.4.3 *Choice and preparation of the indicator organism*

The indicator organism must give zones of suitable size (not too large or small) over the range of concentrations to be measured under the conditions of the assay, and should give sharp zone edges. For assays of clinical samples, it must grow quickly enough to give readable inhibition zones when a result is required, often $4-5$ h. Every effort should be made to keep constant the inoculum and quality of indicator organism in any single type of assay. This can be done by storing vegetative cultures at low temperature ($-70°C$ or over liquid nitrogen), or spore suspensions at $4°C$. The preparation of these are given in *Tables 4* and *5* respectively.

5.4.4 *Choice and use of assay dishes*

Agar can be poured into small round (9 cm diameter) or square plates (10 cm or 25 cm). For the method of pouring plates see *Table 6*. Twenty-five cm^2 plates are preferable,

Table 3. Steps in performing an agar plate assay.

1.	Choose and prepare the agar.
2.	Select and prepare the correct indicator organism.
3.	Pour the plate.
4.	Inoculate the plate with the indicator organism.
5.	Apply the dose of standards and unknowns.
6.	Incubate.
7.	Measure the zones.
8.	Calculate the results.

Table 4. Preparation of a vegetative bacterial suspension.

1.	Prepare a pure culture on a plate of an appropriate medium. This should usually be non-selective, but antibiotic-containing medium may be necessary to maintain a resistant culture.
2.	Inoculate a single colony in 20 ml of an appropriate broth in a container of 250 ml size and incubate at 37°C overnight.
3.	Add 80 ml pre-warmed broth and incubate for a further 3−4 h, with shaking. Add sterile glycerol to a final concentration of 10%, mixing well.
4.	Dispense into 1 ml amounts in tubes suitable for the type of storage to be used and store in a −70°C freezer or, better, over liquid nitrogen.
5.	For use, thaw at room temperature and dilute in sterile water to give the appropriate inoculum[a].

[a]This method will give a consistent inoculum over a long period of time and, in the case of *Klebsiella* spp. growing on Oxoid DST agar, will give readable zones in 4 h at 37°C.

Table 5. Preparation of a spore suspension.

1.	Choose a suitable organism, such as *Bacillus subtilis* (NCTC 10400) and ensure that the culture is pure by incubating a spread culture on a non-selective agar. Then suspend 1 colony in a small amount of sterile water.
2.	Prepare an agar plate (blood agar base will suffice) containing 300 mg l^{-1} of $MnSO_4$ to promote sporulation and place a sterile membrane filter on the surface of the agar. Inoculate the suspension evenly over it with a sterile swab.
3.	Incubate for 3 days at 37°C and then check for sporulation by taking a sample on to a glass slide, heat-fixing, and staining appropriately for visualizing spores. If there is not a high degree of sporulation continue incubation for up to 7 days.
4.	Transfer the membrane filter to 100 ml of sterile water and shake well to make a thick bacterial suspension.
5.	Heat at 56°C for 30 min and from a small aliquot of the suspension prepare three 10-fold dilutions.
6.	Inoculate molten agar (1:100) at 90°C with each suspension, pour, set and incubate at 37°C for 18 h.
7.	Run a trial assay with the antibiotic used in the concentrations inherited for the working standards and use the weakest suspension giving a confluent growth and clear zone edges for assays.
8.	Dilute all the suspension to that for working use and store at 4°C. If it gives hazy or double zone edges after storage the suspension may be contaminated with vegetative bacteria, in which case repeat the heating in step 5.

Table 6. Pouring plates.

1.	Level the plate using a tripod with adjustable legs (Autodata Ltd). The tops of the legs must rest on the glass or plastic bottom of the plate and not the frame.
2.	Place a short spirit level on the bottom of the plate and use it to level the plate in two planes at right-angles to one another. The level must be previously sterilized on its lower surface by putting it inverted under a germicidal UV lamp.
3.	Pour the molten agar (typically 100 ml for a 25 × 25 cm dish) into the dish and spread evenly while it is still fluid by quickly, but gently, tipping the dish in each direction. Then leave undisturbed, with lid partially off, to set at room temperature until fully firm.
4.	Before use, dry the plate in an incubator for 45−60 min at 37°C with its lid off.
5.	If the plate is not required immediately, store it without drying at 4°C for up to 4 days. Since the plate will slowly dry out, less drying will be needed before use.

since all the requisite replicates of standards, controls and tests can be on a single plate, thus removing the inter-plate errors caused by the different concentrations of the same standard curve being on a number of plates. Large plates can be plastic (Gibco-Biocult

Table 7. Instructions for re-using assay dishes.

1.	Clean the plate as soon as possible after use, since drying of the agar and serum will make it difficult to achieve a reasonable standard of cleanliness.
2.	Loosen the edges of the agar to be discarded with a spatula and tip the agar out into a disposal container. Sterilize the spatula, and autoclave the waste agar before discarding.
3.	Put a generous layer of hypochlorite sanitizer in the plate and its lid, and leave for 20 minutes.
4.	Wearing gloves, scrub the inside of the plate with a soft brush until no residues remain.
5.	Wash the plate thoroughly under running water and then with de-ionized water. Dry the plate.
6.	Put the plate with its lid off and the inverted lid under a germicidal UV light for 30 min.
7.	Store the plate with the lid on.

Table 8. Inoculation of an assay plate.

A. *Surface inoculation*

1.	Fully dry the plate; this takes 45−60 min at 37°C (*Table 6*).
2.	Prepare the correct density of inoculum in 20 ml sterile water and tip it on to the plate, quickly distributing the suspension evenly over the whole surface of the plate.
3.	Tip off any excess into a discard jar and allow to drip for 30 sec. Then re-dry for 10 min at 37°C with the lid off.

B. *Incorporation of an inoculum into agar*

1.	Prepare the bacterial suspension either from a stock suspension of spores held at 4°C, or from a culture frozen at −70°C or over liquid nitrogen.
2.	Either:
	(i) if using spores, add the appropriate volume (*Table 5*) directly to the assay agar at 90°C. The high-temperature assists exsporulation. Cool the inoculated agar to 56°C before pouring[a];
	(ii) if using a vegetative suspension, cool the agar to 50°C. Add the correct volume of suspension for the volume of agar, and also any heat-labile additive at this point.
3.	After pouring, setting and drying (*Table 6*), kill the bacteria (spores or vegetative forms) on the surface by a short exposure to UV light[b].

[a]This avoids distorting plastic dishes or cracking glass ones; very hot agar will also lose excessive amounts of water.
[b]This avoids two types of growth (surface and deep) giving double zone edges.

Ltd) or glass-bottomed with raised stainless steel edges (Mast Labs Ltd or Tissue Culture Services). The latter are preferable, since plastic can be distorted by very hot agar. Although plastic plates can be chemically disinfected and re-used, this is difficult to do satisfactorily. Glass plates may be easily cleaned and disinfected, and with care can be re-used indefinitely (*Table 7*).

5.4.5 *Inoculating plates*

It is necessary to apply a very constant and even inoculum of bacteria to the agar for the consistency of any method. The details are given in *Table 8* for surface and incorporated inocula, respectively. For incorporated inocula the agar layer should not be too thick since it may grow significantly more slowly in the depth of the agar, giving bigger zones near to the base of the plate. The volume of agar in which the organism is inhibited would thus be a truncated cone which, when viewed through the agar, would give a poorly defined zone edge. If a thick layer of agar is needed for the conditions of the assay it is better to have two layers, one with the inoculum in it, and another without inoculum over- or underlying it.

5.4.6 *Replication and randomization of doses*

Because of natural variation in the biological response the standard and test samples must each be put on the plate more than once. Experience has shown that triplicate replications give accuracy adequate for clinical assays. Up to 64 doses in an 8 column × 8 row pattern can be accommodated on a 25 × 25 cm plate, but limiting the number to 45 gives more space between doses and so reduces the possibility of large zones merging, and also avoids zones near the edge of the plate where they seem to be subject to greater variability. It is also easier for the less experienced assayist to work with, and still has space for 10 tests and controls and the usual 5 standards.

The replicate doses for any standard or test are not put next to one another but are scattered on the plate so that they are represented in each area of it. A reason for this is to avoid some influence on the zone diameter (such as being on the edge, a variation in agar thickness, or uneven warming, moisture content or inoculum) being present for all the replicates of a single standard or test. It also makes it more difficult for the person reading the zone sizes to anticipate what they should be on the basis of replicates previously read. The ultimate randomization is the latin square, in which every standard and tests occurs only once in each column or row. This is, however, inconvenient for clinical assays where the number of tests is variable and only 3 replicates are needed. Random patterns which have worked well in my laboratory are given for 30 and 45 dose plates in *Figure 1*.

5.4.7 *Templates*

Doses must be placed accurately on plates. To do this, a card is placed under the plate to be dosed on which the pattern of the doses is marked, 6 columns × 5 rows for 30 doses and 5 columns by 9 rows for 45 doses. The positions of the doses are best marked by bold numbers so as to identify them.

5.4.8 *Applying the doses*

Nowadays, only two methods of dosing the standards and samples to the plate are used for clinical assays. The first, wells cut in the agar and filled with doses, gives larger zone sizes for a given concentration of antibiotic than the second, paper discs soaked in the doses, blotted and applied to the surface of the agar. Both methods are capable of similar precision in practised hands, but the disc method is quicker; unfortunately, its poor sensitivity makes its use infrequent for many clinical assays. The two methods are described in *Tables 9* and *10* respectively. Multi-tine punches are available for the well method, but are expensive and require practice for good results; they are not therefore recommended for the occasional user. Wells may be filled with a Pasteur pipette to the surface of the agar (*Table 9*) or with a fixed volume using an automatic pipette and disposable tip. With practice the former gives as accurate results as the latter and has the virtues of compensating for any slight variations in the thickness of the agar sheet. Surprisingly, the doses rarely seem to leak under the agar layer from the bottom of wells, which is fortunate since this produces zones of irregular shape.

		30-dose (Code 1)			30-dose (Code 2)		
Standard	A	1	13	25	5	19	26
	B	7	20	21	9	12	29
	C	5	12	23	3	16	27
	D	4	15	22	7	14	22
	E	3	19	27	1	18	24
Test	1	6	17	28	10	11	23
	2	2	14	26	4	17	30
	3	8	11	30	8	20	21
	4	9	16	24	2	13	25
	5	10	18	29	6	15	28
		45-dose (Code 1)			45-dose (Code 2)		
Standard	A	3	22	33	11	24	35
	B	13	27	40	5	28	34
	C	11	24	34	1	23	32
	D	9	17	44	4	20	36
	E	2	23	42	7	19	43
Tests	1	5	28	37	2	29	38
	2	1	19	43	14	16	42
	3	10	26	39	15	17	39
	4	7	25	41	3	27	39
	5	12	30	38	9	21	33
	6	4	16	32	6	30	31
	7	14	21	35	13	26	44
	8	6	29	45	10	18	41
	9	15	18	36	12	25	37
	10	8	20	31	8	22	45

Figure 1. Randomization for 30- and 45-dose assay plates. A − E are working standards covering a 16-fold range of concentration. Code 1 and code 2 are alternative designs for each size of assay.

5.4.9 Incubation

Assay plates should be incubated at an even temperature on level shelves. If more than one plate is used for a batch of assays they should not be piled up since the plates in the middle will heat more slowly and mainly from their edges, which means that the indicator organism will grow more quickly there. The incubation temperature is usually 35−37°C, but some bacteria grow better at lower temperatures (30°C for *Sarcina lutea*) and others at higher temperatures (41°C has been used to encourage the rapid growth of *Klebsiella edwardsii* so as to give the earliest possible result (9)). Zone sizes, and hence sensitivity of an assay, can often be increased by a period of pre-diffusion of 1−2 h in the cold, either in the refrigerator or at room temperature. It is rarely needed for clinical assays. *K.edwardsii* NCTC 10896 taken from liquid nitrogen will give readable zones in 4 h when grown on Oxoid DST agar at 37°C, although not on the more alkaline agars recommended by some workers. For most assays 18 h incubation is used.

Table 9. Applying doses by wells cut in the agar.

The inoculum must be applied before dosing.

1. Choose a clean, sharp cork borer of a diameter appropriate for the method in use, and flame and cool it before use.
2. Place the dish over the template (see Section 5.4.7) showing where the wells are to be punched. Make sure that the surface of the agar is readily accessible to your hand with your elbows resting on the bench.
3. With a single movement exactly perpendicular to the plate cut a well with the cork borer to the base of the plate in each position. Usually the plug of agar remains in place because of its surface tension to the base of the plate.
4. Remove each plug with the tip of a small scalpel. This is best done by 'spearing' the plug near to, but not on, its edge and easing the edge towards the opposite side to open up the cut. The plug can then be lifted out. The process sounds complicated, but can be a quick one with practice.
5. Take a clean glass Pasteur pipette or Pastette (plastic disposable pipette) for each dose. The former are easier to use for accurate filling of the wells. Draw up enough of a dose for all the replicates of that dose, usually 3; about 0.6 ml is generally sufficient.
6. Squeeze the pipette so as the lower meniscus is at its tip and there is no air below the fluid. Put the tip on the base of the plate in the well to be filled and gently fill the well from the bottom. Stop when the meniscus in the well flattens. Do not overfill so that the fluid spills on to the surface of the agar.
7. Remove the pipette, and then fill the wells of the other replicates of the sample or standard.
8. Discard the pipette and repeat steps 5 to 8 for each sample and standard.

Table 10. Applying the dose by paper discs.

The inoculum must be applied before dosing.

1. Place the dish over the template and put out the number of sterile paper discs (Whatman AA 6 mm discs) you are likely to need as a single layer in a sterile Petri dish. Do not pick the discs out of the stock packet with contaminated forceps.
2. With a fine pair of forceps pick up a disc and dip it into the dose to be used. Wait 2 sec. Do not lose it into the dose.
3. Remove the disc and lay it on a double thickness of sterile, clean blotting paper. Leave it there long enough for the excess fluid to be adsorbed (until the ring of fluid in the blotting paper stops expanding).
4. Repeat step 2 with any replicates of the dose, usually 3 in all.
5. Dry the forceps on some blotting paper, especially their inner grips, and pick up each disc in turn and apply it in its correct position, gently pressing it down so that it makes contact with the agar all over its under surface.
6. Dry the forceps again before moving to another disc.

5.4.10 *Zone measurement*

This is a critical step in obtaining accurate results since there may be as little as 10 mm difference in the zone diameter between the top and bottom standards of an assay which differ by 16-fold in concentration. Measuring zones by ruler or callipers and ruler is unacceptable. A better but more time-consuming method is to use vernier callipers; these are set by touching the points to the edge of the zone to be read at its maximum diameter using the naked eye. Even illumination or transillumination of the plate is essential, and the lighting conditions should be optimized to give the sharpest visualizations of the zone edges. Callipers capable of feeding their measurements directly into a small computer are available (Autodata Ltd).

An optical zone reader (Autodata Ltd or Leebrook Instruments Co. Ltd) is essential

30 dose plate (code 1)
Patient I.D................
Antibiotic.................
Date............
Plate No....
Conc of lowest std .... mg/l
Dilution factor between stds.......

	ZONE NO.	Diameter	ZONE NO.	Diameter	ZONE NO.	Diameter	MEAN DIAMETER
STD A	1		13		25		
STD B	7		20		21		
STD C	5		12		23		
STD D	4		15		22		
STD E	3		19		27		
Test 1	6		17		28		
Test 2	2		14		26		
Test 3	8		11		30		
Test 4	9		16		24		
Test 5	10		18		29		

Figure 2. Example proforma for recording and derandomizing zone sizes.

for a laboratory regularly doing plate assays. The plate is transilluminated and an image of a zone magnified 5−10 times is back-projected on to a ground-glass screen with a measuring graticule in it. It is thus possible to read zone diameters accurately to the nearest 0.2 mm. Irregularities of shape can be detected easily.

Zones are read in order, for example each row from left to right, and not according to the nature of the doses. Thus it would be incorrect to read sequentially all the replicates for a standard or test since this would introduce subjective bias. A pre-prepared form is used to record the zones and then to de-randomize and aggregate the replicates for each sample and standard. An example proforma is given in *Figure 2*.

5.4.11 *Determining the results (Table 11)*

Fitting a curve to plotted points involves subjectivity, and the best method of producing a best-fit line is by calculation based on the polynominal formula

$$Y = a + bx + cx^2$$

as described by Bennett *et al.* (10). A more general method has been developed by Perkins (11) applicable to 4 to 7 standards, inclusive, with any constant dilution factor between them. The method of calculation is complex and should only be done on a routine basis using a calculator or computer programmed to solve the various equations. The program can also be used to de-randomize the zones, so zones may be entered

Table 11. Determining the results.

1.	Calculate the mean zone sizes for each standard or test.
2.	Plot the mean zone sizes against the logarithm of the concentration of the standards. Alternatively, rather than calculating the logarithms, use 2-cycle semi-logarithmic graph paper, with the concentrations on the ordinate and zones sizes on the abscissa.
3.	Join the points with a flexible rule. A less satisfactory method is to join adjacent points with a series of straight lines. Do not join all the points with a single straight line as the best fit for a 16-fold difference in concentration is usually a gentle curve.
4.	Ignore a single point which blatantly does not fit on the chosen line, although this may well reduce the accuracy of the results. If there is more than one point not fitting on the line, repeat the assay, although an approximate and provisional result for a test may be obtainable in an emergency.

in the order in which they are read. When the dilution factor between the standards and the concentration of the lowest of them are also entered, the program can calculate the concentration of the unknown samples. It can also give a value for the goodness of fit of the observed mean zone sizes of the standards.

5.5 Dealing with mixtures of antibiotics

The presence of an antibiotic other than that to be assayed may be apparent for the following reasons.

(i) The laboratory may be told about it by the requesting clinician. Unfortunately, it is not widely appreciated that antibiotics may persist in the body long after their administration has ceased, particularly if renal failure is present.

(ii) The results are pharmacologically impossible, that is, they are too high for the dose given. Usually this is only readily apparent if the error is gross.

(iii) Atypical zone edges may be seen, such as indistinct edges when they should be sharp, or double zone edges.

It is important to try to ascertain the identity of the second antibiotic from the patient's records, since the nature of the action to circumvent its presence will depend on it.

5.5.1 *Methods*

It is often difficult to make a microbiological assay entirely selective. The best method of dealing with a mixture is therefore to use a completely different method, such as an immunologically based assay or HPLC, and this should be done if at all possible. Selective microbiological assay may be achievable as follows.

(i) By removing unwanted antibiotics through enzymatic degradation. This is the preferred method since it is more reliable than using a selectively resistant indicator organism (see below). The enzyme is added to the sample and not to the assay agar so that the antibiotic is completely removed before the assay begins. A typical example is the use of β-lactamase to degrade β-lactam antibiotics (see *Table 12*).

(ii) By antagonizing the activity of antibiotics. In this type of method the antibiotic remains in the sample and diffuses into the agar, but is prevented from inhibiting the indicator organism by a chemical antagonist in the agar. The antagonist is not added to the sample. The inhibition may be by chemically binding the an-

Table 12. Degradation or inactivation of unwanted antibiotics in a microbiological assay.

Unwanted antibiotic	Method
Aminoglycoside	Sodium lauryl sulphate 2% or sodium polyanethol sulphonate 0.6-1%, in the assay agar
Amphotericin B	Heat sample to 100°C for 45 min, and ultrafilter
β-Lactam agents	20% of a suitable β-lactamase in sample
Cycloserine	D-Alanine, 20 mg l^{-1} in agar
Flucytosine	Cytosine in agar
Polymyxin	Sodium polyanethol sulphonate, 1% in agar
Sulphonamide	p-Aminobenzoic acid 50 mg l^{-1} and thymidine 5 mg l^{-1} in agar
Trimethoprim	Thymidine 5 mg l^{-1} in agar
Tetracycline	$MgSO_4$ 50 g l^{-1} in agar

tibiotic and rendering it inactive (for example tetracycline with $MgSO_4$) or by acting at the subcellular level on the organism's metabolism (for example trimethoprim and thymidine). Further examples are in *Table 12*.

(iii) By removal of antibiotic from the sample by binding. Aminoglycosides can be removed from serum samples on to an insoluble binding agent, such as phosphocellulose powder or an ion exchange resin. For doses applied on paper discs, an elegant method is to use 9 mm diameter phosphocellulose paper discs (Whatman P81 ion-exchange paper). This will remove clinically encountered concentrations of aminoglycosides while allowing most other antibiotics to diffuse freely into the agar. Since the dose is restricted to 9 µl the sensitivity of the method is limited. The sensitivity can be increased by putting clean P81 discs on the positions of the doses and dosing the plate with Whatman AA discs (which hold about 25 µl) on top of them, 'top hat' fashion. The use of acid or basic ion exchange resins to remove antibiotics from samples is described by Reeves and Holt (12).

(iv) By the use of a selectively resistant indicator organism. For dealing with a known mixture it may be possible to select an indicator organism with total resistance to the second antibiotic at the concentration encountered, for example, a *Streptococcus pyogenes* to assay penicillin in the presence of gentamicin. For selecting between some antibiotics, indicator organisms may be used which have acquired, as opposed to inherent, resistance. These strains require considerable care to ensure that resistance (for example, encoded by a plasmid) is not lost, and they should be subcultured on antibiotic-containing media. This type of method in particular requires very careful control (see Section 5.5.2).

(v) By separation of mixtures before assay. Mixtures of antibiotics can be separated by high voltage electrophoresis in agar and assayed by bioautography (7,12).

5.5.2 Controls

Whichever method is used to circumvent the effect of second antibiotics, it must be adequately controlled. Known concentrations of the antibiotic to be assayed should be spiked with realistic concentrations of the second antibiotic and subjected to the whole process as if they were samples. The method can only be accepted for use if the results are unaffected by the second antibiotics.

Table 13. Basic conditions for the clinical assay of antibiotics.

Antibiotic	Assay agar	Indicator organism	NCTC number	Inoculum[a]	Dosing method (and size in mm)	Range of working standards (mg l[-1])
Ampicillin ⎱ Amoxycillin ⎰	PSA[b]	*B. subtilis*	10400	I	Disc (6)	0.625 – 10
Carbenicillin	PSA	*P. aeruginosa*	10701	S	Well (9)	6.25 – 100
Cephalothin ⎫ Cefamandole ⎬ Cephazolin ⎪ Cephalexin ⎭	PSA	*B. subtilis*	10400	I	Disc (6)	Vary as required
Cefuroxime[h]	PSA	*E. coli*	–	S	Disc (6)	
Cefotaxime	PSA	*M. morgani*	–	S	Disc (6)	2.5 – 40
Ceftazidime ⎱ Cefotetan ⎰	PSA	*E. coli*	10418	S	Well (6) Disc (6)	1.25 – 20 1 – 16
Chloramphenicol	DST[c]	*E. coli*	–	S	Well (6)	2.5 – 40
Clindamycin	PSA	*S. aureus*	6571	I	Disc (6)	1.25 – 20
Flucytosine	YNB[d,e]	*C. pseudotropicalis*	–	S	Disc (6)	0.5 – 8
Gentamicin ⎫ Netilmicin ⎬ Tobramycin ⎪ Amikacin ⎭	DST	*K. edwardsii*[g]	10896	S	Well (9)	1 – 16 2.5 – 40
Penicillin	PSA	*B. subtilis*	10400	I	Disc (6)	0.5 – 8
Rifampicin	DST[f]	*S. aureus*	–	S	Disc (6)	0.125 – 2
Streptomycin	DST	*K. aerogenes* (Southmead strain)	–	S	Well (9)	2.5 – 40
Vancomycin	DST	*B. subtilis*	10400	I	Well (6)	2 – 32

[a]I = incorporated; S = surface.
[b]PSA = Penassay Seed Agar (Difco).
[c]DST = Diagnostic Sensitivity Test Agar (Oxoid).
[d]YNB = Yeast Nitrogen Base (Difco).
[e]Supplemented with 1% glucose and 0.15% asparagine.
[f]Supplemented with KH_2PO_4, 3% of a 1 M solution.
[g]For neonatal samples with small sample volume it may be necessary to use *B. pumilis* to gain sufficient sensitivity; this reduces the selectivity of the assay.
[h]Another assay for cefuroxime uses *B. subtilis* MB235 spore suspension and Oxoid agar No 2 with 0.25% sodium citrate.

5.6 Summary of methodology of agar plate assays

The basic conditions for a number of assays of clinical importance are given in *Table 13*.

6. IMMUNOASSAYS

6.1 General principles

To assay a drug by an immunological method there are two basic requirements: firstly an antibody with specificity for the drug, and secondly, the drug labelled with a measurable or active group, such as a radioisotope, a fluorochrome, or an enzyme.

The labelled drug must still have specificity for the antibody. In an immunoassay, drug in the sample or standard compete with labelled drug for a limited amount of antibody. Within limits, the greater the amount of unlabelled drug introduced into the system in the sample the smaller will be the amount of labelled drug bound to the antibody. The relative amounts of the reagents are adjusted so that there is a graded response in the amount of labelled drug – antibody binding to the desired concentration of drug to be measured. A calibration curve can be plotted by assaying a series of standard concentrations; plotting % binding of the labelled drug against log concentration gives a sigmoid curve which can be straightened to a large extent by log logit transformation.

To measure the amount of labelled drug bound to the antibody, it can be separated from unbound label (a *heterogeneous assay*, such as one with radioisotopes), or the antibody modifies the properties of the label in such a way that binding can be measured without separation (a *homogeneous assay*, such as some enzyme immunoassays). Heterogeneous immunoassays involve an extra step, separation, which can be labour-intensive and may introduce inaccuracy. They are therefore not much used for clinical assays of antibiotics. Homogeneous assays have complex and critical reagents and are therefore only usually available as kits for antibiotic assays. Only three kit assays are in widespread use in the UK and therefore these will be described here. They are EMIT (Syva UK Ltd), an enzyme immunoassay; TDA (Ames Division), a substrate-labelled fluoroimmunoassay; and TDx (Abbott Laboratories Ltd), a polarization fluoro-immunoassay.

6.2 Characteristics of immunoassays

Not surprisingly, immunoassays, exhibit good specificity and are therefore highly suitable for clinical assays where more than one type of antibiotic is often present, although cross-reaction of varying extent can occur between antibiotics of the same general type, such as the aminoglycosides. By the same token, they are sometimes unsuitable for antibiotics which undergo degradation or metabolism, since the products of these processes (metabolates or metabolites, respectively) may resemble closely the parent drug and thus be at least partially immunoreactive to the same antibody. Immunoassays are therefore most suitable for highly stable antibiotics, such as aminoglycosides. They also exist as commercial kits for vancomycin and chloramphenicol, but there have been difficulties in developing a highly specific assay for these, and at least one of the assays measures to some extent vancomycin metabolites as well as vancomycin (see Section 6.3).

Immunoassays can be made very sensitive and, indeed, a first step for clinical assays is usually a large dilution of the sample. A corollary to this is that only a very small sample is required. Homogeneous immunoassays can be very fast, giving answers in a few minutes. Because they have reagents which are difficult to develop, the kits are often expensive, and the precise technical needs of the equipment can make it very costly. In spite of this, they have become the most widely used methods for assaying aminoglycosides in the UK because of their convenience and their ease of obtaining accurate and fast results. The reagents are difficult to develop 'in house', and industry may take some years to produce an assay for a new antibiotic. Thus immunoassays, unlike microbiological and HPLC assays, are not adaptable methods.

6.2.1 *The EMIT assay*

In the EMIT assay the drug (for example gentamicin) is labelled by being covalently bonded to bacterial glucose-6-phosphate dehydrogenase in such a way as to retain enzyme activity and immunospecificity for the anti-drug antibody. Human glucose-6-phosphate in the serum does not interfere because it uses NADP and not NAD as a cofactor. When anti-drug antibody binds to the labelled antibiotic the enzyme is inhibited, and thus the higher the amount of unlabelled drug in the sample or standard, the higher the enzyme activity, since there is less antibody to inhibit the enzyme. The enzyme activity is measured spectrophometrically in a reaction-rate analyser. Since the absorbance of the reaction mixture is changing rapidly, EMIT assays require precise equipment. Equipment options available are:

(i)   the Syva spectrophotometer, to which samples are offered manually;
(ii)   the Syva autocarousel sampler connected to the spectrophotometer;
(iii)   the Syva QST;
(iv)   an automatic analyser on which EMIT reagents are used.

The more automated methods give the most precise results, although the manual spectrophotometer is capable of giving results perfectly acceptable for clinical assays. Detailed protocols will not be given here since they are available from the manufacturers for users of the equipment. It is extremely important that the flow path of the spectrophotometer is kept as clean as possible. At the end of an assay run it must be cleaned with 'Floclean' (Gilford Diagnostics) and then washed through with at least 50 ml of de-ionized water.

6.2.2 *TDA*

This method is also called substrate-labelled fluoroimmunoassay (SLFIA) since the drug is labelled with enzyme substrate, not the enzyme as in EMIT. The reaction is followed in a fluorimeter because its product is fluorescent, and the amount of the product produced is measured at the end of a fixed time period. The drug is bound to a fluorogenic compound, umbelliferyl-β-D-galactoside. The fluorogenic drug reagent (FDR) is not fluorescent but is hydrolysed to a fluorescent product by β-galactosidase. When antibody to the drug binds to the FDR the action of the enzyme is inhibited. Thus the more unlabelled drug there is in the system from a sample or standard, the less antibody is available for binding to the FDR, and the more the enzyme can release the fluorescence, and thus drug concentration is proportional to fluorescence.

The reagents are available in kit form, as is the exact protocol for their use in the equipment designed for the test, the Fluorostat (Ames). The later steps of adding the FDR and measuring the fluorescence require precise timing, since the equipment is not automated.

6.2.3 *TDx*

In the TDx system the drug is labelled with fluorescein. The reagent fluoresces when exposed to polarizing exciting light, but because the drug – fluorescein molecule is small and undergoes rapid rotation in solution, the emitted light is not polarized. Antibody bound to the reagent increases its molecular weight very greatly so that its rotation

Table 14. Cross-reactions between aminoglycosides in immunoassays.

	Can cross-react in an assay for:
Gentamicin	Netilmicin, sissomicin
Netilmicin	Gentamicin
Tobramycin	Kanamycin, amikacin
Amikacin	Tobramycin, kanamycin

is slowed, and some of the emitted light is then polarized. The more unlabelled drug there is in the system, the less antibody is available for complexing to the drug−fluorescein reagent, and the less the emitted polarized light. Thus drug concentration is inversely proportional to the signal, the reverse of the TDA method. The reagents are thus relatively simple but the equipment to measure the change in polarization of the emitted light is very sophisticated and uses an electrically charged liquid-crystal polarizer and considerable computing power. The TDx analyser is highly automated, requiring only the reagents to be inserted and the standards of samples put on a carousel; it gives a very fast result. The protocol given by the manufacturer should be followed. There is a reminder to remove the reagents from this warm environment at the end of a run, and this must be done if they are not to be destroyed.

6.3 **Cross-reactivity**

Because of the chemical similarity of the aminoglycosides it is not surprising that they can cross-react in immunoassays (*Table 14*). Thus care should be taken in clinical assays if there is a possibility of more than one being present; in view of their very long plasma half-life in renal failure, interference from previously prescribed aminoglycosides should be considered. The EMIT assay for chloramphenicol seems to be reasonably specific in spite of the presence of metabolites in human samples. It does not measure the pro-drug administered intravenously, chloramphenicol succinate. The TDx assay for vancomycin gives over-high results in patients with renal failure because the antibody reacts with one of the inactive metabolites which accumulates along with the vancomycin. The newer EMIT assay is more specific for vancomycin, although still not as specific as microbiological or HPLC assay.

7. HPLC

HPLC is the abbreviation for two descriptions intended to mean the same thing, high-performance or high-pressure liquid chromatography.

7.1 **General principles of HPLC**

A mobile phase of solvents is pumped over a fixed stationary phase. A sample in solution is introduced into the mobile phase and is separated by differential retention on the stationary phase, following which the mobile phase passes to a detector where the components in the sample produce a response. The components are identified by their retention time (the time taken for a component to appear following its introduction into the mobile phase), and sometimes, in addition, by their characteristic absorption spectrum; they are quantitated by measuring peak height or area, either on a chart recorder trace or by using an integrator.

7.2 **Characteristics of HPLC**

The analysis of a single sample often takes only a few minutes, although if more than one drug is being assayed simultaneously some will probably have relatively long retention times. The method can give a high precision and usually has sufficient sensitivity to measure the concentrations of antibiotics found in the blood.

A high degree of specificity is possible, by which compounds as closely related as the gentamicin components in the dose form or the epimers of latamoxef can be separated. Usually it is easily possible to separate antibiotics from their often inactive metabolites. It must be remembered, however, that totally unrelated drugs which may be given to a patient can co-elute with antibiotics. HPLC is easily automated by using an autosampler and microprocessor-controlled or computer-controlled data collection. Because analysis is sequential (samples are assayed one after another), HPLC is very time-consuming for high numbers of assays.

7.3 **Equipment for HPLC**

The equipment is shown in *Figure 3*. The first element in the flow path after the reservoir of mobile phase is a pump. This must be capable of delivering up to 10 ml min^{-1} of mobile phase in a pulse-free flow at pressures up to 4000 p.s.i. The injector is used for introducing samples into the mobile phase at pressure. A common sample size is in the range $10-20$ μl. The injector must deliver a very reproducible sample size if imprecision is not to occur. Unpredictable variations in sample size can be compensated for by adding an internal standard to a precisely known concentration in every sample and comparing the response obtained with it to that from the unknown. Detectors may measure UV absorbance, fluorescence, refractive index, electrochemical activity, etc. The first type is by far the most common and may have a fixed (selectable) or variable wavelength at which the absorbance is measured of the portion of mobile phase in the flow cell. Until recently, variable wavelength detectors were inferior in terms of sensitivity and baseline noise, although clearly more versatile. Fixed wavelength detectors (with a choice, for example, of 313, 280, 254, 229 and 214 nm) are stable and sensitive and, being often cheaper than fully variable instruments, are fully adequate for most routine clinical assays of antibiotics. The signal output from the detector is fed to a recording device, usually either a chart recorder or a recording integrator; for a small number of routine assays the former is adequate and cheaper.

7.4 **Principles of separation in HPLC**

Separation of the components of a sample is done on the stationary phase in the analytical column, which is usually a stainless steel tube of approximately 4 mm internal diameter and $10-25$ cm in length. For rapid and efficient separation microparticulate stationary phases are used $(5-10$ μm$)$. The analytical column, which is expensive to buy and very difficult to pack in the laboratory, is protected in biological assays by a guard column which retains irreversibly absorbed molecules. The commonest type of chromatography used in clinical antibiotic assays is called reverse phase because, unlike

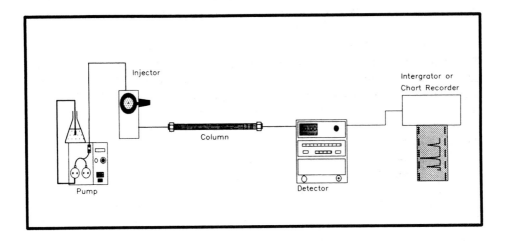

Figure 3. Diagrammatic representation of HPLC equipment.

traditional chromatography, it uses a non-polar stationary phase and a polar (watery) mobile phase. The latter is well suited to biological samples since they are fully miscible with it. A typical column packing uses silica particles with chemically bonded octadecylsilyl ($C_{18}H_{37}Si$; ODS). Acidic antibiotics are assayed in a mobile phase buffered to a low pH which suppresses their ionization and therefore causes them to be held back on the column. They thus elute after the bulk of the contaminating biological material has passed. Basic drugs may require an acidic ion-pairing reagent in the mobile phase because high pH mobile phases can damage the packing. In ion-pair (IP) chromatography a hydrophobic counter-ion (such as heptanesulphonic acid) is used to pair ionically with the drug to be assayed, the heptane moiety having affinity for the packing and thus causing the drug to be retained.

For a given stationary phase, the desired separation may be achieved by adjusting the mobile phase. This usually consists of a mixture of water and an organic solvent (such as methanol) with a modifier (such as buffer, IP reagent) to give the required selectivity. Generally speaking, increasing the proportion of organic solvent decreases the retention time of a given solute. The aim is to have the shortest possible retention time compatible with separating the target solute from the other solutes.

7.5 Sample preparation

All particulate matter must be removed and the matrix of the sample must not precipitate in the mobile phase. Thus, to satisfy the latter, serum samples must usually have their protein removed by precipitation (for example, by mixing serum 1:1 with acetonitrile or methanol and centrifuging) or ultrafiltration. Urines may simply require centrifugation and dilution.

7.6 **Calibration**

As with other assays, working standards are required. These are treated in the same way as samples. Usually a linear standard curve with an intercept of zero will result if the standard concentrations are plotted against detector response (peak height or area). When drugs are assayed in serum which is precipitated the percentage recovery over a range of relevant concentrations must be established. If the recovery is reproducible, accurate calibration is possible. An internal standard may help in improving the precision of an assay.

7.7 **Methods for individual antibiotics**

It is clearly not possible to give the full scope of methods here, but those for most antimicrobials can be found in Reeves and Ullmann (13). Just two methods will be given here as an example and because they are the most common HPLC assays used clinically. Most microbiologists are unfamiliar with HPLC, and, since it is an intensely practical technique, I recommend anyone wishing to use it to attend an appropriate course or to spend some time in a department where it is used routinely.

7.7.1 *Chloramphenicol*

Chloramphenicol is given orally as the palmitate. The parenteral formulation is the microbiologically inactive chloramphenicol succinate which is hydrolysed by esterases to chloramphenicol. Its plasma half-life is $2-5$ h in adults, but may be as long as 28 h in neonates. Most chloramphenicol is conjugated with glucuronic acid; small amounts are converted to other metabolites. Since the conversion of the succinate to chloramphenicol can be slow, measurement of the 'peak' blood level should be delayed to 2 h after an intravenous dose. If chloramphenicol succinate is also measured by the method used, its concentration must not be summated with chloramphenicol for the purpose of reporting.

The method used in our own laboratory (L.O.White, unpublished) uses a μBondapak C18 Z-module column (Waters Associates) and a mobile phase of water:methanol: phosphoric acid $(80-88:12-20:1)$ pumped at up to 5 ml min^{-1}. Two fixed-wavelength detectors are used sequentially at 254 and 214 nm. The ratio of absorbance at the two wavelengths acts as a check on the specificity since chloramphenicol has a peak size at 254 nm of about half that at 214 nm, whereas phenobarbitone, a not uncommon interfering drug with a rather similar retention time, has only a tiny peak at 254 nm compared to 214 nm. Many cephalosporins have similar retention times to chloramphenicol. β-Lactamase can be added to samples to remove interference from β-lactam antibiotics. The injection volume is only 20 μl, making it ideally suited to monitoring concentrations in neonates.

7.7.2 *Benzylpenicillin*

Being a weak acid, this antibiotic is well-suited to reverse-phase separation. It is not particularly UV absorbent and requires a detector with a low wavelength (214 nm) for sufficient sensitivity for clinical assays. In the body benzylpenicillin breaks down spontaneously to the analogous penicilloate, which elutes quicker than the parent. A simple, rapid assay for benzylpenicillin uses Hypersil 5-ODS with a mobile phase of methanol:water:phosphoric acid (35:64:1) with UV detection at 214 nm.

7.7.3 *Other antibiotics*

The antibiotics most frequently assayed clinically, the aminoglycosides, are not well suited to HPLC assay because they lack both a chromatophore and a fluorophore. Derivatization is therefore necessary, but is complex to use with serum samples. Most β-lactams and any stable metabolites can be readily assayed by HPLC. A newer use has been for the fluoroquinolones, particularly ciprofloxacin. By using a simple preparation step, vancomycin can be readily assayed. Other clinical assays which are best done by HPLC are trimethoprim, sulphonamides, nitroimidazoles, flucytosine, and ketoconazole.

8. QUALITY ASSURANCE

Quality assurance (QA) may be internal and external, and is the process by which quality is measured by controls and corrected if necessary. It also covers the institution of good working practices.

8.1 **Internal controls**

These are samples containing in known concentration the analyte to be assayed. They can be locally prepared or may come as part of a commercial assay kit. When they are prepared locally, the primary source of material should preferably be separate from that used to prepare working standards, otherwise inaccuracies may be perpetuated. Similarly the preparation must be kept entirely separate, although it follows the same lines on that for stock (Section 5.2) and working standards (Section 5.3). Amino-glycosides are sometimes adsorbed on to glass tubes and internal controls are best stored in polypropylene tubes with screw caps (Sarstedt Ltd). Internal controls are stored in small volumes (0.5 − 1 ml), preferably at −70°C.

For any particular assay the range of concentration of internal controls should cover that of the working standards. At least one internal control and preferably two of differing

Table 15. Antibiotic concentrations (mg l^{-1}) in the blood related to possible toxicity and efficacy.

	Accepted effective concentration	*Possibly or known toxic concentrations*
Chloramphenicol	10 − 25	> 40
Aminoglycosides		
Gentamicin	'Peak' > 5(> 8 in	> 2(pre-dose)
Tobramycin	enterobacterial	? > 12('peak')
Netilmicin	pneumonia	
Amikacin	'Peak' > 20	> 10(pre-dose)
		> 32('peak')
Benzylpenicillin	Varies with pathogen	> 100
Vancomycin	25	> 10(pre-dose); > 50(post-dose)
Flucytosine	20 − 50	> 80

concentrations should be used in each batch of assays. They should be coded when prepared with the values for each coded tube kept in a book, so that the person doing the assay does not know the exact value until the assay is complete.

The result of every internal control should be recorded. When a number of values for a control are available, its mean and standard deviation can be calculated and recorded on a chart for ease of reference. When an assay batch is done it should not be accepted if the internal control is outside its mean ± two standard deviations. When no such data are available, a single control should be within ± 10% of its target value for acceptance of the batch. If an internal control is outside the limit of acceptability, the batch should not be reported until the control gives a satisfactory result or a reason established for the errant result.

8.2 External controls

These, as part of external QA, should always be done at regular intervals, and participation in a national or international QA is therefore essential. In the UK, enquiries should be made to DMRQC, Central Public Health Laboratory, Colindale, London. Clearly, poor results in external QA should cause concern and must always be drawn to the attention of the head of the department.

9. INTERPRETATION OF RESULTS

The final step in a clinical assay of an antibiotic is the interpretation of the result into clinical action. The significance of the result should initially be assessed by a properly trained medical microbiologist, who should contact the clinician concerned to initiate appropriate action. Many antibiotic assay results have an immediate and direct relevance to the management of the patient, and should therefore be telephoned and not sent by internal or external post alone. The basis for the relevance of assay results has been discussed in detail elsewhere (1,5) and in this chapter (Sections 2.1.1, 2.1.2).

Pre-dose (trough) concentrations greater than those in *Table 15* should be avoided if possible, although this may be difficult in patients with renal failure if good peak concentrations are required more than once a day. The relationship of so-called peak concentrations, usually measured one hour post dose, to toxicity is less clear (see 2.1.2). Levels greater than those for effective therapy (*Table 15*) should be avoided, however, as a matter of general principle.

10. ACKNOWLEDGEMENTS

I am deeply grateful to my staff, especially Martin Bywater, Alan Holt, Andrew Lovering and Les White, who developed many of the practical details described here and unstintingly gave advice on this chapter.

11. REFERENCES

1. Reeves,D.S. and White,L.O. (1981) In *Therapeutic Drug Monitoring*. Richens,A. and Marks,V. (eds), Churchill Livingstone, Edinburgh, p. 445.
2. Wise,R. (1978) In *Laboratory Methods in Antimicrobial Chemotherapy*. Reeves,D.S., Phillips,I., Williams,J.D. and Wise,R. (eds), Churchill Livingstone, Edinburgh, p. 144.
3. Reeves,D.S. and Paton,J.H. (1987) *Care of the Critically Ill*, **3**, 100.
4. Reeves,D.S. (1985) *Lancet*, **ii**, 1420.

5. Reeves,D.S. (1980) *Infection*, **8** (suppl. 3), S5313.
6. White,L.O. and Reeves,D.S. (1983) In *Antibiotics: Assessment of Antimicrobial Activity and Resistance.* Russell,A.D. and Quesnel,L.B. (eds), Society for Applied Bacteriology Technical Series No. 18, Academic Press, London, p. 199.
7. Reeves,D.S. and Bywater,M.J. (1976) In *Selected Topics in Clinical Bacteriology.* de Louvois,J. (ed.), Bailliere Tindall, London, p. 21.
8. White,L.O. and Reeves,D.S. (1981) In *Therapeutic Drug Monitoring.* Richens,A. and Marks,M. (eds), Churchill Livingstone, Edinburgh, p. 456.
9. Shanson,D.C. and Hince,C. (1977) *J. Clin. Path.*, **30**, 521.
10. Bennett,J.V., Brodie,J.L., Benner,E.J. and Kirby,W.M.M. (1966) *Appl. Microbiol.*, **14**, 170.
11. Perkins,A. (1978) In *Laboratory Methods in Antimicrobial Chemotherapy.* Reeves,D.S., Phillips,I., Williams,J.D. and Wise,R. (eds), Churchill Livingstone, Edinburgh, p. 157.
12. Reeves,D.S. and Holt,H.A. (1975) *J. Clin. Path.*, **28**, 435.
13. Reeves,D.S. and Ullmann,U. (1986) (eds), *High Performance Liquid Chromatography in Medical Microbiology.* Fischer, Stuttgart (ISBN 3-437-10983-9).

CHAPTER 9

Reporting to clinicians, laboratory record-keeping and computerization

PAUL M.COCKCROFT

1. INTRODUCTION

No matter how excellent the science of microbiology practised in a clinical laboratory, for maximum effect the diagnostic and therapeutic information generated depends on a fast and accurate method of transmission to the bedside. Indeed, the laboratory findings may also need sifting and sorting to produce a report that is valuable to the clinician. There is inevitably other information generated which, in itself, does not need passing to the clinician in order to manage the patient, but when collected with information from other cases will form a reservoir of valuable data, for example for use in studying the epidemiology of a particular disease. For this reason it is vital that good laboratory records be kept in an easily accessible form. In recent times the use of computers has made this possible and enabled more rapid recognition of the changing pattern of organisms and related diseases.

2. REPORTING TO CLINICIANS

2.1 Principles and methods

Quite obviously the information reported to the clinician who generated the request should convey as rapidly, concisely and accurately as possible the results of laboratory investigations and should answer the implied question that is being posed by the sending of the specimen. Often the clinical information supplied directly poses a question, for example '? pneumococcal lobar pneumonia'. This report must obviously attempt to answer that question, but may also provide information on the specimen of sputum which has not directly been requested, such as reporting the presence of *Mycobacterium tuberculosis*.

Whichever method of generating reports is chosen, the priority must be to make them clear and concise. The simplest may be a handwritten report on pre-printed paper or on the form used for requesting the investigation, though the latter would not allow the information to be kept by the laboratory unless copies were made. While these require technical and medical staff to have good handwriting, they have the advantage of being relatively rapid to produce. Typed reports are often clearer to read but require transcribing, thus there is the potential for error, and they are also more time-consuming to produce.

Whether or not the report is typed, a copy should be kept in the laboratory for reference. This can be achieved relatively easily by use of double or treble-leaved 'No carbon required' (NCR) paper, or by photocopying the report.

A computerized reporting system gives further flexibility by allowing the production of multiple copies of reports and storage of information, but requires the additional step of entering all the relevant data into the system. There is, however, also the further potential benefit of making information available at source through visual display units (VDUs) sited in clinical areas.

Urgent results must be transmitted by a rapid method, and it is normal for these to be telephoned to the clinician. A reliable method of identification of such results is essential both for results which the requesting doctor considers urgent and those which are urgent by the very nature of the laboratory results. When the results themselves determine that urgent transmission is necessary, laboratory policy should ensure that all staff understand the need to inform a responsible person of them.

Because reporting may take a matter of days to complete, it is important that interim reports are sent out as soon as useful diagnostic information is produced. This is obviously most important in the case of seriously ill hospital patients and reports should not be held back until all tests are completed unless to do so would not affect the clinical management of the patient. Cumulative reports of a series of specimens can be particularly helpful to follow the changes in certain parameters, as, for example, variations in serological titres.

2.1.1 *Standardization*

Standardization of the format of written reports is useful and may consist of the use of rubber stamps to list the presence or absence of the recognized pathogens sought from a specimen (e.g. 'Trichomonas not seen; *Candida* species not isolated', reported for a vaginal swab), or to list the antibiotics against which an isolate has been tested. It aids the legibility of the report and the ease by which information can be assimilated by the experienced clinician. Alternatives to rubber stamps may be the use of pre-printed adhesive labels or pre-printed report forms which can incorporate lists of antibiotics to which the results of sensitivity tests are added. The actual choice of antibiotics to be tested is a complex process which is discussed in individual chapters.

2.1.2 *Interpretative reporting*

Such is the complexity of modern-day medical practice that the clinical specialist is unlikely to be an expert in pathology too. The medical microbiologist, therefore, plays an important role in interpreting the laboratory results and providing the clinician with a judgement on the significance of the various findings from a specimen. These are usually judged on the basis of clinical information on the request form, but when advising on the results of diagnostic specimens from seriously ill patients a full knowledge of all relevant factors should be obtained by visiting the patient and talking to the clinician. It is, however, reasonable to lay down simple principles of reporting. For example, the clinician will be confused by a long list of the bacteria constituting the normal flora of the mouth from a swab sent to determine the presence of a fungal superinfection. All that is required is a report stating the answer to his question, for example 'Heavy growth of *Candida* sp. isolated'. Such simple principles can easily be followed by scientific staff, but medical opinion should be readily available to advise on unusual results and decide appropriate structuring of the report. Similarly, rules (applied with a degree of flexibility, in cases of doubt) can be set to determine which organisms from which specimens are likely to be pathogens and therefore require sensitivity tests to be performed. In general, this kind of uniformity, not only in the format of the report but in the contents, will tend to avoid confusion within the laboratory and maintain its credibility. Any such principles set out, however, depend on receiving concise but comprehensive clinical information about the patient.

The range of antibiotics tested for a specific organism isolated from each type of specimen can be standardized, based on the preferred choice of the microbiologist and clinicians. Varying the tests performed, depending on an individual clinician's preferences, may well give rise to confusion. Certainly a choice of sensitivity results should be offered to allow for the possibility of, for example, allergy to an agent. There are good reasons for providing a limited choice, perhaps reporting fewer agents than have been tested in the laboratory. This approach allows the microbiologist to influence prescribing habits, encouraging the use of the more efficacious or less expensive drugs, or those less likely to select for antibiotic-resistant bacteria. In this way a hospital antibiotic policy can be promoted. Antibiotics tested but not reported act as a reserve for when the first choice fails clinically and also allow epidemiological data to be collected by the laboratory on sensitivity patterns.

Often a clinician regards a list of sensitivity results as automatic advice that the organism requires treatment. Sensitivity results should not therefore be reported routinely, but only where it is probable that such treatment is necessary. Suitable comments can be added to the report where there is doubt in this matter, as for example, 'Please consult microbiologist if treatment considered'. Such comments will clarify the degree of importance which the microbiologist attributes to any particular laboratory finding.

2.1.3 *Validation and authorization*

The importance of accurate laboratory results can never be overemphasized, since the consequences of error can be tragic. For this reason it is essential that work performed by junior staff in training is supervised by more experienced workers and results are validated. No matter which method of reporting is used, it also can generate further errors. For this reason the final report itself should be checked and, if correct, authorization given for its release to the clinician. This latter function is best performed by a medical microbiologist who, in the light of the clinical information provided, can amend or comment upon a report, or who may request further testing of the specimen in order to give the clinician the most useful information for patient management. Where this approach is impractical, validation by non-medical staff may be used for certain types of specimen while those of more serious nature, such as blood cultures or cerebrospinal fluids, should be selected for medical authorization. It is important that the clinician should know the level at which the results have been checked, so it is desirable that reports bear the name or signature of the individual who has checked them.

2.1.4 *Report form design*

Report forms may be specific for microbiology, or perhaps a single design may be used by all pathology departments. Whichever is chosen, the report must clearly carry information to identify the patient (including a unique patient identification number), information to identify the specimen (including its type and the date it was collected), the laboratory results themselves (including any comments added at the authorization stage), and the name of the person validating the report. Clinical details can be reproduced on the report, but must be clearly distinct from result data to avoid any confusion. Obviously if NCR forms are used this information is already there.

3. MANUAL RECORD-KEEPING IN THE LABORATORY

Regrettably, being complex institutions, hospitals suffer from the problem of paper-work going astray or failing to keep up with the movement of patients. While not perhaps a legal requirement, it is advisable that the laboratory keeps records of all results generated for a reasonable period of time. Telephone enquiries will be made for interim results before formal reports are produced and thus there is a need for a mechanism to locate work in progress. Appropriately structured files of records will also facilitate the production of workload statistics, stores stock control and epidemiological and infection control information.

3.1 **Work records**

A laboratory daybook is often used to record the arrival of specimens in the laboratory. If this is simply a chronological list of all specimens, it is difficult to use for quickly confirming specimen receipt. More useful are bench books with chronological lists of specimens of given types or of related types, which will facilitate telephone enquiries. In order to simplify labelling of culture plates, slides and other specimen-related material, many laboratories give each specimen a laboratory accession number, which is unique over a period of time, perhaps for 6 months or a year. A prefix or suffix which designates the type of specimen (or group of related specimens) or the month of receipt, helps keep the accession number to a manageable size.

It is necessary to record laboratory test results and workings in addition to the information sent to the clinician. These can be recorded on the request form or written directly into the bench book. If the request form is photocopied to provide the report, laboratory test results can be written on the reverse of the form while the final report is written on the front. The advantage of recording both test results and the final report in a bench book is that they are readily available for retrospective analysis, but it is cumbersome to manage.

3.2 **Statistical data**

3.2.1 *Workload information*

In order to plan and organize resources efficiently, it is necessary to have an accurate knowledge of the work passing through the laboratory. Workload statistics are valuable to monitor changing demands on laboratory services and the effects on workload of changes in policy or methods of patient management by clinicians. It may be necessary to produce a breakdown of work undertaken by specimen type, ward, hospital, requesting clinician or any combination of these. Suitably designed bench books can facilitate this kind of analysis. The efficient planning of resource distribution regionally and nationally may also depend on workload records. Manual extraction of such data is, however, time-consuming to perform.

3.2.2 *Cost analysis*

Part of the evaluation of new laboratory methods and tests, and comparisons with established ones, necessitates itemizing consumable equipment and labour costs in order to assess cost-effectiveness. While secondary to technical assessment, this is nonetheless an important part of any evaluation. Such itemization depends on keeping detailed records of tests done on specimens processed. This gives accurate costings for patient accounts or for clinical budgeting. Simple costings can be based solely on specimen type, but accurate figures require recording of all tests performed. While this can be done continuously it is time-consuming, and specimens may thus be 'sampled', for example by counting tests on one day only per month, varying the day of the week from month to month. Over a period of time an average figure can be produced for the number (and type) of tests performed on each specimen and the average cost of processing each specimen type calculated.

3.2.3 *Stores stock control*

As with the efficient running of a retail store, a laboratory must not run out of items necessary to continue its work, so it is essential that adequate stocks are kept to cover short-term increases in demand. It is valuable to keep records of the levels of stocks which are constantly updated as items are removed for use. For each type of item a re-order level should be established which will allow for replenishment of stocks before their exhaustion, with a margin of safety to cover unforeseen delays. This type of stock control record may perhaps be kept in a card-index system but could instead be managed using a microcomputer. The essential feature, however, is that records are constantly updated to present the current situation.

3.2.4 *Hospital infection control and epidemiology*

Surveillance to detect episodes of cross-infection relies on the recognition of 'alert' organisms which require some kind of remedial action. Cross-infection is more readily recognized if isolations of bacteria are recorded according to organism, clinician, ward, hospital, or perhaps in the case of early post-operative wound infection, even the operating theatre used. Manual records are labour-intensive and time-consuming but necessary if a proportion of nosocomial infections are to be prevented. Obviously a computerized system of analysis can reduce the time spent on this, especially if laboratory results are already recorded on computer for other purposes.

In addition to hospital infection control, microbiologists need to know the incidence of isolation of different species of bacteria in order to detect changes. Data published from other laboratories may reflect only the local incidence and may be significantly affected by the medical specialities that they serve. A hospital with a large neurosurgical unit may have a very different pattern of infective agents than one with a renal dialysis and urology centre. Advice on antibiotic therapy must be based on a detailed knowledge of the local environment in terms of common infecting organisms and their likely antimicrobial susceptibilities. The number of isolations of different organisms and their antibiotic sensitivity patterns need to be recorded, perhaps by hospital or community origin or even smaller sources, such as wards or specialities. Any changes with time can be noted, trends predicted and, of course, the effects of changes in patient type, or choice of antibiotic therapy assessed. It is hard work using a manual system to record all these data and sampling by recording all organisms for perhaps just one month of each year, or by selecting certain 'problem' organisms and studying them continuously, can provide valuable information. While a microcomputer in this kind of study aids statistical analysis, there remains still the burden of entering the data. A fully computerized reporting system, however, has the information fed in only once and permits various types of statistical analysis to be carried out alongside the production of clinical reports. Such systems, if also used to record the antimicrobial agents the patient is receiving, can also be used to assess the effects of changes in antibiotic prescribing trends on bacterial resistance patterns.

3.2.5 *Research*

The research applications of data abstracted from laboratory records are diverse, although constrained by the needs for storing information and for it being in a form which makes it retrievable for analysis. With manual records, only limited amounts of data are normally kept and selected data are often difficult to extract to answer specific research questions. Storage on a computer allows easier and more rapid retrieval. Prospective studies require detailed planning about which data to keep and over what period data access will be needed. Ideally, all information on patients, laboratory methods and results would be stored in case it should later prove to be useful. This is, however, an impractical approach even using computers and a judgement has to be made at some stage as to what information should be kept, depending on labour and financial resources. The problem is to find the right balance between the investment in time and capital and the potential future value of such records.

3.3 **Filing systems**

While there is no statutory requirement for laboratories to keep copies of results in the UK, a better service can be given to the clinician if they are kept. Copies permit telephone enquiries to be readily answered and also duplicate reports to be issued if originals are misfiled or lost. Indeed, legal opinion advises that records be kept for a minimum of 7 years, as this is the average time taken for a case of litigation to reach the courts in the United Kingdom.

The most common system is based on an alphabetical filing of laboratory reports by patient name. Access is most frequently needed in the first few weeks after a report is issued, so it is essential that it is easily available during that time. If space and staffing permit, it is advantageous to have records for the previous few months immediately available, keeping together all the results generated during most current episodes of illness. Serial results may enable better microbiological advice to be given than when it is based on an isolated result. Archiving of information can be helped by creating a separate file each month and, as a new month starts, the oldest month's records can be removed. The disadvantage of this system, however, is that a patient's records may span several months and therefore may be stored in several different files. Filing the results of a whole year in a single file will keep patient's records together but will require a large amount of storage space in the laboratory office and increases the amount of time required for filing and retrieving.

Records can be indexed in other ways, such as by specimen type or by ward, thus allowing certain kinds of data analysis to be performed more easily, but this will make telephone enquiries difficult to answer and may prevent an overview of all the records relating to an individual patient.

4. COMPUTERIZED SYSTEMS OF RECORD-KEEPING

In terms of the space necessary for data storage, the rapidity with which data can be recalled and the speed and flexibility in analysing information, the computer is a more efficient system of record-keeping than any manual method. It will, however, be a more expensive system to install and operate. It is difficult to prove an overall cost benefit from adopting a computerized reporting system but its real value comes from the vastly increased versatility that such a system provides, especially in terms of data analysis.

4.1 Type of computer system

Data can be stored and analysed using a microcomputer which employs 'floppy' discs for storage and a visual display unit and printer for the provision of hard copy. The main limitations of a microcomputer are the amount of data that can be stored, and therefore made accessible from a single disc, and the processing power, which determines the speed of response. Several microcomputers can be interconnected to form a networked system, which improves the volume of accessible data, but there still remains the problem of speed of response.

'Mini' systems have more accessible data and improved response times, but a complete laboratory reporting system for a large department, with rapid data retrieval and the full range of statistical analysis is likely to need a mainframe computer to provide sufficient processing power. A series of further benefits ensue from the choice of a mainframe computer. It is possible to integrate several departments together on a single system with a shared database, reducing the amount of data input by each department, as for example in a total pathology services computer system. For example, patient identification details entered by one department would be accessible to all and recalled by entering perhaps only a patient identification number. A patient's record can be examined across the disciplines so that, for example, aminoglycoside assay results reported from the microbiology laboratory can be interpreted in the light of information on renal function from the biochemistry department. A total patient administration system which includes not only results of diagnostic investigations but also details of outpatient attendances, admissions and diagnosis further promotes efficient patient management.

4.2 Workfiles

Computer-generated lists of specimens, subdivided according to the tests requested, can aid the efficient organization of work schedules within the laboratory. These obviously lend themselves best to tests where the result is a numerical value. Such results can be added by hand to the workfile and the results entered on to the computer as a batch. It is also useful for such tests as mycobacterial culture or blood cultures, where there may be a long delay between specimen receipt and the production of a report and where workfiles can list all specimens received for this investigation each day or each week and can be used as a 'bench book' to record interim information before processing is completed. A computer system can also allow 'flags' to be added to specific specimens which could, for example, highlight on a workfile those specimens which constitute a biohazard or those which are urgent. The latter can automatically be placed at the head of the next workfile to be printed. Workfiles collected chronologically will also act as a daybook recording receipt of specimens and act as a source of interim results for answering telephone enquiries. Routine bacteriological cultures do not always lend themselves to the use of workfiles for recording results; further tests are often necessary as a result of preliminary findings. The request form may then be used to record results instead, although a workfile listing still can have a role as a record of specimen receipt. Workfiles are most useful in situations where the tests to be performed can be precisely specified at the commencement of processing.

4.3 **Data entry**

There are a variety of methods by which data can be written into a computer file. The versatility of the system and the range of uses to which the data can be put depend upon storage of large amounts of data of various kinds, including information on the patient, the diagnosis, other clinical information and details of antibiotic therapy, together with the specimen type, tests and results. For the process of data input to be efficient, the chosen method must be rapid and preferably easily learnt. The use of punched cards or optical marks on cards requires special hardware dedicated to this function, unlike a keyboard system. In this, the keyboard can be used for entry and retrieval of data. In its simplest form this can be free text, perhaps with word processing functions incorporated, or simple numerical results. Faster data entry can be achieved by using coded information which can be echoed back on the screen in decoded form as confirmation of the correct input. Numerical codes are simple but require reference lists or a good memory. Mnemonic codes alleviate to some extent the need for reference lists, allow a more rapid learning process for new operators, and also reduce the risk of errors in the information which is being entered. Strings of data used frequently in association can be pre-coded into the system using 'macros' which are automatically decoded, first into a string of codes and then further into text.

Where standard results are frequently reported on multiple specimens, batch entry of results is a valuable tool for facilitating rapid data entry. For example, a specimen may be called on to the screen by keying in the laboratory accession number, the result added, then the next specimen called and, by pressing a single key, the identical result added to it. Alternatively, a whole series of specimens could be called by their numbers (or even by numerical ranges) and the results added to all of them, entering the results once only. Simple results such as numerical values or short comments such as 'Positive' or 'Negative' could be entered onto a table displayed on the screen with, for example, the tests performed listed as column headings and the laboratory numbers of the specimens listed horizontally. Cursor movements would then allow results to be added rapidly to each position in the table.

Barcodes are becoming commonplace and represent a very fast method of data input. A barcode reader 'wand' could easily read patient identification, specimen details and perhaps even standard result information. Obviously such a system requires a barcode printer to generate coded labels, but is a very efficient approach, especially when incorporated into an integrated or perhaps even a 'whole-hospital' computer system. Voice recognition is an area of current development which may well see laboratory application in the future. Computer interfaces allowing direct loading of results from automated equipment are likely to be used more often.

4.4 Authorization of results

Like manual reporting systems, there is a need for reports from a computer to be validated. The system can be programmed to compare current with previous results. There are a variety of ways in which authorization of results can take place and the actual method chosen will to some extent depend on the availability of senior staff for this process. Where such staff are not available, results can obviously be entered on to the computer and reported directly to the clinicians. Ideally results should be checked by senior members of the laboratory staff, either in batches or as individual reports. It is possible to programme the system so that some results are reported directly, some are listed for authorization as a batch, while others are queued for individual scrutiny and authorization. Abnormal results can be automatically flagged.

Batch authorization is a rapid process and can be performed by producing a printed listing of results which are quickly authorized at a VDU by a few simple keystrokes. Such lists, however, can accommodate only a limited amount of data about patient and the specimen, or they may become too complex to be read efficiently. Results for individual authorization can be queued and then authorized by a few keystrokes at the terminal. Comments may be added at this stage using either codes or free text. The system should also allow comments to be added to results which are authorized in batch mode, with the facility to add comments to an individual report or to the whole batch. If a personal code is used by the authorizor when calling up an authorization programme, the computer can add the authorizor's name to the report. In addition to adding comments, the authorizor should have the ability to suppress data.

4.5 Report generation

The use of computers to generate laboratory reports has important advantages. The reports are legible and do not rely on handwriting or typing skills (except where results are entered as free text). Typing errors in coded data entry will be rejected by the system and must be corrected before the result is accepted and the report produced. There is an additional benefit in that the computer can arrange the reports into a pre-determined order of destination before printing, thus obviating the need for clerical staff to sort the reports. Interim reports can also be put on a single list for all the patients on each ward for whom specimens have been reported. Final reports may be cumulated onto a single sheet for each patient so that changes in result are more readily recognized. This is particularly valuable in the case of numerical results, so that trends are more apparent. This option also has the advantage of reducing the number of report sheets and therefore the bulk of paper added to a patient's case-notes. Where visual display units are provided in clinical areas, results once authorized are immediately available and so the clinician need not wait for the printed report to be delivered. 'Slave' printers in these locations would allow hard copy to be produced in the ward.

4.6 Data analysis

A computer used for reporting laboratory results has the data entered only once allowing report generation, storage of records and data analysis without duplication of effort. Analysis carried out at regular intervals can then, with very little manual intervention, produce listings for epidemiological surveillance and infection control purposes, quality control statistics, lists of isolations for intra-laboratory and inter-laboratory communications, and searches for research and other special purposes.

4.7 Computerized data displays

In addition to displaying results as single reports or lists, it is simple to programme the system to display serial results in specialized formats either on the VDU or as hard copy. Examples of such displays would be histograms or graphical representations. This might be used for results of serological tests or antibiotics sensitivities. An integrated pathology computer could be programmed to display aminoglycoside serum levels in graphical form alongside serum creatinine or urea results.

4.8 Laboratory management functions

Besides epidemiological and research analyses, computerized laboratory reporting can be used in laboratory management. It is easy to provide a regular listing of the numbers and types of specimen received and the tests performed, perhaps further indexed by hospital department or requesting clinician. Graphical display of such results against time will allow the variations in workload patterns to be easily recognized. Disposition of staff and purchasing of reagents and equipment can then be planned in anticipation of future work patterns.

Where there is devolution of hospital budgets to departments or individual clinicians, workload statistics can be developed. Tests performed in the laboratory can be allocated costings, generating notional accounts for each consumer, who can then be informed at regular intervals of the laboratory resources he has used. Where such management functions are carried out not by the laboratory but by a hospital finance department, data may be off-loaded to a computer within the finance department. Laboratory tests may also be allocated an average time period within which they might normally be expected to be completed. The computer can then generate on a regular basis a list of those specimens which are overdue for reporting. This will highlight reports which have been overlooked, or perhaps those for whom there are reference laboratory results still outstanding.

4.9 Data security

Medical information held on a computer is confidential information between the patient and his clinician, and great care must be taken to ensure that it is secure. The data should be factually correct, adequate for the purpose and yet not excessive, and be kept in confidence, accessible only to those who need it. Security can be maintained by ensuring hardware access to authorized users only, and data access by passwords. These can be constructed in a hierarchical manner allowing access to different programs by level of password. The clinician need only be able to enquire of authorized results, while laboratory staff need to access unauthorized data.

Authorization and validation programs should be restricted to senior laboratory staff who hold 'high-level' passwords. Access to the 'housekeeping' programs should be restricted to computer management staff only. System checks can also be incorporated where not only are abortive attempts to log on to the system recorded, but where, after perhaps three failed attempts, the computer 'disconnects' the peripheral. Unauthorized use can also be prevented by defining to which programs each terminal may gain access, so that, for example, a ward enquiry terminal cannot be used to write laboratory results to the computer, and one department in a multidisciplinary system cannot add to or alter results of a different department.

4.10 System management ('housekeeping' programs)

There are a number of 'housekeeping' activities which are necessary to maintain a computer system running efficiently. These include security disc copying, archiving of data to 'history' files, checking files for errors and the correction of those errors. It is also essential in any large system that both hardware and software are covered by a maintenance contract which provides urgent assistance in case of hardware or software failure. Inevitably any system, however reliable, may eventually fail and it is prudent to plan fall-back manual methods of working and reporting which can be readily and quickly adopted.

4.11 Archiving data

As files are filled with data there comes a point where they have to be archived, when they are removed from the discs used for current working and copied to 'history' files. Discs holding the history files would then only be loaded and run when required. The response time of the computer will increase as files fill up and the system has to search more data. It is therefore necessary to decide how much data should be made readily available and which data are infrequently needed and can therefore be accessible for limited periods only. Microbiology records are most frequently consulted during the 1 or 2 weeks after the specimen has been processed and thereafter relatively rarely. However, if the system permits, it is worthwhile keeping up to a full year of records 'on-line' for immediate continuous access. An advantage of this is that analysis for workload, epidemiology and antibiotic sensitivity patterns can be easily performed. Alternatively searches could be run perhaps monthly and the results stored on disc. The results of the same search for subsequent months are added so that the long-term surveys are produced by cumulation rather than by a single search of the whole time period.

Archived data should probably be kept for a minimum of 7 years, and as the information is much less bulky to accommodate in disc or streamer-tape form than as paper reports, it is not inconvenient or extravagant to keep archive discs indefinitely, perhaps storing 1 or 2 years of records on each disc.

Paperwork associated with specimens, such as request forms and worklists, need only to be kept short-term, for example as a reference source of results where a specimen is listed by the computer as overdue for reporting due to a clerical error in failing to input the report information into the computer. Once the final report has been authorized and all data are stored on disc, the worklists can be destroyed. If, however, only selected information is recorded on the computer system, there may be a need to retain the paperwork so that the additional information can be retrieved. This would be the case where it was desirable to analyse the biochemical profiles of certain organisms, but the computer only recorded the report data, that is the names of the isolates, but not the actual results of the laboratory tests.

CHAPTER 10

Quality control

WILLIAM A.HYDE

1. INTRODUCTION

The European Committee for Clinical Laboratory Standards document on quality control for microbiology states (1):

> Internal quality control is the set of procedures undertaken by the staff of a laboratory for the continual evaluation of laboratory work and the emergent results, in order to decide whether they are reliable enough to be released to clinicians or epidemiologists. External quality assessment, which is a term that should be used in preference to 'external quality control' (since it is not a system for exerting control), refers to an objective system of retrospectively comparing results from different laboratories by means of an external agency.

A more comprehensive definition of quality control would be the method by which an organization ensures that the product or information it provides is as near to perfection as possible, given the constraints of time, budget and the ability of the staff employed.

Good quality control in the pathology laboratory begins with recruitment policies and ends with report validation. This chapter will outline some of the factors which combine to affect the results obtained in a microbiology laboratory and detail methods to overcome them.

2. PERSONNEL AND VALIDATION PROCEDURES

2.1 Recruitment policies and training

Quality control should encompass all aspects of the organization and management of the department. Traditional procedures have concentrated on methodology and have neglected personnel function and training. It is counter-productive to have a highly-trained medical laboratory scientific officer (MLSO) pouring culture plates, except as part of a training and induction programme. Similarly, it is dangerous to have a laboratory aide reporting Gram stain results from important specimens.

As part of the training of apprentices in industry, a log book is kept of all techniques learned. When they have acquired a certain level of skill in a task, details are entered by the trainee and countersigned by the supervisor. This not only provides a useful reference book for the trainee of tasks performed infrequently, but also helps the supervisors to ensure that all aspects of training, including health and safety, have been covered adequately. This type of record-keeping should be undertaken when training all new staff in the laboratory.

All methods used in the laboratory should be described in detail in a procedure manual which has been written by senior staff with current bench experience which should be regularly updated (2,3). Rapid rotation, so that staff are 'trained' for on-call commitments, should be avoided. The training given to new staff should be supervised by senior staff and should be incorporated into the routine work of the department. A rotation system of 4−6 weeks on each section of the laboratory can play a part in this, so that the new entrant can within a few months easily fit into any gap, created at their level, caused by sickness or holidays.

The organization of a department has clear implications for the quality of the results produced. The responsibilities of all senior members of staff must be understood. This departmental senior team should meet regularly to discuss all organizational and methodology changes before they are implemented. These senior meetings need to be backed up by full departmental meetings, when necessary, to allow staff the chance to comment on changes. Many pearls of wisdom can sometimes be gleaned from the most junior staff. This arrangement will promote good staff relations, and improve the working atmosphere, leading to better quality results.

2.2 Specimen and report validation

Many laboratories now have computerized booking systems, some a fully computerized reporting system. If these computers are connected to hospital patient systems, they can be used to check patient details on request cards against patient records. They cannot cope with the wrong specimen with the wrong form; thus this has to be checked manually. The training given on induction should emphasize the need to check specimen details against request card information; clerical errors are responsible for many mistakes.

The main concern here is to make sure that the report reflects the test results obtained and is consistent with previous reports. Computers can help by easy access to previous reports; important when reporting antibiotic sensitivity patterns. Where this method is not available, a level of awareness instilled by thorough training will help detect anomalies. All reporting staff should be aware of possible anomalous results which could affect the report, for example, penicillin-resistant group G streptococci, which are probably D-G antigen variants of enterococci (4). Anomalies should not be edited without investigation for new bacterial variants, mis-identification, media or antibiotic disc failure.

3. SUPPLIES

The Chief MLSO in the department must have a clear idea of the rate at which materials are used. This will help to control stocks, prevent deterioration and monitor the budget. Stock control programs are available with most mini- and microcomputers, but simple record sheets showing supplier, minimum order level, unit size, cost and, if necessary, expiry dates can be used. Decentralization of stock control to Senior MLSO level has the following advantages.

(i)   It gives the responsibility of keeping up stocks to the users.
(ii)   It ensures that users know the costs involved, thus preventing wastage.
(iii)   It should free the Chief MLSO to monitor bench work.

Adequate storage space and correct storage conditions are important to ensure easy access to materials and accurate monitoring and to prevent deterioration.

Table 1. Deterioration of SS agar (LabM) stored in various conditions for 6 months.

Storage conditions	Moisture gain, %	Recovery of salmonellae, %
Unopened bottle stored in cool, dark, dry conditions	0	100
Loose cap, stored in light on bench	1.1	47
Loose cap, stored in light in autoclave room	4.4	22

3.1 Storage conditions of dried and prepared media

Dried media are sensitive to heat, light and especially moisture; the data in *Table I* illustrate this. Dry powder media stored under optimal conditions will keep for 2−3 years in an unopened pot and for up to 6 months after first opening. It is good practice to repeat quality control on media older than 2 years before use. Media which have visibly deteriorated (appearing discoloured or lumpy) should not be used.

Culture plates can be identified on a daily basis by drawing lines down the edges of the stacks of plates using coloured marker pens, or using supermarket price labels. Triple-vented plates can be dried by standing them overnight inverted at room temperature. Single or non-vented plates need to be dried in a cabinet. All plates are stored at $+4°C$. Most plates will keep for up to 10 days, but selective plates can begin to deteriorate after this time due to drying and concentration of chemicals, which can cause them to become inhibitory. Degradation of antibiotics can produce the opposite effect. Bottled or tubed liquid media need to be kept in the dark, otherwise inhibitory peroxides will be formed. Rarely-used sugar media can be stored at $−20°C$ for up to 1 year without deterioration.

Manufacturers' instructions for the storage of kits must be followed precisely, especially regarding storage temperatures and expiry dates.

4. PREPARATION OF CULTURE MEDIA

It is essential to observe manufacturers' instructions when preparing culture media, especially those instructions regarding sterilization, as unnecessarily prolonged auto-claving of acid media will result in degradation of the agar. Certain media such as XLD or DCA are sterilized by boiling, and, if overheated, the sodium deoxycholate precipitates, producing a turbid medium. These types of media should be boiled in quantities of not more than 1 litre, cooled immediately, then poured when the temperature has fallen to less than 56°C. Preparators with efficient cooling systems have been used to produce larger volumes, but care must be used with the instrument settings on these machines.

5. CULTURE MEDIA QUALITY CONTROL

There are two levels of control used in the media laboratory:

(i) evaluation of large batches of routine media to be used over a period which requires comprehensive quality control;

(ii) day-to-day control to ensure that correct procedures of preparation and sterilization have been followed.

Media purchase decisions should never be made on administrative or budgetary criteria alone; different manufacturers' media vary, and serious problems can occur if media are changed without due consideration of their performance. Frequently used media are best purchased on a yearly basis, after first requesting a sample from a manufacturer's batch. This can be quality controlled in detail in the user's laboratory and accepted, or rejected. This gives the laboratory confidence in the subsequent performance of that batch, and also allows the user to limit the amount of week-to-week quality control performed to ensure proper procedures have been carried out in its preparation and the addition of selective agents. It is essential that this testing be carried out quickly so that manufacturers are not holding large reserves which cannot be sold. When requesting media from a manufacturer for evaluation, it is important to ascertain that sufficient media of that batch can be reserved for your order, together with a request for a copy of the manufacturer's quality control record on that batch. This evaluation of large batches of media needs to be carried out carefully.

(i)   The media laboratory should put up the tests but the results should be read by a senior member of staff, not part of the media section.

(ii)   The evaluation should consist of a comparison of the new material against the material in use. The organisms used should be both clinical and stock strains of National Collection type cultures or others of known performance. A number of suitable culture collection strains are described in *Table 2*. The techniques used in the evaluation can be those outlined for daily control, but with more emphasis on semi-quantitative techniques, and a selection of fresh isolates in addition to NCTC strains.

Table 2. Culture collection strains for quality control.

QC organisms	ATCC	NCTC
Acinetobacter calcoaceticus	15309	5866
Bacteroides fragilis	25285	9343
Campylobacter jejuni	–	11168
Candida albicans	18804	–
Clostridium perfringens	13132	11229
Corynebacterium diphtheriae	19409	3984
Enterobacter cloacae	13047	10005
Escherichia coli O:111	–	9111
Haemophilus influenzae	–	10479/11931
Neisseria gonorrhoeae	19424	8375
Proteus mirabilis	25933	–
Pseudomonas aeruginosa	27853	10662
Salmonella senftenberg	–	10384
Serratia marcescens	13880	10211
Staphylococcus aureus	25923	657
S.epidermidis	14990	11047
Streptococcus faecalis	–	775
S.pneumoniae	–	10319
S.pyogenes		8198
Vibrio fluvialis	–	11218

5.1 Daily quality control of solid media

This can be done most simply by using a modification of Mossell's ecometric technique (5) as described in *Table 3*.

This technique is very simple; though it requires care to carry it out properly, it gives

Table 3. Use of the ecometric technique to control selective agar media.

1.	Inoculate 10 ml Brain Heart Infusion Broth with the organism(s) to be used in the test and incubate for 4 h.
2.	Divide the plate of media to be tested into quadrants as shown in *Figure 1*.
3.	Charge a 1 μl wire loop with 4 h culture.
4.	Spread plate as in *Figure 1*, going from A1→B1→C1→D1→A2→B2 etc.
5.	Spread a non-inhibitory plate in similar manner and incubate for 18 h.
6.	Note the segment at which growth last occurs on the selective and non-selective plate (the end point).
7.	Calculate the Absolute Growth Index (AGI) by assigning a segment index value from the end point as follows:

A1 = 5	B1 = 10	C1 = 15	D1 = 20
A2 = 25	B2 = 30	C2 = 35	D2 = 40
A3 = 45	B3 = 50	C3 = 55	D3 = 60
A4 = 65	B4 = 70	C4 = 75	D4 = 80
A5 = 85	B5 = 90	C5 = 95	D5 = 100

The AGI is then calculated by the following formula:

$$\frac{\text{Index of test}}{\text{Index of control}} \times 100$$

8.   *Worked example*: continuous growth on test was shown to be up to segment B line 4, index = 70, and on the control plate (non-selective) with same organism D line 4, index = 80.

Then AGI = $\dfrac{70}{80} \times 100 = 87.5$.

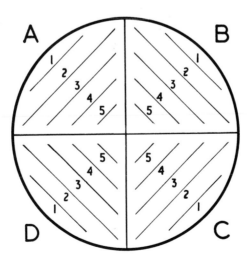

Figure 1. Pattern for spreading agar plates when using the ecometric technique.

Table 4. Suggested quality control organisms for daily control of media.

Medium	Incubation[a] conditions	Test organism	Expected result
Blood agar bases	37°C in O_2	*Streptococcus pyogenes*	Good growth, β-haemolysis
		Str.pneumoniae	Good growth
CLED (Sandy's or Bevis)	37°C in O_2	*Staphylococcus aureus* *Str.faecalis*	Good growth and distinction
		Escherichia coli	Typical colony lactose +ve
		Proteus mirabilis	No swarming blue
Hoyles medium	37°C in O_2	*Clostridium diphtheriae* (non-toxinogenic)	Typical colonies
		Staphylococcus aureus	No growth
MacConkey agar No. 2	37°C in O_2	*E.coli*	Typical pink colonies
		P.mirabilis	Pale colonies, no swarming
		Staphylococcus aureus	Pink colonies, good growth
		Streptococcus faecalis	Deep red colonies, good growth
Mannitol salt	37°C in O_2	*Staphylococcus aureus*	Good growth, yellow colonies
		E.coli	No growth
Sabouraud agars[b]	37°C in O_2	*Candida albicans*	Good growth
		E.coli	Poor growth
TCBS	37°C in O_2	*Vibrio* Group F	Typical yellow colonies
		P.mirabilis	No growth
Sensitivity test agar	37°C in O_2	*Staphylococcus aureus* NCTC 6571	Sensitive to: trimethoprim, sulphonamide, tetracycline, nitrofurantoin, gentamicin
		Pseudomonas aeruginosa NCTC 10662	Gentamicin, colistin, ceftazadime
		E.coli NCTC 10418	Trimethoprim, sulphonamide, ampicillin, nitrofurantoin, cephalexin
			Look for good growth, adequate and reproducible zone sizes which should be recorded
Selective media for *Neisseria gonorrhoeae*	37°C in CO_2	*Candida albicans*	No growth
		Staphylococcus aureus	No growth
		Proteus sp. (trimethoprim-sensitive, NCTC)	No growth
		Pseudomonas aeruginosa	No growth
		N.gonorrhoeae	Good growth, small colonies
Chocolate agar	37°C in 10% CO_2	*Haemophilus influenzae*	Good growth
DNase agar	30°C in O_2[c]	*Staphylococcus epidermidis*	Negative
		Staph.aureus	Positive

Table 4. (*Continued*)

Medium	Incubation[a] conditions	Test organism	Expected result
Campylobacter medium	44°C in 6% O_2 (Skirrow) 37°C in 6% O_2 (blood-free)	*Campylobacter jejuni* *Staph.aureus* *E.coli*	Good growth No growth No growth
Gentamicin or neomycin blood agar	37°C, no O_2 10% CO_2	*Bacteroides fragilis* *E.coli*	Good growth No growth
Nalidixic acid Tween blood agar		*Staph.aureus*	Good growth

[a] All media are incubated for 18 h at 37°C.
[b] Medium should not be dark, gel must be firm. Chloramphenicol should be added to make it more selective.
[c] Very few false positive results are found following incubation at 30°C.

more information than simple plating out and a record can be kept using the semi-quantitative data produced. A spiral plater (Spiral Systems Inc.) may be used to produce plates in a similar fashion. Daily quality control needs to be carried out on all batches of media to which the media room has to add selective agents, for example antibiotic plates. This is to ensure that the appropriate agent has been correctly added. This is performed by dividing a plate into sections so that appropriate organisms can be plated on to each segment (*Figure 1*). The more selective agents in the cocktail, the more organisms need to be used in quality control, see *Table 4*.

5.2 Routine batch quality control of bottled or tubed media

As batches of these media are produced, they should be held in stock prior to satisfactory performance in the quality control tests in *Table 5*.

6. EQUIPMENT MONITORING

6.1 Temperature monitoring

Monitoring of the temperature of media during autoclaving can be achieved by the use of a floating thermocouple, introduced into the bottle of medium in the centre of the load. Example chart records showing the required cycles should be displayed near the recorder or, better still, a transparent overlay photocopied from the charts obtained at commissioning can be used to compare runs. Older autoclaves may have a threaded port into which can be screwed a floating thermocouple. Failing this, satisfactory results can sometimes be obtained by introducing the thermocouple protected by thin PVC tape through the door of the machine. These thermocouples can be connected to an electrical thermometer (Comark Electronics).

Chemical indicator tubes (Browne's tubes, obtained from Albert Browne Ltd) can also be introduced into the flasks. These will indicate if the sterilizing temperature and time have been achieved; they will not indicate if the medium has been overheated. These tubes need to be kept in a refrigerator to prevent the chemicals from deteriorating and giving false readings. Some early agar preparators present problems for external monitoring and these can be partially overcome by the use of Browne's tubes attached to the paddles.

Table 5. Tests for quality control of bottled or tubed media.

Medium	Incubation temp.	Incubation time	Organism	Result
Cooked meat	37°C	18 h	*Clostridium perfringens*	Good growth; gas production
Enteric media (e.g. selenite broth, Rappaport's, Muller, Kauffman)	37°C or 44°C	18 h	*Salmonella senftenberg* *Escherichia coli* O:111	After subculture, increased growth Not increased
Arginine dihydrolase	37°C	48 h	*Enterobacter cloacae* *Proteus mirabilis*	Positive Negative
Lysine decarboxylase	37°C	48 h	*Serratia marcescens* *Enterobacter cloacae*	Positive Negative
Ornithine decarboxylase	37°C	48 h	*Ser.marcescens* *Enterobacter cloacae*	Positive Negative
O.F. Medium + glucose (Leifsons) (minus oil)	37°C	24 h	*Pseudomonas aeruginosa* *Acinetobacter calcoaceticus*	Yellow surface Negative
Thioglycollate including Brewers FAB[a], etc.	37°C	18 h	*Bacteroides fragilis* *Streptococcus pneumoniae*	Good growth Good growth
Transport media	20°C	48 h	*Neisseria gonorrhoeae* *B.fragilis*	Recovered after 48 h
Urea media	37°C	18 h	*Proteus mirabilis* *E. coli*	Positive Negative

[a]If used for GLC, either request manufacturer's quality control record or run baseline and standard organisms.

All temperature-controlled equipment needs to have a separate means of temperature reading, other than that supplied by manufacturers. Some of these can be installed by the user, such as maximum and minimum thermometers screwed into, or stuck with Araldite® on to, the inside of refrigerators or incubators. Uniformity of temperature within an incubator should also be monitored. Multiple temperature monitoring can be carried out using thermocouples connected to an electronic thermometer via a switching mechanism, the results recorded on a chart recorder (Comark Electronics). Another useful method is to use an infra-red thermometer (Horiba Ltd). This device can also be used for measuring the temperature of sterilized agars before adding blood etc.

As with any aspect of quality control, this monitoring is useless unless someone reads the instruments, records the results, understands all the implications and takes action accordingly. A Senior or Chief MLSO should have clear responsibility to carry out this study. It should be instilled into staff that thermometers are to be read automatically every time they open the door of the incubator.

6.2 pH meter electrodes

The best electrodes for media are those which are 'unbreakable', for example glass embedded in resin, such as Sensorex type 5200C, or a flat-ended type for agar plates, such as Orion type 450C/B (Orme Scientific). Between uses the electrodes should be washed in distilled water, then kept in a pH 4 buffer, to prevent the growth of contaminants. The instrument needs to be checked *every time it is used*, using two buffers, pH 7 and pH 4. Colour-coded buffers work well and contain a preservative (BDH Ltd). If a setting of pH 4 cannot be attained, the electrode should be immersed in a solution of pepsin overnight (approximately 2 mg pepsin in 20 ml of 1 M HCl), then washed well in distilled water before recalibration. The meter should also be fitted with a thermistor to compensate automatically for temperature variation. If not, the medium is cooled to room temperature, or the temperature of media is taken and the meter set to that temperature, though this method can sometimes give inaccurate results. It should be noted that pH values shown on media formulations are the pH at 20°C.

6.3 Anaerobic cabinet control

Bacteriological indicators of oxygen contamination require overnight incubation and are too slow to detect oxygen in the cabinet before the damage to oxygen-sensitive organisms has occurred. The atmosphere in the cabinet is best monitored using the chemical indicator in *Table 6*. The blue colour with this indicator may persist for up to 12 h when first installed. This can be overcome by putting the tube into the cabinet while warm, but not too hot, as the vacuum on the interchange chamber can cause it to boil.

If the humidity in cabinets is not controlled, or if the cabinet is in a room which cools during the night, condensation can occur. Cabinets are then liable to become contaminated with bacteria, even aerobes such as *Proteus* spp. and *Pseudomonas* spp. Spreading clostridia are particularly difficult. These can be removed using a wash down with a glutaraldehyde solution.

(i)   Remove the catalysts and the desiccators.
(ii) Spray glutaraldehyde solution (Gigasept®, 10%) through the cabinet using a hand-mist spray while wearing gloves.
(iii) Leave the cabinet overnight.

Table 6. Procedure for making an anaerobiosis indicator stock powder.

To prepare stock powder:

1. Using a mortar and pestle, crush 20 mg methylene blue crystals to a fine powder.
2. Add 50 g glucose and 500 g NaHCO$_3$ in small amounts until the methylene blue is evenly distributed.
3. Place the dry powder mixture into an airtight labelled jar.

To use the stock powder:

1. Fill a 16 × 100 mm test tube with the stock powder to a depth of 2.5 cm.
2. Half fill the test tube with distilled water, stopper the tube and mix the contents until the powder is completely moist.
3. Place the mixture in the work chamber and unstopper the tube.
4. The mixture will slowly become clear if the chamber is anaerobic. Once clear, if the indicator begins to turn blue, oxygen is present in the work chamber.

    This indicator should be replaced weekly.

(iv)   Connect the outlet pump to a piece of tubing and place in the open air or into a dilute ammonia solution in a bucket to remove the glutaraldehyde.
(v)   Flush the cabinet with gas as in the procedure given in the manual for start-up.
(vi)   Keep a stock of anaerobic jars and active catalysts ready to use when the cabinet is out of action.

The cabinet catalysts and desiccators are dated with a pencil when first used, and should be changed daily. They should be dried thoroughly after use and discarded after 6 months. The cabinet should be wiped out thoroughly once a week, and the anaerobic indicator changed.

7. AUTOCLAVES

Laboratory autoclaves have undergone considerable changes from the original simple downward displacement machines with inlet valve and exhaust valve, and no electronics to go wrong! The best autoclaves now in use are extremely complex machines, often incorporating pulsed evacuation, air ballasting, condensate containment and fully automatic cycles. They cost little more than conventional machines, rarely block, and should conform to possible future legislation and new working practices in maintenance departments regarding 'permission to work certificates'. This is important in view of the report that older autoclave exhausts can become contaminated with organisms from the chamber, making these regulations difficult to comply with (6). These new autoclaves require considerable maintenance and quality control.

Commissioning new machines with the manufacturers present should be part of the task of the microbiologist. The type of loads and vessels to be used in that department in day-to-day working should be used in the tests, which should not be based on another laboratory's experience of how they run their autoclaves. In this way, the automatic cycles can be set to the loads relevant in the laboratory, especially the culture media cycles. These must be controlled using a 'floating' thermocouple placed inside a flask or bottle with the same material as the load in the centre of the load, and not a 'standard' bottle as found in many pharmacy autoclaves. The slow heating of agar-containing media makes this precaution imperative if good results are to be obtained.

8. PIPETTES

The automatic pipettes in the media room and throughout the laboratory also need to be checked monthly. This can most easily be done by weighing replicate amounts on a balance accurate to 3 decimal places. If there is any deviation beyond the original specification of the pipette, the pipette can be stripped, lubricated and re-checked.

9. MAINTENANCE AND STORAGE OF CONTROL ORGANISMS

The two conflicting requirements of a storage system are:

(i)   the long-term preservation of organisms in conditions which will maintain their characteristics;
(ii)   ready access to the organisms for day-to-day use.

9.1 Long-term storage

Freeze-drying is perhaps still the best, though the most tedious, technique for long-

Table 7. Preservation of bacteria using a modified glass bead technique.

1. Grow the organisms on an appropriate solid medium until a heavy growth is obtained. Use several plates with organisms forming small colonies.

2. Remove growth from plate using a sterile cotton swab and emulsify in 10% v/v glycerol in Brain Heart Infusion Broth.

3. Carefully pipette the suspension on to sterile glass beads with a hole for threading, then place them in a plastic freezer tube. Replace the cap and tap the bottle to remove the bubbles from bead centres.

4. Pipette off the excess fluid into phenolic disinfectant in a discard jar. Cap the tube, label and place in freezer.

5. To recover the organisms, remove the beads using forceps, roll on an appropriate medium and streak out to obtain single colonies.

   There are potential problems with this technique which can be avoided.

   (i) The tubes should be duplicated and then stored in separate pots — one for routine access, the other as a back-up in a separate freezer.

   (ii) The frozen beads will soon defrost on the bench. A block of aluminium or copper drilled out to take the plastic tubes will prevent thawing. The block is kept in the freezer along with the beads, and removed wearing a glove.

term preservation. This technique has been described in detail many times elsewhere (7). Other approaches are the gelatin disc method of Stamp (8), the paper strip method of Hawkey (9) and the bead system of Feltham *et al.* (10). These methods all require the purchase of expensive equipment such as $-70°C$ freezers or freeze dryers, or are tedious (gelatin disc). A method using glass beads and a domestic freezer ($-20°C$), successfully used at the author's laboratories for over 18 months, is described in *Table 7.* After recovery from the beads, the majority of aerobic bacteria can be kept on appropriate non-selective media on Petri dishes. This technique works well for most organisms, including delicate anaerobes, but losses can occur with *Campylobacter* spp. and *Haemophilus* spp. Recent reports suggest that polystyrene beads may be better for some species such as *Legionella* spp. These can be kept at 4°C and subcultured on a weekly basis. Anaerobes and *Campylobacter* spp. are maintained for a short time in cooked meat broths if kept at 37°C. *Neisseria* spp. and *Haemophilus* spp. need to be kept on chocolate agar in an atmosphere of 5% CO_2.

10. QUALITY CONTROL OF KITS AND IDENTIFICATION SYSTEMS

It is expensive and unnecessary to quality-control most identification systems on a regular basis. Sometimes, however, either on receipt of a new batch, or if there is some doubt about results, a suitable set of organisms needs to be used. Some companies such as API System S.A. give details of suitable quality-control organisms as part of their instructions for use. These organisms can be valuable for other quality-control work. It must be borne in mind, however, that certain manufacturers use different enzyme substrates to test for the same enzyme, and this can lead to problems of interpretation (11).

11. UNITED KINGDOM NATIONAL EXTERNAL QUALITY ASSESSMENT SCHEME (UKNEQAS)

This voluntary scheme, organized by the PHLS Division of Microbiological Reagents and Quality Control (DMRQC), is an exercise not so much in quality control but in comparing the results obtained from various laboratories in the UK. This type of quality control can be effective only if it is presented to the laboratory staff in the same way as any other clinical sample. In many laboratories, however, the exercise is carried out by the most senior MLSO, and bears little relation to routine investigations. A major advantage of the scheme is its exposure of laboratories to rare pathogens which can be used as a training exercise. Those laboratories which consistently perform badly are offered help confidentially. As almost all laboratories in the UK participate, DMRQC has a unique opportunity to compare the results of different methods.

Similar schemes exist in the USA, such as the Quality Assurance Service of the College of American Pathologists.

12. QUALITY CONTROL OF STAINING TECHNIQUES

Staining techniques can fail, either when the stain does not give correct reactions, or if the stains themselves become contaminated with organisms, resulting in misleading results. Gram stains, especially crystal violet, can become contaminated with *Pseudomonas* spp., which will adhere to films, especially smears of CSF or blood, causing false results to be reported (12). The source of these organisms is often the de-ionized water used to make up the stains. These problems may be avoided by making small batches from concentrated stains and by ensuring that de-ionized water is used while fresh and is not allowed to stand around in large containers for long periods. Similar problems have occurred with contamination of water by saprophytic mycobacteria and false results have been reported in Ziehl−Neilson stains (13).

Dyes themselves can cause problems; if, for instance, acid fuchsin is substituted for basic fuchsin in the Ziehl−Neilson stain, it will not work. Some manufacturers' dyes do not contain what the label claims (14) and testing of batch samples is advisable.

13. REFERENCES

1. European Committee for Clinical Laboratory Standards (1985) *Part 2: Internal Quality Control in Microbiology*, Vol. 2, No. 4., ECCLS, Lund.
2. Natural Committee for Clinical Laboratory Standards (1980) *Tentative Guidelines for Clinical Laboratory Procedure Manuals*. Villanova, PA, USA.
3. Miller,J.M. (1985) In *Methods for Quality Control in Diagnostic Microbiology*. Miller,J.M. and Wentworth,B.B. (eds), American Public Health Association, Washington, DC, p. 1.
4. Birch,B.R., Keaney,M.G.L. and Ganguli,L.A. (1984) *Lancet*, **1**, 856.
5. Mossel,D.A.A., Van Rossem,F., Koopmans,M, Hendriks,M., Verouden,M. and Eelderink,I. (1980) *J. Appl. Bacteriol.*, **49**, 439.
6. Scruton,M.W. (1986) *Hospital Engineering*, **40**, (9)24.
7. Lapage,S.P. and Redway,K.F. (1974) *Preservation of Bacteria with Notes on other Micro-organisms*. Public Health Laboratory Service Monograph Series, 7, HMSO, London.
8. Stamp,Lord (1947) *J. Gen. Microbiol.*, **1**, 251.
9. Hawkey,P.M., Bennett,P.M. and Hawkey,C.A. (1984) *J. Med. Microbiol.*, **18**, 277.
10. Feltham,R.K.A., Power,A.K., Pell,P.A. and Sneath,P.H.A. (1978) *J. Appl. Bacteriol.*, **44**, 313.
11. Heltberg,O., Busk,H.E, Bremmelgaard,A., Kristiansen,J.E. and Frederiksen,W. (1984) *Eur. J. Clin. Microbiol.*, **3**, 241.
12. Walsh,D.M. and Eberiel,D.T. (1986) *J. Clin. Microbiol.*, **23**, 962.
13. Collins,C.H. and Yates,M.D. (1979) *Instit. Med. Lab. Sci. Gaz.*, 578.
14. Gadsdon,D.R. (1986) *Med. Lab. Sci.*, **43**, Suppl. I, S77.

CHAPTER 11

Laboratory investigation of nosocomial infection

PETER M.HAWKEY

1. INTRODUCTION

Whilst most hospital microbiology laboratories are very busy processing the large numbers of specimens detailed in the previous chapters, they will also periodically be required to investigate and direct the control of episodes of cross-infection. Although this chapter will concentrate on hospital-acquired infection (nosocomial infection), some laboratories will be involved with community cross-infection problems. Most of the techniques described here will be suitable for use in community outbreaks but some may require different application and interpretation. The techniques for the isolation and identification of organisms responsible for diseases which predominantly cause problems in the community are dealt with under the appropriate sections elsewhere in this book (bacterial meningitis, Chapter 2, Section 3; diphtheria, Chapter 3, Section 2.3; food poisoning, Chapter 6; cholera, Chapter 6, Section 5.3). Although the microbiology of food and water is of little interest to laboratories dealing exclusively with specimens from hospital patients, it may on occasions be necessary for those laboratories to examine such specimens. This chapter will not give specific methods but rather refer the reader to specialist publications on water (1) and food (2−4). Most Public Health Laboratories can also offer assistance and advice.

The investigation of suspected nosocomial infection must be undertaken in a logical and unbiased fashion, not by hasty assumptions of the nature of sources and routes of transmission. Details of an approach to the investigation of a suspected outbreak which will allow sound epidemiological and statistical analysis are given elsewhere (Chapter 12, Section 5). In the end it is the aim of every investigation to identify the source(s), the mode(s) of transmission and the portal of entry into the patient.

1.1 Administration

No description of the role of the laboratory in the investigation of nosocomial infection would be complete without a system for the administration of the control of nosocomial infection. In the UK the earlier official guidelines for the management of nosocomial infection, issued in 1959 (5), have been updated (6) as a result of the findings of the enquiry reports of outbreaks of infections due to legionellae (7) and salmonellae (8). Administrative arrangements in the USA differ slightly from the UK (9), mainly as a result of the lack of an equivalent to the clinical microbiologist, that role being taken by a hospital epidemiologist in the USA. However, in both countries the major decision-making body is the Infection Control Committee (ICC), and practical support is provided by the Infection Control Practitioner (nurse) (ICN), both of whom have direct equivalents in the UK system.

In the UK the Infection Control Doctor (ICD) is an important member of the Infection Control Team (ICT), who provides leadership for the team. The post should be held by the Consultant Microbiologist who will be in a position to command respect from clinical colleagues and therefore be able to advise and lead the ICT and advise the Health Authority in the control of hospital infection. The ICD will ensure that the policy made by the Control of Infection Committee is put into action. In some hospitals the ICN will be a Medical Laboratory Scientific Officer, in which case that individual will need to be sensitive to the needs and problems of the nursing staff. The ICT will therefore consist of the ICD, ICN, Consultant Microbiologist (if not already the ICD) and a representative of management, who need not liaise on a day-to-day basis. Should an episode of cross-infection be identified, then the ICT may decide to deal with it themselves or, if it is a major problem, expand the ICT to an action group (AG). The AG is the ICT plus relevant clinicians, a senior nurse and a community physician. The AG will ensure that all steps to control the outbreak are taken, communicate with all affected groups, prepare a report for the ICC (ideally within 48 h), review progress and finally analyse the outbreak, making recommendations for prevention.

The Infection Control Committee will consist of the ICD, ICN, General Manager, District Medical Officer, Medical Officer for Environmental Health and representatives of the medical and nursing staff including occupational health. The ICC may also co-opt or invite representatives from any other section of the hospital administration particularly from hotel services, pharmacy, engineering services and operating theatres. It must meet at least twice a year to advise the Health Authority and formulate policies and programmes.

2. SAMPLE COLLECTION

2.1 **Surveillance**

Surveillance as applied to nosocomial infection is an ill-defined term which implies some degree of effectiveness in the control of nosocomial infection. However, there is very little evidence to suggest this, particularly in the USA where some hospitals pursue extensive ward-based surveillance programmes with little reduction in nosocomial infection rates (10).

A compromise would be limited laboratory-based surveillance in which the ICN visits the laboratory every morning and identifies likely isolates of bacteria causing nosocomial infection. This work can be reduced if the laboratory uses a computer-based reporting system as infection control programs are often available (Chapter 9, Section 3.2.4). If this surveillance is backed up by frequent visits to the wards and discussion with ward staff, existing and undiscovered episodes of nosocomial infection will be brought to light for the ICT to consider.

It may be appropriate sometimes to carry out limited surveys of the prevalence of particular nosocomial infections, but these should always have a purpose, such as the discovery of an occult source.

A marked increase in the isolation rate of a bacterium usually indicates a problem of cross-infection, although obviously an increase in the prevalence in the community may lead to increased admissions to hospital. It must also be remembered that 'pseudo-outbreaks' of bacteria may arise from contaminated anticoagulants being introduced into blood cultures via splashes (see Chapter 2, Section 2.2.6).

Routine monitoring of the environment by culture is *not* indicated, except during the investigation of an outbreak. Evidence collected in the USA suggests that, although many fewer unnecessary environmental cultures are now taken, there is still room for reduction (11).

2.2 Sampling protocols

2.2.1 *Patients and staff*

With the possible exception of patients on high-risk wards such as neonatal and adult intensive-care units, there is no value in performing routine surveillance cultures on patients. Some laboratories may wish to survey patients on intensive-care units for the carriage of gentamicin-resistant coliforms, *Pseudomonas aeruginosa*, *Staphylococcus aureus* (including MRSA where it is thought to be a problem on adjoining wards). The coliforms and *P.aeruginosa* are best detected using rectal swabs, staphylococci by nasal swabs and/or perineal swabs plated on to appropriate selective media, see *Table 1*. Suggested guidelines for the management of MRSA infection in hospitals in the UK have been published (12). It should be borne in mind that the information gained from these cultures is unlikely to benefit the individual patient, so it should be regarded as a measure of the level of cross-infection in that unit.

Sampling of patients during outbreaks will be determined by the bacteria involved. Screening of patients on a regular basis (at least on admission and 1 or 2 times per week) at the most likely carriage site(s) will identify asymptomatic carriers and give accurate pictures of the spread of the organism which will assist in epidemiological investigations.

Screening of staff for nosocomial bacteria is an emotive subject and should not be undertaken unless there are likely to be tangible benefits to the patients and the action to be taken with those members of staff that are colonized is clear. It is, however, sometimes valuable to take hand-impression plates whilst investigating an outbreak of nosocomial infection. Two purposes will be served, firstly a common potential route of cross-infection for many nosocomial bacteria will be identified, and secondly the nursing and medical staff will be reminded of the importance of hand-washing (13).

2.2.2 *Therapeutic substances*

The microbiologist investigating an episode of nosocomial infection where administration of the infecting bacteria in a therapeutic substance is possible is usually presented with a bewildering array of substances. The degree of sterility deemed appropriate for each type of substance ranges from the absolute in intravenous fluids to the relative in liquidized enteral feeds.

Whilst it is a cardinal rule that the sterility of no substance should be assumed, it is often appropriate to examine the non-sterile or easily contaminated sterile products first. In the case of chronic, episodic cases of nosocomial infection, careful use of survey techniques such as case-control and cohort studies will be vital (Chapter 12, Section 4). The routine sampling of commercially prepared substances labelled as sterile, and the in-use testing of disinfectants and antiseptics is inappropriate.

Creams and solids can be emulsified in a quantity of nutrient broth using a vibrating mixer and then either plated directly or enriched by incubating overnight, followed by plating on a suitable selective and non-selective medium. Heavily contaminated fluids can be plated directly on to solid selective media, but it is always useful to have a quantitative count for lightly contaminated fluids to help distinguish chance contamination. Traditionally this was achieved by preparing 10-fold dilutions of the fluid in sterile saline and then dropping duplicate 20 μl drops on to solid media and counting the colony-forming units. This is a time-consuming process; the alternative is vacuum filtration of a known volume of the fluid through a sterile 0.45 μm cellulose ester filter held in a suitable holder, such as the Sterifil Aseptic System [Millipore (UK) Ltd]. The filter is placed on the surface of a suitable selective agar medium and incubated for 18 h at 37°C. This method will allow large numbers of fluids to be processed in a very short time.

2.2.3 *Equipment*

The method of sampling equipment will be determined by the nature of the equipment. Most sites on equipment can be sampled with a cotton swab soaked in saline or nutrient broth. Containers and the lumens of tubes can be sampled as follows.

(i)   Place 10−15 ml of nutrient broth in the article to be examined.
(ii) Close by whatever means are available and vigorously agitate for 30 sec.
(iii) Pour the nutrient broth out into a sterile container and either filter the whole volume or count an aliquot of the broth using 10-fold dilutions (see Section 2.3.2 above).

Intravascular catheters should be cultured using the semi-quantitative technique of Maki *et al.* (14).

(i)   Clean the skin surface in the region of the intravascular catheter with an alcohol-soaked pledget and withdraw the catheter using sterile forceps. After withdrawal apply pressure to the puncture site.
(ii) Cut the distal 5 cm of the catheter off with sterile scissors and place in a dry, sterile container; transport to the laboratory as soon as possible.
(iii) Whilst applying downward pressure with sterile forceps, roll the section of catheter back and forth across a blood agar plate at least 4 times.
(iv) Incubate the inoculated plate at 37°C for 18 h.
(v)   The presence of ≥15 colony-forming units on the area inoculated indicates colonization of the catheter; confluent growth is often associated with catheter-related septicaemia. Colony counts of <15 CFU should be ignored, as they usually represent skin contamination.

It should be remembered that colonization of the non-sterile ports of intravascular devices such as arterial pressure-transducer monitoring ports may result in hand contamination and infection of the intravascular line itself (15).

2.2.4 *Environment*

It is not necessary to routinely sample the environment unless an episode of environmentally derived cross-infection is suspected to have occurred. Quantitative or semi-quantitative sampling of the environment is essential, as comparisons between results

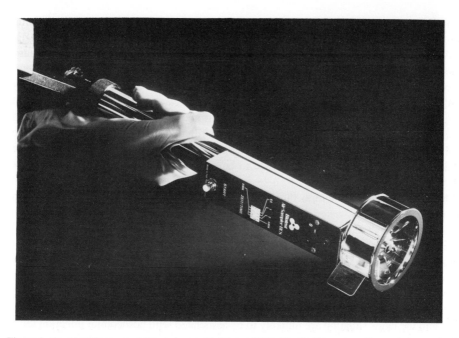

Figure 1. Hand-held Reuter centrifugal air sampler (Biotest RCS). The flexible agar medium strip is contained in the circular housing surrounding the impeller blades.

from different sites can then be made.

The airborne spread of nosocomial bacteria is a comparatively rare event, so routine sampling of air will achieve little. However, if cross-infection is suspected to have occurred, then sampling with settle plates or a more sophisticated mechanical air sampler will be required. Although settle plates are an inexpensive way of enumerating airborne organisms, air turbulence will greatly affect sampling. Also, in conditions of low humidity, particles ≤3 μm will remain suspended and not therefore be collected on a settle plate. Withstanding these limitations, a 9 cm petri dish exposed for 15 min in still air will sample particles from approximately 1 cubic foot (16). Should a more rapid sampling technique, which can also sample from specific points, be required, then the hand-held Reuter centrifugal sampler (Biotest RCS, Biotest Folex Ltd) will fulfil that role (*Figure 1*). It is a hand-held instrument with a battery-operated electric motor that drives a multi-bladed impeller. Air is captured between the impeller blades and particles deposited by centrifugal force onto a flexible plastic strip containing wells of agar medium around the periphery of the impeller blades. The device performs poorly when sampling particles with a diameter of approximately 1 μm, unlike the cumbersome, noisy Casella slit sampler. The manufacturers' stated sampling rate of 40 litres min^{-1} is also an underestimate, 100 litres min^{-1} being a more accurate assessment (17). As most airborne-bacteria-bearing particles found in hospitals are 4−20 μm in size, the Reuter instrument is the most practical one for routine hospital infection control procedures (18). Although standards for the level of microbial contamination of air have been suggested, they have not been widely adopted because agreement on the correlation of infections with levels of airborne contamination cannot be agreed (19).

251

The best use of air sampling would seem to be during commissioning and servicing of clean areas and the investigation of specific episodes of nosocomial infection.

Whilst floors and other surfaces such as work tops and refrigerator doors are easy to sample, the value of such data is questionable, particularly when undertaken routinely. Smooth surfaces can be sampled using a moistened cotton swab; a sterilized card mask will enable a pre-determined area to be sampled, take care to rub in a direction at right angles to the first used. A more precise quantitation of contamination may be obtained using Rodac plates, which are small petri dishes filled with 16.5 ml of a non-selective medium, thus providing a meniscus of medium which protrudes from the dish. The plate is pressed against the dry surface to be sampled and the colonies counted after incubation.

Most water supplies within the hospital will be chlorinated, although it is worth remembering that hot water will lose all if not most of the chlorine present in it before heating. Water (and melted ice) can either be examined for evidence of faecal contamination (1), or, more usefully, in the hospital environment for the presence of nosocomial bacteria. This is most readily achieved by filtering 100 ml of water (less if heavily contaminated) through a 0.45 μm cellulose acetate filter using the technique described in Section 2.3.2 of this chapter. Bacteria, notably *Pseudomonas aeruginosa*, will sometimes be found growing around tap outlets and in sink water traps. Whilst those in the latter situation are unlikely to be associated with nosocomial infection (20), tap nozzles can be sampled with a cotton swab. Organisms can be eluted by vortex mixing if a semi-quantitative result is required, otherwise plate the swab directly on to a suitable selective medium.

3. SPECIMEN PROCESSING

3.1 Criteria for organism identification

The extent to which isolates of bacteria in a clinical laboratory are identified is always a matter for debate. Whilst a report of 'coliform' is perfectly adequate in an uncomplicated urinary tract infection, patently it is not appropriate for a blood culture isolate. Obviously problems can arise from differences in the level of identification when organism identities are used to collect surveillance data. Failure to sufficiently sub-divide isolates may obscure cross-infection caused by a species. In addition, failures in procedures may cause 'pseudo-outbreaks'; if for instance an error occurs in the reading of coagulase tests, then coagulase-negative staphylococci will be misreported as *Staphylococcus aureus* (21).

In general terms, if an episode of nosocomial infection is suspected, then isolates related to the causes should be as fully identified as possible. If a number of isolates belong to the same species, then some form of further sub-division must be used, such as typing.

3.2 Use of selective and differential media

Once the bacterium suspected of causing nosocomial infection has been identified, it will be necessary to thoroughy delineate the occurrence of that bacterium. The use of appropriate selective media will ensure that even small numbers of the cross-infecting bacterium will be identified, ensuring that all sources, routes of transmission and portals

Table 1. Suggested selective and differential media for the isolation of commonly occurring nosocomial bacteria.

Bacterium	Medium	Commercial Supplier[a]	Components and principle
Staphylococcus aureus	Mannitol salt agar (MSA)	B, D, G, L, O	7.5% NaCl inhibits bacteria other than most staphylococci, S.aureus usually ferments mannitol (yellow colonies), sometimes after 48 h. Coagulase tests performed directly from medium may give erroneous results. May not grow all strains of S.aureus.
S.aureus (methicillin resistant, MRSA)	MSA + 4 mg l^{-1} methicillin[b] Blood agar + 4 mg l^{-1} methicillin[b] salt, phenolphthalein, methicillin agar (SPMA)[b,c] (22)		May not support growth of all MRSA strains. MRSA may be overgrown but all strains will grow. 5% salt, less inhibitory than MSA, not all S.aureus phosphatase positive (sodium phenolphthalein diphosphate split to give free phenolphthalein detected by exposure to NH$_3$, pink colour).
Streptococcus spp. and Staphylococcus spp.	Azide blood agar	B, D, G, O	5% NaCl and 0.2% NaN$_3$ inhibit all organisms except Streptococcus spp. and Staphylococcus spp.
Streptococcus spp., including Lancefield gp A	Colistin, oxolinic acid, blood agar (COBA) (23)	L, O	Colistin 10 mg l^{-1} and oxolinic acid 3 mg l^{-1} provide good selection for streptococci, blood adds nutrients and provides indication of haemolysis.
Lancefield gp B streptococci	Granada medium[d] (24)		Trimethoprim provides the selection, horse serum, starch and anaerobic atmosphere ensures red pigment production.
Lancefield gp D streptococci	Kanamycin aesculin azide agar (25)	O	Developed for foods, but useful if enterococci thought to be causing nosocomial infection. Kanamycin and azide selective agents, enterococci hydrolyse aesculin causing black precipitate around colonies.
Clostridium difficile	Cycloserine-cefoxitin agar[d] (26)	D, G, O	Antibiotics provide selection. Characteristically green/yellow fluorescent colonies seen under long-wave (360 nm) UV light, smelling of p-cresol.

Table 1. (continued)

Bacterium	Medium	Commercial Supplier[a]	Components and principle
Klebsiella spp.	MacConkey, inositol, carbenicillin[c] agar (MICA) (27) with pre-enrichment in Koser's citrate broth		Few species of the *Enterobacteriaceae* ferment inositol, klebsiella do so, appear as pink colonies, 10 mg l^{-1} carbenicillin inhibits most other bacteria. Pre-enrichment in Koser's citrate broth will increase recovery of small numbers.
Serratia marcescens	Deoxyribonuclease, toluidine blue[c] cephalothin agar (DTBCA) (28)		Most Gram-negative bacilli are DNase negative, *Serratia* is usually positive and is routinely resistant to cephalothin (cephradine or cefazolin may be substituted). Toluidine blue is a metachromatic dye which is pink in the presence of free nucleotides and blue with intact DNA.
Enterobacter spp.	Desoxycholate citrate, crystal violet, cefazolin, rhamnose[c] agar (DCCR) (29)		Not all *Enterobacteriaceae* ferment rhamnose, all species of *Enterobacter*, except a few strains of *E. agglomerans*, do. Cefazolin, crystal violet and DCA are selective agents.
Proteus spp., Providencia spp. and Morganella spp.	Proteeae identification[c] medium (PIM) (30)		Medium contains tryptophan which *Proteeae* degrade to a brown melanin-like pigment, they also degrade the fine crystals of tyrosine in the medium producing clear zones around brown colonies. Cindamycin 5 mg l^{-1} inhibits Gram-positive bacteria and 100 mg l^{-1} of colistin will inhibit most Gram-negative bacteria. (N.B. 10% of *Proteeae* also inhibited.)
Pseudomonas aeruginosa	Nalidixic acid, cetrimide agar[c] (31) (various commercial formulations)	B, D, G, L, O	Cetrimide 300 mg l^{-1} in original formulation (32) supports the growth of many bacteria, however the addition of nalidixic acid (15 mg l^{-1} after sterilization) and 200 mg l^{-1} cetrimide provides a more selective agar. *P. aeruginosa* produces a blue-green pigmentation (pyocyanin), yellow fluorescence under UV light (fluorescein) and rarely pink/maroon pigment (pyrubin). Further tests needed to confirm identity.
	Phenanthroline, C-390[c] agar (PCA) (33)		Combination of phenanthroline and C-390 (see Appendix II) is highly selective for *P.aeruginosa*, no other Gram +ve or −ve bacteria growing on the medium (33).

254

Organism	Medium	Supplier	Comments
Pseudomonas spp. (other than *aeruginosa*)	Pseudomonas C-F-C agar[b] (34)	L, O	Very low concentration of cetrimide 10 mg l^{-1} allows *Pseudomonas* other than *P.aeruginosa* to grow, selection increased with cephaloridine 50 mg l^{-1} and fusidic acid 10 mg l^{-1}.
Achromobacter spp.	Cetrimide agar (32)	B, D, G, L, O	If used *without* nalidixic acid all strains of *Achromobacter* should be recovered as non-pigmented/fluorescent, oxidase positive colonies (35). N.B. This medium is not particularly selective, check identity of all colonies carefully.
Acinetobacter spp.	Herellea agar (36)[c] N.B.: maltose in original formulation replaced by sucrose	D, G	Selection achieved by addition of bile salts, *Enterobacteriaceae* ferment sucrose or lactose in the medium. *Acinetobacter* spp. appear as pale lavender colonies as they ferment neither. N.B. *Pseudomonas* spp. produce grey-green colonies, screen with oxidase test (*Acinetobacter* spp. negative).
Aeromonas hydrophila	Xylose desoxycholate citrate[c] agar (XDCA) with pre-enrichment in alkaline peptone (37)		This medium was designed to recover *A.hydrophila* from faeces, but can easily be used for water and other samples. *Aeromonas* spp. appear as non-xylose fermenters. Check presumptive colonies as other bacteria can give a similar appearance to *Aeromonas* spp.

[a] Commercial suppliers: B, BBL Microbiology Systems; D, Difco; G, Gibco; L, Lab M; O, Oxoid.
[b] Incubate for 48 h at 30°C in air.
[c] These media are described in detail in Appendix II.
[d] Incubate for 20 h at 37°C in anaerobic conditions.

of entry are known. If the suspected epidemic strain is resistant to an antibiotic that the species is generally sensitive to, then the antibiotic can be incorporated into a suitable medium. It will be necessary to determine the MIC of the strain in question and check that it will grow on media containing the chosen selective concentration of antibiotic.

If an individual microbiologist has not had direct experience of investigating a particular nosocomial bacterium, then he or she may be uncertain as to the best selective medium. The information is widely distributed in the literature. *Table 1* is an effort to bring that information together in an easily used form.

4. BACTERIAL TYPING SYSTEMS

4.1 **Principles and use of bacterial typing systems**

Most nosocomial infections are caused by a relatively limited number of bacterial species. This means that identification of bacterial isolates to species level will not allow the detection of cross-infecting strains and hence recognition of their source and route of transmission. Obviously the isolation of two or more epidemiologically related isolates of an unusual species such as *Salmonella cubana* strongly suggests cross-infection or a single source; the same cannot be said for two isolates of *Pseudomonas aeruginosa*.

Over the years a large number of different methods of subdividing species of bacteria (typing) have been developed and applied to many different species. No single typing system is perfect, and it is important to appreciate the strengths and weaknesses of the method that is used. An 'ideal' typing system for a bacterial species should perform well when judged by the following criteria.

(i) *Typing ability*. A method should be able to distinguish bacteria which are biologically or genetically similar but not identical, so that an additional method is unnecessary. If a method for example only types 50% of the strains encountered then it is a poor method.

(ii) *Discrimination*. A typing method which exhibits a high degree of typability may well only divide the bacteria examined into a very small number of strains. The method would then be regarded as having poor discrimination or sensitivity. A method which exhibits good discrimination should recognize a reasonable number of types which correlate well with other methods and with epidemiological findings.

(iii) *Reproducibility*. This is an important characteristic, as a method will be used over a long period of time and in different centres. However, the good performance of a method such as bacteriophage typing in other areas may outweigh a lack of stability. The technical complexity of a method will have a bearing on reproducibility as well as biological variations.

(iv) *Applicability*. It is possible to develop a typing system using a laboratory collection of bacteria which has no value when used on clinical isolates of the same bacterial species. A typing method should therefore always be tested in field trials. The method should not be too complicated or expensive, as it will not be used by microbiologists. Centralization in reference laboratories will help improve availability of occasionally used methods.

Judgement should be exercised when deciding whether to type an isolate. Some laboratories may choose to type all isolates of bacteria commonly causing nosocomial infection, e.g. *Staphylococcus aureus* and *Pseudomonas aeruginosa*, particularly as methods may be used which can be automated to a certain extent. Smaller laboratories will rely on reference laboratories to carry out their typing so they may choose to be more selective. Good surveillance methods linked to epidemiological studies by infection control personnel would reduce the amount of typing done (see Section 2.1, this chapter).

A brief description of the various typing methods follows. Many of the methods are appropriate to the reference or research laboratory and are therefore not described in detail. The availability of methods for individual species will vary greatly from country to country and an attempt to collate those methods has been published elsewhere (38). The typing methods described in detail here are those that might reasonably be attempted by a moderately large clinical microbiology laboratory.

When typing isolates from sites (such as environmental sources) where a range of subtypes can be expected, it will be necessary to type more than one colony of the bacterial species to identify the epidemic strain. Obviously very large numbers of colonies cannot be typed, due to limitations on time and materials. However it should be remembered that if 5 colonies are typed then there is a 90% probability of detecting 2 equifrequent types. The probability falls rapidly if more than two types are present (39).

4.2 Biotyping

Most laboratories now use a disposable, commercially-prepared gallery of biochemical tests to identify important bacterial isolates, such as the API 20E which utilizes 20 different biochemical tests. The use of this method will therefore provide a biochemical profile, in which different biotypes may be noticed such as urease-positive *Providencia stuartii* or indole-negative *Escherichia coli*. However, variations in the inoculum and duration of incubation can affect the results, so methods should be carefully standardized (40). The characters used in biotyping isolates are not always stable and can often be encoded on plasmids which are transferable and sometimes lost from strains, such as urease-positive *P.stuartii* (41). Finally, biotyping is rarely useful, as most bacterial species are divided into a very small number of types and in some cases, e.g. *Staphylococcus epidermidis*, not divided into any useful sub-groups.

4.3 Antibiogram and resistogram typing

The determination of the pattern of susceptibility of a bacterium to a range of antimicrobial agents has been used many times to type organisms. It has advantages, as most laboratories will generate the new data as a by-product of the reporting of useful antimicrobial sensitivities to clinicians. When this information is handled in a computer (if MICs are used then sensitivity will be improved), then the various infection control programmes can 'flag' recurring patterns. This then is the main area of use for antibiogram typing; it has no value in comparative studies, as stability (particularly if plasmids are involved) is a problem, and because only a small number of agents are going to give different results, discrimination will be poor. Resistograms utilize the sensitivity of strains to different chemicals, thus building up a similar pattern to antibiograms. The same limitations apply as for antibiograms, and because of the small

Table 2. Bacteriophage typing of *Staphylococcus aureus*.

It is important that a batch of medium is used which is suitable for bacteriophage typing. Difco 'Bacto' nutrient broth and Oxoid nutrient broth should usually be suitable. The medium must not be too firm and should contain a high concentration of calcium ions.

Typing procedure

1.   Add 7.5 g l^{-1} of agar-agar and 5 g l^{-1} NaCl to the manufacturer's suggested weight of dehydrated broth base and, after sterilization, sufficient CaCl$_2$ to give a minimum concentration of 400 μg ml^{-1}. The correct level of Ca^{2+} is usually achieved by adding 2.5 ml of filter-sterilized 32% w/v CaCl$_2 \cdot$2H$_2$O solution to the molten sterile agar. As some batches of CaCl$_2$ vary in Ca^{2+} content, assay may be necessary if poor bacteriophage typing results are obtained.

2.   Pick strain for typing into 5 ml of nutrient broth and incubate overnight at 37°C. Use the culture to flood a lightly dried bacteriophage typing agar plate, remove excess culture either with a pipette or a pipette attached by tubing to a Buchner flask and vacuum pump arranged to act as a trap for the excess culture. The tubing and flask can then be autoclaved prior to cleaning.

3.   To each plate apply one drop (usually about 10 μl) of each of a full set of phages (*Table 3*) at Routine Test Dilution (RTD is the highest dilution which just fails to give confluent lysis with homologous propagation strains), using either an automated replication machine (LEEC Ltd) (*Figure 2*) or a fine pipette. Care must be taken not to touch the agar surface to avoid transfer of staphylococci from plate to plate, as liberation of lysogenic phages from the transferred strain may cause non-specific lysis. Some laboratories prefer to type using RTD ×100.

4.   Dry the plates for about 30 min at room temperature and incubate at 37°C overnight.

5.   Read the plates with a 10× hand-lens and record the results as follows.

1 − 19 plaques	±
20 − 50 plaques	+
> 50 or confluent lysis	+ +

Any that do not show at least one + + reaction should be retyped with RTD × 100 using the remains of the broth culture, when confluent lysis with secondary growth may be seen as well as inhibition reactions (see footnote to *Table 3*).

6.   Results should be reported as those phages that give a + + result. Minor variations of lesser reactions can give rise to inconsistent typing results if they are reported, but may be of local epidemiological significance. Variations in results mean that a fixed 'type' could be ascribed to a strain. Guidance on the likelihood of two very similar strains being identical must be given by the microbiologist.

Standardization of phage lysates

Phage lysates should be obtained from a reference laboratory (in the UK, the Staphylococcus Reference Laboratory will supply lysates at RTD × 1000). As the RTD has been obtained in the reference laboratory, it will be necessary to re-titrate using the reagents and strains in the user's laboratory as follows.

1.   Make serial 10-fold dilutions of each phage preparation in nutrient broth, by adding 100 μl of phage suspension to 900 μl broth and so on to provide a suitable series of dilutions.

2.   Apply each of the dilutions to a lawn of the propagating strain as described above.

3.   Every 7 days or so, spot a drop of phage lysate at RTD on an area of agar previously inoculated with the propagating strain. This will provide a quick check on the strength of the phage lysate.

number of species for which systems have been developed, it is not worthwhile for a diagnostic laboratory to set it up as a routine procedure.

4.4 Serotyping

This is one of the oldest typing methods, which is still used extensively today. The *Enterobacteriaceae* is the group of bacteria most commonly typed by serotyping, and schemes have been produced for almost all the genera and species. Serotyping to identify

Figure 2. Mechanical inoculator for phage typing (LEEC Ltd). The machine incorporates small gas jets to rapidly sterilize each of the inoculating loops, preventing carry-over of bacterial strains.

O and H antigens is the basis of salmonella identification according to the Kauffman – White scheme (see Chapter 6, Section 4.5). Serotyping schemes for *Enterobacteriaceae* associated with nosocomial infection are described in detail elsewhere (42). As the availability of such schemes will vary greatly from country to country, the problem should be discussed with the national reference laboratory. Serotyping can be applied to many different bacteria, and is one of the commonly used methods for typing *Pseudomonas aeruginosa*. Although there are problems with standardization of methods and production of antisera, serotype appears to be one of the most stable markers in bacteria. For this reason serotyping is still widely used, but not normally in the clinical laboratory, isolates being referred to specialized reference laboratories.

4.5 Bacteriophage typing

Bacteriophages are viruses capable of replication within the bacterial cell, leading in some cases to subsequent destruction of the bacterial cell (lysis) and release of infective bacteriophage particles. Typing schemes are developed by isolating a range of bacteriophages active against the bacterial species concerned (often from filtered sewage). The bacteriophage is purified and its activity against a large number of bacterial strains determined, and a set of bacteriophages is then selected to provide the maximum sensitivity for differentiating strains of bacteria. The technique has the advantage that it can be applied to a wide range of bacteria, many of which are not typable by other means. It is also a highly sensitive method, but suffers from being complex technically (environmental conditions can affect the sensitivity of bacteria to infection by

259

Table 3. Phage pattern of *Staphylococcus aureus* propagating strains.

Phage no.	NCTC no.	Result at RTD[a]
29	8331	29[b] (80)[c]
52	8507	52, 52A±(++)[b], 80+(++)
52A/79	8363	52±(++), 52A, 79, 80±(++)
80	9789	80, 81
3A	8319	3A, (3C), 55±(++), 71±(++)
3C	8327	(3A), 3C, 55, 71
55	8358	(3A), 3C, 55, 71
71	9315	3C, 55, 71
6	8509	6, 42E±(++), 47, 53, 54, 75, 77, 83A, 84, 85, 81±(++)
42E	8357	42E, (53+), (85+), 81±(++)
47	8325	(29+), (52+), (52A±), (79+), (80), 47, 53, (54), 75, 77, 84, 85
53	8511	53, 54, 75, 77, 84, 85
54	8329	(42E), 47, 53, 54, 75, 77, 84, 85, 81±(++)
75/76	8354	(79±) (47)[c], 53, 75, 77, 84, 85
77	8356	(47), (53), 77, 84±(++), 85+(++)
83A	10039	(52+), (52A±), (79±), (80+), 6, (42E+), 47, 53, 54±(++), (77), 83A, 84, 85, (81)
84	10455	(77±), 84, 85
85	10457	(75±), (77±), 84, 85
81	9717	80, 81
94	10970	94, 96
95	10971	(79±), 95
96	10972	94, 96

[a]Additional reactions to RTD for RTD × 100 are shown in brackets.
[b]Reactions are all ++ at both dilutions unless otherwise shown.
[c]Indicates an inhibition reaction which is a thinning of the lawn in the area of the phage spot and can be confused with confluent lysis. Titration of the relevant phage will not give separate plaques as in a genuine confluent reaction.

bacteriophages) with many variables to be controlled. There is also a need to maintain the bacteriophage typing set in a viable state by serial passage. For these reasons, bacteriophage typing has largely remained in the province of the reference laboratory. It is particularly useful for further subdividing serotypes of *Pseudomonas aeruginosa* and salmonellae. Bacteriophage typing remains the major typing method for *Staphylococcus aureus*, which is a common nosocomial pathogen. Some larger hospital laboratories undertake bacteriophage typing of *S. aureus* as they have sufficient isolates to make the investment in materials and labour worthwhile. A method for bacteriophage typing *S. aureus* is given in *Table 2*, which is based on the method of Blair and Williams (43). Smaller laboratories will probably refer isolates to a reference laboratory. The phage pattern of *S. aureus* propagating strains is shown in *Table 3*.

4.6 Bacteriocin typing

Bacteriocins are antibiotic-like, bactericidal substances (often proteins) which inhibit different strains of bacteria (44). The strain producing the bacteriocin is usually resistant to its action but, rarely, may be sensitive. By selecting suitable producer strains, isolates can be typed according to their sensitivity to a particular bacteriocin. Strains may also be typed by their ability to produce bacteriocins. Bacteriocins share many of the

Table 4. Rapid pyocin typing method for *Pseudomonas aeruginosa* (45).

1.	Inoculate the field strains of *P. aeruginosa* to be tested (including control strains that are known to give positive results with the producer strains used) on to nutrient agar plates to produce single colonies after overnight incubation at 37°C.
2.	The following day, using the overnight culture prepare suspensions of each strain in sterile physiological saline (10^8 to 10^9 CFU ml^{-1}, absorbance 0.5 at 550 nm).
3.	Use a multipoint inoculator (Model A400, Denley Instruments Ltd) with a 21-pin head and 2-mm diameter pins to deliver 1 μl of each suspension on to the surface of 13 9 cm Petri dishes, each containing 10 ml of Tryptone Soy agar (Oxoid). This enables 21 strains to be typed simultaneously against each of the 13 indicator strains. Remember to mark the plate to show the correct orientation (alternatively, use a marker pin instead of the 21st strain).
4.	When the spots are dry incubate the plates for exactly 6 h at 30°C. Impregnate 5 cm diameter filter paper discs with chloroform and invert the incubated plates over them for 15 min to kill the field strains. Expose the plates to the air for a further 15 min to allow residual chloroform vapour to evaporate.
5.	Cultures of the 13 indicator strains should be prepared earlier in the day by inoculating 2 ml of nutrient broth no. 2 (Oxoid) with 1 or 2 colonies from an agar plate culture. Incubate the broth cultures for 4 h at 37°C without shaking (should be approximately 10^7 CFU ml^{-1}). 100 μl of the broth culture is added to 2.5 ml of molten (45°C), semi-solid agar (1% peptone Difco Laboratories) 0.5% agar (Oxoid) and poured as an overlay, one indicator strain per plate.
6.	When the overlays are set incubate the plates at 37°C for 18 h.
7.	The plates are read as follows.
	— No inhibition of the indicator strain over the position of the field strain.
	+ Inhibition of growth of indicator strain either within the area of field strain growth (5−7 mm R or F-type pyocins, sharp edge) or inhibiting extending well beyond the field strain (9−12 mm, S-type pyocins, edge diffuse).
	Phage activity—mottled inhibition zone.
8.	Depending on the pattern of inhibition observed with the indicator strain 1−8 and A−E, a specific pyocin type number can then be assigned to each field strain by reference to *Tables 5* and *6*, e.g. 29/f. Differences in S-pyocin activity can be used to further subdivide strains.

Table 5. Inhibition patterns of pyocin types of *Pseudomonas aeruginosa* using the method of Fyfe *et al.* (45).

Pyocin type	Inhibition of indicator strain no.							
	1	2	3	4	5	6	7	8
1	+	+	+	+	+	−	+	+
2	−	+	−	−	−	−	−	−
3	+	+	+	−	+	−	+	−
4	+	+	+	+	+	−	−	+
5	−	−	−	−	+	−	−	−
6	+	+	+	+	+	−	+	−
7	+	+	+	−	−	−	+	+
8	−	+	+	+	−	−	+	−
9	−	−	−	−	+	−	+	−
10	+	+	+	+	+	+	+	+
11	+	+	+	−	−	−	+	−
12	+	+	−	+	+	−	−	+
13	−	−	−	+	−	−	−	+
14	−	−	+	−	+	−	+	−
15	−	+	−	−	+	−	+	−
16	+	−	+	+	−	−	+	+
17	−	−	+	−	−	−	+	−
18	+	−	+	+	+	−	+	+
19	−	−	+	+	−	−	+	−
20	−	−	−	−	+	+	−	−
21	−	+	−	+	+	−	−	−
22	+	+	+	−	+	+	+	−
23	+	−	−	−	+	−	+	−
24	−	−	+	+	+	−	+	+
25	+	−	+	−	−	−	+	−
26	+	−	−	−	−	−	+	−
27	+	−	+	−	+	−	+	−
28	−	−	−	+	−	−	+	−
29	−	+	−	−	+	−	−	−
30	−	+	+	−	−	−	−	−
31	−	−	−	−	−	−	+	−
32	−	−	−	+	+	−	−	+
33	+	+	+	+	+	+	+	−
34	−	−	−	−	−	−	−	+
35	+	+	−	−	+	−	+	−
36	−	+	−	+	−	−	−	+
37	−	+	+	+	+	−	+	−
38	−	+	+	−	−	−	+	−
39	−	+	+	+	−	−	+	+
40	+	+	−	−	+	−	−	−
41	−	+	+	−	+	−	+	−
42	−	−	+	−	−	−	+	+
43	−	+	+	+	+	−	+	+
44	+	+	+	−	+	−	−	−
45	+	+	+	−	+	−	+	+
46	+	+	+	+	−	−	+	−
47	−	−	+	−	−	+	+	−
48	+	+	−	−	+	+	+	−
49	−	−	+	−	+	−	−	−
50	−	−	+	−	−	−	−	−
51	+	+	+	+	−	−	−	+

52	+	+	−	−	+	+	−	−
53	−	+	−	+	+	−	−	+
54	−	+	+	+	−	−	−	−
55	+	−	−	−	−	−	−	−
56	+	−	−	−	+	−	−	−
57	−	+	+	+	−	−	−	+
58	+	+	+	−	−	−	−	−
59	+	−	+	−	−	−	−	−
60	+	+	−	−	−	−	+	−
61	+	−	−	+	−	−	−	+
62	+	+	+	−	−	+	+	−
63	+	−	+	+	+	−	+	−
64	−	−	+	−	−	−	−	+
65	−	−	+	+	−	−	−	+
66	−	+	+	−	+	−	−	−
67	−	−	−	−	−	+	+	−
68	−	−	−	+	−	−	−	−
69	−	+	+	−	−	+	+	−
70	−	+	−	+	−	−	−	−
71	−	+	−	+	−	−	+	−
72	−	+	−	−	+	+	−	−
73	−	+	−	−	−	+	−	−
74	−	+	+	−	−	−	+	+
75	+	−	+	+	−	+	+	−
76	+	+	−	+	+	+	+	−
77	−	+	+	−	−	−	−	+
78	−	+	−	+	−	+	+	+
79	−	−	−	+	+	+	+	+
80	−	+	−	+	−	−	+	+
81	−	+	−	−	+	−	−	+
82	−	+	−	−	+	−	+	+
83	−	−	−	+	+	−	+	+
84	−	+	−	−	−	−	+	−
85	−	+	−	−	−	−	+	+
86	−	+	+	−	−	+	−	−
87	−	+	+	+	−	+	−	+
88	+	−	−	−	+	−	−	+
89	−	+	+	+	−	+	−	−
90	−	−	+	+	−	−	−	−
91	−	−	+	+	−	+	−	−
92	−	−	+	+	+	−	+	−
93	+	−	−	+	−	−	−	−
94	+	−	−	+	+	−	−	+
95	+	−	+	−	−	+	+	−
96	+	−	+	+	−	−	−	−
97	+	−	+	+	+	−	−	+
98	+	−	+	+	−	−	+	−
99	+	−	+	+	+	+	+	+
100	+	+	−	−	−	+	+	−
101	+	+	−	−	+	−	−	+
102	−	−	−	+	−	+	+	−
103	−	−	−	+	+	+	−	+
104	−	−	−	+	−	−	+	+
105	+	+	+	+	−	−	+	+

+ = inhibition; − = no inhibition.

Table 6. Inhibition patterns of subtypes of common pyocin types using the method of Fyfe *et al.* (45).

Pyocin subtype[a]	Inhibition of indicator strain				
	A	B	C	D	E
a	+	+	+	+	+
b	−	+	+	+	+
c	−	−	+	+	+
d	+	−	+	+	+
e	−	+	+	−	+
f	−	−	−	−	−
g	−	−	+	−	+
h	−	+	−	+	+
j	+	−	−	−	+
k	−	−	−	−	+
l	−	+	+	−	−
m	+	+	+	−	−
n	+	+	+	−	+
o	−	+	−	−	−
p	+	−	+	+	−
q	+	−	+	−	+
r	+	−	−	+	−
s	−	−	+	+	−
t	+	−	+	−	−
u	−	+	−	+	−
v	−	−	−	+	−
w	+	+	+	+	−
x	−	−	−	+	+
y	−	−	+	−	−
z	+	−	−	−	−

+ = inhibition; − = no inhibition.
[a]Strains in these subtypes are designated as type 1/a, 5/f, UT/k, etc.

properties of bacteriophages, except they cannot replicate. Sensitivity to many bacteriocins is encoded on transferable plasmids, so stability of the method may sometimes be suspect. The method is also rather labour-intensive, particularly if cross-streaking is used. However, if a method is used which uses automated inoculation and it is applied to a bacterial species that is frequently encountered as a nosocomial pathogen, then the large clinical laboratory will benefit from routine bacteriocin typing. The rapid method for pyocin typing *Pseudomonas aeruginosa* of Fyfe *et al.* (45) is just such a method, described in detail in *Tables 4−6*. Bacteriocin typing has also been applied to *Shigella* spp., *Proteeae*, *E.coli* and *Enterobacter* spp. amongst others.

4.7 Molecular typing methods

A large number of potentially useful molecular typing methods have been developed recently, such as plasmid, chromosome and cell protein analysis. These techniques are reviewed elsewhere (46); plasmid analysis is the only one which is easily adopted in the clinical microbiology laboratory. A variety of rapid plasmid isolation methods have been described. The method given in *Tables 7* and *8* (47) is reliable and has the advantage that the plasmid DNA prepared by the method can be digested with restriction

Table 7. Reagents used in the rapid plasmid DNA isolation method.

Reagent	Description	Component	Amount
Reagent 1	50 mM glucose, 10 mM EDTA, 25 mM Tris HCl, pH 8.0	Glucose	901 mg
		Tris-HCl[a]	222 mg
		Tris-Base[a]	133 mg
		Na$_4$EDTA	372 mg
		Distilled water to 100 ml	
Reagent 2[b]	1% SDS in 0.2 M NaOH	NaOH	0.8 g
		SDS	1.0 g
		Distilled water to 100 ml	
Reagent 3	3 M sodium acetate pH 4.8	Dissolve 24.6 g sodium acetate in 50 ml distilled water, add glacial acetic acid until pH 4.8, add water up to 100 ml	
Reagent 4	50 mM Tris HCl, 100 mM sodium acetate	Tris-HCl[a]	0.44 g
		Tris-Base[a]	0.265 g
		Sodium acetate	0.82 g
		Distilled water to 100 ml	
Phenol reagent	Add 40 ml of distilled water, 6 ml of 1 M Tris HCl[a] buffer at pH 8.0 and 5 ml of 2 M NaOH to 100 g of crystalline phenol ('Analar' grade), leave until phenol has dissolved		
TEB buffer	40 mM Tris HCl[a], 1 mM EDTA, 50 mM Boric acid pH 8.2	Make ×10 and then dilute for use. To make 1 litre of ×10:	
		Tris-Base[a]	60.5 g
		Na$_4$EDTA	3.7 g
		Boric acid	31.0 g
		Distilled water to 1 l	
		Check pH 8.2	
Loading buffer	40% w/v sucrose, 0.5 M Na$_4$EDTA, 0.5% w/v bromophenol blue	Na$_4$EDTA	16.5 g
		Sucrose	40 g
		Bromophenol blue	0.5 g
		Distilled water to 100 ml	

[a]Weights of Tris-Base and Tris-HCl refer to Trizma® compound supplied by Sigma Chemical Co Ltd.
[b]This reagent should be freshly prepared every 4 weeks.

265

Table 8. A rapid method for the isolation of bacterial plasmid DNA.

1.	Inoculate 5 – 10 ml of Nutrient broth No. 2 (Oxoid) or similar medium in sterile 20 ml universal containers with the bacteria to be typed by plasmid profile.
2.	Incubate with shaking at an appropriate temperature overnight (usually 37°C).
3.	Harvest the bacteria by centrifuging 1.5 ml at maximum speed in a microcentrifuge (MicroCentaur, MSE Scientific Instruments Ltd) for 4 min using a 1.8 ml polypropylene Eppendorf-type tube. A pellet at least the size of a rice grain should be obtained. With some bacteria, such as coagulase-negative staphylococci, it will be necessary to decant the supernatant, refill with fresh culture and re-centrifuge until a large enough cell pellet is built up.
4.	After decanting the supernatant, resuspend the pellet in 100 μl of reagent 1 to which 1 mg ml^{-1} of lysozyme (Sigma Chemical Co. Ltd) has been added just before use. Lysozyme should be used when examining Gram-negative bacteria. For Gram-positive bacteria 1 mg ml^{-1} of lysostaphin (Sigma Chemical Co. Ltd) is added instead, also just before use.
5.	Incubate at room temperature for 15 min (Gram-negative bacteria) or 20 min at 37°C (Gram-positive bacteria).
6.	Add 200 μl of reagent 2 to achieve complete lysis of the cells, mix by gently inverting the tube 2 or 3 times; at this stage the solution will become clear and viscous.
7.	After a period of 5 min at room temperature add 150 μl of reagent 3 and mix by inversion. The chromosomal DNA has now been precipitated. This is removed by centrifugation at 12 800 g^a for 5 min.
8.	Using a pipette, carefully remove 400 μl of the clear supernatant to a clean Eppendorf tube, taking care not to remove any chromosomal DNA.
9.	Add 1 ml of ethanol and mix by inverting several times. Place the Eppendorf tube in liquid N$_2$ for 20 – 30 sec until a white condensate *just* starts to appear. An alternative method is to hold at −20°C for 1 h. Centrifuge for 2 min. It is important to ensure that the hinges of the tubes are on the outside of the rotor so that the position of the feathery pellet can be predicted, thus avoiding damage to it.
10.	Decant the ethanol, taking care not to disturb the pellet, and resuspend in 400 μl of reagent 4.
11.	Add 400 μl of the phenol reagent and mix briefly using a vortex mixer. Centrifuge for 2 min and carefully remove the *upper* phase into a clean tube, taking care not to take any phenol over.
12.	Precipitate the DNA using ethanol as in steps 9 and 10, but do not resuspend the pellet.
13.	Gently add 200 μl of diethyl ether to wash the pellet and centrifuge for 15 sec, decant the ether and leave the tube inverted to allow any residual ether to evaporate.
14.	Dissolve the DNA pellet in 20 μl of sterile distilled water and mix with 10 μl of loading buffer. The DNA can then be subjected to electrophoresis in either a vertical or slab agarose gel electrophoresis system. Many workers use TEB buffer to both make the gel (0.8% w/v) and fill the apparatus. Stain the gel for about 20 min with TEB buffer or water containing a small amount of ethidium bromide (1 mg l^{-1}).
15.	Examine the gel on a UV transilluminator (302 nm, UV Products Ltd). Bands may be recorded on a Polaroid camera for convenience using an orange filter.

^{a}All centrifugation is carried out at approx. 12 800 g which represents maximum speed on an MSE MicroCentaur centrifuge.

endonucleases as follows.

(i)   Add to the ether-washed pellet from step 13, *Table 8*, 2 μl RNase solution (10 mg ml^{-1} boiled to destroy nuclease activity), 1 μl of core buffer (varies according to restriction endonuclease used, manufacturers often supply buffer with the enzyme preparation) and 7 μl of sterile distilled water.

(ii) Spin for 15 sec in a microcentrifuge to mix.

(iii) Add restriction endonuclease in manufacturer's recommended amounts (5 – 10

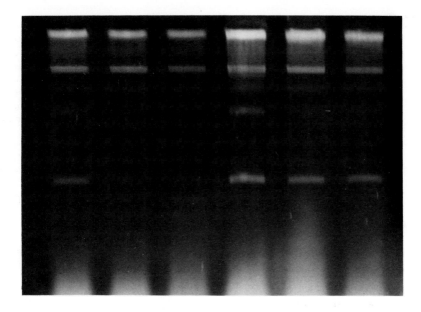

Figure 3. Plasmid profiles from isolates of *Salmonella typhimurium* made during an outbreak of food poisoning. Lanes **1**, **5**, and **6** show identical profiles of 2 plasmids and were all from faecal isolates from cases eating pork pies. Lane **4** is the blood isolate from the patient whose faecal isolate is in Lane **5**, it shows a slightly smaller deletion derivative of the larger plasmid. The isolates in Lanes **2** and **3** were from cases not eating pork pies and show different profiles to the pork-pie associated strain (they were phage type 204 and 49 respectively; the isolates in lanes **1**, **4**, **5** and **6** were all phage type 12). The band attributable to chromosomal DNA is indicated (**C**). The faint band below the chromosomal DNA in Lane 4 is the open circle form of the small plasmid, the majority of which is present in the covalently closed form.

units will usually give a complete digestion) and incubate for 2 h at the recommended temperature.

Plasmid analysis can be applied to any bacterial species provided that they have plasmids which are stable. It is a valuable method for typing coagulase-negative staphylococci. The routine laboratory will also find the method useful for subdividing serovars of food poisoning salmonellae; the gel in *Figure 3* is taken from the investigation of such an outbreak.

4.8 Miscellaneous typing methods

4.8.1 *Dienes phenomenon*

This unusual typing method can be applied only to swarming *Proteus* spp.. It relies on both the sensitivity of a strain to a specific bacteriocin and that strain's ability to produce a bacteriocin (48). When differing strains of *Proteus* spp. swarm towards each other and meet, a 'ditch' is produced between the two strains into which neither strain will swarm. It is a simple method which can easily be applied in the smallest laboratory and the results confirmed by serotyping or bacteriocin typing in a specialist laboratory. A suggested method is given in *Table 9*.

Table 9. Dienes typing method for *Proteus mirabilis* and *P. vulgaris*.

1. Inoculate the strains to be tested on to two blood agar plates in the positions indicated in *Figure 4* (6 strains A−F are shown in the figure). The inoculum can either be a small amount of a colony or a loopful of broth culture. Always include a strain from a different source to act as a positive control.
2. Incubate for 18 h at 30°C; slow-spreading strains may require a longer incubation time.
3. Examine the plates under reflected light for lines of incompatibility. If the recommended pattern is used, all strains will be exposed to each other. Some strains may not swarm and become overrun by a neighbouring strain. Observing the origin of the contours of swarming growth will help recognize this problem.

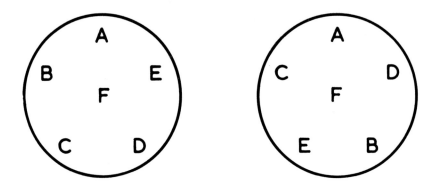

Figure 4. Positions of inocula for testing the Dienes compatibility of six strains of *Proteus* spp. in all combinations.

6. REFERENCES

1. Department of Health and Social Security (1983) *The Bacteriological Examination of Drinking Water Supplies 1982*. Reports on Public Health and Medical Subjects. No. 71. HMSO London.
2. International Commission on Microbiological Specifications for Foods (1978) *Microorganisms in Foods (Their Significance and Methods of Enumeration)*. Vol. 1: University of Toronto Press, Toronto.
3. International Commission on Microbiological Specifications for Foods (1986) *Microorganisms in Foods* Vol. 2: *(Sampling for Microbial Analysis: Principles and Specific Applications)*. 2nd edn Blackwell Scientific Publications Ltd, Oxford.
4. Hayes,P.R. (1985) *Food Microbiology and Hygiene*. Elsevier Applied Science Publishers, London.
5. Ministry of Health (1959) *Staphylococcal Infection in Hospitals*. Report of the Sub-Committee. HMSO, London.
6. Department of Health and Social Security (1988) *Hospital Infection Control*. HMSO, London HC(88)33.
7. Department of Health and Social Security (1986) *Public Inquiry into the Cause of an Outbreak of Legionnaires Disease in Staffordshire*. HMSO, London.
8. Department of Health and Social Security (1986) *The Report of the Committee of Inquiry into an Outbreak of Food Poisoning at Stanley Royd Hospital*. HMSO, London.
9. Goldmann,D.A. (1986) *J. Hosp. Infect.*, **8**, 116.
10. Casewell,M.W. (1980) *J. Hosp. Infect.*, **1**, 293.
11. Mallison,G.F. and Haley,R.W. (1981) In *Nosocomial Infections*. Dixon,R.E. (ed.), Yorke Medical Books, New York.
12. Report (1986) *J. Hosp. Infect.*, **7**, 193.
13. Millar,M.R., Keyworth,N., Lincoln,C., King,B. and Congdon,P. (1987) *J. Hosp. Infect.*, **10**, 187.
14. Maki,D.G., Weise,C.E. and Sarafin,H.W. (1977) *New Engl. J. Med.*, **296**, 1305.
15. Donowitz,L.G., Marsik,F.J., Hoyt,J.W. and Wenzel,R.P. (1979) *JAMA*, **242**, 1749.
16. Gröschel,D.H.M. (1980) *Ann. N.Y. Acad. Sci.*, **353**, 230.
17. Clark,S., Lach,V. and Lidwell,O.M. (1981) *J. Hosp. Infect.*, **2**, 181.

18. Casewell,M.W., Desai,N. and Lease,E.J. (1986) *J. Hosp. Infect.*, **7**, 250.
19. Whyte,W.,Lidwell,O.M., Lowbury,E.J.L. and Blowers,R. (1983) *J. Hosp. Infect.*, **4**, 133.
20. Levin,M.H., Olson,B., Nathan,C., Kabins,S.A. and Weinstein,R.A. (1984) *J. Clin. Path.*, **37**, 424.
21. Weinstein,R.A. and Mallison,G.F. (1978) *Am. J. Clin. Path.*, **69**, 130.
22. Wilson,P.A. and Petts,D.N. (1987) *Lancet*, **i**, 558.
23. Petts,D.N. (1984) *J. Clin. Microbiol.*, **19**, 4.
24. De La Rosa,M., Villareal,R., Vega,D., Miranda,C. and Martinezbrocal,A. (1983) *J. Clin. Microbiol.*, **18**, 779.
25. Mossel,D.A.A., Ellderink I.de Vor, H, and Keizer,E.D. (1976) *Lab. Practice*, **25**, 393.
26. Borriello,S.P. and Honour,P. (1981) *J. Clin. Path.*, **34**, 1124.
27. Cooke,E.M., Brayson,J.C., Edmondson,A.S. and Hall,D. (1979) *J. Hyg. (Camb.)*, **82**, 473.
28. Farmer,J.J., Silva,F. and Williams,D.R. (1973) *Appl. Microbiol.*, **25**, 151.
29. Flynn,D.M., Weinstein,R.A., Nathan,C., Gaston,M.A. and Kabins,S.A. (1987) *J. Infect. Dis.*, **156**, 363.
30. Hawkey,P.M., McCormick,A. and Simpson,R.A. (1986) *J. Clin. Microbiol.*, **23**, 600.
31. Goto,S. and Enomoto,S. (1970) *Jpn. J. Microbiol.*, **14**, 65.
32. Lowbury,E.J.L. and Collins,A.G. (1955) *J. Clin. Path.*, **8**, 47.
33. Campbell,M.E., Farmer,S.W. and Speert,D.P. (1988) *J. Clin. Microbiol.*, **26**, 1910.
34. Mead,G.C. and Adams,B.W. (1977) *Brit. Poult. Sci.*, **18**, 661.
35. Holmes,B., Snell,J.J.S. and Lapage,S.P. (1977) *J. Clin. Path.*, **30**, 595.
36. Mandel,A.D., Wright,K. and McKinnon,J.M. (1964) *J. Bacteriol.*, **88**, 1524.
37. Millership,S.E. Curnow,S.R. and Chattpadhyay,B. (1983) *J. Clin. Path.*, **36**, 920.
38. Aber,R.C. and Mackel,D.C. (1981) *Am. J. Med.*, **70**, 899.
39. Hedges,A.J., Howe,K. and Linton,A.H. (1977) *J. Appl. Bacteriol.*, **43**, 271.
40. Murray,P.R. (1978) *J. Clin. Microbiol.*, **8**, 46.
41. Grant,R.B., Penner,J.L., Hennessy,J.N. and Jackowski,B.J. (1981) *J. Clin. Microbiol.*, **13**, 561.
42. Ewing,W.H. (1986) *Edwards and Ewing's Identification of Enterobacteriaceae*. 4th edn, Elsevier Science, New York.
43. Blair,J.E. and Williams,R.E.O. (1961) *Bull. World Health Org.*, **24**, 771.
44. Reeves,P. (1965) *Bact. Rev.*, **29**, 25.
45. Fyfe,J.A.M., Harris,G. and Govan,J.R. (1984) *J. Clin. Microbiol.*, **20**, 47.
46. Hawkey,P.M. (1987) *J. Hosp. Infect.*, **9**, 211.
47. Bennett,P.M., Heritage,J. and Hawkey,P.M. (1986) *J. Antimicrob. Chemother.*, **18**, 421.
48. Senior,B.W. (1977) *J. Gen. Microbiol.*, **102**, 235.

CHAPTER 12

Epidemiological methods in the investigation of acute bacterial infections

STEPHEN R.PALMER

1. INTRODUCTION

Epidemiology is the study of the occurrence and causes of disease in populations. In contrast to the clinical situation when an individual patient is the focus of concern, the epidemiological approach relates the disease in the individual to the occurrence or risk of disease in others within the relevant population. This means taking into account not only the microbiological, but all personal, environmental and social factors which influence the occurrence and presentation of the disease. A well-defined methodology exists (1), which demands specialized skills, but every clinical microbiologist will need to be familiar with certain basic concepts and methods (2) and to take an epidemiological perspective from time to time. Examples include the investigation of sources and modes of transmission in outbreaks (3), applying public health measures to the control of outbreaks (4), preventing the spread of sporadic cases of certain infections (such as diphtheria, typhoid, meningococcal meningitis) (4), and devising preventive strategies, for instance for nosocomial Legionnaires' disease (5).

2. BASIC CONCEPTS IN INFECTIOUS DISEASE EPIDEMIOLOGY

2.1 Reservoir of infection

This is the principal habitat of the infectious agent from which it may spread to cause disease. Examples of reservoirs of bacteria are man (example: *Corynebacterium diphtheriae*); animals (*Campylobacter* spp.); soil (*Clostridium tetani*) and water (*Legionella* spp.).

2.2 Source of infection

Infection may be endogenous (caused by the patient's own flora) or exogenous (acquired from another source). The source of an exogenous infection may be different from the reservoir. Thus, in an episode of salmonella food poisoning the reservoir of infection may be commercially reared chickens. However, utensils and surfaces used for preparation of the poultry may cross-contaminate other foods which, when eaten, become the source of infection. When the source of infection is inanimate, such as food or water, it is termed the *vehicle* of infection.

2.3 Mode of transmission

The mechanism by which an infectious agent passes from the reservoir or source of infection to the person is called the mode of transmission. The major categories are:

(i)   *Person-to-person* spread from the *primary* case to the *secondary* cases who are *contacts* of primary cases. Within this category possible transmission routes include:

       (a)   faecal−oral spread (e.g. shigellosis);
       (b)   sexual transmission (e.g. syphilis);
       (c)   direct inoculation of blood (e.g. hepatitis B);
       (d)   airborne-droplet nuclei (e.g. tuberculosis);
       (e)   droplets (e.g. streptococcal pharyngitis);
       (f)   transplacental and perinatal (e.g. syphilis, gonorrhoea).

(ii)   *Food- and waterborne* (e.g. salmonella food poisoning, cholera). 'Food poisoning' is usually applied to incidents in which the organism multiplies in the food vehicle before transmission (*Clostridium perfringens*), although all suspected foodborne infection is statutorily notifiable.

(iii)   *Insect-borne* transmission via the bite of an infected insect (e.g. Lyme disease caused by *Borrellia burgdorferi* from a tick bite).

(iv)   *Direct contact* with animals or their products or with the agent in the environment (e.g. anthrax, leptospirosis).

(v)   *Airborne* droplet nuclei and aerosols (e.g. Legionnaires' disease) or dust (e.g. ornithosis).

2.4 Occurrence

Cases may be *sporadic* (not known to be related to other cases) or clustered in *outbreaks* (two or more related cases suggesting the possibility of transmission or a common source). Two measures of occurrence of infection are the *incidence rate* (the number of new cases in a defined population over a specific time period expressed as a proportion of the total population, e.g. 10 cases per 100 000 persons per year), and *prevalence* (all cases existing at a point or period in time in a defined population). The *attack rate* during an outbreak is the proportion of the population at risk who were ill during the period of the outbreak. The *secondary attack rate* is the attack rate in the contacts of primary cases due to person to person spread.

An infection which is continuously present in a population is said to be *endemic*, and an increase in incidence above the endemic level is described as an *epidemic* or *pandemic*.

2.5 Incubation period

The time from infection to the onset of symptoms is called the incubation period. For each organism there is a characteristic range within which infecting dose, and portal of entry as well as host factors (such as age) may introduce individual variability.

2.6 Host response

This will depend upon infecting dose, susceptibility (age, sex, other concurrent disease, immunity) as well as existence of other *risk factors* (for example smoking for Legionnaires' disease). In any outbreak of infection there will usually be a spectrum of clinical response ranging from no symptoms to fulminant disease and death.

2.7 Communicability

The infectious agent may be passed to others over a variable time, the *period of communicability*; in some infections even from symptomless temporary or chronic carriers (for example in *Salmonella typhi*).

3. EPIDEMIOLOGICAL METHODS

3.1 Descriptive methods

The investigation and control of both sporadic cases and outbreaks of infection begins with a thorough epidemiological history of the index patients. Routine medical records are seldom sufficient and a careful clinical interview should be undertaken if possible. Data should be recorded accurately, in detail, and retained for future reference.

3.1.1 *Clinical interview*

The data to be collected will be determined by the natural history of the particular infection. In newly recognized infections where the natural history is poorly understood, the questions will have to be wide-ranging and open-ended. Patients should be asked if they have kept diaries, calendars or even notes of events and exposures (for example restaurants visited on holiday). When more than one related case is to be interviewed, the main subject headings should be used to draw up a pro-forma to be used for interviews so that a standard history is obtained from each case. Informal questioning should follow the structured interview to explore possible leads. The following broad categories should be considered when drawing up a data collection form:

Name	*Date of admission*
Address	*Hospital no.*
Sex	*Ward and bed*
Age/date of birth	*Attending physician*
Occupation	*Investigations*
Place of work	*Treatment*

Clinical description of disease (nature, onset, severity, duration).

Predisposing factors. Other medical history, smoking, antibiotics, history of immunizations.

Contacts. History of illness in contacts. Identify household and other contacts by name and address for subsequent follow-up if necessary.

Travel history. Dates, places, hotels, flight numbers.

Social and *recreation.* Functions attended, other activities, hobbies, sports, use of recreational pools, etc.

Sexual history. Sexual orientation, names and addresses of partners for contact tracing if appropriate.

Food and drink. Document all food and drink consumed within the period immediately before onset which corresponds to the maximum incubation period for the suspected infection. Before interviewing prepare a checklist of categories of foods e.g. meats, dairy produce, tins. Record brand names and batch numbers if appropriate.

Exposure to animals. Pets, farm animals, zoos, wildlife.

3.1.2 *Questionnaire design and administration*

In large outbreaks it will not be practicable to interview in depth all persons affected. Usually a few patients, say 5–10, should be interviewed in depth to explore all possible exposures. Use these data to draw up a questionnaire (Appendix IV) for subsequent interviews. In some situations it is not possible to interview patients personally, and self-administered questionnaires can be given or posted to patients with a stamped addressed envelope for return. Such questionnaires require especially careful wording to avoid ambiguities. Before administration, try out questionnaires by asking colleagues or office staff to complete them, and then revise the questionnaire. In some studies, telephone interviews have proved to be satisfactory.

3.2 **Analysis and presentation of case data**

Data from patients must be summarized and compared to identify possible common exposures or risk factors. To do this, a line listing is prepared as in *Table 1*, which is taken from the outbreak investigated using the questionnaire in Appendix IV. Each question of interest on the questionnaire should form a column, and if possible, for each case the data should be recorded as 'Yes', 'No' or 'Not known'. Descriptive data should be summarized by time, place and person.

3.2.1 *Time*

The time of crucial importance is the time of onset of disease, since from this and a knowledge of the incubation period of the infection the period of exposure to infection can be determined. Do not confuse (as is often done) the date of hospital admission, date of specimen or date of laboratory test with the date of onset of symptoms. In an outbreak, the dates of onset in cases should be presented graphically, usually in the form of a histogram (*Figure 1*), though this is called an *epidemic curve*. The scale of the *x* axis will be determined by the incubation period: hours for *Staphylococcus aureus*, days for salmonellae and most other bacterial infections. The epidemic curve should be drawn immediately data become available, and updated during the course of the outbreak.

The epidemic curve is the most useful and immediate means of assessing the type of outbreak. In point-source outbreaks in which all cases are exposed at a given time (such as a wedding reception), onset of symptoms of all primary cases will cluster within the range of the incubation period (e.g. 6–72 h for salmonella food-poisoning). An epidemic curve which extends beyond a single incubation period suggests either a continuing or recurring source of infection, or the possibility of secondary transmission

Table 1. Part of a line listing of cases in an outbreak based upon data collected using the questionnaire in Appendix IV.

Case	Age	Sex	Deck	Dormitory	Onset of Symptoms	Visit to Naples				Visit to Haifa		
						Food bought	Drinks	Fruit	Ices	Ate Chicken	Extra Chicken	Fruit
1	13	M	A	2	4/2	√	–	–	–	√	√	–
2	13	F	B	4	4/2	–	–	–	–	√	–	√

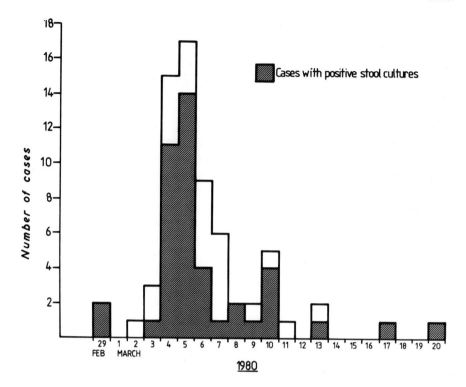

Figure 1. Epidemic curve of an outbreak of *Salmonella typhimurium* infection in a students' hall of residence (6). The major wave of illness from 4–7 March was shown to be due to consumption of cottage pie served March 3 and 4. Subsequent cases which spread out over several incubation periods were thought to be due to person-to-person spread.

(see *Figure 1*). In outbreaks propagated from person to person, the occurrence of cases will be spread over several incubation periods. Mixed outbreaks may also occur. The onset of diseases should be related to other events in the environment which may thereby be implicated as possible sources of infection, for example reduction in hot-water temperatures in a hospital just before a cluster of nosocomial Legionnaires' disease (7).

3.2.2 Place

Cases clustering in a particular place of work or neighbourhood, for example, may indicate the existence of a point source of infection or of person-to-person spread. Plotting cases by place of residence or work on a map as a scatter plot, or for example, by hospital ward, may reveal such patterns. In nosocomial outbreaks, movement of patients between wards may hide clusters and therefore it is necessary to identify and plot location at the time of likely exposure.

3.2.3 Person

In communicable diseases, most relevant patient characteristics and exposure factors will be discrete variables (for example sex) rather than continuous variables (for example white blood cell count), and will be analysed as proportions of cases or controls with a factor, or as a ratio (for example male:female). Analysis of patient characteristics

275

and histories of exposures (age, sex, medical history, occupation, travel history), may suggest hypotheses about the source and mode of infection. For example, the predominance of patients with gastro-intestinal dysfunction in a hospital outbreak of *Salmonella cubana* led to identification of carmine dye used in investigations as the vehicle of infection (8).

4. ANALYTICAL METHODS

Descriptive data may suggest hypotheses about the source or mode of transmission of an infection, but they are not always a sufficient basis for introducing control measures. Furthermore, caution is needed in the analysis and interpretation of data from cases, especially data about place and person. For example, in an outbreak of *Salmonella paratyphi* B bacteriophage type 3a var.4, extending over 4 years, which exclusively affected holidaymakers visiting Portugal (9), all cases except the last 3 had eaten at one restaurant in one small village. This restaurant had therefore been considered the most likely source of infection for the first 3 years, although screening of food handlers failed to identify a carrier. However, when local data was eventually obtained, it was found that the particular restaurant was the only one actually sited on the resort beach and that most if not all visitors would eat at the restaurant. The probable source of infection was found to be raw sewage which was contaminating the beach from a faulty sewer drain. Thus, observations on the cases have to be set against what is expected in the population from which they come: in the example above, all holidaymakers visiting the resort would be expected to eat at the restaurant.

Analytical methods are required to test the hypotheses generated from descriptive data. Broadly, there are two complementary approaches; the microbiological (for example culturing foods remaining from a meal thought to have caused food-poisoning) and the epidemiological. Even when microbiological investigations reveal contamination (contaminated food left over from a reception, or legionellae in a hospital cooling tower), this does not in itself identify the source of infection. Epidemiological evidence is still necessary to demonstrate an association between, for example, the contaminated food or the cooling-tower drift and the occurrence of illness. Since, for example, most water stored in large buildings will yield legionellae, but outbreaks are relatively rare, the significance of environmental isolates will need to be determined epidemiologically (5). Essentially the epidemiological approach is to compare the characteristics of infected persons (cases) with those of a similar group of uninfected persons (controls). Two principal study designs are used, the case-control (10) and the cohort (11) method. Choice of method in practice is usually determined by what is feasible. The case-control study will often be the easiest to perform but will yield less information than a cohort study.

4.1 Case-control studies

The use of these should be confined to testing hypotheses which have been raised by careful descriptive epidemiology. They are seldom useful if a prior hypothesis has not been clearly and precisely defined. Although relatively quick and cheap to perform, their design and analysis can be complex, and the practicalities of investigating acute incidents may not allow the ideal design to be followed. Even so, such imperfect studies are often of great help in arriving at answers rapidly during acute episodes. The essential feature of case-control studies is that data on possible sources and risk factors are elicited from both cases and controls retrospectively. Choice of controls is often problematical, but should be determined by the hypothesis being tested. For example, to test the hypothesis that a food item served at a reception was the vehicle of infection, controls would be selected from those attending the function, but who were well. If the vehicle of infection was turkey, then the proportion of cases eating turkey would be predicted to be higher than the equivalent proportion of controls.

The following aspects of case control studies need to be carefully considered.

4.1.1 *Case definition*

With a well-known infection which is readily confirmed microbiologically, case definition is straightforward. However, with newly-recognized diseases this can be difficult. In an investigation of an outbreak of haemorrhagic colitis, a newly recognized disease eventually attributed to infection with *E.coli* 0:157 H7 (12), cases were defined positively by the presence of gross blood in stools, severe abdominal pain and no fever, and negatively by the absence of other known pathogens in stools. Since it was likely that *E.coli* 0:157 H7 produced a spectrum of illness, probably only the severe end of the spectrum was identified by this definition. In a case-control study it is preferable to use such a strict narrow definition of a case.

4.1.2 *Possible misclassification of cases and controls*

In an outbreak of *Salmonella typhimurium* in a university hostel, a vehicle of infection was not detected by comparing food histories from well and ill persons (6). In this investigation stool samples were obtained from well persons as well as cases, and only when symptomless excretors had been grouped with the ill persons instead of as controls did a statistically significant difference in food histories emerge. To help overcome this problem, controls should be asked about symptoms over the appropriate period and those who may have been unrecognized cases excluded from the study. The feasibility of serotesting, swabbing or otherwise testing controls to exclude asymptomatic infected persons should be considered in all case-control studies.

4.1.3 *Selection of cases and controls*

Cases and controls should be representative of the infected and uninfected population from which the cases came. Possible biases in detection of cases, such as considering only those admitted to hospital, may exclude cases who have died of fulminant disease or who have mild illnesses. Risk factors identified on a biased sample may merely reflect those factors which caused the bias, for example admission to hospital.

Similarly, controls should be representative of the population, and this can be achieved by selecting controls randomly from the well population. However, in practice, taking every *n*th person on a list (systematic sampling) is often sufficient. A list of persons from which a sample can be chosen is the sampling frame, and sampling frames commonly used include:

(i)   rates or electoral register;
(ii)   hospital admissions;
(iii)   GP age/sex registers;

(iv)   hotel, reception guest lists;
(v)   family members of cases;
(vi)   neighbours of cases;
(vii) acquaintances nominated by cases;
(viii) persons investigated by the laboratory but who were negative for the disease in question.

The choice of sampling frame will depend upon the hypothesis being tested.

4.1.4 *Data collection*

The major drawback of case control studies is that accurate and complete data may not be available retrospectively. Medical records are notoriously incomplete, and patient recall may be faulty. This latter problem is lessened in acute incidents since there is usually little delay between the event and the interview. One particular problem is that of rumination bias; because of their illness, cases will have gone over possible exposures in their minds and recall may be biased by their own preconceptions. Also, cases may have been interviewed on many occasions, and this may introduce bias from suggestions made by interviewers as well as prompting a more detailed recall. Therefore, to ensure a systematic approach to questioning cases, and to ensure that controls are given an equal chance of recalling events, cases and controls should be interviewed in the same way, by interview or postal questionnaire, and with the same care. Prompts should be used to encourage recall in controls, for example relating time periods about which controls are being questioned to notable events.

4.1.5 *Response rate*

The loss of cases or controls because of refusal to be interviewed or failure to trace patients can seriously bias survey results. Exposures in those groups may not be similar to those of the responding group. Every attempt should be made to obtain a good response rate ($>85\%$), since poor response rate may invalidate a study. Reminders to study participants by letter or telephone should be considered if the response rate is poor.

4.1.6 *Confounding factors and matching*

A *confounding factor* is one which is not the source of infection, but which is associated both with the cases and independently with the hypothesized source. The association with the occurrence of disease may lead to a misinterpretation of the source of the infection. In the paratyphoid outbreak previously discussed, eating at the beach restaurant was shown to be a confounding factor. When confounding factors can be reasonably predicted, they may be excluded by matching controls with cases on those factors. It is usual in case-control studies of acute incidents to match controls for sex and age (usually for adults within 5 years of the case) and often for neighbourhood of residence. Confounding factors may only be identified after the study is completed, but can often be assessed by appropriate analysis.

4.1.7 *Number of controls*

Often only a small number of cases are identified. To increase the statistical power of the study, the number of controls per case can be increased up to 5 before the efficiency of the study falls. The number of controls is usually determined by practical constraints.

4.2 Example: A case-control study (13) of Legionnaires' disease associated with a whirlpool

Epidemiological interviews of 2 patients with Legionnaires' disease implicated a single hotel as a possible common source of infection. Retrospective review of illness in guests reported to hotel staff identified 21 further cases of pneumonia over a 4-month period, 16 of whom had serological evidence of recent infection; 7 other persons met the case definition for Pontiac fever (fever, aches and pains, without pneumonia and a convalescent indirect fluorescent antibody titre of ≥ 64). Interview with these cases suggested the hypothesis that use of the hotel whirlpools or swimming pools might be the source of infection. Control data was needed to test this hypothesis. In order to distinguish between use of whirlpools and other possible hotel-associated risk factors, such as showering and bathing in the hotel rooms, controls would have to be taken from the population of hotel guests, and the use of whirlpools by cases and controls compared. The sampling frame used to select controls was therefore the hotel booking list. In addition, it was considered possible that age, sex and week of stay could be related both to risk of Legionnaires' disease and independently to the use of whirlpools, and could therefore be confounding factors. To overcome this possibility, 2 control groups were selected, one of which was matched for these 3 possible confounding factors.

The need for matching can be explained as follows. If, for example, age and sex were true confounding factors and cases happened to be older than controls and to have a higher proportion of men, differences between cases and controls in use of the whirlpools could possibly be due to (say) older men having a greater susceptibility to *Legionella* and also independently being more likely to use the whirlpools. Without taking into account the possible association of age, sex and whirlpool use, a false identification of the source might be made. Similarly, if controls were not matched for week of stay, then perhaps if the whirlpools were out of use or a more attractive recreation was available during the time when more controls than cases were at the hotel, a spurious association between cases and whirlpool use would have been produced.

The procedure for selection of matched controls was to define the matching parameters, list all eligible guests from the particular week's records, and then to choose every *n*th name to give 5 controls per case. A standard questionnaire was applied to each case and control. Misclassification of controls was a potential problem, since a number of controls reported symptoms which could have been due to *Legionella* infection, and these were excluded from analysis. Asymptomatic infection could only have been excluded by serotesting all controls, and this was not considered feasible. However, including infected persons as controls would tend to bias results against the hypothesis being tested and would not bias the study to produce falsely positive associations.

The results of the study showed that 17 of 21 cases had used the whirlpools but only 20 of 67 controls had done so (*Table 2*). This difference was highly statistically significant. There were no significant differences between cases and controls in the use of domestic baths or showers. The whirlpools were taken out of use and no further cases occurred.

Table 2. History of exposure to possible sources of *Legionella* infection investigated by a case-control study.

Exposure	Cases		Control		Odds ratio
	Exposed	Not exposed	Exposed	Not exposed	
Whirlpool	17	4	20	47	10
Bath	11	9	37	15	0.5
Shower	2	17	14	39	0.3
Drinking tap water	8	12	37	35	0.6

4.3 Cohort studies

The essential difference between a case-control study and a cohort study is that the case-control study begins by identifying people with and without the infection and then retrospectively tries to identify factors associated with disease. In cohort studies, groups of people are identified other than by the presence of disease, and then information on disease occurrence is sought. Cohort studies may be prospective, when the disease occurs after the study has begun and the population characteristics have been identified; or retrospective, as is usually the case in investigation of acute incidents. For example, in a food-poisoning outbreak at a medical conference, all delegates (the cohort) attending the conference were easily identified and names and addresses obtained from the organizers. Delegates were contacted by postal questionnaire, and data on exposures and illness collected.The total cohort was then divided into two groups according to their exposure to a particular meal. Attack rates in those eating the meal and those not eating the meal were calculated. Once the meal responsible for the food-poisoning was identified, attack rates in persons eating particular food items were compared with attack rates in those not eating the items.

As in a case-control study, the hypothesis to be tested by a cohort study will determine the study design. In the outbreak of food-poisoning, each food item on the menu was hypothesized to be the vehicle of infection. Each member of the cohort (those attending the meal) was asked about consumption of each food. The attack rate in these persons eating the food (exposed) was then compared with those not eating the food (not exposed). The method can be applied to any hypothesized vehicle of infection and to hypothesized risk factors (factors which are not necessarily the source of the infection but contribute to the likelihood of infection). In addition to the factors also relevant to case-control studies (Sections 4.1.1−4.1.5) the following need to be carefully considered.

4.3.1 Defining the population at risk

The descriptive epidemiological enquiry will reveal the population at risk for the infection. Thus, in the previous example, interviews with the first cases of food-poisoning revealed that the population at risk was delegates attending a particular conference. In outbreaks where a specific at-risk group cannot be identified, the case-control approach may be more appropriate.

4.3.2 Sampling

If the at-risk population is large, a sample can be investigated and results extrapolated to the total population. In order to do this the sample must be representative. Ideally a random sample should be taken by applying random number tables to the sampling frame. In outbreaks in institutions, a complete list of the population can readily be obtained. An alternative to random number sampling is to select every *n*th person from the list. Cluster or stratified sampling may sometimes be appropriate (1).

4.3.3 *Case definition*

It is usual in cohort studies to seek information on symptoms and to classify persons as cases or not cases according to a predetermined definition. Symptoms will need to be precisely defined (e.g. 'by diarrhoea we mean at least three or more loose or water stools in a 24-h period') so that all respondents understand the questions in the same way. It is seldom practical to confirm a diagnosis microbiologically in such population surveys, and a clinical definition based solely on reported symptoms is usually used.

4.4 **Example: Cohort studies of an outbreak of *Campylobacter* infection in a residential school (14)**

Following a report of an outbreak of *Campylobacter* infection in a residential school, preliminary interviews with a few cases excluded raw milk and foods consumed outside of the school as possible sources of infection. Investigation of the domestic water revealed an unchlorinated borehole supply as a possible source. To test the hypothesis that infection was waterborne, two cohort studies were conducted. All teachers were asked to complete a questionnaire which recorded symptoms and water consumption in the school. The dates of onset of illness in most staff were not sufficiently recent for stool isolation of *Campylobacter* to provide the definition of a case. Instead, a case of illness was defined as the reporting of diarrhoea or abdominal pain for at least 24 h during the school term. The attack rate in staff drinking water from the suspected source was significantly greater than in the remainder. The pupils were resident in several houses, some of which were supplied with a chlorinated water supply. Cohorts of pupils from the different houses were surveyed by self-administered questionnaire. Attack rates by house corresponded to the distribution of the suspected water supply (*Table 3*).

4.5 **Statistical analysis of case-control and cohort studies**

In both types of study the basic analysis is by a comparison of proportions. For example, in the cohort study (Section 4.3.4) the proportion of staff drinking the unchlorinated water who were ill was 21/39 compared with 2/18 who did not drink the water. The data can be presented in a contingency table (*Table 4*).

Table 3. Attack rates in cohorts of pupils according to water supply to residential houses (14).

Water supply	Total	Ill	Attack rate	Relative risks[a]
Unchlorinated	299	153	51%	3.2
Mixed supply	198	60	30%	1.9
Chlorinated	128	21	16%	–

[a]Compared with chlorinated mains supply.

Table 4. Contingency table of a cohort study (Section 4.3.4). Letters in parenthesis show derivation of values.

	Drank water (exposed)	Did not drink (not exposed)	Total
Ill	21 (a)	2 (c)	23 (a+c)
Well	18 (b)	16 (d)	34 (b+d)
Total	39 (a+b)	18 (c+d)	57 (a+b+c+d)

In cohort studies the ratio of $a/a+b$ is the attack rate of the exposed group. The ratio $(a/a+b)/(c/c+d)$, the ratio of the attack rates in exposed and unexposed groups, is called the *relative risk*. The size of the relative risk is an indication of the causative role of the factor concerned. In case-control studies the ratio $a/a+b$ is not meaningful, since b is an unknown fraction of the total well population who were exposed. However, the cross-product ratio ad/bc, called the *odds ratio*, approximates to the relative risk.

The methods to determine the statistical significance of the comparisons depends on the study design (15). In unmatched case-control studies χ^2 is appropriate. The basic principle is to estimate an expected value for each cell in the contingency table, assuming that both exposed and unexposed have the same proportion who were ill and well, by using the marginal totals. Thus the expected value for the exposed ill persons is

$$\frac{(a+c)\times(a+b)}{(a+b+c+d)}$$

For each cell the following expression is calculated:

$$\frac{(\text{observed} - \text{expected})^2}{(\text{expected})}$$

and the sum over all cells gives the χ^2 value.

A formula for χ^2 with Yates' correction is

$$\frac{[ad-bc-\frac{1}{2}(a+b+c+d)]^2(a+b+c+d)}{(a+b)(c+d)(a+c)(b+d)}$$

If $(a+b+c+d)$ is <20, or if the expected value of any cell is <5, then it is advisable to use exact probabilities (e.g. Fisher's exact test) rather than χ^2 (16). When controls have been matched to cases, matched analysis should be performed using McNemar's test or the exact binomial probability (15). Ignoring the matching and using a χ^2 will give a rough estimation of the significance of the differences in proportions. Statistical analysis is usually performed using statistical packages available for microcomputers, but the advice of a statistician should be sought when designing research studies or before using unfamiliar statistical tests.

Multiple 2 × 2 analyses may reveal more than one factor to differ significantly between cases and controls. These factors may be causally related to the infection, or they may be confounding factors. These possibilities may be assessed by stratifying the data by the suspected confounding factor. Thus, in the cohort study above, drinking water was associated with eating food prepared in the school kitchen. When examined individually, both factors were associated with illness. However, stratification by whether food was eaten produced the following table:

| | Food eaten | | No food | |
	Ill	Total	Ill	Total
Water	20	37	1	2
No water	0	9	2	9

Once the effect of eating food from the school kitchen is controlled, the association of illness with drinking water remains significant. Statistical estimates of the stratified data may be carried out by Cochran's test (15) or by the Mantel−Haenszel test (16). More sophisticated analyses using multivariate and log-linear model fitting methods are now being used routinely in analyses of such data. Appropriate analysis of matched case-control studies uses the case-control set as the unit of observation, rather than case versus control groups. McNemar's test, the Mantel−Haenszel test and log-linear model approaches are frequently used (15).

5. A PRACTICAL APPROACH TO THE INVESTIGATION OF AN ACUTE INCIDENT

The administrative aspects of this approach in hospitals are described in Chapter 11, Section 1.2. This section describes the practical aspects of the investigation.

5.1 Identification and confirmation of the problem

5.1.1 Checking information

Inadequate history-taking or clinical examination and investigation, as well as errors in recording and reporting data, can lead to false information being circulated. All epidemiological data should be confirmed by independent enquiry as thoroughly and quickly as possible before action is taken. These data should be accurately recorded and retained for future reference (including possible use as legal evidence).

5.1.2 Checking diagnosis

The possibility of laboratory mistakes, and of equivocal results with some laboratory techniques, requires that laboratory methods should be reviewed and, where appropriate, isolations confirmed by a reference laboratory, which may also be able to help with typing. Isolates and sera should be saved for further typing (Chapter 11, Section 4).

5.1.3 Confirming an outbreak exists

Changes in diagnostic techniques and clinical habits and population structure can cause artifacts in surveillance data, and the media can cause inappropriate public alarm. Prevalence and incidence studies may need to be carried out to confirm a problem exists, and laboratory results reviewed. One useful index of a new problem is the percent positivity. In an outbreak, not only will the number of cases increase, but the proportion of all tests done which are positive will also increase. An increase in investigations due for example to a new interest or concern of clinicians should only increase the total number of samples submitted. When a problem has been confirmed, interim control measures to be instituted should be considered. At this stage, environmental samples (water, food) which may be required later should be taken (Chapter 11, Section 2.3.3/4).

5.1.4 *Communication and designation of responsibilities*

It is essential that everyone who needs to know about an acute incident is given early accurate information and knows what tasks they are expected to perform. Professionals and organizations to be considered are:

(i)   Infection Control Doctor;
(ii)   Control of Infection Nurse;
(iii)   management;
(iv)   Public Health Physician;
(v)   Local Authority Environmental Health Department;
(vi)   PHLS Communicable Disease Surveillance Centre;
(vii)   Governmental Health Departments.

5.1.5 *Patient interviews* (See Sections 3.2.1 and 3.2.2)

In large outbreaks, it will not be practical to interview all cases in depth. A small number of cases (5 – 10) should first be interviewed in depth to explore possible exposures. It may be helpful to interview a few unaffected persons from the at-risk population as well as any atypical cases or persons with very limited exposures. From these interviews, the population at risk will be defined, and hypotheses of the cause of the outbreak will be generated. An appropriate questionnaire can then be designed (Section 3.2.2).

5.1.6 *Defining population at risk*

Often this will be obvious: those attending a single function or reception or those living in an institution. Less easy to define are those outbreaks occurring in the general community. Definition of the population is essential in epidemiology, since all investigations and results should be referable to that group and as a preliminary step for case-searching.

5.1.7 *Case-searching*

Cases presenting at the point of recognition of an outbreak are seldom typical. Vigorous case-finding will be necessary to measure the size of the outbreak, and to increase the power of any proposed case-control study. A preliminary step is to decide on a case definition. This may be approached in two stages. In the first place, a broad case definition is used (pneumonia developing in hospitalized patients); laboratory investigation is then used to reclassify possible cases as confirmed or unconfirmed, for example on the basis of *Legionella* serology). Methods of case-finding, both retrospective and prospective, include:

(i)   review of medical records (GP, hospital, occupational);
(ii)   soliciting clinical reports (GPs, hospital doctors, nurses) and statutory notifications;

(iii)   review of laboratory data;

(iv)   survey of population.

5.1.8 *Analysis of case data and formulating a hypothesis*

Data should be analysed by time, place, person and by cross-tabulations, keeping an open mind since new vehicles and new modes of transmission may be identified for old pathogens.

5.1.9 *Hypothesis testing*

Hypotheses may be tested:

(i)   epidemiologically by case-control or cohort studies;

(ii)   microbiologically (testing food samples);

(iii)   by searching for environmental and other data, e.g. history of water pollution, engineering data or catering practices.

5.1.10 *Monitoring and evaluation of control measures*

Microbiological methods such as the use of sewer swabs or water sampling; direct observations, such as kitchen inspection; and epidemiological surveillance should be considered. Many surveillance systems collect only numerator data which therefore have to be interpreted cautiously (17). National surveillance of infectious diseases in England and Wales is the responsibility of the PHLS Communicable Disease Surveillance Centre, and the main source of data is the laboratory reporting scheme (18).

6. REFERENCES

1.   MacMahon,B. and Pugh,T.F. (1970) *Epidemiology. Principles and Methods.* Little Brown, Boston.
2.   Gregg,M.B. (1985) In *Oxford Textbook of Public Health.* Vol. 3, Holland,W.W., Detels,R. and Knox,G. (eds), Oxford University Press, Oxford, p. 284.
3.   Galbraith,N.S. (1985) In *Oxford Textbook of Public Health.* Vol. 4, Holland,W.W., Detels,R. and Knox,G. (eds), Oxford University Press, Oxford, p. 3.
4.   Benenson,A.S. (ed.) (1985) *Control of Communicable Diseases in Man.* 14th edn, American Public Health Association, Washington, DC.
5.   Bartlett,C.L.R., Macrae,A.D. and Macfarlane,J.T. (1986) *Legionella Infections.* Edward Arnold, London.
6.   Palmer,S.R., Jephcott,A.E., Rowland,A.J. and Sylvester,D.G.H. (1981) *Lancet,* i, 881.
7.   Palmer,S.R., Zamiri,I., Ribeiro,C.D. and Gajewska,A. (1986) *Brit. Med. J.,* **292**, 1494.
8.   Lang,D.J., Kunz,L.J., Martin,A.R., Schroeder,S.A. and Thomson,L.A. (1967) *New Engl. J. Med.,* **276**, 829.
9.   Anonymous (1982) *Brit. Med. J.,* **284**, 1125.
10.   Schlesselman,J.J. (1982) *Case-Control Studies: Design, Conduct, Analysis.* Oxford University Press, New York.
11.   Feinleib,M. and Detels,R. (1985) Cohort studies In *Oxford Textbook of Public Health.* Vol. 3, Holland,W.W., Detels,R. and Knox,G. (eds), Oxford University Press, Oxford, p. 101.
12.   Riley,L.W., Remis,R.S., Helgerson,S.D., McGee,H.B., Wells,J.G., Davis,B.R., Hebert,R.J., Olcott,E.S., Johnson,L.M., Hargrett,N.T., Blake,P.A. and Cohen,M.L. (1983) *New Engl. J. Med.,* **308**, 681.
13.   Bartlett,C.L.R., Personal communication.
14.   Palmer,S.R., Gully,P.R., White,J.M., Pearson,A.D., Suckling,W.G., Jones,D.M., Rawes,J.C.L. and Penner,J.L. (1983) *Lancet,* i, 287.
15.   Tillett,H.E. (1986) *Int. J. Epidemiol.,* **15**, 126.
16.   Armitage,P.L. (1971) *Statistical Methods in Medical Research.* Blackwell Scientific, Oxford.
17.   Galbraith,N.S. (1982) In *Recent Advances in Community Medicine.* Smith,Alwyn (ed.), Churchill Livingstone, Edinburgh, p. 127.
18.   Galbraith,N.S. and Young,S.E.J. (1980) *Community Medicine,* **2**, 135.

Staining procedures

1. GRAM'S STAIN (PRESTON AND MORRELL'S MODIFICATION)

This modification is recommended because it gives reliable results without the need to take great care adjusting the length of decolorization.

1.1 Solutions required

Ammonium oxalate crystal violet

Crystal violet	20 g
Methylated spirit (640P)	200 ml
Ammonium oxalate 1% in water	800 ml

Iodine solution

Iodine	10 g
Potassium iodide	20 g
Distilled water	1000 ml

Liquor iodi fortis (BP)

Iodine	10 g
Potassium iodide	6 g
Methylated spirit (740P)	90 ml
Distilled water	10 ml

Iodine-acetone

Liquor iodi fortis	35 ml
Acetone	965 ml

Dilute carbol fuchsin

Ziehl – Neelsen's (strong) carbol fuchsin	50 ml
Distilled water	950 ml

1.2 Staining procedure

(i)   Flood the slide with ammonium oxalate crystal violet and leave for about 30 sec.

(ii) Pour off and wash freely with iodine solution. Cover with fresh iodine solution and leave for about 30 sec.

(iii) Pour off the iodine solution and wash freely with iodine – acetone. Cover with fresh iodine – acetone and leave for about 30 sec.

(iv) Wash thoroughly with water.

(v)   Counterstain with dilute carbol fuchsin for about 30 sec.

(vi) Wash with water and blot dry.

The slide must be flooded with each reagent in turn and the previous reagent must be removed thoroughly at each step. Gram-positive organisms stain blue and Gram-negative stain pink.

Other counterstains may be used such as:

Neutral red solution

Neutral red	1 g
1% acetic acid	2 ml
Distilled water	1000 ml

Safranin

Safranin, saturated alcohol solution (about 2.5 g/100 ml of 95% alcohol)	10 ml
Water	90 ml

2. GIEMSA STAIN

2.1 **Solutions required**

Stock solution

Giemsa powder	0.5 g
Methyl alcohol, absolute, acetone-free	33 ml

Mix thoroughly, allow to sediment and store at room temperature.

Buffered water, pH 7.2

Solution A. Prepare 0.067 M Na_2HPO_4 by adding 9.5 g of anhydrous salt to 1 l of distilled water.

Solution B. Prepare 0.067 M NaH_2PO_4 by dissolving 9.2 g of anhydrous salt to 1 l of distilled water.

Mix 72 ml of solution A with 28 ml of solution B and 900 ml of distilled water.

Working solution

Stock solution	1 part
Buffered water, pH 7.2	40 or 50 parts

2.2 **Staining procedure**

(i)   Air dry the smear and fix with absolute methanol for at least 5 min and dry again.

(ii) Cover the slide with the working Giemsa solution (freshly prepared the same day) for 1 h.

(iii) Rinse rapidly in 95% ethyl alcohol to remove excess dye. Dry the slide and examine.

3. STAINS FOR ACID FAST BACILLI

3.1 **Auramine phenol**

3.1.1 *Solutions required*

Staining solution

Auramine 'O'	0.3 g
Phenol	3.0 g
Distilled water	97.0 ml

Decolorizing solution

75% industrial alcohol containing 0.5% NaCl and 0.5% HCl.

Counterstain

Potassium permanganate solution 1 in 1000.

3.1.2 *Staining procedure*

(i)   Stain a smear of sputum (or other appropriate material) with auramine staining solution for 15 min.
(ii) Rinse with water and decolorize for 5 min with acid alcohol.
(iii) Wash well with water and apply potassium permanganate solution for 30 sec.
(iv) Wash well with water and allow to dry.

Examine the film dry with an 8 mm objective lens and a high-power eyepiece. Mycobacteria are seen as yellow luminous organisms in a dark field. When such bacilli are seen with the low-power objective check their morphology by observing them under the oil-immersion objective. The method has the advantage that large areas of a film can be scanned in a short time.

3.2 **Ziehl – Neelsen**

3.2.1 *Solutions required*

Carbol fuchsin

Basic fuchsin	0.3 g
Ethyl alcohol (95%)	10.0 ml
Phenol, melted crystals	5.0 ml
Distilled water	95.0 ml

Dissolve the basic fuchsin in the alcohol; dissolve the phenol in the water. Mix the two solutions and let it stand for several days before use.

Acid alcohol

Ethyl alcohol (95%)	97 ml
Hydrochloric acid, concentrated	3 ml

Methylene blue, counterstain

Methylene blue	0.3 g
Distilled water	100 ml

3.2.2 *Staining procedure*

(i)   Flood the slide with carbol fuchsin and heat slowly until steaming. Use low or intermittent heat to maintain steaming for 3–5 min, and then allow to cool.
(ii) Wash briefly with water and decolorize with acid alcohol until no more stain comes off.
(iii) Wash with water and counterstain for 30 sec with methylene blue.
(iv) Wash with water, blot dry and examine.

Acid fast organisms are red; the background and non-acid fast organisms are blue.

3.2.3 *Modification of Ziehl–Neelsen procedure for Nocardia spp.*

The method is the same as 3.2.2 with the exception of the decolorization step. Decolorize with 0.5% sulphuric acid instead of acid alcohol. Cultures of some *Nocardia* spp. will appear acid fast when decolorized in this way.

3.3 Kinyoun's acid fast stain

3.3.1 *Solutions required*

Kinyoun carbol fuchsin

Basic fuchsin	4 g
Ethyl alcohol (95%)	20 ml
Concentrated phenol	8 ml
Distilled water	100 ml

Acid alcohol

Hydrochloric acid, concentrated	3 ml
Ethyl alcohol (95%)	97 ml

Methylene blue counterstain

Methylene blue	0.3 g
Distilled water	100 ml

3.3.2 *Staining procedure*

(i)   Flood the slide with Kinyoun carbol fuchsin and let it stain for 2 min.
(ii)   Wash with water and decolorize with acid alcohol until no more dye is removed.
(iii) Wash with water and counterstain with methylene blue for 30 sec.
(iv)   Wash with water, blot dry and examine.

Acid fast organisms stain red; the background and non-acid fast organisms stain blue.

4. STAINS FOR METACHROMATIC (VOLUTIN) GRANULES

4.1 Loeffler's methylene blue

4.1.1 *Solutions required*

Methylene blue	1 g
Ethyl alcohol (95%)	100 ml

Staining solution

Potassium hydroxide 1% aqueous solution	1 ml
Distilled water	99 ml
Ethanolic methylene blue	30 ml

Mix the reagents in this order. The final reagent must be ripened by oxidation, a process taking several months to complete, but it can be hastened by aeration.

4.1.2 *Staining procedure*

(i)   Heat fix the smear with gentle heat and then flood the slide with the stain.
(ii)   Leave the stain for 1 min and then wash briefly with water, blot dry and examine.

Metachromatic granules appear dark blue in a light blue cytoplasm.

4.2 **Albert's stain, modified**

4.2.1 *Solution required*

Malachite green	0.2 g
Toluidine blue	0.15 g
Ethyl alcohol (95%)	2 ml
Glacial acetic acid	1 ml
Distilled water	100 ml

Dissolve the dyes in the ethyl alcohol. Mix the acid with the water and add to the dye solution. Allow to stand for 24 h and filter.

4.2.2 *Staining procedure*

(i)   Stain with Albert's stain for $3-5$ min.
(ii)   Wash with water and blot dry.
(iii) Stain with Lugol's iodine solution for 1 min.
(iv)   Wash with water, blot dry and examine.

The cytoplasm appears light green and the granules blue-black.

4.3 **Neisser's stain**

4.3.1 *Solutions required*

Solution A

Methylene blue	0.1 g
Ethyl alcohol (95%)	5 ml
Glacial acetic acid	5 ml
Distilled water	100 ml

Dissolve the dye in the water and add the acid and ethyl alcohol.

Solution B

Crystal violet	0.33 g
Ethyl alcohol (95%)	3.3 ml
Distilled water	100 ml

Dissolve the dye in the ethanol$-$water mixture. For use mix 20 ml of solution A with 10 ml of solution B.

4.3.2 *Staining procedure*

(i)   Stain with Neisser's stain for 10 sec.
(ii)   Rinse rapidly with water.
(iii) Stain with 0.2% Bismarck brown.
(iv)   Wash rapidly with water, drain and blot dry.

The cytoplasm appears light brown and the granules blue-black.

5. SPORE STAIN (SCHAEFFER AND FULTON'S METHOD)

5.1 **Staining procedure**

(i)   Flood the slide with 5% aqueous malachite green and steam for 1 min.

(ii)   Wash under running water.
(iii)   Counterstain with 0.5% aqueous safranin for 15 sec.
(iv)   Rinse the slide with water, blot dry and examine.

Bacterial bodies stain red and spores stain green. This method can be used as a cold stain by allowing the malachite green to act for 10 min.

Bacteriological media not usually commercially available

1. TRANSPORT MEDIA

1.1 *Chlamydia* transport medium

The medium described below is that of Richmond (1). Prepare a 0.2 M sucrose buffer as follows:

Sucrose	342.3 g
Dipotassium hydrogen phosphate	10.44 g
Potassium di-hydrogen phosphate	5.44 g

Make up to 5 l and distribute into 500 ml volumes and autoclave at 10 psi for 15 min and store at 4°C or less. The transport medium itself is dispensed in 2 ml aliquots in screw-capped bottles; it may be stored frozen at −20°C. Prepare the medium for dispensing aseptically as follows:

0.2 M sucrose phosphate buffer	500 ml
Streptomycin*	50 μg/ml^{-1}
Vancomycin*	100 μg/ml^{-1}
Amphotericin B*	5 μg/ml^{-1}

*Filter sterilized before addition or prepared using sterile water. An alternative medium which contains foetal calf serum is described below (Dr A.E.Jephcott, personal communication).

Earle's saline containing	
10% sorbitol w/v	100 ml
Sodium bicarbonate 4.4% w/v	8 ml
Foetal calf serum	10 ml

The components are mixed together, filter sterilized and dispensed aseptically into 2 ml aliquots and stored at −20°C until required.

2. SELECTIVE/DIFFERENTIAL MEDIA

2.1 Desoxycholate citrate, crystal violet, cephazolin, rhamnose agar (DCCR)

A selective and differential medium for the isolation of *Enterobacter cloacae*. Most members of the genus *Enterobacter* including *E. cloacea* and *E. aerogenes* are resistant to cephazolin and ferment rhamnose present in the medium. The medium was originally used with a selective enrichment broth, the composition of which was not described (2). Presumptive *E. cloacae* will appear as pink colonies, sometimes mucoid.

Formula	Grams per litre
'Lab-Lemco' powder	5.0
Peptone	5.0
Yeast extract	1.0
Rhamnose	20.0

Sodium citrate	8.5
Sodium thiosulphate	5.4
Ferric citrate	1.0
Sodium desoxycholate	1.0
Neutral red	30 mg
Crystal violet	1 mg
Agar	13.5

pH 7.3 ± 0.2

Suspend ingredients in 1 l of sterile distilled water and bring to the boil over a flame using a gauze to prevent rapid heating. The medium should be agitated to prevent charring and *not* autoclaved as the constituents are heat labile. When cooled to 50°C, 10 mg l^{-1} cephazolin should be added before pouring the plates.

2.2 Deoxyribonuclease, toluidine blue, cephalothin agar (DTBCA)

This is a selective and differential medium for the isolation of *Serratia marcescens* relying on cephalothin or cephazolin for its selective action. Although members of the genera *Klebsiella, Enterobacter, Citrobacter* and *Providencia* are not DNase positive, *S. marcescens* and *S. liquefaciens* are, and this characteristic is detected with toluidine blue dye which is pink in the presence of free nucleotides and blue with intact DNA (3). Strains of *Serratia* spp. will be surrounded by a pink halo, the medium being royal blue in colour. Different batches of toluidine blue vary in their dye content so alteration of the amount used in the medium may be necessary (4).

Formula	Grams per litre
DNase agar (Oxoid)	39.0
Toluidine blue O (Sigma Chemical Co. Ltd)	50 mg*
Autoclave at 121°C for 15 min, pH 7.2	

*May be added as 5 ml of an appropriate stock solution. After autoclaving and cooling 1 g l^{-1} of cephalothin or cephazolin is added before pouring.

2.3 Herellea agar

A selective and differential medium for the isolation of *Acinetobacter calcoaceticus* which has four varieties: *anitratus, lwoffi, haemolyticus* and *alcaligenes*. On conventional media, *A. calcoaceticus* mimics non-lactose fermenting members of the *Enterobacteriaceae*. The bile-salts in Herellea agar provide selection and the sucrose and lactose differentiation as most members of the *Enterobacteriaceae* ferment one or other of the sugars present. The original formulation had maltose in place of sucrose (5). *Acinetobacter calcoaceticus* produces pale lavender colonies, *Pseudomonas* spp. grey-green colonies and *Enterobacteriaceae* yellow colonies with yellow zones surrounding them (NB *Proteeae* can produce similar colonies to *A. calcoaceticus*).

Formula	Grams per litre
Casein peptone	15.0
Soy peptone	5.0
Lactose	10.0
Sucrose	10.0

Sodium chloride	5.0
Bile salts no. 3	1.25
Bromocresol purple	0.02
Agar	16.0

Autoclave at 121°C for 15 min, pH 6.8 ± 0.2

2.4 MacConkey, inositol, carbenicillin agar (MICA)

Klebsiella spp. are among some of the few genera of the family *Enterobacteriaceae* that can ferment inositol. Most members of the genus also possess a chromosomally encoded β-lactamase that is capable of breaking down carbenicillin. The medium described here was originally developed for isolating *Klebsiella* spp. from faeces, but is equally successful in isolating them from other specimens (6). Colonies of presumptive *Klebsiella* spp. will appear as pink colonies on the medium; carbenicillin-resistant bacteria incapable of fermenting inositol will form translucent colonies. To achieve the highest rate of isolation swabs should be pre-enriched by incubation overnight in Koser's citrate broth, available from most commercial media manufacturers.

Formula	Grams per litre
Sodium taurocholate	5.0
Peptone	20.0
Inositol	10.0
Agar	15.0
Neutral red	50 mg

Autoclave at 121°C for 15 min, pH 7.5
When cooled to 50°C add 10 mg l^{-1} of sodium carbenicillin.

2.5 Nalidixic acid, cetrimide agar

Cetrimide (*N*-cetyl-*N*,*N*,*N*-trimethyl-ammonium bromide) inhibits the growth of a wide range of Gram-positive and Gram-negative bacteria. *Pseudomonas aeruginosa* and some other species of *Pseudomonas* are resistant. Incorporating magnesium sulphate and dipotassium phosphate (King's Agar Medium A) enhances the production of pyocyanin by *Ps. aeruginosa*. The addition of nalidixic acid inhibits a number of Gram-negative bacteria such as *Serratia* spp. that are resistant to cetrimide, *Ps. aeruginosa* being unaffected by nalidixic acid (7). Care must be exercised in the type of peptone used as only some types (e.g. Bacto-Peptone) enhance pyocyanin production. Not all strains of *Ps. aeruginosa* will elaborate pigment on this medium, so any oxidase positive colonies appearing should be identified even if not surrounded by the blue-green colour of pyocyanin. Different batches of cetrimide vary in their inhibitory action as commercial preparations are not always pure.

Formula	Grams per litre
Meat peptone	20.0
Dipotassium phosphate K_2HPO_4	0.3
Magnesium sulphate $MgSO_4$ $7H_2O$	0.3
Cetrimide	0.2
Agar	15.0

Autoclave at 121 °C for 15 min, pH 7.4−7.6

After sterilization add 15 mg l^{-1} of sterile nalidixic acid (best added as a solution, dissolved with a small amount of dilute NaOH).

2.6 Phenanthroline, C-390 agar

This is the most selective agar currently available for *Pseudomonas aeruginosa*; generally the only bacteria growing on it will be *Ps. aeruginosa* (8). As no indicator is included in the medium further identification of presumptive colonies is advisable, although current indications are that resistance to C-390 is a characteristic only found in *Ps. aeruginosa*.

Formula	Grams per litre
Columbia agar	39
C-390*	30 mg
o-Phenanthroline	30 mg

Autoclave at 121 °C for 15 min, pH 7.3

*9-Chloro-9-[4-(diethylamino)phenyl]-9, 10-dihydro-10-phenylacridine hydrochloride (Norwich Eaton Pharmaceuticals).

2.7 *Proteeae* identification medium

This medium relies on the ability of all species of *Proteeae* (except occasional strains of *Morganella morganii*) to produce a melanin-like pigment from tryptophan, which leads to the development of brown colonies (9). *Proteeae* also degrade tyrosine, although this is not a characteristic uniquely found in *Proteeae*, like the ability to produce the brown pigment. Clindamycin is used to eliminate Gram-positive bacteria and colistin can be used to inhibit almost all species of Gram-negative bacteria (approximately 10% of *Proteeae* will also be inhibited). To prevent swarming extra agar is incorporated in the medium.

Formula	Grams per litre
DL-Tryptophan	5.0
L-Tyrosine	4.0
Agar	8.0
Tryptone soy agar (Oxoid)	40.0

Autoclave at 121 °C for 15 min, pH 7.3

When cooled to 50 °C add 5 mg l^{-1} clindamycin sulphate and if desired 100 mg l^{-1} colistin (both as filter sterilized solutions). An alternative method of adding selective antibiotics VCN Selectatabs (Diamed Diagnostics Ltd) can be used. Final concentrations of antibiotics are 3 mg l^{-1} vancomycin, 7.5 mg l^{-1} colistin and 12 500 units l^{-1} nystatin; the tyrosine may also be omitted without a great loss of differential properties (10).

2.8 Salt, phenolpthalein, methicillin agar (SPMA)

This medium is an alternative to the more commonly used media for isolating methicillin resistant *Staphylococcus aureus* listed in Chapter 11, *Table 1*. Rather than relying on mannitol fermentation, colonies of *Staph. aureus* are detected by the action of phosphatase on sodium diphenolpthalein diphosphate in the medium, the free phenolpthalein being detected by exposing the plate to ammonia. Selection is provided by 5% Nacl (7.5% is usually used in MSA) and 4 mg l^{-1} methicillin (11). Pre-enrichment in Oxoid no. 2 nutrient broth containing 8% NaCl has been found to be a useful method of increasing isolation rates (12). Multiple swabs from a patient may be examined together in the same container of medium and incubation for longer than 24−48 h may yield extra positive cultures.

Formula	Grams per litre
Sodium chloride	50.0
Columbia agar	39.0

Autoclave at 121°C for 15 min, pH 7.3

When cooled to 50°C add 4 mg l^{-1} methicillin and 100 mg l^{-1} sodium phenolpthalein diphosphate as filtered sterile solutions (phenolpthalein phosphate can be purchased ready prepared from Oxoid Ltd). Incubate inoculated plates for 18 h and expose to ammonia by placing a few drops of strong ammonia solution (SG 0.880) in the lid of the Petri dish. Presumptive colonies of *Staph. aureus* are pink after exposure for about 1 min and can be subcultured for confirmation of identity. This method is useful for detecting small numbers of MRSA amongst large numbers of coagulase negative staphylococci.

2.9 Toluidine blue deoxynucleic acid agar (TDA)

This medium is used in conjunction with the rapid test for heat stable nuclease. The dye toluidine blue is metachromatic which means that it is blue in the presence of intact DNA and pink with free nucleotides.

Formula	Grams per litre
Deoxyribonucleic acid	0.3 g
Agar	10.0
NaCl	10.0

Add the components to 1 litre of 0.05 M Tris buffer pH 9.0. Add 1 ml of 0.01 M anhydrous $CaCl_2$ and boil until dissolved. Cool to 45°C and add 3 ml of 0.1 M toluidine blue O dye (Sigma Chemical Co.), then pour the plates. The plates can be used for up to 60 days if stored at 4°C wrapped in a plastic bag. They should be warmed to 37°C for 1 h before inoculating; positive and negative controls should be used.

2.10 Xylose desoxycholate citrate agar (XDCA)

Aeromonas hydrophila does not ferment xylose unlike many species of *Enterobacteriaceae*. The desoxycholate provides a selection for enteric bacteria. It is essential to use enrichment in alkaline peptone water for 18 h, the top layer is then subcultured onto XDCA (14). Ampicillin may also be added to this and other selective media for the isolation of *A. hydrophila* to increase the selectivity. If 30 mg l^{-1} is used nearly all strains of *A. hydrophila* will be recovered (15).

Formula	Grams per litre
Nutrient broth (Oxoid no. 2)	12.5
Sodium citrate	5.0
Sodium thiosulphate	5.0
Ferric ammonium citrate	1.0
Sodium desoxycholate	2.5
Agar	12.0
Xylose	10.0
Neutral red (1% sterile aqueous solution)	2.5 ml
pH 7.0	

Add 1 litre of sterile distilled water to the ingredients and gently heat to 100°C; simmer at that temperature for 20 sec and cool to 50°C before pouring the plates.

3. REFERENCES

1. Richmond,S.J. (1987) In *Sexually Transmitted Diseases, a Rational Approach to their Diagnosis.* Jephcott,A.E. (ed.), Public Health Laboratory Service, London, p. 48.
2. Flynn,D.M., Weinstein,R.A., Nathan,C., Gaston,M.A. and Kabins,S.A. (1987) *J. Infect. Dis.,* **156**, 363.
3. Farmer,J.J., Silva,F. and Williams,D.R. (1973) *Appl. Microbiol.,* **25**, 151.
4. Waller,J.R., Hodel,S.L. and Nuti,R.N. (1985) *J. Clin. Microbiol.,* **21**, 195.
5. MacFaddin,J.F. (1985) *Media for Isolation − Cultivation − Identification − Maintenance of Medical Bacteria.* Williams and Wilkins, Baltimore.
6. Cooke,E.M., Brayson,J.C., Edmondson,A.S. and Hall,D. (1979) *J. Hygiene (Camb.),* **82**, 473.
7. Goto,S. and Enomoto,S. (1970) *Jpn. J. Microbiol.,* **14**, 65.
8. Campbell,M.E., Farmer,S.W. and Speert,D.P. (1988) *J. Clin. Microbiol.,* **26**, 1910.
9. Hawkey,P.M., McCormick,A. and Simpson,R.A. (1986) *J. Clin. Microbiol.,* **23**, 600.
10. Haynes,J. and Hawkey,P.M. (1989) *Br. Med. J.,* **298**, in press.
11. Wilson,P.A. and Petts,D.N. (1987) *Lancet,* **i**, 558.
12. Cookson,B.D., Webster,M. and Phillips,I. (1987) *Lancet,* **i**, 696.
13. Barry,A.L., Lachica,R.V.F. and Atchison,F.W. (1973) *Appl. Microbiol.,* **25**, 496.
14. Millership,S.E., Curnow,S.R. and Chattopadhyay,B. (1983) *J. Clin. Path.,* **36**, 920.
15. Richardson,C.J.L., Robinson,J.O., Wagener,L.B. and Burke,V. (1982) *J. Antimicrob. Chemother.,* **9**, 267.

APPENDIX III

Principles of biochemical tests for the identification of bacteria

1. INTRODUCTION

The following sections describe some of the biochemical tests used to identify medically important bacteria. Most laboratories now use disposable prepared galleries of tests which are read from a colour chart then encoded to give a profile number for use with a computer data base. It is still important to understand the underlying principles of the test used to enable any problems encountered to be both recognized and solved.

1.1 Catalase test

Most cytochrome-containing aerobic and facultative anaerobic bacteria possess the enzyme catalase. The major exceptions to this rule are *Streptococcus* spp. which lack the catalase enzyme and the alternative enzyme capable of breaking down hydrogen peroxide, peroxidase, which is usually found in anaerobic bacteria.

In the presence of catalase two molecules of hydrogen peroxide react: one molecule acts as the substrate and is reduced by hydrogen atoms supplied by the other molecule to produce two molecules of water, the donor molecule being oxidized to one molecule of gaseous oxygen. The reaction is detected by trapping the bubbles of oxygen formed in the hydrogen peroxide solution in contact with the bacteria under a coverslip or in a capillary tube.

1.1.1 *Precautions*

(i)   Red blood cells contain catalase, so care must be taken not to take any medium with the bacteria (chocolated blood does not contain catalase).
(ii)   Do not use platinum loops as they will cause a false positive result.
(iii)   Hydrogen peroxide solution (30%) is caustic; spills on skin should be quickly washed with 70% ethanol.
(iv)   Always use fresh hydrogen peroxide and check it with a positive control. Occasional catalase negative strains can be encountered [e.g. *Staphylococcus aureus* (1)].
(v)   Routine testing can liberate aerosols so use a method to minimize this such as the capillary tube method.

1.2 Citrate test

This is a test to determine whether a bacterium can utilize citrate as a sole carbon source for growth. It is usually used to help identify Gram-negative bacteria, particularly *Enterobacteriaceae*. Some bacteria can, in the absence of fermentation of sugars or lactic acid production, use citrate as a sole source of energy. An enzyme, citrate demolase, cleaves citrate to yield oxaloacetate and acetate which can then enter the Krebs cycle. Normally coenzyme A is required to enable citrate to enter the cycle. Pyruvate is then formed which in acid conditions will yield acetate, CO_2 and lactate or acetoin and CO_2, and in alkaline conditions acetate and formate. Media for the detection of citrate utilization contain ammonium salts which the growing bacteria use as a sole source of nitrogen. These when broken down yield ammonia with alkalinization of the medium. The further utilization of the organic acid produces carbonates and bicarbonates on subsequent decomposition. A typical medium used is Simmon's citrate medium which contains magnesium sulphate (required for activity of citrate demolase), ammonium dihydrogen phosphate, dipotassium phosphate, sodium citrate, sodium chloride, agar, bromothymol blue and water. The uninoculated medium is green and bacteria unable to utilize citrate as a sole carbon source do not change their colour. A positive result is indicated by a deep Prussian blue colour.

1.2.1 *Precautions*

(i)   A heavy inoculum might give a pale yellow colour in the start; this is *not* a positive result.
(ii)   When multiple tests are being inoculated glucose or other nutrients may be carried over; therefore flame the loop before inoculating the citrate medium.
(iii) If the test is performed in screw-capped tubes the tops should not be tightened down as anaerobic conditions may develop leading to a poor colour change. Some bacteria may require long incubation periods before a colour change develops.

1.3 **Decarboxylase and dehydrolase tests**

These tests detect enzymes which decarboxylate amino acids yielding alkaline amines. Bacteria possess numerous decarboxylase enzymes with specific substrates. The three enzymes used in identification are ornithine and lysine decarboxylase (ODC and LDC) and arginine dehydrolase (ADH). The process occurs under anaerobic conditions and some of the products such as cadaverine and putrescine are stable when produced under these conditions (2). The alkaline amines produced are detected with pH indicators (in the Møller version of the test bromocresol purple and cresol red). A variety of media exist for the detection of these enzymes (3), Møller's version of the test is the most frequently used.

$$
\begin{array}{ccc}
NH_2 & & NH_2 \\
| & & | \\
CH_2 & & CH_2 \\
| & \xrightarrow[\text{decarboxylase}]{\text{Lysine}} & | \\
(CH_2)_3 & & (CH_2)_3 + CO_2 \\
| & & | \\
CH_2 & & CH_2 \\
| & & | \\
NH_2 & & NH_2 \\
| & & \\
COOH & & \text{Cadaverine} \\
\text{L-Lysine} & &
\end{array}
$$

$$NH_2-(CH_2)_3-CH(NH_2)-COOH \xrightarrow[\text{decarboxylase}]{\text{Ornithine}} CH_2NH_2-(CH_2)_2-CH_2NH_2 + CO_2$$

L-Ornithine → Putrescine

$$\text{L-Arginine} \xrightarrow[\text{dehydrolase}]{\text{Arginine}} \text{L-Citrulline} \xrightarrow[\text{ureidase}]{\text{Citrulline}} \text{L-Ornithine} + 2NH_3 + CO_2 \xrightarrow[\text{decarboxylase}^*]{\text{Ornithine}} \text{Putrescine} + CO_2$$

L-Arginine:
$$NH=C(NH_2)-NH-(CH_2)_3-CH(NH_2)-COOH$$

L-Citrulline:
$$NH=C(OH)-NH-(CH_2)_3-CH(NH_2)-COOH$$

L-Ornithine:
$$NH_2-(CH_2)_3-CH(NH_2)-COOH + 2NH_3 + CO_2$$

Putrescine:
$$CH_2NH_2-(CH_2)_2-CH_2NH_2 + CO_2$$

*This pathway only occurs if ODC is present as well as ADH.

1.3.1 *Precautions*

(i) Always inoculate a control tube which lacks any added amino acid; it should remain yellow. A positive colour (purple) invalidates the test.

(ii) Always layer sterile paraffin oil over the tubes immediately after inoculation and do not attempt to read the tests before they have been incubated for 24 h. Under anaerobic conditions organic acids cannot be oxidized so peptones present in the medium cannot be deaminated; however decarboxylases are active under anaerobic conditions so any pH rise is due to those enzymes' activity.

1.4 **Hippurate hydrolysis test**

Sodium hippurate can be hydrolysed by some bacteria (e.g. *Streptococcus agalactiae* and *Campylobacter jejuni*) to yield glycine and benzoic acid. Both benzoic acid or glycine can be detected in different versions of the test. The former is usually detected with $FeCl_3$ and glycine with ninhydrin when a deep purple colour is produced (4).

$$\text{Hippuric acid} + H_2O \xrightleftharpoons[\text{hydrolysis}]{\text{Hippurate hydrolase}} \text{Benzoic acid} + \text{Glycine}$$

Hippuric acid: $C_6H_5-C(=O)-NHCH_2-COOH$

Benzoic acid: C_6H_5-COOH

Glycine: CH_2NH_2-COOH

1.4.1 *Precautions*

(i)   When using ninhydrin reagent do not incubate for longer than 30 min after adding the reagent as false positive results can occur.

1.5 **Hydrogen sulphide test**

Sulphur-containing amino acids such as methionine and cysteine can be degraded by some bacteria to liberate hydrogen sulphide. In some cases sodium thiosulphate can also be metabolized to liberate H_2S. Hydrogen sulphide is detected by its ability to react with metal ions and produce insoluble black sulphides. Ferric ions can be incorporated into media but if lead ions are used (gives increased sensitivity) in the form of lead acetate it is placed on a filter paper strip above the growing bacteria. This is because lead acetate is highly toxic to bacteria.

1.5.1 *Precautions*

(i)   Sucrose in media will suppress the enzyme systems producing H_2S (5), so Triple Sugar Iron agar may give negative results for H_2S production for some species of the H_2S positive salmonellae.

(ii)   Lead acetate is very toxic to bacteria and paper strips containing it should *not* be allowed to touch the medium.

1.6 **Indole test**

This test determines the ability of a bacterium to cleave the indole ring from tryptophan. Indole positive bacteria possess a series of enzymes collectively known as 'tryptophanase'. These enzymes oxidize tryptophan to intermediates such as indole pyruvic acid which is deaminated to indole, and indole acetic acid which is decarboxylated to skatole (methyl indole). Indole and its related compounds such as skatole and indole acetic acid are detected with an aldehyde in the reagent which causes a condensation of the pyrrole structure present in indole to give rise to an intense red coloured quinoidal compound. The most commonly used reagent is *p*-dimethyl aminobenzaldehyde (DMABA). Because this compound will react with a wide range of indole-containing compounds, DMABA is dissolved in amyl alcohol which extracts only indole and skatole. A rapid spot test can be performed using *p*-dimethylaminocinnamaldehyde (DMACA) which is the most sensitive reagent (6).

L-Tryptophan   Indole   Pyruvic acid

1.6.1 *Precautions*

(i) Certain batches of peptone are low in tryptophan and should be checked for their ability to give a positive test with a positive control bacterium (*E. coli*).

(ii) Some bacteria (e.g. *Clostridia* spp.) decompose indole as fast as it is produced and will give a false negative result.

(iii) Media for indole testing must not contain any glucose as the acid produced can inhibit tryptophanase (as can media with a low pH); the addition of tryptophan induces the enzyme.

1.7 **Methyl red and Voges−Proskauer test**

Fermentative bacteria such as the *Enterobacteriaceae* derive their energy from the conversion of sugars such as glucose to pyruvic acid via the Embden−Meyerhof pathway. Pyruvic acid is then utilized usually by either the mixed acid fermentation or the butylene glycol pathway. A simplified scheme of these pathways is shown below. The methyl red test detects the large amount of mixed acids produced by bacteria using that pathway as methyl red changes colour from orange to red at pH 4.4; above a pH of 6.0 it is yellow. A positive result is indicated by the appearance of a distinct red colour at the surface of the medium after 48 h incubation. A rapid version of the test giving a result after 24 h incubation has been described (7).

The Voges−Proskauer test detects acetoin which is an intermediate produced by bacteria in which butylene glycol (2,3-butanediol) is the major end product of glucose fermentation, rather than organic acids. Voges−Proskauer (VP) positive bacteria include *Klebsiella* spp., *Enterobacter* spp. and *Serratia* spp. which also give a negative result in the methyl red test. Bacteria which are positive in the methyl red test are not usually positive in the VP test as one pathway only is used (*Proteus mirabilis* and *Hafnia alvei* are exceptions and positive in both tests.) Acetoin is detected by KOH oxidizing it to diacetyl which then reacts with the guanidine nucleus present in the meat peptones in the media to produce a pinkish-red colour. The α-naphthol enhances the colour as does gentle shaking to expose the media to atmospheric oxygen.

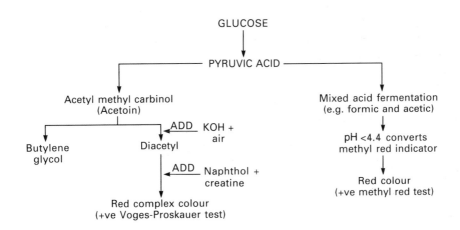

1.7.1 *Precautions*

(i)   Rarely some bacteria known to produce acetoin give a negative VP test; warming the test will give a positive reaction.

(ii)   Some bacteria can destroy acetoin when it is produced making the test unreliable. It should not be used as the sole test for identification.

1.8 Nitrate reduction test

This test determines the ability of a bacterium to reduce nitrate to nitrite, or free nitrogen gas. All members of the *Enterobacteriaceae* are nitrate positive (except strains of *Enterobacter agglomerans* and *Erwinia* spp.). The test is also used in identifying members of the genera *Neisseria*, *Branhamella* and *Haemophilus*. In the test bacteria extract oxygen from nitrate to form nitrite and in some cases nitrites are further reduced to N_2, NH_3 or N_2O. The nitrites formed in the process are detected with α-naphthylamine and sulphanilic acid when a red dye (*p*-sulphobenzeneazo-α-naphthylamine) is formed. If on adding the two reagents no colour develops it is possible that either the nitrates have been fully reduced to nitrogen or other products that have escaped or that nitrate has not been reduced and is still present in the medium. The presence of unreduced nitrate is confirmed by adding a small amount of zinc dust which reduces any nitrate present to nitrite with the concomitant development of the red colour. Should the nitrate have been fully reduced no colour will develop on the addition of the zinc dust.

1.8.1 *Precautions*

(i)   The red colour produced fades quickly so the results must be interpreted immediately.

(ii)   The test is very sensitive so always test an uninoculated tube of media to confirm no nitrites are present.

(iii) α-Naphthylamine is carcinogenic so the alternative reagent N,N-dimethyl-α-naphthylamine should be substituted whenever possible.

(iv)   Do not add too much zinc dust as the hydrogen liberated can reduce the nitrite present to NH_3 and give a false negative result.

1.9 ONPG (*o*-nitrophenyl-β-D-galactopyranoside) test

Bacteria capable of fermentating lactose (an important characteristic in identifying *Enterobacteriaceae*) possess two enzymes: β-D-galactosidase (intra-cellular) which cleaves the β-glycosidic linkage between the glucose and galactose residues of lactose and β-galactosidase-permease which transports the lactose into the cell. Whilst lactose together with a pH indicator can be used to detect the activity of β-D-galactosidase in bacteria with the permease, some bacteria (late lactose fermenters) lack the permease and will not produce a colour change in 24 h as mutants with the enzyme arise on prolonged incubation (8). An alternative substrate ONPG does not require the permease and will detect any bacteria possessing β-D-galactosidase. When ONPG is cleaved in alkaline conditions the yellow product *o*-nitrophenyl (ONP) is formed.

o-Nitrophenyl-β-D-galactopyranase (ONPG, colourless)

o-Nitrophenol (ONP, yellow)

Galactose

1.9.1 *Precautions*

(i)   The ONPG solution must be colourless before use and of the correct pH $(7.0-7.5)$ or the ONP formed will be colourless. Before use the solution must be placed in a 37°C water bath to re-dissolve the phosphate buffer which crystalizes out of solution on storage at 4°C.

(ii)   A heavy inoculum must be used or insufficient pre-formed enzyme will be present.

1.10 Oxidase test

This test determines the presence of the cytochrome oxidase system of enzymes which activate the oxidation of reduced cytochrome by molecular oxygen which then acts as an electron acceptor in the last stage of electron transfer. The enzyme by definition is only found in some bacteria capable of utilizing ozygen as a final hydrogen acceptor to reduce molecular oxygen to H_2O_2 (aerobic, microaerophilic or facultative anaerobes). All members of the *Enterobacteriaceae* are negative, whereas some *Pseudomonas* spp., *Neisseria* spp., *Campylobacter* spp. and others are positive. Anaerobic bacteria are invariably negative in the oxidase test. The most frequently used reagent is tetramethyl-*p*-phenylenediamine which produces an intense blue/purple colour (Wurster's blue). An alternative reagent is dimethyl-*p*-phenylenediamine which produces indophenol blue. Both reagents are usually placed on filter paper or a cotton wool swab and the colonies dabbed onto them. A purple colour should appear in 10 s.

1.10.1 *Precautions*

(i)   Never use a nichrome wire loop to handle bacteria to be tested for oxidase activity as traces of iron present will catalyse the oxidation of the reagent. Platinum loops can be used but it is better to use paper or cotton wool.

(ii)   Media containing glucose inhibit oxidase activity. Selective and differential media may also interfere with oxidase activity. Only test colonies from non-selective/differential media, e.g. blood agar, nutrient agar, trypticase soy agar, etc.

(iii) The reagents auto-oxidize rapidly so ascorbic acid should be added and the reagent replaced frequently.

1.11 **Phenylalanine deaminase test**

A small number of bacteria including all the members of the *Proteeae* can deaminate the aromatic amino acid phenylalanine to produce phenyl pyruvic acid. This end product is detected by adding ferric chloride which chelates with the phenyl pyruvic acid to produce a green colour. The colour fades rapidly so the test must be examined immediately. The API-20E system detects the similar enzyme tryptophan deaminase which has a similar distribution amongst bacteria to phenylalanine deaminase.

Phenylalanine → Phenylpyruvic acid
(Detected by the addition of FeCl₃ when a green colour develops on exposure to air)

$$CH_2\text{-}CH\text{-}COOH \text{ (NH}_2) + \bar{O} \xrightarrow[\text{flavoprotein}]{-2H} CH_2\text{-}C\text{-}COOH \text{ (O)} + NH_3$$

1.12 **Urease test**

Urease enzymes are widely distributed amongst bacteria and are diverse in their relationships (9). They all catalyse the hydrolysis of urea to form ammonia and carbon dioxide. The ammonia produced causes the medium to become alkaline and this can be detected with a pH indicator. Ureases vary greatly in their rate of hydrolysis of urea and use is made of these differences in buffering the medium used. Stuart's urea broth is highly buffered and so only the urease positive *Proteeae* will produce sufficient ammonia to overcome the buffering system. Christensen's medium is much less buffered than Stuart's medium and urease positive bacteria other than the *Proteeae* will produce a colour change in 24 h (*Proteeae* should produce a positive result in 1−6 h). It is important to remember that only a pH change is being detected and utilization of peptones in the medium may raise the pH in Christensen's medium to give a false positive result. To eliminate this error if it is thought to have occurred, inoculate a control tube of the medium *without* urea.

$$H_2N{-}C{=}O{-}NH_2 + 2HOH \xrightarrow{\text{urease}} CO_2 + H_2O + 2NH_3$$

2. REFERENCES

1. Tu,K.K. and Palutke,W.A. (1976) *J. Clin. Microbiol.*, **3**, 77.
2. Møller,V. (1955) *Acta Pathol. Microbiol. Scand.*, **36**, 158.
3. MacFaddin,J.F. (1980) *Biochemical Tests for Identification of Medical Bacteria,* 2nd edition, Williams and Wilkins, Baltimore and London.
4. Hwang,M. and Ederer,G.M. (1975) *J. Clin. Microbiol.*, **1**, 114.
5. Bulmarsh,J.M. and Fulton,M.D. (1964) *J. Bacteriol.*, **88**, 1813.
6. Lowrance,B.L., Reich,P. and Traub,W.H. (1969) *Appl. Microbiol.*, **17**, 923.
7. Barry,A.L., Bernsohn,K.L., Adams,A.P. and Thrupp,L.D. (1970) *Appl. Microbiol.*, **20**, 866.
8. Lowe,G.H. (1962) *J. Med. Lab. Technol.*, **19**, 21.
9. Jones,B.D. and Mobley,H.L.T. (1987) *Infect. and Immun.*, **55**, 2198.

Epidemiological questionnaire

A questionnaire used in the investigation of an outbreak of salmonella infection in school children aboard an ocean-going cruise liner.

S.S.UGANDA ENQUIRY

School ....

Name............................Age.............................Sex............................

Deck no.............Dormitory name............Bunk no.............Group no.............

Did you have any of the following symptoms whilst you were on the cruise or within one week of returning from the cruise?

Tick each symptom you suffered and give the date it started. Please be as accurate as possible.

If you suffered more than one bout of illness please give the dates for each one.

SYMPTOMS	Please tick as appropriate			Date of onset of symptoms
Vomiting	Yes ☐	No ☐	Don't know ☐	....
Diarrhoea	Yes ☐	No ☐	Don't know ☐	....
Headache	Yes ☐	No ☐	Don't know ☐	....
Abdominal pain	Yes ☐	No ☐	Don't know ☐	....
Fever/temperature	Yes ☐	No ☐	Dont know ☐	....

If you were unwell on the cruise please put an X or Xs along the line below to show when your illness(es) started.

Put an X along
the dotted
line to show
when illnesses
started

24th   25   26   27   28   1   2   3   4   5   6   7   8   9   10   11

February   March

<u>At Naples</u>:   <u>Please tick as appropriate</u>

Did you buy food in the town?   Yes ☐   No ☐   Don't know ☐

Did you drink water or fruit juice in the town?   Yes ☐   No ☐   Don't know ☐

Did you eat locally bought fruit?   Yes ☐   No ☐   Don't know ☐

Did you eat ices/lollipops?   Yes ☐   No ☐   Don't know ☐

<u>Messina</u>:

Did you go ashore?   Yes ☐   No ☐   Don't know ☐

Did you buy food in the town?   Yes ☐   No ☐   Don't know ☐

Did you drink water or fruit juice in the town?   Yes ☐   No ☐   Don't know ☐

Did you eat locally bought fruit?   Yes ☐   No ☐   Don't know ☐

Did you eat ices/lollipops?   Yes ☐   No ☐   Don't know ☐

<u>Alexandria</u>:

Did you go ashore?   Yes ☐   No ☐   Don't know ☐

Did you eat all your packed lunch?   Yes ☐   No ☐   Don't know ☐
(Pork pie, etc.)
If not, what did you not eat? ....

Did you eat anyone else's pork pie?   Yes ☐   No ☐   Don't know ☐

Did you use your drink token?   Yes ☐   No ☐   Don't know ☐

Haifa:

Did you go ashore? Yes ☐ No ☐ Don't know ☐

Did you eat all your packed lunch? (Chicken) Yes ☐ No ☐ Don't know ☐
If not, what did you not eat? ....

Did you eat anyone else's chicken? Yes ☐ No ☐ Don't know ☐

Did you eat any local fruit? Yes ☐ No ☐ Don't know ☐
If yes, what was it?..

Limassol:

Did you go ashore? Yes ☐ No ☐ Don't know ☐

Did you eat all your packed lunch? Yes ☐ No ☐ Don't know ☐
(Chicken and bacon pie)
If not, what did you not eat? ....

Did you eat anyone else's pie? Yes ☐ No ☐ Don't know ☐

Did you eat any local fruit? Yes ☐ No ☐ Don't know ☐
If yes, what was it?..

Nauplia:

Did you go ashore? Yes ☐ No ☐ Don't know ☐

Did you eat all your packed lunch? (Sausage rolls) Yes ☐ No ☐ Don't know ☐
If not, what did you not eat? ....

Did you eat anyone else's sausage rolls? Yes ☐ No ☐ Don't know ☐

Did you eat any local fruit? Yes ☐ No ☐ Don't know ☐
If yes, what was it?..

Split:

			Don't
Did you eat food in the town?	Yes ☐	No ☐	know ☐

(Please say what you ate, including ice-cream)

....

....

			Don't
Did you have anything to drink?	Yes ☐	No ☐	know ☐

(Please say what drank)

....

On board ship: Please tick as appropriate

			Don't
Did you drink water from the water fountain?	Yes ☐	No ☐	know ☐

If yes, how many times each day on average

....

			Don't
Did you drink tap water?	Yes ☐	No ☐	know ☐
Did you swim in the pool?	Yes ☐	No ☐	know ☐

For breakfast did you have milk on your cereal?

Every day ☐   Usually ☐   Sometimes ☐   Never ☐

For lunch or dinner did you eat chicken: Twice ☐   Once ☐   Never ☐

			Don't
Did you eat lamb?	Yes ☐	No ☐	know ☐
beef?	Yes ☐	No ☐	know ☐
shepherd's pie?	Yes ☐	No ☐	know ☐
sausages?	Yes ☐	No ☐	know ☐
fish?	Yes ☐	No ☐	know ☐
salads?	Yes ☐	No ☐	know ☐
soup?	Yes ☐	No ☐	know ☐
ice-cream?	Yes ☐	No ☐	know ☐
cakes?	Yes ☐	No ☐	know ☐

			Don't
fruit?	Yes ☐	No ☐	know ☐

			Don't
Did you ever have more than one portion per meal?	Yes ☐	No ☐	know ☐

If you did, what were the foods? ....

			Don't
Did you share towels or soap with your friends?	Yes ☐	No ☐	know ☐

			Don't
Did any of your close friends or dormitory	Yes ☐	No ☐	know ☐

neighbours have diarrhoea?

Communicable Disease Surveillance Centre   26th March 1981
61 Colindale Avenue   S.R.P.
Colindale
London NW9 5EQ

APPENDIX V

Manufacturers' addresses

Abbott Laboratories Ltd, Abbott Diagnostics Division, Abbott House, Moorbridge Road, Maidenhead, Berks SL6 8XZ, UK

American Hospital Supplies, Station Road, Didcot, Oxfordshire OX11 7NP, UK

Ames Division, Miles Laboratories Ltd, PO Box 35, Stoke Court, Stoke Poges, Slough, Bucks SL2 4LY, UK

Amicon Ltd, Upper Mill, Stonehouse, Gloucestershire GL10 2BJ, UK

Analytab (API), 200 Empress Street, Plainview, New York, NY 11803, USA

API Laboratory Products Ltd, Grafton Way, Basingstoke, Hampshire RG22 6HY, UK

API Systems SA—see API Laboratory Products Ltd

Anbodata Ltd, 80 Walsworth Road, Hitchin, Herts SG4 9SX, UK

BBL Microbiology Systems—see Beckton Dickinson

BDH Ltd, Broom Road, Poole, Dorset BH12 4NN, UK

Beckton Dickinson UK Ltd, Between Towns Road, Cowley, Oxford OX4 3LY, UK

Biotest (UK) Ltd, Unit 21A Monkspath Business Park, Stratford Road, Shirley, Solihull B90 4NY, UK

Boots Celltech Diagnostics Ltd, 240 Bath Road, Slough, Berks SL1 4ET, UK

Albert Brown Ltd, Chancery House, Abbey Gate, Leicester LE4 0AA, UK

Cambridge Biomedical Ltd. Alternative supplier: Alpha Laboratories Ltd, 40 Parham Drive, Eastleigh, Hampshire SO5 4NV, UK

Chance Propper Ltd, Spon Lane, Smethwick, Warley, UK

Cheeseborough Ponds Ltd, London NW10 6NA, UK

Cormark Electronics, Dominion Way, Rustington, West Sussex BN16 3QZ, UK

DMRQC, Central Public Health Laboratory, Colindale Avenue, London NW9 5HT, UK

Denley Instruments Ltd, Natts Lane, Billingshurst, Sussex RH14 9EY, UK

Diamed Diagnostics Ltd, Mast House, Derby Road, Bootle, Merseyside L20 1EA, UK

Difco Laboratories, PO Box 14B, Central Avenue, East Moseley, Surrey KT8 0SE, UK

Du Pont (UK) Ltd, MCD Dept, Wedgewood Way, Stevenage, Herts SG1 4QN, UK

Du Pont de Nemours Inc., Clinical Systems Division, Wilmington, DE 19898, USA

Dynatech Laboratories Ltd, Daux Road, Billingshurst, West Sussex RH14 9SJ, UK

Gen Probe Inc., 9889 Campus Point Drive, San Diego, CA 92121, USA

Gibco Biocult Ltd, 3 Washington Road, Sandyford Industrial Estate, Paisley PA3 4EP, UK

Gilford Diagnostics, 16035 Industrial Pathway, SW, Cleveland, OH 44135, USA

Glaxo Laboratories Ltd, Greenford, Middlesex UB6 0HE, UK

C A Hendley Ltd, Oakwood Hill Industrial Estate, Loughton, Essex, UK

Horiba Ltd, 1 Harrowden Road, Brackmills, Northampton NN4 0EB, UK

Innovative Diagnostic Systems Inc., 3404 Oakcliff Road, Suite C-1, Atlanta, GA 30340, USA

Key-Med (UK) Ltd, Key-Med House, Stock Road, Southend-on-Sea, Essex SS2 5QH, UK

LIP Ltd, 111 Dorkfield Road, Shipley, West Yorkshire BD17 7AS, UK

LEEC Ltd, Private Road No 7, Colwick Industrial Estate, Nottingham NG4 2AJ, UK

Lab M Ltd, Topley House, PO Box 19, Bury, Lancs BL9 6AV, UK

Leebrook Instruments Co. Ltd, Claylands Cottage Works, Claylands Road, Bishops Waltham, Hampshire, UK

Lumac Systems Inc., PO Box 2805, Titusville, FL 32780, USA

MSE Scientific Instruments Ltd, Bishop Meadow Road, Loughborough, Leics LE11 0RG, UK

Mast Diagnostics, Mast Laboratories Ltd, Mast House, Derby Road, Bootle, Merseyside L20 1EA, UK

Medical Wire and Equipment Ltd, Potley, Corsham, Wiltshire, UK

Millipore (UK) Ltd, 11–15 Peterborough Road, Harrow, Middlesex HA1 2YH, UK

National Collection of Type Cultures, Central Public Health Laboratory (NCTC), Colindale Avenue, London NW9 5HT, UK

Norwich Eaton Pharmaceuticals Inc., Norwich, New York NY 13815, USA

Nunc—from Gibco BRL Ltd, Unit 4, Cowley Mill Trading Estate, Longbridge Way, Uxbridge, Middlesex UB8 2YG, UK

Orbec Ltd, 87 Limpsfield Road, Sanderstead, Surrey CR2 9LE, UK

Organon Teknika Ltd, Science Park, Milton Road, Cambridge CB4 4FL, UK

Orme Scientific, PO Box 3, Stakehill Industrial Park, Middleton, Manchester M24 2RH, UK

Oxoid Ltd, Wade Road, Basingstoke, Hampshire RG24 0HW, UK

Perkin-Elmer Ltd, Post Office Lane, Beaconsfield, Bucks HP9 1QA, UK

Pharmacia Ltd, Pharmacia House, Midsomer Boulevard, Milton Keynes, MK9 3HP, UK

Pye-Unicam, York Street, Cambridge CB1 2PX, UK

Rainin Instrument Co. Inc., Woburn, Massachusetts, USA

Roche Products Ltd, Diagnostics Division, PO Box 8, Welwyn Garden City, Herts AL7 3AY, UK

Sarstedt Ltd, 68 Boston Road, Beaumont Leys, Leicester LE4 1AW, UK

Sensititre UK, Imberhorne Lane, East Grinstead, West Sussex RH19 1QX, UK

Seward Medical, 131 Great Suffolk Street, Southwark, London SE1 9UG, UK

Sigma Chemical Co. Ltd, Fancy Road, Poole, Dorset BH17 7NH, UK

Southern Group Laboratories, Hither Green Hospital, Hither Green Lane, London SE13 6RU, UK

Spiral Systems Inc., 4853 Cordell Avenue, Suite A-11, Bethesda, MD 20814, USA

Sterilin Ltd, Lampton House, Lampton Road, Hounslow, Middlesex TW3 4EE,UK

Supelco Chromatography Supplies Inc., Supelco Park, Bellefonte, PA 16823-0048, USA

Syva UK Ltd, Syntex House, Maidenhead, Berkshire SL6 1RD, UK

Tissue Culture Services, 10 Henry Road, Slough, Bucks SL1 2QL, UK

UV Products Ltd, Science Park, Milton Road, Cambridge CB4 4FH, UK

Varian Associates, 24−28 Manor Road, Walton-on-Thames, Surrey KT12 2BF, UK

Vitek Systems Inc., 595 Anglum Drive, Hazlewood, MO 63042, USA

Waters Millipore (UK) Ltd, Waters Chromatography Division, Peterborough Road, Harrow, Middlesex HA1 2YH, UK

Wellcome Diagnostics, Temple Hill, Dartford, Kent DA1 5AH, UK

Whatman Biochemicals Ltd, Springfield Mills, Maidstone, Kent ME14 2LE, UK

Don Whitley Scientific Ltd, 14 Otley Road, Shipley, West Yorkshire BD17 7SE, UK

INDEX